# American Urban Politics in a Global Age

page 392

# American Urban Politics in a Global Age

## The Reader

FIFTH EDITION

EDITED BY

**Paul Kantor**
*Fordham University*

**Dennis R. Judd**
*University of Illinois at Chicago*

PEARSON
Longman

New York  San Francisco  Boston
London  Toronto  Sydney  Tokyo  Singapore  Madrid
Mexico City  Munich  Paris  Cape Town  Hong Kong  Montreal

Editor-in-Chief: Eric Stano
Executive Marketing Manager: Ann Stypuloski
Production Manager: Bob Ginsberg
Project Coordination, Text Design, and Electronic Page Makeup:
  Carlisle Publishing Services
Cover Design Manager: John Callahan
Cover Designer: Maria Ilardi
Cover Photos: *(left)* Homestead Steel Works Plant © H.C. White/CORBIS;
    *(center)* Abandoned Buildings in the Bronx © Owen Franken/CORBIS;
    *(right)* Times Square © Michael N. Paras/AGE Fotostock America, Inc.
Manufacturing Manager: Mary Fischer
Printer and Binder: RR Donnelley & Sons Company/Crawfordsville
Cover Printer: RR Donnelley & Sons Company/Crawfordsville

Library of Congress Cataloging-in-Publication Data

American urban politics in a global age : the reader / edited by Paul Kantor, Dennis R.
  Judd.--5th ed.
     p. cm.
   Includes bibliographical references.
   Contents: Pt. 1. Globalization and the economic imperative -- pt. 2. Governing the
multi-ethnic metropolis -- pt. 3. Governing the fractured metropolis.
   ISBN 0-205-55371-0
   1. Urban policy--United States. 2. Municipal government -- United States. 3.
Metropolitan government--United States. I. Kantor, Paul. II. Judd, Dennis R.

HT123A6664 2008
320.8'50973--dc22
                                                                          2006052533

Visit us at www.ablongman.com

ISBN-13: 978-0-205-55371-6
ISBN-10:     0-205-55371-0

12345678910—DOC—10 09 08 07

*To the lovely Desmond Women—Anna, Mary, Eileen, Joan, and Nora—
and to Stephen. How fortunate I am to share your world.*

—Paul Kantor

*To my grandchildren, Dylan, Miranda, Jennifer, Jake, Weston, Wyatt,
and Eliza: you make the world go round!*

—Dennis R. Judd

# CONTENTS

*Section 1 less than one page* "Annotated Bibliography"

*single spaced*

viii    Contents

PART TWO  *Governing the Multi-Ethnic Metropolis*

*March 24*

## PART THREE *Governing the Fractured Metropolis*

*March 31*

*April 7*

# PREFACE

In this book we have assembled readings that highlight the historic changes occurring in urban America as a result of globalization: the intense competition among cities in the international marketplace; the new attention given to urban culture in promoting cities; the fears and rivalries among groups over efforts to privatize public spaces; the political competition over new issues of race, ethnicity, and inequality arising in suburbs as well as cities; the emergence of a multiethnic metropolis resulting from international immigration; efforts to address the consequences of urban sprawl; and the attempts by political leaders to prepare for terrorist attacks or natural disasters. Our efforts to incorporate these features led us to reconceive this, the fifth edition of our reader. *American Urban Politics in the Global Era* departs significantly from earlier editions.

To fully understand the changes of the global era, we take pains to acknowledge the degree to which many of the "new" urban issues are actually rooted in the past. In previous editions of the book, we included several historical selections for this purpose. This time, however, nearly all of the readings treat global issues. To place issues of the global age in historical context, our introductory essay emphasizes historical continuities as well as sharp departures. In that essay we trace urban America through three periods of development. In the first century, cities were spread across the frontier, engaged in a frenetic competition for primacy and power, coping with the political effects of massive immigration. During the second period, which spans the late nineteenth century to the global era in the twentieth century, central cities emerged as economic powerhouses and then slid into decline as a result of the postwar movement to the suburbs.

In the global era, mobile capital moves with lightening speed from place to place makes it imperative that every city undertake entrepreneurial strategies to boost local economies. Cities are increasingly on their own, partly because the federal government has withdrawn from urban programs. American cities have always had to rely upon their own resources in comparison to cities in Europe and elsewhere; thus the promotion of local prosperity has been a dynamic driving urban politics for a long time. American cities possess significant powers, but nothing of consequence can be done without the participation and cooperation of the private institutions of the market. Political tensions arise from the division between state and market. On one hand, marketplace institutions supply capital and jobs that make local economies work. In recent decades, cities have expended huge resources in their efforts to keep and attract investors and firms.

Quite often these efforts provoke protests that governments care a lot more about business than anyone else.

On the other, democratic norms require that public officials respond to the demands of the many groups competing for political influence; failure to do so means they may have very brief political careers. The immigration flows of the global age mean that "identity" politics involving race, ethnicity, and gender have become a central feature of international, national, and local political arenas. In metropolitan areas, concern has also emerged about regional issues. Interestingly, the imperatives of democracy and of economic prosperity give energy to this concern. Local governments compete vigorously with one another for shopping malls, big-box retailers, and high-level residential development (often facilitated by gated communities). The question of whether such competition undermines metropolitan communities is the subject of spirited debate. At the same time, many scholars assert that social, racial, and ethnic divisions are made worse by the patchwork pattern of metropolitan governance. Recently, concern about regional governance has taken on urgency. Because we consider these issues to be so important, we end the volume with two chapters on regional governance.

Since the 9/11 terrorist attacks and the disaster visited on New Orleans by Hurricane Katrina, intergovernmental relations have become of paramount importance. The federal government and New York City Mayor Giuliani teamed up to organize an effective response to the attack of 9/11. By contrast, the policy response to Katrina was disastrous. What is the proper relationship between the federal government and the cities? Do cities possess the capacity to respond to all problems that may face them? Hurricane Katrina and the terrorist attacks offer a mixed message. With sufficient national attention and effective local leadership, the response can be impressive; without either of these two, large-scale disasters are magnified.

This book is intended to add depth and scope to a main text or to stand alone as a resource book in urban politics and related courses; in particular, it works as a companion to Dennis R. Judd and Todd Swanstrom's *City Politics*, a textbook also published by Longman Publishers. By reading the sources that textbooks and scholarly works draw from, students are able to delve deeper into the vital issues of urban politics. Although the Internet and electronic libraries provide ready access to information about urban politics, students often find these sources overwhelming. Worse, they are lacking in selectivity and context. This volume overcomes these deficiencies. It brings together a selection of readings that represent some of the most important trends and topics in urban scholarship today. These are placed in context by means of editors' essays placed at the beginning of each chapter. These essays explain how each reading fits into the thematic context of the book.

We wish to thank Eric Stano, our Longman political science editor, for championing this book. His interest, ideas, and encouragement were essential to this enterprise. We also wish to thank the professional referees for their helpful comments on this and prior editions: John Bretting, University of Texas;

Michael Coulter, Grove City College; Aubrey Jewett, University of Central Florida; Kenneth Fernandez, University of California; Tim Mead, University of North Carolina; Platon Rigos, University of South Florida; Linda Shafer, Allegheny College; and Allan Wallis, Colorado University.

PAUL KANTOR
DENNIS R. JUDD

# American Urban Politics in a Global Age

# GOVERNING THE METROPOLIS IN THE GLOBAL ERA

In many respects, urban politics in our global era differs dramatically from the past. The politics of local communities everywhere has been reshaped by the accelerating movement of people, capital, information, and goods around the globe. Cities have been thrown into intense interurban competition because investors send their money to wherever it yields the highest profits. People from low-wage parts of the world are moving in large numbers to places that afford opportunity; frequently, this means they move to cities. So many travelers and tourists move about each year that they have become a permanent fixture of the local landscape and the economies of all larger cities. The media, the Internet, and air travel accelerate these movements. Cities and urban regions are at the center of these globalization processes and are deeply affected by them. If "all politics is local," as a congressman famously observed decades ago, the phrase can now be interpreted to mean that the processes of globalization can be understood best by the imprint they leave on local communities.

Yet the politics of cities in the global age do not constitute a clean rupture from the past. The continuities are as striking as the differences, considerable though they may be. Throughout American history, the governance of cities has required urban leaders to nurture and promote local prosperity, and at the same time to manage the conflicts that arise from racial, ethnic, and social diversity. In the global age, as in the past, America's urban politics is driven in equal measure by an economic and a political logic.[1] Economic logic requires elected officials to use governmental authority and resources to promote local prosperity; political logic requires them to attend to the demands of the many interest groups that participate in the democratic process. Successful urban leaders become adept at balancing these two imperatives.

The logic of the marketplace treats cities solely as locations for private economic activity—commerce, industry, finance, land investment, and jobs. The economic behavior of business and entrepreneurs is rarely, if ever, influenced significantly by a concern for the public at large because the discipline of the market does not reward—and may actually penalize—business for doing so. Aside from occasional philanthropy, citizens do not look to the marketplace and business to address the problems of society; ultimately, the business of business is to make profits.

1

The political logic of democratic institutions motivates public officials to maintain and expand political support for what they do; otherwise, they will not remain in office for long. City governments are mechanisms for arbitrating among the groups and factions that make up the local polity, a task as difficult today as it ever was in the past. Democratic procedures invest those who govern with the legitimacy to act in the name of citizens collectively. Governmental authority springs from the right to "make and apply decisions that are binding upon any and all segments of society."[2] At the same time that city officials must satisfy investors, they must also satisfy voters. City officials can preserve their claim to authority only as long as they seem sufficiently responsive to a large enough proportion of the urban population.

Balancing economic and political imperatives is an extremely challenging task in the global era. On one hand, the competition for business and investment of every kind forces public officials to give high priority to policies that will keep them connected to global circuits of investment and capital. These priorities can be read by observing the transformation of city skylines. In recent decades, restored waterfronts and historic buildings, gleaming office towers, luxury hotels, convention centers, sports stadiums—and the list goes on—have sprung up in central cities everywhere. In the suburbs it is, more often, big-box stores, shopping malls, and office campuses. Much of this infrastructure has been underwritten, in part, by public subsidies. Such activities draw critical comments in the letters sections of local newspapers because it often appears that local governments do little else but support physical development.

On the other hand, a multiethnic metropolis has emerged that requires a high degree of political dexterity to manage the demands made by various groups. In recent decades, minorities have become increasingly incorporated into local politics. This is a historic development because it helps to channel demands and grievances into the political system and away from the streets. Part of the bargain is that the political system must at least give the appearance of being representative and democratic. The extreme fragmentation of governments within metropolitan areas complicates governance. It is impossible to speak of a metropolitan community. There are many communities. Some groups will become incorporated into the politics; others will meet opposition and hostility. One of the great challenges of the global era is how to effectively govern metropolitan regions that are politically divided.

But some urban residents seem to be opting out of the demands of governance altogether by retreating from the public realm into protected, privatized enclaves. Enclaves have proliferated in suburbs just as they have in central cities. A large proportion of urban residents commute from subdivisions, gated communities, townhouse developments, and condominium complexes to high-rise downtown office buildings or suburban office parks, drive to enclosed malls and mall complexes for shopping, and commute to entertainment and tourist bubbles to enjoy themselves.[3] For many urban residents, the urban experience has turned into a series of enclosures, each connected by a transportation corridor.

Globalization has intensified competition among cities, quickened the pace of immigration, and changed spatial relationships within metropolitan areas.

Each of these developments has reshaped the politics of the metropolis, bringing in its wake problems as well as opportunities. The service-sector employment of the globalized economy has contributed to the revival of some central cities and made up for the loss of industrial jobs—but has also brought about high levels of inequality. Immigrants have been essential to the growth of metropolitan economies—but they have also complicated the task of governance. The new urban form has made the suburbs racially and ethnically diverse—but the metropolis is also being fractured into a complex enclave geography. These are the issues of the globalized metropolis.

It is important to note, however, that the issues of the global era are not as different as one might suppose. The politics of growth, governance, and urban space always have been central features of America's urban politics; they are not peculiar to the global age.

# The Globalized City in Historical Perspective

If we place today's urban politics in historical context, the differences as well as the continuities come into focus. During the nineteenth century, fierce interurban competition provided a main dynamic of urban politics. Local elites actively promoted town growth and shaped their circumstances. They were indefatigable promoters of local growth because they instinctively understood that some cities—but not all—would prosper in the market system that was emerging during the preindustrial age. Before industrialization, the major obstacles to local economic growth were physical barriers that impeded the exchange of goods between a rural hinterland and the city, and between the city and other commercial centers. With the coming of railroads in mid-century, competition among cities became truly national in scope. Cities everywhere, big or small, new or old, could use railroad lines to penetrate their hinterland in the expectation that they could gather up the trade of the back country and channel it through to their own commercial streets. Individual cities, as public corporations, provided massive assistance to railroad companies that agreed to build connecting lines.

There is a close parallel with the politics of growth in today's cities. As in an earlier era, today's civic boosters are fired with the conviction that the fate of their cities cannot be left to chance. This time, rather than helping to build railroads, cities have expended great resources to build an infrastructure to support the economic sectors of the global economy. They also market themselves through such events as auto races, music festivals, and special museum exhibits. These ventures may be expensive, but urban leaders realize they cannot afford to stand on the sidelines watching other cities grab a bigger share of the global tourism industry.

The emergence of mass political participation introduced a second fault line into the politics of cities in the late nineteenth century; indeed, by late century the pressures of governance had replaced interurban competition as the main dynamic in local politics. In part, this momentous change occurred because the urban hierarchy had become well defined, and individual cities occupied unique niches within it. Labor, capital, and transportation links converged at the center of industrial cities. So compelling were the competitive advantages of larger central cities that business and investment activities became firmly anchored there, and were not going to be easily dislodged. Chicago became a powerhouse in meat-packing, agricultural commodities, and diverse manufacturing; later, Detroit emerged as the dominant center for automobile manufacturing, whereas Pitts-burgh specialized in steel production. The economic security of cities became relatively stable. At the same time, the immigrant floodtide that made prosperity possible guaranteed that governance would become a pressing priority.

A rapidly expanding urban electorate became an enduring fixture in the poli-tics of cities. This development radically changed the complexion of local poli-tics. By the 1840s, property qualifications to vote were abolished almost every-where, a reform that enhanced the influence of immigrant voters. After the Civil War, city populations exploded when waves of immigrants from abroad and mi-grants from rural areas came in search of jobs in the factories. Wide-open politi-cal struggles began to replace oligarchic control by business elites. A new gener-ation of politicians learned how to mobilize the urban electorate by buying loyalty and favors with cash, jobs, contracts, and other material inducements. Whatever their merits or shortcomings, the machines gave the immigrants a voice in local politics. This new-found influence became the lightening rod for a reform movement dedicated to restoring the influence of the white, Protestant, middle-class electorate.

The parallels with urban politics today are plain to see. An immigrant flood-tide has made cities and urban regions more racially and ethnically diverse than ever before. A power struggle is taking place between newly arrived immigrants, African Americans, and middle- and upper-class residents. But there are also sig-nificant differences between the industrial and the global era. In the earlier pe-riod, most of the immigrants crowded into the industrial cities; now they are lo-cating throughout urban regions. Today, jobs and populations are widely dispersed.

It is important to note, as well, that the regional character of urban politics to-day contrasts sharply with the metropolitan politics of the twentieth century. In the years after World War II, images of race, poverty, crime, and slums came to symbolize the inner cities, while at the same time the suburbs became identified, in the popular imagination, with tranquil subdivisions with cul-de-sacs and green expanses of lawn. Two great migrations created the stark divide between city and suburb: the movement of millions of African Americans from the South to north-ern cities, and white flight to the suburbs. In the two decades between the cen-suses of 1950 to 1970, approximately five million blacks left the South for north-ern cities; over the same period, suburban populations grew by 35 million people. The movements into and out of the cities created a nearly unbridgeable social chasm that threatened to rend the fabric of American society. The civil dis-order that swept through cities and the segregation that separated blacks in the central cities from whites in the suburbs became enduring symbols of the urban crisis of the twentieth century.

Cities sought help from the federal government to remedy the problems that came in the wake of their declining fortunes. From the present perspective, it may be difficult to recall a time when strong political support existed for programs to help cities. From Franklin Roosevelt's election in 1932 until its decline and final collapse in the 1980s, the New Deal coalition counted on blacks and blue-collar voters in the inner cities to help send Democrats to Congress and to the presidency. For a few decades, urban leaders looked to the federal government rather than to a politics of growth to solve their problems. This strategy fell apart when federal programs dried up in the 1980s, which only exacerbated the problems cities already faced when industrial jobs began to move elsewhere. In the years since, cities have returned to a locally driven politics of urban development with a vengeance; indeed, this competition has become a hallmark of the global age.

Cities occupied distinct niches in the urban hierarchy of the industrial age. Globalization has torn that system apart. New technologies in computers, communications, materials, production, and business organization have enabled businesses to disperse many of their activities to far-flung locations in suburbia, the Sunbelt, and foreign production sites. Many traditional industrial activities that once were undertaken in cities, such as steel making and garment and appliance manufacturing, have migrated to lower-cost locations in foreign countries in the Asian rim, the Caribbean, Mexico, and South and Central America. The so-called global office has become commonplace, a manifestation of the fact that large corporations have concentrated their headquarters' activities in major cities while decentralizing all other business operations to a multitude of sites.

Globalization has catalyzed massive population movements. More immigrants came to the United States in the 1990s than in any previous decade in the nation's history, and the flow is certain to continue well into the twenty-first century. The social and political effects of large-scale population movements are dramatically evident in big global cities such as Miami, New York, Chicago, and San Francisco. In these cities—and even in some smaller places—the new immigration has taken place in tandem with the rise of a highly mobile, very affluent global elite.

The global economy has also favored investments in postindustrial business sectors such as finance, real estate, insurance, and a variety of service activities. In global cities all over the world, layer upon layer of highly educated white-collar professionals—for example, corporate managers, management consultants, legal experts, accountants, computer specialists, financial analysts, media and public relations specialists—work in clusters of downtown skyscrapers.[4]

Cities of all sizes, including those in the suburbs, must compete for the sectors of the new economy; as in the past, they can ill afford to leave their fortunes to chance. Central cities commonly try to attract investment by offering such lures as historic tax credits, tax subsidies, and public improvements; surrounding suburbs try to outdo one another to influence the location of malls and office parks. To attract the most affluent workers in the globalized service economy, all cities must offer a high level of urban amenities.[5] At the same time, all but the most homogeneous and prosperous local communities must manage a complex politics marked by racial, ethnic, and class differences. The tensions between the economic and political imperatives of urban governance shape the unique contours of urban politics in the global era.

# The Political Contours of the Global Era

To trace the main contours of today's urban politics, we have organized *American Urban Politics in a Global Era* into three parts. Part One contains selections highlighting how the economic imperative drives contemporary urban politics. Part Two is made up of selections dealing with the governance imperative: How are the politics of race, space, and ethnicity negotiated in contemporary cities and urban areas? Finally, the selections in Part Three comment on the fragmentation of power and governmental authority in America's urban regions. In the remainder of this essay, we summarize the major topics the selections are meant to address.

## Part One: Globalization and the Economic Imperative   *driving urban politics*

### The Politics of Urban Development

The globalized economy has precipitated a competitive struggle for economic survival that has enormous implications for local politics and public policy. Individual cities must try to find a place within the new urban system. The competitive environment of globalization makes the arguments advanced by the urban scholar Paul Peterson highly relevant. Peterson maintains that economic or market standing is so fundamentally important to cities that citizens should do nothing that might compromise the possibility of achieving economic success. In Peterson's formulation, all residents of a city share a "unitary interest" in promoting growth; accordingly, city officials should adopt policies that make the city a good environment for business and affluent residents.[6]

Whatever arguments or counterarguments may rage over Peterson's view, the political leaders of cities generally act as if they agree with it. Cities are constrained to emphasize economic development because of the place they occupy in the U.S. intergovernmental system, which forces them to compete with other cities, and because of the powerful role that investors play in the ability of cities to borrow and spend. Cities are expected to provide a high level of services and also to promote local prosperity, yet they rely on property owners and investors for their revenues. Because there is no easy way for public officials to escape the economic imperative, it is the axis around which city politics rotates. Accordingly, in virtually all cities the most reliable allies of city hall are found in the business community, and vice versa. No other political coalition comes together as often or in so many cities as the city hall–business alliance.

### Cities in the International Marketplace

In the global era, the competition among cities takes on a particular shape, with cities dependent on the decisions made by highly mobile, transnational corporations. Globalization keeps local officials fixated on economic matters for the simple reason that the rules of the game are constantly changing. Yesterday it was manufacturing; today it is a complex mix of services and the economic benefits flowing from tourism and culture. All cities try to get their share, but the options available to them vary greatly from city to city as well as from one country to another.

There is great variation in the policies that cities pursue—and that are available to them—in this struggle. In the United States, virtually all cities offer a mix of tax benefits, direct subsidies, and investment in public amenities to lure investors. In part, these policies reflect the fact that U.S. cities are left on their own; they cannot expect much help from the federal government. In other countries, direct assistance from the national government is available, and therefore a high degree of coordination of development efforts is normal. It is difficult to identify a mix of policies or governmental arrangements that work best for attracting capital. If pure markets were the answer, cities in the United States would be beating all comers. If coordinated government intervention worked best, all U.S. cities would be losers. Evidence seems to show there is no "best" model; every city arrives at the solution that maximizes its unique advantages and that fits its particular context.[7] Even though the international marketplace drives urban economies, local choices matter.

### The Political Economy of Urban Culture

The breakup of the old urban pattern does not guarantee that the racial and ethnic segregation that has long characterized urban America will become a thing of the past. Within cities, affluent downtown and gentrified neighborhoods are sharply separated from the neighborhoods inhabited by the urban poor. This patterns shows up most starkly in the global cities and, in fact, in all cities that have attracted highly paid workers connected to the global economy. High-rise condominium and townhouse developments sometimes sit only a block or two from neighborhoods with extreme levels of poverty.

High levels of social polarization are especially obvious in the cities tied most closely to the global economy. Large global cities attract an extraordinarily diverse profile of immigrants.[8] Jobs are the lure. The concentration of multinational businesses, financial services corporations, and the businesses connected to them draw well-educated workers from all over the globe. But the greatest demand for jobs (at least expressed in numbers) is found at the other end of the labor market. Lower-status service workers are indispensable to the working of a global city. Clerical workers, janitors and cashiers, nannies, cooks and busboys, maintenance and security workers, hotel maids, and a multitude of personal-service specialists from masseuses to personal shoppers and dog-walkers: Jobs at this end of the employment structure are taken by immigrants and minorities disproportionately. Though the consequences are amplified in cities, these employment patterns have contributed to rising inequality in U.S. society.

Affluent empty-nesters and young professionals are moving back downtown. Central cities are once again becoming hotspots for culture, nightlife, and fun. Urban culture has become fundamental to local economic prosperity because the affluent professionals who work in the globalized economy will not choose to live in a dull place. Urban culture is also political because it is nurtured by local policies meant to support it—especially the provision of a high level of public amenities. In sum, urban culture has become a key component of the local political economy and of local politics.

## Part Two: Governing the Multiethnic Metropolis

### The Politics of Space, Race, and Ethnicity: The Cities

Issues of race and ethnicity became contentious, even explosive, issues in the 1960s, and they have remained crucially important ever since. In the 1960s and 1970s, mayors looked to Washington in the hope that social and urban programs financed by the federal government could help them cope with the racial turmoil and social problems that confronted them. Since the withdrawal of the federal government from the cities in the 1980s, their task has been challenging, to say the least. Maintaining a minimal degree of social cohesion has become a delicate task.

Cities are contested arenas within which groups jostle for political influence and advantage. In central cities, a politics made of a complex mixture of engagement, negotiation, and marginalization has unfolded. The old politics that pitted white-dominated power structures against African-American aspirations has been replaced by struggles among various groups fighting for a share of the pie. In some cities, the "insider" group is just as likely to be nonwhite as not, and the ability of ethnic groups to cooperate is variable.

The tensions between economic and political logic guarantees that the policies pursued by city governments will often be inconsistent and even contradictory. Affirmative action policies in hiring and contracting (to the extent accepted by courts) may coexist with policies that have the effect of segregating affluent residents from everyone else. Competition to control valued spaces adds to this. High-end residential and tourist enclaves exist in virtually all cities whatever their racial and ethnic makeup, and policies to promote such developments are nearly universal. Issues concerning jobs, housing, neighborhoods, and even routine city services are often infused with conflicts over group identity, national origin, race, and class.

### The Politics of Space, Race, and Ethnicity: The Suburbs

Immigrants from Asia, Latin America, the Caribbean, and Eastern and Central Europe now constitute a substantial and growing proportion of the residents of America's cities and of its suburbs. The political consequences of this development are far-reaching. For decades, the urban crisis was defined as the segregation between blacks in the central cities and whites in the suburbs. What is different now is that the tensions of urban society have spread to the suburbs; conflicts over race and ethnicity are no longer located primarily in central cities. They take place on many different territorial scales.

Many suburbs are becoming multiethnic, and in some of these a politics has evolved that looks similar to the central cities. The movement of racial and ethnic minorities to the suburbs seems to promise a greater degree of racial and ethnic integration than in the past. But the overall pattern of metropolitan growth seems to be going in a different direction, with affluent residents moving into privatized enclaves that separate and protect them from ethnic minorities and lower-income residents. Wherever this happens, political incorporation tends to be replaced by political escape. It is difficult to predict if this impulse will define the metropolitan future because the construction of enclaves and some degree of residential integration are happening at the same time.

## The New Politics of Space

Are metropolitan regions becoming more or less segregated? On one hand, it is easy to observe the proliferation of barriers and privatized spaces. Neighborhoods and the downtowns of large cities are often demarcated and defended from surrounding land uses that might seem threatening. The barriers that protect downtowns come in various forms, including office towers, shopping centers, entertainment districts, and tourist enclaves. Visitors to central cities now commonly fly into an airport, take a taxi or a light rail to a downtown hotel, and stay within the well-defined tourist area, never seeing or even becoming aware of the larger city around them.

In seeming contradiction to these trends, the old patterns of residential segregation seem to be breaking down. In the 1990s, Asians and Latinos settled in the suburbs in large numbers, but a large proportion of both groups now live in ethnic enclaves that are more separated from whites than before.[9] Residential segregation levels for Latinos and Asians increased slightly in the 1990s,[10] but these groups were less segregated in the suburbs than in the central cities.[11] Some suburbs and enclaves are segregated, but others provide housing opportunities for minorities and immigrants, especially if they earn middle-class incomes.

It is difficult to read the spatial future of the suburbs from present patterns. There can be no doubt that suburbs have opened to minorities and to the poor. The immigration of Asians, Latinos, and other groups has made most metropolitan areas, including their suburbs, multiethnic rather than biracial. For example, during the 1990s two parallel streams moved to Orange County, California, just outside Los Angeles: highly educated professionals and foreign-born immigrants. The two streams could hardly have been more different: high-income families making more than $150,000 per year jumped by 184 percent in the county, but at the same time the number of foreign-born immigrants increased by 48 percent.[12] Commenting on these trends, a noted demographer said the county could go in two directions: either a "mostly gated-community-type mentality" or "Immigrants start integrating into middle-class areas, so you have a blended suburbia."[13]

## Part Three: Governing the Fractured Metropolis

### Urban Sprawl and the New Regionalism

In recent years, urban sprawl has blossomed as an important public policy issue. But the sprawled metropolis has spawned a set of highly publicized issues including traffic congestion and gridlock, uncontrolled development, air pollution, the loss of open space and farmland, and polluted water. Urban scholars have long been preoccupied with tracing another problem long associated with metropolitan decentralization—the governmental fragmentation of America's urban regions. In the past, reformers who were concerned about regional problems advocated the regional consolidation of governments, but attempts to achieve this goal failed decade after decade. Though a few people still hold out hope for comprehensive reform, more realistic reformers have embraced the modest goal of achieving cooperative agreements among governments.

The New Urbanism offers another remedy for sprawled development. For the New Urbanists, much of the solution for tract housing developments, big-box retailing, and expressways are planned developments that mix uses and design traffic grids, streets, and neighborhoods to human scale. But it should be noted that not everyone agrees that sprawl is a problem at all; if it is not a problem, it does not need fixing. For them, sprawl is little more than an expression of people's desires for adequate housing and amenities, as is the character of urban design. The logic that drives both is the marketplace.

## Federal-City Relations and the Capacity to Govern

The slow and inadequate response to the devastation wrought on New Orleans by Hurricane Katrina in August 2005 raised important questions about the complicated governmental system of the United States. The terrorist attacks of September 11, 2001, also raised the alarm. It is not only regions that are fragmented; the governmental structure of the nation is as well, and as the disaster revealed, it was difficult for national, state, and local authorities to work together. What is the proper relationship between the federal government and the cities? Do cities possess the capacity to respond to all problems that may face them? Since the withdrawal of federal urban programs in the 1980s, cities have been on their own. At the same time, there are signs of creeping federal regulation and mandates, but often without adequate funding to assist local governments in meeting their obligations. For the most part, local governments have stepped up to the daunting challenge posed by of revitalizing local economies at a time of limited federal assistance. But large-scale disasters pose a different kind of problem that may require a closer relationship between cities and federal government. The nation's federal system is in flux, and its future evolution will dramatically shape the capacity of cities to govern.

## NOTES

1. Todd Swanstrom, "Semisovereign Cities: The Politics of Urban Development," *Polity* 21 (Fall 1988): 83–110.
2. Eric Nordlinger, *On the Autonomy of the Democratic State* (Cambridge, MA: Harvard University Press, 1981).
3. Dennis R. Judd, "Enclosure, Community, and Public Life," in Dan A. Chekki (ed.), *Research in Community Sociology: New Communities in a Changing World* (Greenwhich, CN: JAI Press, 1996), pp. 217–238.

4. Saskia Sassen, *The Global City: New York, London, Tokyo,* 2nd ed. (Princeton, NJ: Princeton University Press, 2001).

5. Richard Florida, *The Rise of the Creative Class* (New York: Basic Books, 2002).

6. Paul Peterson, *City Limits* (Chicago: University of Chicago Press, 1981), p. 22.

7. Hank H. V. Savitch and Paul Kantor, *Cities in the International Marketplace* (Princeton, NJ: Princeton University Press, 2002).

8. Mark Abrahamson, *Global Cities* (New York: Oxford University Press, 2004).

9. John R. Logan, "The New Ethnic Enclaves in America's Suburbs," a report by the Lewis Mumford Center for Comparative Urban and Regional Research (Albany, NY: 2002), pp. 1–2.

10. Ibid., p. 253.

11. William A. V. Clark and Sarah A. Blue, "Race, Class, and Segregation Patterns in U.S. Immigrant Gateway Cities," *Urban Affairs Review* 39, 6 (2004): 667–688.

12. Jim Hinch and Ronald Campbell, "Gated Enclaves One Future for Orange County," *Orange County Register*, May 15, 2002 (www. ocregister. com).

13. Ibid., quoting William Frey, a demographer in the Milken Institute of Los Angeles.

# CHAPTER 1

# THE POLITICS OF URBAN DEVELOPMENT

## ENTREPRENEURIAL CITIES

Cities are commonly referred to as if they were people, capable of independent thought and action. Such a construction is more than a mere rhetorical flourish because, in fact, as public corporations, cities are invested with significant public powers that can be used for a variety of purposes. As Paul E. Peterson points out in Selection 1, there are constant debates about the "public interest" that cities ought to pursue. Some people might demand that cities spend their public resources on "redistributive" policies designed to help those most in need. Others might promote the view that city governments should do little more than provide the services necessary to make the city a healthy and functional environment. Peterson's view is that cities must at all costs avoid policies that redistribute resources from businesses and affluent residents to those with fewer resources. Instead, he argues, cities have no choice but to support policies that will stimulate economic growth. Such policies, he says, respond to a "unitary interest" that all urban residents hold in local economic vitality: "It is in the city's interest . . . to help sustain a high-quality local infrastructure generally attractive to all commerce and industry." This logic dictates that even the social health of a city depends upon its economic prosperity: "When a city is able to export its products, service industries prosper, labor is in greater demand . . . tax revenues increase, city services can be improved, donations to charitable organizations become more generous, and the social and cultural life of the city is enhanced."

In Peterson's analysis, the leaders of cities cannot leave economic growth to chance because cities compete with one another. City governments are unable to control the movement of capital and labor across borders. In contrast to the national government, they lack the authority to regulate immigration, currency, prices, and wages, or the import or export of goods and services. City governments, therefore, are constrained to compete for capital investment or suffer decline in the economic well-being of the community. Cities occupy a particular space, but businesses can move; therefore, if the local business environment is not pleasing to them, investors and businesses will go elsewhere. This logic drives cities to minimize taxes, avoid expensive regulations, and offer a variety of subsidies to business. If they heed Peterson's injunction, politicians will resist the clamor of all political interests that might compromise the preferences of business in any way.

The book from which the Peterson selection is taken ignited a controversy among urban scholars—a controversy that has not died down completely even after more than two decades. (Peterson's book was published in 1981.) Many scholars took Peterson to task for his apparent assertion that growth benefits everyone. Others accused him of ignoring the complexities of local politics by pointing out that the mix of local policies differs substantially from city to city depending on population demographics, the political influence and the degree of political participation of various groups, and governmental powers and structures. The importance of local prosperity is likely to always be high on the agenda, but politicians must also mobilize sufficient political support to remain in office; in other words, they must win elections. Mayors must often perform a delicate balancing act that requires them to protect and enhance the economic base of a city while at the same time mobilizing sufficient political support to remain in office and implement their policies.

A literature on "urban regimes" has introduced a much more subtle and nuanced understanding of the relationship between political and business leaders. Local regimes are comprised of both political and economic actors who constantly negotiate settlements among political factions and interests. As described by Clarence N. Stone in Selection 2, the two most powerful components of urban regimes include city hall—the officials who are most motivated by electoral concerns—and the city's business elite. Governmental officials lack the resources to do much on their own. Likewise, the business community requires a local government capable of maintaining a level of amenities and services necessary for a pleasant urban environment. In Clarence Stone's account of politics in Atlanta, he notes that, "What makes governance in Atlanta effective is not the formal machinery of government, but rather the informal partnership between city hall and the downtown business elite. This informal partnership and the way it operates constitute the city's regime; it is the same means through which major policy decisions are made." Note that Stone's use of the term *partnership* suggests cooperation rather than control. If regime participants learn to work together to accomplish mutual goals, all are empowered in the sense that they can accomplish things that none of them working alone can do.

The interurban competition noted by Peterson is a basic fact of life in the global era. But competition among cities goes back a long way. The spirit of this intercity rivalry is captured in Selection 3 by Richard C. Wade, who portrays the commercial struggles among frontier cities in the first decades of the nineteenth century. In this selection, Wade notes that in these contests, the rewards for winning might be considerable, and the penalties for losing could be devastating: "the economically strongest survived and flourished . . . smaller places were trampled in the process, some being swallowed up by ambitious neighbors, others being overwhelmed before they could attain a challenging position." In the attempts to attract new businesses and residents, local boosters bragged about their (alleged) cultural sophistication, natural advantages, and the energy of local entrepreneurs and residents.

Things have not changed much. In Selection 4, Mark Douglas Lowes explains why Vancouver, British Columbia, has been willing to spend large amounts of public money to host an annual Indy Car Race. In his account, the media coverage of the race portrays Vancouver has playing on a "world stage," an image reinforced by the lifestyles and cash brought by famous teams, drivers, and their sponsors and promoters. Lowes points out that "in the climate of relentless interurban competition, spending on image-making and public relations is often perceived to be as important as spending on urban infrastructure and other tangible upgrades." The importance of an Indy race expresses this priority because it plays up an image of fun and lifestyle that has become so important to Vancouver's downtown and its regional economy. Cities throughout North America are fighting for a similar image.

# 1

## *Paul E. Peterson*

## THE INTERESTS OF THE LIMITED CITY

Like all social structures, cities have interests. Just as we can speak of union interests, judicial interests, and the interests of politicians, so we can speak of the interests of that structured system of social interactions we call a city. Citizens, politicians, and academics are all quite correct in speaking freely of the interests of cities.[1]

## Defining the City Interest

By a city's interest, I do not mean the sum total of the interests of those individuals living in the city. For one thing, these are seldom, if ever, known. The wants, needs, and preferences of residents continually change, and few surveys of public opinion in particular cities have ever been taken. Moreover, the residents of a city often have discordant interests. Some want more parkland and better schools; others want better police protection and lower taxes. Some want an elaborated highway system; others wish to keep cars out of their neighborhood. Some want more inexpensive, publicly subsidized housing; others wish to remove the public housing that exists. Some citizens want improved welfare assistance for the unemployed and dependent; others wish to cut drastically all

such programs of public aid. Some citizens want rough-tongued ethnic politicians in public office; others wish that municipal administration were a gentleman's calling. Especially in large cities, the cacophony of competing claims by
diverse class, race, ethnic, and occupational groups makes impossible the determination of any overall city interest—any public interest, if you like—by
compiling all the demands and desires of individual city residents.

Some political scientists have attempted to discover the overall urban public interest by summing up the wide variety of individual interests. The earlier
work of Edward Banfield, still worth examination, is perhaps the most persuasive effort of this kind.[2] He argued that urban political processes—or at least
those in Chicago—allowed for the expression of nearly all the particular interests within the city. Every significant interest was represented by some economic firm or voluntary association, which had a stake in trying to influence
those public policies that touched its vested interests. After these various
groups and firms had debated and contended, the political leader searched for
a compromise that took into account the vital interests of each, and worked out
a solution all could accept with some satisfaction. The leader's own interest in
sustaining his political power dictated such a strategy.

Banfield's argument is intriguing, but few people would identify public
policies as being in the interest of the city simply because they have been formulated according to certain procedures. The political leader might err in his
judgment; the interests of important but politically impotent groups might
never get expressed; or the consequences of a policy might in the long run be
disastrous for the city. Moreover, most urban policies are not hammered out after great controversy, but are the quiet product of routine decision making.
How does one evaluate which of these are in the public interest? Above all, this
mechanism for determining the city's interest provides no standpoint for evaluating the substantive worth of urban policies. Within Banfield's framework,
whatever urban governments do is said to be in the interest of their communities. But the concept of city interest is used most persuasively when there are
calls for reform or innovation. It is a term used to evaluate existing programs
and to discriminate between promising and undesirable new ones. To equate
the interests of cities with what cities are doing is to so impoverish the term as
to make it quite worthless.

The economist Charles Tiebout employs a second approach to the identification of city interests.[3] Unlike Banfield, he does not see the city's interests as a
mere summation of individual interests but as something which can be ascribed
to the entity, taken as a whole. As an economist, Tiebout is hardly embarrassed
by such an enterprise, because in ascribing interests to cities his work parallels
both those orthodox economists who state that firms have an interest in maximizing profits and those welfare economists who claim that politicians have an
interest in maximizing votes. Of course, they state only that their model will assume that firms and politicians behave in such a way, but insofar as they believe
their model has empirical validity, they in fact assert that those constrained by
the businessman's or politician's role must pursue certain interests. And so does
Tiebout when he says that communities seek to attain the optimum size for the

efficient delivery of the bundle of services the local government produces. In his words, "Communities below the optimum size seek to attract new residents to lower average costs. Those above optimum size do just the opposite. Those at an optimum try to keep their populations constant."[4]

Tiebout's approach is in many ways very attractive. By asserting a strategic objective that the city is trying to maximize—optimum size—Tiebout identifies an overriding interest which can account for specific policies the city adopts. He provides a simple analytical tool that will account for the choices cities make, without requiring complex investigations into citizen preferences and political mechanisms for identifying and amalgamating the same. Moreover, he provides a criterion for determining whether a specific policy is in the interest of the city—does it help achieve optimum size? Will it help the too small city grow? Will it help the too big city contract? Will it keep the optimally sized city in equilibrium? Even though the exact determination of the optimum size cannot presently be scientifically determined in all cases, the criterion does provide a useful guide for prudential decision making.

The difficulty with Tiebout's assumption is that he does not give very good reasons for its having any plausibility. When most economists posit a certain form of maximizing behavior, there is usually a good commonsense reason for believing the person in that role will have an interest in pursuing this strategic objective. When orthodox economists say that businessmen maximize profits, it squares with our understanding in everyday life that people engage in commercial enterprises for monetary gain. The more they make, the better they like it. The same can be said of those welfare economists who say politicians maximize votes. The assumption, though cynical, is in accord with popular belief—and therefore once again has a certain plausibility.

By contrast, Tiebout's optimum size thesis diverges from what most people think cities are trying to do. Of course, smaller communities are often seeking to expand—boosterism may be the quintessential characteristic of small-town America. Yet Tiebout takes optimum size, not growth or maximum size, as the strategic objective. And when Tiebout discusses the big city that wishes to shrink to optimum size, his cryptic language is quite unconvincing. "The case of the city that is too large and tries to get rid of residents is more difficult to imagine," he confesses. Even more, he concedes that "no alderman in his right political mind would ever admit that the city is too big." "Nevertheless," he continues, "economic forces are at work to push people out of it. Every resident who moves to the suburbs to find better schools, more parks, and so forth, is reacting, in part, against the pattern the city has to offer."[5] In this crucial passage Tiebout speaks neither of local officials nor of local public policies. Instead, he refers to "economic forces" that may be beyond the control of the city and of "every resident," each of whom may be pursuing his own interests, not that of the community at large.

The one reason Tiebout gives for expecting cities to pursue optimum size is to lower the average cost of public goods. If public goods can be delivered most efficiently at some optimum size, then migration of residents will occur until that size has been reached. In one respect Tiebout is quite correct: local governments must concern themselves with operating local services as efficiently as possible in order to protect the city's economic interests. But there is little evidence that there is an optimum size at which services can be delivered with greatest efficiency. And even if such an optimum did exist, it could be realized only if migration occurred among residents who paid equal amounts in local taxes. In the more likely situation, residents pay variable prices for public services (for example, the amount paid in local property taxes varies by the value of the property). Under these circumstances, increasing size to the optimum does not reduce costs to residents unless newcomers pay at least as much in taxes as the marginal increase in costs their arrival imposes on city government.[6] Conversely, if a city needs to lose population to reach the optimum, costs to residents will not decline unless the exiting population paid less in taxes than was the marginal cost of providing them government services. In most big cities losing population, exactly the opposite is occurring. Those who pay more in taxes than they receive in services are the emigrants. Tiebout's identification of city interests with optimum size, while suggestive, fails to take into account the quality as well as the quantity of the local population.

The interests of cities are neither a summation of individual interests nor the pursuit of optimum size. Instead, policies and programs can be said to be in the interest of cities whenever the policies maintain or enhance the economic position, social prestige, or political power of the city, taken as a whole.[7]

Cities have these interests because cities consist of a set of social interactions structured by their location in a particular territorial space. Any time that social interactions come to be structured into recurring patterns, the structure thus formed develops an interest in its own maintenance and enhancement. It is in that sense that we speak of the interests of an organization, the interests of the system, and the like. To be sure, within cities, as within any other structure, one can find diverse social roles, each with its own set of interests. But these varying role interests, as divergent and competing as they may be, do not distract us from speaking of the overall interests of the larger structural entity.[8]

The point can be made less abstractly. A school system is a structured form of social action, and therefore it has an interest in maintaining and improving its material resources, its prestige, and its political power. Those policies or events which have such positive effects are said to be in the interest of the school system. An increase in state financial aid or the winning of the basketball tournament are events that, respectively, enhance the material well-being and the prestige of a school system and are therefore in its interest. In ordinary speech this is taken for granted, even when we also recognize that teachers, pupils, principals, and board members may have contrasting interests as members of differing role-groups within the school.

Although social roles performed within cities are numerous and conflicting, all are structured by the fact that they take place in a specific spatial location that falls within the jurisdiction of some local government. All members of the city thus come to share an interest in policies that affect the well-being of that territory. Policies which enhance the desirability or attractiveness of the territory are in the city's interest, because they benefit all residents—in their role as residents of the community. Of course, in any of their other social roles, residents of the city may be adversely affected by the policy. The Los Angeles dope peddler—in his role as peddler—hardly benefits from a successful drive to remove hard drugs from the city. On the other hand, as a resident of the city, he benefits from a policy that enhances the attractiveness of the city as a locale in which to live and work. In determining whether a policy is in the interest of a city, therefore, one does not consider whether it has a positive or negative effect on the total range of social interactions of each and every individual. That is an impossible task. To know whether a policy is in a city's interest, one has to consider only the impact on social relationships insofar as they are structured by their taking place within the city's boundaries.

An illustration from recent policy debates over the future of our cities reveals that it is exactly with this meaning that the notion of a city's interest is typically used. The tax deduction that homeowners take on their mortgage interest payments should be eliminated, some urbanists have argued. The deduction has not served the interests of central cities, because it has provided a public subsidy for families who purchase suburban homes. Quite clearly, elimination of this tax deduction is not in the interest of those central city residents who wish to purchase a home in the suburbs. It is not in the interest of those central city homeowners (which in some cities may even form a majority of the voting population), who would then be called upon to pay higher federal taxes. But the policy might very well improve the rental market in the central city, thereby stimulating its economy—and it is for this reason that the proposal has been defended as being in the interest of central cities.

To say that people understand what, generally, is in the interest of cities does not eliminate debate over policy alternatives in specific instances. The notion of city interest can be extremely useful, even though its precise application in specific contexts may be quite problematic. In any policy context one cannot easily assert that one "knows" what is in the interest of cities, whether or not the residents of the city agree. But city residents do know the kind of evidence that must be advanced and the kinds of reasons that must be adduced in order to build a persuasive case that a policy is in the interest of cities. And so do community leaders, mayors, and administrative elites.

# Economic Interests

Cities, like all structured social systems, seek to improve their position in all three of the systems of stratification—economic, social, and political—characteristic of industrial societies. In most cases, improved standing in any one of these systems helps enhance a city's position in the other two. In the short run, to be sure, cities may have to choose among economic gains, social prestige, and political weight. And because different cities may choose alternative objectives, one cannot state any one overarching objective—such as improved property values—that is always the paramount interest of the city. But inasmuch as improved economic or market standing seems to be an objective of great importance to most cities, I shall concentrate on this interest and only discuss in passing the significance of social status and political power.

Cities constantly seek to upgrade their economic standing. Following Weber, I mean by this that cities seek to improve their market position, their attractiveness as a locale for economic activity. In the market economy that characterizes Western society, an advantageous economic position means a competitive edge in the production and distribution of desired commodities relative to other localities. When this is present, cities can export goods and/or services to those outside the boundaries of the community.

Some regional economists have gone so far as to suggest that the welfare of a city is identical to the welfare of its export industry.[9] As exporters expand, the city grows. As they contract, the city declines and decays. The economic reasoning supporting such a conclusion is quite straightforward. When cities produce a good that can be sold in an external market, labor and capital flow into the city to help increase the production of that good. They continue to do so until the external market is saturated—that is, until the marginal cost of production within the city exceeds the marginal value of the good external to the city. Those engaged in the production of the exported good will themselves consume a variety of other goods and services, which other businesses will provide. In addition, subsidiary industries locate in the city either because they help supply the exporting industry, because they can utilize some of its by-products, or because they benefit by some economies of scale provided by its presence. Already, the familiar multiplier is at work. With every increase in the sale of exported commodities, there may be as much as a four- or fivefold increase in local economic activity.

The impact of Boeing Aircraft's market prospects on the economy of the Seattle metropolitan area illustrates the importance of export to regional economies. In the late sixties defense and commercial aircraft contracts declined. Boeing laid off thousands of workmen, the economy of the Pacific Northwest slumped, the unemployed moved elsewhere, and Seattle land values dropped sharply. More recently, Boeing has more than recovered its former position. With rapidly expanding production at Boeing, the metropolitan area is enjoying low unemployment, rapid growth, and dramatically increasing land values.

The same multiplier effect is not at work in the case of goods and services produced for domestic consumption within the territory. What is gained by a producer within the community is expended by other community residents. Residents, in effect, are simply taking in one another's laundry. Unless productivity increases, there is no capacity for expansion.

If this economic analysis is correct, it is only a modest oversimplification to equate the interests of cities with the interests of their export industries. Whatever helps them prosper redounds to the benefit of the community as a whole—perhaps four and five times over. And it is just such an economic analysis that has influenced many local government policies. Especially the smaller towns and cities may provide free land, tax concessions, and favorable utility rates to incoming industries.

The smaller the territory and the more primitive its level of economic development, the more persuasive is this simple export thesis. But other economists have elaborated an alternative growth thesis that is in many ways more persuasive, especially as it relates to larger urban areas. In their view a sophisticated local network of public and private services is the key to long-range economic growth. Since the world economy is constantly changing, the economic viability of any particular export industry is highly variable. As a result, a community dependent on any particular set of export industries will have only an episodic economic future. But with a well-developed infrastructure of services, the city becomes an attractive locale for a wide variety of export industries. As older exporters fade, new exporters take their place and the community continues to prosper. It is in the city's interest, therefore, to help sustain a high-quality local infrastructure generally attractive to all commerce and industry.

I have no way of evaluating the merits of these contrasting economic arguments. What is important in this context is that both see exports as being of great importance to the well-being of a city. One view suggests a need for direct support of the export industry; the other suggests a need only for maintaining a service infrastructure, allowing the market to determine which particular export industry locates in the community. Either one could be the more correct diagnosis for a particular community, at least in the short run. Yet both recognize that the future of the city depends upon exporting local products. When a city is able to export its products, service industries prosper, labor is in greater demand, wages increase, promotional opportunities widen, land values rise, tax revenues increase, city services can be improved, donations to charitable organizations become more generous, and the social and cultural life of the city is enhanced.

To export successfully, cities must make efficient use of the three main factors of production: land, labor, and capital.[10]

## Land

Land is the factor of production that cities control. Yet land is the factor to which cities are bound. It is the fact that cities are spatially defined units whose boundaries seldom change that gives permanence to their interests. City residents come and go, are born and die, and change their tastes and preferences. But the city remains wedded to the land area with which it is blessed (or cursed). And unless it can alter that land area, through annexation or consolidation, it is the long-range value of that land which the city must secure—and which gives a good approximation of how well it is achieving its interests.

Land is an economic resource. Production cannot occur except within some spatial location. And because land varies in its economic potential, so do the economic futures of cities. Historically, the most important variable affecting urban growth has been an area's relationship to land and water routes.

On the eastern coast of the United States, all the great cities had natural harbors that facilitated commercial relations with Europe and other coastal communities. Inland, the great industrial cities all were located on either the Great Lakes or the Ohio River–Mississippi River system. The cities of the West, as Elazar has shown, prospered according to their proximity to East-West trade flows.[11] Denver became the predominant city of the mountain states because it sat at the crossroads of land routes through the Rocky Mountains. Duluth, Minnesota, had only limited potential, even with its Great Lakes location, because it lay north of all major routes to the West.

Access to waterways and other trade routes is not the only way a city's life is structured by its location. Its climate determines the cost and desirability of habitation; its soil affects food production in the surrounding area; its terrain affects drainage, rates of air pollution, and scenic beauty. Of course, the qualities of landscape do not permanently fix a city's fate—it is the intersection of that land and location with the larger national and world economy that is critical. For example, cities controlling access to waterways by straddling natural harbors at one time monopolized the most valuable land in the region, and from that position they dominated their hinterland. But since land and air transport have begun to supplant, not just supplement, water transport, the dominance of these once favored cities has rapidly diminished.

Although the economic future of a city is very much influenced by external forces affecting the value of its land, the fact that a city has control over the use of its land gives it some capacity for influencing that future. Although there are constitutional limits to its authority, the discretion available to a local government in determining land use remains the greatest arena for the exercise of local autonomy. Cities can plan the use of local space; cities have the power of eminent domain; through zoning laws cities can restrict all sorts of land uses; and cities can regulate the size, content, and purpose of buildings constructed within their boundaries. Moreover, cities can provide public services in such a way as to encourage certain kinds of land use. Sewers, gas lines, roads, bridges, tunnels, playgrounds, schools, and parks all impinge on the use of land in the surrounding area. Urban politics is above all the politics of land use, and it is easy to see why. Land is the factor of production over which cities exercise the greatest control.

## Labor

To its land area the city must attract not only capital but productive labor. Yet local governments in the United States are very limited in their capacities to control the flow of these factors. Lacking the more direct controls of nation-states, they are all the more constrained to pursue their economic interests in those areas where they do exercise authority.

Labor is an obvious case in point. Since nation-states control migration across their boundaries, the industrially more advanced have formally legislated that only limited numbers of outsiders—for example, relatives of citizens or those with skills needed by the host country—can enter. In a world where it is economically feasible for great masses of the population to migrate long distances, this kind of restrictive legislation seems essential for keeping the nation's social and economic integrity intact. Certainly, the wage levels and welfare assistance programs characteristic of advanced industrial societies could not be sustained were transnational migration unencumbered.

Unlike nation-states, cities cannot control movement across their boundaries. They no longer have walls, guarded and defended by their inhabitants. And as Weber correctly noted, without walls cities no longer have the independence to make significant choices in the way medieval cities once did.[12] It is true that local governments often try to keep vagrants, bums, paupers, and racial minorities out of their territory. They are harassed, arrested, thrown out of town, and generally discriminated against. But in most of these cases local governments act unconstitutionally, and even this illegal use of the police power does not control migration very efficiently.

Although limited in its powers, the city seeks to obtain an appropriately skilled labor force at wages lower than its competitors so that it can profitably export commodities. In larger cities a diverse work force is desirable. The service industry, which provides the infrastructure for exporters, recruits large numbers of unskilled workers, and many manufacturing industries need only semiskilled workers. When shortages in these skill levels appear, cities may assist industry in advertising the work and living opportunities of the region. In the nineteenth century when unskilled labor was in short supply, frontier cities made extravagant claims to gain a competitive edge in the supply of ordinary labor.

Certain sparsely populated areas, such as Alaska, occasionally advertise for unskilled labor even today. However, competition among most cities is now for highly skilled workers and especially for professional and managerial talent. In a less than full-employment economy, most communities have a surplus of semiskilled and unskilled labor. Increases in the supply of unskilled workers increase the cost of the community's social services. Since national wage laws preclude a decline in wages below a certain minimum, the increases in the cost of social services are seldom offset by lower wages for unskilled labor in those areas where the unemployed concentrate. But even with high levels of unemployment, there remains a shortage of highly skilled technicians and various types of white collar workers. Where shortages develop, the prices these workers can command in the labor market may climb to a level where local exports are no longer competitive with goods produced elsewhere. The economic health of a community is therefore importantly affected by the availability of professional and managerial talent and of highly skilled technicians.

When successfully pursuing their economic interests, cities develop a set of policies that will attract the more skilled and white collar workers without at the same time attracting unemployables. Of course, there are limits on the number of things cities can do. In contrast to nation-states, they cannot simply forbid entry to all but the highly talented whose skills they desire. But through zoning laws, they can ensure that adequate land is available for middle-class residences. They can provide parks, recreation areas, and good-quality schools in areas where the economically most productive live. They can keep the cost of social services, little utilized by the middle class, to a minimum, thereby keeping local taxes relatively low. In general, they can try to ensure that the benefits of public service outweigh their costs to those highly skilled workers, managers, and professionals who are vital for sustaining the community's economic growth.

# Capital

Capital is the second factor of production that must be attracted to an economically productive territory. Accordingly, nation-states place powerful controls on the flow of capital across their boundaries. Many nations strictly regulate the amount of national currency that can be taken out of the country. They place quotas and tariffs on imported goods. They regulate the rate at which national currency can be exchanged with foreign currency. They regulate the money supply, increasing interest rates when growth is too rapid, lowering interest rates when growth slows down. Debt financing also allows a nation-state to undertake capital expenditures and to encourage growth in the private market. At present the powers of nation-states to control capital flow are being used more sparingly and new supranational institutions are developing in their place. Market forces now seem more powerful than official policies in establishing rates of currency exchange among major industrial societies. Tariffs and other restrictions on trade are subject to retaliation by other countries, and so they must be used sparingly. The economies of industrialized nations are becoming so interdependent that significant changes in the international political economy seem imminent, signaled by numerous international conferences to determine worldwide growth rates, rates of inflation, and levels of unemployment. If these trends continue, nation-states may come to look increasingly like local governments.

But these developments at the national level have only begun to emerge. At the local level in the United States, cities are much less able to control capital flows. In the first place, the Constitution has been interpreted to mean that states cannot hinder the free flow of goods and monies across their boundaries. And what is true of states is true of their subsidiary jurisdictions as well. In the second place, states and localities cannot regulate the money supply. If unemployment is low, they cannot stimulate the economy by increasing the monetary flow. If inflationary pressures adversely affect their competitive edge in the export market, localities can neither restrict the money supply nor directly control prices and wages. All of these powers are reserved for national governments. In the third place, local governments cannot spend more than they receive in tax revenues without damaging their credit or even running the risk of bankruptcy. Pump priming, sometimes a national disease, is certainly a national prerogative.

Local governments are left with a number of devices for enticing capital into the area. They can minimize their tax on capital and on profits from capital investment. They can reduce the costs of capital investment by providing low-cost public utilities, such as roads, sewers, lights, and police and fire protection.

They can even offer public land free of charge or at greatly reduced prices to those investors they are particularly anxious to attract. They can provide a context for business operations free of undue harassment or regulation. For example, they can ignore various external costs of production, such as air pollution, water pollution, and the despoliation of trees, grass, and other features of the landscape. Finally, they can discourage labor from unionizing so as to keep industrial labor costs competitive.

This does not mean it behooves cities to allow any and all profit-maximizing action on the part of an industrial plant. Insofar as the city desires diversified economic growth, no single company can be allowed to pursue policies that seriously detract from the area's overall attractiveness to capital or productive labor. Taxes cannot be so low that government fails to supply residents with as attractive a package of services as can be found in competitive jurisdictions. Regulation of any particular industry cannot fall so far below nationwide standards that other industries must bear external costs not encountered in other places. The city's interest in attracting capital does not mean utter subservience to any particular corporation, but a sensitivity to the need for establishing an overall favorable climate.

In sum, cities, like private firms, compete with one another so as to maximize their economic position. To achieve this objective, the city must use the resources its land area provides by attracting as much capital and as high a quality labor force as is possible. Like a private firm, the city must entice labor and capital resources by offering appropriate inducements. Unlike the nation-state, the American city does not have regulatory powers to control labor and capital flows. The lack thereof sharply limits what cities can do to control their economic development, but at the same time the attempt by cities to maximize their interests within these limits shapes policy choice.

## Local Government and the Interests of Cities

Local government leaders are likely to be sensitive to the economic interests of their communities. First, economic prosperity is necessary for protecting the fiscal base of a local government. In the United States, taxes on local sources and charges for local services remain important components of local government revenues. Although transfers of revenue to local units from the federal and state governments increased throughout the postwar period, as late as 1975–76 local governments still were raising almost 59 percent of their own revenue.[13] Raising revenue from one's own economic resources requires continuing local economic prosperity. Second, good government is good politics. By pursuing policies which contribute to the economic prosperity of the local community, the local politician selects policies that redound to his own political advantage. Local politicians, eager for relief from the cross-pressures of local politics, assiduously promote goals that have widespread benefits. And few policies are more popular than economic growth and prosperity. Third, and most important, local officials usually have a sense of community responsibility. They know that, unless the economic well-being of the community can be maintained, local business will suffer, workers will lose employment opportunities, cultural life will decline, and city land values will fall. To avoid such a dismal future, public officials try to develop policies that assist the prosperity of their community—or, at the very least, that do not seriously detract from it. Quite apart from any effects of economic prosperity on government revenues or local voting behavior, it is quite reasonable to posit that local governments are primarily interested in maintaining the economic vitality of the area for which they are responsible.

Accordingly, governments can be expected to attempt to maximize this particular goal—within the numerous environmental constraints with which they must contend. As policy alternatives are proposed, each is evaluated according to how well it will help to achieve this objective. Although information is imperfect and local governments cannot be expected to select the one best alternative on every occasion, policy choices over time will be limited to those few which can plausibly be shown to be conducive to the community's economic prosperity. Internal disputes and disagreements may affect policy on the margins, but the major contours of local revenue policy will be determined by this strategic objective.

## NOTES

1. Flathman, R. E. 1966. *The public interest* (New York: John Wiley).
2. Banfield, E. C. 1961. *Political influence* (Glencoe, Illinois: Free Press). Ch. 12.
3. Tiebout, C. M. 1956. A pure theory of local expenditures. *Journal of Political Economy* 64: 416–424.
4. Ibid., p. 419.
5. Ibid., p. 420.
6. Bruce Hamilton, "Property Taxes and the Tiebout Hypothesis: Some Empirical Evidence," and Michelle J. White, "Fiscal Zoning in Fragmented Metropolitan Areas," in Mills, E. S., and Oates, W. E. 1975. *Fiscal zoning and land use controls* (Lexington, Massachusetts: Lexington Books). Chs. 2 and 3.
7. See Weber, "Class, Status, and Power," in Gerth, H. H., and Mills, C. W., trans. 1946. *From Max Weber* (New York: Oxford University Press).
8. For a more complete discussion of roles, structures, and interests, see Greenstone, J. D., and Peterson, P. E. 1976. *Race and authority in urban politics.* Phoenix edition (Chicago: University of Chicago Press). Ch. 2.
9. Cf. Thompson, W. R. 1965. *A preface to urban economics* (Baltimore, Maryland: Johns Hopkins University Press).
10. I treat entrepreneurial skill as simply another form of labor, even though it is a form in short supply.
11. Elazar, D. J. 1976. *Cities of the prairie* (New York: Basic Books).
12. Weber, M. 1921. *The city* (New York: Collier Books).
13. United States Department of Commerce, Bureau of the Census. 1977. *Local government finances in selected metropolitan areas and large counties: 1975–76.* Government finances: GF 76, no. 6.

# 2

## *Clarence N. Stone*

# URBAN REGIMES

What makes governance in Atlanta effective is not the formal machinery of government, but rather the informal partnership between city hall and the downtown business elite. This informal partnership and the way it operates constitute the city's regime; it is the means through which major policy decisions are made.

The word "regime" connotes different things to different people, but in this [selection] regime is specifically about the *informal arrangements* that surround and complement the formal workings of governmental authority. All governmental authority in the United States is greatly limited—limited by the Constitution, limited perhaps even more by the nation's political tradition, and limited structurally by the autonomy of privately owned business enterprise. The exercise of public authority is thus never a simple matter; it is almost always enhanced by extraformal considerations. Because local governmental authority is by law and tradition even more limited than authority at the state and national level, informal arrangements assume special importance in urban politics. But we should begin our understanding of regimes by realizing that informal arrangements are by no means peculiar to cities or, for that matter, to government.

Even narrowly bounded organizations, those with highly specific functional responsibilities, develop informal governing coalitions.[1] As Chester Barnard argued many years ago, formal goals and formal lines of authority are insufficient by themselves to bring about coordinated action with sufficient energy to accomplish organizational purposes,[2] commitment and cooperation do not just spring up from the lines of an organization chart. Because every formal organization gives rise to an informal one, Barnard concluded, successful executives must master the skill of shaping and using informal organization for their purposes.

Attention to informal arrangements takes various forms. In the analysis of business firms, the school of thought labeled "transaction cost economics" has given systematic attention to how things actually get done in a world full of social friction—basically the same question that Chester Barnard considered. A leading proponent of this approach, Oliver Williamson,[3] finds that what he terms "private orderings" (as opposed to formal and legal agreements) are enormously important in the running of business affairs. For many transac-

"Urban Regimes: A Research Perspective" from *Regime Politics: Governing Atlanta, 1964–1988* by Clarence N. Stone, pp. 3–12, 238–245. Copyright © 1989 by the University Press of Kansas. Reprinted by permission of the publisher.

tions, mutual and tacit understanding is a more efficient way of conducting relations than are legal agreements and formal contracts. Williamson quotes a business executive as saying, "You can settle any dispute if you keep the lawyers and accountants out of it. They just do not understand the give-and-take needed in business."[4] Because informal understandings and arrangements provide needed flexibility to cope with nonroutine matters, they facilitate cooperation to a degree that formally defined relationships do not. People who know one another, who have worked together in the past, who have shared in the achievement of a task, and who perhaps have experienced the same crisis are especially likely to develop tacit understandings. If they interact on a continuing basis, they can learn to trust one another and to expect dependability from one another. It can be argued, then, that transactions flow more smoothly and business is conducted more efficiently when a core of insiders form and develop an ongoing relationship.

A regime thus involves not just any informal group that comes together to make a decision but an informal yet relatively stable group *with access to institutional resources* that enable it to have a sustained role in making governing decisions. What makes the group informal is not a lack of institutional connections, but the fact that the group, *as a group,* brings together institutional connections by an informal mode of cooperation. There is no all-encompassing structure of command that guides and synchronizes everyone's behavior. There is a purposive coordination of efforts, but it comes about informally, in ways that often depend heavily on tacit understandings.

If there is no overarching command structure, what gives a regime coherence? What makes it more than an "ecology of games"?[5] The answer is that the regime is purposive, created and maintained as a way of facilitating action. In a very important sense, *a regime is empowering.* Its supporters see it as a means for achieving coordinated efforts that might not otherwise be realized. A regime, however, is not created or redirected at will. Organizational analysis teaches us that cognition is limited, existing arrangements have staying power, and implementation is profoundly shaped by procedures in place.[6] Shrewd and determined leaders can effect purposive change, but only by being attentive to the ways in which existing forms of coordination can be altered or amplified.[7]

We can think of cities as organizations that lack a conjoining structure of command. There are institutional sectors within which the power of command may be much in evidence, but the sectors are independent of one another.[8] Because localities have only weak formal means through which coordination can be achieved, informal arrangements to promote cooperation are especially useful. *These informal modes of coordinating efforts across institutional boundaries are what I call "civic cooperation."* In a system of weak formal authority, it holds special importance. Integrated with the formal structure of authority into a suprainstitutional capacity to take action, any informal basis of cooperation is empowering. It enables community actors to achieve cooperation beyond what could be formally commanded.

Consider the case of local political machines. When ward politicians learned to coordinate informally what otherwise was mired in institutional fragmentation and personal opportunism, the urban political machine was created and proved to have enormous staying power.[9] "Loyalty" is the shorthand that machine politicians used to describe the code that bound them into a cohesive group.[10] The political machine is in many ways the exemplar of governance in which informal arrangements are vital complements to the formal organization of government. The classic urban machines brought together various elements of the community in an informal scheme of exchange and cooperation that was the real governing system of the community.

The urban machine, of course, represents only one form of regime. In considering Atlanta, I am examining the governing coalition in a nonmachine city. The term "governing coalition" is a way of making the notion of regime concrete. It makes us face the fact that informal arrangements are held together by a core group—typically a body of insiders—who come together repeatedly in making important decisions. Thus, when I refer to the governing coalition in Atlanta, I mean the core group at the center of the workings of the regime.

To talk about a core group is not to suggest that they are of one mind or that they all represent identical interests—far from it. "Coalition" is the word I use to emphasize that a regime involves bringing together various elements of the community and the different institutional capacities they control. "Governing," as used in "governing coalition," I must stress, does not mean rule in command-and-control fashion. Governance through informal arrangements is about how some forms of coordination of effort prevail over others. It is about mobilizing efforts to cope and to adapt; it is not about absolute control. Informal arrangements are a way of bolstering (and guiding) the formal capacity to act, but even this enhanced capacity remains quite limited.

Having argued that informal arrangements are important in a range of circumstances, not just in cities, let me return to the specifics of the city setting. After all, the important point is not simply that there are informal arrangements; it is the particular features of urban regimes that provide the lenses through which we see the Atlanta experience. For cities, two questions face us: (1) Who makes up the governing coalition—who has to come together to make governance possible? (2) How is the coming together accomplished? These two questions imply a third: What are the consequences of the *who* and *how?* Urban regimes are not neutral mechanisms through which policy is made; they shape policy. To be sure, they do not do so on terms solely of the governing coalition's own choosing. But regimes are the mediating agents between the ill-defined pressures of an urban environment and the making of community policy. The *who* and *how* of urban regimes matter, thus giving rise to the further question of *with what consequences.* These three questions will guide my analysis of Atlanta.

## Urban Regimes

As indicated above, an urban regime refers to the set of arrangements by which a community is actually governed. Even though the institutions of local government bear most of the formal responsibility for governing, they lack the resources and the scope of authority to govern without the active support and co-operation of significant private interests. An urban regime may thus be defined as the *informal arrangements by which public bodies and private interests function together in order to be able to make and carry out governing decisions*. These governing decisions, I want to emphasize, are not a matter of running or controlling everything. They have to do with *managing conflict* and *making adaptive responses* to social change. The informal arrangements through which governing decisions are made differ from community to community, but everywhere they are driven by two needs: (1) institutional scope (that is, the need to encompass a wide enough scope of institutions to mobilize the resources required to make and implement governing decisions) and (2) cooperation (that is, the need to promote enough cooperation and coordination for the diverse participants to reach decisions and sustain action in support of those decisions).

The mix of participants varies by community, but that mix is itself constrained by the accommodation of two basic institutional principles of the American political economy: (1) popular control of the formal machinery of government and (2) private ownership of business enterprise.[11] Neither of these principles is pristine. Popular control is modified and compromised in various ways, but nevertheless remains as the basic principle of government. Private ownership is less than universal, as governments do own and operate various auxiliary enterprises from mass transit to convention centers. Even so, governmental conduct is constrained by the need to promote investment activity in an economic arena dominated by private ownership. This political-economy insight is the foundation for a theory of urban regimes.[12]

In defining an urban regime as the informal arrangements through which public bodies and private interests function together to make and carry out governing decisions, bear in mind that I did not specify that the private interests are business interests. Indeed, in practice, private interests are not confined to business figures. Labor-union officials, party functionaries, officers in nonprofit organizations or foundations, and church leaders may also be involved.[13]

Why, then, pay particular attention to business interests? One reason is the now well-understood need to encourage business investment in order to have an economically thriving community. A second reason is the sometimes overlooked factor that businesses control politically important resources and are rarely absent totally from the scene. They may work through intermediaries, or some businesses may even be passive because others represent their interests as property holders, but a business presence is always part of the urban political scene. Although the nature of business involvement extends from the direct and extensive to the indirect and limited, the economic role of businesses *and the resources they control* are too important for these enterprises to be left out completely.

With revived interest in political economy, the regime's need for an adequate institutional scope (including typically some degree of business involvement) has received significant attention. However, less has been said about the regime's need for cooperation—and the various ways to meet it.[14] Perhaps some take for granted that, when cooperation is called for, it will be forthcoming. But careful reflection reminds us that cooperation does not occur simply because it is useful.

Robert Wiebe analyzed machine politics in a way that illustrates an important point: "The ward politician . . . required wider connections in order to manage many of his clients' problems. . . . Therefore clusters of these men allied to increase their bargaining power in city affairs. But if logic led to an integrated city-wide organization, the instinct of self-preservation did not. The more elaborate the structure, the more independence the ward bosses and area chieftains lost."[15] Cooperation can thus never be taken as a given; it must be achieved and at significant costs. Some of the costs are visible resources expended in promoting cooperation—favors and benefits distributed to curry reciprocity, the effort required to establish and maintain channels of communication, and responsibilities borne to knit activities together are a few examples. But, as Wiebe's observation reminds us, there are less visible costs. Achieving cooperation entails commitment to a set of relationships, and these relationships limit independence of action. If relationships are to be ongoing, they cannot be neglected; they may even call for sacrifices to prevent alienating allies. Forming wider connections is thus not a cost-free step, and it is not a step that community actors are always eager to take.

Because centrifugal tendencies are always strong, achieving cooperation is a major accomplishment and requires constant effort. Cooperation can be brought about in various ways. It can be induced if there is an actor powerful enough to coerce others into it, but that is a rare occurrence, because power is not usually so concentrated. More often, cooperation is achieved by some degree of reciprocity.

The literature on collective action focuses on the problem of cooperation in the absence of a system of command. For example, the "prisoner's dilemma" game instructs us that noncooperation may be invited by a number of situations.[16] In the same vein, Mancur Olson's classic analysis highlights the free-rider problem and the importance of selective incentives in inducing cooperation.[17] Alternatively, repeated interactions permit people to see the shortcomings of mutual noncooperation and to learn norms of cooperation.[18] Moreover, although Robert Axelrod's experiments with TIT FOR TAT computer programs indicate that cooperation can be instrumentally rational under some conditions, the process is not purely mechanical.[19] Students of culture point to the importance of common identity and language in facilitating interaction and promoting trust.[20] Size of group is also a consideration, affecting the ease of communication and bargaining among members; Michael Taylor, for example, emphasizes the increased difficulty of conditional cooperation in larger groups.[21]

What we can surmise about the urban community is thus twofold: (1) cooperation across institutional lines is valuable but far from automatic; and (2) cooperation is more likely to grow under some circumstances than others. This conclusion has wide implications for the study of urban politics. For example, much of the literature on community power has centered on the question of control, its possibilities and limitations: to what extent is domination by a command center possible and how is the cost of social control worked out.

The long-standing elitist-pluralist debate centers on such questions. However, my line of argument here points to another way of viewing urban communities; it points to the need to think about cooperation, its possibilities and limitations—not just any cooperation, but cooperation of the kind that can bring together people based in different sectors of a community's institutional life and that enables a coalition of actors to make and support a set of governing decisions.

If the conventional model of urban politics is one of social control (with both elitist and pluralist variants), then the one proposed here might be called "the social-production model." It is based on the question of how, in a world of limited and dispersed authority, actors work together across institutional lines to produce a capacity to govern and to bring about publicly significant results.

To be sure, the development of a system of cooperation for governing is something that arises, not from an unformed mass, but rather within a structured set of relationships. Following Stephen Elkin, I described above the basic configuration in political-economy terms: popular control of governmental authority and private ownership of business activity. However, both of these elements are subject to variation. Populations vary in characteristics and in type of political organization; hence, popular control comes in many forms. The economic sector itself varies by the types of businesses that compose it and by the way in which it is organized formally and informally. Hence there is no one formula for bringing institutional sectors into an arrangement for cooperation, and the whole process is imbued with uncertainty. Cooperation is always somewhat tenuous, and it is made more so as conditions change and new actors enter the scene.

The study of urban regimes is thus a study of who cooperates and how their cooperation is achieved across institutional sectors of community life. Further, it is an examination of how that cooperation is maintained when confronted with an ongoing process of social change, a continuing influx of new actors, and potential break-downs through conflict or indifference.

Regimes are dynamic, not static, and regime dynamics concern the ways in which forces for change and forces for continuity play against one another. For example, Atlanta's governing coalition has displayed remarkable continuity in the post-World War II period, and it has done so despite deep-seated forces of social change. Understanding Atlanta's urban regime involves understanding how cooperation can be maintained and continuity can prevail in the face of so many possibilities for conflict.

## Structure, Action, and Structuring

Because of the interplay of change and continuity, urban regimes are perhaps best studied over time. Let us, then, take a closer look at historical analysis. Scholars make sense out of the particulars of political and social life by thinking mainly in terms of abstract structures such as democracy and capitalism. Although these are useful as shorthand, the danger in abstractions is that they never capture the full complexity and contingency of the world. Furthermore, "structure" suggests something solid and unchanging, yet political and social life is riddled with contradictions and uncertainties that give rise to an ongoing process of change and adjustment. Much of the change that occurs is at the margins of basic and enduring relationships, making it easy to think in terms of order and stability. Incrementalists remind us that the present is the best predictor of the near future. But students of history, especially those accustomed to looking at longer periods of time, offer a different perspective. They see a world undergoing change, in which various actors struggle over what the terms of that change will be. It is a world shaped and reshaped by human efforts, a world that never quite forms a unified whole.

In historical light, social structures are less solid and less fixed than social scientists have sometimes assumed. Charles Tilly has argued that there is no single social structure. Instead, he urges us to think in terms of multiple structures, which "consist of shifting, constructed social relations among limited numbers of actors."[22] Philip Abrams also sees structures as relationships, relationships that are socially fabricated and subject to purposive modification.[23]

Structures are real but not fixed. Action does not simply occur within the bounds set by structures but is sometimes aimed at the structures themselves, so that a process of reshaping is taking place at all times. Abrams thus argues that events have a two-sided character, involving both structure and action in such a way that action shapes structures and structures shape actions. Abrams calls for the study of a process he labels as "structuring," by which he means that events occur in a structured context and that events help reshape structure.[24]

Abrams therefore offers a perspective on the interplay of change and continuity. This continuity is not so much a matter of resisting change as coping with it. Because the potential for change is ever present, regime continuity is a remarkable outcome. Any event contains regime-altering potential—perhaps not in sudden realignment, but in opening up a new path along which subsequent events can cumulatively bring about fundamental change.[25] The absence of regime alteration is thus an outcome to be explained, and it must be explained in terms of a capacity to adapt and reinforce existing structures. Events are the arena in which the struggle between change and continuity is played out, but they are neither self-defining nor free-formed phenomena. They become events in our minds because they have some bearing on structures that help shape future occurrences. It is the interplay of event and structure that is especially worthy of study. To identify events, one therefore needs to have some conception of structure. In this way, the researcher can focus attention, relieved of the impossible task of studying everything.

There is no escaping the necessity of the scholar's imposing some form of analysis on research. The past becomes known through the concepts we apply. Abrams sees this as the heart of historical sociology: "The reality of the past is just not 'there' waiting to be observed by the resurrectionist historian. It is to be known if at all through strenuous theoretical alienation."[26] He also reminds us that many aspects of an event cannot be observed in a direct sense; too much is implicit at any given moment.[27] That is why the process, or the flow of events over time, is so important to examine. That is also why events are not necessarily most significant for their immediate impact; they may be more significant for their bearing on subsequent events, thus giving rise to modifications in structure.

## Prologue to the Atlanta Narrative

Structuring in Atlanta is a story in which race is central. If regimes are about who cooperates, how, and with what consequences, one of the remarkable features of Atlanta's urban regime is its biracial character. How has cooperation been achieved across racial lines, particularly since race is often a chasm rather than a bridge? Atlanta has been governed by a biracial coalition for so long that it is tempting to believe that nothing else was possible. Yet other cities followed a different pattern. At a time when Atlanta prided itself on being "the city too busy to hate," Little Rock, Birmingham, and New Orleans pursued die-hard segregation and were caught up in racial violence and turmoil. The experience of these cities reminds us that Atlanta's regime is not simply an informal arrangement through which popular elections and private ownership are reconciled, but is deeply intertwined with race relations, with some actors on the Atlanta scene able to overcome the divisive character of race sufficiently to achieve cooperation.

Atlanta's earlier history is itself a mixed experience, offering no clear indication that biracial cooperation would emerge and prevail in the years after World War II. In 1906, the city was the site of a violent race riot apparently precipitated by inflammatory antiblack newspaper rhetoric.[28] The incident hastened the city's move toward the economic exclusion and residential segregation of blacks, their disenfranchisement, and enforcement of social subordination; and the years after 1906 saw the Jim Crow system fastened into place. Still, the riot was followed by modest efforts to promote biracial understanding, culminating in the formation in 1919 of the Commission on Interracial Cooperation.

Atlanta, however, also became the headquarters city for a revived Ku Klux Klan. During the 1920s, the Klan enjoyed wide support and was a significant influence in city elections. At this time, it gained a strong foothold in city government and a lasting one in the police department.[29] In 1930, faced with rising unemployment, some white Atlantans also founded the Order of Black Shirts for the express purpose of driving blacks out of even menial jobs and replacing them with whites. Black Shirt protests had an impact, and opportunities for blacks once again were constricted. At the end of World War II, with Atlanta's black population expanding beyond a number that could be contained in the city's traditionally defined black neighborhoods, another klanlike organization, the Columbians, sought to use terror tactics to prevent black expansion into previously all-white areas. All of this occurred against a background of state and regional politics devoted to the subordination of blacks to whites—a setting that did not change much until the 1960s.

Nevertheless, other patterns surfaced briefly from time to time. In 1932, Angelo Herndon, a black Communist organizer, led a mass demonstration of white and black unemployed protesting a cutoff of work relief. Herndon was arrested, and the biracial following he led proved short-lived. Still, the event had occurred, and Atlanta's city council did in fact accede to the demand for continued relief.[30] In the immediate postwar period, a progressive biracial coalition formed around the successful candidacy of Helen Douglas Mankin for a congressional seat representing Georgia's fifth district. That, too, was short-lived, as ultra-conservative Talmadge forces maneuvered to reinstitute Georgia's county-unit system for the fifth district and defeat Mankin with a minority of the popular vote.[31]

It is tempting to see the flow of history as flux, and one could easily dwell on the mutable character of political alignments. The Atlanta experience suggests that coalitions often give expression to instability. Centrifugal forces are strong, and in some ways disorder is a natural state. What conflict does not tear asunder, indifference is fully capable of wearing away.

The political incorporation of blacks into Atlanta's urban regime in tight coalition with the city's white business elite is thus not a story of how popular control and private capital came inevitably to live together in peace and harmony. It is an account of struggle and conflict—bringing together a biracial governing coalition at the outset, and then allowing each of the coalition partners to secure for itself an advantageous position within the coalition. In the first instance, struggle involved efforts to see that the coalition between white business interests and the black middle class prevailed over other possible alignments. In the second instance, there was struggle over the terms of coalition between the partners; thus political conflict is not confined to "ins" versus "outs." Those on the inside engage in significant struggle with one another over the terms on which cooperation will be maintained, which is one reason governing arrangements should never be taken for granted.

Atlanta's urban regime therefore appears to be the creature of purposive struggle, and both its establishment and its maintenance call for a political explanation. The shape of the regime was far from inevitable, but rather came about through the actions of human agents making political choices. Without extraeconomic efforts by the city's business leadership, Atlanta would have been governed in a much different manner, and Atlanta's urban regime and the policies furthered by that regime might well have diverged from the path taken. History, perhaps, is as much about alternatives not pursued as about those that were. . . .

# The Political Ramifications
## of Unequal Resources

From Aristotle to Tocqueville to the present, keen political observers have understood that politics evolves from and reflects the associational life of a community. How people are grouped is important—so much so that, as the authors of the *Federalist* essays understood, the formation and reformation of coalitions [are] at the heart of political activity. Democracy should be viewed within that context; i.e., realizing that people do not act together simply because they share preferences on some particular issue.

Overlooking that long-standing lesson, many public-choice economists regard democracy with suspicion. They fear that popular majorities will insist on an egalitarian redistribution of benefits and thereby interfere with economic productivity. As worded by one economist, "The majority (the poor) will always vote for taxing the minority (the rich), at least until the opportunities for benefiting from redistribution run out."[32] In other words, majority rule will overturn an unequal distribution of goods and resources. This reasoning, however, involves the simple-minded premise that formal governmental authority confers a capacity to redistribute at the will of those who hold office by virtue of popular election. The social-production model of politics employed here offers a contrasting view. Starting from an assumption about the costliness of civic cooperation, the social production model suggests that an unequal distribution of goods and resources substantially modifies majority rule.

In operation, democracy is a great deal more complicated than counting votes and sorting through the wants of rational egoists. In response to those who regard democracy as a process of aggregating preferences within a system characterized by formal equality, a good antidote is Stein Rokkan's aphorism, "Votes count but resources decide."[33] Voting power is certainly not insignificant, but policies are decided mainly by those who control important concentrations of resources. Hence, governing is never simply a matter of aggregating numbers, whether for redistribution or other purposes. . . .

Of course, the election of key public officials provides a channel of popular expression. Since democracy rests on the principle of equal voting power, it would seem that all groups do share in the capacity to become part of the governing regime. Certainly the vote played a major role in the turnaround of the position of blacks in Atlanta. Popular control, however, is not a simple and straightforward process. Much depends on how the populace is organized to participate in a community's civic life. Machine politics, for example, promotes a search for personal favors. With electoral mobilization dependent upon an organizational network oriented toward patronage and related considerations, other kinds of popular concerns may have difficulty gaining expression.[34] The political machine thus enjoys a type of preemptive power, though the party organization is only one aspect of the overall governing regime.

On the surface, Atlanta represents a situation quite different from machine politics. Nonpartisan elections and an absence of mass patronage have characterized the city throughout the post-World War II era. Yet it would hardly be accurate to describe civic life in Atlanta as open and fluid. Nonpartisanship has heightened the role of organizations connected to business, and the newspapers have held an important position in policy debate. At the same time, working-class organizations and nonprofit groups unsupported by business are not major players in city politics.

Within Atlanta's civic sector, activities serve to piece together concerns across the institutional lines of the community, connecting government with business and each with a variety of nonprofit entities. The downtown elite has been especially adept at building alliances in that sector and, in doing so, has extended its resource advantage well beyond the control of strictly economic functions. Responding to its own weakness in numbers, the business elite has crafted a network through which cooperation can be advanced and potential cleavages between haves and have-nots redirected.

Consider what Atlanta's postwar regime represents. In 1946, the central element in the governing coalition was a downtown business elite organized for and committed to an active program of redevelopment that would transform the character of the business district and, in the process, displace a largely black population to the south and east of the district. At the same time, with the end of the white primary that same year, a middle-class black population, long excluded from power, mobilized its electoral strength to begin an assault on a firmly entrenched Jim Crow system. Knowing only those facts, one might well have predicted in 1946 that these two groups would be political antagonists. They were not. Both committed to an agenda of change, they worked out an accommodation and became the city's governing coalition. The alliance has had its tensions and even temporary ruptures, but it has held and demonstrated remarkable strength in making and carrying out policy decisions.

To understand the process, the Atlanta experience indicates that one must appreciate institutional capacities and the resources that various groups control. That is why simple preference aggregation is no guide to how coalitions are built. The downtown elite and the black middle class had complementary needs that could be met by forming an alliance, and the business elite in particular had the kind and amount of resources to knit the alliance together.

Politics in Atlanta, then, is not organized around an overriding division between haves and have-nots. Instead, unequally distributed resources serve to destabilize opposition and encourage alliances around small opportunities. Without command of a capacity to govern, elected leaders have difficulty building support around popular discontent. That is why Rokkan's phrase, "Votes count but resources decide," is so apt.

## Unequal Resources and Urban Regimes

Regimes, I have suggested, are to be understood in terms of (1) who makes up the governing coalition and (2) how the coalition achieves cooperation. Both points illustrate how the unequal distribution of resources affects politics and what differences the formation of a regime makes. That the downtown elite is a central partner in the Atlanta regime shapes the priorities set and the trade-offs made. Hence, investor prerogative is protected practice in Atlanta, under the substantial influence of the business elite *within* the governing coalition. At the same time, the fact that the downtown elite is part of a governing coalition prevents business isolation from community affairs. Yet, although "corporate responsibility" promotes business involvement, it does so in a way that enhances business as patron and promoter of small opportunities.

Similarly, the incorporation of the black middle class into the mainstream civic and economic life of Atlanta is testimony to its ability to use electoral leverage to help set community priorities. The importance of the mode of coop- eration is also evident. Although much of what the regime has done has gener- ated popular resistance, the black middle class has been persuaded to go along by a combination of selective incentives and small opportunities. Alliance with the business elite enabled the black middle class to achieve particular objec- tives not readily available by other means. This kind of enabling capacity is what gives concentrated resources its gravitational force.

The pattern thus represents something more than individual cooptation. The black middle class as a group benefited from new housing areas in the early postwar years and from employment and business opportunities in re- cent years. Some of the beneficiaries have been institutional—colleges in the Atlanta University system and a financially troubled bank, for example. Be- cause the term "selective incentives" implies individual benefits (and these have been important), the more inclusive term "small opportunities" provides a useful complement. In both cases, the business elite is a primary source; they can make things happen, provide needed assistance, and open up opportuni- ties. At the same time, since the downtown elite needs the cooperation of local government and various community groups, the elite itself is drawn toward a broad community-leadership role. Although its bottom-line economic interests are narrow, its community role can involve it in wider concerns. Selective in- centives, however, enable the elite to muffle some of the pressure that might otherwise come from the larger community.

Once we focus on the regime and the importance of informally achieved cooperation, we can appreciate better the complex way in which local politics actually functions. Public-choice economists, fearful that democracy will lead to redistribution, misunderstand the process and treat politics as a causal force operating in isolation from resources other than the vote. That clearly is unwar- ranted. Atlanta's business elite possesses substantial slack resources that can be and are devoted to policy. Some devotion of resources to political purposes is direct, in the form of campaign funds, but much is indirect; it takes on the char- acter of facilitating civic cooperation of those efforts deemed worthy.

The business elite is small and homogeneous enough to use the norms of class unity and corporate responsibility to maintain its cohesion internally. In interacting with allies, the prevailing mode of operation is reciprocity, rein- forced in many cases by years of trust built from past exchanges. The biracial insiders have also been at their tasks long enough to experience a sense of pride in the community role they play. Even so, the coalition is centered around a combination of explicit and tacit deals. Reciprocity is thus the hallmark of At- lanta's regime, and reciprocity hinges on what one actor can do for another. In- stead of promoting redistribution toward equality, such a system perpetuates inequality.

Reciprocity, of course, occurs in a context, and in Atlanta, it is interwoven with a complex set of conditions. The slack resources controlled by business corporations give them an extraordinary opportunity to promote civic cooperation. Where there is a compelling mutual interest, as within Atlanta's downtown elite, businesses have the means to solve their own collective-action problem and unite behind a program of action. Their resources also enable them to create a network of cooperation that extends across lines of institutional division, which makes them attractive to public officials and other results-oriented community groups. In becoming an integral part of a system of civic cooperation, Atlanta's business elite has used its resource advantage to shape community policy and protect a privileged position. Because the elite is useful to others, it attracts and holds a variety of allies in its web of reciprocity. The concentration of resources it has gathered thus enables the elite to counter demands for greater equality.

## Social Learning versus Privilege

Instead of understanding democratic politics as an instance of the equality (redistribution)/efficiency (productivity) trade-off, I suggest an alternative. Policy actions (and inactions) have extensive repercussions and involve significant issues that do not fit neatly into an equality-versus-efficiency mold. There is a need, then, for members of the governing coalition to be widely informed about a community's problems, and not to be indifferent about the information. That is what representative democracy is about.

For their part, in order to be productive, business enterprises need a degree of autonomy and a supply of slack resources. It is also appropriate that they participate in politics. However, there are dangers involved in the ability of high-resource groups, like Atlanta's business elite, to secure for themselves a place in the governing coalition and then use that inside position along with their own ample resources to shape the regime on their terms. Elsewhere I have called this "preemptive power,"[35] and have suggested that it enables a group to protect a privileged position. The ability to parcel out selective incentives and other small opportunities permits Atlanta's business elite to enforce discipline on behalf of civic cooperation by vesting others with lesser privileges—privileges perhaps contingently held in return for "going along."

The flip side of discipline through selective incentives is a set of contingent privileges that restrict the questions asked and curtail social learning. Thus, one of the trade-offs in local politics can be phrased as social learning versus privilege. Some degree of privilege for business may be necessary to encourage investment, but the greater the privilege being protected, the less the incentive to understand and act on behalf of the community in its entirety.

The political challenge illustrated by the Atlanta case is how to reconstitute the regime so that both social learning and civic cooperation occur. The risk in the present situation is that those who govern have only a limited comprehension of the consequences of their actions. Steps taken to correct one problem may create or aggravate another while leaving still others unaddressed. Those who govern can discover that only, it seems, through wide representation of the affected groups. Otherwise, choices are limited by an inability to understand the city's full situation.

No governing coalition has an inclination to expand the difficulties of making and carrying out decisions. Still, coalitions can be induced to attempt the difficult. For example, Atlanta's regime has been centrally involved in race relations, perhaps the community's most difficult and volatile issue. Relationships within the governing coalition have been fraught with tension; friction was unavoidable. Yet the coalition achieved a cooperative working relationship between the black middle class and the white business elite. In a rare but telling incident, black leaders insisted successfully that a 1971 pledge to build a MARTA spur to a black public-housing area not be repudiated. The newspaper opined that trust within the coalition was too important to be sacrificed on the altar of economizing. Thus the task of the governing regime was expanded beyond the narrow issue of serving downtown in the least expensive manner possible; concerns *can* be broadened.

Although no regime is likely to be totally inclusive, most regimes can be made more inclusive. Just as Atlanta's regime was drawn into dealing with race relations, others can become sensitive to the situations of a larger set of groups. Greater inclusiveness will not come automatically nor from the vote alone. Pressures to narrow the governing coalition are strong and recurring. Yet, if civic cooperation is the key to the terms on which economic and electoral power are accommodated, then more inclusive urban regimes can be encouraged through an associational life at the community level that reflects a broad range of perspectives. The problem is not an absence of associational life at that level but how to lessen its dependence on business sponsorship, how to free participation in civic activity from an overriding concern with protecting insider privileges, and how to enrich associational life so that nonprofit and other groups can function together as they express encompassing community concerns.

This step is one in which federal policy could make a fundamental difference. In the past, starting with the urban-redevelopment provision in the 1949 housing act and continuing through the Carter administration's UDAG program, cities have been strongly encouraged to devise partnerships with private, for-profit developers, thus intensifying already strong leanings in that direction. Since these were matters of legislative choice, it seems fully possible for the federal government to move in another direction and encourage nonprofit organizations. The federal government could, for example, establish a program of large-scale assistance to community development corporations and other nonprofit groups. Some foundations now support such programs, but their modest efforts could be augmented. Programs of community service required by high schools and colleges or spawned by a national-level service requirement could increase voluntary participation and alter the character of civic life in local communities. It is noteworthy that neighborhood mobilization in Atlanta was partly initiated by VISTA (Volunteers in Service to America) workers in the 1960s and continued by those who stayed in the city after completing service with VISTA. This, however, is not the place to prescribe a full set of remedies; my aim is only to indicate that change is possible but will probably require a stimulus external to the local community.

# Summing Up

If the slack resources of business help to set the terms on which urban governance occurs, then we need to be aware of what this imbalance means. The Atlanta case suggests that the more uneven the distribution of resources, the greater the tendency of the regime to become concerned with protecting privilege. Concurrently, there is a narrowing of the regime's willingness to engage in "information seeking" (or social learning). Imbalances in the civic sector thus lead to biases in policy, biases that electoral politics alone is unable to correct.

A genuinely effective regime is not only adept at promoting cooperation in the execution of complex and nonroutine projects, but is also able to comprehend the consequences of its actions and inactions for a diverse citizenry. The promotion of this broad comprehension is, after all, a major aim of democracy. Even if democratic politics were removed from the complexities of coordination for social production, it still could not be reduced to a set of decision rules. Arrow's theorem shows that majority choices cannot be neutrally aggregated when preference structures are complex,[36] as indeed they are bound to be in modern societies.

Democracy, then, is not simply a decision rule for registering choices; it has to operate with a commitment to inclusiveness. Permanent or excluded minorities are inconsistent with the basic idea of equality that underpins democracy. That is why some notion of social learning is an essential part of the democratic process; all are entitled to have their situations understood. Thus, to the extent that urban regimes safeguard special privileges at the expense of social learning, democracy is weakened.

Those fearful that too much community participation will lead to unproductive policies should widen their own understanding and consider other dangers on the political landscape. Particularly under conditions of an imbalance in civically useful resources, the political challenge is one of preventing government from being harnessed to the protection of special privilege. The social-production model reminds us that only a segment of society's institutions are under the sway of majority rule; hence, actual governance is never simply a matter of registering the preferences of citizens as individuals.

The character of local politics depends greatly on the nature of a community's associational life, which in turn depends greatly on the distribution of resources other than the vote. Of course, the vote is significant, but equality in the right to vote is an inadequate guarantee against the diversion of politics into the protection of privilege. If broad social learning is to occur, then other considerations must enter the picture. "One person, one vote" is not enough.

## NOTES

1. James G. March, "The Business Firm as a Political Coalition," *Journal of Politics* 24 (November 1962): 662–678.
2. Chester I. Barnard, *The Functions of the Executive* (Cambridge, Mass.: Harvard University Press, 1968).

3. Oliver E. Williamson, *The Economic Institutions of Capitalism* (New York: Free Press, 1985).

4. Ibid., 10.

5. See Norton E. Long, "The Local Community as an Ecology of Games," *American Journal of Sociology* 64 (November 1958): 251–261.

6. Cf. Graham T. Allison, *Essence of Decision* (Boston: Little, Brown, 1971).

7. See Philip Selznick, *Leadership in Administration* (New York: Harper & Row, 1957).

8. Cf. Bryan D. Jones and Lynn W. Bachelor, *The Sustaining Hand* (Lawrence: University of Kansas Press, 1986).

9. See especially Martin Shefter, "The Emergence of the Political Machine: An Alternative View," in *Theoretical Perspectives on Urban Politics,* by Willis D. Hawley and others (Englewood Cliffs, N.J.: Prentice-Hall, 1976).

10. Clarence N. Stone, Robert K. Whelan, and William J. Murin. *Urban Policy and Politics in a Bureaucratic Age,* 2d ed. (Englewood Cliffs, N.J.: Prentice-Hall, 1986, 104).

11. Stephen L. Elkin, *City and Regime in the American Republic* (Chicago: University of Chicago Press, 1987).

12. Ibid.

13. Cf. Jones and Bachelor, *The Sustaining Hand,* 214–215.

14. But see Elkin, *City and Regime;* Martin Shefter, *Political Crisis/Fiscal Crisis: The Collapse and Revival of New York City* (New York: Basic Books, 1985); and Todd Swanstrom, *The Crisis of Growth Politics* (Philadelphia: Temple University Press, 1985).

15. Robert H. Wiebe, *The Search for Order, 1877–1920* (New York: Hill and Wang, 1967), 10.

16. Russell Hardin, *Collective Action* (Baltimore: Johns Hopkins University Press, 1982); and Michael Taylor, *The Possibility of Cooperation* (Cambridge, Mass.: Cambridge University Press, 1987).

17. Mancur Olson, Jr., *The Logic of Collective Action* (Cambridge, Mass.: Harvard University Press, 1965).

18. Hardin, *Collective Action.*

19. Robert Axelrod, *The Evolution of Cooperation* (New York: Basic Books, 1984).

20. Hardin, *Collective Action;* and David D. Laitin, *Hegemony and Culture* (Chicago: University of Chicago Press, 1986).

21. Taylor, *Possibility of Cooperation.*

22. Charles Tilly, *Big Structures, Large Processes, Huge Comparisons* (New York: Russell Sage Foundation, 1984), 27.

23. Philip Abrams, *Historical Sociology* (Ithaca, N.Y.: Cornell University Press, 1982). For a similar understanding applied to urban politics, see John R. Logan and Harvey L. Molotch, *Urban Fortunes* (Berkeley and Los Angeles: University of California Press, 1987).

24. Cf. Anthony Giddens, *Central Problems in Social Theory* (Berkeley and Los Angeles: University of California Press, 1979).

25. Cf. James G. March and Johan P. Olsen, "The New Institutionalism," *American Political Science Review* 78 (September 1984): 734–749.

26. Abrams, *Historical Sociology,* 331.

27. Ibid.

28. Michael L. Porter, "Black Atlanta: An Interdisciplinary Study of Blacks on the East Side of Atlanta, 1890–1930" (Ph.D. diss., Emory University, 1974); Walter White, *A Man Called White* (New York: Arno Press and the New York Times, 1969); and Dana F. White, "The Black Sides of Atlanta," *Atlanta Historical Journal* 26 (Summer/Fall 1982): 199–225.

29. Kenneth T. Jackson, *The Ku Klux Klan in the City 1915–1930* (New York: Oxford University Press, 1967); and Herbert T. Jenkins, *Forty Years on the Force: 1932–1972* (Atlanta: Center for Research in Social Change, Emory University, 1973).

30. Charles H. Martin, *The Angelo Herndon Case and Southern Justice* (Baton Rouge: Louisiana State University Press, 1976); Kenneth Coleman, ed., *A History of Georgia*

(Athens: University of Georgia Press, 1977), 294; and Writer's Program of the Works Progress Administration, *Atlanta: A City of the Modern South* (St. Clairshores, Mich.: Somerset Publishers, 1973), 69.

31. Lorraine N. Spritzer, *The Belle of Ashby Street: Helen Douglas Mankin and Georgia Politics* (Athens: University of Georgia Press, 1982).

32. John Bonner, *Introduction to the Theory of Social Choice* (Baltimore: Johns Hopkins University Press, 1986), 34.

33. Stein Rokkan, "Norway: Numerical Democracy and Corporate Pluralism," in *Political Oppositions in Western Democracies,* ed. Robert A. Dahl (New Haven, Conn.: Yale University Press, 1966), 105; see also [Steven Erie, *Rainbow's End: Irish-Americans and the Dilemmas of Urban Machine Politics, 1840–1985* (Berkeley: University of California Press, 1988)].

34. Matthew A. Crenson, *The Un-Politics of Air Pollution* (Baltimore: Johns Hopkins University Press, 1971); see also Edwin H. Rhyne, "Political Parties and Decision Making in Three Southern Counties," *American Political Science Review* 52 (December 1958): 1091–1107.

35. Clarence N. Stone, "Preemptive Power: Floyd Hunter's 'Community Power Structure' Reconsidered," *American Journal of Political Science* 32 (February 1988): 82–104.

36. Norman Frohlich and Joe A. Oppenheimer, *Modern Political Economy* (Englewood Cliffs, N.J.: Prentice-Hall, 1978), 19–31.

# 3

## *Richard C. Wade*

## THE URBAN FRONTIER

Part of Philadelphia's appeal to towndwellers was its leadership among the nation's cities, for nearly every young metropolis . . . coveted a similar primacy in the West. Indeed, one of the most striking characteristics of this period was the development of an urban imperialism which saw rising young giants seek to spread their power and influence over the entire new country. The drive for supremacy, furthermore, was quite conscious, infusing an extraordinary dynamic into city growth, but also breeding bitter rivalries among the claimants. In the ensuing struggles, the economically strongest survived and flourished, while the less successful fell behind. Smaller places were trampled in the process, some being swallowed up by ambitious neighbors, others being overwhelmed before they could attain a challenging position. The contest, however, produced no final victor. In fact, the lead changed three times, and though Cincinnati commanded the field in 1830, Pittsburgh, Louisville, and St. Louis were still in the running.

"Conclusion: The Urban Dimension of Western Life" reprinted by permission of the publisher from *The Urban Frontier: The Rise of Western Cities* by Richard C. Wade, pp. 322–336, Cambridge, Mass.: Harvard University Press, Copyright © 1959 by the President and Fellows of Harvard College.

The rivalries developed very early. Lexington jumped off to a quick start, but by 1810 Pittsburgh, enjoying a commercial and manufacturing boom, forged ahead. The postwar depression undermined its leadership, however, and Cincinnati moved forward to take its place. The fierce competition led to widespread speculation about the outcome. Most of the prophecy was wishful, stemming from the hopes of boosters and involving doubtful calculations. In 1816, for instance, a Pittsburgher summed up many of the elements of this competition in a table (with ratings presumably on a scale of excellence from one to ten) designed to illustrate the inevitability of the Iron City's supremacy.[1] Not only did the author work out the estimates in scientific detail, but he also predicted that the totals represented the population (in thousands) which each would reach in 1830.

| | Pittsburgh | Lexington | Cincinnati |
|---|---|---|---|
| Situation for inland trade and navigation | 9 | 2 | 6 |
| Adaptness for manufacturers | 9 | 3 | 5 |
| Fertility of surrounding soil | 2 | 7 | 4 |
| Salubrity | 9 | 7 | 5 |
| Pleasantness and beauty | .3 | 1 | .6 |
| Elegance of scite [sic] and environs | 1 | .3 | .6 |
| | 30.3 | 20.3 | 21.2 |

Before a city could hope to enter the urban sweepstake for the largest prize, it had to eliminate whatever rivals arose in its own area. In many instances the odds in these battles were so uneven that smaller places gave in quickly. In others, a decision came only after a bitter and prolonged struggle. Edwardsville, Illinois, fell easily before St. Louis, but Wheeling's submission to Pittsburgh followed a decade of acrimony. Sometimes defeat meant the end of independence for a town. Louisville, for example, ultimately annexed Shippingport and Portland, while Pittsburgh reached across the river to take in Allegheny. In other cases, the penalty for failure was the lessening of power and prestige. Steubenville and Wheeling, unable to sustain their position against Pittsburgh in the Upper Ohio, had to settle for a much reduced pace of development. The same fate befell Ste. Genevieve, an early challenger of St. Louis's domination of the Mississippi and Missouri. Occasionally a victor reduced its competitor to a mere economic appendage. This is what happened to Jeffersonville and New Albany, Indiana, after Louisville captured the trade of the Falls.

Though struggles for regional primacy characterized the urban growth of the entire West, the most celebrated was Pittsburgh's duel with Wheeling. Both were situated on the Ohio and both hoped to capture its flourishing commerce. Wheeling's great advantage lay in its down-river position, where it outflanked the shoals and rapids which dominated the approach to Pittsburgh. During the late summer, low water made navigation difficult and at times impossible, inducing some merchants to use the Virginia town as a transshipment point to the East. This fact alone made Wheeling a competitor, for in no other department could it match the Iron City. Pittsburgh's detractors saw this situation as early as 1793, when the Army considered establishing a post at Wheeling. Isaac Craig complained that "this new arrangement, . . . has Originated in the Brain of the Gentlemen in Washington who envy Pittsburgh, and . . . have represented to General Knox, that Navigation is practicable from Wheeling in the dry season."[2] The same consideration made Wheeling a stop in the mail route to the West and the Ohio River terminus of the National Road.

Despite these advantages, Wheeling's population barely reached 1,000 by 1815, while Pittsburgh had become the new country's leading metropolis. A serious rivalry seemed almost ridiculous. But the postwar depression, felling the Iron City, gave its smaller neighbor the hope of rising on the ruins. This prospect brightened in 1816, when, after many abortive attempts to change the terminus, the National Road was completed to Wheeling. Optimism about the town's future abounded throughout the valley. A Steubenville editor caught the spirit in verse:

> Wheeling has secured her roads,
> Come waggoners, come and bring your loads.
> Emigrants, come hither, and build a town,
> And make Wheeling a place of renown.

By 1822, 5,000 wagons were arriving annually in the booming settlement. "Wheeling is a thriving place," a traveler observed; "it bids fair to rival Pittsburgh in the trade of the Western country."[3]

The Iron City, troubled by a stagnant economy and worried about its future, warily watched the progress of this upstart. Actually, Wheeling's challenge was only a small part of Pittsburgh's total problem, but its very ludicrousness made the situation all the more intolerable. "A miserable Virginia country town, which can never be more than two hundred yards wide, having the mere advantage of a free turnpike road and a warehouse or two, to become rivals of this *Emporium* of the West!" exclaimed the incredulous editor of the *Statesman*. As Wheeling continued to prosper, Pittsburgh accused its competitor of unfair practices, particularly of circulating the rumor that ships could not go up the river to "the Point." "They have taken to lying," the *Statesman* snapped. "We cannot believe this report," the *Gazette* asserted with more charity; "the citizens with whom we are acquainted in that place, are too honorable to countenance such childish, hurtless falsehood," especially since "everybody acquainted with the river knows that the water is as good if not better above than for 100 miles below."[4]

Civic leaders in Wheeling, feeling their oats and certain that the National Road provided a secure base for unlimited growth, continually goaded the stricken giant. "Strange that a 'miserable Virginia Country Town,' a 'mere village,' should have attracted so much attention at the 'emporium of the West,'" the *Northwestern Gazette* observed. Moreover, it asserted that the difficulty of navigation on the Upper Ohio was not mere rumor. "During the drier part of the season the greater part of the Western Merchants order their goods to Wheeling and *not* to Pittsburgh. This fact is a stubborn and decisive one. It speaks volumes. It is a demonstration." A patronizing condescension expressed an increasing confidence. "Pittsburgh may, if she will, be a large and respectable manufacturing town. She may also retain a portion of the carrying trade," the same source graciously conceded. There seemed no limit to Wheeling's assurance. Travelers reported that its residents were "actually doing nothing but walking about on stilts, and stroking their chins with utmost self-complacency. Every man who is so fortunate as to own about 60 feet front and 120 feet back, considers himself . . . snug."[5]

The next few years demonstrated, however, that history was only teasing. Wheeling's hopes for greatness were soon dashed. The National Road proved disappointing as a freight carrier, and Pittsburgh recovered from its depression, once again becoming the urban focus of the Upper Ohio. Though the Virginia town could boast over 5,000 inhabitants in 1830, its rate of growth lagged and its future prospects dimmed. To some shrewd observers the outcome was not unexpected. A Steubenville editor, consoling his readers in 1816 after their efforts to get the National Road had failed, asserted that cities could not be reared on mere highway traffic. "Rely on agriculture and manufactures," he counseled," and you will do well without the mail or the turnpike bubble—it is not the sound of the coachman's horn that will make a town flourish."[6]

Though Pittsburgh beat back Wheeling's challenge, it could not maintain its Western leadership. Cincinnati, less affected by the postwar collapse, surged by the Iron City and established its primacy throughout the new country. It was not content, however, to win its supremacy by another's injury. Rather it developed its own positive program to widen its commercial opportunities and spread its influence. In fact, the city was so alive with ideas that one visitor referred to it as "that hot bed of projects," and another observed "great plans on foot; whenever two or three meet at a corner nothing is heard but schemes." In broad terms the object of Cincinnati's statesmanship was threefold: to tap the growing trade on the Great Lakes by water links to the Ohio, to facilitate traffic on the river by a canal around the Falls, and to reach into the hinterland with improved roads. Later another canal—this time down the Licking "into the heart of Kentucky"—a bridge across the Ohio, and a railway to Lexington were added.[7] Success would have made the entire valley dependent upon this urban center, and given the Ohio metropolis command of the strategic routes of trade and travel.

This ambitious program caused great concern in Pittsburgh. "We honestly confess," the *Gazette* admitted, that "a canal from the lakes either into the Ohio or the Great Miami . . . adds another item to the amount of our present uneasiness." By tipping the commerce of the valley northward, Cincinnati would substantially reduce the Iron City's importance as the central station between East and West. "Without this trade," the *Statesman* warned, "what can Philadelphia and Pittsburgh become but deserted villages, compared with their great rivals?"[8] Pennsylvania responded to this threat by improving the turnpike between its urban centers and ultimately constructing an elaborate canal across the mountains. In addition, Pittsburgh proposed to head off Cincinnati by building a water route to Lake Erie or tying into the Ohio system below Cleveland.

The challenge to Cincinnati's supremacy, however, came not only from a resurgent Pittsburgh, but also from a booming downriver neighbor, Louisville. As early as 1819 a visitor noted this two-front war. "I discovered two ruling passions in Cincinnati; enmity against Pittsburgh and jealousy of Louisville." In one regard the Falls City was the more serious rival, because as a commercial center it competed directly with the Ohio emporium. In fact, guerilla warfare between the two towns for advantage in the rural market began early in the century.[9] But the great object of contention was the control and traffic on the river—the West's central commercial artery.

In this contest Louisville held one key advantage. Its strategic position at the Falls gave it command of both parts of the Ohio. All passengers and goods had to pass through the town, except during the few months of high water when even large vessels could move safely over the rapids. It was a clumsy system, and from the earliest days many people envisaged a canal around the chutes. Nothing came of these plans until the coming of the steamboat immensely expanded traffic and made the interruption seem intolerable. Though nearly every shipper favored a canal, it was not until Cincinnati, anxious both to loosen river commerce and weaken a rival city, put its weight behind the improvement that any real activity developed.

Cincinnati had a deep stake in this project. A canal would not only aid the town generally but also advance the interests of some powerful groups. The mercantile community was anxious to get freer trade, and many residents had large investments in companies which hoped to dig on either the Kentucky or Indiana side of the Falls.[10] Others owned real estate in the area. William Lytle, for example, had large holdings around Portland of an estimated value of between $100,000 and $500,000.[11] Moreover, ordinary Cincinnatians had come to the conclusion that a canal would serve a broad public purpose. Hence in 1817 a town meeting was called to discuss the issue. An editor provided the backdrop: "No question was ever agitated here that involved more important consequences to this town." And from the beginning Louisville was cast as the villain of the piece. *Liberty Hall* referred to it as "a little town" trying to make "all the upper country tributary to it, by compelling us to deposit our goods in its warehouses and pay extravagant prices for transportation around or over the Falls."[12]

Since the Falls City could frustrate any project on Kentucky soil, Cincinnati's first move was to build on the opposite side. The Indiana legislature incorporated the Jeffersonville Ohio Canal Company in 1817, empowering it to sell 20,000 shares of stock at $50 apiece, and authorizing a lottery for $100,000 more. From the outset it was clear that the scheme stemmed from the Queen City. Not only did that town provide more than half the concern's directors, but also the campaign for funds emphasized its role. "The public may be assured that the wealth, influence, enterprise and talents of Cincinnati are at the head of this measure," *Liberty Hall* declared in 1818. Moreover, advocates underlined the stake of the Ohio metropolis, warning residents that if they did not support the drive they "deserved to be hewers of wood and drawers of water" for Louisville. In May 1819 a prominent Cincinnatian gave the ceremonial address as digging began on the Indiana side.[13]

Louisville hesitated to support any canal. The city had flourished on the transportation break, and many inhabitants felt that facilitating travel over the rapids would destroy the very *raison d'être* of the place. That view was probably extreme, but in the short run no one could deny that certain interests were jeopardized. "It must be admitted that the business of a portion of our population would be affected," the *Public Advertiser* confessed. "The storage and forwarding business would probably be diminished—and there might be less use for hacks and drays."[14] Tavern and hotel owners shared this anxiety, while the pilots who guided the ships through the chutes faced almost certain unemployment.

Unwilling to sacrifice these interests and uneasy about the town's future, Louisville leaders tried to deflect the mounting enthusiasm for a canal. Their first strategy was to suggest a small cut around the Falls which would accommodate keelboats and lesser craft. This expedient found few supporters, and Louisville next tried to reduce the pressure by paving the road to Portland and Shippingport, thus, facilitating the transshipment process.[15] But this, too, was inadequate, and within a few years the clamor for a canal became irresistible.

Yet the city still hoped to salvage something out of defeat, to find some compensation for the loss of its strategic position. In 1824 a local editor laid down the conditions. "It is true that we could feel but little interest in opening a canal merely for the purpose of navigation," he conceded. "A canal to be useful . . . should be constructed to give us ample water power, for various and extensive manufacturing establishments; and a sufficient number of dry docks for the building and . . . repair of nearly all the steamboats employed on western waters, should be constructed as necessary appendages." If the project included these items, he declared, then "the citizens of Louisville will be found among its most zealous advocates."[16]

The Falls City could afford to take its pound of flesh, because building on the Indiana side was much less feasible than the Kentucky route. The engineering problems were immensely more complicated, and the cost was nearly three times as great. In 1819 an official committee, comprised of delegates from Virginia, Pennsylvania, Ohio, and Kentucky, estimated the expense of the northern plan at $1,100,000 and the southern one at $350,000.[17] Hence few people acquainted with the situation took seriously the Jeffersonville Ohio Canal Company's enterprise. Yet the disadvantages of the Indiana route were not insurmountable, and Louisvillians realized that in the long run the Falls would be skirted on one side or the other. If they dragged their feet too much, their opponents would press for action regardless of the cost or difficulty. This possibility ultimately brought the Kentucky emporium to its knees.[18]

While Louisville reluctantly yielded at the Falls, Cincinnati pursued the rest of its expansion program. By 1822 the Miami Canal to Dayton was open, and work had begun on the state system which ultimately connected the Great Lakes with the Ohio River. Though the Queen City could claim less success in the Kentucky area, its economic supremacy in the West was not questioned. The new country's largest urban center, it had corralled the bulk of the region's mounting commerce and become the nexus of trade lines that reached from the Atlantic Ocean to the Gulf of Mexico.

Cincinnati's economic primacy, however, did not yet carry with it cultural leadership. This honor still belonged to Lexington, whose polish and sophistication were the envy of every transmontane town. "Cincinnati may be the Tyre, but Lexington is unquestionably the Athens of the West," *Liberty Hall* conceded in 1820. This admission reflected a sense of inadequacy which constantly shadowed the Queen City and compromised its claim to total supremacy. One resident suggested an ambitious lecture program to overcome the deficiency and "convince those persons at a distance who pronounce us as a *Commercial* people alone, that we have here, both the *Tyre* and the *Athens* of the West." Another observer, though not armed with a remedy, made the same point. "It may be well for us," he counseled, "when we can catch a moment from the grovelling pursuits of commercial operations, to cull and admire the varied sweets of those literary and scientific effusions, which have stamped Lexington as the headquarters of *Science and Letters* in the Western country."[19]

The establishment and success of Transylvania University [in Lexington] aggravated this inferiority complex. Not only did it lend prestige to another place, but it also lured local youths to its classrooms. The *Western Spy* admitted that it was "particularly mortifying to see the College of a neighboring state attract both Students and Professors" from the Ohio metropolis. In the early twenties Cincinnati countered with a medical school which it hoped would become a "powerful rival" and "ultimately go beyond" the Kentucky institution.[20] But it was not until financial difficulties and fire brought down Transylvania that the Queen City could claim cultural parity with its Blue Grass rival.

Lexington's position also bred jealousy in Louisville. Though the larger and more prosperous of the two by 1825, the Falls City had to concede that intellectual primacy rested with its Kentucky neighbor. This admission was not easy to make, because the two towns had been bitter foes for many years. They contended for political leadership in the state; earlier, in fact, each had hoped to become its capital. Moreover, their economic interests often collided, with Lexington depending upon manufacturing and protection and Louisville emphasizing commerce and wanting freer trade. Neither yielded readily to the other on any issue. Yet the cultural leadership of the Blue Grass town was too obvious to be denied, and, from the Falls City viewpoint, it was certainly too important to be permanently surrendered.

There was, however, something of a family quarrel about this rivalry. Despite their differences, both professed love for mother Kentucky, and occasionally one deferred to the other out of filial pride. In 1820, for example, Louisville's *Public Advertiser* supported state aid to Transylvania, explaining that "distinguished institutions of learning in our own state, where education from its cheapness, shall be within the reach of the poor, is the *pivot* on which the grandeur of the state depends." In addition, the Falls City stood to gain by its success. "Louisville cannot be jealous of Lexington," the same newspaper declared; "her future interest is measurably blended with that of Transylvania University; for as that flourishes Lexington will become a more extensive and important customer to her in a commercial point of view." Likewise, when Lexington tried to get money for a hospital, its old foe offered support, but for perhaps less elevated reasons. If the Blue Grass got such an institution, "one of the same kind at this place cannot, consistently, be refused," the editor observed.[21]

And nothing forced the two to discover common interests more quickly than the appearance of a hostile outsider. When Cincinnati planned a medical school to compete with Transylvania, Louisville stood behind the testimony of the university, whose spokesman urged the state to give additional money to the institution. Otherwise, he warned, "in the struggle that must ensue, we of Transylvania will be compelled to enter the lists naked and defenceless, our opponents of Cincinnati being . . . armed. The issue of such a conflict cannot be doubted. We shall certainly be vanquished and your young men will . . . repair to the eastern schools for medical education, or Kentucky must become tributary to the state of Ohio."[22] Lexington reciprocated when the Queen City threatened a canal on the Indiana side of the river.

Kind words were few, however, and mutual aid sporadic. Usually the two communities did little to conceal their animosity. In fact, Louisville had no sooner supported Transylvania's expansion than it began again its vicious barrage on the school and its town. The attack stemmed from a mixture of political, economic, and urban motives, but it centered on the university because it was at once the symbol of Lexington's importance and its most vulnerable spot. The city's economy never recovered from the postwar depression and only its cultural renaissance kept stores and shops open. If the college failed, all failed. This was understood in the Falls City. Indeed, the *Public Advertiser* noted that the "ablest and best citizens" of the Blue Grass metropolis had tried to give a "new impetus" to the place by the encouragement of its "literary establishments."[23] Knowingly, then, Louisville struck at Lexington where it would hurt most.

Nor was there anything gentle about the tactics. In 1816, during the first debate over state assistance to Transylvania, John Rowan from the Falls City argued that the institution ought to be moved elsewhere to keep it from "improper influence" and the "many means of corrupting the morals of youth," which existed in the town. Four years later the criticism had become more barbed. "If you wish to jeopardize every amiable trait in the private character of your son, send him to Lexington," the *Public Advertiser* contended, linking the college to radical politics. "If you wish him to become a Robespierre or a Murat, send him to Lexington to learn the rudiments of Jacobinism and disorganization." By 1829 a Louisville editor was warning parents that at the university their children would be "surrounded by political desperadoes" and that "the very atmosphere of the place has been calculated to pollute the morals and principles of the youth attending it.[24]

Lexington, though an old veteran of urban rivalries, had not anticipated this bitterness. "We thought of all our institutions, it was the pride and boast of the town; and the least calculated to excite the envy, and stir up the opposition of any individual or section of the country." But the assault threatened the city's very life, and it fought back. The defense was generally constructive, detailing the achievements of Transylvania and extolling its influence on students and the new country. Graduates wrote testimonials and local citizens publicized the healthfulness and "literary atmosphere" of the community, while officials dispelled rumors about the snobbery of the college.[25]

The case was good, but Lexington strategists bungled in several respects. In 1829 not a single Jacksonian was appointed to the Board of Trustees, and not enough was done to quiet the uneasiness of either the farmers or the highly religious.[26] As a result, when Transylvania needed support most, it was almost friendless. By 1830 the campaign instituted by Louisville had destroyed Kentucky's brightest ornament and pulled the most substantial prop from Lexington's economy.

Even before Transylvania's demise Lexington felt itself slipping economically, and it tried to steady itself by better connections with the trade of the Ohio River. Canals and roads proved either impractical or inadequate, and in 1829 civic leaders planned a railroad. The act of incorporation in the next year left the northern terminus undecided, with the understanding that it would be either Louisville or Cincinnati. The uncertainty set off a curious kind of competition between those two cities. Neither could foresee the impact that a railroad might have on its own importance, yet they equally feared that it would give their rival a substantial advantage.

Louisville was especially wary. This looked like the canal issue in another form, and many people thought it wise to wait for the results of the first project. Moreover, some of the same local interests seemed to be threatened. The hack and dray owners protested that their $125,000 business would be jeopardized. And since the railroad would pass through the city and continue on to Portland, others feared the growth of a "rival town" on the western end of the Falls. The city council, walking gingerly because of this opposition, appointed a committee to look into the question, and called a public hearing to sound out local opinion. The meeting attracted over three hundred people, and after a lively debate, it voted to keep the tracks out of Louisville.[27]

Very quickly, however, civic leaders realized that any alternative terminus was more perilous to the Falls City than the possible dislocations occasioned by accepting the railroad. Thus "S" wrote that if "we are to have a rival town, the nearer to us the less dangerous," and a "Gentleman in Lexington" warned that its "great rival, Cincinnati," was "straining every nerve" to induce the company to build in that direction. By December 1830 the tide had turned, and the council invited the Lexington and Ohio Railroad to come to Louisville.[28]

Cincinnati, despite its official policy, had many qualms about a railroad from Lexington. "Why should the citizens of Cincinnati be so anxious to create a rival town across the river?" asked the editor of the *Advertiser*. Yet the same logic which drove Louisville to change its mind sustained the Queen City's original decision. On December 7, 1830, a public meeting declared that the project "would conduce to the prosperity of this city, in an eminent degree," and a committee of prominent civic leaders invited the company's directors to come to Cincinnati to discuss details.[29] These events, coupled with Louisville's acceptance, brought great rejoicing to Lexington, for it now looked as though the railroad would bring it a share of the Ohio's commerce and arrest at last the economic decay which had brought the "Athens of the West" to the very brink of disaster.

The struggle for primacy and power—and occasionally survival—was one of the most persistent and striking characteristics of the early urban history of the West. Like imperial states, cities carved out extensive dependencies, extended their influence over the economic and political life of the hinterland, and fought with contending places over strategic trade routes. Nor was the contest limited to the young giants, for smaller towns joined the scramble. Cleveland and Sandusky, for example, clashed over the location of the northern terminus of the Ohio canal, the stakes being nothing less than the burgeoning commerce between the river and the lakes. And their instinct to fight was sound, for the outcome shaped the future of both.

Like most imperialisms, the struggle among Western cities left a record of damage and achievement. It trampled new villages, smothered promising towns, and even brought down established metropolises. Conflicting ambitions infused increasing bitterness into the intercourse of rivals, and made suspicion, jealousy, and vindictiveness a normal part of urban relationships. Yet competition also brought rapid expansion. The fear of failure was a dynamic force, pushing civic leaders into improvements long before they thought them necessary. The constant search for new markets furnished an invaluable stimulus to commercial and industrial enterprise. And, at its best, urban imperialism bred a strong pride in community accomplishment. As one resident put it, "there exists in our city a spirit . . . which may render any man proud to being called a Cincinnatian."[30]

# NOTES

1. *Pittsburgh Mercury,* February 3, 1816.
2. I. Craig to J. O'Hara, June 15, 1793, MS, Isaac Craig Papers, Carnegie Library of Pittsburgh.
3. C. B. Smith, "The Terminus of the Cumberland Road on the Ohio River" (M.A. Thesis, University of Pittsburgh, 1951), 69; *Western Herald* (Steubenville), April 12, 1816; Smith, "Cumberland Road," 71; Woods, *Illinois Country,* 75.
4. *Pittsburgh Statesman,* June 2, 1821; *Pittsburgh Gazette,* May 4, 1821.
5. *Northwestern Gazette* (Wheeling), June 16, 1821; *Pittsburgh Gazette,* December 18, 1818.
6. Smith, "Cumberland Road," 69; *Western Herald* (Steubenville), September 20, 1816.
7. *Pittsburgh Gazette,* January 22, 1819; February 5, 1819; *Liberty Hall* (Cincinnati), January 21, 1823; November 25, 1825.
8. *Pittsburgh Gazette,* January 22, 1819; *Pittsburgh Statesman,* November 26, 1818.
9. *Pittsburgh Gazette,* February 5, 1819; *Louisville Public Advertiser,* June 21, 1820.
10. For example, see the account of the Ohio Canal Company in *Liberty Hall* (Cincinnati), March 24, 1817.
11. The William Lytle Collection in the Historical and Philosophical Society of Ohio library includes a series of letters which explain his stake in the canal. He owned most of the land in the Portland area through which the canal ultimately passed. For a statement of its value, see D. McClellan to W. Lytle, October 21, 1817. Lytle Collection.

12. *Liberty Hall* (Cincinnati), December 29, 1817; March 26, 1817.
13. *Liberty Hall* (Cincinnati), June 5, 1818; February 26, 1818; May 20, 1818; May 6, 1818; May 14, 1819.
14. *Louisville Public Advertiser,* February 7, 1824.
15. *Liberty Hall* (Cincinnati), March 18, 1816; *Louisville Public Advertiser,* October 16, 1819.
16. *Louisville Public Advertiser,* January 21, 1824.
17. *Louisville Public Advertiser,* November 17, 1819.
18. *Louisville Public Advertiser,* February 7, 1824.
19. *Liberty Hall* (Cincinnati), May 27, 1820; December 17, 1819; May 27, 1820.
20. *Western Spy* (Cincinnati), October 13, 1817; *Liberty Hall* (Cincinnati), January 14, 1823.
21. *Louisville Public Advertiser,* September 20, 1820; September 27, 1820; December 20, 1820.
22. *Louisville Public Advertiser,* November 27, 1820.
23. *Louisville Public Advertiser,* August 23, 1820.
24. *Kentucky Reporter,* February 14, 1816; *Louisville Public Advertiser,* September 9, 1820; October 13, 1829.
25. *Kentucky Reporter,* March 7, 1827; March 10, 1823; February 21, 1827; September 8, 1828.
26. For these problems see, for example, *Louisville Public Advertiser,* October 29, 1829.
27. *Louisville Public Advertiser,* December 8, 1830; November 2, 1830; Louisville, City Journal, October 20, 1830; October 29, 1830; *Louisville Public Advertiser,* November 4, 1830.
28. *Louisville Public Advertiser,* November 3, 1830; November 5, 1830; Louisville, City Journal, December 3, 1830.
29. *Cincinnati Advertiser,* December 11, 1830; *Liberty Hall* (Cincinnati), December 10, 1830.
30. *Liberty Hall* (Cincinnati), January 9, 1829.

# 4

## *Mark Douglas Lowes*

# INDY DREAMS AND URBAN NIGHTMARES

In media coverage of the Molson Indy Vancouver, a recurrent theme is that the race puts Vancouver on 'the world stage'—a sensibility frequently captured by reference to the argument that hosting this spectacular international event could make Vancouver 'the Monaco of North America, Canada's Monte Carlo.' This allusion draws on all the glitz and glamour of Monaco: the high-flying royal family and its Hollywood connections through the late Grace Kelly, its palaces and mansions, posh hotels and casinos, breathtaking Mediterranean landscape, a playground for globetrotting financial power players, and not least—Monaco's annual Formula One race, the Monaco Grand Prix, one of the most prestigious and anticipated stops on the F-1 circuit.

Like its Monte Carlo referent, the Molson Indy Vancouver event and its spectacular False Creek site are saturated with meaning, with connotations of greatness, of European chic. Promoters argue that the Molson Indy brings all that to Vancouver—the international lifestyle of elite motorsport racing, its flashy drivers from all over the world, including Brazil, Argentina, and Spain. 'The Molson Indy Vancouver has gotten to the point where it's more than just a race. It has become a world-class event,' declared the chair of Tourism Vancouver at the 1995 event. The MIV brings all this to Vancouver every year. In this sense, to civic boosters the Molson Indy is a *signifier* of Vancouver's arrival as a world-class city. 'It is Canada's Monte Carlo, pure and simple, a stunning setting where the Coast Range meets the Pacific Ocean.'[1]

Vancouver's distant claim to 'Monte Carlo–ness' arises from its international pretensions as an emerging player on the world stage, its celebration of affluent lifestyle pursuits: the large concentration of art galleries, trendy clothing and accessory boutiques, hair salons, New Age bookstores, and many branches of Starbucks that saturate the False Creek area. Moreover, the Molson Indy gives the city international exposure through its coverage by the media, the media hordes spending up to four and five days in the city, covering not only the actual race but also various general interest stories about Vancouver and its surrounding region. In such coverage the city is typically represented as a world-class place. 'It puts Vancouver on the map, both as a major destination and a city that knows how to throw a party.'[2]

I asked a city engineer responsible for the Molson Indy file to explain what is in it for the city, hosting the Indy race. He answered unequivocally that the primary motivation for the city's support of the event is 'global exposure.' He explains: 'The city itself doesn't really make any money off the Molson Indy, [not directly]. Coverage of the race, it puts the city out to the world. It's exposure.' This international exposure, the argument runs, translates into economic windfall primarily through increased tourism. This is the apparent payoff for Vancouver and its business community. The city engineer I spoke to continues, explaining: 'You see how it works: you give away the television rights, if you want to pick it up in Brazil, South Africa, Mexico, Australia—then go ahead and do it. You put it on the tube over there and—Hey, there's Vancouver. Look at those mountains, wouldn't that be a nice place to visit, do some skiing. You see? . . . It's great for promoting Whistle-Blackcomb. The Molson Indy Vancouver has, several times, been reported as *the Monaco of North America,* alluding to the Formula One racing event held there each year, a major and really glamorous event that is known around the world.'

Jerry Krull, a long-time motor sport enthusiast and promoter, elaborates this notion of Vancouver as Monaco: 'Monaco is a Formula One race. There's always the naysayers that show up in the local media there. If they took that race out of there, not only would the mystique be gone, so would that influx of cash that event generates once a year. But it's also a part of their culture, a key element of Monaco's identity as a glamorous international city. And that's what I'd like to see happen in Vancouver with the Molson Indy. There's a lot of public support for the race. It adds something significant, a big celebrity event, to the local area each year.'

Along these same lines, the MIV's media relations director explains in so many words that the Indy is a key promotional signifier of Vancouver's world-class standing. He acknowledges that 'from a technical point of view we are a nuisance. We close roads, we close bridges, the cars are very noisy.' Nonetheless, he argues that 'overall, the community supports the race because its good for the city, its good profile, it's a lot of fun . . . the race fills up the entire city. It's hard to find a hotel room for that long weekend in September. It brings a billion [television] viewers to Vancouver—and how do you put a number on that, in terms of promoting tourism or whatever? *It just reinforces Vancouver's standing as an international city'* (my emphasis).

Crucial to this imaging function of the Molson Indy is that organizers must site the race in a place that has 'a downtown, international feel . . . You can't stick the event just anywhere.' This is why, notes one MIV staffer, False Creek is such a perfect location: 'Down there, the race site is right beside the water. You've got the posh condo residences and office towers there, people in their yachts and whatnot, moored in the east False Creek basin. I mean, it's a very pretty sight, a very picturesque sight, which is another reason why the Indy group was pushing so hard to keep the race in Vancouver . . . Burnaby and Surrey, they just aren't the same as False Creek, as downtown Vancouver. You know, Vancouver is a world-class city and that means a lot when you're hosting an event like this. For example, the Detroit Grand Prix—not to take anything away from their event, but its held at Detroit's old airport. It's not a pretty race they have there; it doesn't have any, uh, luster.'

False Creek delivers this spectacular visual and physical landscape. As we shall see in the following chapters, so does Hastings Park, which is why it was the site organizers wanted to move to when they lost False Creek.

This express concern for image and the crucial role it plays in civic boosterism and urban growth strategies is not entirely a new phenomenon. Richard Gruneau and David Whitson make the point that image has *always* been important in the making of modern industrial cities. 'Boosterism,' they write, 'combines a promoter's professional optimism with a competitiveness that is presented simply as an instinct for survival.' At the beginning of the twentieth century the wide-open, entrepreneurial atmosphere of Canadian capitalism, for instance, found local boosters typically working hard to distinguish their nascent community from countless others like it. Western Canada, in particular, attracted 'dreamers and promoters' and those 'dreams (and investments) could quickly turn to dust if not enough people could be persuaded to share in them by settling in your community rather than somewhere else . . . The presence of more settlers in a locale might make a trader set up a store or a doctor establish a medical practice. In turn, the presence of businesses and services that attracted farmers to do their business at one crossroads rather than another served to attract other businesses and more settlers to the area.'[3]

In this sense, the Canadian urban landscape was a highly contested promotional terrain. Whether an area would develop as an important urban centre or 'turn to dust' depended very much on the ability of its civic leaders to attract industry, jobs, and attractive urban recreations for its citizens. In this context, it was necessary to cultivate and disseminate an image of prosperity, of the area's entrepreneurial drive and boldness of vision.

The presence of 'community life' was very important to constructing this image of a prosperous area, and for distinguishing it from other areas competing for the same investment capital and settlers. Gruneau and Whitson argue that a positive image of community life was significant not only because it made a difference to the happiness of settler or labourer families, but also because it 'reinforced the image of a vital (and hence probably growing) community.'[4] It became common practice for business people and others who had an interest in promoting their communities to throw their support behind a variety of community associations and organizations. Sports teams in particular emerged as extremely popular promotional vehicles for spreading a town's reputation—especially the ones that beat their neighbours' teams at fairs and regional competitions.[5]

The organized sports that emerged in Canada during the last two decades of the 1800s and into the early twentieth century became very powerful vehicles for expressing community aspirations, spirit, pride, and prosperity. Throughout this period, the representative character of spectacular sports entertainment provided a new way of speaking metaphorically about the relationships between civic identities, status, and power in Canadian social life. When local athletes or teams began to represent their communities, the significance of winning or losing increased dramatically. Initially, when athletes came from or resided in their home communities, Gruneau and Whitson argue, it could be credibly claimed that the quality of a team's performance actually said something about the community that produced it—'not only about the skill levels of its players, but also about the character of its people.'[6]

This representational dynamic was a constitutive element in the early urbanization and industrialization of Canada. It emerged at a time when the first brush strokes mapping the country we recognize today were drawn: a map featuring well-established centres of population and commerce, and substantial road, rail, and telecommunications networks to service them. In this context, sports and fairs, and the spectacular architecture often associated with them, joined together in a celebration of industrial modernity: discourses of technology, progress, and prosperity were articulated through a community or region's agricultural fairs, exhibitions, sports teams—and their venues. The driving motivation behind this was to make a bold statement about a city, to attract attention and business into its fold.

Vancouver's Pacific National Exhibition (PNE), for instance, was inaugurated at Hastings Park early in the twentieth century as a major agricultural fair, featuring the latest developments in farming and industrial machinery, as well as facilities for thoroughbred horse racing and other amusements. For the city's business and political leaders, the broader objectives behind establishing the annual exhibition were to distinguish Vancouver from its regional neighbours as an industrial city with a strong entrepreneurial drive and spirit—precisely the sort of civic image that confers an advantage in competitions for industrial investment capital and population growth.[7]

Civic image continued to play a vital role in the growth strategies of major North American cities over the course of the twentieth century. Nevertheless, over the past three decades things have changed somewhat from the processes of urbanization and settlement just described. There is a considerable agreement in the social sciences that the period since the early 1970s represents a transition of sorts from one distinct phase of capitalist development to a new one—known variously by host of terms, such as 'post-industrialism,' 'post-Fordism,' and 'flexible accumulation.' In this transition there has been a shift from a centralized manufacturing base, featuring mass production, government regulation, and mass markets, towards more technologically versatile and 'flexible' modes of organizing production. Accompanying this, the argument runs, in the face of the widespread deregulation of industry and markets, and given new communications technologies, there has also been widespread fragmentation of mass markets into more specialized niches.

It is easy to over-draw these changes. They do appear, however, to have had a significant impact on older industrial cities, resulting in massive economic and social restructuring and, in some cases, collapse and decay.[8] We are now in a time of 'bewildering transformation and change' in the structure and organization of modern Western economy and society.[9] Capitalism is 'at a crossroads' . . . in its historical development signaling the emergence of forces—technological, market, social and institutional—that will be very different from those which dominated the economy after the Second World War.' There is a pervasive sense that these are times of 'epoch-making transformation' in the very forces that drive, stabilize, and reproduce the capitalist world.

In contrast to the unprecedented economic expansion of the immediate postwar period, the 1960s and 1970s saw a series of changes in the relative wealth, power, and status of cities and regions across North America—notably, shifts of wealth and people away from once-powerful industrial centres into other kinds of economic activity and other locales.[10] In addition, widespread deficit reduction strategies by national and regional governments put increased pressure on the budgets of municipal governments through such strategies as the "offloading" of the debts of higher levels of government onto municpal governments. In this context, both growing and declining cities have found themselves in a ruthless competition for new forms of investment, for specific capital investments, as well as for relative position in relation to other cities. This has fomented intense inter-urban competition on a global scale, far exceeding in scope the state of affairs in the early part of the twentieth century. On this point, Gruneau and Whitson remark: 'As civic governments have competed for new kinds of investment beyond older industrial investments, they've become more self-consciously "entrepreneurial." These "entrepreneurial cities" now compete to be financial centres, administrative centres, and . . . cultural and entertainment centres.[11]

In response to this new phase of capital accumulation and its dramatic impacts on industrial centres, civic elites have sought to revitalize the city through growth strategies primarily centred on investment and construction aimed at remodelling or rebuilding a portion of the urban environment to accommodate more profitable activities, and expanded opportunities for consumption, particularly in the form of high-density condominium housing and upscale shopping and office boutiques for an upper middle class. In other words, areas of the city are upgraded for 'higher' social and economic uses—those activities that generate the greatest profits based on location.[12]

Urban revitalization projects have always changed both the physical form and the image of the city, the ways in which it is perceived and experienced, and the emotional relationships between people (both local residents and visitors) and urban settings. However, the issue of civic image has taken on special prominence in major cities over the past three decades. The goal has become to upgrade the image of the city—to replace perceptions of the city as a place of disinvestment, deterioration, crime, and poverty. If civic boosters in western nations have long promoted images of progress, growth, vitality, and prosperity, such promotions now seem to have taken on a pressing urgency. In this context, the 'image of the vigorous, renascent city is carefully nurtured as the seed of the future material city.'[13]

More precisely, it is a 'world-class' image of the city that civic elites now strive self-consciously to construct. Researchers have argued that the primary force driving this is inter-urban competition for the major public and private investments that contribute to economic growth.[14] For example, David Harvey argues that cities now take much more care to create a positive and high quality *image of place*, and they seek an architecture and forms of urban design that respond directly to such need. 'That they should be so pressed . . . is understandable, given the grim history of deindustrialization and restructuring that left most major cities in the advanced capitalist word with few options except to compete with each other, mainly as financial, consumption, and entertainment centres.'[15] For civic boosters, it seems that now, more than ever before, *image is everything*.

In a climate of relentless inter-urban competition, spending on image-making and public relations is often perceived to be as important as spending on urban infrastructure and other tangible upgrades. The more that a city such as Vancouver can appear 'on the same stage' or 'in the same league' with New York, Tokyo, and Los Angeles, the stronger its civic leaders believe their chances will be of growing and prospering, rather than remaining simply as a regional or provincial centre on the margins of world business, political, and cultural affairs.

Spectacular consumption spaces are vital signifiers conveying this image of the world-class city. Shopping megamalls, gentrified downtowns, waterfront retail districts with hotel and convention centres, high-density condominium and office complexes, upscale clothing boutiques, sports stadiums—these are the spectacular 'consumption palaces' through which the city is now imaged. It is around these spaces that promotional discourses concerning the city's identity and future development trajectory are constructed and disseminated. Imaging a city through the organization of spectacular consumption-biased spaces has become a dominant means for attracting capital and people (of the desired affluence) in this period of intensified inter-urban competition and urban entrepreneurialism. Not only are these the city's premier consumption sites, but most significantly these places function as the city's key *symbolic* places; it is through these places that the city is imaged and marketed as a world-class place.

What is more, it is not just the built and physical environment that is crucial to imaging the city: the *lifestyles* that can be pursued in these spaces through recreation and leisure activities are also vital to a city's image. For it is in these spectacular consumption-biased spaces that people circulate and, through their various consumption activities, form personal and collective identities—in what amounts to a widespread desire to invest personal resources (time, money, and effort) in the *pursuit of lifestyle*. Indeed, a serious engagement with contemporary urban living must appreciate that lifestyles and consumption activities constitute the emergence of new personal and collective identities. In these terms, cultural consumption must be treated as an active and committed production of both *self* and *public culture*. Consumption activities of this nature necessarily include the social patterns of leisure and new expectations for the control and use of time and space in personally meaningful ways.

A major theme in the literature suggests that the way consumption spaces are organized in today's cities has become at least as important in people's lives as the organization of production spaces (factories, warehouses, and dock- and railyards).[16] This basic assertion leads me to emphasize the importance of the leisure and entertainment industries—the so-called culture industries—in urban political economy. With a continued displacement of manufacturing and increasing development of the service, financial, and non-profit sectors of the urban economy, cultural production and consumption is now so much of what major cities are all about. 'Culture' in this sense is both a commodity and a public good, a base of economic growth and a means of framing the city and its public life.[17] If we want to understand what is happening to urban public culture today, then we have to look at what is happening to the city's most prominent spaces for public consumption.

## NOTES

1. Mike Beamish, 'Concord Pacific Place: Creating a Course,' *Molson Indy Vancouver Program,* 1995, 8.
2. Ted Laturnus, 'Concord Pacific Place: Creating a Course,' *Molson Indy Vancouver Program* 1995, 60.
3. Richard Gruneau and David Whitson, *Hockey Night in Canada: Sport, Identities and Cultural Practices* (Toronto: Garamond, 1993), 210–11.
4. Ibid., 211.
5. For an excellent analysis and discussion of the emergence of organized sport in late eighteenth-century Canada, see Alan Metcalfe, *Canada Learns to Play: The Emergence of Organized Sport, 1807–1914* (Toronto: McClelland and Stewart, 1987), Chapter 3. See also, Bruce Kidd, *The Struggle for Canadian Sport* (Toronto: University of Toronto Press, 1996).
6. Gruneau and Whitson, *Hockey Night,* 67.

7. David Breen and Kenneth Coates, *Vancouver's Fair* (Vancouver: University of British Columbia Press 1982).

8. Sharon Zukin, *Landscapes of Power: From Detroit to Disney World* (Berkeley: University of California Press, 1991); Harvey, *The Condition of Postmodernity* (Oxford: Blackwell, 1989); Neil Smith and Peter Williams (eds.), *Gentrification of the City* (Boston: Allen and Unwin, 1986); David Ley, *A Social Geography of the City* (New York: Harper and Row, 1983); H. Holcomb and Robert Beauregard, *Revitalizing Cities* (Washington, DC: Association of American Geographers, 1981).

9. Ash Amin, 'Post-Fordism: Models, Fantasies and Phantoms of Transition,' in Ash Amin (ed.), *Post-Fordism: A Reader* (London: Blackwell, 1994), 1–40.

10. David Harvey, 'Flexible Accumulation through Urbanization: Reflections on "Post-Modernism" in the American City.' *Antipode,* 19(3), 1987.

11. Gruneau and Whitson, *Hockey Night in Canada,* 235–6.

12. On this point, two articles by Neil Smith are instructive: 'Gentrification and Uneven Development,' *Economic Geography* 58, (1982), 139–55; 'Gentrification and the Rent Gap,' *Annals of the Association of American Geographers* 77, (1987), 462–78.

13. Holcomb and Beauregard, *Revitalizing Cities,* 52.

14. B. J. Friedan and L. B. Sagalyn, *Downtown Inc.: How America Rebuilds Its Cities,* Cambridge, Mass.: MIT Press, 1989).

15. Harvey, *The Condition of Postmodernity,* 91–2.

16. Zukin, *The Cultures of Cities* and *Landscapes of Power.*

17. Zukin, *The Cultures of Cities,* 260.

# CHAPTER 2

# CITIES IN THE INTERNATIONAL MARKETPLACE

## THE NEW URBAN ECONOMY

Three changes in global capitalism have transformed urban economies: the replacement of industrial with service-sector jobs, the deconcentration of business activities and urban residents, and the emergence of an international competition among cities. In Selection 5, H. V. Savitch and Paul Kantor trace these developments. They argue that the radical deconcentration of businesses and population began around the middle of the twentieth century as changes in communication, technology, transportation, and production processes enabled more and more businesses to leave central cities in favor of lower-cost locations in suburbia and the Sunbelt. Where jobs went, people followed. By the end of the century, these movements had transformed the United States into a predominantly suburban nation.

Savitch and Kantor also show that the deindustrialization of urban economies changed how Americans make a living. The United States has become less dependent on industry and hard goods production because business activity has shifted decidedly into services. Where cities once pursued smokestack industries, they now are converting old warehouse, seaport, and industrial districts to tourist destinations, downtown malls, and office centers. In places where armies of blue-collar workers in factories fueled city growth, today it is more likely to be driven by white-collar managers and technicians meeting face-to-face in downtown offices, business parks, and upscale restaurants. Finally, the authors describe how globalization has made cities, suburbs, and even whole regions part of an international marketplace. The latter is characterized by rapid communication, transnational business activities, and a complex linkage among workers, managers, and cultures all over the world.

Savitch and Kantor argue that this "great transformation" is a source of new political challenges for cities of all kinds. Older as well as newer urban centers must compete on a wider playing field as places to work and live. Those who lose in this game of competition struggle to find ways of coping with their diminished fate. Yet the authors do not conclude that local governments are prisoners of the forces of internationalization. Rather, they believe that local choices about the kind of community citizens want to live in remain important because there are many possible responses to external challenges. While some cities may give high priority to fast business growth, others may not, or they may choose a different strategy for enhancing the economic health of the community, such as promoting culture and amenities—schools, parks, and libraries—that affect the quality of life.

The other two readings in this chapter describe the strategies used by urban governments to compete for economic growth; each selection also raises questions about who benefits from these policies. There is evidence that citizens often come up empty-handed in the end or that public officials give away far too much in the deal-making that goes on between business and government. Selection 6, by Richard Foglesong, illustrates this point. In his brief story of the coming of Disney World to Winter Park, Florida, Foglesong describes how the transformation of that community by America's entertainment giant was dominated by private purposes and unexpected public consequences. Although Disney promised to build a model city for people to live in, what eventually materialized was a megacomplex entertainment center that is run purely as a business. This was possible in part because the Disney Corporation managed to win the legal right to incorporate itself as a virtual city-state controlled by the company while enjoying regulatory powers and privileges normally reserved by law to popularly elected local governments. Without a resident citizen population, the government of Epcot became—to use Foglesong's phrase—"a Vatican with mouse ears." As such, company executives could make key decisions without having to answer to any local residents other than a handful of their own employees.

In Selection 7, Paul Kantor and H. V. Savitch argue that local officials can sometimes gain considerable influence in guiding their own development even though the pressures to compete are intense. Scholars have sometimes depicted cities as junior partners to business in the global development game. In theory, business investors have many cities and regions to choose from; cities are often desperate to attract their money and employees. In their comparative analysis of cities in the United States and Western Europe, Kantor and Savitch show that the real world is not always so one-sided. The authors describe how city bargaining advantages relative to business are not uniform; sometimes business actually is the junior partner. The explanation is that the bargaining advantages of cities can be enhanced by market conditions, local political systems, and national urban policies. For example, some city governments have the advantage of a very favorable market environment for attracting or keeping business; not all are desperate to chase every dollar investors offer. Sometimes this is because there are businesses—entertainment parks, for example—with such large sunk costs that they cannot easily move elsewhere.

Alternatively, some global cities, such as London, Tokyo, and New York, serve as global anchors for industries like financial services; this limits the economic competition they face from smaller cities. Still others may have such highly diversified economies that jobs that are lost are easily replaced. In all these circumstances, economic advantages can favor cities, not investors. This, in turn, makes it possible for these city governments to act with greater independence and promote development policies that generate more community benefits than others can.

As the authors note, bargaining advantages are not always economic in nature. Cities that have highly democratic political systems are better able to resist business demands. Cities with access to assistance from national governments that take an active role in urban affairs also are better able to extract concessions from the private sector and limit business power. Savitch and Kantor's comparative research suggests that the role of national governments in supporting their cities may be pivotal. U.S. cities tend to have fewer bargaining advantages than their counterparts in Western Europe—largely because of the limited role of the federal government in regulating local economic development activity.

# 5

## H. V. Savitch and Paul Kantor

## CITIES IN THE INTERNATIONAL MARKETPLACE

An enormous transformation engulfs the industrial world. The rapidity and consequences are unparalleled. The change is breathtaking. The ancient world lasted for three thousand years, the medieval age for less than a millennium, and the industrial era for about a century. Our postindustrial society has been brought about in roughly three decades, and its pace is quickening. This new revolution has already remade the economic fabric of society, radically altered the behavior of capital, broken down national boundaries, and is remodeling government.

This transformation is particularly profound within liberal democratic states in North America and Western Europe. Since 1970, these states have shed their older industrial capacity and have become societies dominated by the tertiary sector—business, professions, services, high technology, and government. Within these societies capital has changed its configuration. It is more nimble and more multinational.[1] "Flexible production" and "just-in-time inventory" are not only techniques for quick action but they have also changed the operations of capitalism. Corporate ownership is not confined solely to a single nation but can span the globe, putting management in the hands of unlikely collaborators. Archrivals continue their rivalries but also find themselves in partnership with one other; fiercely competing one day and collaborating the next. The giant plane-manufacturer Airbus is a case in point. Its operations are a product of a European high-tech faceoff with America. At the same time, it buys products from its American nemesis, Boeing, and 40 percent of Airbus components are made in the United States.

Migration is another part of the story. Counting refugees alone, one finds that within the last decade 4.3 million have flocked into Germany, France, Italy, and the United Kingdom. Over one million have turned to the United States and Canada.[2] Recent immigrants now make up roughly 10 percent of these last two societies. While North America is regarded as the traditional immigrant haven, the numbers in Western Europe have exploded. During the past decade European officials expected that more than 25 million legal or illegal immigrants would settle on that continent.[3] Meanwhile birth rates of nationals within most Western countries have flattened or declined. The birth rate crisis is most acute in France and Italy, where the newborn cannot keep pace with the rate of mortality. As those birthrates continue to plummet, Europeans will have to rely on even more immigrants to support high living standards and generous pensions.

On the political front transnational pacts have nurtured the transformation by facilitating the movement of goods, people, and common policies across boundaries. The most prominent of these pacts are in the West and include the European Union (EU), which comprises fifteen nations, and the North American Free Trade Association (NAFTA), composed of the United States, Canada, and Mexico.[i] The EU already has a supranational government and bureaucracy that imposes policy on member nations. NAFTA is not that far advanced, but it has begun to affect political life in North America by forcing choices over freer trade, currency supports, and labor policy.

Technology plays a central role in this transformation. Just as previous periods may have been driven by steam locomotion (1780–1840), rail transportation (1840–90), electric power (1890–1930), or petroleum energy (1930–70), so the current era is propelled by the transmission of information. The last quarter of the twentieth century was appropriately called "the information age," and it portended revolutionary technological achievements into this millennium.

By now it may be a commonplace observation that warrants repeating. Ordinary people are communicating faster, they are more directly in touch with events, and they often exchange information person to person. The new world of cyberspace is just one technology that allows this. At the dawn of the postindustrial age, during the mid-1970s, just 50,000 computers existed in the world. That number has now rocketed to 556 million, giving common individuals access to each other across the globe. More than half of Americans and more than a quarter of Western Europeans own computers. In North America and Western Europe, big and small cities are hard-wired for instant communication. Carriers, like BBC or CNN, have established global news networks, allowing the world to witness the same events at the same time. Impressions are created instantly, and reactions occur swiftly. The decreasing cost of telephone service and the spread of fiber optic cables (simultaneously transmitting 1.5 million conversations within the diameter of a human hair) catapulted personal information to new levels. By the year 2000 international telephone calls reached an all-time high of 100 billion minutes.[4] None of these developments can create democracy, but collectively they assure wider dissemination of information, they facilitate freer exchange among people, and they hold potential for greater accountability between rulers and the ruled. Under these conditions, it becomes increasingly difficult to monopolize information, control public opinion, or ignore citizen demands.

The combination of economic, demographic, technological, and political change is cumulative, and will continue to impact the social order. No society encapsulates this transformation more than urban society. Cities are the crucibles through which radical experiments become convention. They are concentrated environments in which people adapt and their resilience is tested. They are the world's incubators of innovation—made possible by critical mass, diversity, and rich interaction. And cities have steadily grown over the centuries to fulfill that role. In the tenth century one of the world's largest cities, Cordoba, held just 300,000 people. Later Constantinople became the leading metropolis and held half a million people. By the eighteenth century London had surpassed every other Western city with one million inhabitants. In the twentieth century New York rose to ascendancy with several million people. Now in the twenty-first century Tokyo, São Paulo, and Mexico City have climbed above ten million inhabitants.

What is more, cities have complemented their role as global innovators with geophysical centrality. Despite enormous changes in technology, cities remain at the juncture of world transportation, as transit points for business, science, and travel of every stripe. This puts cities at the very pivot of transformation. Few statistics demonstrate this better than air traffic. . . .

In just nine short years average passenger traffic jumped by 51 percent while cargo increased by 131 percent. Already a global transit point, Paris more than doubled both its air passengers and cargo, Seoul showed a similar doubling in passengers and cargo, while Amsterdam and London also showed impressive gains. All told, every one of these cities registered gains, and we note that these advance have been made on very substantial bases. Cities are continuing to grow in this global transformation, and indeed are at its very heart. Despite the dip in passenger air traffic after September 11, that transformation is likely to continue and cities will resume their station at the junctures of air travel.

This tells us something not only about the future, but also about the recent past. Cities have been the terrain on which technological, social, and global transformation has taken place. Cities hold the machinery that furnishes each era with a distinct product; they are the progenitors of national culture; and, they are the great mixing cauldrons that supply a unique human hybrid. In providing all of these functions, cities continually remake themselve, reconstruct their productive base, and adapt their physical environment to the necessities of the time.

We examine this transformation . . . (along three distinct trajectories: 1) the deindustrialization of urban economies, 2) the deconcentration of older cities,  and 3) the globalization process. As we shall see, cities are not necessarily the passive recipients of this change, but have the capacity to guide it and shape its impact. . . .

## Deindustrialization: For What?

Just thirty years ago, cities in North America and Europe were bustling with factories, workshops, warehouses, and open air markets. While the great primate cities of New York, London, and Paris had always held financial houses and corporate headquarters, they also were balanced by textile manufacture, light industry, chemical production, and warehousing.[ii]

At the same time, secondary cities took on the heavy lifting. Cleveland, Pittsburgh, Birmingham, Newcastle, Essen, Lille, and Turin were centers for tool and dye making, automobile manufacture, and steel production. These industrial towns were complemented by cities of passage. New Orleans, Liverpool, Marseilles, Hamburg, and Naples were glorious ports, which boasted the world's finest bistros and bawdiest night life.

Secondary cities were the workshops of the industrial world. They also housed large numbers of blue-collar families in a rich social milieu. From London's East End to New Orleans's Garden District, neighborhoods anchored the social life of the city. To be sure, the housing was often substandard and the neighborhoods overcrowded, but they spawned a host of vibrant institutions. Labor unions, shops, schools, churches, and social clubs bound communities together, allowed citizens to connect to public institutions, and gave the city meaning.

The bulk of those factories are now gone and many of the ports are closed. Some workers hold on to remnants of the old economy, some have joined the ranks of the unemployed, and others have found jobs elsewhere. While some working-class neighborhoods are intact, others have been gentrified and enriched with boutiques and expensive specialty shops. Still other inner-city neighborhoods now accommodate immigrants who bring with them a new culture, different foodstuffs, and an altogether distinct way of life (from tea salons to mosques). A substantial number of old neighborhoods, mostly in America and Great Britain, have not been recycled for the gentry or for immigrants. Instead they have fallen into disuse: the houses are abandoned, stores are boarded up, sidewalks are littered, and streets are dangerous. Many social institutions are gone—either they have disappeared or taken new form in the suburbs. . . .

Deindustrialization is generating uneven development and social imbalance. . . . Some cities remain in decay while others have succeeded in remaking themselves. Chicago, Cleveland, Madrid, and Rotterdam saw the collapse of blue-collar employment. Some of these same cities (Madrid and Rotterdam) made up their losses in manufacture through white-collar employment. Other cities like Cleveland, Philadelphia, and St. Louis have not yet recovered from this trauma. The crises of transformation is more widespread in Anglo-American cities than on the European continent. American cities were particularly hard hit, and account for the bulk of those that have yet to recover. In part, this is due to the nineteenth- and early-twentieth-century genesis of American central cities as locations for heavy industry. This is also true for some British cities (Newcastle, Liverpool, Glasgow). Continental cities mostly developed in the trading eras of the seventeenth and eighteenth centuries, and wealth was largely vested in the urban core. Thus, the ecological structure of European cities permitted them to shift more easily to tertiary economies.[iii]

By and large, primate cities did well. London emerged as the banking center where capital could be concentrated, New York as a producer of financial instruments where loans and mergers could be consummated, and Paris as a seat for corporate headquarters and professional services where deals could be struck. Each of these cities carved out niches for themselves as command posts in a larger world economy.[5] In large measure London, New York, and Paris became the forerunners of postindustrialism and established the pace for others.[6] To be sure, these cities already had thriving nests of banks and corporate headquarters, and they were able to build upon economies of agglomeration. Yet primate cities are complex, and during the 1950s high finance made up just a fraction of their economies. Manufacture, ports, and warehousing held the bulk of employment, and losses in these sectors were enormous. After deindustrialization struck, London, New York, and Paris had to refill huge holes in their economies just to stay even.

Secondary cities show greater variation in outcome. Cleveland experienced fiscal collapse in 1978, and nearly 40 percent of its residents are now below the poverty line.[7] Detroit and countless other rustbelt cities in America suffered a similar fate.[8] By contrast, Pittsburgh guided its shrinkage, revived its economy through research and technology, and kept its downtown healthy. In France, grimy, industrial Lille was rebuilt as the crossroads for Northern Europe. Industrial Glasgow has acquired a new downtown, but the rest of the city remains mired in decline.

Port cities have also turned out differently from one another. New Orleans and Liverpool fell into deep decline and have yet to recover. For a while, Hamburg reeled under successive economic blows, but recovered by modernizing its port and diversifying its industry. Today it is one of Europe's success stories and exults in the fact that it has more millionaires per capital than any other city on the continent.[9] Rotterdam, too, managed a partially successful transition by retaining its role as Europe's leading port and by building commercial linkages with Amsterdam and Utrecht.

Deindustrialization has also paved the way for new types of cities. So-called new-age boomtowns or sunbelt cities owe their urban form to late-twentieth-century technology.[10] Their economies usually are based on computers, software, electronics, space technology, or other emerging economic sectors. Their social structure is founded on middle-class outlooks, small families, and private housing. Especially in North America, new-age boomtowns enjoy an abundance of space, and their development spreads out along the corridors of modern freeways.

The United States has a concentration of these cities in its southwest and counts among them Phoenix, Houston, Albuquerque, and San Diego. Canada's boomtowns are found in its westerly open spaces and include Calgary and Vancouver. Boomtowns are not as common in Europe, which is already highly urbanized and lacks much vacant land. Nevertheless, European versions of these cities can be found in Southeast London (Croydon) and Oxford, in Grenoble and Montpellier, in Bavaria (Munich), and in the smaller towns of Italy's Northeast.

In America these boomtowns grew rapidly during the late 1960s and through the 1970s. Upheavals in petroleum and real estate sometimes threw cities like Houston into shock. But Houston recovered and continues to grow. In Canada, Vancouver is fueled by investments from Hong Kong, and it continues to lead that nation. The picture in Europe is hazy, though cities like Oxford and Grenoble have embraced high technology and believe that they are Europe's answer to the Silicon Valley.

In a nutshell, cities in North America and Europe changed substantially during the previous three decades. While the most successful became postindustrial, that status represented a dominant layer of activity, superimposed upon a diminished base of manufacture, shipping, and skilled trades. Less successful cities underwent shrinkage, though many of these managed to secure some postindustrial activity (small downtowns, tourism, stadiums, and exhibition centers). New-age boomtowns thrived on a combination of office employment, services, electronics, and light industry—set in the midst of universities, research centers, and low density development.

This reshuffling of the urban hierarchy has brought old and new cities into a competitive scramble to secure their economic well-being. As old industries decline and new investment patterns emerge, citizens and politicians are drawn into finding a niche for their communities in the new economic order. In the process, cities may be gripped by a certain angst—internal conflicts over means and ends, a belief that if a community does not grow it will surely die, and a rush to move faster.

## Deconcentration: The Spreading Urban Landscape

The great transformation has also influenced human settlement and mobility. Overall, central cities have lost population. This deconcentration of population encompasses a range of different demographic processes, some healthy for cities, others not. Deconcentration entails movement away from places. This includes a movement out of healthy central cities, which allows remaining residents more space and gives departing residents more economical accommodations. We call this *dedensification*. Of course, dedensification also involves movement toward other places. This includes a burgeoning of low-density, metropolitan peripheries, brought about by rising living standards and a desire for single-family housing in the suburbs. It can also mean an entry into newer boomtowns and a search for fresh opportunities and economic betterment (new migration). This kind of movement can facilitate prosperity. On the other hand, deconcentration can also entail an exodus from urban cores because of decaying conditions, leaving these cities as segregated reservations for the poor. We refer to this as *decline*. In this case, population loss usually leaves cities in deeper distress.

Just as population loss does not necessarily mean decline, population growth does not always mean prosperity. Impoverished growth can occur when people move off rural land in search of opportunities elsewhere and fail to find them. We label this *impaction*. Migration into or around cities can also be accompanied by poorer living conditions and unemployment. The upshot has been massive growth without commensurate development. While this experience is uncommon among more mobile North Americans, it does occur in Africa and Latin America. A few European cities have grown while living conditions deteriorated. Whether accompanied by affluence or poverty, new migration and impaction create sprawling urban regions or megalopoli.[11]

In the United States, deconcentration often meant urban decline. As cities lost employment and neighborhoods decayed, some people escaped to the suburbs, while others remained behind in segregated ghettos. Even major cities that managed to remake themselves incurred the ravages of decline because whole neighborhoods feel apart. New York and Chicago did manage population gains during the past decade, but white residents continued to flee and the gains were due to immigration from Latin America or Asia. Population decline was rampant in secondary cities, where immigration was marginal and could not offset losses. Detroit, Cleveland, and St. Louis, once cities with close to or above a million residents, shrunk to less than half that size. Even after devastating losses of the 1970s and 1980s, the past decade was scarcely better, with those cities losing between 5 and 10 percent of their population.[12]

At the same time, urban deconcentration brought enormous prosperity to sunbelt boomtowns and swelled their suburbs. Boomtowns are the paragons of what we think of as urban *growth*. These areas experienced dramatic increases in residential populations, which gave rise to new shopping malls, office complexes, and single-family houses. The transformative years saw a virtual upheaval of inner-city populations, a massive shift of the white middle class into new settlements, and the trek of blacks and Hispanics into what remained of the urban cores.[13]

Some cities in Europe also suffered urban decline and now resemble their American counterparts. For the most part, however, European deconcentration was more genteel, taking the form of urban dedensification. Having begun in the Middle Ages and matured in the industrial era, Europe's cities were already overcrowded. Families often lived in small apartments within congested communities where shopping, recreation, schools, and factories were tightly clustered. Some urban theorists hailed this as the realization of community, but the relatives were less quaint.[14] Space was scarce, private bathrooms often absent, and sanitary conditions dubious. By the 1970s, if people could afford to live in the city, they bought extra space and renovated. If not, they moved out.

A push-pull operated in European cities to shift populations around. The rich, the upwardly mobile, and the single people stayed. Modest income families left because of financial pressures, but were also attracted by the ease of living outside the central city. In contrast to the United States, suburbs were built for those who could not afford to live closer to the center. The best of these were in outlying villages, in "new towns," or further away in new-age boomtowns; and they accommodated middle-class citizens. They were clean, spacious, and featured supermarkets, playgrounds, and schools woven into the residential fabric. The worst, were low-income projects built in segregated edges or as extensions to impacted cities. They were massive, dingy concrete blocks that accommodated immigrants.

In sum the great transformation produced massive population shifts with different kinds of consequences. . . . Despite differences in geography, size, and population, major cities across the industrial West have undergone economic restructuring, brought on by similar forces. On both continents, populations spread throughout metropolitan areas. Suburbs and boomtowns radically expanded and urbanization proceeded apace. Rural areas shrank and fewer people earned their living through agriculture. Distant towns and rural villages lost population and, in some instances, fell into near vacancy. All told, we see substantial variation among these cities. The ramifications are deeply political. Citizens face a new set of urban challenges, driven by deindustrialization, migration, and a need to adapt.

## Global Sweep, Local Brooms

Globalism is an encompassing concept; it covers a broad range of activities, and it has brought both positive and negative results. Foremost among its characteristics is free trade. Open markets rest on a theory of competitive advantage, whereby each locale finds it beneficial to produce goods or services it can most efficiently turn out and to use international markets to acquire products that are best made elsewhere. This has sharpened and refined the division of labor among nation-states. The upshot is an explosive process, in which productivity, consumption, and participation rise at exponential rates. As we have seen and will continue to explore, urban growth has been nothing short of colossal, but it has also been accompanied by deep inequalities and paradoxes.[15]

Fundamentally, globalism and its attendant free trade are derived from a technological revolution that has shrunk time and distance. We have already mentioned the revolutionary effects of instant communication, and here we amplify how that technology allows nations to achieve deeper levels of economic integration within competitive markets. By now, advanced technology moves $1.5 trillion around the world each day. In the United States international flows of bonds and equities are fifty-four times higher today than in 1970. The comparable figures for Germany and Japan are sixty and fifty times higher. Other research has shown that international trade sustains the global patterning and has brought about changes in economic relationships, social structure, and the significance of geographical place.[16]

A corollary characteristic is standardization. Once goods and information are alike, they become recognizable and interchangeable. Common standards of measurement, universal criteria, interchangeable parts, and identical symbols are essential for globalization. Just as the grid system of streets helped land-development, so too does standardization facilitate globalization. This includes a common currency, established procedures for registering and enforcing patents, and compatible mechanical or electronic equipment. Licenses and professional certification have also become standardized in order to allow human resources to flow across boundaries. Even sports has become standardized. The Olympic Games and Olympic committees legitimate certain sports and sanction rules through which athletic contests are held. Traditionally, American baseball has been capped by the misnomer of a "World Series." Up until recently this was entirely an American affair, but increasingly players and even some teams have been drawn from other nations. The progressive universality of sports today is incontrovertible.

Another wave of global change is heavily political. Globalization has magnified the intercourse between states, localities, and social movements across the world.[17] Signs of this are visible in the rise of multilateral organizations, regional pacts, and talk of a borderless world. States, localities, nongovernmental organizations, and labor increasingly ignore old boundaries and are driven more than before by the seemingly contradictory stimuli of cooperation and competition. For some this has opened new worlds of opportunity, where masses of people can be mobilized for democratic ends. This interaction, both on site and across cyberspace, makes government more accountable and also more replaceable. For others, globalism signifies a concentration of wealth and power, and a treat of lower living standards. This has led to a perilous instability and a thunderous reaction from both left- and right-wing protestors.[iv]

An additional wave of globalization is sociocultural. This involves diffusion of a more open, multipolar, and multicultural society in which migration is a major by-product.[18] What distinguishes current migration from preceding movements is its truncated and temporary patterns of settlement. Commonly, single men live abroad for lengthy periods, while sending remittances to the homeland. When whole families do migrate, they often are treated as long-term aliens, rarely assimilating, and even children born in the host country may not acquire citizenship. Indeed, the telecommunications revolution has given permanency to this temporary status. Cheap, efficient technology compresses space and time, enabling groups to retain homeland ties and preserve indigenous culture. Overseas, ethnic culture are now said to thrive in "transnational space" in which language, habit, and tradition continue regardless of geography.[19]

These aspects of globalization also foster a greater sense of mutual vulnerability. Free trade and competitive advantage have made societies more efficient, but they have also made societies more fragile and susceptible to crisis. In a matter of minutes, turmoil in a single great bank can upset finance at the other end of the world. Currency fluctuations can overturn decades of progress, hitting those at the bottom of the economic scale hardest. As economies become more integrated, localities share more closely both the good and bad times of globalization. Through the 1990s Taipei, Tel Aviv, and Santiago experienced an unprecedented boom. After 2000 the global economy was hit by recession and those cities went bust. The more integrated and the more synchronized the locality with globalization, the greater the upturn and the steeper the downturn.

Vulnerability has many dimensions. Disease travels as swiftly as airline flights and has acquired an international character. The recent exuberance and then depression of stock markets as well as the AIDS epidemic are unfortunate examples of this exposure. Still another dark side of globalism is the spread of terrorism.[20] The ease of travel, instantaneous communication, and quick transfer of money make it possible for terrorists to do their work and attack fragile international linkages.[v] International terror most vividly illustrates the underside of global interdependence. The multinational character of its actors and the slippery content of its operations are especially well suited for porous boundaries. . . . It was at the seams of globalization where international cities and international terror were tragically joined on September 11.

How do cities fit into this overall picture? One might suppose that global-ization makes cities less important, as they are swept into a common world of economic competition and social interchange. Presumably, people could be lo-cated anywhere, and conduct business via the Internet from a mountaintop re-treat.[21] In fact, the opposite is true—at least for some cities. A knowledge-based economy has accelerated face-to-face and informal contact. It has increased an appetite for conferences, seminars, and annual meetings. Additionally, busi-ness searches for that extra edge that comes from personal contact.

Globalization also has generated a need for central direction in which finan-cial, legal, and professional services are concentrated within a common locale. Cities have made free trade much easier to accomplish, they have facilitated a new international division of labor, and they have absorbed waves of migration.[22] While not all cities have been blessed with these advantages, many are still effi-cient and enormously productive work stations for the postindustrial era. Whether one selects a handful of global cities, a larger number of primate cities, or a sampling of regional ones, urban centers lead national productivity, and their to-tal output in goods and services has quickened during the last few decades.[23]

Rising urbanization has occurred concomitantly with globalization and is associated with rising GDP. Metropolitan areas of Europe and North America grew rich during the transformation, though clearly as the process matures the rate of urbanization flattens. . . .

Globalization has not made all urban places alike. Where you live and work matters more than ever in accessing jobs, income, public amenities, schools, and green space. These things are contingent upon "place." Location does make a huge difference. Neat suburban residential enclaves, edge cities, busy commercial downtowns, urban ghettos, vacated industrial areas, and campus-like office parks are all part of a complex urban fabric that differenti-ates opportunities. Some cities have taken advantage of those opportunities and the enormous wealth that springs from global trade. By the end of the mil-lennium, Foreign Direct Investment (FDI) had reached an all-time high of $865 billion. While it is not possible to trace that investment to every locality, an overwhelming proportion of it went to advanced industrial nations, mostly lo-cated in the West. Banks held that money and facilitated investments, and al-most all of these institutions were located in major cities. Moreover, along with investment flows, banking assets have gushed over the last few decades. . . .

Even during this short period, most banks substantially increased their holdings. In some cases the aggregation of capital crested by over 300 percent. Place often shapes perspective, and location cannot help influencing decisions. More than ever, cities serve as the command and control centers of those deci-sions. They have benefited not just from saturated white-collar employment and offshoot industries, but also from their strategic placement in international capital markets. Not all of this has produced salutary results. There are always paradoxes and contradictions connected to change, and the impact of global-ization on cities is no exception.

One paradox is that while most metropolitan areas have become wealthier, they also contain rising numbers of the poor. In Western Europe 10 percent of city residents are classified as poor, while the percentage rises in suburbs to roughly 20 percent. The United States reverses these proportions, so that central cities and suburbs respectively hold 21 percent and 9 percent of residents who fall below the poverty line.[24] Quite expectedly, migrants searching for opportunities in cities account for a substantial portion of the poor. More than 50 percent of the populations in New York and Toronto are classified as either ethnic minorities or foreign born. In Paris, the percentage is above 15 percent.

Another paradox is that urban transformation has both expanded the sphere of central cities and shrunk it. In some ways deconcentration has extended central cities by making suburbanites dependent upon them for income, investment, jobs, and culture. One can see this in the huge numbers of commuters pouring into urban cores each day as well as in the many monetary transactions (mortgages, business loans, venture capital) that occur between city financial institutions and the hinterlands. In other ways, deconcentration has also meant an escape from the central city and has created an altogether new urban form. Green cities have sprung up in the more distant countryside and eliminated distinctions between urban and rural life. A newer urban life is built around asphalt, glass, trees, and grass, and it functions apart from traditional central cities.

Still another oddity is that while transformation has made cities into hardworking centers of productivity, it has also made them into sites of gluttonous leisurely consumption. Scholars often write about the dichotomy between investment and consumption whereby different locales tend toward one or the other.[25] Postindustrial cities have united these dichotomies. Complementing an enormous white-collar apparatus of producer services is a burgeoning industry in leisure and consumption. The rise of the office-complex city has been accompanied by the rise of the tourist city. Cities are today in the midst of what Judd and Fainstein describe as a "tourist bubble," whose growth is among the fastest in the world.[26]

Put in historical perspective, these paradoxes are not unusual. Cities have always grown or shrunk alongside technological advance. The introduction of elevators and steel framing allowed for skyscrapers but broke up traditional neighborhoods. Metro lines were a boon for central business districts, but a bust for out-of-the-way small towns. Invention is often a conveyance for what Schumpeter called "creative destruction"[27] and brought about very different results. . . .

## "Glocal" Choices

Deindustrialization, deconcentration, and globalization have put cities on trajectories of change. It is this unusual blend of global challenge and local response that confronts us, and this combination is sometimes denoted by the inelegant terms "glocal" or "glocalization."[28] Like the industrial revolution before it, this revolution can be decisively influenced by government as well as other social institutions.[29] Governments have responded to these challenges in diverse ways. First, leaders and citizens have made strategic decisions about *what kind of community* they want. Some political leaders look to the marketplace for strategic direction, placing a high priority on gaining a competitive advantage for their communities. They ask, how can we find our niche in the regional, national, or world market? What can we do best? Where can we garner capital investment? How can we grow by helping business operate more efficiently? For cities that choose competition, answers to these questions have produced a variety of strategic responses. We see cities remaking waterfronts into tourist attractions, refurbishing downtowns with office towers and convention halls, and trying to attract big bang events such as the World Cup, Expo, or Olympic games, as well as revenue sources such as sports teams, theme parks, or gaming casinos.

Cities then do not just react to the movement of capital but act upon these forces. Although local governments have only limited control over the marketplace, they use public power to engage it. They do so whenever land is recycled, development rights are granted, housing is built, taxes are collected, or capital is borrowed. Moreover cities can profoundly affect factors of production. They can lower overhead costs by building bridges, ports, and airfields. They can tighten up or loosen controls over air pollution. Cities can even affect labor costs by making it easier or more difficult for individuals to access welfare benefits.[30] In making decisions over these issues, cities struggle to resolve an array of problems and influence their own restructuring.

Some leaders try to induce capital investment by reducing risks for business. They may put up bonds that guarantee the building of stadiums or convention halls, they may underwrite loans to potential investors, and they may find themselves forming public private-partnerships in order to assure private investors of unified backing.[31] Cities also aggressively solicit business by lobbying for private capital, bidding for company headquarters, or establishing international offices to stimulate trade.

Cities seeking competitive advantages may also tolerate increased migration, allow informal economies to flourish, and facilitate the supply of cheap goods and services. They may countenance permissive building codes, lax licensing, and an abundance of substandard housing. These newfound resources explain the partial resurgence of textile manufacture in some cities, where old-fashioned sweatshops arise and where illegal immigrants are exploited as low-cost labor. The upscale life-style of postindustrial cities generates a demand for low-paying service jobs. A virtual night shift of unskilled workers commutes into downtowns to clean the office towers, staff the restaurants, and drive the taxicabs. The "reverse commute" of marginal workers into affluent suburbs also helps to maintain an attractive low cost of living.

Alternatively, cities sometimes defy the swells of the marketplace. Local leaders can remain politically sensitive and rely on a logic of populist, anti-growth policies.[32] This logic may well clash with the rationality of the marketplace. Cities may resist the lure of growth and opt for preservationist or caretaker strategies.[33] They may want to protect historic neighborhoods, guard surrounding farmland, or prohibit large discount outlets and suburban malls. Some fear higher taxes and increased congestion. They may want to remain as quiet residential communities.

Large and small cities have resisted economic growth by invoking moratoria on the construction of office towers, using zoning exactions to force concessions from developers, adopting strict architectural codes, requiring underground facilities for automobile parking, and setting aside large tracts for open space.[34] In Western Europe the upsurge of "green parties" has affected urban policies. Green legislators have placed controls on housing costs, limited the price of apartment rentals, and closed off streets to automobiles. Reciprocally, they have used public funds to renovate housing, protected rights of squatters, and reserved sections of the streetscape for bicycles. Populist movements have sometimes arisen to challenge the power of corporate decision makers in places such as Cleveland, Ohio, the Mon Valley in Pennsylvania, and Liverpool, England.

There is variation in the response to globalization. In important ways, world competition has sparked a quest for capital investment and growth. In other ways, the free exchange of ideas and possibilities for collaboration has enabled groups to mobilize. Some scholars have found evidence of a new urban politics based on social issues, increased diversity, and a concern for the environment.[35] They also envision globalized cities as hothouses for the spread of postmaterialist values with its emphasis on citizen activism.[36] The concerns of migrant workers coupled to environmental and populist sentiment could generate counterpressures. Whatever the outcomes, globalization is not a leveling process, and it has created new alternatives.

Who makes decisions over what is another question of choice. This ultimately depends upon the existence of assets and the distribution of power within a city. Some scholars argue that urban decision-making is shaped by economics, and they stress growth and competition as the predominant force. From this perspective, cities must give priority to economic growth because they are disciplined by a market that punishes them with loss of jobs and tax revenue.[37] Other scholars argue that political preferences matter more than economic pressures. They see powerful leaders, coalitions, regimes, and growth machines operating to shape economic preferences.[38] There is something to both interpretations. Cities are certainly limited by the assets at their disposal, and they cannot deal with global change unless they have the wherewithal to do so. By the same token, dealing with change requires initiative, and coalitions must be built by political entrepreneurs who mobilize groups and classes.

The important questions deal not only with differences of alternatives taken, but also with the reasons why some cities might be able to chose particular alternatives. Are there structural characteristics that are common to cities choosing similar strategic alternatives? If so, can they be identified and how do they interact? Likewise, do cities that share similar strategic responses to globalism also share similar cultural or political characteristics. If so, what are these and how do they operate? Can we make sense of these varying influences on choice and put them into some logical schema? Finally, what are the lessons learned from this inquiry? Does the international marketplace have a tendency to homogenize cities so that they become alike, or are cities becoming more dissimilar? Given the tension between the global and the local, can one decide which side, if any, prevails? . . .

The classic development conflict occurs between "anti-growth" and "pro-growth" coalitions, and includes such debates as whether to adopt building moratoria and preserve historic districts or aggressively recruit private investors and turn downtowns into rows of towering office complexes. This conflict often encompasses a political component where the sides are poised for battle—neighborhood groups, preservationists, and environmentalists on one side versus developers, chambers of commerce, and media boosters on the other. Pro-growth impulses are often driven by a desire to standardize development (trade centers, office towers, tourist attractions) and expand the contributions of multinational firms in the local economy. Anti-growth impulses frequently stem from a desire for citizen participation and local autonomy.[39] These tensions reflect the degree to which local development agendas are influenced by the international market.

Looking at the situation more broadly, we can appreciate that issues of international import are fought on local battlegrounds, and that ultimately these conflicts change the character of cities. Many local challenges and responses have global proportions; decisions flow to and from an international marketplace. This marketplace can either saturate cities with massive investment and political pressure or marginalize them. Either way, cities must respond by accommodating, managing, or resisting these forces.

## NOTES

i. Other parts of the world have also formed transnational associations, including the Association of South East Asian Nations (Brunei, Indonesia, Malaysia, Philippines, Singapore, Thailand, and Vietnam) and Mancusor (Argentina, Brazil, Paraguay, and Uruguay).

ii. Primate cities are giant entities, at least twice as large as the next largest city in the nation, and not infrequently they hold 20 percent or more of a nation's population. While primate cities are not always at the nexus of the global economy, they are central to a national economy and generate a substantial portion of its GDP.

iii. There are also cultural, social, and geographical reasons for this. Anglo-American traditions favor country and low-density living, while Continental traditions are more disposed to high-density or clustered environments. In America, the availability of greater space and racial enmity contributed to middle-class white flight.

iv. Instances of both democratic and antidemocratic movements can be traced in some ways to globalization. In 1999 the overthrow of the Indonesian government was made possible by Internet communication in that nation's archipelago. Within the next year, populist, protest movements held large-scale demonstrations in Seattle and Washington, D.C. Populist demonstrations against Iran's repressive theocracy have also been held and gained resonance through telecommunications. On the other side, in the United States neo-Nazi and racist groups have been able to mobilize followers through the Internet. Also, marginal political parties in both America and Europe have capitalized on a reaction against global trade (in the U.S., Patrick Buchanan's Reform Party; in France, Jean-Marie Le Pen's National Front; in Italy Gianfranco Fini's neofascists).

v. Every action has its reaction, and globalism is no different. Vulnerability also has a more fortunate side that can be found in cross-national cooperation and synergy. This kind of complementary interdependence has brought about cooperation in regulating currencies, controlling AIDS and combating terrorism.

1. Knight and Gappert, *Cities in a Global Society;* Judd and Parkinson, *Leadership and Urban Regeneration.*
2. Population Action International, *Global Migration.*
3. Stoltz, "Europe's Back Doors."
4. A.T. Kearney, Inc., "Globalization Index."
5. Sassen, *Cities in World Economy.*
6. Savitch, *Post-industrial Cities;* Sassen, *Global City.*
7. Swanstrom, "Semisovereign Cities"; Hill, "Cleveland Economy."
8. Gappert, *Future of Winter Cities.*
9. Dangschat and Obenbrugge, "Hamburg."
10. Bernard and Rice, *Sunbelt Cities;* Ruble, Tulchin, and Garland, "Globalism and Local Realities."
11. Gotttman, *Megalopolis.*
12. U.S. Bureau of the Census, "Population of the 100 Largest Cities"; State of the Cities Census Data Systems.
13. Sternlieb and Hughes, *Post-industrial America;* Kantor with David, *Dependent City;* Kantor, *Dependent City Revisited,* chap. 6.
14. Mumford, *City in History;* Jacobs, *Death and Life of Great American Cities;* Garls, *Urban Villagers.*
15. Savitch, "Global Challenge."
16. Sassen, *Global City, Cities in a World Economy;* A.T. Kearney, Inc., "Globalization Index."
17. Held, "Democracy."
18. Knight and Gappert, *Cities in Global Society;* United Nations Centre for Human Settlements, *Indicators Newsletter.*
19. Smith, *Transnational Urbanism.*
20. Savitch and Ardashev, "Does Terror Have an Urban Future?"
21. Webber, "Order in Diversity."
22. Kresl, "North American Cities International"; Sassen, *Cities in World Economy;* Glickman, "Cities and International Division of Labor."
23. Prud'homme, "Les sept plus grandes villes du monde"; Savitch, "Cities in a Global Era."
24. European Foundation for the Improvement of Living and Working Conditions, *Living Conditions* (1986); Baugher and Lamison-White, *Poverty.*
25. O'Connor, *Fiscal Crisis of State;* Saunders, "Central Local Relations."
26. Judd and Fainstein, *Tourist City.*
27. Schumpeter, *Capitalism, Socialism and Democracy.*
28. Swyngedouw, "Mammon Quest"; Ascher, *Metapolis ou l'Avenir des Villes.*
29. Polanyi, *Great Transformation.*
30. Logan and Molotch, *Urban Fortunes.*
31. Rubin and Rubin, "Economic Development Incentives."
32. Mollenkopf, *Contested City.*
33. Williams and Adrian, *Four Cities;* Swanstrom, "Semisovereign Cities."
34. Muzzio and Bailey, "Economic Development"; Clavel, *Progressive City.*
35. Clark and Inglehart, "New Political Culture"; Clark, "Structural Realignments."
36. Miranda, Rosdil, and Yeh, "Growth Machines."
37. Peterson, *City Limits.*
38. Stone and Sanders, *Politics of Urban Development;* Stone, *Regime Politics;* Swanstrom, "Semisovereign Cities"; Logan and Molotch, *Urban Fortunes.*
39. Leo, "City Politics"; Clarke and Gaile, *Work of Cities.*

# 6

## *Richard Foglesong*

## WHEN DISNEY COMES TO TOWN

"It was as though they'd put a gun to our head," said the director of tri-county planning. "They were offering to invest $600 million. And there was the glamour of Disney. You could hardly say no to that. We were all just spellbound."

They had come from around the state to hear, finally, what Disney's new East Coast theme park would look like. The new Republican governor and most of his cabinet were there. So was half the legislature. Bankers, developers and a planeload of reporters filled out the audience. Everyone was clamoring to hear Disney's proposal, but the politicians, in particular, were anxious to know what the giant entertainment company would demand of the state legislature.

The project was Walt Disney World; the year was 1967; the place was Winter Park, Fla., outside Orlando, where the pooh-bahs had gathered to hear Disney's plans for a regional theme park. There are significant differences between 1960s Florida and 1990s Virginia, of course—Floridians were relatively untutored in the consequences of urban growth, while Virginians today are not so naive—yet the odd familiarity of the Winter Park scene highlights some of the more striking parallels between Disney's Orlando project and its present-day plans for a park in Haymarket. Then, as now, Disney's proposal was accompanied by hardball lobbying from the company, hoopla from business interests, enthusiastic support from a Republican governor and a struggle over the financing of roads. Then—as now—the Walt Disney Co. proved more powerful than local critics or media skeptics, hiring the right lobbyists and nurturing the right legislators. Then—as now—Disney got what it wanted from the state.

Given these similarities, it's instructive to consider the disparity between the plan that Disney laid out on that heady day in Winter Park and what actually transpired in Central Florida. Simply put, the California company proposed one kind of development, which it used to gain special governmental powers, and then built something else. And yet Floridians, blinded by the pixie dust, hardly noticed. Then—as now?—people were mesmerized by the Disney mystique.

The big news about the Florida project, initially, was its much-vaunted plan for a model city where ordinary people would make their homes and go about their lives in an idealized setting. This was a concept that had been brewing for some time: Two years before the Winter Park presentation, Walt Disney, speaking at a Florida press conference, rhapsodized about building a "City of Tomorrow." In the following months, the City of Tomorrow became an obsession with Walt,

---

"When Disney Comes to Town," by Richard Foglesong, as appeared in *The Washington Post Magazine*, May 15, 1994. Richard Foglesong is Professor of Politics at Rollins College in Florida. Reprinted by permission of the author.

according to Disney biographer Bob Thomas. The company already knew how to build an amusement park, Walt insisted; so he focused his attention on what he was soon calling "an experimental prototype community of tomorrow"—or Epcot.

But the company's commitment to Epcot depended on the creative leadership of one man—Walt himself. In the fall of 1966, Orlando banker and power broker Billy Dial flew to California to meet with the 64-year-old Disney. Worried about the showman's health, he asked over lunch: "Mr. Disney, if you walked out of this restaurant and were hit by a truck, what would happen to the Orlando project?" Walt responded: "Absolutely nothing. My brother runs this company, I just piddle around."

Dial was unpersuaded, and with good reason: Three weeks later, he was in New York at the Bankers Trust Co. when he received a hurried phone call from Disney executive Donn Tatum, who said simply, "Walt is dead." It was December 15, 1966, and Walt Disney had died from lung cancer before almost anyone realized he was ill. His death left the company directionless—creatively at least—and Epcot, which had existed mostly in his head, in a state of flux. Roy Disney, the company's financial mastermind and Walt's older brother, was 73 and had already announced his plans to retire.

Roy agreed to stay on and, after polling senior executives, gave the East Coast project his blessing and directed that it be called *Walt* Disney World as a tribute to his brother. Disney execs knew little of Walt's Epcot plans, however, so they focused instead on building a Disneyland-type amusement park; as Disney Vice President Card Walker would later observe, "It was the thing we knew best."

Indeed, Walt's comments on a May 23, 1966, memo suggest that he himself had privately backed away from the model city vision before he died. In the memo, which was found in Walt's desk and is now kept at the Disney Archives in Burbank, Calif., Florida attorney Paul Helliwell sketched out the problem of allowing permanent residents at Epcot. If people lived there, they would vote there, diluting the company's political control of the property. It seems that Walt's thoughts were headed in a similar direction: On the memo, every time Helliwell referred to "permanent residents," Walt crossed it out and substituted "temporary residents/tourists."

Yet the company persisted in hyping Epcot as the centerpiece of Walt Disney World. When, shortly after Walt's death, Roy addressed that SRO crowd in Winter Park, he touted Epcot. The highlight of the press conference was a 25-minute color film, Walt's last screen appearance, in which he described Epcot as the "heart" of the Florida project, a vibrant community where people would "live and work and play." In the film and in the accompanying press release, the company said Epcot would "serve a new population of 20,000."

Following the Winter Park press conference, Roy and Republican Gov. Claude Kirk flew to Jacksonville, where they filmed a joint presentation that was shown along with the Epcot film on statewide television. Floridians thus saw Walt, in a posthumous appearance, describing Epcot as a working community that would always be on the cutting edge of technology and urban design. The film was unequivocal in this depiction; yet, a decade later, a Disney spokesman would state that the model city concept was "only one visual presentation of one way to go." The film was likewise shown to the Florida legislature as it began work on the Disney legislation.

If, after Walt's death, the company was uncommitted to building a true residential community, why did company officials present this as the crux of their proposal? In part it was because the Epcot film was so visually compelling—with Walt alive on screen, offering his futuristic vision of Epcot and appealing for lawmakers' support. But it was also for legal reasons best explained in the Helliwell memo.

In that memo, Helliwell expressed concern about state and local laws that might limit the company's "freedom of action" in developing its 43-square-mile property. He proposed a Disney-controlled government with regulatory powers "superseding to the fullest extent possible under law state and county regulatory authorities." There was just one hitch: Under Florida law, as Helliwell explained, planning and zoning authority could only be exercised by a  popularly elected government. To escape external land-use controls, the company had to submit to control by voters. Disney attorneys, however, found a clever way to avoid this fate.

Their proposed legislation called for a two-tier system of government. The top tier, embracing an area twice the size of Manhattan, was the Reedy Creek Improvement District. It would be controlled by the landowner, its board of supervisors elected on the principle of one acre equals one vote. Since Disney owned the land, Disney would elect the board. The bottom tier consisted of two municipalities, Bay Lake and Lake Buena Vista, each having a handful of residents who would be trusted Disney employees living in company housing. Officially, planning and zoning authority was vested in these two municipalities. Their residents would elect a government and then—ingeniously—transfer administrative responsibility for planning and zoning to the Reedy Creek District.

By this legal magic, the company was able to comply with the law and still enjoy regulatory immunity. The charter made it possible for the Reedy Creek government to regulate land use, provide police and fire services, license the manufacture and sale of alcoholic beverages, build roads, lay sewer lines, construct waste-treatment plants, carry out flood projects—even build an airport or nuclear plant, all without local or state approval. The company was creating a sort of Vatican with Mouse ears: a city-state within the larger state of Florida, controlled by the company yet enjoying regulatory powers reserved by law for popularly elected governments.

To acquire such powers, the company had to convince the Florida legislature that Epcot would be a bona fide community. Paul Helliwell, acting as lobbyist, frequently used the term "resident" in describing the company's plans. Disney lobbyists also told lawmakers that Disney would include "public school sites and other public needs in their two cities," according to an April 22, 1967, article in the Orlando Sentinel-Star. And Helliwell told legislators, few of whom had read the thick Reedy Creek charter, that the company was not asking for anything "that had not been done before." At best the statement was half-true: The charter combined the powers available in three kinds of special districts. But Florida had not combined those powers in one district before.

In persuading the legislature to adopt this legislation, the California company ably plied the old-boy system. A good example is a meeting between J. J. Griffin, a former state representative who became a Disney lobbyist, and the powerful president of the Senate, Verle Pope. Griffin had started a long-winded explanation of the weighty Reedy Creek charter when Pope stopped him. "J. J.," he said, "I just have one question. Is this good for Florida?" Griffin answered, "Yes, sir, I believe it is." Whereupon Pope said, "Well, that's good enough for me." (The anecdote is recounted by Griffin in the film "Florida's Disney Decade," produced by Disney.)

With Pope's blessing, the legislation sailed through the Senate, passing unanimously and without debate. In the House there was one dissenting vote, from Miami. Less than an hour after the vote, the State Road Board approved emergency funding for Disney's road requests. And finally, the Florida Supreme Court ruled in 1968 that the Reedy Creek District was legally entitled to issue tax-free municipal bonds. The bonding power would "greatly aid Disney interests" but would nevertheless benefit the "numerous inhabitants of the district," the court ruled.

What about those "numerous inhabitants" today? How fares the city where 20,000 would "live and work and play"? Sure enough, in 1982, 11 years after the turnstiles began spinning at Disney World, the company opened something called Epcot. Yet today, there are more hotels than homes on Disney property. Between the two cities of Bay Lake and Lake Buena Vista, there are 43 residents living in 17 mobile homes—all nonunion Disney supervisors and their families, who safeguard the company's political control of its property.

Disney is also designing a huge mixed-use development called "Celebration," billed as a further realization of Walt's urban vision. While some permanent housing is scheduled for Celebration, it will be de-annexed from the Reedy Creek District—making it impossible for homeowners to vote in Disney elections. Celebration will also have time-share units, whose temporary occupants will not have voting rights. The model city described by Walt, promoted by Roy and dangled before Florida lawmakers by Disney lobbyists has never come about; the promises of 1967 are the stuff of history.

# 7

## Paul Kantor and H. V. Savitch

## CAN POLITICIANS BARGAIN WITH BUSINESS?

In the summer of 1989, United Air Lines announced it was planning a new maintenance hub that would bring nearly a billion dollars in investment and generate over 7,000 jobs for the region lucky enough to attract it. Within a few short

Paul Kantor and H. V. Savitch, "Can Politicians Bargain with Business? A Theoretical and Comparative Perspective on Urban Development," *Urban Affairs Quarterly,* Vol. 29(2), pp. 230–255, copyright © 1993 by Sage Publications, Inc. Reprinted by permission of Sage Publications, Inc.

months, officials in over 90 localities were competing for the bonanza and were tripping over one another in an effort to lure United. Denver offered $115 million in incentives and cash, Oklahoma City sought to raise $120 million, and localities in Virginia offered a similar amount. The competition for United was so keen that cities began to bid against one another and asked that their bids be kept secret.

United was so delighted at the level of bidding that it repeatedly delayed its decision in anticipation the offers would get even better. Nearly two years later, city officials in nine finalists were enhancing their incentives, courting United executives, and holding their breaths. Reflecting on the competition, Louisville Mayor Jerry Abramson quipped, "We haven't begun to offer up our firstborn yet, but we're getting close. Right now we are into siblings."[1]

Except for the extremity of the case, there is nothing new about cities questing for private capital. Cities compete with one another for tourism, foreign trade, baseball franchises, and federal grants. Yet, there is another side to this behavior. Although 93 cities competed for the United hub, many others did not, and some cities would have resisted the corporate intrusion (Etzkowitz and Mack 1976; Savitch 1988). When United stalled and raised the ante, Kentucky's governor angrily withdrew, complaining that he would "not continue this auction, this bidding war. There is a point at which you draw the line" ("Governor turns down UAL," Courier-Journal, 18 October 1991). In Denver, the legislature's majority leader protested, saying, "United has a ring and is pulling Colorado by the nose." With those remarks and heightening resentment, public opinion began to pull the state away from the lure of United ("UAL bidding goes on," Courier-Journal, 22 October 1991).

Such cases do not seem uncommon. Although many cities are willing to build sports stadia, others have turned down the opportunity. For instance, when Fort Wayne, Indiana, declined to go beyond its offer of a short-term low-interest loan to obtain a minor-league baseball team, the franchise was taken elsewhere (Rosentraub and Swindell 1990). Although officials in some cities trip over one another in efforts to attract business by lowering taxes, officials in others raise them. Over the last three years, Los Angeles, New York, and Denver have increased business taxes. Notwithstanding high taxes and locational costs, business continues to seek out such cities as San Francisco, Tokyo, London, Toronto, and Frankfurt.

Nevertheless, the literature on urban politics has not systematically examined such "nondecisional" cases (Bachrach and Baratz 1962) to probe the precise circumstances under which local governments can influence the capital investment process. . . .

. . . We propose that questions of how, when, and why local government can influence economic development are best answered by treating political control as something that springs from bargaining advantages that the state has in political and economic exchange relationships with business. Variations in local-government influence are strongly tied to the ways in which the larger political economy distributes particular bargaining resources between the public and private sectors.

Following Lindblom (1977), we find that it is useful to regard this context as a liberal-democratic system in which there is a division of labor between business and government (Kantor 1988; Elkin 1987). The private sector is responsible for the production of wealth in a market system in which choices over production and exchange are determined by price mechanisms. For its part, the public sector is organized along polyarchal lines (Dahl 1971; Dahl and Lindblom 1965) in which public decisions are subject to popular control. Public officials may be viewed as primarily responsible for the management of political support for governmental undertakings; business leaders can be considered essentially managers of market enterprises.

This perspective suggests that even though public and private control systems are theoretically separate, in reality they are highly interdependent. So far as government is concerned, the private sector produces economic resources that are necessary for the well-being of the political community—including jobs, revenues for public programs, and political support that is likely to flow to public authorities from popular satisfaction with economic prosperity and security. For business, the public sector is important because it provides forms of intervention into the market that are necessary for the promotion of economic enterprise but that the private sector cannot provide on its own. Such interventions include inducements that enable private investors to take risks (tax abatements and tax credits), the resolution of private conflicts that threaten social or economic stability (courts, mediation services), and the creation of an infrastructure or other forms of support (highways, workforce training).

Conceptualized in this manner, business and government must engage in exchange relationships (bargaining) to realize common goals. This is done by using bargaining advantages that derive from three dimensions or spheres of interdependence: market conditions, popular-control systems, and public-intervention mechanisms. . . .

Our analysis suggests that there is substantial variation among local governments in their ability to bargain. We also suggest that bargaining advantages tend to be cumulative—that is, the more advantages a city holds, the greater its ability to bargain. Finally, we suggest that because bargaining is a product of political and economic circumstance, so is urban development. Although it may not be possible for a city to manipulate all the variables affecting its bargaining position, most cities can manipulate some and thereby shape its own future. . . .

# Markets and Public Control
# of Urban Development

There is little doubt that businesses' greatest bargaining resource in urban development is its control over private wealth in the capital investment process. It is this dimension of business-government relations that Peterson's (1981) market-centered model of local politics describes. The logic of this model is that cities compete for capital investment by seeking to attract mobile capital to the community; failure to meet the conditions demanded by business for investment leads to the "automatic punishing recoil" (Lindblom 1982) of the marketplace as business disinvests. This notion has been variously interpreted to suggest that business inherently holds a dominant position (Fainstein et al. 1986; Mollenkopf 1983; Logan and Molotch 1987; Jones and Bachelor 1986; Kantor 1988).

Although the market-centered model is a powerful tool for analyzing development politics, it does not fully capture the bargaining relationships that logically derive from it. Specifically, the market perspective tends to highlight only those advantages that accrue to business. Yet, the marketplace works in two directions, not one. If we look at specific market conditions and bargaining demands, it becomes apparent that government also can use the market to obtain leverage over business. Thus we will present a number of common market-centered arguments and show their other side.

## The Cities-Lose-If-Business-Wins Argument

In the market model, public and private actors represent institutions that compete to achieve rival goals. Business pursues public objectives only insofar as they serve private needs; if important business needs are not met, local government experiences the discipline of the marketplace as capital and labor seek alternative locations.

Yet, in this description of market dynamics, cases in which local government and business may also share the same goals (as distinct from the same interests) are ignored; in such instances the market model no longer indicates business advantage in the development process. Thus a local government may have an interest in raising public revenue by increasing retail sales while shopkeepers and investors have an interest in maximizing profits. Though their interests are different, they may share the common goal of bringing about higher sales through expanded development. When this happens, bargaining between government and business shifts from rivalry over competing goals to settling differences over how to facilitate what already has been agreed on. This kind of scenario enhances the value of bargaining resources that are mostly owned by the public sector. Development politics focuses on such things as the ability to amass land, grant legal privileges and rights, control zoning, provide appropriate infrastructure, and—not least—enlist public support. Because alternative means of promoting growth are important choices (Logan and Swanstrom 1990), substantial bargaining leverage over development outcomes is placed in the hands of those who manage the governmental process, a point that Mollenkopf (1983) underscored in his study of urban renewal politics.

Yet, this partial escape from the market often is not recognized. Peterson (1981) considered the sharing of interests and goals to be one and the same. Other scholars have often assumed that there is an inherent conflict between private and public goals (Stone and Sanders 1987; Logan and Swanstrom 1990; Swanstrom 1986). However, a strong case can be made that business and government often share common goals. Although they cannot logically share interests, public officials, motivated by different stakes, frequently choose to pursue economic objectives that are also favored by business (Cummings 1988). Although some critics reject progrowth values, these values tend to be supported broadly by local electorates (Logan and Molotch 1987, 50–98; Vaughn 1979; Crenson 1971).

To take a different tack on former head of General Motors Charles Wilson's aphorism, scholars may be too anxious to suggest that if it is good for General Motors, it must be bad for Detroit. Yet, local officials and their publics do not always share this logic. When government and business perceive common goals, such perceptions can have a powerful effect on opportunities for political control over the urban economy. Under these conditions, the ability of political authorities to create political support for specific programs and their willingness to use public authority to assist business can become important bargaining resources for achieving their own interests. At the very least, the extent to which agreement between business and local government is a byproduct of political choice rather than of economic constraint should be a premise for empirical investigation instead of an a priori conclusion.

## The Capital Mobility Argument

This argument encompasses an assumption that bargaining advantages accrue to business as it becomes more mobile. Historically, private capital was more dependent on the local state than it is today (Kanto 1988). Technological advances in production, communications, and transportation have enhanced the ability of business to move more easily and rapidly. Changes in the organization of capital, especially the rise of multilocational corporations, have increased business mobility and made urban locations interchangable. Automation, robotics, and the postindustrial revoultion are supposed to enhance capital mobility. Fixed capital has been nudged aside by a new postindustrial technology of flexible capital (Hill 1989; Parkinson, Foley, and Judd 1989).

It would seem to follow that increasing capital mobility must favor business interests. Yet, this conclusion does not always follow, if one considers specific cities and businesses that are caught up in this process of economic globalization. Capital is, in fact, not always very portable. Although cities are frequently viewed as interchangeable by some corporations, many cities retain inherent advantages of location (e.g., Brussels), of agglomeration (e.g., New York), of technological prowess (e.g., Grenoble), or of political access (e.g., Washington, D.C.). The dispersion of capital has triggered a countermovement to create centers that specialize in the communication, coordination, and support of far-flung corporate units. Larger global cities have captured these roles. Much of postindustrial capital has put enormous sunk costs into major cities. One of the more conspicuous examples is the Canadian development firm of Olympia and York, which has invested billions of dollars in New York, London, Ontario, and a host of other cities. As Olympia and York teeters on the edge of collapse, banks, realty interests, and mortgage brokers are also threatened. It is not easy for any of these interests to pull up stakes.

There has been a fairly stable tendency for corporate headquarters operations, together with the ancillary services on which headquarters depend, to gravitate to large cities that have acquired the status of world business centers (Sassen 1988; Noyelle and Stanback 1984). New York's downtown and midtown, London's financial district and its docklands, Paris's La Defense, and Tokyo's Shinjuku are some outstanding examples of postindustrialism that [have] generated billions in fixed investments. Movement by individual enterprises away from such established corporate business centers is unlikely for various reasons, including that this kind of change imposes costs on those owning fixed assets in these locations and disrupts established business networks.

Cities that have experienced ascendant market positions have not been reluctant to cash in on this. When property values and development pressures rose in downtowns, local politicians used the advantage to impose new planning requirements and demand development fees. In San Francisco, a moratorium on high-rise construction regulates the amount and pace of investment (Muzzio and Bailey 1986). In Boston and several other large cities, linkage policies have exacted fees on office development to support moderate-income housing (Dreier 1989). In Paris, differential taxes have been placed on high-rise development and the proceeds used to support city services (Savitch 1988). One should also recognize that market conditions are not immutable.

Local governments may be subject to the blandishments of business at an early stage of development, when there is great eagerness for development and capital has wide investment choices. However, once business has made the investment, it may be bound for the long term. Thus bargaining does not stop after the first deal is struck, and the advantages may shift.

This occurred in Orlando, Florida, where Disney World exacted early concessions from the local governments, only to be faced with new sets of public demands afterward (Foglesong 1989). Prior to building what is now a vast entertainment complex near Orlando, Disney planners capitalized on their impending investment and won huge concessions from government (including political autonomy, tax advantages, and free infrastructure). However, as Disney transformed the region into a sprawling tourist center, local government demanded that the corporation relinquish autonomy and pressured it to pay for physical improvements. Disney struggled to defeat these demands but eventually conceded. With huge sunk investments, Disney executives had little choice but to accommodate the public sector.

So although some industries have grown more mobile, others have not. The issue turns on the relative costs incurred by business and by government when facilities, jobs, and people are moved. How relative costs are assessed and the likelihood that businesses will absorb them influence the respective bargaining postures of business and government.

## The City-Cannot-Choose Argument

In the market model, business makes investment choices among stationary cities; because cities cannot move, powerful bargaining advantages accrue to business in the urban development process and supposedly this enables them to exact what they want from local governments. Although this is sometimes the case, it is also true that local communities may have investment choices as well. Some local governments can make choices among alternative types of business investment. In particular, economic diversification enables local political authorities to market the community in a particular economic sector (e.g., as a tourist city, as a research or technical center, or as a sound place in which to retire). Furthur, economic diversification enhances a locality's ability to withstand economic pressure from any particular segment of the business community. This has occurred in cities as far ranging as Seattle, Singapore, and Rome, enabling them to maintain powerful market positions for years, despite profound changes in the world and national economies.

Experience teaches city officials to sense their vulnerabilities and develop defenses against dominance by a single industry. Through diversification, these cities can gain a good deal of strength, not only in weathering economic fluctuations but in dealing with prospective investors. Houston's experience after oil prices crashed moved city leaders to develop high-technology and service industries (Feagin 1988). Pittsburgh's successful effort to clean its air gave that city a new economic complexion. Louisville's deindustrial crisis was followed by a succession of new investments in health services, a revival in the transportation industry, and a booming business in the arts (Vogel 1990). Diversification, which was so instrumental in strengthening the public hand, was actually made possible by government coalitions with business.

The advantages of diversification are most apparent when these cities are compared to localities that are prisoners of relatively monopolistic bargaining relations with business. Officials in single-industry towns are strongly inclined to accommodate business demands on matters of development because they lack alternative sources of capital investment. Crenson (1971) found this pattern in Gary, Indiana, where local officials resisted proposals for pollution control because they feared that U.S. Steel would lay off workers. Similarly, Jones and Bachelor (1986) described how Detroit leaders weakened their market position when they sought to preserve the city's positions as a site for automobile manufacturing. When worldwide changes in the auto industry eroded Detroit's traditional competitive advantages, political leaders fought to subsidize new plants and to demolish an otherwise viable residential neighborhood.

Neither Gary's steel-centered strategy nor Detroit's auto-centered strategy has stemmed their economic decline. The lesson for urban politicians is clear: Instead of vainly hanging on to old industry, go for new, preferably clean business. More than most politicians, big-city mayors have learned well and are fast becoming major economic promoters (Savitch and Thomas 1991).

## The City-Maximizes-Growth Argument

Although the market model is built on the supposition that it is in the interest of cities to promote economic growth, not all localities seek to compete in capital markets. To the extent that communities ignore participation in this market, they do not have to bargain with business over demands that they might choose to bring to the bargaining table. Santa Barbara, Vancouver, and Stockholm are cities that have insisted growth and instituted extensive land-use controls. These cities are in enviable positions as they deal with business and developers.

Aside from major cities, there are smaller communities that do not seek to compete for capital investment such as suburban areas and middle-size cities that after years of expansion, now face environmental degradation. Even if these localities have a stake in maintaining competitive advantages as bedroom communities or steady-state mixed commercial/residential locales, their bargaining relationship with business is more independent than in relatively growth-hungry urban communities (Danielson 1976). University towns, in which a self-sustaining and alert population values its traditions, have managed to resist the intrusions of unwanted industry. Coastal cities, which seek to preserve open space, have successfully acquired land or used zoning to curtail development.

Moreover, there are cities in which governmental structures reduce financial pressure and are able to resist indiscriminate development. Regionalism and annexation have enabled cities to widen their tax nets, so that business cannot easily play one municipality off against another. Minneapolis-St. Paul, Miami-Dade, and metro Toronto furnish examples of localities banding together to strengthen their fiscal positions and turn down unwanted growth. In Western European and other non-American nations, cities are heavily financed by central government, thereby reducing and sometimes eliminating the pressure to attract development. For these cities, growth only engenders liabilities.

# Popular-Control Systems and Urban Development

Democratic political institutions not only provide means of disciplining public officials, but they constrain all political actors who seek governmental cooperation or public legitimation in the pursuit of their interests. The reality of this is suggested by the fact that business development projects frequently get stopped when they lack a compelling public rationale and generate significant community opposition. This has occurred under varying conditions and in different types of cities. In Paris, neighborhood mobilization successfully averted developers (Body-Gendrot 1987); in London, communities were able to totally redo urban renewal plans (Christensen 1979); in Amsterdam and Berlin, local squatters defied property owners by taking over abandoned buildings; after the recent earthquake in San Francisco, public opinion prevailed against the business community in preventing the reconstruction of a major highway. The existence of open, competitive systems of elections and other polyarchal institutions affords a means by which nonbusiness interests are able to influence, however imperfectly, an urban development process in which business power otherwise looms large.

But do institutions of popular control afford political authorities with a valuable bargaining resource in dealing with business? Are democratic institutions loose cannons that are irrelevant to political bargaining over economic development? From our bargaining perspective, it would appear that these institutions can provide a resource upon which political leaders can draw to impose their own policy preferences when the three conditions described in the following paragraphs are satisfied.

First, public approval of bargaining outcomes between government and business must be connected to the capital-investment process. This is often not the case because most private-sector investment decisions are virtually outside the influence of local government. Even when the characteristics of private projects require substantial public-sector cooperation, many decisions are only indirectly dependent on processes of political approval. Economic-development decisions have increasingly become insulated from the mainstream political processes of city governments as a result of the proliferation of public-benefit corporations (Walsh 1978; Kantor 1993). As power to finance and regulate business development has been ceded to public-benefit corporations, the ability of elected political leaders to build popular coalitions around development issues has shrunk because it makes little sense to appeal to voters on matters that they cannot influence.

On the other hand, the importance of this bargaining resource increases as issues spill over their ordinary institutional boundaries and into public or neighborhood arenas. When this occurs, elected political authorities gain bargaining advantages by putting together coalitions that can play a vital role in the urban development game. Consequently, even the most powerful public and private developers can be checked by politicians representing hostile voter coalitions.

In New York, Robert Mose's slide from power was made possible by mounting public discontent with his later projects and by the intervention of a popular governor who capitalized on this to undercut Moses's position (Caro 1974); Donald Trump's plans for the Upper West Side of Manhattan incurred defeats by a coalition of irate residents, local legislators, and a hostile mayor (Savitch 1988); a major highway (Westway) proposal, sponsored by developers, bankers, and other business interests, was defeated by community activists who skillfully used the courts to question the project's environmental impact.

Second, public authorities must have the managerial capability to organize and deliver political support for programs sought by business. Credible bargaining requires organizing a stable constituency whose consent can be offered to business in a quid pro quo process. However, political authorities clearly differ enormously in their capacity to draw on this resource. In the United States, the decline of machine politics, the weakening of party loyalties and organizations, and the dispersal of political power to interest groups have weakened the capacity of elected political authorities. To some extent, this has been counterbalanced by grassroots and other populist-style movements that have provided a broad base for mayors and other political leaders (Swanstrom 1986; Dreier and Keating 1990; Savitch and Thomas 1991; Capek and Gilderbloom 1992).

In contrast, in Western European cities, the stability and cohesion displayed by urban party systems more frequently strengthen political control of development. In Paris, extensive political control over major development projects is related to stable and well-organized political support enjoyed by officials who dominated the central and local governments (Savitch 1988). In London, ideological divisions between Conservative and Labour parties at the local and national levels limit the ability of business interests to win a powerful role, even in cases involving massive redevelopment such as Covent Garden, the construction of motorways, and the docklands renewal adjacent to the financial city. For example, changes in planning the docklands project were tied to shifts in party control at both the national and local levels. Given the political significance of development issues to both major British parties, it was difficult for nonparty interests to offer inducements that were capable of splitting politicians away from their partisan agendas (Savitch 1988).

Similarly, even highly fragmented but highly ideological political party systems seem capable of providing a powerful bargaining resource to elected governmental authorities. In Italy, many small parties compete for power at the national and local levels. Although this is sometimes a source of political instability, the relatively stable ideological character of party loyalties means that elected politicians are assured of constituency support. Consequently, this base of political power offers substantial bargaining advantages in dealing with business. According to Molotch and Vicari (1988), this enables elected political authorities to undertake major projects relatively free from business pressure. In Milan, officials planned and built a subway line through the downtown commercial district of the city with minimal involvement of local business.

Third, popular-control mechanisms are a valuable bargaining resource when they bind elected leaders to programmatic objectives. If political authorities are not easily disciplined for failure to promote programmatic objectives in development bargaining, business may promote their claims by providing selective incentives (side payments), such as jobs, campaign donations, and other petty favors, to public officials in exchange for their cooperation. When this happens, the bargaining position of city governments is undermined by splitting off public officials from their representational roles—and the process of popular control becomes more of a business resource.

In America, where partisan attachments are weak and where ethnic, neighborhood, and other particularistic loyalties are strong, political leaders are inclined to put a high value on seeking selective benefits to the neglect of programmatic objectives. Although populist mayors have sometimes succeeded in overcoming these obstacles (Swanstrom 1986; Dreier and Keating 1990), the need to maintain unstable political coalitions that are easily undermined by racial and ethnic rivalries limits programmatic political competition. For example, in Detroit and Atlanta, black mayors have relied heavily on economic development to generate side payments that are used to minimize political opposition; this is facilitated by the symbolic importance that these black mayors enjoy among the heavily black electorates in the two cities. Consequently, they have been able to hold on to power without challenging many business demands (Stone 1989; Hill 1986). In contrast, in Western Europe, where political party systems more frequently discipline public officials to compete on programmatic grounds, bargaining with business is less likely to focus on side payments. As suggested earlier, in France, Italy, and Britain, votes are more often secured by partisan and ideological loyalties and reinforced by progammatic competition than by generating selective incentives for followers.

In sum, city governments vary enormously in their capacity to draw on the popular-control process in bargaining over development. The proximity of electoral competition to development, the capability of officials to organize voter support, and the extent of competition over programmatic objectives are crucial factors that weaken or enhance the resources of city governments.

# State Intervention and Urban Development

. . . Ironically, integrated national governmental systems appear to enhance local governmental control of urban development, and political structures that decentralize the regulation of market failures afford less local governmental influence. Political systems that accord a powerful urban regulatory role for the national government limit local political authority in urban planning, of course. Yet, these more centralized systems can often work to enhance local governmental bargaining power with the private sector; they do this by making it easier for governments to contain capital movement (overriding private decision making), as well as by permitting localities to draw on the resources, regulatory apparatus, and political support of higher levels of government.

Contrasts between American and some Western European cities illustrate the different bargaining implications of each system. The United States is unique in the degree to which urban public capital investment is highly decentralized. Although the national government provides grants to support highway and other capital projects, this aid is spotty and unconnected to any system of national urban planning. Most important, responsibility for financing most local infrastructure is highly decentralized. Consequently, local and state governments have little choice but to find an administrative means of extracting revenues from the private sector that gives priority to satisfying investor confidence. To market long-term debt, public corporations must contend with investor fears that borrowed funds might be diverted to satisfy political pressures, rather than used for debt repayment. Consequently, major urban infrastructure development is in the hands of public corporations that are only indirectly accountable to urban electorates. These corporations are well known for courting private investors and treating them as constituents rather than as bargaining rivals (Caro 1974; Walsh 1978).

The European experience is quite different. There, most capital expenditures are supported by the central government. In France, upwards of 75% of local budgets are financed by central government; in Holland, the figure is 92%. This relieves some of the pressure on local authorities to compete with one another for capital investment to finance basic services. Local governments in Europe are capable of dealing with business from a position of greater strength. Beyond this, national government is not as dependent on private capital as local government is and can turn to vast financial and regulatory powers to reinforce public bargaining on the part of national and local governmental authorities.

The case of La Defense, just outside of Paris, is instructive of how state-business relations have been managed in Western Europe. During the 1960s, the national government planned to build another central business district for Paris on the vacant fields of La Defense. Despite skepticism by private investors, funds were allocated by the national government. Just as the project was launched, it was confronted by a fiscal crisis. French business looked on as La Defense reeled from one difficulty to another, and the enterprise was mocked as a "white elephant." The national government responded quickly, infusing the project with funds from the treasury, from nationalized banks, and from pensions. To buttress these efforts, the government clamped down on new office construction within Paris and used other carrots and sticks to persuade corporations that La Defense was the wave of the future. The effort worked, and La Defense became a premier site as an international business headquarters.

La Defense was not built in unique circumstances. To the contrary, it demonstrates the cumulative effect of centralized policy intervention on urban development. It is not unusual for governments throughout Western Europe to pour infrastructure into a particular development area, to freeze the price of surrounding land to prevent speculation, to construct buildings in the same area by relying on public corporations, and to design all the structures in the development site. The last public act is usually to invite private investors to compete for the privilege of obtaining space. Only then does bargaining begin.

Comparison of ... two antipodal cities [—Amsterdam and Detroit—] permits us to illustrate the cumulative consequences of differences in bargaining resources for political control of business development. To begin with market conditions, Amsterdam has a highly favorable market position because it is at the center of Holland's economic engine—a horseshoe shaped region called the Randstad. The cities of the Randstad (Amsterdam, Utrecht, Rotterdam, and the Hague) form a powerful and diversified conurbation that drives Holland's economy, its politics, and its sociocultural life. Amsterdam itself is the nation's political and financial capital. It also holds light industry, is a tourist and historic center, and is one of northern Europe's transportation hubs. Although Amsterdam has gone through significant deindustrialization (Jobse and Needham 1987) and has lost 21% of its population since 1960, it has transformed its economy to residential and postindustrial uses and is attractively positioned as one of the keystones of a united Europe.

Detroit's market conditions are dramatically less favorable. It is situated in what was once America's industrial heartland and what is now balefully called the Rustbelt. Known as America's Motor City, its economy revolved around automobile manufacture. Deindustrialization and foreign competition have taken a devastating toll. In just three decades, Detroit lost more than half its manufacturing jobs and 38% of its population (Darden et al. 1987). Nearly half the population lives below the poverty line, and one quarter is unemployed (Nethercutt 1987). Detroit has tried to come back to its former prominence by rebuilding its downtown and diversifying its economy for tourism and banking. But those efforts have not changed the city's market posture. Jobs and the middle class continue to move to surrounding suburbs, and any possible conversion of the Rustbelt economy appears slim when viewed against more attractive opportunities elsewhere.

The differences in popular control of these two cities are equally stark. Amsterdam is governed by a 45-member council that is elected by proportional representation (the council also elects a smaller body of aldermen) and is well organized and easily disciplined by the voters. Political parties have cohesive programs geared to conservative, social democratic, centrist, and leftwing orientations. Political accountability is reinforced by a system of elected district councils that represent different neighborhoods of the city. These councils participate in a host of decentralized services including land use, housing, and development.

In contrast, Detroit's government is poorly organized in respect to promoting popular control of economic development. A nine-member city council is elected at large and in nonpartisan balloting. Detroit's mayor [in 1993], Coleman young, has held power for 16 years and has based his administration on distributing selective benefits, especially city jobs and contracts, while focusing on downtown project development (Hill 1986; Rich 1991). The system affords scant opportunity for neighborhood expression, and the city's singular ethnic composition (Detroit is 75% black) is coupled to a politics of black symbolism that impedes programmatic accountability and pluralist opposition. Indeed, one scholar has described Detroit as ruled by a tight-knit elite (Ewen 1978); two other researchers believed that the city's power was exercised at the peaks of major sectors within the city (Jones and Bachelor 1986).

The two cities also differ dramatically in respect to modes of policy intervention. Like many European cities, Amsterdam is governed within an integrated national planning scheme. The Dutch rely on three-tier government, at the national, regional, and municipal levels. Goals are set at the uppermost levels, master plans are developed at the regional level, and allocation plans are implemented at the grass roots. A municipalities fund allocates financial support based on population, and over 90% of Amsterdam's budget is carried by the national treasury.

By contrast, Detroit stands very much alone. While "golden corridors" (drawn from Detroit's former wealth) have sprung up in affluent outskirts, the suburbs now resist the central city. Attempts at creating metropolitan mechanisms to share tax bases or to undertake planning have failed (Darden et al. 1987). Over the years, federal aid has shrunk and now accounts for less than 6% of the city's budget (Savitch and Thomas 1991). State aid has compensated for some of Detroit's shortfalls, but like most states, Michigan is at a loss to do anything about the internecine struggles for jobs and investment.

Given the cumulative differences along all three dimensions, the bargaining outcomes for each city are dramatically opposite. Under the planning and support of national and regional authorities, Amsterdam has managed its deindustrialization—first by moving heavy industry to specific subregions (called *concentrated deconcentration*) and later by locating housing and light commerce in abandoned wharves and depleted neighborhoods. The Dutch have accomplished this through a combination of infrastructure investment, direct subsidies, and the power to finance and build housing (Levine and Van Weesop 1988; Van Weesop and Wiegersma 1991). Amsterdam's capacity to construct housing is a particularly potent policy instrument and constitutes a countervailing alternative to private development. Between 50% and 80% of housing in Amsterdam is subsidized or publicly built. This puts a considerable squeeze on private developers, who face limitations of and availability as well as zoning, density, and architectural controls. As a condition of development, it is not uncommon for commercial investors to agree to devote a portion of their projects toward residential use (Van Weesop and Wiegersma 1991).

Indeed, the bargaining game in Holland is titled toward the public sector in ways that seem unimaginable in the United States. Freestyle commercial development in Amsterdam has been restricted, so that most neighborhoods remain residential. Because of massive housing subsidies, neighborhoods have lacked the extremes of wealth or poverty. Even squatting has been declared legal. Abandoned buildings have been taken over by groups of young, marginal, and working-class populations—thus leading to lower-class gentrification (Mamadouh 1990).

All this compares very differently to the thrust of development outcomes in Detroit. The case of Poletown provides a stark profile of Detroit's response to bargaining with the private sector (Fasenfest 1986). When General Motors announced that it was looking for a new plant site, the city invoked the state's "quick take" law, allowing municipalities to acquire property before actually reaching agreement with individual owners. To attract the plant and an anticipated 6,000 jobs, the city moved more than 3,000 residents and 143 institutions (hospitals, churches, schools, and businesses) and demolished more than 1,000 buildings. To strike this bargain, Detroit committed to at least $200 million in direct expenditures and a dozen years of tax abatements. In the end, the bargaining exchange resulted in one lost neighborhood and a gain of an automobile plant—all under what one judge labeled as the "guiding and sustaining, indeed controlling hand of the General Motors Corporation" (Jones and Bachelor 1986).

In many respects, Poletown reflects a larger pattern of bargaining. The city is now trying to expand its airport. At stake are 3,600 homes, more than 12,000 residents, and scores of businesses. The city and a local bank also have their sights set on a venerable auditorium called Ford Hall. The arrangement calls for razing Ford Hall and granting the developers an $18 million no-interest loan, payable in 28 years. When citizen protests stalled the project, developers threatened to move elsewhere. Since then, Detroit's city council approved the project (Rich 1991).

The polar cases of Amsterdam and Detroit reveal something about the vastly different development prizes and sacrifices that particular cities experience as a result of their accumulated bargaining advantages. Amsterdam is able to use public investment to extract concessions from investors and enforce development standards in a process conducted under public scrutiny. Detroit offers land, money, and tax relief to attract development in a process managed by a tight circle of political and economic elites.

## Political Control of Urban Development

By examining urban development from a state-bargaining perspective, we are able to identify some critical forces that influence local governmental control over this area of policy. From this vantage point, public influence over urban development appears to be tied to differences in market conditions, popular control mechanisms, and public policy systems because these interdependent spheres powerfully affect the ability of politicians to bargain with business. . . .

By using our bargaining perspective, future researchers may be able to overcome the limitations of extant theory and better understand the actual political choices of local communities in economic development.

### NOTE

1. Urban Summit Conference, New York City, 12 November 1990.

### REFERENCES

Almond, G. 1988. The return to the state. *American Political Science Review* 82:853–874.

Bachrach, P., and M. Baratz. 1962. The two faces of power. *American Political Science Review* 56:947–952.

Body-Gendrot, S. 1987. Grass roots mobilization in the Thirteenth Arrondissment: A cross national view. In *The Politics of urban development* edited by C. Stone and H. Sanders, 125–143. Lawrence: University Press of Kansas.

Capek, S., and J. Gilderbloom. 1992 *Community versus commodity* Albany: State University of New York Press.

Caro, R. 1974. *The power broker.* New York: Vintage.

Christensen, T. 1979. *Neighborhood survival.* London: Prism Press.

Crenson, M. 1971. *The un-politics of air pollution.* Baltimore, MD: Johns Hopkins University Press.

Cummings, S., ed. 1988. *Business elites and urban development.* Albany: State University of New York Press.

Dahl, R. 1971. *Polyarchy.* New Haven, CT: Yale University Press.

Dahl, R., and C. E. Lindblom. 1965. *Politics, economics, and welfare.* New Haven, CT: Yale University Press.

Danielson, M. 1976. *The politics of exclusion.* New York: Columbia University Press.

Darden, J., R. C. Hill, J. Thomas, and R. Thomas. 1987. *Race and uneven development.* Philadelphia: Temple University Press.

Dreier, P. 1989. Economic growth and economic justice in Boston. In *Unequal partnerships,* edited by G. Squires, 35–58. New Brunswick, NJ: Rutgers University Press.

Dreier, P., and W. D. Keating. 1990. The limits of localism: Progressive housing policies in Boston, 1984–1989. *Urban Affairs Quarterly* 26:191–216.

Eisinger, P. 1987. *Rise of the entrepreneurial state.* Madison: University of Wisconsin Press.

Elkin, D. 1987. State and market in city politics: Or, the real Dallas. In *The politics of urban development,* edited by C. Stone and H. Sanders, 25–51. Lawrence: University Press of Kansas.

Etzkowitz, H., and R. Mack. 1976. Emperialism in the First World: The corporation and the suburb. Paper presented at the Pacific Sociological Association meetings, San Jose, CA, March.

Ewen, L. 1978. *Corporate power and the urban crisis in Detroit.* Princeton, NJ: Princeton University Press.

Fainstein, S. S., N. I. Fainstein, R. C. Hill, D. Judd, and M. P. Smith. 1986. *Restructuring the city.* 2nd ed. New York: Longman.

Fasenfest, D. 1986. Community politics and urban redevelopment. *Urban Affairs Quarterly* 22:101–123.

Feagin, J. 1988. *Free enterprise city.* New Brunswick, NJ: Rutgers University Press.

Foglesong, R. 1989. Do politics matter in the formulation of local economic development policy: The case of Orlando, Florida. Paper presented at the annual meeting of the American Political Science Association, Atlanta, GA, September.

Governor turns down UAL. 1991. *Courier-journal,* 18 October, 1.

Hill, R. C. 1986. Crisis in the motor city: The politics of urban development in Detroit. In *Restructuring the city,* 2d ed., by S. S. Fainstein, N. I. Fainstein, R. C. Hill, D. Judd, and M. P. Smith. New York: Longman.

———. Industrial restructuring, state intervention, and uneven development in the United States and Japan. Paper presented at conference: The tiger by the tail: Urban policy and economic restructuring in Comparative perspective. State University of New York, Albany, October.

Jobse, B., and B. Needham. 1987. The economic future of the Randstad, Holland. *Urban Studies* 25: 282–296.

Jones, B., and L. Bachelor. 1986. *The sustaining hand.* Lawrence: University Press of Kansas.

Kantor, P. 1993. The dual city as political choice. *Journal of Urban Affairs* 15 (3): 231–244.

Kantor, P. (with S. David). 1988. *The dependent city.* Boston, MA: Scott, Foresman/Little, Brown.

Levine, M., and J. Van Weesop. 1988. The changing nature of urban planning in the Netherlands. *Journal of the American Planning Association* 54:315–323.

Lindblom, C. 1977. *Politics and markets.* New Haven, CT: Yale University Press.

———. 1982. The market as a prison. *Journal of Politics* 44:324–336.

Logan, J., and H. Molotch. 1987. *Urban fortunes.* Berkeley: University of California Press.

Logan, J., and T. Swanstrom, eds. 1990. *Beyond the city limits.* Philadelphia: Temple University Press.

Mamadouh, V. 1990. Squatting, housing, and urban policy in Amsterdam. Paper presented at the International Research Conference on Housing Debates and Urban Challenges, Paris, July.

Mollenkopf, J. 1983. *The contested city.* Princeton, NJ: Princeton University Press.

Molotch, H., and S. Vicari. 1988. Three ways to build: The development process in the United States, Japan, and Italy. *Urban Affairs Quarterly* 24:188–214.

Muzzio, D., and R. Bailey. 1986. Economic development, housing, and zoning. *Journal of Urban Affairs* 8:1–18.

Nethercutt, M. 1987. *Detroit twenty years after: A statistical profile of the Detroit area since 1967.* Detroit, MI: Center for Urban Studies, Wayne State University.

Noyelle, T., and T. M. Stanback. 1984. *Economic transformation of American cities.* New York: Conservation for Human Resources Columbia University.

Parkinson, M., B. Foley, and D. Judd. 1989. *Regenerating the cities.* Boston, MA: Scott, Foresman.

Peterson, P. 1981. *City limits.* Chicago: University of Chicago Press.

Rich, W. 1991. Detroit: From Motor City to service hub. In *Big city politics in transition,* edited by H. V. Savitch and J. C. Thomas, 64–85. Newbury Park, CA: Sage Publications.

Rosentraub, M., and D. Swindell. 1990. "Just say no"? The economic and political realities of a small city's investment in minor league baseball. Paper presented at the 20th annual meeting of the Urban Affairs Association, Charlotte, NC, April.

Sassen, S. 1988. *The mobility of capital and labor.* Cambridge: Cambridge University Press.

Savitch, H. V. 1988. *Post-industrial cities: Politics and planning in New York, Paris, and London.* Princeton, NJ: Princeton University Press.

Savitch, H. V., and J. C. Thomas, eds. 1991. *Big city politics in transition.* Newbury Park, CA: Sage Publications.

Stone, C. 1989. *Regime politics.* Lawrence: University Press of Kansas.

Stone, C., and H. Sanders, eds. 1987. *The politics of urban development.* Lawrence: University Press of Kansas.

Swanstrom, T. 1986. *The crisis of growth politics* Philadelphia: Temple University Press.

UAL bidding goes on. 1991. *Courier-Journal.* 22 October, 1.

Van Weesop, J., and M. Wiegersma. 1991. Gentrification in the Netherlands. In *Urban housing for the better-off: Gentrification in Europe* edited by J. Van Weesop and S. Musterd, 98–111. Utrecht, Netherlands: Bureau Stedellijke Netwerken.

Vaughn, R. 1979. *State taxation and economic development.* Washington, DC: Council of State Planning Agencies.

Vogel, R. 1990. The local regime and economic development. *Economic Development Quarterly* 4:101–112.

Walsh, A. 1978. *The public's business.* Cambridge: MIT Press.

# CHAPTER 3

# THE POLITICAL ECONOMY OF URBAN CULTURE

## CULTURAL STRATEGIES OF URBAN DEVELOPMENT

Tourism/entertainment, culture, and urban amenities have been extremely important for the revitalization of downtowns and urban economies. Old cities have an advantage in developing these sectors. Jobs are connected to amenities; the affluent residents who live downtown want to commute less but also prefer to live in an environment with exciting street life, nightlife, culture, and entertainment. With their historic architecture, public monuments, redeveloped waterfronts, and older neighborhoods, cities are uniquely positioned to provide an exciting urban culture. Partly for this reason, for the first time in a half century, cities seem to be indispensable to their metropolitan regions.

A leading urban scholar, Richard Florida, has identified the rise of "the creative class" to explain the recent emphasis on tourism, culture, and entertainment. In Selection 8, Florida argues that the creative class, which is composed of highly educated professionals with rarified intellectual, analytic, artistic, and creative skills, frequently regard lifestyle as more important than a particular job in choosing a place to live. The members of this class demand social interaction, culture, nightlife, diversity, and authenticity, which have become identified with historic architecture, renovated buildings, old neighborhoods, special features such as trendy bars and music, and a certain measure of urban grit. Florida indicates that the creative class tends to reject the "canned experiences" associated with tourist enclaves. Instead, the creative class has become the basis for a new political movement that demands a high level of urban amenities, both public and private, in the downtowns and neighborhoods they frequent. The result is a revival of the downtown and of inner-city neighborhoods after decades of decline.

In Selection 9, Elizabeth Strom points out that as the traditional economic base of cities has weakened, culture and the arts have become increasingly important for urban revitalization. Whatever other problems they may face, older cities hold a distinct advantage over suburbs in building a new economy based on culture and arts because of the presence of renovated waterfronts, historic districts, museums, concert halls, opera galleries, and "high culture" assets. Strom describes how a close collaboration between the private and public sectors has emerged to enhance the presence of culture downtown. Promoters of culture and arts seek public funding for their efforts. At the other end of the bargain, city officials perceive cultural and art institutions as industries that can help drive urban revitalization. Strom believes that this close collaboration raises questions: Does the commercialization of culture exclude artistic endeavors that do not draw big crowds or long lines? Does it bias public support for the arts in favor of events that have quick audience potential, but diminish sustained support for museums and concert halls after they are built? Ultimately, is the quality of life in cities improved or degraded by the new culture-development alliance?

In Selection 10, Alison Isenberg calls attention to some of the unsavory aspects of nostalgia that sometimes drive the revitalization of old downtowns and historic buildings. She gives an account of how some visitors to a museum celebrating dime store architecture used the occasion to offer fond memories of the past, including a past that was all-white. In her view, the exhibit encouraged an oversimplified narrative of decline that emphasized social change above all other causes. Isenberg considers an important question: Is today's renovation, with its evocation of an idealized urban past, creating environments that will all be the same, sanitized and cleansed of diversity and difference? Her answer is a decisive "no"; part of the reason is that romanticized notions of the past have become the subject of lively debate and controversy—an element that was generally missing from those same historic venues.

# 8

## *Richard Florida*

# THE POWER OF PLACE: THE CREATIVE CLASS

As I walked across the campus of Carnegie Mellon University on a delightful spring day, I came upon a table filled with young people chatting and enjoying the spectacular weather. Several had on identical blue t-shirts with "Trilogy@CMU" written across them—Trilogy being an Austin-based software company that often recruited our top students. I walked over to the table. "Are you guys here to recruit?" I asked. "No, absolutely not," they answered, seeming taken aback by the very question. "We're not recruiters. We're just hangin' out, playing a little Frisbee with our friends." How interesting, I thought. They've come to campus on a workday, all the way from Austin to Pittsburgh, just to hang out with some new friends.

I noticed one member of the group sitting slouched over on the grass, dressed in a tank top. This young man had spiked multicolored hair, full-body tattoos and multiple piercings in his ears—an obvious slacker. "So what's your story?" I asked. "Hey man, I just signed on with these guys." As I would later learn, he was a gifted student who had just inked the highest-paying deal of any graduating student in the history of his department, right at that table on the grass, with the recruiters who do not "recruit," because of course that would be pushy and not cool.

What a change from my own college days, when students would put on their dressiest clothes and carefully hide any counterculture symptoms, in order to show recruiters that they could fit in. Here the company was trying to fit in with the student. Trilogy had wined and dined this young man over margaritas in Pittsburgh and flown him to Austin for private parties in hip nightspots and aboard company boats. When I called the recruiters to ask why, they answered, "That's easy. We wanted him because he's a rock star." Moreover, "when big East Coast companies trek down here to see who is working on *their* project, we'll wheel him out"—blowing the customers' minds with his skill and coolness.

But something bigger struck me: Here was another talented young person leaving Pittsburgh. That was exactly the problem that had started me on this line of research in the first place. My adopted hometown has a huge number of assets. Carnegie Mellon is one of the world's leading centers for research in information technology. The University of Pittsburgh, right down the street, has a world-class medical center. Pittsburgh attracts hundreds of millions of dollars per year in university research funding and is the sixth largest center for college and university students, on a per capita basis, in the country. It is hardly a cultural backwater. The city is home to three major sports franchises, renowned museums and cultural venues, a spectacular network of urban parks, remarkable industrial-age architecture, and truly great urban neighborhoods with an abundance of charming yet affordable housing. It is a friendly city, defined by strong communities and a strong sense of pride. In the 1985 Rand McNally survey, Pittsburgh was ranked "America's Most Livable City," and it has continued to score high on such lists ever since.

Yet the economy putters along in a middling flat-line pattern. Both the core city and the surrounding metropolitan area lost population in the 2000 census. And those bright young university people keep leaving. Most of Carnegie Mellon's prominent alumni of recent decades—like Vinod Khosla, among the best known of Silicon Valley's venture capitalists, and former faculty member Rick Rashid, now head of R&D at Microsoft—went elsewhere to make their marks. Pitt's vaunted medical center, the place where Jonas Salk created his polio vaccine and the site of the world's premier organ-transplant program, has inspired only a handful of entrepreneurs to build biotech companies in Pittsburgh.

Over the years I have seen the community try just about everything possible to remake itself, and I was personally involved in many of these efforts. The region has launched a multitude of programs to diversify its economy away from heavy industry into high technology. It rebuilt its downtown virtually from scratch, invested in a new airport and developed a massive new sports complex for the baseball Pirates and the football Steelers. It devotes considerable effort to attracting and retaining talented young people. But nothing, it seems, can reverse the tide of people and companies leaving.

I vividly recall the day one of our university's most famous spin-off companies, Lycos, left town. I was on leave at Harvard's Kennedy School and opened the morning paper only to find a story reporting the company's relocation to Boston. Carnegie Mellon researchers had developed the Lycos catalog-and-search technology in the earliest days of the commercial Internet. The technology had then been licensed to the Boston-based venture capital firm CMGI, which built a company around it. At first, Lycos headquarters were in Boston but the engineering offices and the technical operations, a considerable enterprise, were kept in Pittsburgh. But now that was moving as well. According to a number of my colleagues who were close to the situation, the main reason was that Boston offered lifestyle options that made it much easier to attract top managerial and technical talent.

With all of this whirring in the back of my brain, I asked the young man with the spiked hair why he was going to a smaller city in the middle of Texas, a place with a small airport and no professional sports teams, without museums and high-art cultural amenities comparable to Pittsburgh's. The company is excellent, he told me. It has terrific people and the work is challenging. But the clincher was: "It's in *Austin!*" "Why is that good?" I asked. There are lots of young people, he explained, and a tremendous amount to do, a thriving music scene, ethnic and cultural diversity, fabulous outdoor recreation, and great nightlife. That's what mattered—not the symphony or the opera, which he enjoyed but would not feel comfortable attending. What's more, Austin is affordable, unlike Silicon Valley, another place that offered the kinds of work he desired. He was right: Austin ranked as the fourth most affordable place for information-technology workers like him, with a pay differential of more than $18,000 over the San Francisco Bay area, when cost-of-living differences are taken into account.[1]

"I can have a life in Austin," he concluded, not merely a job. When I asked him about Pittsburgh, where he had chosen to go to college, he replied that he had lived in the city for four years and knew it well. Though he had several good offers from Pittsburgh high-tech firms, he felt the city lacked the lifestyle options, cultural diversity and tolerant attitude that would make it attractive to him. As he summed it up, "How would I fit in here?"

Thus a question that lies at the heart of our age, and that would drive much of the research for this book:

> *How do we decide where to live and work? What really matters to us in making this kind of life decision? How has this changed—and why?*

The usual answer is "jobs." That certainly is what most economists would say. People go to places in pursuit of the most attractive positions and the greatest financial rewards. But jobs are not the whole story. People balance a host of considerations in making decisions on where to work and live. What they want today is different from what our parents wanted, and even from what many of us once thought we wanted. And while the young man with spiked hair and impressive tattoos is not representative of everyone in the Creative Class, my research shows that the same basic kinds of things he liked about Austin are representative of the traits many look for in choosing a place to live. A number of consistent themes emerge from my research:

- The Creative Class is moving away from traditional corporate communities, Working Class centers and even many Sunbelt regions to a set of places I call Creative Centers.
- The Creative Centers tend to be the economic winners of our age. Not only do they have high concentrations of Creative Class people, they have high concentrations of creative economic outcomes, in the form of innovations and high-tech industry growth. They also show strong signs of overall regional vitality, such as increases in regional employment and population.
- The Creative Centers are not thriving for such traditional economic reasons as access to natural resources or transportation routes. Nor are they thriving because their local governments have given away the store through tax breaks and other incentives to lure business. They are succeeding largely because creative people want to live there. The companies then follow the people—or, in many cases, are started by them. Creative centers provide the integrated eco-system or habitat where all forms of creativity—artistic and cultural, technological and economic— can take root and flourish.
- Creative people are not moving to these places for traditional reasons. The physical attractions that most cities focus on building—sports stadiums, freeways, urban malls and tourism-and-entertainment districts that resemble theme parks—are irrelevant, insufficient or actually unattractive to many Creative Class people. What they look for in communities are abundant high-quality amenities and experiences, an openness to diversity of all kinds, and above all else the opportunity to validate their identities as creative people.

## Limits of the Conventional View

Several perspectives dominate the debate over the role of place in our economy and society. While not opposed to each other in every respect, they are seldom in agreement. Perhaps the greatest of all the New Economy myths is that "geography is dead." With the Internet and modern telecommunication and transportation systems, the thinking goes, it is no longer necessary for people who work together to *be* together, so they won't be. This end-of-geography theme has been with us since experts predicted that technologies from the telegraph and the telephone to the automobile and the airplane would essentially kill off the cities. In his widely read 1998 book *New Rules for the New Economy*, Kevin Kelly wrote, "The New Economy operates in a 'space' rather than a place, and over time more and more economic transactions will migrate to this new space."[2] Kelly then qualifies this to some degree: "Geography and real estate, however, will remain, well . . . real. Cities will flourish, and the value of a distinctive place, such as a wilderness area, or a charming hill village, will only increase." Still he reiterates that "People will inhabit places, but increasingly the economy inhabits a space." Never has a myth been easier to deflate. Not only do people remain highly concentrated, but the economy itself—the high-tech, knowledge-based and creative-content industries that drive so much of economic growth—continues to concentrate in specific places from Austin and Silicon Valley to New York City and Hollywood, just as the automobile industry once concentrated in Detroit. Students of urban and regional growth from Robert Park and Jane Jacobs to Wilbur Thompson have long pointed to the role of places as incubators of creativity, innovation and new industries.[3] Moreover, the death-of-place prognostications simply do not square with the countless people I have inter- viewed, the focus groups I've observed, and the statistical research I've done. Place and community are more critical factors than ever before. And a good deal of the reason for this is that rather than inhabiting an abstract "space" as Kelly suggests, the economy itself increasingly takes form around real concentrations of people in real places. There are several theories that seek to account for the continued importance of place in economic and social life. Let's take a look.

One view suggests that place remains important as a locus of economic ac- tivity because of the tendency of firms to cluster together. This view builds on the seminal insights of the economic Alfred Marshall, who argued that firms cluster in "agglomerations" to gain productive efficiencies. The contemporary variant of this view, advanced by Harvard Business School professor Michael Porter, has many proponents in academia and in the practice of economic de- velopment.[4] It is clear that similar firms tend to cluster. Examples of this sort of agglomeration include not only Detroit and Silicon Valley, but the *maquiladora* electronics- and auto-parts districts in Mexico, the clustering of makers of disk drives in Singapore and of flat-panel displays in Japan, and the garment dis- trict and Broadway theater district in New York City.

The question is not whether firms cluster but why. Several answers have been offered. Some experts believe that clustering captures efficiencies gener- ated from tight linkages between firms. Others say it has to do with the posi- tive benefits of co-location, or what they call "spillovers." Still others claim it is because certain kinds of activity require face-to-face contact.[5] But these are only partial answers. As I have already noted and will show in greater detail, the real force behind this clustering is people. Companies cluster in order to draw from concentrations of talented people who power innovation and economic growth. The ability to rapidly mobilize talent from such concentrations is a tremendous source of competitive advantage for companies in the time-driven Creative Economy.

An alternative view is based on Robert Putnam's social capital theory. It basically says that regional economic growth is associated with tight-knit com- munities where people and firms form and share strong ties.[6] Putnam and oth- ers have tried to use social capital theory to account for the performance of high-tech industrial clusters like Silicon Valley, arguing that the networks of people and firms in these places constitute a form of social capital. But these high-tech centers do not approximate the classic social capital model. Rather they are centers of loose ties, of economic and social diversity. The Creative Class people I have interviewed in these places do not desire the strong ties and long-term commitments associated with traditional social capital. Rather they prefer a more flexible, quasi-anonymous community—where they can quickly plug in, pursue opportunities and build a wide range of relationships.

## Human Capital and Economic Growth

Over the past decade or so, a potentially more powerful theory for city and regional growth has emerged. The basic idea behind this theory is that people are the motor force behind regional growth. Its proponents thus refer to it as the "human capital" theory of regional development.

Economists and geographers have always accepted that economic growth is regional—that it is driven by and spreads from specific regions, cities or even neighborhoods. The traditional view, however, is that places grow either because they are located on transportation routes or because they have endowments of natural resources that encourage firms to locate there. According to this conventional view, the economic importance of a place is tied to the efficiency with which it can make things and do business. Governments employ this theory when they use tax breaks and high-way construction to attract business. But these cost-related factors are no longer the key to success.

The proponents of the human capital theory argue that the key to regional growth lies not in reducing the costs of doing business, but in endowments of highly educated and productive people. This clustering of human capital is even more important to economic growth than the clustering of companies, because as Ross DeVol of the Milken Institute points out, "You attract these people and you attract the industries that employ them and the investors who put money into the companies." Joel Kotkin captures the essence of the human capital view when he writes that:

> Traditionally, human intelligence tends to cluster in places where industry and commerce draw them. This has been true from the time of ancient Mesopotamia and Rome through early modern Amsterdam and New York. Yet at the same time brainpower could be highly concentrated in certain places—like New England or the Minneapolis region, other regions with more relative brawn—such as industrial Detroit or Buffalo, would still lead economic growth, luring highly skilled workers when needed.... This "brawn to brain" shift profoundly alters the importance of "place." Under the new regime of geography, wherever intelligence clusters evolve, in the small town or the big city, so too will wealth accumulate. Moreover, these clusters are far less constrained by traditional determinants such as strategic waterway location, the abundance of raw materials or the proximity to dense concentrations of populations.[7]

The human capital theory—like many theories of cities and urban areas—owes a debt to Jane Jacobs. For a long time academic economists ignored her ideas, but in the past decade or two, some very prestigious ones have taken them up in earnest and tried to develop empirical proof of their validity.

Decades ago, Jacobs noted the ability of cities to attract creative people and thus spur economic growth.[8] The Nobel Prize-winning economist Robert Lucas sees the productivity effects that come from the clustering of human capital as the critical factor in regional economic growth, referring to this as a "Jane Jacobs externality." In a widely circulated e-mail he went so far as to suggest that she should be considered for a Nobel in economics herself. Building on Jacobs's seminal insight, Lucas contends that cities would be economically infeasible if not for the productivity effects associated with endowments of human capital:

> If we postulate only the usual list of economic forces, cities should fly apart. The theory of production contains nothing to hold a city together. A city is simply a collection of factors of production—capital, people and land—and land is always far cheaper outside cities than inside . . . . It seems to me that the "force" we need to postulate to account for the central role of cities in economic life is of exactly the same character as the "external human capital." . . . What can people be paying Manhattan or downtown Chicago rents for, if not for being near other people?[9]

Studies of national growth find a clear connection between the economic success of nations and their human capital, as measured by the level of education. This connection has also been found in regional studies of the United States. In a series of studies, Harvard University economist Edward Glaeser and his collaborators found considerable empirical evidence that human capital is the central factor in regional growth.[10] According to Glaeser, such clustering of human capital is the ultimate cause of regional agglomerations of firms: Firms concentrate to reap the advantages that stem from common labor pools—not merely, according to Glaeser, to tap the advantages from linked networks of customers and suppliers as is more typically argued. Research by one of Glaeser's Harvard graduate students, Spencer Glendon, shows that a good deal of city growth over the twentieth century can be traced to those cities' levels of human capital at the beginning of the century.[11] Places with greater numbers of highly educated people grew faster and were better able to attract more talent. Research by Patricia Beeson, an urban economist at the University of Pittsburgh, supports this view. Her ongoing work explores how investments in various sorts of infrastructure have affected city and regional growth since the mid-nineteenth century. She finds that investments in higher education infrastructure predict subsequent growth far better than investments in physical infrastructure like canals, railroads or highways.[12]

# Creativity and Place

The human capital theory says that economic growth will occur in places that have highly educated people. This begs the question: Why do creative people cluster in certain places? In a world where people are highly mobile, why do they choose to live in and concentrate in some cities over others and for what reasons?

While economists and social scientists have paid a lot of attention to how companies decide where to locate, they have virtually ignored how people do so. This is the fundamental question I sought to answer. With little in the way of academic studies or literature to guide me, I began simply by asking people how they make their decisions about where to live and work. I started with my students and colleagues at Carnegie Mellon and then turned to friends and associates in other cities. Eventually I began to ask virtually everyone I met about this. The same answer kept coming back. People said that economic and lifestyle considerations both matter, and so does the mix. In reality, people were not making the career decisions or geographic moves that the standard theories said they should: They were not slavishly following jobs to places.

Gradually I came to see my perspective as distinct from the human capital theory. A colleague of mine even gave it a name, the "creative capital theory." Essentially my theory says that regional economic growth is driven by the location choices of creative people—the holders of creative capital—who prefer places that are diverse, tolerant and open to new ideas. It thus differs from the human capital theory in two respects: (1) It identifies a type of human capital, creative people, as being key to economic growth; and (2) it identifies the underlying factors that shape the location decisions of these people, instead of merely saying that regions are blessed with certain endowments of them. . . [L]et me share the findings from my interviews and focus groups that provide invaluable insights on what creative people actually value in locations.

## Thick Labor Markets

When asked about the importance of employment, the people in my interviews and focus groups repeatedly say they are not looking just for a single job but for many employment opportunities. The reason, they tell me, is simple. They do not expect to stay with the same company for very long. Companies are disloyal and careers are increasingly horizontal. To be attractive, places need to offer a job market that is conducive to a horizontal career path. In other words, places have to offer a *thick labor market.*

In this way, place solves a basic puzzle of our economic order: It facilitates the matching of creative people to economic opportunities. Place thus provides a labor pool for companies who need people and a thick labor market for people who need jobs. The gathering of people, companies and resources into particular places with particular specialties and capabilities generates efficiencies that power economic growth. It is for this reason that I say place is becoming the central organizing unit of our economy and society, taking on a role that used to be played by the large corporation.

## Lifestyle

The people in my focus groups tell me that lifestyle frequently trumps employment when they're choosing where to live. Many said they had turned down jobs, or decided not to look for them, in places that did not afford the variety of "scenes" they desired—music scene, art scene, technology scene, outdoor sports scene and so on. Some recounted how they or their friends had taken jobs for economic reasons, only to move elsewhere for lifestyle reasons. In the course of my research, I have come across many people who moved somewhere for the lifestyle and only *then* set out to look for employment there.

People today expect more from the places they live. In the past, many were content to work in one place and vacation somewhere else, while frequently getting away for weekends to ski, enjoy a day in the country or sample nightlife and culture in another city. The idea seemed to be that some places are for making money and others are for fun. This is no longer sufficient. The sociologists Richard Lloyd and Terry Nichols Clark of the University of Chicago note that "workers in the elite sectors of the postindustrial city make 'quality of life' demands, and . . . increasingly act like tourists in their own city."[13] One reason is the nature of modern creative work. Of course people still go away at times, but given their flexible and unpredictable work schedules, they want ready access to recreation on a "just-in-time" basis. When putting in a long day, for instance, they may need an extended break in the middle to recharge their batteries. Many who do this tell me a bike ride or run is a staple of their day-to-day productivity. And for this, a beach house or country getaway spot doesn't do them much good. They require trails or parks close at hand.

Nightlife is an important part of the mix. The people I talked to desired nightlife with a wide mix of options. The most highly valued options were experiential ones—interesting music venues, neighborhood art galleries, performance spaces and theaters. A vibrant, varied nightlife was viewed by many as another signal that a city "gets it," even by those who infrequently partake in nightlife. Interestingly, one of the biggest complaints of my focus groups had to do with cities where the nightlife closes down too early. The reason is not that most of these people are all-night partyers, but with long work hours and late nights, they need to have options around the clock. . . . As one person in a focus group summed it up: "I want the option available, when I want to do it."

A survey by one of my students, Erica Coslor, found that nightlife is indeed an important component of a city's lifestyle and amenity mix. Defining nightlife as "all entertainment activities that happen after dark," Coslor examined what younger Creative Class people (her respondents ranged in age from early twenties into their thirties) desire in urban nightlife. The highest-rated nightlife options were cultural attractions (from the symphony and theater to music venues) and late-night dining, followed by small jazz and music clubs and coffee shops. Bars, large dance clubs and after-hours clubs ranked much farther down the list. Most of her respondents desired a mix of entertainment options and safe and reliable "after-hours transportation." She also identified a strong preference for "on-demand entertainment." A third of Coslor's survey respondents said that "nightlife" plays a role in where they choose to live and work. She found that it takes a variety of activities coming together to create that *gestalt* that is nightlife.[14] Time and again, the people I speak with say these things are signals that a place "gets it"—that it embraces the culture of the Creative Age; that it is a place where they can fit in.

## Social Interaction

People have always, of course, found social interaction in their communities. But a community's ability to facilitate this interaction appears to be more important in a highly mobile, quasi-anonymous society. In his book *A Great Good Place*, Ray Oldenburg notes the importance of what he calls "third places" in modern society. Third places are neither home nor work—the "first two" places—but venues like coffee shops, bookstores and cafés in which we find less formal acquaintances. According to Oldenburg, these third places comprise "the heart of a community's social vitality" where people "hang out simply for the pleasures of good company and lively conversation."[15]

Creative Class people in my focus groups and interviews report that such third places play key roles in making a community attractive. This is because the two other sources of interaction and stability, the family and workplace, have become less secure and stable. People are more likely to live alone, and more likely to change jobs frequently. Third places fill a void by providing a ready venue for acquaintance and human interaction.

The importance of third places also arises from the changing nature of work. More of us do not work on fixed schedules and many of us work in relative isolation—for instance, in front of a keyboard at home, as I often do. Reliable human contact is thus hard to come by, and e-mail or phone interruptions provide only a limited form. So I frequently take a break and head to the coffee shop down the street just to see people on the street; or I take a bike ride to recharge, then head to the cafe to see my associates there. Many people I interview say they do much the same thing.

## Diversity

My focus group and interview participants consistently listed diversity as among the most important factors in their choice of locations. People were drawn to places known for diversity of thought and open-mindedness. They actively seek out places for diversity and look for signs of it when evaluating communities. These signs include people of different ethnic groups and races, different ages, different sexual orientations and alternative appearances such as significant body piercings or tattoos.

Small wonder that when a group of students visited my house recently, and I asked them where they wanted to live after graduation, highly diverse Washington, D.C., was the favorite. A Korean student liked it "because there's a big Korean community," meaning Korean religious institutions, Korean grocery stores and Korean children for his children to play with. Likewise an Indian student favored it for its large Indian population, an African-American for its large black professional class, and a gay student for the community around DuPont Circle.

But there's more at work here than expatriates who only want to be around people like themselves. It's the differences, not just the sameness, that are the benefit. A young female premedical student of Persian descent summarized the many criteria for diversity:

> I was driving across the country with my sister and some friends. We were commenting on what makes a place the kind of place we want to go, or the kind of place we would live. And we tried to list [the factors]. . . . We said: It has to be open. It has to be diverse. . . . It has to have a visible gay community; it has to have lots of different races and ethnic groups. It has to have people of all ages and be open to young people. It has to have people who *look* different.[16]

Like the diverse workplace, a diverse community is a sign of a place open to outsiders. And just as domestic partner benefits convey that a potential employer is open and tolerant, places with a visible gay presence convey the same kind of signal. Some said they oriented their location search to such places, even though they are not gay themselves. Others actively sought out gay neighborhoods for their amenities, energy, safety and sense of community. Younger women in particular said they liked to live in gay neighborhoods because they are "safe." As with employers, visible diversity serves as a signal that a community embraces the open meritocratic values of the Creative Age.

Diversity also means "excitement" and "energy." Creative-minded people enjoy a mix of influences. They want to hear different kinds of music and try different kinds of food. They want to meet and socialize with people unlike themselves, to trade views and spar over issues. A person's circle of closest friends may not resemble the Rainbow Coalition—in fact it usually does not—but he or she wants the rainbow to be available.

An attractive place doesn't have to be a big city, but it has to be cosmopolitan—a place where anyone can find a peer group to be comfortable with, and also find other groups to be stimulated by; a place seething with the interplay of cultures and ideas; a place where outsiders can quickly become insiders. In her book *Cosmopolitan City,* Bonnie Menes Kahn puts it very simply.[17] She says a great city has two hallmarks: tolerance for strangers and intolerance for mediocrity. These are precisely the qualities that appeal to members of the Creative Class—and they also happen to be qualities conducive to innovation, risk-taking and the formation of new businesses.

## Authenticity

Places are also valued for authenticity and uniqueness, as I have heard many times in my studies. Authenticity comes from several aspects of a community—historic buildings, established neighborhoods, a unique music scene or specific cultural attributes. It comes from the mix—from urban grit alongside renovated buildings, from the commingling of young and old, long-time neighborhood characters and yuppies, fashion models and "bag ladies."

People in my interviews and focus groups often define "authenticity" as the opposite of generic. They equate authentic with being "real," as in a place that has real buildings, real people, real history. An authentic place also offers unique and original experiences. Thus a place full of chain stores, chain restaurants and nightclubs is not authentic: Not only do these venues look pretty much the same everywhere, they offer the same experience you could have anywhere. One of my Creative Class subjects, emphasizing the way people are attracted to the authenticity and uniqueness of a city, used the two terms together as a combined phrase.

> I'm thinking in particular of the Detroit Electronic Music Festival. Here was a free concert that drew a million people the first year...and featured a stellar lineup of Detroit and some national performers and DJs, a great boon to the city and its image. This year, they...start to drop Detroit artists in favor of more well-known national acts. So more people come, but the event is losing much of the uniqueness/authenticity that makes people want to come to this event from around the world.[18]

Music is a key part of what makes a place authentic, in effect providing a sound or "audio identity."[19] Audio identity refers to the identifiable musical genre or sound associated with local bands, clubs and so on that make up a city's music scene: blues in Chicago, Motown in Detroit, grunge in Seattle, Austin's Sixth Street. This is what many people know about these cities and the terms in which they think of them; it is also the way these cities promote themselves.

Music in fact plays a central role in the creation of identity and the formation of real communities. Sounds, songs and musical memories are some of the strongest and most easily evoked. You can often remember events in your life by what songs were playing at the time. Simon Frith writes that music "provides us with an intensely subjective sense of being sociable. It both articulates and offers the immediate *experience* of collective identity. Music regularly soundtracks our search for ourselves and for spaces in which we can feel at home."[20]

In fact, it is hard to think of a major high-tech region that doesn't have a distinct audio identity. In addition to Seattle and Austin, consider the San Francisco Bay Area. It was home to perhaps the most creative music scene of the 1960s with the Grateful Dead, Jefferson Airplane, Mamas and the Papas, Haight-Ashbury and the seminal Monterey Pop Festival. Chapel Hill, North Carolina, at the heart of the Research Triangle, was recently named as having one of the best local music scenes in the country. Technology and the music scene go together because together they reflect a place that is open to new ideas, new people and creativity. And it is for this reason that frequently I like to tell city leaders that finding ways to help support a local music scene can be just as important as investing in high-tech business and far more effective than building a downtown mall.

Other kinds of "soundtracks" are important besides music. As Creative Class people like to say, an authentic place has a distinct "buzz." The sociologists Lloyd and Clark write of a sculptor who told them, "I came to Chicago because that was where the conversation was." This kind of soundtrack cannot be dubbed into a place. It is played and sustained by the creative people who live there—who *choose* to live there.

## Identity

Place provides an increasingly important dimension of our identity. Fewer people today find lifelong identity in the company for which they work. We live in a world where many traditional institutions have ceased to provide meaning, stability and support. In the old corporate-driven economy, many people took their cues from the corporation and found their identity there. Others lived in the towns where they grew up and could draw on the strong ties of family and long-term friends. As the Berkeley sociologist Manuel Castells has noted, "the power of identity" has become a defining feature of the insecure, constantly changing postmodern world.[21]

The combination of where we live and what we do has come to replace who we work for as a main element of identity. Forty years ago, some would likely identify themselves by saying "I work for General Motors" or "I'm with IBM." Today our tattooed friend is more likely to identify himself by saying "I'm a software developer and I live in Austin" rather than "I work for Trilogy." I travel by plane a lot and have noticed that the standard conversation-starter has changed. Ten years ago, people were likely to ask, "Where do you work?" Today it's "Where do you live?"

With the demise of the company-dominated life, a new kind of pecking order has developed around places. Place is becoming an important source of status. To some extent, this has always been true. Places like Paris, London and New York City have always been high on the status order. Elsewhere, people were content to substitute the economic status that came from a good job with a prestigious company for the status of place. But now the people in my focus groups and interviews tell me they are likely to move to places that convey high status.

Many Creative Class people I've studied also express a desire to be involved in their communities. This is not so much the result of a "do-good" mentality, but reflects their desire to both actively establish their own identity in places, and also to contribute to actively building places that reflect and validate that identity. In Pittsburgh, for instance, a group of young people in creative fields, ranging from architecture and urban design to graphics and high-tech, has formed a loose association that they dubbed "Ground Zero" (the group was formed and took its name before the World Trade Center tragedy). The group emerged on its own out of a series of brainstorming sessions that I organized in early 2000 to gain insight into the lifestyle and other concerns of young Creative Class people. While the initial impetus for the group was to combat a redevelopment plan that would have replaced an authentic downtown shopping district with a generic urban mall, they quickly began to focus their efforts on shaping the creative climate and identity of the city. Their initial "manifesto" speaks so directly to the nexus of creativity, place and identity that it is worth reproducing here in full.

Creative Friends,
Now is the time for us to come together to Speak Up and Act Up.
We the people who make things, who make the culture of this city, need to connect and engage. We want you to come and join us.

We all hear about how to make Pittsburgh a better place to be a consumer or a sports fan or an entrepreneur. We hear about strategies to suck in the young suburban consumers so they can park their cars, shop and leave.

This isn't us. We are already here. We are actively creating, whether it be food, stories, photographs, music, video games, paintings, buildings, performance or communities. We are making the culture of this city. We already know what makes Pittsburgh unique, interesting and attractive to people of all ages. We want to work to preserve its authenticity as a place; to make it more authentic.

We want to capitalize on what is already here, not destroy, demolish or suppress it. We want City policy that encourages culture to grow from within instead of promoting removal and replacement. We will then work proactively through ALL forms of media to make our voice heard. To make our city better.

We want to provoke awareness, discussion, argument, debate, and maybe even local pride (?) through what we will accomplish. And we want the voice of young creators to be heard loud and clear by those who make public policy.

The Ground Zero people have launched a variety of efforts to realize their vision, from organizing edgy community arts events to working to organize a shuttle-bus system, the "Ultra-Violet Loop," to establish "connectivity" between the various neighborhoods that make up Pittsburgh's street-level cultural mix. In doing so, they have sought to implant their creative identity into the urban fabric of the city.

The role of place in our identity is also evident in the growing struggles over who controls places. Some of the great conflicts of our age are the displacement of existing residents from their communities—their identities. I got a first-hand taste of this on a warm night in Seattle's up-and-coming Belltown neighborhood in May 2000. Walking down newly fashionable First Avenue with its mix of high-tech companies, high-end residences and nice restaurants, our group came upon a rag-tag band banging on drums and bellowing: "Say no to the construction noise." Jolted by the commotion, well-dressed yuppies emerged onto the street to see what it was about. A boisterous debate broke out between them and the protesters over who were the neighborhood's "true" residents.

## Quality of Place

All of the factors that go into Creative Class location decisions are, together, so powerful that I have coined a term to sum them up: *quality of place.* I use the term in contrast to the more traditional concept of quality of life. It refers to the unique set of characteristics that define a place and make it attractive. Generally, one can think of quality of place as having three dimensions:

- *What's there:* the combination of the built environment and the natural environment; a proper setting for pursuit of creative lives.
- *Who's there:* the diverse kinds of people, interacting and providing cues that anyone can plug into and make a life in that community.
- *What's going on:* the vibrancy of street life, café culture, arts, music and people engaging in outdoor activities—altogether a lot of active, exciting, creative endeavors.

The quality of place a city offers can be summed up as an interrelated set of experiences. Many of them, like the street-level scene, are dynamic and participatory. You can do more than be a spectator; you can be part of the scene. And the city allows you to modulate the experience: to choose the mix, to turn the intensity level up or down as desired, and to have a hand in creating the experience rather than merely consuming it. The street buzz is right nearby if you want it, but you can also retreat to your home or other quiet place, or go into an urban park, or even set out for the country. This is one reason canned experiences are not so popular. A chain theme restaurant, a multimedia-circus sports stadium or a prepackaged entertainment-and-tourism district is like a packaged tour: You do not get to help create your experience or modulate the intensity; it is thrust upon you.

Many members of the Creative Class also want to have a hand in actively shaping the quality of place of their communities. When I addressed a high-level downtown revitalization group in Providence, Rhode Island, in the fall of 2001, a thirty-something professional captured the essence of this when he said: "My friends and I came to Providence because it already has the authenticity that we like—its established neighborhoods, historic architecture and ethnic mix." He then implored the city leaders to make these qualities the basis of their revitalization efforts and to do so in ways that actively harness the energy of him and his peers. He said that Creative Class people like him seek places that are themselves a challenge and where they can help craft the future. Or as he aptly put it: "We want a place that's not done."

Quality of place does not occur automatically; rather it is an ongoing dynamic process involving the coming together of several different aspects of a community. The sociologist Richard Lloyd of the University of Chicago provides a vivid description of how this occurred in Chicago's Wicker Park neighborhood.

> Wicker Park was a relatively obscure, low-income neighborhood in the 1980s populated largely by Puerto Rican and Mexican immigrants who struggled against receding opportunities in the postindustrial landscape. With its relatively high crime rates and its abundance of derelict buildings leftover from a bygone era, the neighborhood would have seemed a poor candidate for the current proliferation of high-tech enterprises. However in the 1990s it underwent a striking transition. In 1989, the Northwest Tower lent its nickname to an annual "Around the Coyote" festival, designed to advertise the growing numbers of young artists who lived and worked in the neighborhood. The local rock-and-roll scene gained national recognition in the early part of the decade, leading *Billboard* magazine to anoint Wicker Park "cutting edge's new capital." The concentration of young artists, along with the establishment of associated amenities including boutiques, performance venues, coffee shops and galleries transformed the image of the neighborhood from a space of postindustrial decay to a privileged site of urban culture. This in turn has abetted the development of new profit-generating practices.[22]

It has also given rise to gentrification and displacement of long-term residents as Lloyd notes. . . .

Some of my critics like to argue that many people who work in high-tech industries tend to be blandly conservative and prefer homogeneous communities and traditional lifestyles of the sort found in middle-class suburbs. They find evidence in the fact that so many high-tech people live in suburban enclaves like northern Virginia, the heart of Silicon Valley or the Seattle suburbs. My response is simple. These places are all located within major metropolitan areas that are among the most diverse in the country and offer a wide array of lifestyle amenities. In fact, these places are themselves a product of the openness and diversity of the broader areas. Had the Silicon Valley–San Francisco area not been receptive years ago to offbeat people like the young Steven Jobs, it could not have become what it is.

What people want is not an either/or proposition. Successful places do not provide just one thing; rather they provide a range of quality of place options for different kinds of people at different stages in the life course. Great cities are not monoliths; as Jane Jacobs said long ago, they are federations of neighborhoods. Think about New York City and its environs. Young people, when they first move to New York, live in places like the East Village, Park Slope, Williamsburg or Hoboken, where rents are more affordable and there are lots of other young people. When they get a little older and earn a little more, they move to the Upper West Side or maybe to SoHo; earn a little more and they can go to the West Village or the Upper East Side. Once marriage and children come along, some stay in the city while others relocate to bedroom communities in places like Westchester Country, Connecticut, or the New Jersey suburbs. Later when the kids are gone, some of these people then move back to the city and buy a co-op overlooking the park or a duplex on the Upper East Side.

Members of the Creative Class come in all shapes, sizes, colors and lifestyles; and to be truly successful, cities and regions have to offer something for them all.

# NOTES

1. Adjusted for the costs of living differences, the average salary for an IT worker in Austin was $65,310 compared to $47,173 in San Francisco in 2001 (based on salary data from the *Information Week* Salary Survey adjusted for cost-of-living).
2. Kevin Kelly, *New Rules for the New Economy*, 1998, pp. 94–95.
3. Some classic statements include: Robert Park, E. Burgess and R. McKenzie, *The City*. Chicago: University of Chicago Press, 1925; Jane Jacobs, *The Death and Life of Great American Cities*. New York: Random House, 1961; *The Economy of Cities*. New York: Random House, 1969; *Cities and the Wealth of Nations*. New York: Random House, 1984; Wilbur Thompson, *A Preface to Urban Economics*. Baltimore: The Johns Hopkins University Press, 1965; Edwin Ullman, "Regional Development and the Geography of Concentration." *Papers and Proceedings of the Regional Science Association*, 4, 1958, pp. 179–198.
4. See Michael Porter, "Clusters and the New Economics of Competition." *Harvard Business Review*, November-December 1998; "Location, Clusters, and Company Strategy," in Gordon Clark, Meric Gertler and Maryann Feldman (eds.), *Oxford Handbook of Economic Geography*. Oxford: Oxford University Press, 2000; "Location, Competition and Economic Development: Local Clusters in a Global Economy." *Economic Development Quarterly* 14(1), February 2000, pp. 15–34.

5. The literature on agglomeration economies is vast, for a recent review see Maryann Feld-man, "Location and Innovation: The New Economic Geography of Innovation, Spillovers, and Agglomeration," in Clark, Gertler and Feldman (eds.), *The Oxford Handbook of Economic Geography*, pp. 373–394; Adam Jaffe, "Real Effects of Academic Research." *American Economic Review*, 79(5), 1989; David Audretsch and Maryann Feldman, "R&D Spillovers and the Geography of Innovation and Production." *American Economic Review*, 86(3), 1996; David Audretsch, "Agglomeration and the Location of Innovative Activity." *Oxford Review of Economic Policy*, 14(2), 1998, pp. 18–30.

6. Robert Putnam, *Bowling Alone: The Collapse and Revival of American Community*. New York: Simon and Schuster, 2000.

7. Joel Kotkin, "The New Geography of Wealth." *Reis.com, Techscapes*, December 2001; available on-line at www.reis.com/learning/insights_techscapes_art.cfm?art=1.

8. See Jacobs, *Cities and the Wealth of Nations*.

9. Robert Lucas, Jr., "On the Mechanics of Economic Development." *Journal of Monetary Economics*, 22, 1988, pp. 38–39.

10. See Edward Glaeser, "Are Cities Dying?" *Journal of Economic Perspectives*, 12, 1998, pp. 139–160. The human capital literature has grown large; other important contributions include: Glaeser, "The New Economics of Urban and Regional Growth," in Clark, Gertler and Feldman (eds.), *The Oxford Handbook of Economic Geography*, pp. 83–98; James E. Rauch, "Productivity Gains from Geographic Concentrations of Human Capital: Evidence from Cities." *Journal of Urban Economics*, 34, 1993, pp. 380–400; Curtis Simon, "Human Capital and Metropolitan Employment Growth." *Journal of Urban Economics*, 43, 1998, pp. 223–243; Curtis Simon and Clark Nardinelli, "The Talk of the Town: Human Capital, Information and the Growth of English Cities, 1861–1961." *Emplorations in Economic History*, 33(3), 1996, pp. 384–413. A comprehensive review is provided by Vijay K. Mathur, "Human Capital-Based Strategy for Regional Economic Development." *Economic Development Quarterly*, 13(3), 1999, pp. 203–216.

11. Spencer Glendon, "Urban Life Cycles." Cambridge: Harvard University, Department of Economics, unpublished working paper, November 1998.

12. Patricia Beeson, personal communication with author, winter 2000.

13. See Richard Lloyd and Terry Nichols Clark, "The City as an Entertainment Machine," in Kevin Fox Gotham (ed.), *Critical Perspectives on Urban Redevelopment. Research in Urban Sociology*, Vol. 6. Oxford: JAI Press/Elsevier, 2001, pp. 357–378.

14. Erica Coslor, "Work Hard, Play Hard: The Role of Nightlife in Creating Dynamic Cities." Pittsburgh: Heinz School of Public Policy and Management, Carnegie Mellon University, unpublished paper, December 2001.

15. Ray Oldenburg, *The Great Good Place: Cafes, Coffee Shops, Bars, Hair Salons and Other Hangouts at the Heart of a Community*. New York: Marlowe and Company, 1989.

16. Personal interview by author, spring 2001.

17. Bonnie Menes Kahn, *Cosmopolitan Culture: The Gilt Edged Dream of a Tolerant City*. New York: Simon and Schuster, 1987.

18. Personal interview by author, winter 2001.

19. I am indebted to Lenn Kano, a former Carnegie Mellon student for this term.

20. Simon Frith, *Performing Rites: On the Value of Popular Music*. Oxford: Oxford University Press, 1996, p. 273, italics in original.

21. Manuel Castells, *The Power of Identity: The Information Age: Economy, Society, and Culture*, Volume I. Oxford: Blackwell Publishers, 1997.

22. Richard Lloyd, "Digital Bohemia: New Media Enterprises in Chicago's Wicker Park." Paper presented at the annual conference of the American Sociological Association, August 2001, p. 8.

# 9

## Elizabeth Strom

# CULTURE, ART, AND DOWNTOWN DEVELOPMENT

American cities have rediscovered their cultural resources. During the past two decades, city officials have learned to value the historic communities that their predecessors have been eager to raze; have dubbed desolate, derelict warehouses "arts districts"; and have committed local tax dollars to their museums and performing arts complexes, many newly built or recently expanded. A survey of 65 U.S. cities (those with populations of 250,000 and above) finds that 71 major performing arts centers and museums have been either built or substantially expanded since 1985.[1] From Charlotte's Blumenthal Hall, to Los Angeles' Getty Museum, to Seattle's Benaroya Hall, a cultural building boom is clearly under way.

Of course, cultural facilities have always concentrated in urban areas. What is new and interesting, first, is that so many new facilities have been built in a relatively short time span, and so many have been built outside traditional cultural centers such as New York, Boston, Chicago, and San Francisco.[2] Second, whereas once the arts were considered a luxury, supported by philanthropy and enjoyed by an elite group of connoisseurs, today's cultural institutions are constructed as an explicit part of a city's economic revitalization program. This shift reflects changes both in the political economy of cities and in the organization and mission of highbrow cultural institutions. This article examines these changes and shows how they have led to an increasingly close and mutually beneficial relationship between urban political, economic, and cultural entrepreneurs.

The urban cultural building boom, this article maintains, represents a confluence of three related trends. First, cities seeking to attract businesses with quality-of-life amenities are eager to support the development of cultural institutions, especially in their once moribund centers. They believe that these institutions will increase the city's symbolic capital and catalyze other, unsubsidized commercial activities. Second, cultural institutions are drawn by their own economic needs and by the imperatives of their funding sources to seek broader audiences and exploit more commercial, income-generating strategies. They are able to achieve these goals without completely sacrificing their aesthetic legitimacy because, third, the boundaries between high culture—once their dominant domain—and popular culture have blurred. Cultural institutions today are thus better positioned than those of 100 years ago to become active stakeholders in urban growth politics.

Elizabeth Strom, "Converting Pork into Porcelain: Cultural Institutions and Downtown Development," *Urban Affairs Review,* Vol. 38 (1), pp. 3–21, copyright © 2002 by Sage Publications, Inc. Reprinted by permission of Sage Publications, Inc.

# Culture in the Growth Coalition: Why Business and Political Leaders Need the Arts

Business elites have long recognized that the prestige of high arts institutions could bring economic benefit to their hometowns, but policies explicitly drawing on the arts to achieve economic development goals have only recently become common. The urban renewal projects of the 1950s and 1960s occasionally included cultural institutions—landmarks such as New York's Lincoln Center and Washington's Arena Stage were built on sites cleared of tenement housing with the support of city development officials, business elites, and the cultural institutions that would inhabit them (Toffler 1964, 1973). However, during this period, most city planners and business-people still saw investments in culture as incidental to the main city development goals of industrial retention and office and housing development.

By the 1980s, the dominant urban development policy paradigm had shifted away from "smokestack chasing" in which cities competed for investment by offering lower costs (Bailey 1989). Competing for corporate headquarters and producer service firms, economic development practitioners realized, required more than just abating taxes and improving infrastructure. Clark (2000) maintains that today's educated workers are more likely to choose appealing locations, most notably those with attractive natural and cultural resources, and then consider their employment options. In this model, firms that rely on highly skilled labor have greater incentive than ever to either choose amenity-rich locations or to strive to improve the quality of life in their headquarters city. As cities compete for mobile, skilled workers and the firms that employ them, low taxes may be less important than riverfront parks, sports arenas, and historic districts. Moreover, city officials have become ever more aware of the economic importance of tourism and have put a great deal of energy into building and enlarging convention centers (Sanders 1998), subsidizing new hotels, and attracting major retailers (Friedan and Sagalyn 1989; Hannigan 1998; Judd 1999).

Cultural institutions represent an important element of the recreational infrastructure thought to make a city more appealing to tourists and investors (Eisinger 2000; Hannigan 1998). Corporations have come to see the presence of local arts institutions as a business asset, and their support for such organizations represents good business sense as much as philanthropy. Ford Motor's marketing director, who was asked why his company has nearly single-handedly kept Detroit's opera company solvent, noted that the presence of such an institution made it easier to recruit white-collar employees (Bradsher 1999). Donors to the New Jersey Performing Arts Center made this point as well (Strom 1999).

City governments and place-based business elites have become more intent on marketing their cities. Local boosterism, of course, is hardly new, but today professionals with large budgets have replaced the well-intentioned amateurs of an earlier era (Ward 1998; Holcomb 1993). Moreover, as is true throughout the business world, city promoters have moved from a model of *selling*, where one tries to persuade the buyer to purchase what one has, to *marketing*, where one tries to have what the buyer wants (Holcomb 1993). Marketers do not merely come up with a catchy jingle; they seek to remake the city, or at least the most visible part of the city, to conform to the expectations of the affluent consumers they want to attract. Cultural institutions, associated with beauty, good taste, and higher purpose, become singularly important symbolic assets for image-conscious marketers.

At the same time, development practitioners and scholars began to appreciate that the arts comprise a wealth-generating economic sector, one in which urban areas retain a competitive advantage. Since the 1980s, the economic impact of the arts has received considerable attention. In major cultural capitals like New York, the "culture industry," as the production and consumption of the arts is called, comprises an important economic sector (National Endowment for the Arts 1981; the Port Authority of New York and New Jersey 1993). Even in less obvious places, the culture industry plays a measurable economic role (Perryman 2000).

Cultural projects are valued for more than their direct economic impact. They are built in locations well situated to transform waning downtowns, obsolete factory districts, and disregarded waterfronts. New museums and performing arts centers now feature architectural designs that embrace and enhance their surroundings, rather than isolate their audiences from the city around them, as had been the case in an earlier generation (Russell 1999). And the new projects have been seen as a means of bringing life—and economic impulse—to central cities that are too often deserted after business hours. Philadelphia's Kimmel Center for the Performing Arts, it is hoped, will anchor new economic activity in Center City, where until recently check-cashing businesses and nude dance halls were as common as restaurants and theaters. During the past decade, Seattle has built two major arts facilities downtown: a new home for the Seattle Art Museum, opened in 1991, and Benaroya Hall, a performing arts complex built primarily for the Seattle Symphony, which opened in 1998. Seattle business leaders credit these cultural institutions with a downtown revival that includes the development of several major retail complexes and a 40% increase in the number of people living downtown since 1990 (Byrd 1997).

The arts can also lend greater legitimacy to other urban development efforts. One hundred years ago, urban arts patrons were quite clear about their hope that cultural institutions would serve to placate a growing immigrant working class (Horowitz 1976). As Boston entrepreneur Henry Lee Higginson wrote in 1886, "Educate and save ourselves and our families and our money from mobs!" (Quoted in Levine 1988, 205). The social control function of urban arts institutions today is far subtler. To David Harvey (1989), the contemporary urban spectacle—which includes ephemera like street fairs and festivals, as well as more institutionalized cultural facilities and entertainment districts—has become a way of co-opting the oppositional politics of the 1960s. To others, the presence of culture, especially serious, nonprofit culture, can serve to legitimize urban redevelopment among those who would not normally see themselves as its beneficiaries. Large-scale urban renewal projects can be made more palatable to voters and opinion shapers (if not always to those displaced in their wake) when they are packaged as new cultural centers or filled with public art (Miles 1998). In the words of a National Endowment for the Arts official,

> The arts . . . are like Mom and apple pie; they're consensus-makers, common ground. People can easily focus on the arts activities in a new project, instead of dwelling on the complicated costs and benefits public support for private development activity usually entails. (Quoted in Clack 1983, 13)

Arts organizations therefore represent a significant and unique component of the amalgam of downtown consumption palaces Judd (1999) has labeled the "tourist bubble." Urban scholars have analyzed the actors in the urban tourism and entertainment infrastructure, including retail mall developers, convention center operators, and major-league sports franchises, to understand why they are drawn to participate in downtown real estate projects (Friedan and Sagalyn 1989; Rosentraub 1997; Danielson 1997; Sanders 1998). Cultural institutions, however, have not received similar attention from urban political economists, even though their incorporation into urban growth politics begs explanation. Urban scholars have not asked why an elite cultural institution, whose legitimacy has long been based on its ability to showcase the most serious, academically sanctioned art, might join with those seeking to develop and market the city to the widest possible audience. Today's cultural institutions, however, have been affected by some of the same pressures as city governments. Living in a more competitive environment in which entrepreneurship and marketing are held to be the key to their survival, arts organizations have themselves been transformed.

# Culture, Consumption, and Revitalization: Why Arts Institutions Need Urban Development

Cultural institutions are not just the objects of urban development schemes: They have themselves become active promoters of revitalization and place marketing activities, and they have done so to realize their own institutional goals. Cultural facilities, especially art museums, must expand to remain "competitive" in the art world, and their expansion needs often place them at the center of local development plans. They have at least five important reasons for wanting to be part of the area's revitalization.

First, some of their concerns about the city's economic health may derive from the interests of their trustees (Logan and Molotch 1987). In nearly every city, there is considerable overlap between those who are prominent in the city's highest business circles and those who are active on cultural boards. One study found that 70% of the members of Louisville's most prestigious development organizations also served on the boards of cultural organizations. (In contrast, those active in peak economic development groups were far less likely to be found on human service agency boards, suggesting the unique importance of arts organizations to those most concerned with the city's development) (Whitt and Lammers 1991). It would be a mistake, however, to assume that major cultural organizations are mere extensions of profit-seeking trustees. Cultural board members usually grant the arts professionals a great deal of autonomy in running the institution's operations. Nominations to the most prestigious non-profit institution boards are coveted; those invited to join are unlikely to jeopardize the hard-earned esteem of their peers by asserting a self-serving agenda (Ostrower 1998).[3] The business interests of board members provide a context for institutional decision making, but they are unlikely to be the primary imperative pushing cultural organizations toward a development agenda.

Second, cultural institutions need to bring their customers—the cultural audiences—to them. People are unlikely to visit a place if the surrounding community is thought to be dangerous. Many cultural consumers are not arts aficionados willing to go anywhere to see, say, a particular Rembrandt, but rather those for whom arts events are part of an entertainment experience. Not only will high crime and extensive physical deterioration put a cultural institution at a disadvantage, but so also will a dearth of amenities like good restaurants.

Third, numerous studies indicate the extent to which cultural institutions depend on tourist visits (the Port Authority of New York and New Jersey 1993; McDowell 1997). New York's Museum of Modern Art estimates that two-thirds of its visits are from out-of-towners, and half of those come from overseas.[4] Of those who visited the Los Angeles County Museum of Art Van Gogh exhibition in 1999, 56% came from outside Los Angeles (Morey and Associates 1999). Cultural institutions therefore have a strong interest in the city's overall appeal to tourists.

Fourth, cultural institutions are heavily dependent on the availability of local volunteers (there are 2.5 volunteers for every paid museum staff member, according to the American Association of Museums). Location in an impoverished city or in a declining neighborhood may make it more difficult to recruit volunteers. Fifth, wealthy individuals and corporations, which provide the program funds for many cultural organizations, usually focus their giving in their hometowns. When a corporation fails or relocates, local arts organizations lose an important source of support.

In sum, arts organizations in thriving areas will have more visitors, more volunteers, and greater fund-raising success than those in depressed areas.

It is clear that arts organizations benefit when their cities are economically healthy. Moreover, cultural groups are learning that they can benefit when they are perceived as one of the sources of that economic health. Today, preparing a study of one's economic impact seems to be a staple of large arts organizations and local arts councils. Such studies are of questionable economic merit (Cwi and Lyall 1977)—as Eisinger (2000, 327) notes, "Consultants hired by project proponents often seem to pull their multipliers out of thin air." But their purpose is not rigorous cost-benefit analysis; rather, they are tools used by arts groups in their efforts to gain funding and political support. The claim that flourishing arts institutions are important to the urban economy has given arts advocates a rationale to appeal for government support even when tight budgets and political controversies might make public arts funding difficult to obtain (Wyszomirski 1995).

By emphasizing their importance to local revitalization, arts administrators have also been able to gain access to new funding sources. The construction of the New Jersey Performing Arts Center (NJPAC) was supported by $106 million in state contributions, mostly from funds earmarked for economic development activities. Such a large sum would not have been made available for a cultural project had it not been able to claim an important regional economic impact—New Jersey's entire annual cultural budget has never been higher than $20 million (Strom 1999). Arts projects in Louisville, Seattle, and Philadelphia all received generous capital grants from state governments, grants that were clearly tied to the economic mission of these institutions. Similarly, major arts institutions are receiving support from private sources that are more interested in urban revitalization than in art. New Jersey financier Ray Chambers, a man who had never shown much interest in cultural activities but who was deeply committed to the future of Newark, spearheaded the development of NJPAC. Clothing manufacturer Sidney Kimmel made clear in remarks broadcast on local radio that his $15 million donation to Philadelphia's new performing arts center was in support of the center's urban revitalization promises. Arts institutions can show funders that their contributions are not mere charity but rather serve as investments in the city's economic future.

# New Audiences, New Patrons: Why Today's Cultural Institutions Are Well Positioned to Participate in Urban Development

## Funding and Organizing High Culture

Cultural institutions may have long had a clear interest in the city's economic health, but only recently have they emerged as ideal partners for the sorts of growth-oriented coalitions described in Mollenkopf (1983), Logan and Molotch (1987), and Stone (1989). The participation of cultural institutions in urban development coalitions has been facilitated by far-reaching changes in arts patronage and arts management ongoing at least since the 1960s. If nineteenth-century institutions looked to wealthy families for financial support, since that time the private collector/patron has been largely eclipsed by more institutionalized forms of funding.[5] Many wealthy families now route their donations through foundations, the largest of which have professional staffs. Since the mid-1960s, the single most important patron of high culture has been the government. The National Endowment of the Arts will have a budget of about $115 million in 2001–2002, and the 50 state governments have allocated $447.5 million for arts and cultural programs in fiscal year 2001 (National Association of State Arts Agencies 2001). During the 1970s, corporate funding became an increasingly significant source of support. According to the Business Committee for the Arts, corporate support for culture increased from $22 million in 1967 to $1.16 billion in 1997,[6] and corporate arts funding tripled during the 1975–1985 period (DiMaggio 1986).

Changes in arts funding affect arts programming in ways that have implications for economic development policies. More so than private patrons, government agencies and corporate donors seek programs with broad audience appeal (Zolberg 1983; Alexander 1996). The National Endowment for the Arts (NEA) and the state arts councils are eager to associate with programs whose popularity can translate into political support for their efforts. For businesses, cultural donations are a "highbrow form of advertising" (Alexander 1996, 2), as corporations seek to attach their names to programs that are highly visible and prestigious. A well-placed, $200,000 cultural donation, according to one corporate foundation official, can have the same impact as $50 million in paid advertising.[7] Government and corporate funding influence the form of cultural offerings as well as the content. Few corporations want to fund a museum's operations; they prefer to attach their name to special, traveling exhibitions that attract large crowds in a number of cities. Alexander (1996) correlates the growth of government and corporate funding with the increasing number of special, "blockbuster" exhibits mounted by museums (and there may well be similar parallels in others kinds of arts institutions). Museum managers see such events as opportunities to attract large, paying audiences (many museums charge for such special exhibits) and generate new members who will continue to support the museum once the special exhibit has moved on.[8]

If such big-ticket events bring benefits for museum managers, they also fit well into the marketing strategies of urban development and tourism officials. Indeed, arts advocates, economic development officials, and the tourism industry have, since the mid-1990s, consciously sought to promote "cultural tourism." An estimated 50 cultural tourism programs have been founded in state, county, and local convention and visitors bureaus, and two national networks, Partners in Tourism (which is sponsored by American Express) and the Cultural Tourism Alliance, hold conferences and publish newsletters on cultural tourism. The Los Angeles County Museum of Art Van Gogh exhibition that drew so many out-of-town visitors had been promoted heavily by the Los Angeles Convention and Visitors Bureau, which advertised "Van Gogh weekend packages" in such upscale publications as *The New Yorker*. The convergence of interests is clear: City marketing officials, arts funders, and ultimately publicity-conscious cultural administrators all find benefit in mounting large, well-publicized exhibits or performances that attract big audiences.[9]

## The Shifting Brows

Highbrow arts institutions would have limited value as economic development catalysts, however, if they were catering to a narrow stratum of social elites and art connoisseurs. But a dramatic shift in the way culture is framed and classified has made an expansion of art audiences possible. Boundaries between serious and popular art, and between the audiences who enjoy them, have become increasingly blurred. Of course, even the high-low distinctions that seemed so secure at midcentury were hardly inevitable; rather, scholars have shown them to be largely a product of the mid- to late-nineteenth century

(DiMaggio 1982; Levine 1988). In the earlier part of the nineteenth century, concerts might include pieces by Bach or Haydn as well as popular fare; an evening of Shakespeare might be interspersed with acrobatic performances; and fledgling museums displayed works of established, serious artists next to curios (DiMaggio 1982). Even in the late nineteenth century, museums such as Philadelphia's Pennsylvania Museum unapologetically celebrated industrial design alongside European painting (Conn 1998). Such catholic sensibilities soon vanished in favor of more rigid classification schemes that made some cultural artifacts the exclusive terrain of those with education and money. Cultural objects that had once been universally enjoyed, including Shakespearean plays and Italian operas, were reinterpreted so that their more accessible elements were abandoned, and they became the property of the possessors of cultural capital (Levine 1988). That this reclassification took place in the decades surrounding the turn of the century was not accidental: It represented a response on the part of the upper classes to the growing presence and political strength of an increasingly vocal and politically mobilized working class. Defining an elite culture created a safe haven for the upper classes, who could rely on their association with high cultural goods to legitimize their class position (Horowitz 1976; Bourdieu 1984).

High art and popular culture also became institutionally segregated. Earlier in the nineteenth century, high culture had been marketed through the same commercial mechanisms as popular fare. The Swedish opera singer Jenny Lind made a wildly popular American tour in the 1850s under the sponsorship of P. T. Barnum, and European ballerina Fanny Ellsler, who toured the United States from 1840 to 1842, managed to become the darling of economic and cultural elites while still acquiring a mass following and making good profits selling Fanny Ellsler brand garters, stockings, corsets, and shaving soap (Levine 1988).

By the late nineteenth century, however, high and low art forms each had their own institutional home. Profit-driven entrepreneurs disseminated popular culture. The newly created nonprofit corporation, on the other hand, become the vehicle for disseminating high culture. Museums and orchestras so organized had a mix of public and private purposes that suited their patrons. As private corporations, they remained under the control of their appointed trustees. Because they relied on charitable donations, and not on popular political support, they could maintain high standards of elite culture. And because they were nonprofit, they could make claims to have a broader public purpose than a fully private, profit-seeking operation, thus justifying appeals for public support (DiMaggio 1982). Disseminated through the nonprofit corporation, the artifacts of serious culture could maintain their distance from the marketplace.

Today, however, the distinctions so carefully honed in the nineteenth century have become blurred. Rigid classifications fell under attack from several fronts. Gans (1974, 1999) notes a convergence of tastes dating back to the 1920s. The emergence of the middlebrow provided middle classes with more accessible versions of elite art, and today you do not need highbrow credentials to visit a blockbuster event at an art museum or enjoy a foreign film. At the same time, there was a "gentrification" of lowbrow arts, as elite artists and musicians explored jazz and folk art (Peterson 1997). Today, more modern and accessible art forms like jazz, modern dance, film, and photography can be created and consumed in many different venues and at many different levels, challenging the sorts of hierarchies described by Bourdieu (1984). Moreover, theoretical and empirical evidence suggests that the typical upper-class cultural consumer is no longer the snob, whose consumption of elite culture was linked to his or her rejection of other cultural forms, but the "omnivore," who consumes traditional high culture but also partakes of a variety of popular genres (Peterson and Kern 1996). The possibilities for mixing audiences of different classes and art of different genres are far greater today than they were at the turn of the nineteenth century.

The boundaries separating the organization of elite and popular culture have shifted as well. High culture remains the domain of elite, nonprofit institutions, but it is increasingly marketed with reference to the symbols and presentations of popular culture and supported by commercial market mechanisms. Museum shops no longer merely sell postcards and art books. They now feature a whole range of merchandise, some replicas of objects in their collections, some using motifs from objects in their collection (e.g., famous paintings printed on scarves and umbrellas), and some having little to do with their collections but presumably gaining value just by their association with great art. Museums and performing arts centers boast full-scale, four-star restaurants that become part of a city's lure to tourists, and their staffs include people with the business skills needed to help such enterprises run profitably (Alexander 1996).

The obscuring of cultural boundaries has important implications for the value of culture as an element of urban revitalization. Not only can cultural institutions take advantage of the market for arts-associated products. They can also broaden their programmatic offerings without losing their core constituencies. Today's arts organization trustees, apparently mindful of the need to appeal to broader audiences, are able to accept the use of popularizing techniques and commercial marketing without feeling that their elite status is compromised (Ostrower 1998). The Metropolitan Museum features Hollywood costumes; the Guggenheim showcases motorcycles and the work of fashion designer Armani. They do this while displaying their collections of European paintings and Greek sculpture, retaining their base of upscale donors and remaining highly desirable conveyers of status for those fortunate enough to be named to their boards.

Performing arts institutions have exhibited an even greater eclecticism than museums. Because performances are very time limited, a theater's programming can simultaneously appeal to diverse audiences. Indeed, many of today's performing arts centers, built with the goal of having maximum economic impact, contain multiple performance spaces, so that radically different types of performances can take place on the same evening (Rothstein 1998). One need only peruse the calendars of America's leading performing arts centers to find intriguing juxtapositions, as Broadway shows share the theater complex with symphony orchestras, country fiddlers, and travel lectures. In November 2000, just to offer one example, the Tulsa Performing Arts Center's calendar included the Broadway musical Showboat, Brahms Oratorio music, the Moscow String Quartet, the U.S. Marine Band, and a pops concert of Frank Sinatra hits. On one very busy Saturday in February 1998, West Palm Beach's Kravis Center for the Performing Arts hosted singers Steve Lawrence and Eydie Gorme, the Gospel Gala, and the Emerson String Quartet. This is exactly the mix we might expect given the new relationship between the brows. On one hand, distinctions are maintained—these performances all took place in different halls, most likely attracting different audiences who probably conducted themselves according to different codes of behavior. On the other hand, these audiences apparently did not feel that their enjoyment of their brand of art was compromised by their proximity to others enjoying a different kind of performance. A few may have even come back another night to attend one of the other shows.

As long as cultural institutions could not easily cut across genres, their usefulness as vehicles of economic development was limited. They could function as elite establishments, bringing prestige to their city and perhaps attracting a few well-heeled tourists and an occasional amenity-oriented business. However, they would seldom draw large enough crowds or identify with broad enough consumption opportunities to be considered commercial catalysts. On the other hand, organizations offering popular fare might bring in the crowds but would be less likely to earn the support of political and social elites or serve to improve a city's symbolic capital. But this has changed, as we can see when we observe those performing arts center calendars. The Broadway musicals pay the bills. The ethnically diverse programming assures broader political legitimacy. The European art, the symphonic music, the elegant galas affirm an institution's highbrow bona fides to social and economic elites. Institutions of high culture fulfill their unique role within today's urban growth coalitions precisely because they can catalyze profit-generating activities, while bringing their nonprofit, noncommercial credentials with them.

DiMaggio and Powell have theorized that organizations working together in the same "organizational field" come to share structural characteristics to facilitate their relations in a process that is shaped by resource dependencies as well as shared professional norms (DiMaggio and Powell 1983). Peterson has applied this theory to the study of cultural institutions and arts patrons, noting that arts organizations have become more professionalized (there are now 40 graduate programs in arts administration) and specialized as arts funding has shifted from private patronage to bureaucratic support (Peterson 1986). The organizational field of cultural production and consumption can perhaps today be expanded to include not just arts organizations and their funders but also the local officials who are involved in developing and marketing the city's cultural offerings. The marriage of culture and development is thus facilitated by the shared goals and norms of their advocates, and increasingly it is institutionalized through cultural tourism offices, arts district promotional agencies, or national collaboratives like the Institute for Community Development and the Arts, a project uniting the advocacy group Americans for the Arts with the

United States Conference of Mayors. All are involved in selling an image of an urbane place of cultural sophistication, in which the museum or performance hall lends its panache to the city around it, which reciprocates by creating an atmosphere that promotes the consumption of culture.

## Art and the Economy: A Changing Relationship

The cultural life of American cities has always had a complex relationship to the local political economy. Local cultural landscapes were shaped by social rivalries and boosterist regional competition. Such revered institutions as New York's Metropolitan Opera, for example, were created to display the wealth of newly rich industrialists (Burrows and Wallace 1999); the patrons of Chicago's now renowned art museum and symphony sought to assert their cultural parity with Boston and New York (Horowitz 1976). If late-nineteenth and early-twentieth-century patrons could appreciate the potential benefits that accrued to those who built cultural centers, however, for those founding nineteenth-century museums and concert halls—in contrast to today's cultural entrepreneurs—economic gain remained subtext. Cultural institutions of their era were built to show off wealth, not to generate it. Reporting on the opening of the (at that time very modestly housed) Newark Museum in 1909, the local press proclaimed, "The city is rich! A part of the wealth of its citizens should be invested in paintings, sculpture and other art objects" (Newark Museum 1959, 7). Businessman and arts patron Joseph Choate, speaking at the Metropolitan Museum's opening, stressed the museum's function as an uplifting source of beauty and urged men of wealth to "convert pork into porcelain, grain and produce into priceless pottery, the rude ores of commerce into sculpted marble, and railroad shares and mining stocks ... into the glorified canvas of the world's masters" (Tomkins 1970, 23). Today, the relationship between the city's economy and its cultural institutions is understood very differently. Kicking off a fund-raising drive for the expansion of the Newark Museum—the same museum celebrated as a symbol of local prosperity in 1909—New Jersey Governor Tom Kean touted the museum and other urban cultural assets as "catalysts of rebirth," "creating the kind of public image needed for growth and new jobs" (Courtney 1984). Countless public officials and donors have similarly proclaimed their support for culture as a means of spurring an economic revival (Byrd 1997; Davies 1998).

The association of economic development and culture has by now become commonplace, and commentary on this new relationship is largely laudatory. There have been a few cautionary voices: Some urban scholars have expressed concern that an urban development strategy whose primary goal is to attract outsiders to privatized entertainment spaces can be undemocratic and exclusionary (Eisinger 2000; Judd 1999), diverting public funds from projects of more direct benefit to most urban residents (Strom 1999). Even those cultural facilities deemed successful will never generate the tax revenue and employment to make them appear to be good investments in a cost-benefit analysis (National Endowment for the Arts 1981),[10] giving rise to the same critiques that have been leveled against subsidized sports and convention venues (Sanders 1998; Rosentraub 1997). Of course, unlike convention center and sport stadium proponents, cultural advocates have never argued that they could justify public subsidy purely through their production of direct economic benefits. Rather, the arts are said to increase the value of other products and deliver noneconomic benefits as well. Many museums and performing arts centers have effective outreach and education programs that make them genuinely accessible, Surely no other "tourist bubble" institution can make such a claim.

Cultural institutions themselves may face conflicts when they adapt their mission to that of the city's economic development strategists. Hoping for the biggest possible impact on their central city areas, economic development proponents are eager to build new museums and concert halls, and less concerned with sustaining these institutions once they are built. Individual and corporate donors also like to contribute to capital campaigns, where their largesse can be rewarded with wall plaques and naming opportunities. As a result, bricks and mortar investments may be favored over support for cultural programs; smaller arts organizations may be overlooked in favor of the larger groups better able to document their economic clout.

The need to prove their economic mettle to political allies and funders becomes yet one more pressure on cultural institutions already hard-pressed to disseminate great art while paying their bills. The fine arts can certainly be "popular," drawing large audiences. There is also art that is unlikely to play to full houses or attract long lines because it is difficult or challenging or cutting-edge. If arts institutions are primarily seen as mechanisms for urban revitalization and are valued for their ability to draw large numbers of people to city hotels and restaurants, they may be less willing or able to realize the scholarly or educational aspects of their work. To be sure, urban development stakeholders are hardly the only ones pushing arts institutions toward a more commercial, less scholarly mission. And museum curators have often been clever at mounting the kinds of shows that will draw the crowds and pay the bills to gain resources to support more esoteric or challenging programs (Alexander 1996). However, too much focus on the arts institutions' economic role may obscure the fact that making money for the city can never be their primary purpose.

## NOTES

1. Major performing arts centers are defined as those with 1,000 seats or more. Major museums are those with annual attendance of 50,000 or more. Because this survey looks only at large cultural facilities, it understates the full extent of cultural building.
2. No doubt cultural institution capital campaigns have been aided by the unusually prosperous 1990s. States and cities had budget surpluses, and wealthy individuals could gain prestige and tax benefits by donating stock market gains to nonprofit arts institutions. Many of these projects, however, originated years before the economic boom.
3. Similar comments were made by cultural trustees of cultural organizations interviewed by the author as part of an ongoing study of Newark- and Philadephia-based organizations.

4. Comments of museum administrator made at the Art of the Deal conference, Rutgers University, New Brunswick, 27 March, 2001.
5. Arts administrators report that individual patrons have gained in importance in the late 1990s; individual giving has been fueled by the strong stock market (comments of museum administrator made at the Art of the Deal conference, 2001).
6. Whitt (1987) has questioned the methods by which the Business Committee for the Arts collects its data; as an advocacy group, it could well be inclined to inflate the importance of business contributions.
7. Comments of corporate foundation executive made at the Art of the Deal conference, 2001.
8. This strategy seems to be successful: Many museums point to big jumps in membership during blockbuster exhibits (Dobrzynski 1998).
9. The media play a role in cementing this convergence of interests. A study of newspaper arts coverage found that visual arts get short shrift in most newspapers, except when blockbuster exhibits come to town. Local media, then, become part of the system making highly visible and popular exhibits useful for arts institutions and local development officials (Janeway et al. 1999).
10. The National Endowment for the Arts studied the arts institutions of six cities and found that only in three did they generate as much or more local revenue than they cost the city in subsidies and services. Had these calculations included the costs of state and federal subsidies, the balance sheet would have even looked less favorable.

## REFERENCES

Alexander, V. D. 1996. *Museums and money.* Bloomington: Indiana Univ. Press.
American Association of Museums. 1999. *The official museum directory.* New Providence, NJ: National Register Publishing.
Bailey, J. T. 1989. *Marketing cities in the 1980s and beyond.* Rosemont, IL: American Economic Development Council.
Bourdieu, P. 1984. *Distinction.* Cambridge, MA: Harvard Univ. Press.
Bradsher, K. 1999. A horn of plenty for opera in Detroit. *New York Times,* 28 October, E1, 10.
Burrows, E. G., and M. Wallace. 1999. *Gotham: A history of New York City to 1898.* New York and Oxford, UK: Oxford Univ. Press.
Byrd, J., 1997. Culture at the core. *Seattle Post-Intelligencer,* 9 February, J1.
Clack, G. 1983. Footlight districts. In *The city as stage,* edited by K. W. Green. Washington, DC: Partners for Livable Places.
Clark, T. N. 2000. Old and new paradigms for urban research: Globalization and the Fiscal Austerity and Urban Innovation Project. *Urban Affairs Review 36* (1): 3–45.
Conn, S. 1998. *Museums and American intellectual life, 1876–1926.* Chicago: Univ. of Chicago Press.
Courtney, M. 1984. Newark museum revives growth plans. *New York Times,* 8 April, B1, 4.
Cwi, D., and K. Lyall. 1977. *Economic impact of arts and cultural institutions: A model for assessment and a case study for Baltimore.* Washington, DC: National Endowment for the Arts.
Danielson, M. N. 1997. *Home team.* Princeton, NJ: Princeton Univ. Press.
Davies, P. 1998. Philadelphia could make big gains from Performing Arts Center visitors. *Philadelphia Daily News,* 17 April.
DiMaggio, P. J. 1982. Cultural entrepreneurship in nineteenth-century Boston: The creation of an organizational base for high culture in America. *Media, Culture and Society* 4:33–50.
———. 1986. Can culture survive the marketplace? In *Nonprofit enterprise in the arts,* edited by P. J. DiMaggio, 65–92. New York and Oxford, UK: Oxford Univ. Press.
DiMaggio, P. J., and W. W. Powell, 1983. The iron cage revisited: Institutional isomorphism and collective rationality in organizational fields. *American Sociological Review* 48:147–60.

Dobrzynski, J. 1998. Blockbuster shows and prices to match. *New York Times*, 10 November, El, 13.

Duncan, C. 1995. *Civilizing rituals: Inside art museums*. London, New York: Routledge.

Eisinger, P. 2000. The politics of bread and circuses. *Urban Affairs Review 35* (3): 316–33.

Friedan, B. J., and L. B. Sagalyn. 1989. *Downtown Inc.* Cambridge, MA: MIT Press.

Gans, H. J. 1974. *Popular culture and high culture*. New York: Basic Books.

———. 1999. *Popular culture and high culture*. Rev. ed. New York: Basic Books.

Hannigan, J. 1998. *Fantasy city*. London: Routledge.

Harvey, D. 1989. *The condition of postmodernity*. Oxford, UK: Basil Blackwell.

Holcomb, B. 1993. Revisioning place: De- and re-constructing the image of the industrial city. In *Selling places: The city as cultural capital, past and present*, edited by G. Kearns and C. Philo. Oxford, UK: Pergamon.

Horowitz, H. L. 1976. *Culture and the city*. Lexington: Univ. Press of Kentucky.

Janeway, M., D. S. Levy, A. Szanto, and A. Tyndall, 1999. *Reporting the arts: News coverage of arts and culture in America*. New York: Columbia Univ., National Arts Journalism Program.

Judd, D. 1999. Constructing the tourist bubble. In *The tourist city*, edited by D. Judd and S. Fainstein, 35–53. New Haven, CT: Yale Univ. Press.

Levine, L. W. 1988. *Highbrow/lowbrow: The emergence of cultural hierarchy in America*. Cambridge, MA: Harvard Univ. Press.

Logan, J. R., and H. L. Molotch, 1987. *Urban fortunes*. Berkeley: Univ. of California Press.

McDowell, E. 1997. Tourists respond to lure of culture. *New York Times*, 24 April, D1, 4.

Miles, M. 1998. A game of appearance: Public art and urban development—Complicity or sustainability? In *The entrepreneurial city*, edited by T. Hall and P. Hubbard, 203–24. Chichester, UK: Wiley.

Mollenkopf, J. M. 1983. *The contested city*. Princeton, NJ: Princeton Univ. Press.

Morey and Associates, Inc. 1999. Economic impact analysis of the Los Angeles County Museum of Art and the Van Gogh exhibition. Unpublished report.

National Association of State Arts Agencies. 2001. Retrieved 11 April 2001, from www. nasaa-arts.org.

National Endowment for the Arts. 1981. *Economic impact of arts and cultural institutions*. Washington, DC: National Endowment for the Arts.

Newark Museum. 1959. *The Newark Museum: A fifty-year survey*. Newark: Newark Museum.

Ostrower, F. 1998. The arts as cultural capital among elites: Bourdieu's theory reconsidered. *Poetics* 26:43–53.

Perryman, M. R. 2000. The arts, culture, and the Texas economy. Retrieved 15 April 2001, from www.perrymangroup. com.

Peterson, R. A. 1986. From impresario to arts administrator. In *Nonprofit enterprise in the arts*, edited by P. J. DiMaggio, 161–83. New York and Oxford, UK: Oxford Univ. Press.

———. 1997. The rise and fall of highbrow snobbery as a status marker. *Poetics* 25:75–92.

Peterson, R. A., and R. M. Kern. 1996. Changing highbrow taste: From snob to omnivore. *American Sociological Review* 61:900–907.

The Port Authority of New York and New Jersey and the Cultural Assistance Center. 1993. *The arts as industry: Their economic importance to the New York–New Jersey metropolitan region*. New York: The Port Authority of New York and New Jersey.

Rosentraub, M. S. 1997. *Major league losers*. New York: Basic Books.

Rothstein, E. 1998. Arts centers are changing the face of culture. *San Diego Union-Tribune*, 6 December, E10.

Russell, J. S. 1999. Performing arts centers: Using art to revive cities. *Architectural Record*, May, 223–28.

Sanders, H. T. 1998. Convention center follies. *Public Interest* (summer): 58–72.

Stone, C. N. 1989. *Regime politics*. Lawrence: University Press of Kansas.

Strom, E. 1999. Let's put on a show: Performing arts and urban revitalization in Newark, New Jersey. *Journal of Urban Affairs* 21:423–36.

Toffler, A. 1964. *The culture consumers*. New York: Random House.

———. 1973. *The culture consumers*. Rev. ed. New York: Random House.

Tomkins, C. 1970. *Merchants and masterpieces*. New York: E. P. Dutton.

Ward, S. V. 1998. *Selling places*. New York and London: Routledge.

Whitt, J. A. 1987. Mozart in the metropolis: The arts coalition and the urban growth machine. *Urban Affairs Quarterly* 23:15–36.

Whitt, J. A., and J. C. Lammers. 1991. The art of growth. *Urban Affairs Quarterly* 26 (3): 376–93.

Wyszomirski, M. J. 1995. The politics of arts policy: Subgovernment to issue network. In *America's commitment to culture: Government and the arts*, edited by K. Mulcahy and M. J. Wyszomirski. Boulder, CO: Westview.

Zolberg, V. 1983. Changing patterns of patronage in the arts. In *Performers and performances*, edited by J. B. Kamerman and R. Martorella, 251–68. New York: Praeger.

# 10

## *Alison Isenberg*

# DOWNTOWN CULTURE

In the 1980s and 1990s, as historically themed retailing caught on downtown, developers and retailers were understandably interested in evoking only the most pleasantly stimulating historical topics. The public, however, was more likely to raise and debate controversial issues relevant to the downtown's history. Indicative of festival marketplace goals, a Rouse prospectus for Albuquerque proposed creating a destination that would prompt "nostalgic recall of 'fond' memories of the old downtown." Nationally, investors hoped that almost everybody could find a "fond" memory to draw them downtown—in many cities the "great" era of maritime commerce was a popular theme. Many Americans agreed that stepping into a historically evocative retail environment—whether the scripted festival marketplaces or an old-fashioned Woolworth—was "like passing through a time tunnel and entering a cozy and dependable world."[1]

Yet opening a window onto the past, even a contrived one, implicitly raised the question of how contemporary urban commercial experiences compared with those of the past. Needless to say, retailers could not control people's memories or limit their interest to warm rather than hot topics—a lesson learned many times during the racial protests of the 1960s. In the late twentieth century, as history increasingly shaped investment strategies, consumers did not share a generic sense of nostalgia—and they tended to disagree over the characteristics of the past and future trajectories of urban commerical life.

In 1997–98 a museum exhibit celebrating dime store architecture stimulated conflict among visitors over the meaning of Main Street nostalgia. The National Building Museum in Washington, D.C., staged "Main Street Five-and-Dimes: The Architectural Heritage of S. H. Kress & Co." The show's visitor comment books overflowed with many of the familiar, innocuous personal stories that reporters had gathered when the variety stores closed: remembrances of childhood outings with a grandparent, the independence of a trip downtown, or a first job. A visitor noted concisely, "One word: nostalgia." "It was a rare nostalgic treat," wrote another. The visitors used an exhibit of commercial architecture to reflect upon their own lives and their personal experiences of urban commerce. There were many others who lamented the decline of architectural and business values—not a surprising reaction, given the show's focus on design, artifacts, and a specific company. These visitors characterized commercial design of the early twentieth century as representing pride, integrity, class, elegance, and artistic quality, while approving of Kress's apparent sense of corporate responsibility. Wal-Mart was usually cited to demonstrate how far American commerce had fallen in these respects.[2]

But it was integration—a topic not even raised in the exhibition's interpretive panels, only evident in the photographs—that prompted the most heated debate and quickly revealed nostalgia to be anything but a generic concept. One visitor wrote, "Memories of a happier, kinder world—a world that was safe." This was just the kind of fond sentiment the festival marketplace investors would have appreciated. In this case, someone responded in the margin: "Yes— before all the dangerous negroes ruined everything." On September 8, 1997, a person enthusiastically noted, "Reminded me of my childhood, when you could go into a 5 + 10 with 10¢, buy something, and come out with some change, too!" But the next writer savored something else: "I enjoyed the shots of 'whites only' drinking fountains—the way it should be." Others later added "Nazi pig" and "republican," with arrows pointing to the prosegregation remark. In yet another instance, a museum visitor volunteered that "segregation was good for the country. We should bring it back."[3] Both those warmly remembering innocent childhood experiences *and* those warmly remembering a segregated past evoked the theme of decline in urban commercial life.

Other visitors questioned outright whether America's past commercial life had in fact been better, based on their observation that the experiences of African American consumers (and most patrons) had only improved. Today's Wal-Mart might not be as "beautiful" as Kress, read one entry, "but at least they let everyone drink from the same water fountains and use the same rest-rooms." "The Birmingham store w/o blacks in it made me remember the unfair dual society I put up with in North Carolina," recalled a visitor. While some reminisced about a cherry Coke with grandmother, others also brought up sit-ins and segregated lunch counters— "A reminder of a not so honorable past." Another pointed out, probably to those overwhelmed by "warm fuzzy feeling, " that "some change is good," especially the elimination of colored water fountains. The architectural beauty of the Kress stores featured in the exhibit held little positive value to these visitors if it symbolized a segregated, unfair society.[4]

One exchange in particular captured the debates occurring in the exhibition hall and the comment books and some of the dynamics that prompted guests to challenge oversimplified nostalgic narratives of decline. A visitor wrote: "I enjoyed looking back in time—interesting coincidence shed a bit of depth on it— another visitor commented that it took you back to a simpler time & as I began to agree in my head, I saw the photos of the shiny water fountains marked 'White' and 'Colored.' Simpler perhaps but was it better?" In this interaction one sees how easy it was to slip into vague reverie about the urban past but also how quickly a specific personal experience could induce one to challenge the certainty of decline. The fact that this individual's reassessment was triggered by encountering a historical photograph of what other people remembered from their own lives—segregated water fountains—is suggestive. Adding further "depth" in the margins, someone answered the writer's question: "Yes, it was better then before the Negroes messed everything up." Here again was racist nostalgia agreeing for hateful reasons with unfocused fondness for the past. Responding to a museum exhibit, itself resonant with the museum-like qualities of the dime stores and historically themed marketplaces, visitors welcomed the opportunity to engage with each other over the meaning of urban commerce. Another entry read, "I agree, however, with the person who wrote earlier that some comment or discussion of the very prominently featured segregated water fountains, counters, etc. should accompany those photos." And the issues raised could be debated even without the exhibition, as recognized by the guest who "skipped the exhibit, loved the comment book."[5]

Two visitors wrote still another declension narrative of twentieth-century urban commercial life—drawing undoubtedly unanticipated conclusions from the exhibit. One insisted, "Segregation killed these stores. People moved away to the suburbs. Caldor & K-Mart followed them. If there were black faces in the 1930's photo's, maybe Main St. USA could have been saved . . . The fault lies not in the stores. . . . " Another man claimed that God would not have allowed the Kress chain to survive because of its racist history.[6] According to this interpretation, entirely free of nostalgia, segregation had "killed" Main Street. From this perspective, the 1960s Civil Rights movement indeed remade Main Street too late to save it.

The disagreements over integration provoked by the 1997–98 Kress exhibit in fact confirm that the critical impact of 1960s upheavals on downtown commerce was still unfolding and being negotiated thirty years later. In the 1990s, black consumers weighed the belief that Woolworth supported urban retailing against news reports that blacks faced discrimination by store clerks who scrutinized their credit cards or wrote codes on their checks. Eddye Bexley, an African American, disclosed in 1997 that she had avoided Woolworth for thirty-seven years after participation in a 1960 Tampa protest poisoned her associations with the place. On the ground in a festival marketplace, one might be forgiven for not realizing that a core inspiration for Rouse was the 1960s riots and his belief that a new type of urban commerce could heal the nation's racial rifts. Yet his companies experimented with different ways to foster black entrepreneurship, management opportunities, and patronage. Rouse's Gallery at Market East offered one example of how a revitalized downtown retail economy could build successfully upon an integrated clientele. Rouse's optimistic and idealistic rhetoric was partly what earned his company's projects so much favorable attention.[7]

At the close of the twentieth century, Americans could draw upon and create multiple decline and improvement narratives to understand what was happening on Main Street. Amid the various memories sparked by names like F. W. Woolworth and S. H. Kress, the "warmest remembrances" of Main Street included not only first dates or childhood outings with grandparents but also fond long-ings for segregation. These alternative nostalgic versions, which challenged the simplistic view that urban commerce was somehow better in the past, suggest how the interested public could engage critically with the historical themes employed in late-twentieth-century downtown development. Like the thrifty chain store consumers dismissed by market analysts, these 1990s de-bates over history demonstrate how people turned nostalgia to their own purposes and invested urban commerce with their own meanings. Historic Main Streets and festival marketplaces (no matter how vague, contrived, or inaccurate) have helped keep alive visions of populated and democratic urban commercial life amid exten-sive abandonment and proclamations of decline.[8] Even that 1990s symbol of Main Street decay—the increasingly empty and irrelevant variety store—though unable to financially exploit the nostalgia trends, nonetheless stimulated public interest in how downtowns might be reinvented and what values should be central to a newly imagined urban commercial life. In the early twenty-first century, the bal-ance between democratic and exclusionary ideals is still being negotiated.

# Brick by Brick

Calvin Trillin admitted in 1977 that he enjoyed sampling the historically themed markets, but already he found the old-brick motif to be repetitive and more than a little mind-numbing: "The brick exposed in Ghirardelli Square in San Francisco tended to look like the brick exposed in Pioneer Square in Seattle, which had some similarity to the brick exposed in Old Town, Chicago, or Underground At-lanta or the River Quay in Kansas City or Larimer Square in Denver or Gaslight Square in St. Louis." This criticism—that cities were losing the unique character-istics that distinguished one from another—would only grow in volume over the next twenty-five years. To Trillin and many others it seemed that nostalgic redevelopment projects were homogenizing the urban commercial experience. Just as all suburban shopping malls looked alike, now cities had begun to look alike. The lament over the loss of a presumed diversity of urban environment and urban experience was another powerful assertion of decline.[9]

Yet one need only consider Trillin's list of places to see the general folly of assuming that similar design motifs (like red brick) indicated identical experi-ences. Gaslight Square, as we have seen, took a "sinister and unreal" turn to-ward abandonment in the mid-1960s, as did River Quay in the 1970s. Ghi-rardelli Square, in contrast, has unfailingly brought tourists to the San Francisco waterfront, while Seattle's Pioneer Square remains unusual in its ability to draw upscale customers and tourists without chasing away the down-and-out patrons of the city's public spaces. Although many cities have turned to similar nostalgic strategies since the 1970s, using the same bricks did not give them the same history or the same future.

Downtowns are in no more danger of homogenizing today than they were during the heyday of Main Street postcards, under national chain store leader-ship in the 1920s, or in the wake of urban renewal. Throughout the twentieth century, investors constantly pursued or rejected strategies with national reach. From some angles, the pressures toward conformity appear to have been stronger at the beginning of the twentieth century than at the end of that century. A few hundred or thousand Progressive era Main Street postcards can dull the senses more quickly than 1980s Rouse Company plans. In the details of how clients and artists intervened to create the postcards, one sees the shared downtown improvement ideals of activist club women, early city planners, and Main Street businesses. In creating and circulating so many cards, Americans affirmed that they valued the homogenizing formula as much as they valued each city's distinctive characteristics.

At the end of the twentieth century, downtown investors could draw on more—not fewer—approaches to remaking urban commercial life, from the modest improvements of the Main Street ideal to modernization, demolition and rebuilding, and nostalgic preservation hybrids. Developers and consumers could turn for inspiration or discouragement to a wide array of examples from the past, including 1890s club women (whose work is sometimes compared to that of 1980s–90s business improvement districts), resourceful depression-era appraisers, 1960s looters, or trend-setting business leaders like James Rouse. There were more architectural styles, notably modernism, to borrow from or spurn. Urban renewal, 1960s riots, and even depression-era demolitions have left large and small vacant parcels for new projects. And for all the concern about surveillance and security enforcement in the late twentieth century, the end of segregation provides one example of how downtown development now exerts less control over consumers and investors than it did eighty years ago.[10]

The frequent debates and uncertainty over the future of urban commerce suggest the coexistence of multiple downtown ideals and possibilities, replacing unitary notions that prevailed at different times during the twentieth century—such as presumed centrality and growth, segregation, or decline. The tremendous range of downtown conditions should provide some reassurance that American cities will not become indistinguishable. Some Main Streets languish, virtually abandoned. New immigrants have entirely reinvigorated others. Historic preservation has generated many success stories, while some places have maintained dominant department stores and still others thrive on discount retail. Some are defined by new construction. Big-city downtowns usually have a patchwork of all of the above.

A sampling of how several former Woolworth buildings and sites are used today (and proposals for their future uses) indicates the variety of downtown commercial experiences at the beginning of the twenty-first century. As Main Street in Keene, New Hampshire, rebounded from a 1992 low point (which included the loss of Woolworth), several businesses—Hannah Grimes Marketplace, TCBY, and Church and Main Advertising—moved into the renovated Woolworth structure. In Greenwich, Connecticut, an upscale Saks Fifth Avenue store opened in a Woolworth building, after a complete remodeling. Not too far away in Middletown, Connecticut, citizens debated whether a proposed "high-quality" Salvation Army thrift store would help or hurt downtown's prospects. More acceptable bargain retailers moved into downtown Woolworth sites in

Seattle and Boston, including Ross Dress for Less, Marshalls, T. J. Maxx, and H & M. The owner of a vacant Woolworth building in Buffalo, New York, inspired by other success stories, hoped to attract a factory outlet mall. Nightclubs signed leases for portions of Woolworth buildings in San Diego and Ventura, California. The redeveloper of the Denver Woolworth building (once one of the world's largest) preferred purchasing a vacant structure (it had been empty for five years), because that made it easier to re-fit for the high-tech companies he intended to attract. Educational institutions have also redesigned former retail properties, as in Hartford, where the G. Fox & Company department store was renovated for use by a community college.[11]

Elsewhere, Woolworth buildings were demolished in order to build office towers (Omaha), and hotels (New Orleans). In Houston, numerous old commercial structures like the Kress building were converted for residential lofts during the 1990s, but the Woolworth building in that city was replaced by a twelve-story parking garage including forty thousand square feet of retail. At the other end of the spectrum, the former Woolworth building in Butler, Pennsylvania, collapsed in broad daylight after only four years of vacancy. Despite the obvious neglect that had weakened the structure, the site had an active owner who was trying to find a new tenant. In Camden, New Jersey, the former downtown Woolworth building sits empty and apparently forgotten—representative of all the other empty commercial sites that do not make it into the news.

In 2000 a provocative set of preservation issues swirled around the Greensboro, North Carolina, Woolworth building, site of the February 1960 civil rights sit-ins that drew the national spotlight to the issue of Main Street integration. The now "run-down vacant store" was at the center of yet another controversy—over whether the structure should become a civil rights museum and, if so, who exactly should preserve and interpret that history. Varieties of nostalgia, like various interpretations of history, have been capable of opening up productive debates with many participants, viewpoints, and outcomes. In this sense, nostalgia is not a generic force imposing bland and monolithic narratives on the past, present, or future of urban commercial life.[12]

During the late twentieth century, downtown development strategies that retained, referenced, and reused the past emerged slowly but with great impact, signaling a major reorientation in how people engaged in and profited by urban commercial life. Such historical sensibilities, appearing in unexpected places and used by a great variety of participants, overcame significant resistance to animate the key issues and debates of urban commerce. Downtown vacancy and the ebbing vibrancy of old commercial ways coexisted with experimental new approaches, many of them rooted in nostalgia for the "authentic" commercial experiences that were disappearing. Just as the old red bricks of downtown buildings were relaid in festival marketplaces, this dwindling and simultaneous resurgence were closely related. From organized and professional Main Street historic preservation programs to vacant variety stores, festival marketplaces, and the creative and unorthodox recombination of old building parts by bohemian entrepreneurs, nostalgia in many forms inspired new directions for Main Street while almost always sparking disagreement and negotiation. During these decades, people experimented with the impact of historical themes upon the structures and nature of urban commerce. In the context of redevelopment, then, nostalgia has proved to have multiple and often confusing meanings. Besides the invented nostalgia of festival marketplaces and their precursors, for example, there was also a grassroots public nostalgia for dime stores that defied the pronouncements of the retail market analysts. There was racist nostalgia for segregated downtowns. In recent decades, developer interest in exploiting the past has indeed become an important force in remaking urban commerce, but it is only a small part of the story.

# NOTES

1. Peterson, "Past and Future Collide in Plan for Albuquerque," A14. On store as time tunnel, Silverman, "Woolworth Grows from Its Dime-Store Roots," D22. Jon Goss analyzes the symbolic and commercial function of history at Honolulu's Aloha Tower Marketplace, a festival marketplace that opened in 1994. Goss, "Disquiet on the Waterfront," 221–41. On movements to commemorate more controversial dimensions of history, see Dolores Hayden, *The Power of Place: Urban Landscapes as Public History* (Cambridge, MA: MIT Press, 1995).
2. Visitor Comment Book 2, December 30, 1997, "Main Street Five-and-Dimes: The Architectural Heritage of the S. H. Kress & Co. Stores," National Building Museum Comment Books, May 1997–March 1998. Courtesy of National Building Museum, Washington, D.C. (hereafter cited as Visitor Comment Book 1 and Visitor Comment Book 2). For many, these sentiments underscored the need for historic preservation and the creative reuse of old commercial buildings.
3. Visitor Comment Book 2, October 27, 1997; Visitor Comment Book 1, September 8, June 16, 1997. In a note to the author regarding the September 8 page, NBM staff noted, "This page was removed from the book because of comments in poor taste." Since nostalgia for segregation became a persistent theme, the staff must have decided later that it was impossible to remove all such comments.
4. Visitor Comment Book 1, July 28, 1997; Visitor Comment Book 2, mid-November 1997; January 25, 1998; Visitor Comment Book 1, June 7, 1997; Visitor Comment Book 2, December 6, 1997; Visitor Comment Book 1, October 1, 1997. Some singled out what they regarded as the degradation of women in store paraphernalia. The uninterpreted photographs of segregated store facilities prompted others to request a more complicated understanding of dime store history before they offered their opinions. See esp. Visitor Comment Book 1, July 6, 1997.
5. Visitor Comment Book 1, early July, mid-July, late June 1997.
6. Visitor Comment Book 1, mid-September 1997 (all punctuation, including ellipses, original); Visitor Comment Book 2, November 12, 1997. Although it did not appear in the visitor comment books, nostalgia among African Americans for the once-thriving black business districts (many destroyed by urban renewal and highway programs) offered yet another decline narrative.
7. Ric Kahn, "He's Well Dressed, but Still a Suspect," *Boston Globe,* March 12, 1995, city weekly, 1; Booth Gunther, "Dozens Revisit 1960 Lunch Demonstration," *Tampa Tribune,* January 19, 1997, Florida/metro, 1. For some of the conflicts arising over Rouse's support for black business and interest in black customers, see Metzger, "The Failed Promise of a Festival Marketplace," 44; and especially Stephanie Kay Dyer, "Markets in the Meadows:

Department Stores and Shopping Centers in the Decentralization of Philadelphia, 1920–1980" (Ph.D. diss., University of Pennsylvania, 2000), 334–42. Rouse was a rare developer in his willingness to raise controversial "social" issues. He often brought up the role commercial development could play in healing the racial rifts of American society. His housing investment programs run through the Enterprise Foundation strove to remedy inequalities. Fulton, "The Robin Hood of Real Estate," 4–10. On race politics and preservation in Atlanta and New Orleans, see Reichl, "Historic Preservation and Progrowth Politics in U.S. Cities."

8. Jon Goss explains that "in evoking the desire for genuine openness of the city, the festival marketplace creates a potential space for an urban politics committed to its general realization." Goss, "Disquiet on the Waterfront," 240.

9. Calvin Trillin, "Thoughts Brought On by Prolonged Exposure to Exposed Brick," quoted in Ruth Rejnis, "Interior Use of Brick Is on the Upswing," *NYT*, August 28, 1977, sec. 8, p. 1. He observed these similarities even before national developers and architects like James Rouse and Benjamin Thompson spread the genre.

10. For a comparison between 1890s civic improvement groups and 1990s business improvement districts, see Paul Schreiber, "Life after Woolworth," *New York Newsday,* September 15, 1997, C10. Mike Davis has written a widely read attack on the contemporary obsession with security and control, in *City of Quartz: Excavating the Future in Los Angeles* (New York: Vintage Books, 1990).

11. Pindell, "Keene Reborn," 15; Eleanor Charles, "A Million-Dollar Baby in a 5-and-10-Cent Store," *NYT,* November 19, 1995, sec. 9, p. 11; Bill Daley, "Salvation Army Eyes Main Street Building for Thrift Store," *Hartford (Conn.) Courant,* July 27, 1994, F1; Greg Gatlin, "T. J. Maxx Meets Marshalls," *Boston Globe,* May 21, 2001, 29; "Ross Dresses Up Old Woolworth's for Grand Opening—Injecting Life into Deteriorating Area," *Seattle Times,* October 18, 1995, E1; Bill Locey, "Rock (Star) Hunting," *Los Angeles Times,* March 11, 1999, F46; Frank Green, "Landmark Building to House the Blues," *San Diego Union-Tribune,* December 8, 2000, C1; Brian Meyer, "Ex-Woolworth Store on Main Eyed as Factory Outlet Mall," *Buffalo News,* May 28, 1998, 11A; John Rebchook, "Woolworth Site to Get New Life," *Denver Rocky Mountain News,* January 14, 1999, 1B; John Rebchook, "Blast from the Past," *Denver Rocky Mountain News,* December 12, 1999, business sec., 12G.

12. "Woolworth's Building Razed," *New Orleans Times-Picayune,* August 17, 2000, money sec., 1; Steven Jordan, "Office Building in Works," *Omaha World-Herald,* December 30, 1997, business sec., 21; Ralph Bivins, "Commerce Building Gets New Lease on Life," *Houston Chronicle,* February 12, 1999, business sec., 2; Ralph Bivins, "Buyer Plans Lofts for Kress Building," *Houston Chronicle,* May 14, 1998, business sec., 1; Nancy Welsh, "Building Collapses, Closing 2 Streets in Downtown Butler," *Pittsburgh Post-Gazette,* May 19, 1999, local sec., A12; Chris Burritt, "N.C. Museum Vote Reopens Racial Splits," *Atlanta Journal and Constitution,* November 4, 2000, 13A.

# CHAPTER 4

# THE CITIES: THE POLITICS OF SPACE, RACE, AND ETHNICITY

## CONFRONTATION AND ACCOMMODATION

Competition, conflict, and accommodation along racial and ethnic lines is a key element in the process of globalization, as is the dispersal of all groups to the suburbs. This development has profound consequences for city politics. New and older groups compete for living space and access to jobs, sharpening rivalries among people of different racial, ethnic, and social class backgrounds. In order to govern, political leaders must struggle to mobilize new voter coalitions and attempt to satisfy the political claims of voters who have different priorities and life experiences. Thus, city politics is increasingly dominated by political confrontation and accommodation as diverse populations assert their presence and identity in local political systems.

Rising racial tensions over neighborhood space became a dominant feature of city politics decades ago. This set the stage for interracial political conflicts that  sometimes reached crisis proportions. In Selection 11, Thomas J. Sugrue examines the seeds of racial confrontation in Detroit. Abundant jobs in the industrial cities during World War II drew black workers to northern cities, and once the war was over the migration picked up even more steam. In 1940, blacks made up just 9.3 percent of Detroit's population; by 1970, the proportion had increased to 63 percent. In Sugrue's account, whites attempted to keep blacks from moving into white neighborhoods by organizing homeowners' associations and citizen's groups and by resorting to intimidation and violence. White homeowners felt economically vulnerable to economic downturns and changes in the workplace, and they projected onto blacks their insecurities. The overcrowded slums that blacks were forced to live in projected a real-life image of the problems that whites feared. The resistance to black movement into white neighborhoods assumed some of the aspects of war. Racial change in the neighborhoods occurred in block-by-block skirmishes, with whites making an uneven, slow retreat.

Although the city/suburban racial divide inherited from the past still persists in America's metropolitan areas, things are changing. Newer immigrants are establishing an uneven but growing political presence in urban politics. Early in the last century, some immigrants—in particular, the Irish—were able to find a voice in the party machines. That avenue is no longer available, but the ballot box still gives them powerful leverage. In Selection 12, Reuel Rogers focuses on coalition building in cities where new and old minority immigrant groups compete for power. He wonders whether the newcomers will forge coalitions with their native-born counterparts, particularly African-Americans. In the past, many believed that race-based alliances between nonwhite immigrants and African-Americans were likely since both experienced racial discrimination and frequently share other group characteristics that give them common cause.

Using the case of Caribbean and American-born blacks in New York City, Rogers notes the absence of alliances between these groups over many years. Common racial interests have not been sufficient to overcome a pattern of inter-minority tensions and political competition. Rogers explains that race alone is not a satisfactory foundation for alliance building between these two groups. He finds that competition for political turf frequently divides Caribbean and African-American blacks. Entrenched African-American elites have an interest in resisting the mobilization and inclusion of newer Caribbean blacks in order to preserve their hold on jobs and power. For their part, Caribbean minorities seek political recognition and their leaders give priority to constituency building within their own enclave. Rogers also believes that governmental institutions play a part in dividing these two groups. In particular, he says that New York City's decentralized electoral system rewards mobilization of ethnic groups and targeted appeals that become divisive. In addition, the city's one-party politics and lack of rich networks of community-based organizations encourages political faction. The author concludes that race is unlikely to form a stable foundation for governance in big cities like New York for some time, if ever.

Selection 13, by Harvey Newman, suggests that inequality and racial discrimination are sometimes created by urban policies, even in cities with governments run by minorities. Tourism has become a big business in many cities struggling to find a niche in the global economy. As jobs in the old economy dry up or leave town, city after city has tried to become a tourist destination and to attract business travelers seeking a meeting place for conferences. Looking at Atlanta, Harvey describes such efforts and finds them wanting as a way of providing benefits to the city's black community.

Harvey maintains that the remaking of Atlanta's downtown for tourism has created a "tourist bubble" of segregated enclaves where pedestrians have little contact with the city's residents. Sealed skywalk systems that connect hotels, conference centers, restaurants, and other buildings isolate visitors from the people outside, ensuring little contact with black neighborhoods, businesses, and commercial areas. The city avoids supporting projects that might integrate the economy, as do white investors. A succession of black administrations has hardly wavered from sponsoring tourist bubble projects like those created by white politicians in the past, even though most of the economic benefits bypass black neighborhoods and commercial areas. It is likely that the social effects of Atlanta's tourist bubble strategy are similar to the experience in many other cities.

Political competition based on class, racial, and ethnic differences is likely to remain an enduring feature of city politics as long as other sources of social division remain less important. As populations change and age, new urban political coalitions will be forged, and perhaps racial and ethnic identity will become less prominent. From today's perspective, however, that time appears to be far in the future.

# 11

## *Thomas J. Sugrue*

## RACIAL CONFRONTATION IN POST-WAR DETROIT

## The Rise of the Homeowners' Movement

Between 1943 and 1965, Detroit whites founded at least 192 neighborhood organizations throughout the city, variously called "civic associations," "protective associations," "improvement associations," and "homeowners' associations."[1] Few scholars have fully appreciated the enormous contribution of this kind of grassroots organization to the racial and political climate of twentieth-century American cities.[2] Their titles revealed their place in the ideology of white Detroiters. As civic associations, they saw their purpose as upholding the values of self-government and participatory democracy. They offered members a unified voice in city politics. As protective associations, they fiercely guarded the investments their members had made in their homes. They also paternalistically defended neighborhood, home, family, women, and children against the forces of social disorder that they saw arrayed against them in the city. As improvement associations, they emphasized the ideology of self-help and individual achievement that lay at the very heart of the American notion of homeownership. Above all, as home and property owners' associations, these groups represented the interests of those who perceived themselves as independent and rooted rather than dependent and transient.

The surviving records of homeowners associations do not, unfortunately, permit a close analysis of their membership. From the hundreds of letters that groups sent to city officials and civil rights groups, from neighborhood newsletters, and from improvement association letterheads, it is clear that no single ethnic group dominated most neighborhood associations. Names as diverse as Fadanelli, Csanyi, Berge, and Watson appeared on the same petitions. Officers of the Greater Detroit Homeowners' Association, Unit No. 2, in a blue-collar northwest Detroit neighborhood, included a veritable United Nations of ethnic names, among them Benzing, Bonaventura, Francisco, Kopicko, Sloan, Clanahan, Klebba, Beardsley, Twomey, and Barr. Groups met in public-school

From Thomas J. Sugrue, *The Origins of the Urban Crisis: Race and Inequality in Postwar Detroit.* © 1996 by Princeton University Press. Reprinted by permission of Princeton University Press.

buildings, Catholic and Protestant churches, union halls, Veterans of Foreign Wars clubhouses, and parks. Letters, even from residents with discernibly "ethnic" names, seldom referred to national heritage or religious background. Organizational newsletters and neighborhood newspapers never used ethnic modifiers or monikers to describe neighborhood association members—they reserved ethnic nomenclature for "the colored" and Asians (and occasionally Jews). The diversity of ethnic membership in neighborhood groups is not surprising, given that Detroit had few ethnically homogeneous neighborhoods by midcentury. But the heterogeneity of Detroit's neighborhoods only partially explains the absence of ethnic affiliation in remaining records. Homeowners and neighborhood groups shared a common bond of whiteness and Americanness—a bond that they asserted forcefully at public meetings and in correspondence with public officials. They referred to the "white race," and spoke of "we the white people." Some called for the creation of a "National Association for the Advancement of White People," and others drew from the "unqualified support of every white family, loyal to white ideas."[3]

Detroit was a magnet for southern white migrants, but there is no evidence of a distinctive southern white presence in neighborhood organizations. "Hillbillies," as they were labeled, were frequently blamed for racial tension in the city, but their role was greatly exaggerated. Most of them dispersed throughout the metropolitan area, and quickly disappeared into the larger white population. There were a few concentrations of poor white southerners in the city, like the Briggs neighborhood near Tiger Stadium. Even in these neighborhoods, however, they tended not to form civic or political organizations. Scattered evidence from voter surveys suggests that they tended to vote solidly Democratic; indeed, in 1949 and 1951 they were more likely to support liberal candidates than were Italians and Poles. In addition, as historical anthropologist John Hartigan has shown, southern whites often lived in close proximity to blacks with little long-term resistance. Most importantly, a 1951 public opinion survey found that "Southerners who now live in Detroit express no more negative attitudes about Negroes and are no more in favor of segregation than are people from other parts of the country." The racial politics of Detroit's neighborhood associations were thoroughly homegrown.[4]

Racial exclusion had not always been the primary purpose of neighborhood associations. Real estate developers had originally created them to enforce building restrictions, restrictive covenants and, later, zoning laws. Their members served as watchdogs, gathering complaints from neighbors and informing the City Plan Commission of zoning violations. Frequently, they lobbied city officials for the provision of better public services such as street lighting, stop signs, traffic lights, and garbage pickup. Improvement associations were also social clubs that welcomed new neighbors and brought together residents of adjacent streets for events such as block parties, dinner dances, and excursions to local amusement parks or baseball games. They sponsored community cleanup and home improvement competitions. Their newsletters included admonitions to association members to drive safely, announcements of local dinner dances, neighborhood gossip, and home improvement and homemaking tips.[5]

During and after World War II, these organizations grew rapidly in number and influence, as hundreds of thousands of working-class whites became home-owners for the first time. Detroit's industrial workers had used their relatively high wages, along with federal mortgage subsidies, to purchase or build mod-est single-family houses on the sprawling Northeast and Northwest sides. The proportion of owner-occupied homes in the city rose from 39.2 percent in 1940 to 54.1 percent in 1960.[6] Yet the working-class hold on affluence was tenuous. Many city residents had spent a large part of their life savings to buy a home, and they usually had little else to show for their work. Most Detroiters viewed home-ownership as a precarious state, always under siege by external forces beyond their control. Even those who held steady employment found that mortgage or land contract payments stretched family budgets to the breaking point. In a com-prehensive survey of Detroit residents conducted in 1951, Wayne University soci-ologist Arthur Kornhauser found that white Detroiters ranked housing needs as the most pressing problem in the city. Homeownership required a significant fi-nancial sacrifice for Detroit residents: the most frequent complaint (voiced by 32 percent of respondents) was that the cost of housing was too high.[7] To a gen-eration that had struggled through the Great Depression, the specter of foreclo-sure and eviction was very real. For working Detroiters, the vagaries of layoffs, plant closings, and automation jeopardized their most significant asset, usually their only substantial investment—their homes.

Homeownership was as much an identity as a financial investment. Many of Detroit's homeowners were descendants of immigrants from eastern and southern Europe, for whom a house and property provided the very definition of a family. They placed enormous value on the household as the repository of family values and the center of community life. In addition, for many immi-grants and their children, homeownership was proof of success, evidence that they had truly become Americans. A well-kept property became tangible evi-dence of hard work, savings, and prudent investment, the sign of upward mo-bility and middle-class status.[8]

To white ethnics, homeownership was more than the product of individual enterprise. Detroiters, by and large, lived in intensely communal neighbor-hoods. In Detroit's working-class districts, houses were close together on small lots. Day-to-day life was structured by countless small interactions among neighbors; little was private. Property maintenance, behavior, and attitudes seldom escaped the close scrutiny of neighbors. Reinforcing the ties of proxim-ity were the common bonds of religion. In the mid-1950s, about 65 percent of Detroit's population was Roman Catholic; the white population was probably closer to 75 or 80 percent Catholic. Catholic familial and institutional bonds or-dered urban life in ways that cannot be underestimated. Paul Wrobel, a third-generation Polish American, recalled that life in the heavily Catholic East Side neighborhood of his youth "centered around three separate but related spheres: Family, Parish, and Neighborhood." In largely Catholic neighborhoods, im-provement associations grew out of parish social organizations, frequently held meetings in church halls, and often got material and spiritual support from pastors. Improvement associations in largely Polish neighborhoods on De-troit's East Side, reported the Mayor's Interracial Committee (MIC), "conform to the bounds of Catholic Church parish lines rather than subdivisions." Although many Catholic clergy supported civil rights, priests at some Detroit-area churches encouraged their parishioners to support homeowners' associations, for fear that black "invasions" would hurt parish life. Parishioners at Saint Andrew and Saint Benedict, a large Catholic church in a racially changing southwest Detroit neighborhood, were active in the Southwest Civic Improvement League. MIC officials reported a "prevailing sentiment of antagonism and fear" and a "feeling that this investment [in a new parish school building] and the social life of the church will be affected by the movement out . . . of large numbers of church members."[9] Catholic parishes were not the only bases for homeowners' groups, however. White civic associations also found religious and political support among evangelical Protestants. Many white fundamentalist churches, such as the Temple Baptist Church and the Metropolitan Tabernacle, fostered racial prejudices and often sponsored neighborhood association meetings.[10]

The homeowners' movement, then, emerged as the public voice of proud homeowners who defined themselves in terms of their tightly knit, exclusive communities. But the simultaneous occurrence of economic dislocation and black migration in postwar Detroit created a sense of crisis among homeowners. Both their economic interests and their communal identities were threatened. They turned to civic associations to defend a world that they feared was slipping away. Increasingly, they blamed blacks for their insecurity. In the era of open housing, responding to the threat of black movement into their neighborhoods became the raison d'être of white community groups. One new group, the Northwest Civic Association, called its founding meeting "So YOU will have first hand information on the colored situation in this area," and invited "ALL interested in maintaining Property Values in the NORTHWEST section of Detroit." The Courville District association gathered together residents of a northeast Detroit neighborhood to combat the "influx of colored people" to the area, and rallied supporters with its provocatively entitled newsletter, *Action!* When a black family moved onto Cherrylawn Street on the city's West Side, between six hundred and a thousand white neighbors attended an emergency meeting to form a neighborhood association. The founders of the Connor-East Homeowners' Association promised to "protect the Area from undesirable elements." Members of the San Benardo Improvement Association pledged to keep their neighborhood free of "undesirables"—or "Niggers"—as several who eschewed euphemism shouted at the group's first meeting. Existing organizations took on a new emphasis with the threat of black "invasion." In 1950, Orville Tenaglia, president of the Southwest Detroit Improvement League, recounted his group's history: "Originally we organized in 1941 to promote better civic affairs, but now we are banded together just to protect our homes." The league was engaged in a "war of nerves" over the movement of blacks into the community.[11]

The issues of race and housing were inseparable in the minds of many white Detroiters. Economically vulnerable homeowners feared, above all, that an influx of blacks would imperil their precarious investments. "Stop selling houses to the colored," advocated one white Detroiter. "Where would we move? No place—

poor people have no place to move," he added. "What is the poor people to do?" Speaking for homeowners who felt threatened by the black migration, a self-described "average American housewife" wrote: "What about us, who cannot afford to move to a better location and are surrounded by colored? . . . Most of us invested our life's savings in property and now we are in constant fear that the neighbor will sell its property to people of different race.[12] Kornhauser found that race relations followed a close second to housing in Detroiters' ranking of the city's most pressing problems. Only 18 percent of white respondents from all over the city expressed "favorable" views toward the "full acceptance of Negroes" and 54 percent expressed "unfavorable" attitudes toward integration. When asked to discuss ways in which race relations "were not as good as they should be," 27 percent of white respondents mentioned "Negroes moving into white neighborhoods." 22 percent answered that the "Negro has too many rights and privileges; too much power; too much intermingling." Another 14 percent mentioned "Negroes' undesirable characteristics." Only 14 percent mentioned the existence of discrimination as a problem in race relations.[13]

Whites in Detroit regularly spoke of the "colored problem" or the "Negro problem."[14] In their responses to open-ended questions, Kornhauser's informants made clear what they meant by the "colored problem." Of blacks: "Eighty percent of them are animals," stated one white respondent. "If they keep them all in the right place there wouldn't be any trouble," responded another. "Colored treat the whites in an insolent way," added a third white, "They think they own the city." A majority of whites looked to increased segregation as the solution to Detroit's "colored problem."[15] When asked, "What do you feel ought to be done about relations between Negroes and whites in Detroit?" a remarkable 68 percent of white respondents called for some form of racial segregation—56 percent of whites surveyed advocated residential segregation. Many cited the Jim Crow South as a model for successful race relations.[16]

Class, union membership, and religion all affected whites' attitudes toward blacks. Working-class and poor whites expressed negative views toward blacks more frequently than other respondents to Kornhauser's survey. 85 percent of poor and working-class whites supported racial segregation, in contrast to 56 percent of middle-income and 42 percent of upper-income whites. Union members were slightly "less favorable than others towards accepting Negroes." CIO members were even more likely than other white Detroiters to express negative views of African Americans—65 percent—although more CIO members were also likely to support full racial equality (18 percent) than ordinary white Detroiters. And finally, Catholics were significantly more likely than Protestants to express unfavorable feelings toward blacks.[17]

Neighborhood groups responded to the threat of "invasion" with such urgency because of the extraordinary speed of racial change. Most blocks in changing neighborhoods went from being all-white to predominantly black in a period of three or four years. They also reacted viscerally against the tactics of blockbusting real estate brokers, whose activities fueled their sense of desperation. Whites living just beyond "racially transitional" areas witnessed the rapid black movement into those areas. They feared that without concerted action, their neighborhoods would turn over just as quickly.

White Detroiters also looked beyond transitional neighborhoods to the "slum," a place that confirmed all of their greatest fears. Whites saw in the neighborhoods to which blacks had been confined in the center city area, such as Paradise Valley, a grim prophecy of their own neighborhoods' futures. The rundown, shabby appearance of inner-city housing, the piles of uncollected garbage, and the streets crowded with children and families escaping tightly packed apartments seemed confirmation of whites' worst fears of social disorder. To them, the ghetto was the antithesis of their tightly-knit, orderly communities. They also noticed the striking class difference between blacks and whites. The median family income of blacks in Detroit was at best two-thirds of that of whites between the 1940s and the 1960s. Although the poorest blacks were seldom the first to move into formerly white neighborhoods (in fact black "pioneers" were often better off than many of their white neighbors), whites feared the incursion of a "lowerclass element" into their neighborhoods.[18]

To white Detroiters, the wretched conditions in Paradise Valley and other poor African American neighborhoods were the fault of irresponsible blacks, not greedy landlords or neglectful city officials. Because housing was such a powerful symbol of "making it" for immigrant and working-class families, many Detroit whites interpreted poor housing conditions as a sign of personal failure and family breakdown. Wherever blacks lived, whites believed, neighborhoods inevitably deteriorated. "Let us keep out the slums," admonished one East Side homeowners' group. If blacks moved into white neighborhoods, they would bring with them "noisy roomers, loud parties, auto horns, and in general riotous living," thus depreciating real estate values and destroying the moral fiber of the community. A middle-aged Catholic woman living in a racially changing Detroit neighborhood offered a similar view. Blacks "just destroy the whole neighborhood," she told an interviewer. "They neglect everything. Their way of life is so different from ours."[19] A Northwest Side neighborhood association poster played on the fears of white residents afraid of the crime that they believed would accompany racial change: "Home Owners Can You Afford to . . . Have your children exposed to gangster operated skid row saloons? Phornographic [sic] pictures and literature? Gamblers and prostitution? You Face These Issues Now!"[20]

As black joblessness rates rose in the 1950s, such fears were not totally without basis. As more and more young African American men faced underemployment or unemployment, many spent time hanging out on streetcorners, a scene that whites found threatening. And as the city's economy began its downward spiral in the mid-1950s, rates of burglary, robbery, and murder began to rise. In the city's poorest black neighborhoods, an alternative economy of gambling, drugs, and prostitution flourished. Even though whites were seldom the victims of black-initiated crimes, Detroit's white-owned daily newspapers paid special attention to black-on-white crimes, giving prominent billing to murders and rapes. Often sensationalistic accounts mentioned the race of a black perpetrator, but seldom, if ever, mentioned that of whites.[21]

Whites also commonly expressed fears of racial intermingling. Black "penetration" of white neighborhoods posed a fundamental challenge to white racial identity. Again and again, neighborhood groups and letter writers referred to the perils of rapacious black sexuality and race mixing. The politics of family, home, and neighborhood were inseparable from the containment of uncontrolled sexuality and the imminent danger of interracial liaisons. Neighborhood newsletters ominously warned of the threat of miscegenation. One Northwest Side newspaper praised a Common Council candidate with a banner headline: "Kronk Bucks Mixing Races." Members of the Courville District association discussed "interracial housing," "interracial marriage," and "interracial dancing in our schools and elsewhere." Proximity to blacks risked intimacy. "Do you want your children to marry colored?" asked one woman at an improvement association rally in 1957. At a meeting at Saint Scholastica Catholic Church in northwest Detroit nine years later, fears of racial intermarriage remained the most pressing concern. Parishioners expressed concerns about the supposed sexual potency of black men.[22]

The undistilled sentiments of youth offer a revealing glimpse into the racial attitudes that undergirded Detroit's battles over housing. In the mid-1940s, a teacher at the all-white Van Dyke School in northeast Detroit asked students in a sixth-grade class to write essays on "Why I like or don't like Negroes." The students frequently mentioned cleanliness, violence, and housing conditions as grounds for disliking blacks, and often offered pejorative comments about blacks' living habits. Several students expressed concerns about black neighbors. "They are durty fighters and they do not keep their yardes clean," wrote one sixth-grader. In the words of another student, "they try to mix in with white people when they don't want them." A classmate stated that "they wanted to live out on Van Dyke and we didn't want them to." Another argued (in words that must have come right from his parents), that "if you give them a inch they take a mile and they are sneaky." Mary Conk drew up a list which encapsulated most of her classmates' sentiments:

1. Because they are mean
2. And they are not very clean.
3. Some of them don't like white people
4. They leave garbage in the yard and it smells
5. And in the dark the skare you
6. And they pick you up in a car and kill you. at nite
7. And they start riots

Most of the students at the Van Dyke School had never lived near a black person. Few spoke from experience. But the children, fearful of the prospect of blacks as neighbors, expressed attitudes that they had heard again and again from their parents and friends. As white Detroiters continued to fight against black movement throughout the city, they ensured that subsequent generations of children and adults would share Mary Conk's fears about blacks.[23]

Life was good for Easby Wilson in the spring of 1955. The city was in a recession, but Wilson was still steadily employed on the day shift at the Dodge Main plant. At a time when many of his fellow black workers were being laid off, Wilson was lucky. He had saved enough money so that he, his wife, and their five-year-old son could move from the crowded and run-down Paradise Valley area to the quiet, leafy neighborhood around the Courville School on

Detroit's Northeast Side. The Courville area was popular with Dodge Main workers because it was affordable, attractive, and only three miles from the plant. Wilson could drive from his house to the factory gate in about ten minutes, or take a fifteen-minute bus ride down Dequindre Avenue.[24]

After looking at a few houses in March 1955, the Wilsons chose a modest frame house on Riopelle Street. They knew that the neighborhood was predominantly white and had heard rumors of racially motivated violence in changing Detroit neighborhoods. But their real estate agent reassured him that "the situation" (a euphemism for race relations) "was fine." What the broker failed to tell them was that they were breaching an invisible racial boundary by buying a house west of Dequindre Avenue. The neighborhood to the east of Dequindre had a rapidly growing black population, but only one other black family lived on the blocks to the west. The Wilsons also did not know that over the preceding decade, white residents of the surrounding neighborhood had formed a powerful homeowners' association to resist the black "invasion" of their area, had harassed whites who offered their houses to blacks, and had driven out several black newcomers. Less than two years before the Wilsons bought their house, neighbors in the same block had threatened a white family who put their house on the market with a black broker.[25]

Shortly after the Wilsons closed on the real estate deal, their new house became a racial battleground. Indignant white neighbors launched a five-month siege on 18199 Riopelle. In late April, just before the Wilsons moved in, someone broke into the house, turned on all the faucets, blocked the kitchen sink, flooded the basement, and spattered black paint on the walls and floors. Later that day, after the Wilsons cleaned up the mess and left, vandals broke all the front windows in the house. Despite the noise, no neighbors reported the attack to the police. On Tuesday, April 26, the Wilsons moved in. The onslaught escalated. White members of the Cadillac Improvement Association approached the Wilsons and demanded that they sell the house. That evening, someone threw a stone through the bathroom window. For two straight nights, the phone rang with angry, anonymous calls.

On Friday, after dinner, a small crowd gathered on Riopelle Street in front of the Wilsons' house. They were soon joined by more than four hundred picketing and chanting whites, summoned by young boys who rode their bikes up and down the street, blowing whistles. The crowd drew together a cross-section of neighborhood residents: as Mrs. Wilson reported, "it was children; it was old people; it was teen-agers; in fact all ages were there." Demonstrators screamed epithets. "You'd better go back where you belong!" shouted an angry neighbor. A rock shattered the dining room window. Trapped inside, Easby Wilson could barely contain his rage. "He lost his head" before he was calmed by his wife and a police officer. The following evening, more protesters filled the street in front of the Wilson house; despite police surveillance, someone threw a large rock toward the house so hard that it stuck in the asbestos siding.

In the aftermath of the demonstrations, some of Wilson's friends from UAW Local 3 stood guard occasionally on the Wilsons' porch. The police stationed a patrol car near the house twenty-four hours a day. Gradually the pickets subsided, but over the next two months, hit-and-run vandals launched eggs, rocks, and bricks at the Wilsons' windows, splashed red, black, and yellow paint on the facade of the house, and put several snakes in the basement. An older white woman who lived next door threatened the family and was caught one evening pouring salt on the Wilsons' lawn. "At night," reported Mrs. Wilson, "when the lights are out, you can expect anything." Despite the police protection, the attacks went unabated; in fact many of the attacks occurred while police officers sat in their car nearby. At the end of the second month of the siege, Mrs. Wilson was exasperated. "I don't know whether it's worthwhile. I believe in Democracy; I believe in what my husband fought for [in World War II]. . . . They fought for the peace and I wonder if it's worthwhile. I have a question in my mind: where is the peace they fought for—where is it?"

The beleaguered Wilsons reported a "terrific strain" because of the incidents. Easby Wilson suffered from a mild heart condition that was aggravated by the stress of constant harassment. Their son Raymond, a five-year-old, began having "nervous attacks," waking up in the middle of the night complaining that he felt like "something was crawling over him, maybe ants." Raymond's affliction proved to be the last indignity the Wilsons would suffer. They moved out of their Riopelle Street house when a psychologist warned the Wilsons that Raymond risked "becoming afflicted with a permanent mental injury" because of the relentless attacks. The siege on the Wilsons, and other attacks on black newcomers to the area, served as an effective deterrent to black movement onto the streets west of Dequindre Avenue, between McNichols and Seven Mile Roads. In 1960, almost five years after the Wilsons were driven out, only 2.9 percent of the area's residents were black.[26]

Violent incidents like the attacks on the Wilsons' home were commonplace in Detroit between the Second World War and the 1960s. The postwar era, as a city race relations official recalled, was marked by many "small disturbances, near-riots, and riots." The city "did a lot of firefighting in those days." White Detroiters instigated over two hundred incidents against blacks moving into formerly all-white neighborhoods, including harassment, mass demonstrations, picketing, effigy burning, window breaking, arson, vandalism, and physical attacks. Most incidents followed improvement association meetings. The number of attacks peaked between 1954 and 1957, when the city's economy was buffeted by plant closings, recession, and unemployment, limiting the housing options of many white, working-class Detroiters. Incidents accelerated again in the early 1960s, reaching a violent crescendo in 1963, when the Commission on Community Relations reported sixty-five incidents. A potent mixture of fear, anger, and desperation animated whites who violently defended their neighborhoods. All but the most liberal whites who lived along the city's racial frontier believed that they had only two options. They could flee, as vast numbers of white urbanites did, or they could hold their ground and fight.[27]

The violence that whites unleashed against blacks was not simply a manifestation of lawlessness and disorder. It was not random, nor was it irrational. In the arena of housing, violence in Detroit was organized and widespread, the outgrowth of one of the largest grassroots movements in the city's history. It involved thousands of whites, directly affected hundreds of blacks, mainly those who were among the first families to break the residential barriers of race, and indirectly constrained the housing choices of tens of thousands of blacks fearful of harassment and physical injury if they broke through Detroit's residential color line. The violent clashes between whites and blacks that marred the city were political acts, the consequence of perceptions of homeownership, community, gender, and race deeply held by white Detroiters. The result of profound economic insecurities among working- and middle-class whites, they were, above all, desperate acts of neighborhood self-determination, by well-organized community groups, in response to an array of social and economic changes over which they had little control.

Racial incidents encoded possession and difference in urban space. Residents of postwar Detroit carried with them a cognitive map that helped them negotiate the complex urban landscape. In a large, amorphous twentieth-century city like Detroit, there were few visible landmarks to distinguish one neighborhood from another. But residents imposed onto the city's featureless topography all sorts of invisible boundaries—boundaries shaped by intimate association, by institutions (like public-school catchment areas or Catholic parish boundaries), by class, and, most importantly, by race. As the city's racial demography changed in the postwar years and as blacks began to move out of the center city, white neighborhood organizations acted to define and defend the invisible boundaries that divided the city. Their actions were, in large part, an attempt to mark their territory symbolically and visibly, to stake out turf and remind outsiders that to violate those borders was to risk grave danger.[28]

The sustained violence in Detroit's neighborhoods was the consummate act in a process of identity formation. White Detroiters invented communities of race in the city that they defined spatially. Race in the postwar city was not just a cultural construction. Instead, whiteness, and by implication blackness, assumed a material dimension, imposed onto the geography of the city. Through the drawing of racial boundaries and through the use of systematic violence to maintain those boundaries, whites reinforced their own fragile racial identity. Ultimately, they were unsuccessful in preventing the movement of blacks into many Detroit neighborhoods, but their defensive measures succeeded in deepening the divide between two Detroits, one black and one white. On one side of the ever-shifting, contested color line were insecure white workers who expressed their racial sentiments politically and depended on the most extreme among them to patrol racial borders. On the other side of the line were blacks, initially optimistic about the prospects of residential integration, but increasingly unwilling to venture into territory they justifiably considered hostile.

## Territoriality

For those white Detroiters unwilling or unable to flee, black movement into their neighborhoods was the moral equivalent of war. As the racial demography of Detroit changed, neighborhood groups demarcated racial boundaries with great precision, and, abetted by federal agencies and private real estate agents, divided cities into strictly enforced racial territories. In the postwar years, white urban dwellers fiercely defended their turf. They referred to the black migration in military terms: they spoke of "invasions" and "penetration," and plotted strategies of "resistance." White neighborhoods became "battlegrounds" where residents struggled to preserve segregated housing. Homeowners' associations helped whites to "defend" their homes and "protect" their property.[29]

In defended neighborhoods, white organizations served as gatekeepers by diplomacy and by force. Their goal was nothing short of the containment of Detroit's black population, a domestic Cold War to keep the forces of social disorder, represented by blacks, at bay.[30] White community organizations served the double function of social club and neighborhood militia. On the Lower West Side, homeowners formed the "Property Owners Association" in 1945 to combat the expansion of the black West Side into their neighborhood with "every means at our command."[31] "United Communities are Impregnable," noted founders of the National Association of Community Councils, a grandiosely named "protective, vigilant, American organization" on the West Side.[32]

Most neighborhood improvement associations that battled black newcomers assumed a paramilitary model of organization. The Courville District Association divided the neighborhood into "danger spots," that were "in the process of disintegration by an influx of colored families in the past year." Each section had "captains" and "supervisors" who would lead residents to "retard and diminish this influx, and prevent our white families from exodus."[33] Residents of the De Witt–Clinton area adapted the civil defense system from World War II to their new racial battleground. They formed as "Unit Number 2" of the Greater Detroit Neighbors Association (later renamed the De Witt–Clinton Civic Association) in 1949, a full seven years before the first black family attempted to move into the area. "Block wardens" were responsible for the defense of every street in the area. Residents of other Wyoming Corridor neighborhoods invited De Witt–Clinton officials to help them organize in 1955, 1956, and 1957. They formed a tightly knit network of neighborhood groups that covered every subdivision along the West Side's racial frontier and that shared leadership and passed on information about black movements in the area.[34]

One of the most important roles of improvement associations was to mark the city's racial borders. Frequently, groups used signs to make visible the invisible boundaries of race. In November 1945, for example, white residents of a neighborhood that was beginning to attract blacks to its low-rent apartments posted a sign on a building: "Negroes moving here will be burned, Signed Neighbors."[35] Residents of a West Side street posted "Whites Only" and "KKK" on a house sold to a black family.[36] Blacks seeking homes on American Street in Saint Luke's parish could not miss two large signs at each end of the block that boldly proclaimed "ALL WHITE."[37] Protesters in front of a new house built for an African American in the "white section" of the Seven Mile–Fenelon area carried signs reading, "If you're black, you'd better go back to Africa where you belong."[38] Signs often greeted the first black families who crossed invisible racial lines, warning them of their proper place in the city. The first black family to cross into the Northeast Side neighborhood surrounding Saint Bartholomew's parish in 1963, for example, was greeted with a sign that read "Get back on the other side of 7 Mile."[39] And countless variations on the theme "No Niggers Wanted" (posted on a West Side house in 1957) appeared throughout the city. Signs sometimes conveyed a more subtle message. Some whites in neighborhoods threatened by racial change attempted to stake their turf and deter "blockbusting" real estate agents by posting signs declaring "This House is Not for Sale."[40]

Often protesters chose boundaries as the site of demonstrations. In the Seven Mile–Fenelon area, in November 1948, two men burned an effigy at the corner of Nevada and Conley, only a block from the Sojourner Truth site, on the edge of their threatened white neighborhood. Their ominously simple symbolic act made clear to blacks the risks of crossing racial barriers. When private developers announced plans to construct homes in a formerly all-white section of the area to be sold "on a non-restricted basis," Seven Mile–Fenelon residents tore down signs advertising the new homes and vandalized the houses that breached the racial divide.[41] In the Courville area, residents of Nevada and Marx Streets joined a "car parade," for the purpose of "keeping undesirables out." Led by a sound truck, the paraders ritualistically marked the line that they did not want breached.[42]

In the crucible of racial change, white protesters targeted and stigmatized outsiders whom they believed threatened their communities. The consummate outsiders were blockbusting real estate agents, who violated community boundaries and acted as the catalyst of racial "invasions." In 1948, a coalition of homeowners' organizations published a list of brokers who sold homes to blacks and encouraged members to "Get busy on the phone." Even though the pamphlet asked members to "Never threaten or argue," whites in defended neighborhoods regularly called and harassed offending brokers. Especially galling to white groups was the prominence of blacks and Jews in real estate firms conducting business in changing neighborhoods. Both suffered relentless abuse from members of community groups. When Nathan Slobin, a Jewish real estate agent working in the Lower West Side, sold a home on Poplar Street to a black family, unnamed women barraged him with over a hundred phone calls, many with "obscene and menacing language." Area residents carrying anti-Semitic signs picketed his office and his home. Members of the Seven Mile–Fenelon Association threatened Charles Taylor, a black real estate broker who worked with contractors in the area, and warned him that any new homes for blacks constructed north of Stockton Street "will be burned down as fast as you can build them."[43] In the Courville area, white residents made death threats to a real estate agent who sold a house to a black family. On Woodingham, a crowd catcalled James Morris, a black real estate agent showing a house to a black family. In another incident on Woodingham, the police demonstrated their solidarity with protesting whites when they arrested Morris, after he had requested police intervention to quell the hostile mob that had gathered. On nearby Tuller and Cherrylawn Streets, gangs of youths harassed black real estate agents and their clients.[44]

Equally galling to residents of defended communities were white neighbors who listed their homes with known blockbusting real estate agents. Protesters reserved special venom for white "race traitors" who sold their homes to African Americans. Frequently, threats were ominous. Whites hid behind the cloak of anonymity "to intimidate and terrify white people who might sell to Negroes." In one case, Mrs. Florence Gifford, a Lower West Side white woman who offered her house with a black real estate agent, received a hundred phone calls over a ten-day period in early 1948. All the calls came from women, but only three were willing to identify themselves, all members of the neighborhood improvement association. Callers threatened property damage and offered more vague warnings like "It will be too bad if you sell to Negroes." Protesters also followed blockbusting white sellers to their new neighborhoods and tried to poison their relations with their new neighbors. Lower West Side picketers tracked Edward Brock to his new house on Detroit's far West Side, and circulated copies of his business card to his new neighbors along with a handbill that read: "WATCH ED BROCK ... IS ATTEMPTING TO PUT COLORED IN OUR *WHITE* NEIGHBORHOOD 3420 HARRISON. HE WOULD DO THE SAME TO YOU!!" In 1956, white residents of Ruritan Park followed Mr. and Mrs. Peter Hays to their new suburban Livonia home after they sold their Detroit house to a family suspected to be black. They warned the Hays' Livonia neighbors that the couple was "just the type who would sell a home to Negroes.[45]

Occasionally, community groups sought reprisals in the workplace. In 1955, the president of one neighborhood association gleefully reported that his group "had taken care of the white seller on his job." The owner of the chain store where the seller worked "asked us not to boycott [his] business because of this man." In 1957, protesters on Cherrylawn Street tried a similar tactic, threatening officials at Federals Department Store with a boycott if they did not fire Stella Nowak, a white woman who had sold her house to an African American family. Such threats deterred many whites from being the first on a block to sell to blacks.[46]

Threats were most effective when combined with diplomacy. In well-organized neighborhoods, delegations from improvement associations approached parties involved in the sale of a house to offer them alternatives. Often, community groups offered to purchase the house, usually for a sum greater than the asking price. If they lacked the financial resources, delegations often simply approached buyers and sellers and warned them of the dire consequences of breaching the residential color line. By approaching the offending seller or customer, whites presented a united community front, making clear their determination to preserve the neighborhood's racial homogeneity.[47]

Black resisters were the exception rather than the norm. White-initiated violence or the threat of it was a powerful deterrent to black pioneers. The effect of white resistance was to create a sieve through which a relatively small number of black Detroiters passed. The Seven Mile–Fenelon Association's activity did not fully preserve the racial status quo in the area, but it severely limited the residential options open to black home buyers, and slowed black residential movement.

26 percent of the population in the area was black in 1940, and only 35 percent was black in 1950. Considering that 250 black families had moved into the Sojourner Truth project, black movement to other parts of the neighborhood was at best incremental. 1960 census data make more clear the dynamics of racial transition in the area. Blacks were confined to the section of the neighborhood sandwiched between Conant Gardens and Sojourner Truth and to certain blocks immediately to the east.[48] Whites maintained the invisible boundary of race along Dequindre Avenue and slowed black movement further west. In 1960, the section of Courville west of Dequindre was only 2.7 percent black.[49] The De Witt–Clinton area also preserved its racial homogeneity for nearly fifteen years. Although the neighborhoods to the east steadily gained black population, from 1949, when they formed an association, to 1963, not a single black family successfully moved into the neighborhood.[50] The one exception to the norm was the Lower West Side. The number of blacks living in the area increased between 1940 and 1950, but relatively slowly. Of the entire area, only 11.2 percent of the population was black in 1950; and over one-third of the black population was concentrated in the one census tract closest to the Tireman–Grand Boulevard area. By 1960, however, all but one of the tracts in the former turf covered by the Property Owners Association had a black population of at least 30 percent, but the western part of the district attracted more blacks and fewer whites.[51]

By preoccupying blacks in block-by-block skirmishes, and hastily retreating when blacks finally "broke a block," residents of defended neighborhoods offered a small safety valve to residents of the overcrowded inner city. The rearguard actions of the defended neighborhoods essentially preserved— indeed strengthened—the principle of racial segregation in housing. They protected the homogeneity of all-white neighborhoods beyond the contested blocks. Over the long run, most of the defended neighborhoods became majority black communities. Whites, as one observer noted, "hold 'til the dam bursts, then run like hell." Those whites who remained were, with a few exceptions, older people who could not afford to move.[52]

Detroit was not alone in its pattern of racial violence. Urban whites responded to the influx of millions of black migrants to their cities in the 1940s, 1950s, and 1960s by redefining urban geography and urban politics in starkly racial terms. In Chicago and Cicero, Illinois, working-class whites rioted in the 1940s and 1950s to oppose the construction of public housing in their neighborhoods. White Chicagoans fashioned a brand of Democratic party politics, especially under mayors Martin Kennelly and Richard Daley, that had a sharp racial edge. In Newark, New Jersey, in the 1950s, blue-collar Italian and Polish Americans harassed African American newcomers to their neighborhoods. And in the postwar period, white Philadelphians and Cincinnatians attacked blacks who moved into previously all-white enclaves, and resisted efforts to integrate the housing market.[53] Countless whites retreated to suburbs or neighborhoods on the periphery of cities where they prevented black movement into their communities with federally sanctioned redlining practices, real estate steering, and restrictive zoning laws.[54]

Racial violence had far-reaching effects in the city. It hardened definitions of white and black identities, objectifying them by plotting them on the map of the city. The combination of neighborhood violence, real estate practices, covenants, and the operations of the housing market sharply circumscribed the housing opportunities available to Detroit's African American population. Persistent housing segregation stigmatized blacks, reinforced unequal race relations, and perpetuated racial divisions.

A visitor walking or driving through Detroit in the 1960s—like his or her counterpart in the 1940s—would have passed through two Detroits, one black and one white. Writing in 1963, sociologists Albert J. Mayer and Thomas Hoult noted that blacks in Detroit "live in essentially the same places that their predecessors lived during the 1930s—the only difference is that due to increasing numbers, they occupy more space centered around their traditional quarters."[55] Segregation in housing constrained black housing choices enormously. Whole sections of the city and the vast majority of the suburbs were entirely off limits to blacks. Racial discrimination and the housing market confined blacks to some of Detroit's oldest and worst housing stock, mainly that of the center-city area, and several enclaves on the periphery of the city.[56] Through sustained violence, Detroit whites engaged in battle over turf, a battle that had economic and social as well as political and ideological consequences.

But more than that, it added to Detroit blacks' already deep distrust of whites and white institutions. Speaking to an open housing conference in 1963, the Reverend Charles W. Butler, a prominent African American minister and civil rights advocate, reminded his audience of the anger that seethed among Detroit's blacks. "The desire and ability to move without the right to move," he argued, "is refined slavery." Butler summed up his remarks with a warning that racial segregation "spawned and cultivated the spirit of rebellion. . . . This rebellion is evident in many forms, from nonviolent resistance to vandalism. This rebellion is proof positive that the Negro has grown weary of being the eternal afterthought of America." Racial violence left blacks in neighborhoods increasingly bereft of capital, distant from workplaces, and marginalized politically. In a city deeply divided by racial violence, it was only a matter of time before blacks retaliated. The results of housing segregation, in combination with persistent workplace discrimination and deindustrialization, were explosive.[57]

## NOTES

1. Joseph Coles, a prominent Democratic activist and an appointee to the Detroit Mayor's Interracial Committee (MIC), stated that 155 homeowners' associations existed in Detroit during the Cobo administration. Joseph Coles, Oral History, 15. Blacks in the Labor Movement Collection, ALUA. Coles slightly underestimated the number of associations. At least 171 organizations existed during the Cobo administration and at least 191 organizations thrived in Detroit from the end of World War II to 1965. This figure undoubtedly understates the number of such associations, for many were ephemeral and kept no records. The most important source is: "Improvement Associations of Detroit, List From Zoning

Board of Appeals," July 12, 1955, DUL, Box 43, Folder A7–13, which includes names and addresses of 88 improvement associations. Through a detailed survey of letters and petitions on matters of housing and expressway construction sent to Mayor Albert Cobo, and especially through careful examination of letters in Cobo's separate files of correspondence from "civic associations," I was able to identify another 83 neighborhood groups not included in the 1955 list. See Mayor's Papers (1950) Boxes 2, 3, 5; (1951) Boxes 2, 3; (1953) Box 1, 3, 4; (1954) Box 2; (1955) Boxes 2, 4. The remaining associations were identified in a number of sources: a list of property owners' associations that joined the amicus curiae brief for the plaintiff in *Sipes v. McGhee* before the Michigan Supreme Court in Clement Vose. *Caucasians Only: The Supreme Court, the NAACP, and the Restrictive Covenant Cases* (Berkeley: University of California Press, 1959), 272, n. 41; Richard J. Peck, Community Services Department, Detroit Urban League, "Summary of Known Improvement Association Activities in Past Two Years 1955–1957," 6, in VF, Pre-1960, Folder: Community Organization 1950s; *Michigan Chronicle*. December 4, 1948, August 6, 1955, September 9, 1961; *Detroit News*, July 21, 1962; *Brightmoor Journal*, May 3, 1956, October 29, 1964, June 2, 1966, October 19, 1967, November 16, 1967; letters and brochures in SLAA; MIC, Incident Reports 1949, CCR, Part I, Series 1, Box 6, Folder 49–37; "A Study of Interracial Housing Incidents," January 20, 1949, ibid., Folder 49–3; CCR, Field Reports December 18, 1961, in RK, Box 2, Folder 4.

2. In 1955, housing activist Charles Abrams noted the importance of improvement associations in major cities and the dearth of studies of their activities. See Charles Abrams, *Forbidden Neighbors: A Study of Prejudice in Housing* (New York: Harper, 1955), 181–90. Abrams's call for research has remained largely unheeded, with the important exception of the brilliant discussion of Los Angeles' powerful grassroots homeowners' association movement in Mike Davis, *City of Quartz: Excavating the Future in Los Angeles* (London: Verso, 1990), 153–219.

3. Quotes from *Action!* the Newsletter of the Courville District Improvement Association, vol. 1 (February 15, 1948), attached to Mayor's Interracial Committee Minutes, April 4, 1948, CCR, Part I, Series I, Box 10; *The Civic Voice*, the newsletter of the Plymouth Manor Property Owners Association, vol. 2, no. 9 (September 1962), in CCR, Part III, Box 25, Folder 25–128. For examples of ethnic diversity in Detroit, letters to Mayor Edward Jeffries, regarding the Algonquin Street and Oakwood defense housing projects, in Mayor's Papers (1945), Box 3, Folder: Housing Commission. See also Exhibit A, October 22, 1945, 1–2, attached to Memorandum to Charles S. Johnson et al. from Charles H. Houston, NAACP, Group II, Box B133, Folder: Michigan: *Swanson v. Hayden: Neighborhood Informer*, Greater Detroit Neighbors Association—Unit No. 2 (December 1949), 2, UAW-CAP, Box 4, Folder 4–19. The editor of the *Informer*, it should be mentioned, was a James Sugrue, a first cousin once removed of the author. For derogatory references to Jews, see "Demonstrations Protesting Negro Occupancy of Homes, September 1, 1945–September 1, 1946: Memorandum J," 31, CCR, Part I, Series 1, Box 3; and "Activities of the East Outer Drive Improvement Association," February 8, 1947, ibid., Part III, Box 25, Folder 25–49. For a reference to "niggers, chinamen, and russians," see William K. Anderson to Herbert Schultz, October 17, 1958, SLAA. For housing incidents involving an Indian family, a Chinese family, and a Filipino family moving into white neighborhoods, see Chronological Index of Cases, 1951 (51–31) and (51–58), CCR, Part I, Series 1, Box 13; Detroit Police Department Special Investigation Bureau, Summary of Racial Activities, April 30, 1956–May 17, 1956, DUL, Box 38, Folder A2–26. On the ethnic heterogeneity of Detroit neighborhoods, see Olivier Zunz, *The Changing Face of Inequality: Urbanization, Industrial Development and immigrants in Detroit, 1880–1920* (Chicago, 1982), 340–51. In his examination of arrest records for whites arrested in anti-public

housing riots in Chicago, Arnold Hirsch also found great diversity in ethnic affiliations. See Hirsch, *Making the Second Ghetto: Race and Housing in Chicago, 1940–1960* (New York: Cambridge University Press, 1983), 81–84.

4. See Dominic J. Capeci, Jr. and Martha Wilkerson, *Layered Violence: The Detroit Rioters of 1943* (Jackson: The University Press of Mississippi, 1991); on Briggs, see John M. Hartigan, Jr., "Cultural Constructions of Whiteness: Racial and Class Formations in Detroit" (Ph.D. diss., University of California, Santa Cruz, 1995); Arthur Kornhauser, *Detroit as the People See It; A Survey of Attitudes in an Industrial City* (Detroit: Wayne University Press, 1952), 104. On Southern whites and their organizational affiliations, see Cleo Y. Boyd, "Detroit's Southern Whites and the Store-Front Churches," Department of Research and Church Planning, Detroit Council of Churches, 1958, in DUL, Box 44, Folder A8–25; on their voting patterns, see Handwritten Vote Counts [1949], UAW-PAC, Box 63, Folder 63–2; "Degree of Voting in Detroit Primary," September 11, 1951, and "Indexes of Group Voting for Selected Councilmanic Candidates," September 11, 1951, ibid., Box 62, Folder 62–25. In 1956, Mrs. Cledah Sundwall, a Northwest Side resident and possibly a southern white migrant, called for the creation of a White Citizens Council in Detroit, calling it a "modern version of the old-time town meeting called to meet any crisis by expressing the will of the people. The primary aim of the council is to combat the NAACP and to preserve the upkeep of neighborhoods" (*Brightmoor Journal,* May 3, 1956). There is no evidence that the organization attracted any significant number of adherents in the city, perhaps because of the strength and ubiquity of improvement associations.

5. The South Lakewood Area Association had its humble origins in a protest against a proposal to expand off-street parking for stores on Jefferson Avenue: *East Side Shopper,* April 28, 1955. The SLAA papers offer evidence of the role of the homeowners' association in matters of zoning, traffic control, and parking. The South Lakewood area, on the Southeast Side of the city, was far enough removed from Detroit's black population that race seldom became an issue for the organization. The neighborhood association was concerned about what appeared to be a boarding house at 670 Lakewood, and noted "One colored" among the many boys who played in front of the house. ("Report—July 14, 1958," SLAA, Folder: 1957–1960). For a group concerned with city services, zoning enforcement, and streets and traffic, as well as racial transition, see Interoffice Correspondence, Subject: Meeting of the Burns Civic Association, April 1, 1963, CCR, Part III, Box 25, Folder 25–40. For concern about recreation, garbage pickup, and city services, see "Report on Puritan Park Civic Association Meeting," September 20, 1956, ibid., Folder 25–101. On the role of neighborhood associations in zoning enforcement, planning, and cleanups, see Detroit City Plan Commission, *Planner,* January 1945, 3–4, in the author's possession. Robert J. Mowitz and Deil S. Wright, *Profile of a Metropolis: A Case Book* (Detroit: Wayne State University Press, 1962), 426–29, describe the role of Northwest Side civic associations in battling the construction of the Lodge Freeway extension. For an excellent discussion of civic associations in Queens, New York (which, because of its distance from black populations, did not organize around racial issues in the 1950s), see Sylvie Murray, "Suburban Citizens: Domesticity and Community Politics in Queens, New York, 1945–1960" (Ph.D. diss., Yale University, 1944), esp. 78–131, 181–261.

For an example of the combination of civic uplift and racist rhetoric, see *Action!* vol. 1 (February 15, 1948). The Northwest Home Owners, Inc., met to discuss threats to the community including a city incinerator and "possible Negro residence in the neighborhood." Richard J. Peck, Community Services Department, Detroit Urban League, "Summary of Known Improvement Association Activities in Past Two Years 1955–1957," 6, VF, Pre-1960, Box 2, Folder: Community Organization 1950s. For a discussion of the role that improvement associations played in upholding restrictive covenants, see Herman H. Lond and Charles S. Johnson, *People vs. Property: Race Restrictive Covenants in Housing* (Nashville, Tenn.: Fisk University Press, 1947), 39–55; for examples of similar associations in Chicago, Baltimore, Washington, D.C., Los Angeles, Houston, Miami, and San Francisco, see Abrams, *Forbidden Neighbors,* 181–90.

6. U.S. Department of Commerce, Bureau of the Census, *U.S. Census of Population and Housing, 1940, Census Tracts Statistics for Detroit, Michigan and Adjacent Area* (Washington, D.C.: U.S. Government Printing Office, 1942), Table 4; U.S. Department of Commerce, Bureau of the Census, *U.S. Census of Population and Housing: 1960, Census Tracts, Detroit, Michigan Standard Metropolitan Statistical Area* (Washington, D.C.: U.S. Government Printing Office, 1962), Table H-1.

7. Kornhauser, *Detroit as the People See It,* 68–69, 75, 77–82. Kornhauser's team interviewed 593 adult men and women randomly selected from all sections of the city. For an elaborate discussion of the survey's methodology, see ibid., Appendix B, pp. 189–96.

8. Kenneth T. Jackson, *Crabgrass Frontier: The Suburbanization of the United States* (New York: Oxford University Press, 1985), 49–52, 117–18; on the desire of immigrants to own their own homes, see John Bodnar, Roger Simon, and Michael P. Weber, *Lives of Their Own: Blacks, Italians, and Poles in Pittsburgh, 1900–1960* (Urbana: University of Illinois Press, 1982), 153–83; a succinct synthesis of literature on homeownership and mobility can be found in Eric H. Monkkonen, *America Becomes Urban: The Development of U.S. Cities and Towns* (Berkeley: University of California Press, 1989), 182–205. On high rates of homeownership among ethnic Detroiters, see Zunz, *The Changing Face of Inequality,* 152–61.

9. The National Council of Churches conducted a census of church membership by county in the mid-1950s. It estimated that 65.9 percent of residents of Wayne County, Michigan, were Roman Catholics. Because so few African Americans were Catholic, the percentage of Wayne County whites who were Catholic was probably significantly higher. See National Council of Churches, Bureau of Research and Survey, "Churches and Church Membership in the United States: An Enumeration and Analysis by Counties, States, and Regions," series C, no. 17 (1957), Table 46; Paul Wrobel, "Becoming a Polish-American: A Personal Point of View," in *Immigrants and Migrants: The Detroit Ethnic Experience: Ethnic Studies Reader,* ed. David W. Hartman (Detroit: New University Thought Publishing Company, 1974), 187. "Survey of Racial and Religious Conflict Forces," Interviews with Father Constantine Djuik, Bishop Stephen Wozniak, Father Edward Hickey, in CRC, Box 70; Dominic J. Capeci, Jr., *Race Relations in Wartime Detroit: The Sojourner Truth Housing Controversy of 1942* (Philadelphia: Temple University Press, 1984), 77–78, 89–90; Memorandum Dictated by Major Jack Tierney, October 17, 1945, in NAACP, Group II, Box A505, Folder: Racial Tension, Detroit, Mich., 1944–46; Edward J. Hickey to Edward Connor, May 9, 1944, CHPC, Box 41. In April 1948, the pastors of Saint Louis the King Catholic Church and Saint Bartholomew's Catholic Church reportedly urged parishioners to attend City Council meetings to oppose the construction of houses for blacks on a Northeast Side site: See CCR, Part I, Series I, Box 4, Folder 48–80. Quote on Polish parishes from Mayor's Interracial Committee Minutes, February 19, 1947, 3, ibid., Box 10. On Saints Andrew and Benedict Parish, see Mayor's Interracial Committee Minutes, April 17, 1950, ibid., Part III, Box 25, Folder 25–114. John T. McGreevy, "American Catholics and the African-American Migration, 1919–1970" (Ph.D. diss., Stanford University, 1992) 56–58, 119–20, 159–160; also on the importance of Catholicism in Detroit, see Gerhard Lenski, *The Religious Factor: A Sociological Study of Religion's Impact on Politics, Economics, and Family Life* (Garden City, N.Y.: Doubleday, 1961).

10. See Report on Meeting, Temple Baptist Church, October 25, 1956, and States-Lawn Civic Association, February 14, 1957, DUL, Box 43, Folder A7–13; Metropolitan Tabernacle

pamphlets, MDCC, Part I, Box 9, Folder: Civil Rights Activity Feedback and Box 10, Folder: Housing—Homeowner's Ordinance, Friendly; Jim Wallis, "By Accident of Birth: Growing Up White in Detroit," *Sojourners,* June–July 1983, 12–16.

11. Poster, "OPEN MEETING ... for Owners and Tenants," n.d. [c. 1945], CRC, Box 66, Folder: Property Owners Association; *Action!,* vol. 1 (Feb. 15, 1948), 2; Guyton Home Owners' Association and Connor-East Home Owners Association, leaflets, in SLAA, Folder: 1957–1960; Peck, "Summary of Known Improvement Association Activity," *Southwest Detroiter,* May 11, 1950, copy in Mayor's Papers (1950), Box 5, Folder: Housing Commission.

12. Kornhauser, *Detroit as the People See It,* 62; "Integration Statement," anonymous letter, n.d., in MDCC, Part I, Box 9. For another example of economically vulnerable workers' insecurity about homeownership, see Bill Collett, "Open Letter to Henry Ford II," *Ford Facts,* September 15, 1951.

13. Kornhauser, *Detroit as the People See It,* 95; quotations from Kornhauser's analysis of survey response patterns.

14. The term "colored problem" was used most frequently by whites to describe black movement into their neighborhoods. See, for example, Property Owners Association flyer, 1945, in CRC, Box 66; *Action!,* vol. 1 (Feb. 15, 1948).

15. Kornhauser, *Detroit as the People See It,* 85, 185.

16. Ibid., 100. It should be recalled that there was already virtually complete residential segregation in Detroit when Kornhauser conducted his survey. In 1950, the index of dissimilarity between blacks and whites (a measure of segregation calculated on the percentage of whites who would have to move to achieve complete racial integration) was 88.8; the index of dissimilarity in 1940 had been 89.9. Respondents to the survey then supported even stricter racial segregation than already existed. Figures from Karl E. Taeuber and Alma F. Taeuber, *Negroes in Cities: Residential Segregation and Neighborhood Change* (Chicago: Aldine, 1965), 39.

17. Kornhauser, *Detroit as the People See It,* 87, 90, 91. For findings on the racial conservatism of Detroit Catholics that confirm Kornhauser's data, see Lenski, *The Religious Factor,* 65. On the importance of Catholic parish boundaries in preserving the racial homogeneity of a neighborhood and in shaping Catholic attitudes toward blacks, see McCreevy, "American Catholics and African-American Migration" and Gerald Gamm, "Neighborhood Roots: Institutions and Neighborhood Change in Boston 1870–1994," (Ph.D. diss., Harvard University, 1994).

18. Detroit Housing Commission and Work Projects Administration, *Real Property Survey of Detroit. Michigan,* vol. 3 (Detroit: Bureau of Government Research, 1939), maps and data for Area K. As Northwest Side resident Alan MacNichol complained: "I have watched the area within the Boulevard deteriorate into slums as the character of the neighborhood changed, restrictions were broken, and multiple flats came in," *Brightmoon Journal,* December 22, 1949.

19. Outer-Van Dyke Home Owners' Association, "Dear Neighbor," [1948], CCR, Part III, Box 25, Folder 25–94; Interview with Six Mile Road–Riopelle area neighbors in Incident Report, August 30, 1954, DUL, Box 43, Folder A7–13; William Price, "Factors Which Militate against the Stabilization of Neighborhoods," July 3, 1956, ibid., Box 38, Folder A2–17; woman quoted in Lenski, *The Religious Factor,* 66.

20. Longview Home Owners Association poster, n.d., MDCC, Part I, Box 10, Folder: Housing—Homeowners Ordinance—Friendly. Ellipsis in original.

21. For statistics on crime in Detroit, see Robert Conot, *American Odyssey* (New York: William Morrow, 1974), Statistical Appendix.

22. Alex Csanyi and family to Mayor Jeffries, February 20, 1945, Mayor's Papers (1945), Box 3, Folder: Housing Commission 1945. Ellipsis in original. *Home Gazette.* October 25,

1945: copy in CAH; Gloster Current, "The Detroit Elections: A Problem in Reconversion," *Crisis* 52 (November 1945): 319–21; "Program: General Meeting Courville District Improvement Association," April 2, 1948, CCR, Part III, Box 26, Folder 26–4; *Action!* vol. 1 (February 15, 1948); "Report on Formation of Area B Improvement Association," DUL, Box 38, Folder A2–22; Detroit Urban League Housing Committee, Quarterly Report, April–June 1966, ibid., Box 53, Folder A17–1. For other examples of fears of racial mixing, see John Bublevsky, Tom Gates, Lola Gibson, Victor Harbay, and Sally Stretch, "A Spatial Study of Racial Tension or 'The Walls Come Tumbling Down,'" CCR, Part III, Box 13, Folder 13–20; "Report on the Improvement Association Meeting at Vernor School," September 13, 1955, DUL, Box 43, Folder A7–13; Kornhauser, *Detroit as the People See It*, 28, 37, 101–2.

23. The original essays and a complete typescript are in "Compositions—6B Grade—Van Dyke School," CCR, Part I, Series 1, Box 3, Folder: Community Reports— Supplementing. Accompanying the essays cited were drawings and responses to another assignment, intended to foster racial harmony, on "Why Little Brown Ko-Ko Is My Friend," based on a short story about a black child. The name Mary Conk is a pseudonym.

24. All quotes and details regarding the Easby Wilson case are drawn from the following sources (unless otherwise noted): "Summary of Facts of Case Involving Mr. Easby Wilson," UAW Press Release, July 25, 1955; and "Interview: Housing Discrimination" (Mrs. Easby Wilson and Harry Ross), all in UAW-FP, Box 14, Folder 14–8; *Pittsburgh Courier,* June 18, 1955; *Michigan Chronicle,* July 30, 1955; report on racial incident, in DUL, Box 43, Folder A7–13.

25. See, for example, George Schermer, "Re: Case 52–16, Petition—Courville Improvement Association Members," July 25, 1952, 1, CCR, Part I, Series 1, Box 9, Folder 52–16CP. When a white neighbor on the same section of Riopelle Street had offered his house for sale in the fall of 1953, a crowd of five hundred had gathered on the street to protest. See Incident Report, 18176 Riopelle, October 31, 1953, ibid., Folder 53–38; *Pittsburgh Courier,* October 31, 1953; Incident Report, November 7, 1954, DUL, Box 43, Folder A7–13.

26. U.S. Department of Commerce, Bureau of the Census, *U.S. Census of Population and Housing: 1960, Census Tracts, Detroit, Michigan Standard Metropolitan Statistical Area,* Final Report PHC(1)–40 (Washington: U.S. Government Printing Office, 1962) (hereafter cited as *1960 Census),* data for tract 606.

27. "A lot of firefighting": John G. Feild, oral history, December 28, 1967 (Katherine Shannon, interviewer), 11, Civil Rights Documentation Project, MSRC. The finding guide and interview transcript mistakenly spell Feild as Fields. John Feild, "A Study of Interracial Housing Incidents," January 20, 1949, 4, CCR, Part I, Series 1, Box 6, Folder 49–3, identified five "techniques employed" by improvement associations in the 1940s: warnings, street demonstrations, anonymous threats, picketing, and property damage. I have calculated the number of racial incidents through a comprehensive survey of records in CCR, DNAACP, DUL, and Detroit's African American newspapers, *Michigan Chronicle, Detroit Tribune,* and *Pittsburgh Courier* (Detroit edition). The number of reported incidents ranged from seven in 1953 to sixty-five in 1963. Unfortunately the Commission on Community Relations only kept complete data for a limited number of years.

28. An important discussion of territoriality is Gerald D. Suttles, *The Social Construction of Communities* (Chicago: University of Chicago Press, 1972). Suttles's discussion of defended neighborhoods is rich in its theoretical implications for studies of neighborhood change. But by building on the ecological model of Chicago School sociology, Suttles offers too deterministic a model of "invasion" and "succession," ignoring the political and economic determinants of urban transformation. An important revision that has strongly influenced my own work is Gerald Gamm, "City Walls: Neighborhoods, Suburbs, and the American City" (paper presented to the American Political Science Association, New York, September 1994).

29. *Brightmoor Journal,* October 11, 1945; *Neighborhood informer,* December 1949, 1, 3, copy in UAW- CAP, Box 4, Folder 4–19; Handbill, "Emergency Meeting, March 11, 1950," CCR, Part III, Box 25, Folder 25–107; Ruritan Park Civic Association, "Dear Neighbor," ibid., Folder 25–101.

30. Detroit race relations official Richard Marks used the term "containment" (to describe white resistance to housing integration) in his testimony in the school desegregation case, *Milliken v. Bradley.* See Dimond, *Beyond Busing,* 43–44. For a development of the notion of "domestic containment" (though not applied to race), see Elaine Tyler May, "Cold War, Warm Hearth: Politics and the Family in Postwar America," in *The Rise and Fall of the New Deal Order,* 1930–1980, ed. Steve Fraser and Gary Gerstle (Princeton, N.J.: Princeton University Press, 1988), 153–81.

31. "Demonstrations, 1945–1946," 4.

32. National Association of Community Councils, "To Make a Long Story Short," CCR, Part III, Box 20, Folder 20–37.

33. *Action! The Newsletter of the Courville District Improvement Association,* vol. 1, February 15, 1948, 5–6, CCR, Part I, Series 1, Box 10.: *Michigan Chronicle,* March 6, 1948.

34. *Neighborhood Informer,* December 1949, March 1951, copies in UAW-CAP, Box 4, Folder 4–19; *Brightmoor Journal,* February 10, 1955, March 24, 1955; Richard J. Peck, "Summary of known Improvement Association Activities in Past Two Years, 1955–1957," 1–2, VF—Pre-1960, Box 2, Folder: Community Organization 1950s; "Report on Ruritan Park Civic Association Meeting," 3, September 20, 1956, DUL, Box 43, Folder A7–13; Richard J. Peck, "Report on Formation of Area E Improvement Association," 9, ibid., Box 38, Folder A2–22; "Activities Report, February 1–March 1, 1957, Current Status of Property, Cherrylawn Case," 4, ibid., Folder A2–23.

35. Detroit Police Department, Special Investigation Squad, Memo from Detective Sergeant Leo Mack and Detective Bert Berry to Commanding Officer, Special Investigation Squad, November 7, 1945, CCR, Part I, Series 1, Box 3, Folder: Incidents Housing 1945.

36. *Michigan Chronicle,* November 6, 1948.

37. Memo, n.d. [c. 1955], DUL, Box 43, Folder A7–13.

38. John Feild, "Special Report, Subject: Opposition to Negro Occupancy in Northeast Detroit," April 28, 1950, 3–4, CCR, Part I, Series 1, Box 7, Folder 50–18.

39. Commission on Community Relations, Field Division, Case Reports, January 21, 1963, CCR, Part I, Series 4, Box 4; see also Memo, Classification: Housing, September 27, 1954, DUL, Box 38, Folder A2–13.

40. *Southwest Detroiter,* May 11, 1950, copy in Mayor's Papers (1950), Box 5, Folder: Housing Commission (2); *Michigan Chronicle,* July 16, 1955; Commission on Community Relations, Minutes, June 17, 1957, CCR, Part I, Series 4, Box 2; Commission on Community Relations, Field Division Report, February 20, 1961, ibid., Box 3; McGreevy, "American Catholics and the African American Migration," 122.

41. See "Chronological Summary of Incidents in the Seven Mile-Fenelon Area," attached to John Feild, "A Study of Interracial Housing Incidents," January 20, 1949, CCR, Part I, Series 1, Box 6, Folder 49–3, ALUA.

42. Commission on Community Relations, Minutes, September 21, 1959, ibid., Part I, Series 4, Box 3. Nevada marked the boundary of Saint Rita's parish. See Saint Rita's Parish Boundary File, AAD.

43. *Michigan Chronicle,* December 4, 1948; "Demonstrations, 1945–1946": Memorandum J, 31. John Feild, "Special Report, Subject: Opposition to Negro Occupancy in Northeast Detroit," April 28, 1950, 3–4, CCR, Part I, Series 1, Box 7, Folder 50–18.

44. Thomas H. Kleene, "Report of Incident, Subject: Opposition to Negro Occupancy of Dwelling at 4227 Seventeenth Street (Continued)," ibid., Box 5, Folder 48–124H. On Courville, see Incident Report, November 7, 1954, DUL, Box 43, Folder A7–13. James

Morris, the real estate broker who had originally called the police to the scene on Woodingham Street, was charged with driving with an expired license. The police, who did nothing to disperse the crowd, responded with remarkable efficiency to a neighbor's complaint that Morris's car was obstructing a driveway, the offense that gave occasion to ask Morris for his license. Another black realtist, John Humphrey, testified in the Detroit school desegregation case *Milliken v. Bradley* that he had suffered harassment by the police when he showed houses in predominantly white neighborhoods. See Dimond, *Beyond Busing,* 50–51. CCR Field CCR Field Division, Case Reports, September 18, 1961, in RK, Box 2, Folder 4; on Tuller and Cherrylawn, see CCR Field Division, Case Reports, August 11, 1961, October 23, 1961, ibid. See also *East Side Shopper* clipping, n.d. [September 1952], in CCR, Part I, Series 1, Box 9, Folder 52–30; *Michigan Chronicle,* December 4, 1948; "9423 Meyers," Case Reports for Period August 27–September 23, 1957, CCR, Part I, Series 4, Box 2.

45. John Feild and Joseph Coles, "Report of Incident, Subject: Protest to Negro Occupancy at 3414 and 3420 Harrison Street, August 23, 1948," in CCR, Part I, Series 1, Box 5, Folder 48–124; included in the file are Brock's card and the attached notice; see also "Buyer Beware," *Time* April 16, 1956, 24.

46. Richard J. Peck, "Summary of Known Improvement Association Activity in Past Two Years 1955–1957," 3, in VF—Pre-1960, Box 2, Folder: Community Organization 1950s; see also Report of Second Meeting of Ruritan Park Civic Association, Fitzgerald School, November 29, 1956, DUL, Box 43, Folder A7–13; Commission on Community Relations Minutes, February 18, 1957, CCR, Part I, Series 4, Box 2.

47. Successful purchases include Yorkshire and Evanston (1948), ibid., Series 1, Box 5, Folder 48–120; 7745 Chalfonte and Tracy and Chippewa in 1955, DUL, Box 38, File A2–15; 15550 Robson, *Detroit Free Press,* May 7, 1956; Richard J. Peck, "Summary of Known Improvement Association Activities in the Past Two Years, 1955–1957," pp. 1, 4, in VF—Pre-1960, Box 2, Folder: Community Organization 1950s. Attempts include "Report of Incident: Intimidation of Henry Lyons (Negro) by a White Group at 18680 Caldwell," September 22, 1947, CCR, Part I, Series 1, Box 4, Folder 47–59H; "Protest of Negro Occupancy at 18087 Shields," 1949, ibid., Box 6, Folder 49–33; Detroit Police Department Interoffice Memorandum, Subject: Racial Disturbance at 2966 Greyfriars, August 31, 1953, DSL, Box 20, Folder: Racial—Gang Activities and Complaints (2).

48. *1950 Census,* tract 603; *1960 Census,* tracts 603A, 603B.

49. Ibid., data for tracts 604, 605, 606.

50. *Michigan Chronicle,* September 10, 1955; Incident Report, DUL, Box 38, Folder A2–15. *1960 Census,* tract 261; tracts to the east, 170, 171, 172, 173.

51. *1950 Census* and *1960 Census,* tracts 9, 10, 35, 36, 37, 38, 39, 41.

52. *Detroit News.* October 4, 1961.

53. Hirsch, *Making the Second Ghetto.* 40–99.

54. Kenneth T. Jackson, *Crabgrass Frontier: The Suburbanization of the United States* (New York, 1985), esp. 190–218; Patricia Burgess Stach, "Deed Restrictions and Subdivision Development in Columbus Ohio, 1900–1970," *Journal of Urban History* 15 (November 1988): 42–68.

55. Albert Mayer and Thomas F. Hoult, *Race and Residence in Detroit* (Detroit: Urban Research Laboratory, Institute for Urban Studies, Wayne State University, 1962), 2.

56. A superb overview of patterns of racial segregation in Detroit is Donald R. Deskins, Jr., *Residential Mobility of Negroes in Detroit, 1837–1965* (Ann Arbor: Department of Geography, University of Michigan, 1972). For a perceptive discussion of similar patterns nationwide, see Douglas S. Massey and Nancy A. Denton, *American Apartheid: Segregation and the Making of the Underclass* (Cambridge: Harvard University Press, 1993).

57. Reverend Charles W. Butler, "Message to the Open Occupancy Conference," in *A City in Racial Crisis: The Case of Detroit Pre- and Post- the 1967 Riot.* ed. Leonard Gordon (n.p.: William C. Brown Publishers, 1971), 33. For an earlier statement of black suspicion of white homeowners, vandals, and the police, see *Michigan Chronicle,* September 24, 1955.

# 12

## *Reuel R. Rogers*

# MINORITY GROUPS AND COALITIONAL POLITICS

The current wave of non-White immigrants to American cities has prompted a range of important empirical and normative questions for political scientists to ponder. One of the most widely considered is how these newcomers will alter coalition dynamics in demographically diverse cities such as New York and Los Angeles, where alliances are a do-or-die fact of political life. Some researchers have speculated that the non-White racial status of the immigrants and their vulnerability to discrimination will lead them to forge coalitions with native-born minorities, specifically African-Americans (Jennings 1997; Marable 1994; Henry and Munoz 1991). Combating racial discrimination has long been a central political preoccupation for American-born Blacks. Scholars who subscribe to the "minority group" view believe that it will also be a chief concern for the new, non-White immigrants. Their conclusion is that this shared interest will become a powerful basis for interminority alliances, unifying African-Americans and their foreign-born counterparts. In short, this perspective anticipates a grand rainbow coalition among native-born Blacks and recent non-White immigrants from Latin America, Asia, and the Caribbean.[1]

But in cities with significant numbers of African-Americans and non-White newcomers, race-based alliances among these groups generally have proven to be an elusive political goal. Stable coalitions between native-born Blacks and their foreign-born counterparts have not been much in evidence in cities around the country. In New York, for instance, political figures as varied as Al Sharpton and Fernando Ferrer have tried to foster an alliance between African-Americans and Latinos with only the most limited results (Falcon 1988; Mollenkopf 2003). At the other end of the Atlantic seaboard in Miami, African-Americans and Cubans have been at odds for decades (Warren and Moreno 2003). Tensions also have simmered between African-Americans and Asians in Los Angeles (Sonenshein 2003b). In short, political relations between Blacks and recent non-White immigrants have been marked more often by conflict than by cooperation. Although race-based coalitions among native-born Blacks

From Reuel R. Rogers, "Race-Based Coalitions among Minority Groups: Afro-Caribbean Immigrants and Africa-Americans in New York City," *Urban Affairs Review,* Vol. 39 (3), pp. 283–317, copyright © 2004 by Sage Publications, Inc. Reprinted by permission of Sage Publications, Inc.

and foreign-born minority groups are widely expected, it turns out that they are actually quite rare.

The rarity of such alliances has led some researchers to speculate that African-Americans are more likely to find themselves in grim political isolation than in any grand rainbow coalition with non-White immigrants (Mollenkopf 2003). A few observers even dismiss the idea of race-based alliances altogether as a misguided and losing electoral strategy in increasingly diverse, multiracial cities, where immigration has scrambled the old Black-White, biracial political calculus (Sleeper 1993). Whatever their future prospects, race-based coalitions between African-Americans and non-White immigrants have not had much success to date.

Why have such race-based alliances been difficult to foster? A number of studies have noted the political conflicts between Blacks and non-White immigrants, to be sure. But very few have provided detailed analyses of why the racial commonalities they share have not been enough to override differences and produce stable alliances between them. . . .

# The Case Study

This article takes up that question with a case study analysis of political relations between African-Americans and Afro-Caribbean immigrants in New York City.[2] These two groups of Black New Yorkers—one native and the other foreign born—together furnish a highly instructive case for exploring why the race-based alliances anticipated by the minority group view have not come to fruition. By the logic of the minority group perspective, rainbow alliances among non-Whites should be most likely when the racial commonalities between them are strong and the racial divisions separating them from Whites are pronounced and politically salient. The strategy for this analysis, then, was to identify a case that fully meets those conditions to give the minority group hypothesis a favorable test.

African-Americans and Afro-Caribbean immigrants living in New York City do just that. As Blacks, the two groups share the same ascriptive racial category, encounter similar forms of discrimination and disadvantage, and have a number of political and economic interests in common. True enough, they also have a history of occasional intergroup tensions, which could undermine any potential for a race-based political alliance between them. Yet the minority group perspective would maintain that racial commonalities, shared interests, and the potential benefits of a race-based coalition should override the intermittent interethnic conflicts.

The analysis reveals, however, that Afro-Caribbeans and African-Americans in New York—like non-White groups elsewhere—have not had much success at fostering a sturdy race-based coalition. I find that relations between Afro-Caribbean and African-American leaders typically have deteriorated in the face of interest conflicts over descriptive representation. The critical role that interest convergence plays in coalition building has been well established by scholars (Sonenshein 2003a). When interests are at odds, alliances crumble, or fail to develop for that matter. But rather than leaving the analysis at that conventional wisdom, the article explores why the racial commonalities the two groups share have not compelled them to settle these differences, as the minority group perspective would predict. It would be simplistic not to expect divisions of some kind among non-White groups. The challenge of any coalition is to overcome the inevitable intergroup differences and emphasize commonalities and compromises. Scholars who subscribe to the minority group view believe that race provides much of the incentive to do so.

I offer evidence from a series of interviews with Afro-Caribbean political leaders, however, that race is not always the unifying category that minority group scholars expect it to be. My analysis of the interview data shows that race, despite its potential as a rallying point, has serious limits as a linchpin for coalitions among non-Whites. In fact, it actually may heighten divisions among racial minority groups by emphasizing some interests over others. The analysis specifies and traces the conditions under which such differences tend to manifest, even in the face of strong racial affinities such as the ones shared by Afro-Caribbean and African-American New Yorkers.

I then turn from the internal dynamics between these two groups to consider whether any external factors may also help to explain why they have been unable to capitalize on their commonalities to forge a stable alliance. I argue that two key New York City political institutions—its parties and elections—have tended to undermine the intraracial commonalities between these two constituencies; these institutions, in fact, often have exacerbated the interethnic conflicts over descriptive representation between them. I also speculate that the lack of an institutional vehicle to bring African-American and Afro-Caribbean elites together to emphasize shared racial interests, address disagreements, and find compromises has also made it difficult for them to sustain a coalition. In sum, the article draws two major conclusions from the case study. First, race has serious limits as a site for coalition building among non-White groups. Second, whatever potential it does hold may be undermined by a city's political institutions. More generally, the article suggests that the literature on coalition building among non-White minorities in cities should be more attentive to how the complexities of race play out in intergroup relations and how institutions shape these dynamics.

## The Minority Group Theoretical Perspective

With so few cases of successful race-based alliances between non-White immigrants and African-Americans in the literature, the question is why they are expected to develop at all. Why would scholars who advance the minority group perspective predict such a coalition in light of such limited empirical evidence? First, their expectations rest on the bedrock of dominant historical patterns in American politics. Race has been a long-standing and stubborn dividing line in local, state, and national politics in the United States. "Indeed, throughout American politics, the racial barrier redefined opinions, attitudes, and alignments"

(Sonenshein 2003b, 334). In urban politics, race has been a key axis for the ideological divisions and interest conflicts that dominate campaigns, make and break political alliances, and shape voting preferences. For much of that history, Blacks and Whites have been on opposite sides of the dividing line. But even when groups of Blacks and Whites have managed to forge alliances, racial issues often have been the touchstone for interest and ideological convergence between the two (Browning et al. 2003).

Although some observers believe that the new non-White immigrants will blur and diminish the significance of the racial divide in urban politics, minority group scholars predict that it will hold. Only instead of pitting Whites against Blacks, it will divide Whites and non-Whites. Even with limited empirical evidence to date of race-based coalitions between Blacks and the new immigrants, minority group scholars infer from the long history of racial division in this country that such alliances are still likely to develop. They reason that as non-White newcomers meet racial barriers such as the ones African-Americans have encountered, the probability of their making political common cause with their native-born Black counterparts will increase.

Beyond the dominant patterns of racial division in this country, minority group scholars also take their analytic cues from theories of African-American politics. More specifically, the minority group view draws much of its inspiration from the literature on "linked racial fate" in African-American politics (Dawson 1994a; Tate 1993). Scholars have found that African-Americans remain a unified voting bloc in many cities, despite growing class divisions within the population (Stone and Pieranunzi 1997; Reed 1988). Dawson and others contend that the persistence of the racial divide and anti-Black discrimination in American life are what keep middle- and low-income African-Americans in relatively close political step. African-Americans, the argument goes, share a "linked fate" insofar as they all inevitably confront racial disadvantages. Race is, in short, a powerful political common denominator among African-Americans, trumping the divisions between the middle class and the poor. It is essentially the linchpin unifying middle- and low-income Blacks in an intraracial coalition. Similarly, minority group scholars predict that race will override the differences between African-Americans and the new immigrants and encourage them to forge political alliances.

# The Prima Facie Case for an Afro-Caribbean and African-American Alliance

There are good reasons to expect this prediction to hold for non-White groups in New York City, particularly African-Americans and Afro-Caribbean immigrants. First, racial division and inequality have long been salient features of life in the city. Immigration has increased New York's demographic diversity in recent decades, to be sure: Foreign-born minority groups from Latin America, Asia, and the Caribbean have proliferated, while the numbers of native-born Whites and Blacks have declined. But even in the face of these new patterns of population diversity, familiar racial divisions remain. The city's political and economic sectors are marked by a pronounced racial divide, with well-off Whites often on one side and relatively disadvantaged non-White minorities on the other.

## New York's Racial Divisions

New York's racial minorities have made significant advances in the past few decades, to be sure. Blacks, Latinos, and Asians have gone from having virtually no presence on the city council in the 1970s to a level of representation now almost proportionate to their numbers in the population. Racial minorities likewise have elected their own representatives to the state legislature and Congress, as well as to three of the city's five boroughs presidencies (Mollenkopf 2003). There are also signs of minority progress in the economy. Among the more notable trends from the past decade are the increases in Black incomes, Asian educational progress, and Latino business growth (Lewis Mumford Center for Comparative Urban and Regional Research 2002).

But the picture is not altogether sanguine. Even with these advances by racial minorities, Whites continue to enjoy a disproportionate share of the power, influence, and rewards in both the economic and political spheres of New York life. Table 4.1 indicates that significant disparities remain between the city's White and minority populations on key indicators of economic well-being. White New Yorkers outpace their minority counterparts by a substantial margin in median income. One recent study also uncovered a wide racial gap in neighborhood quality among New York residents (Lewis Mumford Center for Comparative Urban and Regional Research 2002). Whites tend to live in areas of the city with higher incomes, more homeowners, greater numbers of degree holders, and lower poverty rates than their minority counterparts.

Similarly, although New York's minorities have enjoyed considerable political gains in the past two decades, they nonetheless have much less substantive policy influence than Whites do. That is, they have less access to the political levers that actually control policy outcomes. Mollenkopf (2003) noted,

> With the exception of Congressman Charles Rangel . . . none of the city's minority legislators . . . wields great influence within their legislative bodies. . . . The city's minority legislators can and do extract rewards from the White leaders of their bodies, but they do not exert a strong and independent influence on the overall allocation of public benefits. (pp. 121–22)

**Table 4.1   Median Income by Groups in New York City**

| Year | All Groups | Non-Hispanic Blacks | Non-Hispanic Whites | Hispanics | Asians |
|------|-----------|---------------------|---------------------|-----------|--------|
| 2000 | 38,293 | 50,920 | 35,629 | 27,881 | 41,338 |
| 1990 | 38,706 | 47,325 | 31,955 | 20,402 | 41,350 |

*Source:* Data are from Lewis Mumford Center for Comparative Urban and Regional Research (2002).
*Note:* Median income for both years adjusted for 2000 dollars.

At the mayoral level, minorities largely have been at the margins or out-side of the electoral and governing coalitions assembled by New York's chief executive. Several of the elections for the top office have been racially divisive. What is more, the mayoralty has been occupied by a succession of White politi-cians. Aside from the short-lived administration headed by African-American David Dinkins, minorities have not played a leading role in the city's mayoral regimes. Although several have relied on a modicum of minority support, they have been dominated largely by Whites. Blacks, Latinos, and Asians mostly have occupied subordinate positions, if any at all.

## Racial Commonalities between Afro-Caribbeans and African-Americans

Although the divisions separating Whites and non-Whites in New York are pronounced and politically salient, there is no reason to believe that they alone would compel a race-based alliance among the city's minority constituencies. The minority group view holds that such divisions are necessary but not suffi-cient to produce the predicted coalition. According to this perspective, alliances among non-Whites are probable, not only when there is a sharp racial divide in the political system but also when there are strong commonalities among the minority groups. By that logic, minority group scholars perhaps would not be surprised to find that African-Americans have not been able to forge a sus-tained alliance with the city's Latino or Asian constituencies (Falcon 1988; Mol-lenkopf 2003).[3]

After all, there are notable cultural, ideological, economic, and even racial differences between native-born Blacks and these immigrant groups. Many Latinos, for instance, do not identify as non-Whites or racial minorities, unlike African-Americans who largely do. In short, the racial commonalities between African-American New Yorkers and their Asian and Latino counterparts are limited; the differences among these groups arguably match or outweigh the similarities.

For African-Americans and Afro-Caribbean immigrants, however, there is a much stronger argument to be made for racial commonalities. The two groups of Black New Yorkers appear to have considerable mutual interests and incentives for forging a race-based alliance. Consider the prima facie case. First, Afro-Caribbeans and African-Americans obviously share the commonality of Black skin color in a country where discrimination against Blacks has a long history. . . .

The two groups experience higher levels of residential segregation than any other population in New York (Lewis Mumford Center for Comparative Urban and Regional Research 2003). Put another way, both Afro-Caribbeans and African-Americans are confined to overwhelmingly Black sections of the city.[4] The neighborhoods where the two groups live tend to be more economi-cally distressed than majority-White areas. Afro-Caribbeans and African-Americans are exposed to the same neighborhood problems, whether they be failing schools, concentrated poverty, or crime. These two groups thus often have overlapping interests in contests over the distribution of public services and resources to city neighborhoods.

Both Afro-Caribbeans and African-Americans also have had their share of neighborhood-level tensions with Whites. Quite a few of New York's most serious cases of interracial conflict from the past two decades have involved either Afro-Caribbeans or African-Americans and White residents. In the late 1980s and early 1990s, the city was convulsed by a series of violent attacks against Blacks by groups of Whites. All but one of these incidents involved an Afro-Caribbean victim (Waters 1996). The two groups also have had turbulent relations with the city's mostly White police force. There is no need to rehearse individual instances of conflict here. But suffice it to say that there have been complaints about police brutality and misconduct from both the African-American and Afro-Caribbean communities.

Finally, Afro-Caribbean immigrants and African-Americans have similar partisan attachments. The two groups are more heavily Democratic than any other constituency—White or non-White—in the New York City electorate. Although first-generation Afro-Caribbean immigrants do not have the same long-standing, historical ties to the party as their native-born counterparts, they nonetheless have favored the Democratic line almost as much as African-Americans in their voting and registration patterns.

This shared party allegiance does not necessarily mean that Afro-Caribbeans and African-Americans have identical ideological outlooks. Indeed, Afro-Caribbean election districts are consistently several points less Democratic than African-American districts. Although both groups tend to be fairly liberal in their political outlooks, there are shades of difference between them on particular policy questions. Afro-Caribbeans, for instance, are supportive of liberal immigration policies, whereas African-Americans are more ambivalent (Fuchs 1990; Rogers 2000). A few case studies also have suggested that Afro-Caribbeans may be a little less supportive than their native-born counterparts of government solutions to social problems (Rogers 2000; Waters 1999). Still, there is no evidence of deep ideological divisions between these two overwhelmingly Democratic constituencies.

Support for the party has led to gains for African-Americans and Afro-Caribbean immigrants at the elite level. African-Americans have secured leadership positions in the Democratic county organizations. The party also has incorporated a handful of Afro-Caribbean elites in recent years. Even with these gains, both groups have less power within the party than Whites do. In Queens and the Bronx, Whites continue to control a disproportionate share of the leadership positions and influence within the Democratic Party; only in Manhattan, and in Brooklyn to a lesser extent, have African-Americans been able to wield a decisive share of power in the party organization. After many decades of unwavering allegiance to the Democratic Party, then, native-born Blacks still do not match their White counterparts in their level of influence over the organization. Afro-Caribbeans, on the other hand, are marginal players, as the party continues to ignore the vast majority of these immigrants.

All in all, the racial commonalities between African-Americans and Afro-Caribbean immigrants are more than skin deep. The two groups have a number of experiences, interests, and partisan viewpoints in common. They also boast a solid cadre of leaders who regularly interact within New York's Democratic Party. All these factors—common interests, shared ideology, and familiar leadership, coupled with the pronounced racial divide in New York City politics—would appear to pave the way for a race-based alliance between Afro-Caribbean immigrants and African-Americans. This is not to say that there are no potential divisions between the two groups. Yet the minority group view would argue that their commonalities and the strategic appeal of a race-based coalition should override such divisions. This perspective recognizes a clear imperative for these two groups of Blacks to "close racial ranks" and forge a stable political alliance (Kasinitz 1992; Carmichael and Hamilton 1967).

Race-based mobilization represents an alternative route into politics for the thousands of Afro-Caribbean immigrants who have been neglected by the Democratic Party. Outnumbered by African-Americans, these newcomers might find it hard to resist the strategic benefits of combining with their native-born counterparts to build a larger Black constituency and thereby achieve incorporation. Likewise, such mobilization could also serve as a potent source of political leverage for African-Americans seeking to enlarge their share of government resources and influence on the direction of public policy. With their combined numbers, the two groups could comprise a powerful minority bloc of voters with the potential to decide election outcomes.

# The Empirical Case: A Coalition that Never Came

Yet Afro-Caribbean and African-American New Yorkers thus far have been unable to establish a stable coalition. For all their prima facie commonalities, the two groups have been no more successful at fostering a race-based alliance than their non-White counterparts in other cities. There have been instances of political cooperation and common cause between them, to be sure. In 1989, for example, Afro-Caribbean and African-American voters lined up solidly behind Dinkins in his successful first bid for the mayoralty. Together, the two groups were the single largest bloc of voters to support Dinkins in the election (Arian et al. 1991). Since then, these two groups of Black ethnics have also joined together at the voting booth to support high-profile Democratic candidates for state- and citywide office, such as Senator Hillary Clinton and unsuccessful mayoral candidate Mark Green.

Similarly, the episodes of police brutality in Black neighborhoods in the late 1990s galvanized hundreds of Afro-Caribbeans and African-Americans to take to the streets and demand greater police accountability. Both the Dinkins election and the protests against police brutality appealed to the sense of racial solidarity among African-Americans and Afro-Caribbeans. The two instances might well have been viewed as promising precursors to the race-based coalition anticipated by minority group scholars. But these cases of mutual support were episodic and short lived.

## Patterns of Conflict

Relations between Afro-Caribbean immigrants and African-Americans over the past two decades more often have been marked by a stubborn undercurrent of tension. My interviews with Afro-Caribbean elites reveal a pattern of friction in the political relationship between the two groups. The conflicts have not extended to rank-and-file Afro-Caribbean and African-American constituents. Nor have they revolved around anything such as competing economic interests, substantive policy differences, or ideological disagreements. Rather, the conflicts typically have been confined to the elite level and have centered mostly on matters of political turf. More specifically, African-American and Afro-Caribbean leaders have clashed over attempts by the latter group to secure descriptive representation and carve out political influence for a distinct Caribbean constituency. African-American leaders have resisted these efforts, whereas their Afro-Caribbean counterparts have complained about the opposition from their fellow Black leaders.

My interview respondents noted that African-American politicians have long been resistant or lukewarm to the prospect of Afro-Caribbean mobilization. One interviewee (November 22, 1996) conjectured that African-American opposition to Caribbean participation was one impediment to greater electoral representation for the immigrant group. As he explained, Afro-Caribbeans have yet to achieve a level of representation proportionate to their numbers, "partially because there has been opposition from African-American leaders." Caribbean Action Lobby (CAL) member and former state senator Waldaba Stewart (interview, May 2, 1997) recalled that many African-American politicians were either slow or unwilling to acknowledge the emergence of an Afro-Caribbean ethnic constituency in the 1980s.

> Ten, fifteen years ago, African-Americans—many of them—took the position that the only relevant issues were African-American issues, and in many respects ignored the growing Caribbean bloc. . . . In the 1980s, they didn't even want us to run for political office.

Indeed, as Kasinitz (1992) has recounted in his study, African-American politicians consistently opposed or refused to support Afro-Caribbean candidates for elective office in the 1980s.

The pattern continued into the 1990s. Consider former city councilwoman Una Clarke's account of her 1991 bid for a legislative seat. Clarke was seeking to represent a heavily Caribbean district in Brooklyn; her victory made her the first Caribbean-born member of the city council. Her account of the campaign underscores her perception that African-American leaders have often resisted Afro-Caribbean mobilization. The Jamaican-born politician (interview, December 13, 20, 1996) recalled,

> I helped to elect almost every African-American in central Brooklyn, and when my time came to run they were far and few in between that supported me. . . . There

was not a single African-American that considered themselves "progressive" that did not come to me and did not ask for my support, and for whom I gave it. So when my time came, I thought that everybody was gonna rally around me, that there would not even be a campaign. . . . "Look your time has come." . . . Nothing of the sort happened.

In a 1999 interview, the former city councilwoman lamented, "I never saw bias until I ran in 1991. When I entered office the street talk was 'Why do these West Indians feel they have to be in politics?' " (Dao 1999). To be fair, Clarke did have the support of African-American Congressman Major Owens, who perhaps recognized that backing her would carry important symbolic value in his own increasingly Caribbean district. But staunch opposition to Clarke's campaign came from African-American Clarence Norman, Brooklyn's Democratic county leader. Norman ran his own candidate, fellow African-American Carl Andrews, for the council seat and led an ultimately aborted legal challenge to Clarke's victory in the aftermath of the election. Clarke and Norman have managed to build a cordial, if somewhat delicate, relationship since then (*New York Carib News* 1996a).

The former city councilwoman and other elite respondents also noted that African-American leaders generally have been slow to court Afro-Caribbeans as a distinct constituency. When asked whether African-American politicians reach out to Caribbean-American voters, one campaign organizer (interview, November 24, 1996) replied tersely, "Not enough. And when they do, they reach out half-heartedly." Another respondent (interview, July 5, 1997) offered,

> [Clarence] Norman has enormous political clout because he is the head of the Democratic Party in Brooklyn. From time to time, I've heard Caribbean leaders, including Una Clarke, that he would support other people than them. I'm not sure if that's the case. But I would like to see him in more [Caribbean] events. I would like to see him reach out more to the community.

Clarke rated White politicians slightly higher than African-Americans on outreach to the Caribbean population. She (interview, December 13, 20, 1996) elaborated, "I think White politicians [unlike their Black counterparts] feel compelled to do that kind of outreach. Yes. Marty Markowitz is a well-known example. And I can give other examples too."

More recently, some African-American leaders—Dinkins, Owens, Sharpton, and Rangel—have begun to make their own appeals to the immigrant community. Owens and Sharpton have been particularly vocal about incidents of police brutality involving immigrants from the Caribbean, Latin America, and Africa. Their efforts are clearly intended to acknowledge the growing numbers of foreign-born newcomers to the city and perhaps to prevent conservative interests from pursuing divide-and-conquer tactics among New York's minority constituencies. But some of my respondents still characterize these efforts by African-American leaders as begrudging or lukewarm. One (interview, November 22, 1996) recalled Dinkins's early outreach to Caribbean-Americans. "Oh, we had a rough time getting Dinkins out into the Caribbean community. . . . They say that there were some people in Dinkins's camp who were very anti-Caribbean—African-American people." In sum, many Afro-

Caribbean elites remain convinced that some African-American politicians still regard the prospect of Caribbean mobilization with ambivalence or resistance. Key historical episodes in the relations between Afro-Caribbean and African-American political elites tend to support the views of these respondents. One of the most well known instances of conflict between the two groups came during former mayor Ed Koch's 1985 bid for reelection. A group of approximately 150 politically active Afro-Caribbeans established "Caribbeans for Koch" to back the incumbent mayor's campaign. Support for Koch in the Afro-Caribbean immigrant community was hardly widespread or deep. But the group's aim was largely symbolic. That is, to secure greater access to the mayor and City Hall for Afro-Caribbean immigrants—especially since Koch would likely be reelected. Caribbeans for Koch was thus an early attempt by Afro-Caribbean elites to signal the emergence of their immigrant community as a distinctive ethnic constituency with its own aspirations to political power (Kasinitz 1992, 253).

Whatever the motivation, Caribbeans for Koch was met with a torrent of angry criticism from African-American political leaders. Their outrage was fueled by two major concerns. First, anti-Koch sentiment was pervasive in the African-American community. African-American leaders accused the mayor of fomenting anti-Black racism and exacerbating the city's racial problems with his incendiary rhetoric. In their view, then, Caribbeans for Koch showed complete disregard for the mayor's troubling record on race relations; that insensitivity was perhaps all the more incensing to African-American leaders because it came from a group of Black immigrants, who were expected to be equally as outraged by the mayor's record on race as their native-born counterparts.

Second, Caribbeans for Koch was established at the same time that African-American leaders were attempting to "close ranks" and mount an independent political initiative to replace Koch with a Black mayor. The Coalition for a Just New York brought together scores of Black politicians and activists to identify a candidate and support his campaign. The expectation by organizers was that the group would mobilize Blacks and other minority New Yorkers to help ensure electoral victory. The coalition was riven by internal division, though; their African-American candidate ran a poor campaign and lost. Yet many African-Americans strongly criticized Caribbeans for Koch for working at cross-purposes with the coalition, flouting the goals of African-American political leadership, and undermining the larger struggle for Black empowerment. As one of my elite respondents recalled, the African-American leader of the Coalition for a Just New York, Al Vann, publicly reproached Afro-Caribbean leaders for pursuing divisive strategies. "They were not happy with us [Caribbean American leaders]. Al Vann called our attempts to organize on our own tribalism" (interview, November 22, 1996). The supporters of the Coalition for a Just New York essentially saw this attempt at independent Caribbean mobilization as a strain against the tether of racial solidarity.

There have been more recent political conflicts between the two groups involving issues of racial unity and representation. In fact, the tensions have become more palpable as growing numbers of Caribbean politicians run for elective office in the name of a distinct Afro-Caribbean ethnic constituency. As the numbers of Afro-Caribbean New Yorkers have increased steadily over the past two decades, so too has the political viability and likelihood of such ethnically targeted campaigns by Caribbean politicians. These attempts by Afro-Caribbean political entrepreneurs to organize their fellow immigrants into a distinct voting bloc still engender occasional criticism and resistance from some African-American leaders.

A number of Afro-Caribbean candidates joined the fray in the last round of New York City elections by making direct appeals to their coethnics. The most notable instance was the 2000 race for Brooklyn's Eleventh Congressional District seat between nine-term incumbent Owens and former city councilwoman Clarke. Blacks comprise 55% of the district population; more than two-thirds of them trace their roots to the Caribbean. The large numbers of Afro-Caribbeans in the district is a striking example of how immigration has transformed this stretch of central Brooklyn over the past few decades. Despite these demographic shifts, African-American Congressman Owens had held on to his seat since 1982 without a serious electoral challenge. That is, until he faced a fierce test from Clarke in the 2001 Democratic primary. Although Owens won the primary and went on to retain the seat in a lopsided general election victory, the race was one of the most bitter of the campaign season.

Practically none of the rancor between the two candidates was driven by actual issue disagreements. Rather, it was fueled by two very emotionally charged factors. First, there was the underlying tableau of political betrayal. The two were long-time political allies before Clarke announced her candidacy. Owens described himself as a former mentor to the councilwoman (Hicks 2000b). He thus saw her bid to replace him as an act of political betrayal. Clarke, on the other hand, dismissed the talk of betrayal as a distraction from her true motivation for mounting her campaign: that is, to serve the district's constituents. As she put it, "Too much has been made of friendship. It's about leadership and effectiveness. I don't think he's kept up with the needs of the changing community" (Hicks 2000a). Note that Clarke's mention of the "changing community" might be taken as a thinly veiled reference to the increasing numbers of Caribbean immigrants in the district. Her allusion hints at the other factor that fueled the rancor of the contest between these two candidates.

Even more significant than this personal tableau was the pall of interethnic conflict that hung over the race. Clarke made a point of trumpeting her Caribbean roots, appealing directly to her coethnics, and painting her opponent as anti-immigrant. Her goal clearly was to announce the presence of a distinct Caribbean constituency within the majority Black Eleventh District. Even more critically, she sought to emphasize her affinity with these immigrant voters while at the same time raising doubts about the incumbent's sensitivity to their concerns. Owens, in turn, condemned Clarke for couching her campaign in what he described as a divisive ethnic chauvinism (Hicks 2000a). His complaint was echoed by a number of African-American leaders who sent Clarke a letter urging her to abandon her candidacy. The congressman lamented that Clarke's tactics would split Brooklyn's Black community and undermine the larger cause of Black empowerment. His complaints practically echoed those directed against Caribbeans for Koch by African-American leaders more than 15 years earlier.

# Case Study Analysis

The conflicts over descriptive representation between Afro-Caribbean and African-American leaders are striking for how often the question of racial unity is invoked. The fact that racial solidarity has not provided the incentive for the two groups to overcome these differences belies the predictions of the minority group view. The steady recurrence of such conflicts suggests that even racial commonality has its limits as a potential coalition linchpin.

## The Limits of Racial Solidarity

The interviews and historical evidence indicate that African-American politicians have had one prevailing criticism against their Afro-Caribbean counterparts in the conflicts over descriptive representation. They complain that the immigrants' efforts to appeal to a separate Afro-Caribbean constituency are divisive and antithetical to the cause of racial solidarity and greater Black empowerment.[5] This lament typically greets electoral campaigns by Caribbean politicians seeking to rally, mobilize, or acknowledge their coethnics as a distinct constituency. The logic behind this line of criticism is straightforward. Appealing separately to Afro-Caribbean immigrants, the complaint goes, is tantamount to splitting apart Black New Yorkers, which in turn undermines Black political power. African-American political leaders have grown increasingly concerned about these potential divisions over the past decade, as the numbers of non-White immigrants in the city have expanded. Their worry is that conservative political interests will look to exploit or even sow divisions between African-Americans and these new immigrant constituencies, thereby dousing any potential for a liberal rainbow coalition led by Blacks. It is the classic divide-and-conquer strategy. Divisions between native- and Caribbean-born Black New Yorkers, they contend, might be put to those very political designs. In short, some African-Americans argue that the mobilization of Afro-Caribbeans as a distinct constituency is ultimately a threat to Black racial solidarity and empowerment.

Afro-Caribbeans, on the other hand, insist that the opposition from African-American leaders is unfair and that appeals to racial unity are beside the point. More precisely, Afro-Caribbean politicians note that the immigrant community is large enough to warrant its own representatives and has distinctive concerns that cannot be taken for granted or glossed over with appeals to Black racial solidarity. My elite respondents were emphatic on this point. One (interview, December 14, 1996) offered,

> I think because we [Caribbean-Americans] have some separate interests, we have a responsibility to be a distinct bloc, be it around immigration and immigration reform, be it around trade with the Caribbean. I think that we can play a pivotal role. . . . We have that obligation. And I think it's a mistake to use skin color to be the only criterion. To use skin color as the only criterion stifles both African-Americans and Caribbean-Americans.

Another respondent gave a more concise reply to the same question. He (interview, November 23, 1996) explained, "Caribbean-Americans are a distinct bloc. Of course, we share many of the same concerns of African-Americans. But we have our own needs and concerns that you just can't dismiss or take it for granted that they [African-Americans] will understand." A community activist answered the charge that Afro-Caribbean mobilization promotes divisiveness within New York's Black population this way.

> Our comment is that you have different Caucasian or White groups, you have the Irish, the Italian, the this and that. What's wrong with us? Why can't we have that too? Just because we're originally, say from Africa, does that mean we have to think and act the same way? Don't we [Caribbean-Americans] have our own needs and issues? (interview, May 2, 1997)

Furthermore, many resent what they perceive to be African-American leaders' implicit assumption that Afro-Caribbeans will be relegated to junior status in any alliance between the two groups. In a 1996 interview, for example, Clarke bristled when she was asked about African-American county leader Norman's aim to consolidate Black political power in the heavily Caribbean 43rd AD. "There are over 300,000 Caribbean Americans in Central Brooklyn. What consolidation are we talking about here? Nobody will relegate us to second class status" (*New York Carib News* 1996b). It is clear that Clarke's objection is not necessarily to the prospect of a unified Black political bloc; in fact, she and many of the Caribbean-American leaders I interviewed were supportive of the notion of a coalition between the two groups. But her worry is that the political goals and interests of Afro-Caribbean immigrants will be subordinated in any such alliance.

Clarke's concern illuminates an important analytic point about alliances built around the idea of racial solidarity. The former city councilwoman noted that African-American leaders insist on serving as racial agents on behalf of Afro-Caribbean immigrants by appealing to the notion of group unity,[6] but in doing so, they often diminish or ignore the distinctive ethnic interests of their foreign-born counterparts. Appeals to racial group unity or collective racial interests—such as the ones made by Vann, Norman, and Owens more recently—are almost always articulated in an effort to advance very specific agendas, which ultimately favor some interests over others. Vann's Coalition for a Just New York, for instance, invoked the goal of racial group unity to criticize and discourage independent mobilization by Afro-Caribbean politicians. The coalition's expectation was that all Black New Yorkers, native- and foreign-born alike, should fall in line with their hand-picked candidates and issue positions. Their notion of group unity, then, was one in which their agenda took precedence over other interests within New York's Black community, such as Afro-Caribbeans' desire for their own share of political influence.

Of course, racial solidarity in politics does not necessarily prescribe or authorize a particular agenda, set of positions, or slate of candidates. Indeed, calls to racial unity might well be seen as an invitation to discuss and reach negotiated stances on such issues. Yet appeals to racial solidarity often implicitly privilege one set of interests over others without any open debate. Even worse, the resulting bias takes cover beneath the rhetorical gloss of "natural" or "collective" racial interests that benefit the population as a whole. Consequently, interests that ought to be debated or evaluated for how they affect different constituents are instead deemed to be settled and beyond question. The case of African-Americans and Afro-Caribbeans in New York demonstrates that the group that happens to have more influence—whether by virtue of numbers, longer political history, or whatever—has the advantage of framing the agenda in this way. African-American elites in New York thus have often taken the lead in prescribing what is required for a race-based alliance or minority empowerment, even if that agenda is not necessarily conducive to the interests of Afro-Caribbeans or other non-White groups.

Furthermore, the case demonstrates that the notion of racial group unity not only favors specific interests and agendas but also can be used to impose discipline and gatekeeping. Appeals to racial group solidarity are often made in the service of mobilization efforts. But the tensions between African-American and Afro-Caribbean politicians show that racial group unity is a two-edged sword that can also be used to discourage mobilization by particular interests within the Black population, or any minority constituency for that matter. To discipline specific constituencies within the population, dominant elites often stake out certain positions and label them as the ones most in keeping with the aims of racial empowerment and the political preferences of Blacks as a whole.[7] Any interests that appear to deviate from those positions are then conveniently challenged for threatening group unity, the "true" preferences of Blacks, or the cause of empowerment. The criticisms lodged against Caribbeans for Koch by the leaders of the Coalition for a Just New York are an obvious example of this tactic.

Owens employed a similar strategy against Clarke in their 2000 primary battle. The congressman tried to portray the city councilwoman as a supporter of Mayor Rudolph Giuliani, who was notoriously unpopular among Blacks during his tenure in office. He also charged that Clarke had been silent on the issue of police brutality, about which the vast majority of Black New Yorkers were acutely concerned. In contrast, he noted that he had engaged in demonstrations to protest incidents of brutality and had even been arrested (Hicks 2000a). Owens essentially waved his civil rights credentials in support of Blacks, while implying that Clarke had none to show. The strategy served to brand the Caribbean-born candidate as a kind of race traitor, a politician out of step with Black interests and the goal of Black empowerment. Tactics such as these are likely to play a role in the conflicts between Afro-Caribbean and African-American leaders, precisely because questions of racial unity so often come into play.[8]

## Why Interest Conflicts Over Descriptive Representation

The analysis demonstrates why race is not the ultimate unifying category that minority group scholars expect it to be, even for two groups of Blacks. Yet the question that remains is why the interest conflicts between Afro-Caribbean and African-American elites have focused on descriptive representation. African-Americans have achieved higher levels of influence in New York City politics than have Afro-Caribbeans and other non-White groups. As the dominant minority group in the Democratic Party, in fact, African-Americans have been able to control a significant share of the material rewards. Mobilization by Afro-Caribbean newcomers, or any other minority group for that matter, could potentially threaten their hold on these political prizes. Entrenched African-American elites thus have a rational interest in maintaining the status quo and resisting Afro-Caribbean mobilization.

Afro-Caribbeans and African-Americans are concentrated in many of the same election districts. The ascension of an Afro-Caribbean to political office could mean the displacement of an African-American incumbent. Several respondents explained this competitive intergroup dynamic.

> There definitely is competition and conflict between the two groups sometimes, especially in politics. Part of the problem is, if you want to call it, we are fighting for the same political offices in the same election districts. We're fighting for the same piece of the pie. And African-Americans probably think if Caribbean people get elected they will lose out on their share. (interview, November 28, 1996)

The result is often African-American resistance to Caribbean political initiative and organization. As Clarke (interview, December 13, 20, 1996) put it, "The [African-American] attitude is 'don't try passing me. I've been here.' "

Battles over political turf and representation between the two groups thus devolve into zero-sum struggles. The conflicts are not simply over political office but also access to the government jobs and other prizes that come with it. For some African-American politicians, then, the interest in political self-preservation trumps any vision for race-based mobilization and coalition building between them and their Caribbean-born counterparts. Afro-Caribbean elites, on the other hand, worry that their interest in greater descriptive representation and policy influence will be trumped by African-American political prerogatives.

The competition between African-Americans and Afro-Caribbeans is arguably reminiscent of earlier historical conflicts among White ethnic groups. There were, for example, fierce battles over patronage and positions within the Democratic Party between Jewish and Italian New Yorkers. But there is an important distinction between those earlier interethnic conflicts and the current tensions between African-American and Afro-Caribbeans. The earlier competition for patronage and public jobs among Irish, Italian, and Jewish ethnics was diminished, or at least moderated, as one or the other group moved into private-sector employment and up the socioeconomic ladder. Italian politicians, for instance, had less of a stake in holding on to government jobs when their coethnics began to find success in private-sector professions. They were thus gradually inclined to relinquish patronage positions in government to their Jewish rivals.

Today's African-American political elites, however, are much more reluctant to concede public-sector jobs and positions to their Caribbean-born counterparts. Their determination to hold on to these forms of public patronage is not surprising. Discrimination historically has made it difficult for African-Americans to find jobs and move up the career ladder in the private sector.

Government, in contrast, has long furnished them with fair and ample employment opportunities. Indeed, public-sector jobs have helped foster the expansion of a stable African-American middle class in New York and other cities. The incentive to hold on to these public-sector jobs is thus much greater for African-Americans than it was for White ethnics in the past century. To put it more bluntly, the stakes are higher.

African-Americans thus arguably have legitimate reason to worry about Afro-Caribbean political mobilization. Their concern is likely compounded by the widespread perception that Whites often view these foreign-born Blacks more favorably than African-Americans (Waters 1999).[9] Any potential advancement by Afro-Caribbeans essentially raises the specter not only of political displacement but also economic backsliding for African-Americans. By this light, Afro-Caribbeans look less like a racial in-group and potential coalition partner for native-born Blacks and more like a competing out-group that could threaten African-Americans' share of political power and public-sector resources. That threat of competition and displacement calls into question a key assumption of the minority group perspective: that is, that non-White groups are likely to find common cause and grounds for coalition building in their shared racial experiences. For all the galvanizing power that race carries, this has not been the case with African-American and Afro-Caribbean New Yorkers. Clearly, even presumed common racial interests have their limits.

## Electoral Institutions

Another weakness of the minority perspective is a failure to consider how institutional factors might influence the way groups perceive and frame their interests. Racial inequalities and divisions in the political system provide considerable impetus for African-Americans, Afro-Caribbeans, and other non-Whites to forge a race-based alliance, to be sure. But whether groups opt to coalesce and capitalize on common interests—racial or otherwise—or go it alone depends to some degree to the incentive structure of the political system. The prospects hinge on how political institutions frame group perceptions about interests, competition, rewards, and so on. In the case of Afro-Caribbeans, the interviews make it clear that the immigrants are inclined to elect their own coethnics to political office rather than having African-Americans serve as their racial agents. The question is how the immigrants came to value ethnic over racial representation.

It turns out that New York's elective institutions may very well dispose them to do so. The city's electoral structure encourages groups to organize and think of themselves primarily as ethnic cohorts, rather than as racial constituents. Electoral jurisdictions in New York City closely follow the outlines of ethnic neighborhoods. The scores of community board, city council, and state assembly seats in New York are based on districts that often track the boundaries of residential enclaves bearing the unmistakable stamp of particular ethnic groups. It is not too much of an exaggeration, then, to conclude that the basic political jurisdiction in the minds of New York politicians and perhaps its voters is the ethnic neighborhood. It is the fundamental unit of the city's political cartography. New York's "city trenches," to borrow Katznelson's (1981) famous phrase, are its ethnic neighborhoods.

Consider the 40th city council district seat, formerly held by Caribbean-born Una Clarke and now occupied by her daughter. The city created this district in 1991 specifically to accommodate the proliferation of Caribbean immigrant enclaves in central Brooklyn. Most of the pressure to establish the seat came from Afro-Caribbean politicians. The new district essentially gave the ethnic group an opportunity to garner its own share of political representation. As Stewart of CAL (interview, May 2, 1997) put it, "We [Caribbean politicians] noticed that other groups had districts to represent their people, we felt we should have some too." His remark suggests that the decision to push for a heavily Caribbean city council district was not merely the result of constituent pressure or elite initiative. Rather, it was encouraged by politicians' perceptions of the institutional logic of the city's electoral districts. Once institutional arrangements are in place, they tend to influence how elites understand their interests, their ties to constituents, and their relations with other groups. Sure enough, the 40th city council seat has come to be held perpetually and predictably by a Caribbean politician, fulfilling the logic of the district's original design.

More generally, the city's electoral battles are waged from these ethnic neighborhood trenches. The most obvious way for an aspiring politician to build a constituent base in New York is to rally and mobilize voters in ethnic neighborhoods. If a politician can put together a sizable, cohesive bloc of ethnic votes at the neighborhood level, he or she essentially can become a serious player in New York's political game. Politicians are thus often encouraged to make ethnic group appeals. Ethnic politics has long been a staple of political life in American cities, to be sure. The ethnic and immigrant enclaves across New York City are a hard-to-miss source of votes. But the close continuity between the design of the city's electoral institutions and the pattern of its ethnic neighborhoods reinforces this ethnically conscious form of political organization and mobilization. Ethnic appeals are practically dictated by the logic of the city's political jurisdictions.

Some researchers have argued convincingly that this neighborhood-based system of representation serves to regulate and perhaps mute interethnic tensions (Skerry 1993; Mollenkopf 1999). On this view, the system channels interethnic conflicts that might otherwise spill over into the streets and translates them to the bargaining table of the political process where they can be managed or resolved. That may explain why cities like New York and San Antonio, which both boast this kind of neighborhood-based system, have been less susceptible to volatile intergroup clashes than Los Angeles, where no such system exists. Nevertheless, this electoral institutional design simply transfers the potential for interethnic tension from the neighborhood to the elite level, where leaders are often encouraged to position themselves and relate to each other as representatives of particular ethnic groups. The interethnic conflicts thus move from the neighborhood level to the party system, the campaign trail, and the legislature.

It is no wonder, then, that relations between Afro-Caribbean and African-American political elites have been plagued by interethnic tensions over descriptive representation. The potential for interethnic conflict between these two groups of Black leaders is fairly telegraphed in the pattern of Black neighborhood settlement across New York City. Recall that African-Americans and Afro-Caribbean immigrants often live in adjoining neighborhoods or even share the same ones. When these areas are carved up into electoral jurisdictions, they easily become arenas for ethnically tinged, intraBlack bickering over descriptive representation. When a district that was predominantly African-American is somehow redrawn to give growing numbers of Afro-Caribbean immigrants a numerical advantage, the strategic incentive for Caribbean political entrepreneurs to make targeted ethnic appeals is hard to resist.

There are a few who avoid playing the ethnic card in campaigns. State Senator John Sampson is a good example. This second-generation Afro-Caribbean New Yorker has largely refrained from making exclusive appeals to his coethnics.[10] He instead campaigns to Blacks generally and scrupulously avoids the interethnic schisms that have erupted among the city's Black leaders. But most other Afro-Caribbean politicians have followed the ethnic strategy. The price of giving into the temptation is the danger of engendering interethnic conflict with African-American political elites faced with the specter of electoral displacement. The primary battle between Clarke and Owens is just one of the more well-known recent examples. But several cases fit this predicted pattern.

A simple historical comparison helps to demonstrate how the institutional design of New York's electoral districts shapes intergroup dynamics. It is no coincidence that the tensions over descriptive representation between Afro-Caribbean and African-American political elites have emerged only in the past two decades. Prior to 1989, the city council was not composed of the 51 neighborhood-based seats it boasts today. Rather, it consisted of 10 at-large districts, with 2 designated for each of the five boroughs (Macchiarola and Diaz 1993). Council members were elected on a borough-wide basis. Unlike the current neighborhood-based system, the at-large configuration compelled officeholders and candidates to make broad appeals beyond the boundaries of the city's ethnic enclaves.

An Afro-Caribbean politician with aspirations to the city council, for instance, could hardly afford to target only Caribbean voters in select neighborhoods. Minority candidates could win only by making wide cross-ethnic and sometimes cross-racial appeals. Earlier generations of Afro-Caribbean politicians thus refrained from marketing themselves as ethnic representatives of a distinct Caribbean constituency or appealing exclusively to their coethnics. Rather, they attempted to speak for Blacks at large and did not draw a distinction between themselves and their African-American counterparts (Kasinitz 1992; Watkins-Owens 1996). Consequently, there were almost no interethnic tensions over descriptive political representation between the two groups in that earlier era. This is not to say that there were no conflicts at all between Afro-Caribbeans and African-Americans. There were the inevitable cultural clashes and occasional conflicts over jobs when the immigrants first began migrating to New York (Vickerman 1999; Watkins-Owens 1996; Foner 1985; Hellwig 1978; Reid 1939).

Yet the friction between the two groups did not have much of a political dimension.[11] Ethnicity was simply not a major source of division or conflict among Blacks in the electoral sphere. With the shift to neighborhood-based city council seats, however, there is greater electoral incentive for Afro-Caribbean politicians to engage in the kind of ethnically targeted appeals that lead to tensions with African-American leaders. The past two decades have thus seen a marked increase in political conflicts between the two groups. Although this historical shift is not conclusive evidence, it does suggest indirectly that institutional configurations have some casual impact on intergroup racial and ethnic dynamics.

A brief comparison across cities also makes the point. The city of Hartford, like New York, is home to a sizable minority population of American- and Caribbean-born Blacks. Both groups, in fact, comprise roughly similar proportions of the minority population in both cities, although New York fairly dwarfs Hartford in absolute numbers. African-Americans in Hartford, like their counterparts in New York, also have enjoyed greater levels of electoral representation and influence than the city's other minority constituencies. But in the past decade, the other groups have started to make their own serious bids for political power. Afro-Caribbean leaders in Hartford have begun to organize their coethnics to participate in politics, much like their fellow Black immigrants in New York have been doing for the past two to three decades.

Yet these efforts by Hartford's Caribbean-born residents have generated considerably less friction and resistance from African-American leaders there than have the attempts by their counterparts in New York. A number of factors may explain this difference in intergroup dynamics, to be sure. But one important variable may be the design of Hartford's electoral institutions. Unlike New York's neighborhood-based city council districts, Hartford's legislature is composed of at-large seats. By the logic of the at-large electoral design, ethnically targeted campaigning must be balanced by broader appeals to other constituencies, which ultimately may serve to moderate or minimize interethnic conflict. It bears noting that the Hartford comparison is also not conclusive support for the casual impact of electoral institutions on intergroup dynamics, but it is certainly suggestive.

In the New York case, it should be emphasized that the interethnic tensions between these two groups of Black leaders took shape as Afro-Caribbean ethnic enclaves have developed and expanded to proportions large enough to leave an imprint or have an impact on the pattern of neighborhood-based electoral districts in boroughs such as Brooklyn and Queens. Prior to the 1980s, Caribbean settlements in these areas were too small to have much of an influence on the design of the city's system of elective representation or stand alone as a politically viable ethnic constituency. What is more, African-American and Afro-Caribbean political leaders could talk of representing the city's Blacks without drawing any further ethnic distinctions. Representing Blacks essentially meant African-Americans by and large. With the dramatic growth of the

Caribbean immigrant population over the past few decades, however, intra-Black ethnic distinctions have taken on political salience. The potential for intergroup conflict is now reinforced by the city's electoral institutions.

## The Absence of an Institutional Mechanism

Still, a final question remains: Why have the two groups been unable to resolve these interethnic differences over descriptive representation to build a coalition around their intraracial common interests and shared policy concerns? If New York's electoral institutions have encouraged or exacerbated the interethnic conflicts between Afro-Caribbean and African-American political leaders, the absence of certain other kinds of institutions have made those differences difficult to bridge. Sonenshein (2003b) was correct that shared interests, ideological compatibility, personal ties, and strong leadership are all essential for forging sturdy intergroup alliances. But his formulation overlooks one other important building block. Institutions are equally as important as interests, ideology, personal relations, and leadership for cultivating and sustaining coalitions. Viable institutions provide a framework for groups to engage in social learning, that is, articulate shared interests, acknowledge distinct ones, reinforce ideological commitments, solidify personal ties, and identify promising leaders.[12]

Race-based alliances among non-White groups do not simply spring from some essential racial viewpoint or presumptive group interest. Rather, such coalitions require an institutional mechanism for expressing and mobilizing substantive, shared racial interests—a point that proponents of the minority group view sometimes miss or overlook. Blacks in Chicago, for instance, developed a network of community organizations in the early 1980s that proved crucial to the election of the city's first Black mayor in 1983 (Grimshaw 1992). This institutional framework allowed Black Chicagoans to negotiate internal divisions, identify a strong mayoral candidate in Harold Washington, and muster the voter mobilization necessary to win the election. Similarly, institutional networks have been critical to successful intergroup coalition building in cities such as Atlanta (Stone 1989). The absence of such an institutional vehicle for New York's Afro-Caribbean and African-American political leaders largely explains their failure to override interethnic tensions and build an enduring race-based alliance.

The Democratic Party may appear, at first blush, to be a potentially viable institutional site for Afro-Caribbean and African-American elites to organize a race-based movement. By virtue of their combined numbers inside the party, the two groups have the makings of a powerful caucus capable of a reform. The overwhelming attachment of African-American and Afro-Caribbean voters to the Democratic Party also gives these leaders the electoral clout necessary for mounting such a challenge. In fact, a Black reform impulse surfaced in the party's Brooklyn organization in the mid-1970s. But it faded as infighting erupted and many of the erstwhile insurgents made peace with the regular Democratic machine. Since then, there has been no major, viable movement for insurgency by Blacks in Brooklyn or the other borough party organizations.

The failure of African-Americans and Afro-Caribbeans to mount an insurgent movement from within the Democratic Party confirms the long-standing common sense of V.O. Key's (1949) 50-year-old observation about one-party systems. Key argued that one-party systems tend to be breeding grounds for factionalism. Factions, he noted, give rise to personality-driven politics that focus on invidious status or group distinctions and drown out substantive policy issues. Hence, one-party systems, such as New York's Democratic organization, are notoriously unsuitable institutions for launching and sustaining reform movements. It is no wonder then that African-American and Afro-Caribbean leaders have been unable to put together an insurgent coalition from within New York's dominant Democratic party. Their relations within the party show all the symptoms of Key's diagnosis: squabbles over turf between individual politicians and disagreements over descriptive representation that deteriorate into interethnic schisms. Congruent with Key's predictions, tensions between Afro-Caribbean and African-American political leaders in the party tend to obscure the substantive issues in which they may share a common racial interest or mutual understanding.

Despite the dominance of the Democratic Party in New York City politics, there is a modest Republican organization that conceivably could serve as a site for establishing a reformist coalition. Mollenkopf (1992, 89) reminds us that the Republican Party played this role in New York politics for many decades, uniting "discontented elements of the city electorate into potent, if short-lived, fusion movements." But it no longer does so today. The Republican Party has lost much of its organizational muscle and has transformed into a more conservative institution. As Mollenkopf (1997, 105) noted, "The Republican party has forsaken its traditional role as the organizational kernel of reform." Even more significantly, the party has made virtually no effort to court African-American and Afro-Caribbean voters. There is thus little chance that African-Americans and Afro-Caribbeans will mount a race-based movement for reform from either the Republican or Democratic Party.

Parties, however, hardly exhaust the list of potential institutional sites from which Afro-Caribbean and African-American New Yorkers could cultivate and sustain a reformist alliance. In fact, minority group scholars note that insurgent movements for greater racial inclusion typically begin from bases outside the conventional party system. Movements for African-American political empowerment and racial reform, for example, historically have begun in churches, civic groups, and neighborhood-based service organizations. These institutions provide a critical site for African-Americans to delineate their interests, clarify ideology, groom leaders, and strike alliances with other groups (Dawson 1994a).[13] In cities such as Chicago and Atlanta, African-Americans used these sites to forge reformist alliances with liberal Whites (Grimshaw 1992; Kleppner 1985; Stone 1989).

In New York, African-Americans attempted to sustain reform movements from a network of community-based organizations in the 1970s and early 1980s. The short-lived insurgent movement led by Al Vann in the 1970s took root in this network (Green and Wilson 1989). Vann's race-based alliance, the

Coalition for Community Empowerment (CCE), brought together African-American politicians with ties to Brooklyn's Black churches and the community action programs spawned by President Johnson's War on Poverty and Mayor John Lindsay's liberal neighborhood government policies. The alliance included figures such as Congressman Owens and Assemblyman Norman, who traced their political beginnings to this network of community-based institutions. A handful of Afro-Caribbeans were also involved in the coalition, although none in leadership positions. Most of them had ties to community-based institutions, particularly school and community boards.

In the context of this institutional network, alliance members united around a shared vision for greater Black political empowerment, community control, and racial reform. As members were elected to the state and city legislatures, the alliance became a virtual party within Brooklyn's Democratic Party. The movement collapsed in the early 1980s, however, as its institutional base began to decay. The network of community-based agencies that had furnished an organizational framework for the movement was absorbed by the local city government and lost much of its political independence. Many of these agencies fell into disarray in the face of fiscal retrenchment and federal funding cutbacks. The African-American churches that had also supplied leaders for the movement remained an important part of some Brooklyn neighborhoods, but they struggled to attract younger parishioners. Consequently, they were no longer a leading source of leadership for Black politics in Brooklyn. Bereft of its independent institutional base, the CCE began to lose its way. Internal divisions surfaced, former insurgents were absorbed into the regular party organizations, and the push for reform ebbed.

Just as the movement was deteriorating in the 1980s, the CCE came into conflict with Afro-Caribbean elites who were seeking to win seats on the state assembly. Most of these Afro-Caribbean candidates had no ties to the institutional network that had spawned the African-American-led CCE movement. They were largely entrepreneurial lone wolves, such as Trinidadian-born Anthony Agard, or endorsees of immigrant organizations, such as Panamanian-born Stewart of the CAL. In short, they had no institutional ties to the African-American politicians involved in the CCE. The organization fiercely opposed the Afro-Caribbean candidates in their races for the state legislature. Without a shared institutional framework to build trust and dialogue, African-American politicians in the CCE and Afro-Caribbean elites were unable to resolve their differences in the interest of their shared racial goals.

## The Future of Race-Based Coalitions

Not much has changed since then. The absence of an institutional mechanism for uniting and building trust between Afro-Caribbean and African-American elites diminishes the prospects of race-based mobilization. Of course, there have been small pockets of mutual cooperation and attempts at shared institution building in parts of Brooklyn and Queens—in political clubs and elsewhere. Recently, for

example, native and foreign-born Black New Yorkers established a citywide organization to ensure that their numbers in the population are accurately reflected
in the decennial census (John Flateau, personal communication, June 16, 2000). It
is too early, however, to tell if the organization will last, especially since it has yet
to face the difficult challenges posed by the city's electoral politics; reapportion-
ment, for instance, could easily trigger the usual conflicts over descriptive representation. All in all, then, none of these recent organizational efforts have quite
taken firm root; most have been ad hoc and short lived.

One potential institutional network that already has the benefit of
longevity is New York's constellation of public unions. Emerging research on
labor union activity in cities such as New York and Los Angeles over the past
decade suggests that these institutions are beginning to serve a key role in the
political adjustment of new immigrants to the United States (Wong 2000). This
marks a radical break with a long, notorious history of anti-immigrant activity
among American labor unions. Scholars speculate that changing demographic
and economic realities have precipitated this shift. The growing numbers of
non-White immigrants in American manufacturing and service-sector jobs,
coupled with the overall decline in union membership, has compelled labor
leaders to recruit these newcomers (Greenhouse 2000).

What is more, the new generation of labor union leaders are drawn largely
from the ranks of native-born racial minority groups. African-Americans, for
example, are at the helm of several active unions in New York. These native-
born Blacks and their Caribbean-born counterparts, in fact, comprise a significant share of the membership in two of the city's most powerful public
employee unions, Local 1199 of hospital workers and District Council 37 of city
workers. By sharing these institutional vehicles, the two groups can engage in
the kind of social learning and mutual search for shared interests that make
coalition building easier. It may turn out that these unions prove to be the most
promising institutional site for identifying leaders skilled in bridging the intergroup divisions among Afro-Caribbeans, African-Americans, and other racial
minority populations. Still, there is an important caution to bear in mind. Much
like local party machines, unions historically have been prone to internal wars
of ethnic and racial succession (Mink 1986). Whether these union organizations
can navigate those potential pitfalls well enough to become a stable site for a
race-based alliance remains to be seen.

Some observers speculate that the ideological fervor for race-based mobilization has diminished, with the successes of the civil rights movement and
the measurable minority group progress of the past few decades (Sleeper 1993).
Simply put, the claim is that race-based movements are politically passé. Post-
civil rights concerns, the argument goes, do not generate the same sense of urgency and consensus among minorities that fueled the civil rights movement.
The conclusion is that race-based mobilization will be unlikely or difficult to
foster in the current ideological climate. Yet Afro-Caribbean and African-American outrage over issues such as police brutality suggests that there are still
grounds for race-based mobilization.

This study, however, shows that racial commonalities are not enough to generate an alliance of minority groups; indeed, appeals to racial unity actually may privilege some interests over others and thus heighten divisions among non-White groups. What is more, the institutional design of a city's electoral system may exacerbate these differences. To avoid these perverse effects, political leaders looking to foster race-based alliances must turn to neighborhood and community institutions. Without an institutional framework to identify shared issue concerns, acknowledge distinct interests, and generate dialogue, stable coalitions between African-Americans and Afro-Caribbeans or other racial minority newcomers will be difficult to generate.

# REFERENCES

Arian, A., A. Goldberg, J. Mollenkopf, and E. Rogowsky. 1990. *Changing New York City politics.* New York: Routledge.

Browning, R., D. Marshall, and D. Tabb, eds. 2003. *Racial politics in American cities.* 3rd ed, New York: Longman.

Carmichael, S., and C. Hamilton. 1967. *Black power: The politics of liberation in America.* New York: Random House.

Crowder K., and L. Tedrow. 2001. West Indians and the residential landscape of New York. In *Islands in the city: West Indian migration to New York,* edited by Nancy Foner. Berkeley: Univ. of California Press.

Dao, J. 1999. Immigrant diversity slows traditional political climb. *New York Times.* December 28.

Dawson, M. 1994a. *Behind the mule: Race and class in African-American politics.* Princeton, NJ: Princeton Univ. Press.

———. 1994b. A Black counterpublic? Economic earthquakes, racial agenda(s), and Black politics. *Public Culture* 7:195–223.

Falcon, A. 1988. Black and Latino politics in New York City: Race and ethnicity in a changing urban context. In *Latinos and the political system,* edited by F. Chris Garcia. Notre Dame, IN: Note Dame Univ. Press.

Foner, N. 1985. Race and color: Jamaican immigrants in London and New York. *International Migration Review* 19:284–313.

Fuchs, L. 1990. *The American kaleidoscope: Race, ethnicity, and civic culture.* Hanover, NH: Wesleyan Univ. Press.

Green, C., and B. Wilson. 1989. *The struggle for Black empowerment in New York City: Beyond the politics of pigmentation.* New York: Praeger.

Greenhouse, S. 2000. Despite defeat on China bill, labor is on rise. *New York Times,* April 28.

Grimshaw, W. 1992. *Bitter fruit: Black politics and the Chicago machine,* Chicago: Univ. of Chicago Press.

Hellwig, D. 1978. Black meets Black: Afro-American reactions to West Indian immigrants in the 1920s. *South Atlantic Quarterly* 72:205–25.

Henry, C., and C. Munoz Jr. 1991. Ideological and interest linkages in California rainbow politics. In *Racial and ethnic politics in California,* edited by B. Jackson and M. Preston. Berkeley, CA: IGS Press.

Hicks, J. 2000a. Bitter primary contest hits ethnic nerve among Blacks. *New York Times,* August 31.

———. 2000b. Term limits turn old allies into opponents; protege against mentor, backer against incumbent. *New York Times,* March 22.

Holder, C. 1980. The rise of the West Indian politician in New York City. *Afro-Americans in New York Life and History* 4:45–59.

Jackson, J. 2001. *Harlemworld: Doing race and class in contemporary Black America.* Chicago: Univ. of Chicago Press.

Jennings, J. 1997. *Race and politics: New challenges and responses for Black activism.* London: Verso.

Kasinitz, P. 1992. *Caribbean New York: Black immigrants and the politics of race.* Ithaca, NY: Cornell Univ. Press.

Katznelson, I. 1981. *City trenches: Urban politics and the patterning of class in the United States.* New York: Pantheon.

Key, V. O. 1949. *Southern politics in state and nation*. New York: Vintage.

Kim, C. 1999. The racial triangulation of Asian Americans. *Politics and Society* 27(1): 105–38.

———. 2000. *Bitter fruit: The politics of Black-Korean conflict in New York City*. New Haven, CT: Yale Univ. Press.

Kleppner, P. 1985. *Chicago divided: The making of a Black mayor*. Dekalb: Northern Illinois Press.

Lewis Mumford Center for Comparative Urban and Regional Research. 2002. *Separate and unequal: The neighborhood gap for Blacks and Hispanics in metropolitan America*. Albany, NY: Univ. at Albany Press.

Lewis Mumford Center for Comparative Urban and Regional Research. 2003. *Black diversity in metropolitan America*. Albany, NY: Univ. at Albany Press.

Macchiarola, F., and J. Diaz. 1993. Minority political empowerment in New York City: Beyond the Voting Rights Act. *Political Science Quarterly* 108(1): 37–57.

Marable, M. 1994. Building coalitions among communities of color. In *Blacks, Latinos, and Asians in urban America*, edited by J. Jennings. New York: Praeger.

Mink, G. 1986. *Old labor and new immigrants in American political development*. Ithaca. NY: Cornell Univ. Press.

Mollenkopf, J. 1992. *A phoenix in the ashes: The rise and fall of the Koch coalition in New York City*. Princeton, NJ: Princeton Univ. Press.

———. 1997. New York: The great anomaly. In *Racial politics in American cities*, 2nd ed., edited by R. Browning, D. Marshall, and D. Tabb. New York: Longman.

———. 1999. Urban political conflicts and alliances: New York and Los Angeles compared. In *The handbook of international migration: The American experience*, edited by C. Hirschman, P. Kasinitz, and J. DeWind. New York: Russell Sage Foundation.

———. 2003. New York: The great anomaly. In *Racial politics in American cities*, 3rd ed., edited R. P. Browning, D. R. Marshall, and D. H. Tabb, New York: Longman.

*New York Carib News*. 1996a. April 23.

*New York Carib News*. 1996b. October 1.

———. 1988. Black urban regime: Structural origins and constraints. *Comparative Urban and Community Research* 1:138–89.

Reid, I. 1939. *The Negro immigrant: His background characteristics and social adjustments, 1899–1937*. New York: AMS Press.

Rogers, R. 2000. Between race and ethnicity: Afro-Caribbean immigrants, African Americans, and the politics of incorporation, Ph.D. diss., Princeton University.

Skerry, P. 1993. *Mexican Americans: The ambivalent minority*. Cambridge, MA: Harvard Univ. Press.

Sleeper, J. 1993. The end of the rainbow. *New Republic*, November 20–25.

Sonenshein, R. 1993. *Politics in black and white: Race and power in Los Angeles*. Princeton, NJ: Princeton Univ. Press.

———. 2003a. Post-incorporation politics in Los Angeles. In *Racial politics in American cities*, 3rd ed., edited by R. P. Browning, D. R. Marshall, and D. H. Tabb. New York: Longman.

———. 2003b. The prospects for multiracial coalitions: Lessons from America's three largest cities. In *Racial politics in American cities*, 3rd ed., edited by R. P. Browning, D. R. Marshall, and D. H. Tabb. New York: Longman.

Stone, C. 1989. *Regime politics: Governing Atlanta, 1946–1988*. Lawrence: University Press of Kansas.

Stone, C., and C. Pierannunzi. 1997. Atlanta and the limited reach of electoral control. In *Racial politics in American cities*, 2nd ed., edited by R. Browning, D. Marshall, and D. Tabb. New York: Longman.

Tate, K. 1993. *From protest to politics: The new Black voters in American elections*. Cambridge, MA: Harvard Univ. Press.

Vickerman, M. 1999. *Crosscurrents: West Indian immigrants and race*. New York: Oxford Univ. Press.

Warren, C., and D. Moreno. 2003. Power without a program: Hispanic incorporation in Miami. In *Racial politics in American cities*, 3rd ed., edited by R. Browning, D. Marshall, and D. Tabb. New York: Longman.

Waters, M. 1996. Ethnic and racial groups in the USA: Conflict and cooperation. In *Ethnicity and power in the contemporary world*, edited by K. Rupesinghe and V. Tishkov. London: U.N. University.

Waters, M. 1999. *Black identities: West Indian immigrant dreams and American realities*. Cambridge, MA: Harvard Univ. Press.

Watkins-Owens, I. 1996. *Blood relations: Caribbean immigrants and the Harlem community, 1900–1930*. Bloomington: Indiana Univ. Press.

Wong, J. 2000. Institutional context and political mobilization among Mexican and Chinese immigrants. Paper presented at the Immigrant Political Participation in New York City Working Conference, New York, June.

# NOTES

1. I use *non-White* and *minority* interchangeably throughout this article to refer to Blacks, Latinos, and Asians. I distinguish these three groups from Whites, who remain the majority racial population in this country. It should be noted that Latinos, unlike the other groups, are not classified as a distinct racial group by the census. In fact, they may identify as Black, White, or other under the census classification scheme. Most opt for White or other. Yet urban scholars typically define Latinos as a minority group by virtue of their numbers and cultural distinctiveness. This article follows that convention.

2. I use *Afro-Caribbean* to refer to Black immigrants from the Anglophone Caribbean region and to distinguish them from their counterparts from the French- and Spanish-speaking Caribbean. Anglophone Caribbean immigrants are the focus of this study. Although I use the term *Afro-Caribbean,* most of these Black newcomers refer to themselves as *Caribbean American* or *West Indian.* New York's Afro-Caribbean immigrants hail from throughout the Caribbean region, but the largest numbers come from Jamaica, Trinidad, and Guyana.

3. Scholars have puzzled over the absence of a strong minority coalition in New York. The city would seem to be fertile soil for this kind of alliance. The fact that one has yet to take root makes New York a "great anomaly" in the urban politics literature (Mollenkopf 2003).

4. Afro-Caribbean immigrants living in these overwhelmingly Black areas have carved out their own distinctive residential niches, often of marginally higher socioeconomic quality than surrounding African-American neighborhoods (Crowder and Tedrow 2001). Yet this modest economic advantage has not won them access to more integrated neighborhoods, a predicament they share with their middle-class African-American counterparts.

5. The obvious irony of this complaint is that African-Americans view attempts by a group of Black immigrants to achieve political influence as a threat to Black empowerment, rather than a step in that direction.

6. I borrow the term *racial agents* from a conversation with Jack Citrin.

7. The essentialist behavioral notions of racial identity that pervade everyday, commonsense thinking in this country follow the same perverse logic. That is, racial groups are deemed to "behave" or "act" in keeping with an identifiable mold. Blacks, say, are expected to be good dancers, or Asians good students. When group members deviate from the behavioral mold, they are labeled racially inauthentic. For a useful discussion of how this essentialist conflation of racial identity and behavior nonetheless allows for an antiessentialist critique of racial categories, see Jackson (2001).

8. Challenging the racial credentials or commitments of a fellow Black politician in electoral competition is a strategy that surfaces even among African-Americans themselves. The famously acrimonious 2002 race between Newark mayoral incumbent Sharpe James and young upstart Cory Booker is a recent example. Although both men are African-American, questions of racial solidarity and authenticity emerged nonetheless. The James camp took the tactic to bizarre extremes when they began circulating rumors that Booker was actually White and passing as Black to win the support of Newark's mostly Black voters. Such strategies likely will become even more common as the Black population becomes more diverse in cities around the country.

9. For a thoughtful discussion on how White perceptions can engender conflict among subordinate minority groups, see Kim (1999, 2000).

10. Sampson's avoidance of the ethnic strategy may be due to his socialization in the United States. Born to Caribbean parents in New York, his ties to African-Americans run deep. His second-generation experiences and how they influence his political choices may be a precursor to the future of Black politics in New York. He is part of a new, expanding population of second-generation Caribbean New Yorkers. These children of Black immigrants likely will have a significant influence on the city's political future, as they become increasingly involved in the electoral process. It remains to be seen whether they will identify mostly as second-generation Caribbean ethnics or as African-Americans. But whatever the case, they may find coalition building with African-Americans easier than their parents have if they interact regularly with their counterparts in institutional settings.

11. African-American leaders at the time accused White party leaders of playing ethnic favorites by doling out the choicest patronage jobs to Afro-Caribbeans, who tended to be better educated than their native-born counterparts (Watkins-Owens 1996; Hellwig 1978; Holder 1980). But this was more job competition than political conflict, as the party structure was one of the few avenues of social mobility open to Black New Yorkers.

12. Social learning refers to the process by which potential coalition partners acquire knowledge and understanding of each other's interests (Stone 1989).

13. Taken together, these institutions comprise what Dawson (1994b) called the African-American counterpublic.

# 13

## Harvey K. Newman

## RACE AND THE TOURIST BUBBLE

The downtown area of most U.S. cities once functioned as a central business district where a majority of employment and economic activity for the entire city took place. One of the important changes since World War II is the declining significance of these downtowns as cities became sprawling metropolises. Local leaders scrambled to try a variety of strategies that would revitalize the core of their central cities. They constructed expressways to make downtown more accessible to an increasingly suburbanized population, and they used urban renewal funds to clear land of unwanted slum housing and small businesses to make way for new uses. However, finding new economic activities to replace manufacturing, retail, and other types of jobs that were leaving central cities was a challenge for elected public officials and business leaders.

Since the 1960s, the leaders of many cities have adopted tourism as a strategy to attract investment in downtowns and construct space for the enjoyment of visitors. Even cities that lacked natural attractions for tourists could become

Harvey K. Newman, "Race and the Tourist Bubble in Downtown Atlanta," *Urban Affairs Review,* Vol. 37, No. 3, January 2002, pp. 301–321, copyright 2002 by Sage Publications, Inc. Reprinted by permission of Sage Publications, Inc.

what Judd and Fainstein (1999, 266–67) described as "converted cities" by carving out space for tourism. Judd's chapter in this volume suggests that many cities constructed what he calls a "tourist bubble"—that is, a well-defined part of town designed to envelop the traveler and to shield the visitor from the unpleasant aspects of urban living.

In this study, I examine two questions: (1) how the partnership between Atlanta's business and political leaders worked together to create the components of a downtown tourist bubble and (2) how the issue of race affected this tourist space. Stone (1989) described the decision making by Atlanta's coalition of civic leaders as a regime. Although many components of the tourist bubble were created during the tenure of business-oriented white mayors, these officials were willing to sacrifice the residences and small businesses of black Atlantans to convert space for tourism. Another important issue is how this largely segregated white tourist space fared after 1973, when the city elected African-American mayors.

# The Tourist Bubble

The link between downtown regeneration and tourism is an important theme in the research of scholars such as Frieden and Sagalyn (1989), Zukin (1991), Sorkin (1992), and Judd and Fainstein (1999). All these works suggest that city leaders selected tourism as a growth strategy to restore the economic base of downtown areas where decline was evident. If a city could attract tourists, these visitors would bring money to spend in the local economy and create demand for new facilities that would contribute to the improvement of the area. Local residents accepted this process because their leaders promised to produce jobs and taxes as well as improve the image of the city to potential investors (Shaw and Williams 1994).

One city that typifies the "success" of this strategy is Baltimore, where city leaders turned an area of urban decay into the convention and tourism space known as Harborplace. The Harborplace area shelters the 30 million tourists who visit Baltimore each year and protects them from seeing other parts of the city beyond this redeveloped "economic island" that is unconnected to the deteriorating neighborhoods around it (Levine 1987, 118). Judd described this secured, protected, and normalized environment for visitors as a "tourist bubble." Inside this space is an artificial, segregated environment devoted to consumption and play, whereas substantial areas of the city outside the bubble are left to deal with the problems of the loss of industrial employment in the restructuring of the city's economy toward the service sector (Judd and Fainstein 1999).

Frieden and Sagalyn (1989) indicated that the components of downtown tourist spaces are similar in cities throughout the United States. The center of a city's downtown tourist space is usually its convention center. In the competition with other cities to attract the lucrative convention business, cities of all sizes built convention centers. Between 1970 and 1985, U.S. cities constructed more than 100 such centers, and by 1995, there were at least 434 in operation as part of what was a "virtual arms race" of competition among cities for the convention business. Most of these convention centers require annual subsidies for the re- payment of bond debt used for their construction and for operating expenses. Local convention and visitors bureaus also spend heavily to promote the advan- tages of their city to lure large meetings. Yet, despite these costs, cities keep in- vesting in larger and more elaborate facilities just to stay competitive with other places (Judd and Fainstein 1999).

Other expensive items that cities provide for visitors and residents are pro- fessional sports franchises. City leaders consider stadiums and sports arenas as essential for downtown regeneration, so despite their enormous costs, these fa- cilities are an essential signifier of "big league" status. Indeed, the major benefit of professional sports teams to a city may be the intangible quality of the image they provide for civic boosters, as the stadiums and sports arenas are among the most expensive components of a city's tourism infrastructure. The battle to get and keep sports franchises is another aspect of the interurban competition within the tourist industry. Owners are skillful in playing one city off against another with the threat of moving their teams in efforts to extract concessions in the form of new facilities, luxury boxes, and other subsidies. Much of the rev- enue generated from professional sports flows to wealthy owners, making pub- lic subsidies for the facilities a questionable economic investment for cities. The powerful symbolism of "big league sports" keeps the leaders of cities such as Cleveland eager to maintain their town's status despite the limited economic benefits of professional sports to most urban residents (Keating 1997).

Festival malls are another component of the downtown tourist bubble. These are self-contained shopping areas that are promoted to help reverse the long-term decline of downtown retailing. Projects developed in cities through- out the country by James Rouse and Atlanta's John Portman attempt to lure recreational shoppers rather than a resident population seeking mundane necessities. Most are the result of public subsidies and private investments fun- neled through special authorities created to foster these public-private partner- ships. The malls segregate the process of consumption from the routine aspects of daily life in the city in a process influenced by the success of the Disney Cor- poration's projects. As Zukin (1991, 232) suggested, the festival mall is probably more important than any other component of the standardized tourist space in establishing the atmosphere and context of a "utopian visual consumption" that has the potential to make every city, whatever its past function or present condi- tion, a tourist attraction.

The most recent component of the tourist bubble in many cities is casino gambling. Once confined to Las Vegas, casinos have spread rapidly as cities such as Atlantic City, Kansas City, St. Louis, Detroit, and New Orleans sought the revenues available from this form of tourism. Despite questions about the social and economic impacts of casino gambling as well as considerable politi- cal opposition, municipal leaders are scrambling to add these facilities as attractions for tourists to come and spend money in their cities rather than else- where. Despite well-documented negative impacts of casino gambling on cities as diverse as Atlantic City and Central City, Colorado, elected public officials still press for casinos as they search for ways to regenerate urban economies (Hannigan 1998).

Faced with declining financial support from the federal and state governments, leaders in U.S. cities look to tourism revenues to support their fragile local economies. As amusement park operators learned long ago that new rides and attractions keep visitors coming back, city leaders also try to add new baubles to their downtown tourist spaces that will keep visitors returning. Despite enormous costs and intense competition among cities for tourists, business and public leaders feel they cannot be complacent with their tourist areas. However, as Keating (1997) described Cleveland's comeback, a city may promote an image of success in its downtown regeneration by investing in tourist space but fail to provide substantial economic benefits outside the central business district. Atlanta is a city that has likewise attempted to use the components of a tourist bubble to restructure its downtown area.

## Atlanta's Downtown Tourist Bubble

Built along the intersection of rail lines in the Southeast, Atlanta established itself as a crossroads town during the mid-nineteenth century. The transportation connections by train, automobile, bus, and, later, airplane brought a steady stream of visitors to Atlanta. In a region noted for its hospitality, local leaders quickly recognized the commercial importance of tourism as a way of attracting visitors to come and invest in the young town (Newman 1999). By 1895, the partnership of business and political leaders hosted a national convention and a series of three expositions designed to promote their city. Early in the twentieth century, this partnership began shaping the elements of an early tourist bubble. At the urging of white business leaders, local public officials prepared the city to host conventions by constructing a municipal auditorium-armory building that opened in 1909. In November of that year, Atlanta welcomed the National Association of Automobile Manufacturers as it met for the first time in the South.

Preparations for this event showed how Atlanta's business and political partners worked cooperatively to showcase their downtown for visitors. After providing the convention facility as the centerpiece of an early twentieth-century tourist space, the city government also illuminated the sidewalks along the major thoroughfare, Peachtree Street, to form what was called "the Great White Way." Designers of this project attempted to make people feel more secure as they strolled downtown streets to patronize stores, theaters, and hotels. The Great White Way was a public space set aside to appeal to upper-class whites, whereas others were excluded from the amenities offered by the area. With the creation of the Great White Way in 1909, Atlanta's leaders carved out a segregated environment devoted to consumption and play for those white visitors and residents who could afford it. For the next 50 years, the tourist space along Peachtree formed the center of an important convention industry for the city. Typical of the private-sector components of this tourist space was the Weincoff Hotel that opened on Peachtree Street in 1913 and remained a family-operated business until after World War II, appealing to visitors with its proximity to theaters, shopping, and dining.

The partnership between the public and private sectors functioned to make Atlanta an early national leader in the convention business. Local government provided meeting facilities and paid for the illumination of Peachtree Street, and businesses such as hotels, restaurants, theaters, and stores thrived from the visitors attracted to the area. Business leaders in the Atlanta Chamber of Commerce organized a Convention Bureau in 1912 that aggressively solicited groups to hold their meetings in the city. Public officials such as the mayor and the governor further assisted the process by writing letters of invitation extending the warmth of southern hospitality to groups thinking of meeting in Atlanta. The city council's Committee on Auditorium and Conventions provided money to prepare the city for the event, especially if the group brought delegates from throughout the nation in a meeting that meant potential investment in the city. The mayor and council members also offered an official welcome to Atlanta for convention visitors. This pattern of public and private cooperation to shape a downtown tourist space would persist throughout the twentieth century despite many changes in the city.

For more than half of the twentieth century, laws reinforced regional cultural patterns of racial segregation to keep blacks separate from whites. Within this Jim Crow system, the public-private partnership to promote the city's convention industry hosted segregated conventions for African-Americans. In August 1906, for instance, the city welcomed a three-day meeting of the National Negro Business League, led by Booker T. Washington of Tuskegee, Alabama. The city's black hotels, restaurants, bars, and amusements eagerly received the convention delegates, who were greeted by the mayor and president of the all-white Chamber of Commerce. Financial support for the event came from white and black businesses that expected to gain from the money spent by the more than 1,000 visiting delegates. The city's largest black church hosted the meeting, and city government provided the use of a municipal park that was desegregated for the visitors but then closed again to African-Americans following the convention. The requirements of segregation were not allowed to stand in the way of opportunities to attract business and growth with displays of Atlanta's warm hospitality. As Peachtree Street formed the tourist space for whites, segregation pushed African-American tourist businesses into restricted areas, primarily along Auburn Avenue and Decatur Street.

Atlanta's African-Americans promoted their convention business with the same enthusiasm as their white counterparts. Even though the city served as the national headquarters for a revived Ku Klux Klan, blacks advertised for their brothers and sisters to hold meetings in Atlanta and compared the attractions of Auburn Avenue with the bright spots of New York and Chicago. This separate tourist space for African-Americans continued to attract conventions and tourists until after the passage of the 1964 Civil Rights Act that desegregated the city's tourist businesses and facilities. Atlanta's white leaders made political decisions that would also have a dramatic impact on this segregated tourist space.

By 1950, there was a growing awareness among white business and political leaders that the physical condition of downtown Atlanta was deteriorating. First the Depression and then World War II brought the construction of new buildings to a halt. In the years immediately following the war, builders focused their efforts on meeting the demand for suburban housing. The lack of development in downtown Atlanta troubled the city's white power structure. When Hunter (1953, 214–15) conducted his study of "Regional City," he found this elite group most concerned about the issues of growth and development as well as traffic and the "Negro question." The city's leaders made plans to deal with all of these issues at once. Prior to the federal interstate highway program, the city began construction in 1950 on an expressway that curved around downtown, giving whites living in northern and southern suburbs easy access to the central city. White civic leaders designed the expressway not only to relieve traffic congestion but also to serve as a buffer between the central business district and the African-American neighborhood to the east.

The federal urban renewal program provided the Atlanta public-private partnership with the means of clearing the land within the curve in the expressway by relocating black residents and businesses outside the downtown area. The Butler Street urban renewal district provided space for 1,300 new hotel rooms in the downtown area within the curve of the expressway. As initially proposed, this district would have eliminated all of the commercial area of Auburn Avenue, but protests from the black newspaper, the *Daily World*, and African-American leaders succeeded in protecting "Sweet Auburn" (Bayor 1996). The land cleared for the Butler Street area provided space for the Downtown Marriott (now operated as the Sheraton) that opened in 1966. This hotel reflected significant change taking place in the city's hospitality businesses as national corporate ownership replaced local businesses.

The decisions made by the partnership of white business and political leaders during the 1960s guided the redevelopment of Atlanta's downtown tourist bubble. The city still depended on its transportation connections to bring people to the downtown area that was a commercial center of regional and increasingly national importance. Ivan Allen, Jr., a business owner and president of the Chamber of Commerce, campaigned successfully for mayor in 1961 by promising to build a new convention center to replace the outdated Municipal Auditorium. He used the urban renewal program to clear more space for tourism at the site of a new facility known as the Civic Center. A third urban renewal area provided land for the construction of the city's major league sports facility known as the Atlanta-Fulton County Stadium, where a relocated baseball team and a new National Football League franchise played their games.

The local partnership of white business and political leaders used the combination of expressway construction and three urban renewal areas to transform the city's earlier downtown tourist space. The new facilities enabled Atlanta to continue its success as a convention city, but at considerable cost to more than 55,000 African-American residents whose homes were destroyed in the process of reshaping Atlanta's tourist bubble (Eric Hill Associates 1966). Tourists could enjoy the 1,300 new hotel rooms, the Civic Center, and the stadium, but the once-thriving center of African-American commerce along Auburn Avenue was left to deteriorate as a result of the policies pursued by the local regime.

In 1996, Mayor Allen announced that Atlanta was ready to take its place as more than a regional capital and become a city of national importance. As proof, he cited the city's new jet-age airport, a major league stadium, a new convention center under construction, and a doubling of the number of down-town hotel rooms since 1945. In addition, voters approved a referendum for liquor by the drink sales, and plans were under way for a rapid transit system (Pomerantz 1996).

Another important contributor to the development of Atlanta's tourist space was an ambitious young architect, John Portman, who opened a down-town merchandise mart in 1961 to serve as a wholesale shopping center for store owners from throughout the region. The success of the mart in attracting crowds to Atlanta created demand for an adjacent hotel. Portman envisioned the two buildings forming the core of a "Rockefeller Center-type complex" to redevelop an entire section of downtown along Peachtree Street (Crown 1964, 40–41). Portman not only designed the new hotel but also developed the pro-ject, which became known as Peachtree Center. When the Hyatt Regency opened in 1967, its blue glass revolving cocktail lounge served as a landmark in the Atlanta skyline. At the time, architects considered the hotel a revolution in design with a huge atrium of 3 million square feet extending 22 stories high. Exposed tear-shaped glass elevators provided visitors with a ride similar to an amusement park. The Hyatt Corporation and other national chains replicated these novel features, creating a class of atrium hotels in cities throughout the United States ("Downtown Is Looking Up" 1976).

John Portman's Hyatt Regency was a financial success as well, boasting a 95% occupancy rate within three months of its opening. The Hyatt Corporation wanted more rooms, so Portman added 200 more in a cylindrical glass tower built on top of the hotel's ballroom. This design would be replicated in 1976 on a larger scale for the Westin Peachtree Plaza, which became the second hotel in Peachtree Center. The success of the hotel led Portman in 1968 to double the size of the merchandise mart and to construct the first office tower in his Rock-efeller Center-type complex. Eventually, Portman added a third hotel, the Mar-riott Marquis, to Peachtree Center as it occupied all or part of 17 city blocks, making it one of the largest private developments in the world.

John Portman's investments had enormous impact in updating Atlanta's downtown tourist bubble. Peachtree Center reshaped a major portion of down-town, spurring growth northward along Peachtree Street and away from the traditional center of the business district at Five Points. Although Portman gave Atlanta's downtown some of its most distinctive architecture, he also changed the way many tourists experience the city by enclosing a section of downtown. As Judd (1999, 47) observed,

Atlanta has moved indoors, and the city streets have been almost deserted by pedestrian traffic. Shops, hotels and their lobbies, offices, food courts, and atriums are connected by a maze of escalators, skytubes and arcades. The glassed-in skywalks of Peachtree Center isolate its inhabitants from the streets below. A similar isolation characterizes Portman's other developments as well—the Renaissance Center in Detroit, the Hyatt at Embarcadero Center in San Francisco, the Bonaventure Hotel in Los Angeles, and Marriott Marquis in Manhattan's Times Square.

The skywalk system connecting the buildings and the interior space of the Peachtree Center complex was the most controversial aspect of the project. Called "honkey tubes" by many local African-Americans, the skywalks tend to segregate the mostly white visitors within the buildings rather than encouraging them to experience the life of the city outside the buildings. One critic called this design "anti-urban" since the space isolates occupants within the megastructure complex rather than having the buildings relate to the city around them. Travel writer Arthur Frommer (1987, D-1) criticized the exterior design of Peachtree Center's buildings as "fortresses with forbidding walls, opaque exteriors making no contribution and adding no color or light to their city streets, confining guests 'inside the moat,' so to speak, excluding them from Atlanta instead of introducing them to it."

Portman was not the only developer reshaping Atlanta's tourist space. The city's historic preservation commission, organized in 1966, issued a resolution that year calling attention to the downtown area near the railroad tracks under the city's viaducts. The old storefronts and warehouses of late nineteenth-century Atlanta were left behind as a home for derelicts but could be restored for use by tourists as New Orleans did with its French Quarter and St. Louis with its Gas Light Square. By 1969, two young entrepreneurs formed a company, leased space under the viaducts, and called the area Underground Atlanta. The attraction opened that year with 22 tenants providing tourists with a mixture of restaurants, clubs, museums, and shops. Within two years, Underground Atlanta was the best-known and most-visited tourist attraction in the city, offering 65 establishments to appeal to a variety of tastes. Conventioneers and out-of-town visitors were not the only ones who made Underground popular. The location was within walking distance of downtown business and government offices, attracting lunch, happy hour, and evening crowds of residents as well as visitors. The legal drinking age in the state was 18, and the surrounding jurisdictions were legally dry so that Underground Atlanta also attracted large crowds of young people.

Although Underground Atlanta was initially successful, problems soon developed. Souvenir shops charged high prices for cheap goods, and public safety and crime problems from the large crowds of teenage drinkers began to scare off older local residents. Fewer patrons caused a steady decline in the number of businesses in Underground, with the last closing its doors in 1982. The loss of this tourist attraction led hospitality business leaders to begin immediately calling for a revival of Underground Atlanta as an essential component in the city's convention trade.

Atlanta's convention facility, known as the Civic Center, was less than five years old when city leaders realized its size was inadequate to host the meetings of large national organizations such as civic clubs and political parties. Planning began in 1971 for a convention center to keep the city competitive in attracting major events. Fearing a lack of support among voters for the expense of a new facility, Atlanta's business leaders turned to the state government, asking Georgia to create a special authority to build and operate the $20 million building. After intensive lobbying by business leaders and support from a pro-business governor, a reluctant general assembly in 1974 agreed to fund the project whose price had risen to $35 million. When the Georgia World Congress Center opened two years later, its 640,000 square feet of exhibition space made it the "world's largest hall." Chamber of Commerce boosters noted that the new building featured meeting rooms with built-in simultaneous translation facilities so that the city could host meetings of 60,000 or more with delegates from all over the world. This was regarded as an important step in Atlanta's aspirations to become known as an international city. Trade shows such as the textile industry's "bobbin show" became regular events attracting thousands of domestic and international tourists. With the new facility, more than 10,000 downtown hotel rooms, and the city's transportation connections, local business leaders hoped Atlanta could overtake New York and Chicago to become "America's Convention Capital" (Galphin 1975, 74).

Atlanta's aspirations as a "major league" city came true in 1966 when the National League Braves relocated from Milwaukee to occupy the new stadium. Later that year, the city welcomed the new National Football League expansion franchise known as the Atlanta Falcons. Despite fan support for the two teams, gate receipts did not cover the principal and interest on the $18 million debt used to finance the stadium, forcing the city and county to pay almost $500,000 to reduce the debt in 1967 and more than $900,000 the following year (Martin 1987). This type of revenue shortfall is common among cities that are financing expensive sports facilities, leading many urban scholars to question the wisdom of the investment (see Rosentraub 1997). For local boosters in Atlanta, however, the stadium and its two major league teams were a validation of the claim that the city had attained national prominence. They serve as important elements in the city's tourist bubble because professional sports provide a diversion for visitors, attract media coverage, and provide intangible benefits such as an increase in civic pride, community spirit, and collective self-image (Law 1993).

Although public officials in Atlanta liked to take credit for the addition of components to the city's tourist bubble such as the stadium and its professional sports teams (see Allen and Hemphill 1971), private-sector developers made most of the decisions that created space for the tourist industry. Atlanta's largest real estate developers sometimes made investments based on their personal competition with one another. For example, the success of Portman's Peachtree Center caused rival developer, Tom Cousins, to build another project in a different section of downtown. In 1968, Cousins purchased the National Basketball Association's St. Louis Hawks and persuaded the city to construct an arena called the Omni as their home. Four years later, he purchased another sports franchise to play in the Omni, the Atlanta Flames of the National

Hockey League. Cousins also began construction of another multifunction megastructure known as the Omni complex adjacent to the sports arena. It contained the Omni International Hotel, restaurants, shops, an ice skating rink, and a $17 million indoor amusement park called the World of Sid and Marty Krofft. The plan was to lure investment away from Portman's Peachtree Street development toward the Marietta Street location of Cousins's project. After its opening in the spring of 1976, the amusement park closed within six months.

Although given elaborate promotional efforts, the hockey franchise failed to sell out its games or to attract widespread local enthusiasm for a sport that was new to the region. After several years of declining revenues, the team moved to the cooler climate of Calgary in 1980. The hotel and entire complex struggled financially for several years until they were purchased in 1985 by communications mogul Ted Turner, who converted the Omni into CNN Center, which functioned as the studios and headquarters of his media companies. Cousins eventually sold the Atlanta Hawks to Turner, who also bought the Atlanta Braves in order to televise games as part of his nationwide "superstation."

The personal competition between two developers spurred construction of the Omni Complex and additions to Peachtree Center, causing significant impact on downtown Atlanta's tourist bubble. Both megastructures tended to seal visitors within the complexes, reducing pedestrian activity on the city's sidewalks. In 1988, as the city prepared to host the Democratic National Convention and again in anticipation of the 1996 Summer Olympic Games, Atlanta spent millions of dollars in public funds to improve sidewalks by making them more attractive with improved lighting, trees, and art. The enclosed space of the city's two megastructures made the creation of a pleasant outdoor pedestrian environment more difficult.

Despite changes in Atlanta's political leadership, support for tourism as an economic development strategy for downtown remained strong within the longstanding coalition of business and political leaders. Three business groups—the Atlanta Convention and Tourist Bureau, Central Atlanta Progress, and the Chamber of Commerce—were well organized to promote tourism. They also supported a policy research group known as Research Atlanta to analyze policies of importance to the business community. No sooner had the last business in Underground Atlanta closed its doors than business leaders began calling for more entertainment for convention visitors. Research Atlanta published reports in 1982 and 1983 citing the need for downtown entertainment as the greatest weakness in the city's convention business (Research Atlanta 1982, 1983).

Eager to show his cooperation with business leaders, newly elected mayor Andrew Young embraced the proposal to revitalize Underground Atlanta. In a well-coordinated effort, the city joined with Fulton County, the state of Georgia, and the business organization Central Atlanta Progress to fund a $400,000 feasibility study on the revitalization of Underground Atlanta. The American City Corporation (owned by James Rouse, the developer of Harborplace and other festival marketplaces throughout the country) conducted the study that recommended the redevelopment of the Underground area with a mix of restaurants, nightclubs, specialty shops, and public spaces. Many small property owners in the area and some members of the city council were skeptical about the need for the revitalization that reminded them of the old urban renewal program.

In contrast to the rebuilding of Faneuil Hall in Boston (an earlier Rouse project), which required less than 21% public-sector support, the redevelopment of Underground Atlanta was a different kind of partnership, with more than 80% of the $144 million investment coming from a variety of public sources. Although downtown business leaders wanted the project, they were unwilling to assume a large share of the financial risk. There was no doubt that this project carried considerable risk because both the earlier version of Underground and the Omni's entertainment park, the World of Sid and Marty Krofft, failed.

The expectations for the revived Underground Atlanta were great. The mayor regarded the project as a legacy to the city that would provide jobs and tax revenues as well as the potential financial gains from the city's role as entrepreneur. The city council hoped the project would provide opportunities for minority businesses in the construction and operation of the marketplace and stimulate the renewal of the southern edge of downtown through increased economic activity in the area. Tourism officials and other business leaders anticipated that crowds of conventioneers would visit the new attraction.

The celebration of the reopening took place in 1989, and during the first year of operation, an estimated 13 million people visited Underground Atlanta. Only 40% of these patrons were visiting tourists, and the rest were local area residents. Convention delegates came in smaller numbers than anticipated. The major convention hotels were at a considerable distance from the complex, and there was little of the historic Underground left for visitors to experience. As a consequence, the site lacked the authentic qualities to set it apart from similar festival marketplaces in other cities. The original Underground Atlanta was popular in part because it was a historical and architectural signifier of the city's nineteenth-century railroad-era past. With the proliferation of festival marketplaces in cities throughout the country, the new Underground had little novelty to offer visitors.

Rouse Company projections said that Underground Atlanta would generate 3,000 new jobs. Three years after its opening, there were only 969 new jobs in the complex, including 552 full-time and 417 part-time positions. Although the city collected almost a million dollars in additional property, sales, and beverage taxes during 1991, it had the additional expense of providing public safety for the project (Sjoquist and Williams 1992). The fear of crime in the complex caused the city to open a police precinct station in Underground Atlanta that functioned in addition to the private security force of 30 officers. These precautions did not prevent a black gang-related killing in 1990, followed by several other crimes that diminished the number of white suburban visitors to Underground. The result was a $28 million loss during the first five years of operation. In 1994, the Rouse Company's subsidiary, Underground Festival, Inc., which operated the marketplace, asked for and received a restructuring of its debt to the city to continue operations. Shortly after the departure of the crowds of Olympic visitors in 1996, Rouse's management company canceled its contract, forcing the city to hire new managers and raising doubt about the continued viability of Underground Atlanta.

Among the first tenants to close in the new Underground Atlanta were undercapitalized minority-owned businesses that had comprised 27% of the project's tenants at the time of opening. National chain businesses replaced many of these smaller merchants (mostly African-American females), causing racial tensions among the remaining tenants. The presence of the national corporations added to the homogenization of the tourist experience at Underground because the same fudge, T-shirt, and other shops could be found in the festival marketplaces of other cities.

An additional goal of the project was to provide an economic stimulus to downtown and to encourage the revitalization of the south side of the central business district. One year after Underground's reopening, the Coca-Cola Company opened a pavilion known as the World of Coca-Cola, where people could learn about the history of the soft drink in its hometown. From the outset, the Coke exhibit was extremely popular and made its way onto the list of "must-see" attractions in the city, but only a few hundred yards away from its entrance, Underground Atlanta was far less crowded.

With convention delegates avoiding Underground Atlanta, both attendance and revenues were lower than anticipated. This situation provoked a lively debate in the city council over the future of the complex. During 1999, Underground needed a new manager, providing the city council with an opportunity to explore a variety of options. One council member proposed casino gambling as a solution, but a majority voted to give the contract to a company promising to make the complex more attractive to families with children. Meanwhile, Mayor Bill Campbell proposed adding another attraction to the area by investing $75 million in an aquarium located next to Underground Atlanta. No business or foundation stepped forward to provide support for the aquarium project. This portion of Atlanta's tourist space remains without a casino or an aquarium, proving it is often difficult to add new attractions to the theme park city (Sorkin 1992).

## Race and Atlanta's Tourist Bubble

The issue that did not surface in the debate on the future of Underground Atlanta but that affects the project as well as other parts of the downtown tourist bubble is race. Atlanta became a majority African-American city in 1970, and low-income black neighborhoods surround much of the central business district. According to 1990 statistics, the 23 census tracts that form a "U" to the east, south, and west of downtown have a poverty rate more than 35%, and more than 90% of the 50,000 residents in this area are African-American (City of Atlanta 1993). Life for these residents is quite different from the experience of convention delegates and office workers downtown. Like Baltimore, Atlanta's downtown tourist space segregates visitors and office workers inside a bubble that is secured, protected, and normalized (Judd and Fainstein 1999).

Although the convention bureau aggressively recruits as many African-American groups as possible, most of the convention visitors to Atlanta are white. The cultural symbols displayed at Underground Atlanta reflect this dilemma. The original Underground offered tourists a mixture of the real and imagined heritage of southern whites, reaching its nadir in the shop operated by former governor Lester Maddox, who sold autographed pickaxe handles similar to the ones used in 1964 to prevent the integration of his restaurant. This made the other stores selling confederate flags and caps as well as *Gone with the Wind* paraphernalia seem tame.

When the rebuilt Underground project opened in 1989, its cultural symbols were biracial. Although it was still possible to buy confederate flags, there were also pictures and symbols of the civil rights era and black pride T-shirts for sale. This cultural ambiguity contributed to Underground Atlanta's difficulty finding its niche as a tourist attraction. The more white convention visitors perceived Underground as catering to African-American tastes, the less attractive it became to them. On the other hand, Underground lacked authentic cultural experiences of regional cooking, offering fast food and chain operations that catered to mass tastes. Further complicating these cultural issues involving race were concerns over public safety frequently voiced by Underground's management in terms of "loitering" by young black males. The location of a police precinct and the hiring of a private security force discourage this practice, resulting in the privatization of public space described by Sorkin (1992).

If the issue of race played a role in determining the fate of Underground Atlanta, it was the decisive issue in discussions about another of the city's tourist attractions. In the era of segregation, Auburn Avenue was the most important street for Atlanta's African-American cultural institutions, businesses, and entertainment. The combination of expressway construction, urban renewal, and the desegregation of tourist businesses plunged the commercial area of Auburn Avenue into a spiral of decay and neglect. The building of the downtown connector cut a swath through the street, closing many small businesses in its path and separating the largely residential area on the east side of the expressway from the commercial district on the west. The Butler Street urban renewal area destroyed more homes and businesses in the area but created space for new hotels serving the convention trade. After the passage of the Civil Rights Act, blacks were free to eat, sleep, and drink in businesses open to all, but few whites patronized the previously African-American businesses along Auburn Avenue. Small hotels catering to a previously African-American clientele closed first, followed by the gradual decline in the number of restaurants, clubs, and other businesses on the street.

Among the numerous African-American cultural institutions that remain on Auburn Avenue is Ebenezer Baptist Church, where Dr. Martin Luther King, Jr. and his father served as ministers. Also located on the eastern end of the residential portion of this historic street is the house in which Dr. King was born. Near the birth home and church are Dr. King's tomb and the MLK Center for Non-Violent Social Change. Much of this area became a national park, providing funds for the restoration of the houses in the neighborhood. The area draws more than 3 million visitors annually, making the site the most heavily visited tourist attraction in the city. Despite the crowds of tourists and several revitalization efforts, the commercial area of Auburn Avenue located to the west of the expressway continued to deteriorate. A Main Street program attempted to renovate the facades of the storefronts along the avenue. Preparations for the 1996 Olympics included replacing the sidewalks, planting trees, improving the street lighting, and placing interpretive signs along a path designated as the "Freedom Walk" on the entire length of Auburn Avenue. Despite these efforts, the commercial area of the street received no additional private-sector investment. Merchants complain that visitors arrive at the national park area in tour buses, get off, visit the sites, and leave without exploring the historic district's commercial section. Their frustration is much like that resulting from efforts to make Harlem a more important destination for tourists in New York City (Hoffman 1999). The national park area of Auburn Avenue certainly figures as an important element of Atlanta's tourist bubble; however, the issue of race makes the revitalization of the entire avenue a more complicated process. Although public-sector policies have invested in the streets and sidewalks of Auburn Avenue, white business leaders have avoided investments in what is regarded as a black area, leaving it neglected and decaying.

## Tourist Bubble Politics

In 1970, Atlanta became a majority black city, enabling residents to elect the city's first African-American mayor, Maynard Jackson, three years later. Prior to Jackson's election, the partnership between white public officials and business leaders reshaped the city's downtown tourist bubble to provide for the needs of convention visitors at the expense of black neighborhoods and small businesses. How did the change in Atlanta's political leadership affect the longstanding partnership between city government and business leaders to support the city's downtown convention business?

During his initial term as mayor, Maynard Jackson frequently took policy positions that antagonized white business leaders. Jackson argued that the new airport be located on the same site as the old one, providing a symbolic gesture to south-side black voters. He also insisted that airport construction contracts include joint-venture minority partners and affirmative action requirements for companies doing business with the city. After a public dispute with the Constitution and the leadership of Central Atlanta Progress, Jackson made great efforts to restore relationships with the business elite (Newman 2000). This was particularly important in light of the three major hotels (the Peachtree Plaza, Omni, and Downtown Hilton) and the new state-funded convention center scheduled to open in 1976. As part of his efforts, Jackson and the head of the Chamber of Commerce launched a national tour of other cities promoting investment and painting a picture of harmony between the mayor and the Atlanta business community. Addressing an audience in Chicago, Jackson said, "Atlanta can't prosper without city hall and business in bed together" (Teasley

1974, A–1). Adolph Reed (1987) suggested that this accommodation between Mayor Jackson and white business leaders was necessary because of the private-sector control of investments in the city. Many of the largest investments were in the downtown tourist bubble's megastructures and hotels.

To cement his cooperative relationship with the business community during his second term in office, Jackson established an economic development corporation to create public-private partnerships and with its allied organization, the Downtown Development Authority, to finance projects in the city. Among its first efforts was a $9 million industrial development bond financing for the construction of the French-owned Ibis Hotel in downtown. This project was one of many that would enhance the city's tourist bubble. Thus, despite racial change in city government, support for tourism investments in downtown Atlanta continued. This confirms Reed's (1987, 168) observation that black urban regimes are "by and large only black versions of the progrowth regimes that they have replaced."

If Jackson tried to revive the coalition of city government and business leaders, his successor, Andrew Young, fully restored the partnership to promote downtown tourism. His administration worked closely with Central Atlanta Progress to rebuild Underground Atlanta and joined with Fulton County and state government to build a new indoor stadium known as the Georgia Dome for the use of the Falcons of the National Football League. The construction of the Georgia Dome and its parking lots involved displacing a small black neighborhood known as Lightning as well as several African-American churches. As initially proposed, there were no relocation funds for area residents or the churches; however, protests by the city's black clergy finally won $25 million from the state for assistance to those affected.

The building of the Georgia Dome was similar to the city's earlier use of the urban renewal program to expand the downtown tourist bubble at the expense of blacks living near downtown. In this instance, local government support for the development came from the city's African-American mayor. Andrew Young also took an active role in promoting tourism, helping business leaders raise funds for a new promotional campaign to attract conventions. He used his diplomatic skill and international contacts to attract major events to Atlanta such as the 1988 Democratic National Convention and the Olympics. These high-profile events attracted additional international investment in downtown tourist facilities such as hotels and restaurants.

The pattern of decision making in Atlanta throughout most of the twentieth century reflected a close partnership between business and government. Stone (1993) indicated that Atlanta maintained a development regime with tourism as an important strategy to attract attention and promote investment in the city. Incumbent mayor Bill Campbell has attempted to continue this process with the addition of a new sports arena, which opened in 1999 to replace the Omni as the home for the Atlanta Hawks basketball team and an expansion hockey club, the Thrashers. The sports franchises and media empire owned by Ted Turner were purchased by Time Warner, which subsequently merged with America Online

(AOL). This conglomerate signed a 30-year lease on the new sports arena, guaranteeing the repayment on the construction debt and that the teams will play downtown. Continuing the partnership with local government, the city and county financed public improvements around the arena with a new tax on car rentals. The corporate owner of the sports teams also received the right to sell the name of the new arena to Philips, the Dutch electronics firm. The naming rights are reported to be worth $180 million with another $20 million per year from other sponsorship agreements. This more than covers the cost of the sports facility, leaving gate receipts, parking, concessions, and rent from sky boxes as additional sources of profit for AOL–Time Warner (Unger and Poole 1999).

In other efforts, Mayor Campbell has been less successful than his predecessors in promoting private-sector investment in downtown's tourist bubble. For example, he has not attracted investors in a proposed aquarium to be located near Underground Atlanta. With the city of Atlanta representing less than 10% of the metropolitan area's population, business leaders are increasingly focused on suburban areas outside the city. Also, businesses are often owned by international corporations that have little concern for the central city, so in may ways, city government is relegated to the position of a junior partner in the once-flourishing relationship with business leaders.

Yet, despite these changes in the city, Atlanta continues to attract convention visitors. Meeting planners describe the city as convenient because of its airport and rapid rail system. Atlanta also receives high marks for its convention facilities, supply of hotel rooms, and restaurants but is criticized for its safety and lack of interesting sights (Saporta 1990). The issues of crime and the lack of interesting attractions are both related to the city's construction of an enclosed space for tourists in the downtown area. Small businesses and residences were cleared to make way for megastructures such as Peachtree Center and CNN Center. With few people living downtown, the area lacks the 24-hour population as office workers depart for their suburban homes at 5:00 p.m., leaving empty streets and sidewalks. With little regard for historic preservation, older buildings were demolished to make space for newer structures, and the area lacks the character and charm that older buildings would have contributed. Instead, the downtown tourist bubble has been described as "dull and excessively devoted to business and finance" (Frommer 1987, D-1).

Despite these drawbacks, visitors still come to Atlanta because of the city's accessibility, facilities, and relentless promotional efforts. In 1998, the Atlanta Convention and Visitors Bureau reported that the city hosted 3,057 meetings attended by more than 3,423,000 people. This badge-wearing army of convention delegates is an important component of the city's basic economy. Atlanta, along with other cities such as Orlando, Las Vegas, Anaheim, and Phoenix, has fueled its growth with service and leisure-oriented activities instead of more traditional primary and secondary industries. Although older manufacturing centers have declined, these tourism-oriented cities are part of a new emerging hierarchy of urban places. According to Zelinsky (1994), hosting conventions is one of several economic functions that sets the postmodern city apart from its antecedents.

In the case of Atlanta, the city's leaders have used tourism to promote its economic development with expositions and conventions since the nineteenth century. Local business and public officials began constructing the elements of a consumption-oriented tourist space along Peachtree Street in 1909. Economic restructuring in Atlanta did not mean a major shift from manufacturing to service activities such as tourism but did involve rebuilding the downtown tourist space during the 1960s. There were also changes in ownership patterns within the hospitality industry. Smaller family-owned hotels and tourist businesses gave way during the postwar era to national chains and, more recently, to international corporate ownership.

Atlanta's extensive space constructed by private businesses and the public sector for a tourist bubble certainly puts the city among the vanguard of places with downtown areas transformed for purposes of spectacle and consumption. With the hosting of major events such as the 1988 Democratic National Convention, two National Football League "Superbowls," and the 1996 Summer Olympic Games, Atlanta used its tourist space to promote the city as a place worthy of global attention and investment. The only components of the tourist bubble that Atlanta has not added to its theme park downtown are an aquarium and casino gambling. Both have been proposed by public officials but not promoted by business leaders.

The partnership between local government and business that produced Atlanta's tourist bubble still functions to promote downtown convention industry despite racial change at city hall. Nevertheless, the issue of race is evident in the failure of Underground Atlanta and the unrevived commercial section of Auburn Avenue. Although one was built as a $144 million tourist destination that has failed to lure convention visitors, the other has not attracted commercial investment despite the presence of more than 3 million tourists who visit the area each year. The past decisions of the city's public-private partnership created a tourist space that isolates and encloses visitors, giving them little contact with downtown Atlanta outside the hotels and the convention center. As a result, many visitors find Atlanta dull and uninteresting, so they tend not to bring spouses and other family members, nor do convention delegates stay extra days after their meetings (Saporta 1990).

Atlanta's pro-growth regime has used tourism as a strategy to attract investment in downtown. The partnership between business and local government has produced an area devoted to a business-oriented form of tourism, the convention industry. In contrast to New York, Boston, San Francisco, and, especially, European cities where tourist spaces are not isolated from the daily fabric of urban life, Atlanta has a downtown tourist space that is devoted to sports, consumption, and spectacle but encloses its visitors within a secured and protected environment. Within this bubble, business travelers do not mix with a resident population to create an interesting, around-the-clock city (Judd and Fainstein 1999). To the contrary, business and political leaders have not hesitated to move black residents living near downtown. The transition from white to black political leadership did not bring change that benefited African-

Americans. As Reed (1988) observed, black urban regimes usually continue the pro-growth policies of their white predecessors. In Atlanta, this meant support for the continued expansion of the downtown tourist bubble. As the examples of Underground Atlanta, the Georgia Dome, and other projects show, black businesses and residents were moved to make way for an enlarged tourist space. Rather than learn from mistakes made during the urban renewal program, Atlanta continues to repeat them.

# REFERENCES

Allen, I., Jr., and P. Hemphill. 1971. *Mayor: Notes on the sixties.* New York: Simon & Schuster.

Bayor, R. H. 1996. *Race and the shaping of twentieth-century Atlanta.* Chapel Hill: Univ. of North Carolina Press.

City of Atlanta, 1993. *Creating an urban village: Atlanta's community driven vision for the empowerment zone: Vol. I, Strategic development.* Atlanta, GA: Author.

Crown, J. 1964. After forty years: A new hotel. *Atlanta* 3 (February): 40–41.

Downtown is looking up. 1976. *Time,* 5 July, 54–62.

Eric Hill Associates. 1966. *City of Atlanta, Georgia, report on the relocation of individuals, families, and businesses.* Atlanta, GA: Community Improvement Program.

Frieden, B. J., and L. B. Sagalyn. 1989. *Downtown Inc. How America builds cities.* Cambridge, MA: MIT Press.

Frommer, A. 1987. Key to Atlanta's future lies in its past. *Constitution,* 18 January, D-1, D-6.

Galphin, B. 1975. Atlanta's $35 million salesman. *Atlanta* 14 (January): 60–74.

Hannigan, J. 1998. *Fantasy city: Pleasure and profit in the postmodern metropolis.* London: Routledge Kegan Paul.

Hoffman, L. 1999. Tourism and the inner city: Marketing diversity. Paper presented at the annual meeting of the Urban Affairs Association, April, Louisville, KY.

Hunter, F. 1953. *Community power structure: A study of decision makers.* Chapel Hill: Univ. of North Carolina Press.

Judd, D. R. 1999. Constructing the tourist bubble. In *The tourist city,* edited by D. R. Judd and S. S. Fainstein, 35–53. New Haven, CT: Yale Univ. Press.

Judd, D. R., and S. S. Fainstein, eds. 1999. *The tourist city.* New Haven, CT: Yale Univ. Press.

Keating, W. D. 1997, Cleveland: The "comeback" city: The politics of redevelopment and sports stadiums amidst urban decline. In *Reconstructing urban regime theory: Regulating urban politics in a global economy,* edited by M. Lauria, 189–205. Thousand Oaks, CA: Sage.

Law, C. M. 1993. *Urban tourism: Attracting visitors to large cities.* London: Mansell.

Levine, M. V. 1987. Downtown redevelopment as an urban growth strategy: A critical appraisal of the Baltimore renaissance. *Journal of Urban Affairs* 9 (2): 103–23.

Martin, H. H. 1987. *Atlanta and environs: A chronicle of its people and events.* Vol. 3. Atlanta: Atlanta Historical Society and Univ. of Georgia Press.

Newman, H. K. 1999. *Southern hospitality: Tourism and the growth of Atlanta.* Tuscaloosa: Univ. of Alabama Press.

———. 2000. Hospitality and violence: Contradictions in a southern city. *Urban Affairs Review* 35 (4): 541–58.

Pomerantz, G. 1996. *Where Peachtree meets Sweet Auburn: The saga of two families and the making of Atlanta.* New York: Scribner.

Reed, A. L., Jr. 1987. A critique of neo-progressivism in theorizing about local development policy: A case from Atlanta. In *The politics of urban development,* edited by C. Stone and H. Sanders, 199–215. Lawrence: University Press of Kansas.

———. 1988. The black urban regime: Structural origins and constraints. In *Power, community and the city,* edited by M. P. Smith, 138–89. New Brunswick, NJ: Transaction Books.

Research Atlanta. 1982. *The convention industry in Atlanta.* Atlanta, GA: Author.

———. 1983. *Atlanta tourism and convention market: A synopsis of several studies*. Atlanta, GA: Author.

Rosentraub, M. S. 1997. *Major league losers: The real cost of sports and who's paying for it*. New York: Basic Books.

Saporta, M. 1990. GWCC tops list of meeting sites. *Constitution*, 13 March, A-1, A-7.

Shaw, G., and A. M. Williams. 1994. *Critical issues in tourism: A geographical perspective*. Oxford, UK: Blackwell.

Sjoquist, D. L., and L. Williams. 1992. *The Underground Atlanta project: An economic analysis*. Atlanta: Policy Research Center, Georgia State University.

Sorkin, M., ed. 1992. *Variations on a theme park: The new American city and the end of public space*. New York: Hill & Wang.

Stone, C. N. 1989. *Regime politics: Governing Atlanta, 1946–1988*. Lawrence: University Press of Kansas.

———. 1993. Urban regimes and the capacity to govern: A political economy approach. *Journal of Urban Affairs* 15 (1): 1–28.

Teasley, C. 1974. Mayor, Currey deny rift, seek business in Chicago. *Constitution*, 21 November, A-1.

Unger, H., and S. Poole. 1999. Philips arena creating a look: Corporate club. *Constitution*, 12 September, P-13.

Zelinsky, W. 1994. Conventionland USA: The geography of a latterday phenomenon. *Annals of the Association of American Geographers* 84 (1): 68–86.

Zukin, S. 1991. *Landscapes of power: From Detroit to Disney World*. Berkeley: Univ. of California Press.

# CHAPTER 5

# THE SUBURBS: THE POLITICS OF SPACE, RACE, AND ETHNICITY

## IMMIGRATION AND THE SPATIAL MOSAIC OF THE SUBURBS

The suburbs of the contemporary metropolis reflect the dramatic changes wrought by globalization. In the popular imagination, if not always in reality, the suburban population of the twentieth century was made up of white families living on cul-de-sacs with green expanses of lawn. In the twenty-first century, the suburbs have been transformed. Many of them are now multiracial and multiethnic, and new suburban developments run the gamut from row houses and apartment clusters to McMansions to privatized, gated communities. The dramatic differences between one housing development and subdivision and the next gives a visual face to an important new development: the suburbs seem to break up into enclaves that work to separate suburban residents on the basis of class, race, and ethnicity. This trend may become a patchwork of spatial separation, but it is also possible that the movement of immigrants into the suburbs will break down historic patterns of segregation of rich from poor and white from almost everyone else. It is too soon to tell.

But in Selection 14, Andrew Ross is not reassuring on this point. His account of the social life and attitudes of people living in Celebration, a gated community near Disney World run by the Disney Corporation, indicates that residents moved to Celebration precisely to escape from the problems they perceived elsewhere. They took comfort in the one hundred pages of rules and restrictions imposed on them because, they thought, the rules helped to keep order without the burdens of democratic decision making. They also took comfort in the social homogeneity of the development: the high cost of housing kept lower-income people out, and, it was thought, the rules and regulations excluded those who did not share the values of people living there. Though they shared insider jokes about being on the set of *The Truman Show* or *The Stepford Wives* and a few said they sometimes missed the presence of interesting characters, they valued order above all else.

When assessing the ability of immigrants to exert political influence, it is essential to keep in mind the complexity of the recent immigrant streams. Many recent immigrants are focused on just getting by; thus it is their children and grandchildren who will enter the social and political mainstream. Selection 15, which is taken from *Picture Windows*, a book by Rosalyn Baxandall and Elizabeth Ewen, describes the social changes in the suburbs of Long Island, New York. There, recent immigration has exerted immense pressures on housing, schools, and social services. Many of the immigrants work in what the authors call an "underwater economy" of low-pay, informal jobs where they are employed as day laborers, maids, gardeners, babysitters, and the like. The consequences of the low-wage economy are becoming increasingly apparent in the suburbs where the immigrants live. Workers hang out at corners where contractors and other employers drive by to select them as day laborers. To find affordable housing, many of the immigrants crowd into substandard housing. Local health clinics and schools are overcrowded. In these and in other ways, the social consequences of ethnic division and inequality have come to the suburbs of Long Island, and increasingly to suburbs everywhere.

In Selection 16, Eric Avila describes how the past pattern of "chocolate" cities and "vanilla" suburbs is giving way to a complex patchwork that continues to preserve racial, ethnic, and class inequalities. On one end of a spectrum is the high-tech manufacturing district, or "technopolis," which employs the highly skilled and highly paid workers at the top of the global economy. These workers tend to live in exclusive gated communities. At the other end of the spectrum are the low-wage workers who also give energy to the global economy, including people who work in sweatshops, do domestic labor, and work in temporary jobs. They live in older, often deteriorating suburbs. There is, finally, the middle class, who truly are caught in the spatial mosaic of the suburbs. Avila shows that the cultural interpretations of this complex landscape contrast sharply with the cultural legacy from the era of white flight.

Selection 17, from Dolores Hayden's *Building Suburbia*, describes how suburban sprawl is "planned" by political wheeling and dealing among developers, local governments, and other promoters of commercial building projects who take advantage of subsidies and tax breaks as well as laws interpreted in their favor to make such projects viable. Hayden describes how this process has often led to fast-paced growth of low-quality and poorly conceived projects on small and large scale, from vast retail malls, hodge-podge commercial strips, big box stores, and office parks to stand-alone "edge cities" that quickly become obsolete. This commercialization of suburban space often has devastating effects on existing businesses that are threatened by the flight of tenants and shoppers to whatever is new in nearby areas. Hayden concludes that, "For the most part, edge nodes are uncomfortable and ugly places. Building is cheap; depreciation is accelerated; obsolescence is rapid . . . developers . . . design for rapid turnover." Although most of these enclaves of commerce and industry have few defenders and many critics, the political system of suburbia is poorly equipped to change things. Yet the hand of the public sector helps make this style of development possible.

# 14

## *Andrew Ross*

---

## KINDER, GENTLER GOVERNMENT?

"Government, like dress, is the badge of lost innocence."

—Thomas Paine

"Walt wasn't against people voting; he just didn't want them hanging their dirty laundry out. . . . I don't agree. I don't disagree."

—Michael Eisner

"Everyone has made a sacrifice to be here." This belief was an article of faith among Celebrationites, and everyone paid lip service to it. Sacrifice was seen as a built-in condition of pioneerism, stressed routinely in Town Hall newsletters and drummed home in the annual speeches by clergy and managers on Founder's Day.

This perception of selflessness had even helped persuade some retirees to come to Celebration rather than to one of Florida's adult communities. In this category were Jim and Jane Clayman, whose home on the pioneer row of Teal Avenue was crammed with art and artifacts from their working lives in Peru and Brazil and whose porch rockers had once stood on Jane's mother's porch in Kentucky. The Claymans had been attracted by the many young parents they saw at the lottery who seemed willing to forgo creature comforts for a worthier cause. "We'll be eating peanut butter and jelly," one of them had said to the couple, "but this is what we want for our children.". . .

With all of this talk about sacrifice, I might have been excused for inferring that I was living in a training camp for humanitarian workers rather than one of the wealthiest towns in Central Florida. I thought I had surrendered a fair chunk of my own life to go and live in Celebration (among other things, my year out took a fatal toll on the relationship with my girlfriend), but this noble impression would have to be downgraded. Compared to the ordeals of my fellow citizens, my own burdens were a trifle. Living amid so many accounts of great hardship, I needed a regular reality check. Every so often, I would motor out of town in pursuit of places where poverty and hardship were as conspicuous on the ground as Spanish moss was on the trees. In Osceola's trailer parks,

---

Orlando's ghettoes, and all the twilight districts in between, people might have thought they had gotten a raw deal, for which they might have paid dearly. Yet they would probably not have chosen to describe their lives as a condition of self-sacrifice. Sacrifice goes by other names when it is not buttressed by the sense of entitlement that often percolated through Celebration.

But Central Florida's less privileged had one dubious advantage over the Celebrationites. If you do not have the option of living in a pricey, planned community you do not have to agonize over whether to restrict your freedoms in order to abide by the rules. Of all the sacrifices faced by Celebrationites, this was the one that generated the most commentary from outsiders, and the least reflection from residents themselves.

The hundred-page "Declaration of Covenants, Conditions, and Restrictions" signed by all homeowners, and the less weighty, but substantial, document signed by tenants like myself, were generally referred to as "standards" implemented to guarantee the physical upkeep of the houses and streets of Celebration. If these restrictions were of negligible concern to residents, they loomed larger for folks who decided not to move to Celebration, including some who had placed highly on the original lottery draw, and many others who had investigated residency through Celebration Realty. In the course of the year, I ran into several who had decided that the rules and restrictions were too much of an imposition on their personal land use. (Small lot sizes, lack of privacy, and the jitteriness about the school figured among the other reasons.) The chance to build this community would effectively be limited to those willing to regulate their conduct, and perhaps curb their liberties, to safeguard their property values.

One resident, a middle-income manager from a working-class background, explained to me one day that working-class people "don't share the same civic culture as us" and "because they value their freedom of expression too highly, they would not tolerate the deed restrictions." He figured he must "sound like a jerk for saying so," but his comment was little different from the nightmare neighbor scenarios conjured up by many others of unruly, low-class folks with trucks, rundown '83 Buicks; and washing lines in the yard, not to mention garish colors on their window frames.

The "Covenants, Conditions, and Restrictions" are common in planned communities (these days, many bankers will not issue loans without them), but, true to form, Celebration's rulebook got special attention in the media and was widely cited by outsiders as evidence of the company's totalitarian control over residents. One section, in particular, would become quite famous in its own right:

> 6a) Unless the Board of Directors otherwise agrees, the only acceptable coverings that may be affixed to the interior of any windows visible from any street, alley or other portion of the Properties are drapes, blinds, shades, shutters and curtains. The side of such window coverings that is visible from the exterior of any improvements must be white or off-white in color.

Town Hall clocked more phone calls about this one rule than all the others combined. Brent Herrington [Celebrations manager] reminded townspeople, in a Town Hall newsletter in the fall of 1997, that he intended to implement the rule: "I have noticed a couple of residences where the owner has installed colored window coverings, and, unfortunately, these will need to be corrected." For once, at least, the derisory response around town partially echoed the mockery of the media, especially since the warning was accompanied by Herrington's opinion that the colored drapes in question were "icky." Most residents knew that one highly visible window, in a Longmeadow home, had been in violation of the rule for several weeks, and the owners' initial decision to hold out had become a cause célèbre. Since the rule was regarded as a little excessive, many townspeople saw this resident's red drapes as a flag of liberty. In general, however, Celebrationites were quick to fault Town Hall for not cracking down sooner on offending residents. In this town, the developer was perceived to have better taste than the residents, and so homeowners were not happy when management was lax about enforcement.

In response, Herrington encouraged residents to take pride in Town Hall's personal touch. In most planned communities with homeowners associations, negligent residents are sent a formal letter of warning. In kinder, gentler Celebration, they receive an informal phone call. This technique belongs more to the code of friendly customer relations—Disney's field of expertise—than of an inflexible bureaucracy. As far as governance went, everyone understood that the basis for the town's restrictions, perhaps even its "sense of community," lay in the bedrock desire to maintain and promote the value of property investments. It was in bad taste, and antisocial, to remind anyone of this, and besides, it was unnecessary to do so since in Celebration this belief was as natural as breathing.

## Common Interests

Levittown, as Herbert Gans pointed out, was neither a town—which would offer employment—nor a community—which suggests a desire for sharing values. The Levittowners moved there to own a home, most of them for the first time in their lives. Celebration did not yet feel like a town, but it was conceived and populated with the aim of becoming a community as quickly as possible. Between the era of the Levittowns and this new place in Osceola County, the idea of building self-contained communities evolved into a staple of the housing industry in Sunbelt states like Florida. Today, most developers will say they are building communities, not subdivisions.

Historically, most communities were not designed by professionals at all, let alone planned in any systematic way. Community design was the outcome of piecemeal building by artisans, craftsmen, townsfolk, and peasants. Celebration's neighboring lakeside towns of Kissimmee and St. Cloud are typical, modern examples. Most of the great European cities so admired for their urbanity are haphazard hybrids of aristocratic pleasure grounds, sober bourgeois quarters, merchants' commercial enclaves, and proletarian holding tanks. It was not until the onset of rational urban planning at the turn of the century that professionally designed communities would see the light of day as an industrial enterprise.

Originating in Britain, in Ebenezer Howard's blueprint for the Garden City (which rested on cooperative ownership of the land), this planning concept was translated into the American private housing landscape in the form of common-interest development.[1] Today, we know these as planned unit developments, condominiums, or co-ops, where private developers offer buyers commonly shared land. Oftentimes, they are governed by covenants and deed restrictions that "run with the land" and forbid alternative uses of the land in the future. These covenants, which date back to twelfth-century England, protect property value, and, to ensure further protection, homeowners associations offer a form of community governance, at the behest of fellow residents' votes and assessments, which assumes many of the public responsibilities of local government. In the United States, the evolution of these interlocking institutions has given rise to what Roderick McKenzie calls "privatopia," which he describes as a condition of private government currently enjoyed by over 40 million Americans, or about 17 percent of the population.[2] By the year 2000, it is estimated that a quarter of a million homeowner associations will exist, exacting restrictions to guarantee members' property value, and where the only form of participation for homeowning shareholders is to satisfy their contractual obligations by maintaining their mortgage payments.

The privatopian community has become the preferred development for builders of nonurban housing in the last two decades. Lenders are increasingly unlikely to issue mortgages for planned developments unless they have a homeowner association.[3] The flourishing of walled and gated communities—a natural extension of privatopia—arouses widespread concern about a rampant "fortress mentality" in late suburban America, signifying what Robert Reich termed the "secession of the successful" from all public contact with, let alone obligation toward, their less fortunate fellow citizens.[4] One of the most common outsider misperceptions of Celebration is that it is gated, or that its managed ambience is "gated" even in the absence of a physical gatehouse and uniformed guards. On the contrary, the creation of this town is a highly visible counterpunch to the prestige ethos of the gated community. Virtually every resident I met, including many who had lived behind electronic gates before, took pride in the town's open public access and resented the mischaracterization. Should some calamity occur as a result of this openness, the decision about whether to keep the town open will be a real test of residents' commitment to retaining its cherished public character.

In principle, the concept of the homeowner association promises self-government to residents, and in its most shrewdly promoted versions, conjures up the sanctity of ultra-democratic Town Hall meetings, New England-style. In Celebration, Town Hall's information sheets about governance describe membership in the association as "a repressentative form of government similar to our federal system." Yet voting in the association, unlike in the federal system, is restricted to homeowners (not renters), and to one vote per property unit. (In addition, a supermajority of 75 percent is needed to carry any motion.) In most developments like this, the developer will retain control of governance until two-thirds of the lots are sold, and often exercises voting rights thereafter based on continued ownership of parcels of land or other residual rights. When homeowners eventually do take on elected positions, regulating in accordance with the developer's original rules, their zeal often marks them out as "condo nazis," and residents pine for the professional management of the fledgling years.

The governance of Celebration is not exceptional in this regard. The company controls the homeowners association until 25 percent of the units are sold, at which point one out of three board directors are elected by the residents of the town's several villages. After 50 percent, the residents elect two of five directors, and after 75 percent, three of five. One year after this initial "control period" lapses, six of seven directors are elected, and a year later, the developer withdraws all official representation on the board. The 75 percent deadline is nullified if the buildout has not reached this level after forty years. The developer can also withdraw before the deadline at its own discretion. But the "Covenants, Conditions, and Restrictions" also record that nothing can be changed without the decree of the "owners of at least 75% of the total number of Units within the Properties and by the Celebration Company." The latter clause is particularly notable. So long as TCC owns any property or developable land in Celebration, it has veto power over all changes in governance. While they had all read and signed the covenants, the vast majority of residents were unaware of this veto power until an article in the *New York Times* magazine pointed it out. When I asked Herrington to clarify the matter, he professed that although he thought he knew the document very well, he too had not been fully cognizant of this veto power. "In practice," he ventured, "using those kinds of residual powers is a little bit like setting off an atomic bomb in your own underwear," especially for a developer who, at that point, would be "contributing zero to the budget, and has nothing at risk."

For the most part, Celebrationites were content with what they often called their "benevolent dictator" (a phrase that originates in Walt's comment that he wouldn't want to be U.S. president but would "rather be the benevolent dictator of Disney enterprises"[5]). Though if things got too "Orwellian," as one of my tennis partners observed, that would be another matter. It was expected that the company would maintain good order, and so long as the decision making remained benign, TCC would serve residents' private interests better than would any office-bearers elected from their own ranks. Among the townsfolk, I ran into several former presidents of homeowner associations who swore that Town Hall's administering of the rules was much kinder and gentler than in the associations of housing developments they had known, some of which had the power to enter private homes and to restrict the stay of guests. The deed restrictions were no more, and in some cases less, severe than those they had helped to administer elsewhere. Terry Neff, who had served as an association president in nearby Hunter's Creek, even alleged that helicopters had been used there to survey residents' backyards for infractions of the rules, though no one I questioned at Hunter's Creek could confirm this.

If anything, Herrington's light enforcement of the rules drew complaints about the laxity of regulation—"things are not being kept up." Aware of media scrutiny, it's likely that Town Hall sometimes chose to waive some of the micro-rules rather than risk public ridicule in yet another boilerplate press report about the company's suppression of civic liberties. To compensate, residents exercised their own scrutiny, building a groundswell of hearsay that Town Hall could not easily ignore. Many townsfolk were vexed, for example, when homes were not lived in. An ornate, ochre Mediterranean estate home had been lying vacant on Golfpark Drive for as long as I could remember. This violated the residency rule (a home should be occupied for at least nine months of the year), and reinforced conjecture that there was one rule for the wealthy and one for the others. The rumor around town (other than that it belonged to Julia Roberts) was that a rich businessman had bought the home for his wayward son, who decided never to occupy it. On the other hand, there were some decrees that disgruntled residents were happy to see annulled. The rule, established as an anti-speculation deterrent, that no one could profit from sale of a home within one year of closing, was routinely waived if the seller could prove "hardship.". . .

One evening in April, the Osceola County Planning Department called a meeting in Town Hall to solicit residents' feedback for its reappraisal of a comprehensive plan adopted in 1990. Poorly advertised and ill-timed at the dinner hour, the meeting attracted only three residents (it would take a while for residents to feel that their input in county affairs might be a priority). In attendance were myself, Jim Bayley, president of the Celebrators and an inveterate presence at all community events, and Ray Chiaramonte, the Tampa urban planner. It was mostly a red-tape affair for county bureaucrats, but at a late hour, we were asked whether we thought residents would eventually vote to incorporate the town. From the outset, this prospect had been widely discussed among residents, although very few seemed to be aware that the state requires all Community Development Districts to hold a referendum on incorporation when they reach a population threshold—about 9,800, in the case of Celebration.

In response to the question, Bayley summarized the majority view of the "benevolent dictator." If nothing goes too badly amiss, Celebrationites would probably be happier living with the rules laid down by Disney, as interpreted by residents on the board. I summarized another view I had found on residents' lips. Since it had attracted more than its share of independently minded citizens, hungry for true self-government, Celebrationites, I predicted, would incorporate sooner or later. For his part, Ray declared that residents were "more interested in pragmatism than politics," and suggested they would actively resist incorporation for that reason. Of course, there was much more to be said on this topic, and we had not begun to cover the views of all the townsfolk. But these three positions were fairly representative. Jim's opinion displayed a concerned tolerance of the status quo and a general desire to hold the developer to its obligations. Mine was based on evidence of residents' pushing already for more input in decision making, and on their general frustration with outsiders' perception of the community as a Disney-controlled "puppet state." Ray's comment reflected the conviction of many residents who had moved here, in part, to escape from local government politics. It may have also reflected his own professional relish for utilitarian order. Civic politics have a tendency to get in the way of planners' designs.

In truth, none of us had hit on the most likely factor to influence votes on incorporation—the cost of government. Most planned communities figure out whether they will have to pay more or less to assume control over their own destinies. Gary Moyer, the manager of the Celebration Community District, was not able to estimate the financial feasibility for Celebration, but he cited the example of Weston, an Arvida development to the south, where his company is also contracted. Residents there had recently incorporated, and had established what Moyer called "an almost 100 percent contract city," with only three full-time employees. The services of everyone else were contracted. Weston had no mayoral governance structure; it was pure management all the way down.

Many Celebration residents felt they had been promised a "town," with all the municipal trappings that term evoked, but, when the time came, the Weston model might just offer the preferred privatopian alternative—a township with no real public representatives. In the meantime, one sure thing I had learned is that Celebrationites were very defensive about any suggestion—a favorite in the media—that they lived in a less than democratic environment. They knew that they enjoyed the same rights as any other citizen of the republic, and, far from considering the deed restrictions to be an erosion of these rights, they saw the maintenance of community standards as an extra layer of privileges that local government could not otherwise afford. On the other hand, I interviewed several who made a point of speaking passionately about their dislike for "democracy." What could this possibly mean?

John Pfeiffer, the doctor who had moved from Ohio to fulfill a childhood dream of driving a Disney monorail, offered an explanation:

> I'd rather live in a civil than a political society. Here we have a contract with TCC that defines our property rights, and we are not frustrated by bureaucrats with their own agenda. I don't have a contract with politicians. . . . What we have here is a deconstructing of government, a roll-back of politicization. In a civil society you feel a desire to fit into a community and satisfy your neighbors. In a political society, under the heavy hand of government, you expect your neighbors to satisfy you.

Pfeiffer, who looked preternaturally young for his age (he and his wife had fully adult offspring), and who wore a baseball cap backwards to Town Hall meetings, was satisfied that his "contract" gave him more rights than one that was not based on property rights: "We have more self-determination here under a nonpolitical regime than in a political society." His views offered the purest statement of a vision of governance entirely based on property rights. Nor did everyone's property rights appear to be equal. For Pfeiffer, who owned an estate home, there seemed to be a sliding scale, on which owners of smaller lots might have a lesser contract. "If you have less expensive houses, you lose the sense of sacrifice," he explained, adding a new spin to the Celebration ethos of self-sacrifice.

However chilling to behold, these were hardly crankish views in the world of Florida's planned communities. Yet for all the security represented by Pfeiffer's "contract" with the developer, there was little residents could do to stop the company from obtaining a zoning variance to alter its plans for the site, or from blocking a majority resident initiative. As Ray Chiaramonte pointed out, "the developer could decide to put in a Saturn manufacturing plant." At a meeting in June, when TCC unveiled plans for the commercial corridor, several residents loudly expressed dismay at the prospect of twelve-story hotels rising up to obscure their westward views: "We feel it's no longer a small town," one grieved, "it looks like a city, with big buildings." They must have forgotten that they had signed a raft of disclaimers at closing, among which was a waiver of their rights to a view. Pfeiffer's contract could easily turn into a raw deal, and homeowners' rights could often seem like thin, self-addressed envelopes.

Given the legal maze of the "Covenants, Conditions, and Restrictions," it's small wonder there was a general fuzziness in residents' understanding of their internal rights. Most Celebrationites confessed they did not really understand the town's system of governance, and habitually flunked when examined on details regarding the fiduciary responsibilities of entities like the Community Development District. Unlike most master-planned communities, Celebration had as many as four entities of governance: the Residential Owner's Association; a Non-Residential Owner's Association, which represented retailers and owners of apartment parcels; the Community Development District, a quasi-government entity which provided services and was responsible for maintenance of infrastructure (water, sewage, roads, drainage, landscaping) and utilities; and an Enterprise Community Development District, responsible for services to the commercial campus. An over-arching Joint Committee governed all four, and Town Hall functioned as a one-stop home for the whole kit and caboodle. Celebration actually enjoys more of a working distinction between public and private sectors of governance than in most communities with homeowner associations. Here, the municipal functions of government relating to infrastructure are handled by the Community Development District, a unit of special-purpose government created by the Florida Land and Water Adjudicatory Commission, and whose board of supervisors, currently all Disney executives, will eventually be elected by landowners in the district. By contrast, the homeowner association's realm is limited to more private matters such as those relating to architectural review and community standards and restrictions.

Naturally, residents tend to take more of an interest in matters of governance when their property values are on the line. Jim Whelan, the canny psychologist and dedicated cyclist, confessed to me one day: "I didn't think for one minute about the governance structure of the town until I decided to sell the house." After less than a year in town, he and his family had decided to move back to Mahwah, New Jersey. He had only recently discovered that homeowners are not permitted to erect a "For Sale" notice in their yards. In Whelan's view, this helped give the developer a virtual monopoly over the housing market in town. He had begun to suspect that the residency rules helped reinforce the monopoly while masquerading as a deterrent against speculators. Whelan's suspicions in this matter were unconfirmed, but it was significant that his property interest was the factor that galvanized his concern about governance.

In the course of my year in Celebration, at least one hiccup in governmental process did occur, and went entirely unnoticed by residents. The chronic problems caused by the narrowness of the back alleyway increasingly demanded a resolution. At a Community Development District meeting in December, the board members decided they would consider a "one-way" designation for alleys if a majority of the residents on the block petitioned and voted for the measure. There was some discussion about the percentage of votes required: would it be 51 percent, 65 percent, or 75 percent? At several such meetings I attended, no residents were present, and this one was no exception. The meetings were tedious and mostly technical in content, although a period was always set aside on the agenda for public comment. The board decided to implement a 65 percent rule. Several weeks later, residents on Campus Street and Greenbriar were informed in a letter from Town Hall that their alleyways were now one-way streets. No formal votes had been taken, and no one I talked to on those streets had noticed the oversight. It was a small measure, and by all accounts a popular one. Nor was it likely to affect the value of anyone's property. But this had been the first time in Celebration when a residential vote was endorsed, in principle, and yet it had not been solicited.

## Utopia Achieved

Advocates of homeowner associations often argue that their method of community rule keeps at bay the messy intrusion of "politics." Yet there were some Celebrationites, like Larry Haber, a founder of the town's Jewish Council and the Jewish Congregation and whose family had been the town's first official residents, who saw the management structure as a perfect embodiment of their own partisan politics. A busy pioneer, Haber was active in United Way and saw himself as a George Will kind of Republican—social libertarian, fiscal conservative, religious liberal, and fierce opponent of big government. In addition, he was a Disney employee who had no great affection for "big corporate paternalism," a trait shared by many Celebrationites I knew who were also company employees. Haber believed Celebration to be the ideal Republican state in miniature, without government's layers of elected officials to stifle the process of self-determination. In fact, Celebration was pretty close to what Haber saw as a "condition of direct democracy." He said he had liberal friends in town who saw their own politics reflected in Celebration's community values, and he liked to tease them by declaring they were simply "closet Republicans." I never met any liberals who could match Haber's view with a counterclaim, based on their own principles, but it was not inconceivable that they existed in Celebration. In addition, there were residents like Pat Breck, a pro-choice Catholic who attended Presbyterian services, who believed that Celebration was a conservative community in a cultural sense. Conservatives, in her view, are "people people," a "tribe that looks out for another," and she associated liberals with "working mothers and latchkey children."

Haber's view of the town as personifying his own ideal of a pure political utopia was probably exceptional. When people loosely referred to Celebration as a "utopia," they generally meant that it was a good place to start over again, where other places had failed, or that it was a place of general happiness where no one had reason, other than his or her own personal misfortune, to be disenchanted. The use of the phrase had little connection to the venerable American tradition of utopian communities.

In the fanciful European mind, the New World had always been imagined as a utopian place, with apocalyptic dimensions—the end of the world as we know it and the beginning of a new order. The early Puritan settlements, with their own form of community *covenant*, including a New Urbanist–type rule that required residents to live within a mile and half of the meetinghouse, established a model for hundreds of utopian religious communities to follow. These were founded in the seventeenth and eighteenth centuries on the principle of the communal ownership of property by sects like the Shakers, the Rappites, the Moravian Brethren, the Zoar Separatists, and the True Inspirationists of Amana. Some survived for hundreds of years, and a few are still extant. The nineteenth-century versions were mostly secular, like Brook Farm, New Harmony, Fruitlands, Skanateales, Nashoba, Oneida, and the Phalanxes, and were heavily influenced by the anarchist and socialist ideas of Robert Owen and Charles Fourier. More than a hundred sprang up before the Civil War, each with its own polished vision of a new age to come where inhabitants would be truly free to pursue a rational form of the good life.[6] The equivalent in this century were the thousands of hippie communes founded in the late 1960s and early 1970s as living laboratories of a communal freedom that the materialism of consumer society promised but could never deliver. However short-lived, these were all intentional communities, planned as pocket-size correctives to the corruption and inequalities of dominant society. All of them, from the religious to the countercultural versions, experienced the tension between freedom and order that is intrinsic to the planned utopia. . . .

Homeowner's associations have proved an efficient and popular form of common-interest management, and by now they are a semi-permanent feature of the suburban landscape where planners like [Andres] Duany have decided to operate. But the rage to embrace this form of governance and the willingness to salute a corporate monopoly—Duany's "managed market"—troubled folks like myself for whom efficiency, civic order, and exacting management are not overriding goals in and of themselves. When planners accept these forms of management as the price for pushing their own architectural dreams, or as pragmatic compromises in the game of competing with suburban alternatives, some features of their hallowed ideal of civility, freely endorsed by all, are sacrificed. And when citizens are viewed primarily as consumers or as property holders, with no obligations beyond the protection of their own assets, an important line gets crossed.

For one thing, some forms of civic disorder are crucial to the political life of the republic. Without civic disobedience, it has been proved, again and again, that there is little hope of changing unjust laws, discriminatory codes, and exclusive patterns of institutional behavior. The civil rights and life opportunities of a vast percentage of the population have been concessions won from the powerful only after prolonged opposition to the existing rules of civic order. Abiding suspicion of these rules is widespread, whether in the form of distrust of "white justice" or "upper middle class standards," although such distrust is often vilified and blamed for the decline of everything from public manners to the upkeep of housing stock. Moralists see this resistance to civic order as a reflection of laziness and bad character, or as part of a general weakening of respect and refinement. But most of the time it is a result of friction generated between groups who have unequal resources and advantages. In addition, the pattern of most civic disorder reveals that "civility" usually covers a very narrow spectrum of tolerable behavior and is designed as much to exclude as to invite common participation. As if to compensate for all their good civic behavior, some Celebrationites wistfully conjured up a rough-and-ready presence in the streets. One day, as we were sharing a bench, and a slow day, on Market Street, a retiree, and an ex-military man at that, observed: "What we need are a few drunks around this town."

From what I had learned, most Celebrationites were attracted to the efficiency of private government. Many spoke to me of their loss of faith in public institutions and public government, and described democratic public process as laborious, wasteful, and inept. I always found this to be a circular argument, since the capacity of public institutions—especially urban ones—to function efficiently has been decimated by the siphoning away of resources brought about by the rise of suburban privatopias. Tax starvation is one of the reasons it takes a while for someone to answer Andres Duany's phone call at City Hall in Miami. Besides, no one who has tried to be a fully functioning participant in a democratic process ever discovered it to be truly efficient. Just and accountable, perhaps, but never the most economic use of time, energy, or resources. The rage for privatization that has swept the country, and much of the developed world, routinely sacrifices justice and accountability at the altar of efficiency. In practice, the efficiency of most forms of private governance is easily subverted, especially when its member-consumers take legal action. My own apartment in New York City belongs to a co-op, the most minimal form of common-interest development, and I had briefly served as vice president of the co-op board. It was an exhausting term of office, which often involved lengthy weekly meetings with lawyers when a mean-spirited set of residents repeatedly sued the co-op for weather damages to their apartment walls.

As residents found out for themselves, the early, informal attempts at democratic opinion making in Celebration were a messy business, conducted discreetly or semi-publicly among interest groups that had formed around the town's hot spots—primarily the school and home construction. Heedful of their potential labeling as "negative," Celebrationites quickly became aware of the leverage they could command if they "went to the press" to publicly embarrass the company. In this capacity, they wielded a power unavailable to almost any another residential community. Celebration may have been tarred by association with the "Truman effect," and certainly the media had generated no end of caricatures of residents who lived here. But townsfolk learned early on that the threat of media publicity could be their ally. Celebration was, and would always be, like the child of a famous public figure, basking in the warm glow of its birthright or suffering for the sins of its parent. Its private life could be ushered on to the public stage at any moment.[7]

# NOTES

1. Garden Cities literature includes Ebenezer Howard, *Tomorrow: A Peaceful Path to Real Reform* (London, 1898); Raymond Unwin, *Town Planning in Practice* (London, 1911); Robert Fishman, *Urban Utopias in the Twentieth Century* (New York: Basic Books, 1977); Daniel Schaffer, *Garden Cities for America: The Radburn Experience* (Philadelphia: Temple University Press, 1982); Clarence Stein, *Towards New Towns for America* (New York: 1951); Henry Wright, *Rehousing Urban America* (New York: Columbia University Press, 1935); Lewis Mumford, *The Culture of Cities* (New York: Harcourt, Brace, 1938); Catherine Bauer, *Modern Housing* (Boston: Houghton Mifflin, 1934). Jane Jacobs blasts away at the Garden City tradition in *The Death and Life of Great Cities.*
2. Evan MacKenzie, *Privatopia: Homeowner Associations and the Rise of the Residential Private Court* (New Haven: Yale University Press, 1994).
3. MacKenzie points out that, for large developers, the common-interest development was an efficient and profitable solution to the rising cost of land in the late 1970s, and the growing demand for common amenities like golf courses, swimming pools, and recreational areas. More residents could be squeezed onto smaller lots, common open space would be an attractive feature of the consumer package, restrictive covenants could be drawn up to favor the lender and the developer, and professional community managers would be employed to mediate any conflicts between uppity residents and the developers themselves.
4. Edward Blakeley and Mary Gail Snyder, *Fortress America: Gated Communities in the United States* (Washington, D.C.: Brookings Institution Press, 1997).
5. Quoted in Richard Schickel, *The Disney Version: The Life, Times, Art, and Commerce of Walt Disney* (New York: Simon & Schuster: 1968), p. 158.
6. Dolores Hayden, *Seven American Utopias: The Architecture of Communitarian Socialism, 1780–1975* (Cambridge, MIT Press, 1976); Arthur Bestor Jr., *Backwoods Utopias* (Philadelphia: University of Pennsylvania Press, 1950); *Heavens on Earth: Utopian Communities in America* (New York: Dover, 1966); Y. Ovel, *Two Hundred Years of American Communes* (New Brunswick, N.J.: Transaction Books, 1988).
7. In February 1999, a monthly newspaper—the *Celebration Independent*—made its debut in a community that was already information rich. Published by resident Alex Morton, the first issue carried a front-page story excoriating BFI garbage disposal company for its deficient recycling program and for its use of large trucks that ravaged the grass on back alley lawns. A cautious editorial in the second issue applauded the "changes" at Celebration School. Most of the other stories boosted events and personages around town. Neither issue alluded to the ongoing history of construction problems.

# 15

## *Rosalyn Baxandall and Elizabeth Ewen*

## NEW IMMIGRANTS IN SUBURBIA

## New Immigrants

Beginning in the 1980s many older white residents began leaving Long Island suburbs for more rural places or warmer climes. At the same time, a mosaic of immigrants, mainly from Central America but also from South America, the subcontinent of India, Asia, and the Middle East, were moving to Long Island. Japanese, Iranians, Koreans, Cubans, Haitians, and Vietnamese, as well as Indians, Pakistanis, Guatemalans, and Salvadorans, were part of a national trend in immigration. No one knows exactly how many new immigrants live on Long Island. Even the Immigration and Naturalization Service cannot estimate the number. Some experts point to the growth of the Salvadoran population as an indication of the extent of the surge: "In 1979 before civil war broke out in El Salvador, there were as few as 5,000 Salvadorans living on the island. Today according to immigrant groups and outreach workers, the number is well over 100,000."[1]

Unlike their turn-of-the-century predecessors, these immigrants were not of one class. They were wealthy, educated, middle class, working class, uneducated, and poor. Traditionally families moved to suburbs to escape metropolitan exigencies and acquire a private house, with a car in the garage and a yard on a quiet, uncluttered street where children can roam freely. For poor immigrants this is not the case; they live and work in situations that rival the worst turn-of-the-century sweatshops and tenements, exposed by muckrakers like Jacob Riis and Lewis Hines. Few muckrakers today expose the suburban underbelly. Omar Enriquez, organizer for the Workplace Project, suggested, "The problem is much bigger on Long Island than most people will admit. We have a dirty secret here."[2]

Generally poor and unacculturated, the new immigrants challenge the suburban image while their labor helps to preserve and enhance it.[3] "With unemployment at 2.8 percent in Nassau and 3.7 percent in Suffolk, experts and local officials say many of these [low-paying] jobs would not get done without immigrant labor."[4] Nonetheless, some older residents—especially those who live near the immigrants—just don't want them in their backyards. As Vincent Bullock, seventy-five, of Farmingdale, Long Island, said, "[The] long and short of it [is], they're knocking down my property values and I'll be damned if I'm paying a dime to help them do it."[5]

Part of the problem is that many suburbanites and public officials see the issue as cultural rather than economic. Older residents, white and black, complain about men hanging out in groups on suburban street corners, talking and listening to loud music until late at night; yet none of them bother to ask why these new residents are out on the street.

One of the factors that had always differentiated suburbs from cities is the absence of street culture. Front porches and stoops rarely were found. Street life for new suburban immigrants, however, is a result of cultural traditions and overcrowding. As one longtime Freeport resident explains, "Suburbia does not like the idea of people congregating fifteen to twenty of them on suburban street corners, sitting on top of their cars blaring their big radios."[6]

Long Island villages need to both familiarize immigrants with the tacit customs of the suburbs and get longtime residents to accept the different mores of their new neighbors. The village of Glen Cove issued a short flier explaining what is and is not considered acceptable: public drinking is against the law, but outdoor gatherings are not illegal, unless they block the street.[7]

Another striking difference is that most newer immigrants bypass the city and go directly from the airport to the suburbs, a pattern that had begun in the late 1950s, when the majority of suburban immigrants were Puerto Ricans. Cubans joined them in the 1960s and 1970s; in the 1980s Dominicans, Haitians, Jamaicans, Salvadorans, and others arrived from the Caribbean. Jennifer Gordon, organizer of the Workplace Project in Hempstead, makes the point that, "Long Island has become a center for Central Americans in the New York Metropolitan area and is home to more of them than New York City or any other urban area."[8]

Advertisements promising cheap property, jobs in farms, greenhouses, nurseries, factories, and domestic service brought many rural Central Americans to the United States. Others, mainly from El Salvador and Guatemala, came because of political oppression and violent civil wars. Rural families tended to be attracted to Suffolk, while those from cities came to work in the non-unionized light industries of the South Shore of Nassau County, to towns such as Freeport, Rockville Center, Westbury, Glen Cove, and Hempstead.[9]

By the late 1980s pressures began to mount over issues related to the new immigrant presence in schools, housing, jobs, and suburban culture. Long Island, like other suburban areas, had little experience in dealing with newly arrived, diverse immigrant populations. Recession, budget cuts, a skyrocketing real estate market, and anti-immigrant sentiment all conspired against integration into the existing culture. Unlike large cities, suburbs have few local governmental agencies, social services, or homeless shelters to accommodate immigrants. Since many are not eligible to vote, politicians have no motivation to help these groups. Nonprofit advocacy organizations such as the Community Advocates in Nassau, the Central American Refugee Center, and the Workplace

Project in Hempstead—an impressive center that assists immigrants with legal problems, holds classes in English and legal rights, and helps Hispanic residents in organizing labor co-ops—along with many churches have attempted, sometimes successfully, to fill the void. Like other pioneers to suburbia, immigrants rely on each other, their extended families, and informal networks.

Central American immigrants depend on an unconventional, illegal, and mostly informal economy—so hidden and secret that "Salvadorans call it by the Spanish phrase, *baja del agua* [underwater]. . . . In this economic underwater of Long Island there is nothing extraordinary about a suburban home doubling as a dental office or a restaurant, or a makeshift pharmacy in a bodega."[10] Most immigrants have to make use of this underwater economy. Sara Mahler, anthropologist, describes why: "You cannot survive on Long Island with the wages they are earning. In El Salvador, they hear they can make six dollars an hour and translate the worth to their home country. When they get here, they are shocked by the cost of living." In Hempstead, Westbury, and Brentwood,

> a licensed dentist charges about $55 dollars for tooth extraction, in the underwater, the bill comes to $25 dollars. A Main Street restaurant asks $1.25 for Salvadoran pupusas [made of thick tortillas and meat] but underwater cooks charge 75 cents. You can get your laundry done for two dollars and pharmaceuticals for about a dollar a pill.[11]

Although such networks offer the advantages of familiarity, language, and costs, they have disadvantages, too. Consumers have no legal recourse if service is shoddy or deleterious. Sometimes you get what you pay for, sometimes you don't.

The only work available to recent immigrants, who speak little English and sometimes are undocumented, is badly paid and erratic, with long hours and poor conditions. Immigrants often work as day workers doing landscaping or construction for local contractors. Some have more regular jobs in light manufacturing, building, cleaning, maintenance, and restaurants, or work as cashiers, stockroom clerks, gas station attendants, and domestics. Most of these jobs place immigrants at a disadvantage, because "They often take place outside the realm of the law. Employers are rarely registered with the appropriate authorities: many of them neither comply with labor laws nor pay taxes to the government and often, they fail to participate in mandatory insurance programs such as workers compensation or disability."[12]

Maria Luisa Paz (who used a pseudonym because she feared giving her own name) was undocumented and worked in a commercial laundry with 300 other Central American workers. Their work consisted of disinfecting, washing, pressing, and folding mounds of hospital linen. Her job was to fold the sheets that came off the presses. The damp sheets were scalding hot and seldom was she given anything to protect her hands. After a recent Occupational Health and Safety Organization (OSHA) inspection, the company was forced to hand out a few pairs of thin uninsulated gloves.

In the room where Paz worked the temperature was often 100 degrees. After a few weeks Paz's gloves had holes burned in every finger and her fingers were covered with large, watery blisters. Her shirt was splattered with blood from frequent heat-related nosebleeds, and her arms and legs were flecked with white chemical stains. She was not alone. Other workers had been injured as well: one man lost half a finger, another was severely burned on the chest by chemical water that had boiled over, and a woman fainted on the job from heat and fumes. When Paz complained, the owners responded, "We didn't do anything wrong; those health problems are your fault." She then was asked to produce work authorization and was fired when she couldn't. Paz then contacted OSHA about filing a discrimination complaint, but was discouraged because the OSHA investigator told her he couldn't do much for illegals like her.[13]

Suburbia would like simply to ignore these new faces, but often they become all too visible. One way they obtain work is by lining up along major thoroughfares in the morning so that work trucks can fetch them. This creates a problem for local residents, who resent this unsightly practice and gripe to the police, who then try to enforce local ordinances against loitering. In Glen Cove one policeman warned a group of men who had strayed into the street, "It's against the law to hang out in the street in groups, that's from the Mayor himself. We'll have to give you an appearance ticket or jail at worst, if we see you hanging around." When this message had been translated into Spanish, the full meaning sank in. Francisco Martinez, a Hempstead resident from El Salvador, "raised his hand and spoke, 'One question! We don't have the right to buy a coffee? If we go to buy a coffee, they are going to think we are hanging around'."[14] After much ruckus Glen Cove resolved the visibility issue by creating an unobtrusive location for the shape-up (work truck pickup). There are at least five other similar shape-up stops scattered throughout Nassau and Suffolk counties.

In another Long Island town, Inwood, residents in 1994 attempted to remove workers from the corner where they were lined up waiting for employment. The residents complained that the workers were disrupting the neighborhood. Workers were videotaped, verbally harassed, and physically threatened by townspeople who eventually had the police blockade the street. With the help of the Workplace Project, the workers negotiated a settlement for a better place to wait. If towns see these gatherings as disruptive, organizers find them useful for making workers aware of their rights and helping them set new wage standards.[15]

Another hazard immigrant workers face is being cheated out of their wages by fly-by-night companies. Raoul Melendez (a pseudonym) waited on a street corner in the town of Franklin Square with sixty other Latino men at six in the morning. Melendez thought himself lucky to find a job with a landscape company that employed him at first for a few days, then for two weeks. He began to relax waiting for his first paycheck.

Unfortunately, his hand was badly cut by a lawn mower. His employer drove him to the hospital promising to return, but never did. Melendez was not paid for any of his work and was sorely in need of Workers' Compensation—but the company that hired him was not listed in the phone book and not registered with the Chamber of Commerce. Melendez was never paid.[16]

One of Raoul's friends at the Franklin Square street corner, Miguel Gueverra (also an assumed name) was not paid for nine days of work with another landscape company. He tried to confront the boss, who told him that the owner of the house didn't pay him and "when I don't get paid, you don't get paid." Gueverra, along with other workers and the Workplace Project, devised a strategy. They figured out where the landscape boss was working and went to the job site to confront him. Disturbed by the noise, the owner of the house came out and witnessed the confrontation. The home owner was horrified and the landscaper embarrassed by being caught. The boss agreed to pay the money because the home owner said to Gueverra, "If he doesn't pay you the rest like he promised, I won't be paying him what I promised either." The next week the debt was paid in full.[17]

In order to circumvent these irresponsible employment practices, the Workplace Project has set up a landscaping cooperative. The Cooperative Landscaping Innovation Project (CLIP) serves over fifty private clients and a church. Workers are responsible for both the administration of the business and the landscaping itself. Everyone votes on the issues and owns a part of everything. They make $12 an hour, far more than the going wage. As Jose Martinez, who fled the war in El Salvador, where he worked as an electrician, exclaimed, "The miracle is happening. After nine years as a day laborer, I have become my own boss."[18] Another sign of the Workplace Project's success is the passage of the Unpaid Wages Prohibition Act in New York State. This bill creates penalties for nonpayment or payment under the minimum wage. Enforcement remains spotty.[19]

Even when there are laws and redress agencies, enormous problems remain. The Hempstead office of the New York State Department of Labor

> seems designed to discourage immigrants from filing claims of non-payment of wages. A Spanish speaking interviewer is only available for three hours once every two weeks. Moreover because no one who answers the phone—if it is answered at all—speaks Spanish, it is impossible for Spanish-speaking workers to learn the hours of the Spanish-speaking interviewer.[20]

Also, many wage claims that are filed are not investigated for long periods of time, sometimes as long as eighteen months.

The New York State Division of Human Rights, charged with enforcing antidiscrimination laws, takes up to five years to investigate and decide discrimination cases. These practices, combined with requests for documentation concerning taxes, witnesses, and authorization of work "effectively turn a blind eye to the entire underground economy, the arena of the greatest labor abuses."[21]

Another often invisible occupation taken by immigrants is domestic work. In the hierarchy of domestic work, living with an employer is considered the lowest rung of the ladder. Women are isolated without transportation and often are compelled to work hours without defined limits. Hidden in the homes of upper-middle-class suburbs are immigrant women who work up to fifteen-hour shifts six days a week for wages amounting to $2 an hour. The popular Spanish term for this job, *encerrado*, "gets to the heart of the matter—locked up."[22]

Some domestics work by the day cleaning, doing laundry, and taking care of children. These female workers face problems similar to those of their male counterparts: working long hours for less than minimum wage, being subjected to the whims of employers, and having little guarantees of payment or benefits. Dina Aguirre worked for three weeks for a family in Garden City without getting paid. "I worked from seven in the morning until seven at night and sometimes until 11. I asked the woman to pay me and she said, 'I don't owe you anything, because you ruined my blouse.' She said, 'Give me your address and I will send you a bill for all that you owe me.'" Aguirre was finally paid, but only after suing in small claims court. Even when domestic workers go to court for back wages, often they remain unpaid. Yanira Juarez worked for an employer in Bellport, where she won her claim in court for more than $2,000 in back wages, but she was never actually paid. "I returned and returned again, with a friend who spoke English to tell her that I needed the money. She took my address and said, I will send it, I'm still waiting."[23] Other employers deny even having employed the worker, or falsely accuse them of stealing.[24]

The Workplace Project is organizing domestic workers by circulating an advice book about scornful bosses and their overworked maids, as well as forming Justice Committees of domestic workers who will appear at employers' homes to show their court orders and demand back wages. They plan to follow this up with a cooperative for domestic workers.

These low-paid, tenuous employment practices make decent housing for immigrants hard to find, especially in suburbia, where there is little inexpensive housing and a market that favors single-family homes. Most communities have laws limiting the number of unrelated people sharing a home. Town and village officials do not have nearly enough inspectors to handle even a fraction of the hundreds of thousands of illegal apartments believed to exist on Long Island.[25]

Often then, immigrants are forced to live in substandard, illegal makeshift housing with five or six other families who share a single kitchen and bathroom. The situation is even worse for undocumented immigrants, who have no legal recourse and sometimes are forced into renting beds by the day or night. Often "an extra bed in someone's home is rented in shifts to day and night laborers who pay $300 dollars a month and call them hot beds because they are rarely without a warm body."[26] Landlords frequently let small rooms at inflated rents, from $250 to $500 a month; they can get as much as $5,000 a month leasing a house. In 1988 the Long Island Regional Planning Board estimated that there were at least 90,000 illegal apartments, "which is obviously an underestimation considering the massive new immigration and the difficulty in detection."[27]

Suburban neighborhoods by day present a tidy picture. By nightfall, when residents come home from work, the streets change to reveal telltale cracks in the suburban facade. Cars on lawns, groups of people walking because they can't speak enough English to get a driver's license, loud music, cookouts on the street, and general noise are signs that homes meant to house a family have now become rental tenements. Only catastrophe makes this situation fully apparent: a fire, a raid, or a fight.

In May 1999 in Huntington Station a fire engulfed a single-family house crowded with thirty-three Salvadoran immigrants, killing three people and leaving sixteen injured and thirty homeless.[28] Jose Santos Fuentes died of exposure in 1997, after falling into a creek next to his bed under a Glen Cove overpass.[29] Another fire, in Freeport in 1996, revealed twenty-two people, most of them Central American immigrants, crammed into makeshift cubicles of plywood and cardboard on every floor, from the basement up to the third-floor attic. A raid by police and building inspectors in Hicksville turned up nearly 100 immigrants living in a hodgepodge of one- and two-story buildings. The building's residents all worked, but they were living on the edge. Some, like the Delgado family, had pooled their income to pay $2,700 a month to house fifteen people in an office suite that had been converted into seven tiny bedrooms, two small kitchens, two bathrooms, and a tattered former reception area that served as a living room. The Delgado family still lives in this office suite, but now their bags are always packed in case of a raid.[30]

Even when inspections are made, there is no guarantee that living conditions will improve. Huntington's public safety director, Bruce Richards, said that in 1994,

> "inspectors found men living in outdoor sheds on property, and more people living in two apartments carved illegally out of the garage. The sheds were removed and the owner, Estrella Martinez, paid $375 in fines." In 1997 Mr. Richards checked out a report of an overflowing cesspool on the same property and discovered at least 15 people—all of them, apparently undocumented, living on the property: in a camper parked next to the garage; in four rooms in the cellar, two of which he likened to crawl space; and in an upstairs attic.[31]

The house was declared unfit for occupants and Ms. Martinez fined $1,100, but in January 1998 inspectors returned to investigate another complaint and found people again occupying illegal apartments and the cellar. She was given a summons and told to report to court. This situation is not unusual. Landlords calculate the fines in their cost of doing business.

As Marge Rogatz, president of the nonprofit Community Advocates in Nassau County, explained, "We are turning our backs on the low income people working in our communities. We need them to run all kinds of enterprises, but we are perfectly willing to have them come to work from living in a place we don't want to know about."[32]

The black market in housing is a result of the unwillingness to build low-income housing, or to change the zoning regulations that only allow single-family dwellings. The situation persists because of "the extraordinary collusion of landlords, tenants, real estate brokers and contractors tacitly abetted by judges and bureaucrats who are partly unwilling and partly unable to stop it."[33] Without new laws and protections, safety and health conditions cannot be assured.

The integration of this new population into the schools has also been difficult. Since 1990 Long Island has the highest level of students with limited English in New York State. Most of these limited-English districts are on the South Shore of Long Island. Some Long Island districts report that students speak thirty or more languages and dialectics.[34] Non-English-speaking students are expensive to educate; they need bilingual classes. Some school districts have tried to incorporate bilingual education into their curricula, at least for Hispanic students. The financial strain is greatest in poor districts that already are underfunded.

One solution is to place non-English-speaking students into special education classes, intended officially for the learning disabled. A 1994 special education report on teaching English as a second language noted that "the over representation of minorities and the foreign born in special education classes was not restricted to . . . Long Island. It reflects the failure of suburban school systems nationwide to adapt as their populations have changed." The report indicated that in many schools there is only "forty-five minutes of English instruction daily for students expected to master high school level mathematics, biology and history."[35]

One science teacher in Westbury, Long Island, taught twenty Haitian Creole-speaking students with no assistance. Eventually he became so frustrated that he slammed the door on a fourteen-year-old boy's finger, severing the tip. He landed in jail. The Haitian community then pressed school officials for Creole-speaking teachers and aides, but the Westbury school did not respond. Creole-speaking teachers were available, but the Haitian parents hadn't enough clout to ensure that their children's needs were met.[36]

Stringent residency requirements make it difficult for immigrant students to attend school. In many Long Island schools and other suburban districts in the country, one needs to prove residency by showing "lease contracts, mortgage statements and notarized letters from absentee landlords." Nine-year-old Daniel Amaya, whose family did not have these precious documents because they lived in a doubled-up dwelling, where such documents are difficult to attain, was barred from a Hempstead public school. Mrs. Amaya stated, "I have no idea who the owner is. I live with my two sisters." A meeting was arranged for immigrant women and children to explain the requirements. Unfortunately the Salvadoran group spoke no English and no official came to translate. Daniel Amaya captured the essence of this frustration when he said, "I don't understand anything they are saying, but they are really angry at all of us."[37]

In spite of these cultural skirmishes, the new immigrants have had an impact on Long Island. Street signs in a town such as Brentwood are in Spanish and English. In a delicatessen in Patchogue, a sign advertises a *cerveza light*. "The nearby mainstreet market sells baccaloo (dried cod fish) as well as t-bone steaks. Across the street at La Vida Christiana children receive religious instruction and adults learn English."[38] You can buy *platanos* (bananas used for cooking), Jamaican meat patties, curries of all varieties, and *Kim Chee* (Korean pickled cabbage). Video stores carry films in Indian dialects, Spanish, and Chinese.

> In Hicksville, a little India has developed encompassing a five block area offering food markets, restaurants, an Indian-owned hair salon and a duplex movie theatre showing only Indian films. The two biggest annual events [in Brentwood] ... are the St. Patrick's Day Parade in March and the Adelante Day Parade, which celebrates Hispanic struggle, in June.[39]

There is such variety now that ethnic neighbors don't automatically bond. "Twenty years ago, if you saw a Hispanic person, you held him and said, 'I'm Spanish,'" Roberto Portal explained. "Now we are so many that if we see a Hispanic, we go across the street."[40]

Suburbs are now becoming—albeit not always willingly—multiclass, multiethnic, and multiracial. This assimilation continues to be knotty and remains in flux. Can older suburbs accommodate these new ethnic groups, or will outmoded decentralized government structures and prejudice keep them hidden *baja del agua*—underwater? Will these new populations revitalize the dream and energize suburbia to change once again?

# NOTES

1. Charlie LeDuff and David Halbfinger, "Wages and Squalor for Immigrant Workers," *New York Times*, 5 May 1999.
2. *New York Times*, 24 July 1997.
3. Sara Mahler, "First Stop Suburbia," *NACLA* [North American Committee on Latin America] *Report on the Americas* 26, 1 (July 1992): 19.
4. LeDuff and Halbfinger, "Wages and Squalor."
5. Ibid.
6. Norman Appelton, interview by authors, January 1991.
7. Doreen Carvajal, "New York Suburbs Take on a Latin Accent," *New York Times*, 29 July 1993.
8. Jennifer Gordon, "We Make the Road by Walking: Immigrant Workers, the Workplace Project and the Struggle for Social Change," *Harvard Civil Rights Civil Liberties Law Review* (Summer 1995): 411.
9. Mahler, "First Stop Suburbia," 20–48.
10. Doreen Carvajal, "Making Ends Meet in a Nether World," *New York Times*, 13 December 1994.
11. Mahler, "First Stop Suburbia," 20–24.
12. Gordon, "We Make the Road by Walking," 412–13.
13. Ibid., 408, 418, 419.
14. Doreen Carvajal, "Out of Sight, Out of Mind, But Not Out of Work," *New York Times*, 8 July 1995.
15. Ibid.
16. Gordon, "We Make the Road by Walking," 408–9.
17. Ibid., 432.
18. Evelyn Nieves, "Day Laborer Stakes Out His Own Patch," *New York Times*, 10 May 1998.
19. *New York Times*, 24 July 1997; *New York Times* editorial, 31 August 1997; *New York Times*, 19 September 1997.
20. Gordon, "We Make the Road by Walking," 420–21.
21. Ibid., 418–21. See also Kenneth C. Crowe, "The Big Payback," *Newsday*, 7 January 1996.
22. Doreen Carvajal, "For Immigrant Maids, Not a Job But Servitude," *New York Times*, 25 February 1996.
23. Ibid.
24. *New York Times*, 24 July 1997.
25. LeDuff and Halbfinger, "Wages and Squalor."

26. Doreen Carvajal, "Making Ends Meet"; idem, "A Mayor Asks Help on Illegal Tenancies," *New York Times*, 11 October 1996.
27. Ibid., "A Mayor Asks Help"; LeDuff and Halbfinger, "Wages and Squalor."
28. Robert McFadden, "Fire in a Crowded Home of Immigrants Kills 3 and Injures 16 on L.I.," *New York Times*, 2 May 1999.
29. LeDuff and Halbfinger, "Wages and Squalor."
30. McFadden, "Fire in a Crowded Home."
31. Ibid.
32. Bruce Lambert, "Raid on Illegal Housing, Shows the Plight of Suburbs Working Poor," *New York Times*, 7 December 1996.
33. Frank Bruni, with Debra Sontag, "Behind a Suburban Facade in Queens, A Teeming Angry Urban Arithmetic," *New York Times*, 8 October 1996.
34. John Rather, "New Immigrants Transforming the Population," *New York Times*, 17 March 1996, Long Island edition.
35. Diana Jean Schemo, "Education as a Second Language," *New York Times*, 25 July 1994.
36. Doreen Carvajal, "Cultures Clash in Suburbs, Schools Struggle to Cope With Influx of Immigrant Students," *New York Times*, 8 January 1995.
37. Doreen Carvajal, "Immigrants Fight Residency Rules, Blocking Students in Long Island Schools," *New York Times*, 7 June 1995.
38. Sylvia Moreno, "Long Island Census Shows 3.9% Hispanic," *Newsday*, 27 April 1981.
39. Patrick Boyle, "Brentwood's a Melting Pot of Promise," *Newsday*, 1 December 1996; Lyn Dobrin, "The Spice Root in Hicksville." *Newsday*, 16 October 1995.
40. Ibid.

# 16

## *Eric Avila*

# FEAR AND FANTASY IN SUBURBAN LOS ANGELES

In our present age of accelerated globalization, Los Angeles is undergoing yet another round of economic restructuring and demographic upheaval . . . another new Los Angeles has taken shape, and the cultural matrix of chocolate cities and vanilla suburbs is giving way to new social interactions that mirror the striking changes that have transformed the region since the postwar period. The city's capacity for rapid change and incessant innovation has perforated the physical and cultural boundaries that distinguished white space from black space, and although the noir city and its heterosocial interactions have made a certain comeback in recent decades, race continues to shape the cultural geography of the contemporary urban landscape in more powerful and less subtle ways. Once more, the cultural landscape of Southern California's ever-expanding urban region holds clues to the countervailing forces of twenty-first-century urbanism.

Furthering the extremes between white wealth and nonwhite poverty, the demographic transformation of Los Angeles and its environs poses a powerful challenge to the regional hegemony of suburban whiteness. Since 1970, the vast influx of immigrant populations into Southern California has transformed the region from a bastion of middle-class whiteness into a Third World citadel. In 1970, 71 percent of Los Angeles County's population was non-Hispanic white or Anglo, and the remaining 29 percent of the population was divided among Latinos (15 percent), African Americans (11 percent), and Asian/Pacific Islanders (3 percent). By 1980, the non-Hispanic white population had dropped to 53 percent, and ten years later it had fallen further to 41 percent. Throughout the 1970s, large-scale immigration from Latin America and Asia, coupled with a moderate growth in the African American population, inflated the region's nonwhite population. Immigration to the region continued to expand throughout the following decade as the population of Asians and Latinos swelled. By 1990, Latinos comprised 36 percent of the city's population; African Americans and Asians constituted 11 percent respectively. Today's Los Angeles ranks among the most diverse urban regions in the world and the city once heralded as the "nation's white spot" now mirrors the polyglot diversity that defines the city and even its past.[1]

Fueling and fueled by demographic growth, economic restructuring in Southern California simultaneously enforces and enervates existing patterns of racial and ethnic inequality. Since the 1970s, the increasingly transnational currents of economic exchange have positioned the Los Angeles urban region to emerge as a "nodal point" within a new global economy. The manifestations of economic globalization in Southern California have furthered the sociospatial extremes of progress and poverty that have been manifest throughout every stage of capitalist urbanization. On the one hand, the region shelters a growing number of high-tech manufacturing districts, or "technopoles," which extend to the furthest corners of the urban region. In the southernmost portions of Orange County and the western fringes of the San Fernando Valley, where gated communities and high-end subdivisions guard the latest incarnation of suburban whiteness, high-tech manufacturers such as Hughes Aircraft Missile Systems Group, Micropolis, and Rocketdyne further the industrial and residential sprawl that began in earnest during the early 1940s. The region's high-tech economy, which has penetrated the entertainment industry to a certain extent, sustains the class standing of a highly skilled group of managers, business executives, scientists, engineers, designers, and celebrities who continue to reap the rewards of the region's economic prosperity.[2]

At the other end of the economic spectrum and concentrated within the region's multiple urban centers, a low-skill, low-wage, nonunionized workforce, comprising mostly women and undocumented Latino and Asian immigrants, has been taking shape alongside the growth of the manufacturing sector since the 1970s. In contrast to the high unemployment and economic decline that befell other major American cities through the phase of deindustrialization during the

1970s and 1980s, Los Angeles' manufacturing economy grew steadily through-out the 1970s and intensified during the following decade, when the infusion of Asian capital into the regional economy bolstered the production of manufac-tured goods such as apparel, furniture, jewelry, and machinery. Such growth, however, entails mixed consequences for Southern California's expanding im-migrant populations, who are drawn by the prospects of job availability but face new depths of exploitation. The sweatshop has made a comeback within Southern California's industrial landscape in recent decades, providing an of-ten overlooked reminder that the "new" Los Angeles runs on the sweat of im-migrant labor.[3]

Between these extremes, the great white middle class, which dominated the image and reality of the postwar urban region, is making its departure. Throughout the Reagan era, the flight of major manufacturing firms from the region's industrial geography dislodged whites from their suburban neighbor-hoods, creating space for new concentrations of racialized poverty. This trans-formation was most visible in the communities of Southeast Los Angeles, which nurtured the suburban white identity explored in previous chapters: South Gate, Huntington Park, Maywood, Bell, Bell Gardens, Vernon, and Cud-ahy. The departure of industrial giants such as General Motors, Firestone Tires, Weiser Lock, Bethlehem Steel, Dial, and Oscar Meyer from this area during the 1980s entailed a set of profound social consequences that undermined the cul-tural order of the postwar urban region. White workers and their families, who enjoyed full benefits and union representation, have taken flight, and, in their stead, recent arrivals from Mexico and Central America find work in the ex-panding low-wage, non-union sector and take shelter in cities crippled by shrinking tax bases and reduced services.[4]

While the brand of suburban whiteness that took shape within the cultural transition from the centralized, industrial city to the postwar urban region be-comes a relic of the past, its legacy continues to shape California politics. The politics of white home ownership remains a powerful force in the state and its triumphs in recent decades have profound implications for the quality of race relations in the United States. In 1978, the passage of Proposition 13 marked a major victory for white homeowners and their brand of "identity politics" in California, much like the two-term presidency of Ronald Reagan. In the 1990s, California voters passed a series of measures that targeted immigrant groups and racial minorities. Looking back to the buoyant expressions of suburban whiteness that highlighted the cultural landscape of the postwar urban region, the current strategies to preserve white hegemony reflect a brazen attempt to maintain some semblance of the precarious social order that enjoyed a brief life span between the midcentury manifestation of the noir city and the current de-nouement of a Third World urbanism.

Film noir underscored the imperatives of suburban home ownership as a bulwark against the crisis of the public city; Propositior 13 surfaced in 1978 as a measure to secure that imperative for millions of California homeowners. The unbridled growth that swept across the region entailed a mixed set of conse-quences for suburban homeowners. On the one hand, the unceasing demand for homes generated higher property values, but, on the other hand, higher home prices brought higher property taxes, which basically doubled every few years. At the same time, the recession of the mid-'70s heralded a stagnation of real income and frustrated consumer efforts to live the suburban good life that California symbolized. Proposition 13, a measure that would lower property taxes by 60 percent, won by an overwhelming majority in California and inspired a similar set of homeowners' revolts in other states. In Los Angeles, Proposition 13 won by overwhelming majorities in white council districts, while it failed by a similar majority in the city's only black district.

Proposition 13 cannot be understood in isolation from the larger cultural context that dawned on Southern California during the postwar period. When Yvonne de Carlo warns Burt Lancaster in the climactic scene of the film *Criss Cross*, "You have to watch out for yourself; I can't help it if people don't know how to take care of themselves," she recites the creed that suburban homeowners adopted in their insular political outlook that disavowed any connection to other urban constituencies. Instead, the supporters of Proposition 13 campaigned with slogans such as "Vote for yourself! Vote for Proposition 13!" Proposition 13 upheld what Clarence Lo describes as a consumer model of citizenship, which is predicated upon the relentless pursuit of commodities that sustained popular idealizations of suburban domesticity. Such idealizations informed the dominant cultural narratives of Southern California's postwar urban region and guided the ascendance of tax-cutting conservatism that disavowed the interdependency of social groups and instead promoted self-interest as a primary goal of political struggle. Proposition 13 drastically reduced property taxes at the expense of public services such as schools, libraries, and police and fire protection, services that racial minorities have been increasingly forced to rely on. In this capacity, Proposition 13 continued the privatization of social life that began during the postwar period and widened the spatial and racial divide between chocolate cities and vanilla suburbs.[5]

Many proponents of Proposition 13 also endorsed the concurrent antibusing movement, in which white suburban parents sought to preserve the postwar racial order by resisting state efforts to send their children to schools in black and Latino neighborhoods. In suburban communities of both the San Fernando Valley and Orange County, where Proposition 13 won overwhelming support, local organizations such as the PTA marshaled opposition to busing programs, sponsoring constitutional amendments to limit busing, challenging busing in court, and seeking to elect public officials who opposed busing. The racist underpinnings of the antibusing campaign during the mid-'70s were not self-evident, but against the official effort to elide the racial geography of the postwar urban region through school desegregation, white suburban families defended their distance from the racialized city and, with it, the right to maintain school policies that sent white middle-class children to white schools in white neighborhoods.[6]

The political culture that sustained both Proposition 13 and the antibusing movement is essentially the same as that which bestowed two consecutive presidential terms on Ronald Reagan, who championed the rights of homeowners and consumers in their pursuit of privatized self-interest. Reagan's victory in the White House confirmed Southern California's prominence within the national political culture, not unlike the proliferation of homeowners' revolts throughout the nation following the success of Proposition 13 in 1978. The triumph of the New Right by the late 1970s was made possible by the support of various regional constituencies, but the course of political events in Southern California—beginning with the 1950 defeat of Helen Gahagan Douglas, bolstered by the simultaneous victory against public housing, and gaining further momentum with the 1964 cancellation of the Rumford Fair Housing Act—prefigured the subsequent victories of a new brand of Republican conservatism predicated upon the values enshrined in places like Disneyland. By the mid-1980s, at the height of the Reagan era, the brand of suburban whiteness that first took shape within Southern California's cultural landscape had entered the symbol iconography of the American Way and remained under the stewardship of a countersubversive coalition that targeted civil rights crusaders, feminists, antiwar demonstrators, and gay activists as culpable for the social ills and economic malaise wrought by economic restructuring, deindustrialization, and the dismantling of the welfare state.[7]

Reagan's legacy endured through the 1990s and found powerful expressions in the culture and politics of California. One year after the end of the Reagan-Bush-era and on the heels of the Rodney King uprising of 1992, the film *Falling Down* engendered controversy among national audiences for its neonoir portrayal of the white man's identity crisis in contemporary Los Angeles. "D-Fens," an unemployed engineer suffering a nervous breakdown, begins a killing spree as he walks from downtown Los Angeles to the beach. In the tradition of noir's white male antihero, D-Fens trudges through the racialized milieu of the city, attacking a Korean market, a fast-food outlet, a Chicano gang, and a neo-Nazi. The city that once resonated with compelling expressions of suburban whiteness is now alien territory for D-Fens, an inhospitable non-Anglo landscape that renders white male identity obsolete.

That filmmakers could market the fin de siècle crisis of white male identity as entertainment points to the very real challenge to whiteness posed by the demographic transformation of California and Los Angeles at the end of the twentieth century. In this context, California voters approved a series of measures that extended a note of nativist hostility to people of color. In 1994, Proposition 187 triumphed at the polls, denying public services to undocumented workers and their families. Although the measure's implementation has been indefinitely delayed by the courts, it targets California's immigrant population as a scapegoat for the economic woes that befell the state during the recession of the early 1990s. The specter of white identity politics surfaced twice again in the remainder of the decade. In 1996, as if the racial wrongs of the past had been righted, Proposition 209 brought a decisive end to affirmative action in both public service contracts and higher education, and in 1998, Proposition 227 terminated bilingual education programs in public schools to advocate "English only" as state law. The causes and consequences of these measures have been explored elsewhere; suffice it to say here that they signal last-ditch attempts to preserve what vestiges of suburban whiteness remain at the outset of the twenty-first century.[8]

Popular culture in the age of white flight thus maintains a powerful legacy, and although the future of that legacy is uncertain, the current phase of demographic upheaval in Southern California annihilates the racial identities imposed on the spaces of the postwar urban region. Watts, for example, no longer symbolizes the geographic core of black Los Angeles, as a massive in-migration of Latino immigrants dissolves the postwar boundary between white and black Los Angeles. South Gate and Huntington Park, where Southern California's Dust Bowl migrants reinvented themselves in the image of middle-class whiteness after World War II, are the current epicenter of *México de afuera*, as Mexican immigrants reestablish communal ties in the wake of deindustrialization and white flight. A large and expanding Koreatown lies just west of downtown Los Angeles, a new suburban Chinatown centered on Monterey Park has taken shape to the east, and a band of Cambodian and Vietnamese communities has grown to the south, extending from the older Japanese community of Gardena to Long Beach and into Orange County, where the city of Westminster is now known as Little Saigon.[9]

Perhaps even more striking, the San Fernando Valley now shelters a heterogeneous mix of Mexicans, Salvadorans, Guatemalans, Armenians, and African Americans. For a generation of white Americans in search of suburban domesticity, the Valley offered affordable housing and homogeneous neighborhoods, and its location on the northern side of the Santa Monica Mountains promised a comfortable distance from a Los Angeles mired in the mythology of film noir. The landscape of today's Valley, however, reveals a striking record of the demographic changes that have ensued over the past thirty years. On Van Nuys Boulevard, once the heart of white suburbia, Spanish has displaced English as the unofficial language of public signage. All around the Van Nuys business district, travel agents advertise discount tickets for international travel carriers such as Avianca and Aeroméxico. The native fare of El Salvador, Peru, India, Armenia, and a dozen other nations is served in the boulevard's myriad storefront diners. Most institutions that catered to the Valley's original white constituency are now gone: department stores have been replaced by *pupuserias* and *mueblerias*, the First Presbyterian Church closed after its English-speaking constituency plummeted, and the *San Fernando Daily News*, founded as the *Van Nuys Call* in 1911, left for tonier quarters in Woodland Hills. The "New Valley" harbors scant traces of the suburban good life that dominated the cultural imagery of postwar Los Angeles, and its public settings now echo the cultural dissonance of the polyglot noir city.

Amid the browning of the San Fernando Valley, homeowners there are mobilizing a campaign to authorize the secession of the Valley from the city of Los Angeles, in what would be the largest municipal divorce in national history. Valley VOTE (Voters Organized toward Empowerment), a grassroots organization established in 1998, has gathered sufficient signatures on petitions to push the secession drive to its most advanced stage ever. Whether or not the proponents of secession will have their way, the current move to secede from the city of Los Angeles inherits a tradition of municipal discord in Southern California and reflects a long-standing antipathy to the urban behemoth on the southern side of the Santa Monica Mountains.

The social, economic, political, and spatial transformations that engulf today's Los Angeles entail a set of cultural expressions that reflect both the extension and the extinction of popular culture in the age of the white flight. On the one hand, recent scholarship illuminates the cultural manifestations of contemporary urbanism by looking to Los Angeles as a window onto the "theming" of American culture and society. Through the disparate points of Southern California's urban expanse, scholars cite the most spectacular examples of the privatization of public life: From the selfcontained citadel that has become downtown Los Angeles—including the cylindrical glass towers of John Portman's Bonaventure Hotel—to the gated communities of Orange County's "exopolis," to the ersatz urbanism of City Walk, Los Angeles and its environs support the many "variations on a theme park" that condition the experience of urban life at the outset of the twenty-first century. While generally eschewing the broader historical context that sanctions such cultural formations and often ignoring their immense popularity among white and nonwhite consumers alike, such observations generally deplore the corporate sponsors of contemporary public culture, emphasizing the manipulative and coercive strategies built into the design of contemporary public space.[10]

On the other hand, by looking "way, way below" the glass and neon facades of the contemporary metropolis, one can identify competing cultural expressions that emanate from the city's diverse neighborhoods. During the 1980s, amid the deindustrialization of South Central Los Angeles, black youth forged a cultural style that centered upon the distinctively West Coast sounds of hip-hop music. Gangsta Rap made its debut on the streets of Los Angeles through the innovative sounds of Ice-T, Eazy-E and NWA, Ice Cube, Snoop Doggy Dogg, and Dr. Dre, who drew upon African American cultural traditions such as descriptive storytelling and funk music, while utilizing samplers, drum machines, engineering boards, and other components of the latest in digital technology. Gangsta Rap of the late 1980s and early 1990s, as Robin Kelley and Tricia Rose point out, spoke to the realities of ghetto life for young black heterosexual men in postindustrial America, and proffered a genre of black popular culture that proved overwhelmingly popular not only in chocolate cities, but also, if not especially, in vanilla suburbs.[11]

Although the cultural palimpsest of contemporary urbanism supports the musical expressions of young black men, it also reflects the cultural stylings of the city's Mexican and Latino populations. A striking preference for big cities among Latinos brings a transformative energy to the texture of daily life in a "Latino metropolis" such as Los Angeles. As the old barrio of East Los Angeles gives way to the exponential growth of Spanish-speaking neighborhoods and subdivisions, the symbols and signs of *Mexicanidad* are visible throughout the urban region. Immigrant homeowners from Mexico and Central America are investing "sweat equity" in their homes, using paint and inexpensive landscaping materials to reverse the deterioration of urban neighborhoods crippled by deindustrialization and white flight. Bohemian enclaves of Chicano communities in East Los Angeles and the San Gabriel Valley support the proliferation of bilingual cafés and bookstores. Accustomed to the convivial spaces of *plazas* and *mercados* in Latin American cities, Latino immigrants and their children make vital use of playgrounds, parks, squares, libraries, and other endangered public spaces that their more affluent counterparts in the city tend to ignore. Amid the current re-Mexicanization of Los Angeles, with the addition of other Latino populations, we are witnessing an ethnic transformation of the urban landscape on a scale unparalleled in history.[12]

So what's left of popular culture in the age of white flight? What remains of the cultural institutions explored in this book, and how have they fared in light of recent social transformations? Hollywood continues to fixate upon Los Angeles in its dystopian spectacles of urban decadence, and film noir and science fiction maintain their popularity at the box office. In the early 1970s, at the outset of an economic recession and in the wake of the turbulent 1960s, Los Angeles occupied a starring role in a brief noir revival, climaxing with *Chinatown* by Roman Polanski, whose tragic and bizarre encounter with the Manson family in 1969 inspired his dark and morbid vision of Los Angeles and its past. Disaster films such as *Earthquake* and *The Towering Inferno* also kept the spotlight on Southern California, portraying Los Angeles as an epicenter of the moral catastrophe that dawned in the era of Watergate. The following decade witnessed *Blade Runner*, rendering its futuristic nightmare of a Los Angeles dominated by global capital and teeming with Third World populations, while a spate of neonoir films of the late 1980s and early 1990s, most notably *The Grifters*, *The Player*, *Reservoir Dogs*, *Pulp Fiction*, *Short Cuts*, and *L.A. Confidential*, keeps a tight focus on the darkness lurking behind the sunny façade of the Los Angeles landscape.

More striking, however, is the recent arrival of new voices that add their own distinct inflection to the canons of film noir and science fiction. With a nod to Chester Himes, Walter Mosley established his presence in American literature with the 1990 success of *Devil in a Blue Dress*, which portrays the investigations of Easy Rawlins, a black private detective in 1940s Los Angeles who unravels the depths of white racism at the core of Southern California's black city. In a similar vein, Octavia Butler brings a black feminist perspective to her futuristic vision of Los Angeles in *Parable of the Sower*, which renders a bleak portrait of a city overcome with violence and fear in the year 2027. Like all durable genres of American popular culture, film noir and science fiction have incorporated new perspectives that extend and broaden their appeal over time; while Los Angeles, ravaged by successive episodes of racial violence throughout the second half of the twentieth century, remains a favorite site for collective fantasies of urban despair.

Meanwhile, Hollywood finds new ways to recycle its former glory as a means to urban redevelopment. Responding to a cycle of decline throughout the 1980s and 1990s, Hollywood developers have enlisted the support of Los Angeles' Community Redevelopment Agency to bring consumers and tourists back to Tinsel Town. Their most recent *coup de main* has been the Hollywood and Highland Redevelopment Project, built by the Canadian developer Trizec Hahn, the nation's largest owner of downtown office space. At a price of 615 million dollars, the Hollywood and Highland complex occupies one and a half city blocks of downtown Hollywood, containing a mazelike 425,000-square-foot retail mall, a two-thousand-seat multiplex cinema, and an auditorium designed as a permanent home for future Academy Awards ceremonies. With architectural references to the glories of old Hollywood, including a partial reconstruction of the extravagant movie set from D.W. Griffith's 1916 film, *Intolerance*, Hollywood is now reclaiming its former glamour as a means of reversing decades of urban decline.[13]

Disneyland is alive and well, though its constant renovation and ongoing expansion illustrate the extent to which today's audiences have outgrown the thematic imagery and cultural stereotypes that dominated the park's landscape in its postwar heyday. Racial difference no longer supplies a central theme of Disneyland. Aunt Jemima's Pancake House is now the River Belle Terrace and the grinning mammy has been retired from the kitchen. Audio Animatronic animals singing country music have replaced the Indians who once performed at Frontierland. And though Disneyland remains a cornerstone of "family entertainment," this did not preclude park officials from ignoring the vehement protests of the Christian Right and extending domestic-partner benefits to employees in 1995. Moreover, the recent successes of Disney films such as *Mulan* and *Pocahontas* indicate an openness to new stories and images that include the perspectives of racial minorities and women.[14] Would Walt Disney have approved of these changes? That question is impossible to answer, but the business acumen and sensitivity to the changing moral climate that Disney exhibited throughout his career would seem to imply his willingness to make such modifications in the midst of a rapidly changing world.

The Walt Disney Company's more sensitive portrait of racial and ethnic diversity, however, parallels the ongoing Disneyfication of public and private space. Today, Disneyland rests alongside Downtown Disney, a shopping and entertainment complex that presents Southern Californians with a neon-lit simulacrum of the noir city that Orange County residents shunned a generation earlier. While Disney executives repackage the noir city as their latest "attraction," American cities and suburbs today increasingly weave the themed experiences of Disneyland into the fabric of daily life. The brand of suburbanism that took shape in locales such as Orange County during the 1950s now extends its reach into the archetypal noir metropolis. In New York City, under the patronage of Mayor Rudolph Giuliani, the Walt Disney Company spearheaded an effort to revitalize Times Square, investing thirty-two million dollars in the renovation of the New Amsterdam Theater on Forty-second Street. Enticed by a slew of tax breaks and zoning incentives, Disney and other entertainment conglomerates—Nike, Warner Brothers, Virgin—are struggling against the presence of homeless vagrants and porn dealers to rescue Times Square from its previous noir incarnation.[15]

An even more portentous example of how Disney continues to blur urban fantasy and reality, Celebration, U.S.A., reflects the Disney Company's latest effort to establish its definition of community. Celebration, U.S.A., south of Orlando, Florida, extends across five thousand acres, complete with its own school, post office, downtown, pool, and parks. There is also a "town hall" designed by the noted architect Philip Johnson, though it serves no political function since the Disney Company retains the powers of planning and governance for Celebration's first twenty years. Not unlike the planners of Lakewood and countless other suburban housing developments, Disney and Osceola County arranged a mutually beneficial deal to keep low-income housing out of Celebration, U.S.A. Such an arrangement allows for larger profits on the sale of homes and higher property tax revenues, but, in the suburban tradition, minimizes racial diversity and severely limits civic experience.[16] If Celebration, U.S.A., maintains some remnants of suburban whiteness in Florida, Southern California harbors other reminders of Disney's cultural roots. Recently, the Ronald Reagan Presidential Library in Simi Valley, California, featured the exhibit "Walt Disney: The Man and His Magic."

The Dodgers retain their popularity among diverse Southern California baseball fans, and Dodger Stadium endures in the Chavez Ravine. Whatever ill will lingered between the Dodgers and local Chicanos over the Arechiga evictions, the arrival of a rookie pitcher from Etchohuaquila, Sonora, in 1981 sparked an intense passion for Dodger baseball among Chicanos and Mexican baseball fans alike. In his first year of pitching for the Dodgers, Fernando Valenzuela led his team to its fifth World Series victory, and with that, "Fernandomania" descended upon the Spanish-speaking world. Valenzuela's overwhelming popularity demonstrated the new cultural flavor of major-league baseball and illustrated how popular cultural institutions can reinforce distinct cultural identities, even as they appeal to broader audiences. The particular appeal of Dodgers baseball for the city's diverse constituencies continues, as Asian Americans also enjoy a special claim to the Dodgers in recent years. Representing the recent advances by Korean players in the major leagues, Chan Ho Park signed a ten-million-dollar contract with the Dodgers in 2001. Park follows in the footsteps of Hideo Nomo, who pitched for the Dodgers between 1995 and 2000, arousing the loyalties of Southern California's Japanese American community, which maintains an enduring enthusiasm for the game of baseball, dating as far back as the war years, when baseball games provided a momentary distraction from the indignities of internment. Today, as during the postwar period, the Dodgers continue to model interracial cooperation on the field before the city's diverse constituencies in the stands.[17]

Meanwhile, civic officials elsewhere look to Dodger Stadium as an example of how not to build a ballpark. On April 11, 2000, San Franciscans celebrated Opening Day for Pacific Bell Park (now known as SBC Park), a throwback to Boston's Fenway Park and its generation of urban ballparks. In contrast to the sprawling, 250-acre site of Dodger Stadium, SBC Park sits upon a mere 13 acres in the city's South of Market neighborhood, a newly gentrified area adjacent to downtown. Designed by Joe Spear of HOK Sport, the architect of Baltimore's Camden Yards and Cleveland's Jacobs Field, SBC Park offers a more modest— albeit more nostalgic—alternative to the monumentality of Dodger Stadium. Garbed in ivy, brick, and limestone, SBC Park rejects the solemn gray concrete that clothes Dodger Stadium, and its expansive view of the San Francisco Bay delivers a scenic connection to the surrounding region. Most unlike Dodger Stadium, however, SBC Park maintains a mere five thousand parking spaces, one fifth of which are usually empty during any given home game. The park's accessibility to public transportation and its close proximity to the city's many neighborhoods diminish the necessity for the automobile. While it might be unfair to compare SBC Park to a stadium built four decades ago, its success suggests that the designers of Ebbets Field, Fenway Park, and Wrigley Field just may have had it right all along.

Finally, although Southern Californians continue to exercise their preference for the private automobile, the freeway's benefit to urban life is more suspect than ever. Traffic congestion remains an enduring civic nightmare, and with recent population gains and a growing number of commuters willing to drive longer distances to work, today's freeways now more than ever fail to provide rapid access to the disparate points of the urban region. Freeway construction continues, though the master plan for freeways established by the Division of Highways in 1958 remains only half completed. Local residents are far more vocal in their opposition to highway construction, as the recent controversy surrounding the extension of the 710 Long Beach Freeway through South Pasadena illustrates. In the 2001 mayoral campaign, candidate Antonio Villaraigosa won the support of that community by announcing his opposition to the completion of the 710 project, denouncing that freeway as "a throwback to another era."

Growing frustration with the freeway and the automobile has intensified the search for alternative forms of public transportation. Today, the Metropolitan Transit Authority maintains its effort to build an extensive rail transit system throughout the urban region. The Blue Line from Los Angeles to Long Beach opened in 1990, and parts of the Green Line (from Norwalk to Hawthorne) and the Red Line (from downtown to the San Fernando Valley) have followed suit. Whether the vast majority of Southern Californian commuters will relinquish their automobiles in favor of rail transit remains uncertain, but hundreds of millions of dollars continue to pour into a transit system that may or may not alleviate traffic congestion on the region's freeways. Meanwhile, working-class communities of color continue to depend on the city's overcrowded and inadequate bus system. The Bus Riders' Union, a grassroots organization dedicated to improving bus service, continues its fight against fare increases and route cancellations. During the age of the freeway, Los Angeles has sustained a kind of "transit apartheid" in which the experience of moving through urban space remains contingent upon class and color.[18]

The age of the freeway may be passing, but the street is making a comeback within the city's diverse communities. Los Angeles' emergence as the nation's preeminent Latino metropolis brings the street-oriented culture of Chicanos and Mexican immigrants to the very center of a new civic life. The city streets support the informal economy that relies upon the public display of goods and services. Day laborers congregate on sidewalks or parking lots, looking for a day's work in the vicinity of paint and hardware stores. *Vendedores* and *vendedoras* sell produce and flowers at freeway off-ramps and along median islands. Although such public interactions are commonplace within Latino neighborhoods, they are new to more affluent neighborhoods. Westside communities are taking their cue from their Eastside counterparts and learning to enjoy the pleasures of street life. Farmers' markets draw large crowds throughout the city's diverse neighborhoods, offering a weekly festival for adults and children. In the posh quarters of West Hollywood, planners have recently completed a massive redevelopment project to enhance street life along Santa Monica Boulevard. Sunset Strip and its more modest imitations throughout the Southern California metropolis continue to attract increasingly diverse crowds in search of the city's nightlife. Contrary to popular stereotypes about the freeway metropolis, the street is reclaiming its place at the center of a changing public life.

The cultural forms that nurtured a suburban white identity during the postwar period now include alternative perspectives and experiences. Since the postwar period, whiteness and white flight no longer have been the master narratives that shape the texture of American cultural life, at least in cities on the cutting edge of social transformations. Other narratives have been inserted into the built environment since the postwar period, and their vitality points to a new definition of urban life at the outset of the twenty-first century. Whether or not the recent appreciation of multiculturalism and diversity will empower marginal social groups, however, is an open question. If cultural expressions of suburban whiteness inaugurated a greater disparity between white suburban affluence and nonwhite urban poverty during the postwar period, can we expect the current incarnation of Los Angeles as a "world city" to bring about a more equitable reconfiguration of urban social relations? As whites have become a demographic minority in the Los Angeles urban region, new forms of urban popular culture model new configurations of race and space and encompass even more diverse cultural expressions. As the urban landscape mirrors the city's great diversity in more equitable ways, whiteness will lose its saliency as a defining principle of urban culture and identity. Once again, Los Angeles, a city often recognized as a cultural trendsetter, may be the first to model this development. Though the city once supported powerful expressions of suburban whiteness, it may be, in the not too distant future, that to imagine a white identity in a region teeming with nonwhite peoples will be to conjure a historical fiction from the city's past.

# NOTES

1. William A. V. Clark, "Residential Patterns: Avoidance, Assimilation and Succession," in *Ethnic Los Angeles*, ed. Roger Waldinger and Mehdi Bozorgmehr (New York: Russell Sage Foundation, 1996), 115.
2. Allen J. Scott, "High-Technology Industrial Development in the San Fernando Valley and Ventura County: Observations on Economic Growth and the Evolution of Urban Form," in *The City: Los Angeles and Urban Theory at the End of the Twentieth Century*, ed. Allen J. Scott and Edward W. Soja (Berkeley: University of California Press, 1996), 293.
3. Janet Abu-Lughod, *New York, Chicago, Los Angeles: America's Global Cities* (Minneapolis: University of Minnesota Press, 1999), 364–65.
4. Raymond A. Rocco, "Latino Los Angeles: Reframing Boundaries/Borders," in *The City: Los Angeles and Urban Theory at the End of the Twentieth Century*, ed. Allen J. Scott and Edward W. Soja (Berkeley: University of California Press, 1996), 374–75.
5. Clarence Y. H. Lo, *Small Property versus Big Government: Social Origins of the Property Tax Revolt* (Berkeley: University of California Press, 1990).
6. Ibid., 57–60; Abu-Lughod, *New York, Chicago, Los Angeles*, 379–82.
7. Michael Paul Rogin and John L. Shover, *Political Change in California: Critical Elections and Social Movements, 1890–1966* (Westport, Conn.: Greenwood Publishing Corporation,

1970), 173–78; George Lipsitz, *The Possessive Investment in Whiteness: How White People Profit from Identity Politics* (Philadelphia: Temple University Press, 1998), 136–38.

8. Abu-Lughod, *New York, Chicago, Los Angeles*, 383–85.

9. Edward W. Soja, "Los Angeles, 1965-1992: From Crisis-Generated Restructuring to Restructuring-Generated Crisis," in *The City: Los Angeles and Urban Theory at the End of the Twentieth Century*, ed. Allen J. Scott and Edward W. Soja (Berkeley: University of California Press, 1996), 443.

10. Michael Sorkin, ed., *Variations on a Theme Park: The New American City and the End of Public Space* (New York: Hill and Wang, 1992); Edward W. Soja, *Postmetropolis: Critical Studies of Cities and Regions* (Oxford: Blackwell Publishing, 2000), 233–63.

11. Robin D. G. Kelley, *Race Rebels: Culture, Politics and the Black Working Class* (New York: Free Press, 1996), 183–227. See also Tricia Rose, *Black Noise: Rap Music and Black Culture in Contemporary America* (Hanover, N.H.: University Press of New England, 1994).

12. Mike Davis, *Magical Urbanism: Latinos Reinvent the U.S. City* (London: Verso, 2000). See also Victor M. Valle and Rodolfo D. Torres, *Latino Metropolis* (Minneapolis: University of Minnesota Press, 2000); Gustavo Leclerc, Raul Villa, and Michael J. Dear, *Urban Latino Cultures* (Thousand Oaks, Calif.: Sage Publications, 1999); and Marta López-Garza and David R. Diaz, *Asian and Latino Immigrants in a Restructuring Economy: The Metamorphosis of Southern California* (Stanford, Calif.: Stanford University Press, 2001).

13. "Can Hollywood Get Its Glitz Back?" 12 November 2001, www. businessweek.com/ magazine/ content/01_46/b3757018.htm.

14. Jim Rawitsch, "Moving Right Along," *Los Angeles Times Magazine*, 13 July 1986, 1.

15. Samuel R. Delany, *Times Square Red, Times Square Blue* (New York: New York University Press, 1999); Ada Louise Huxtable, "Reinventing Times Square: 1990," in *Inventing Times Square: Commerce and Culture at the Crossroads of the World*, ed. William R. Taylor (Baltimore: Johns Hopkins University Press, 1991), 356–70.

16. Dana Cuff, *The Provisional City: Los Angeles Stories of Architecture and Urbanism* (Cambridge, Mass.: MIT Press, 2000), 334–35; Andrew Ross, *The Celebration Chronicles* (New York: Ballantine Books, 1999); Douglas Frantz and Catherine Collins, *Celebration, U.S.A.: Living in Disney's Brave New Town* (New York: Henry Holt, 2000).

17. Samuel O. Regalado, *Viva Baseball! Latin Major Leaguers and Their Special Hunger* (Urbana: University of Illinois Press, 1988), 122–28.

18. Roger Keil, *Los Angeles: Globalization, Urbanization, and Social Struggles* (New York: John Wiley and Sons, 1998) xxxi–xxxii; Kelley, *Race Rebels*, 232–33.

# 17

## *Dolores Hayden*

# "PLANNED SPRAWL" AND THE RISE OF THE MALL

The greatest beneficiaries of federal highway programs and commercial real estate subsidies were the developers of shopping malls. Well-designed, small

From *Building Suburbia* by Dolores Hayden, pp. 168-180 , 274–276, copyright © by Dolores Hayden. Used by permission of Pantheon Books, a division of Random House, Inc.

shopping areas had been part of earlier elite picturesque enclaves, such as Lake Forest, Illinois, Roland Park, Maryland, and the Country Club Plaza in Kansas City. Small strip shopping areas had also emerged on many suburban arterials in the 1920s. By the 1940s architects such as Victor Gruen were promoting "shopping towns" with anchor stores and smaller stores surrounded by parking.[1] Gruen was a Viennese émigré who worked on luxury boutiques in Manhattan before developing a firm in Southern California. Gruen designed the first fully enclosed mall at Southdale, near Minneapolis, in 1956, and prospered as a specialist in retail malls.[2]

Malls in the late forties and early fifties were risky. Suburban customers still believed in making major purchases in the central business districts of cities and towns, where they expected to find the greatest selection of merchandise and the most competitive prices. After the tax laws of 1954, this changed. Shopping mall developers were among the biggest beneficiaries of accelerated depreciation, and they most often located projects where the older strips met the new interchanges of major highways. With the new tax write-offs, over 98 percent of malls made money for their investors.[3] Together, the tax breaks and the new roads explain the orgy of commercial real estate built in automotive configurations after the mid-1950s. According to Hanchett, tax incentives helped spur the construction of many more shopping centers than would otherwise have been started.[4] Frequently state and local governments also subsidized malls with "economic development" grants, infrastructure such as local access roads, and abatements of local taxes.[5] The culture of land use planning became very corrupt in many places, with both elected officials and paid staff in local governments receiving handouts from speculators, builders, and bankers in exchange for tens of millions in subsidies.

In a landmark study of the late 1970s, *Planned Sprawl*, sociologist Mark Gottdiener looked at the largest township in Suffolk County, Long Island, to analyze the planning behind roadside suburban development. He challenged observers who called the landscape chaotic, showing that physical disorder resulted from planned and systematic profit-seeking by builders, developers, and banks. He documented one case where a developer sought and received rezoning for a project called Dollarhaven Mall from local politicians. In general, Gottdiener noted many ways for developers to promote deals: "buying blocks of tickets to party functions," "purchasing a service from a business" (such as a local newspaper, construction firm, or car dealership associated with a political boss, his associates, or a councilman), and making campaign contributions.[6] Other writers railed against *The Great Land Hustle* and the *Mortgage on America*.[7] Although some academics and politicians advocated more effective regional planning, metropolitan government, and environmental regulation, little was done to halt the federal, state, and local subsidies for growth channeled to real estate developers.

Between the mid-1950s and the late 1970s about 22,000 suburban shopping centers were built. By the late 1990s there were 43,000.[8] They included thousands of strip malls, euphemistically called "neighborhood or community shopping centers," with one large store such as a supermarket, drugstore, or low-cost department store and a line of little stores facing parking. There were hundreds of "regional malls" like the Connecticut Post Mall in Milford, Connecticut. Regional malls were sited on at least thirty acres, usually enclosed, with multiple shops and at least one big anchor store including 100,000 square feet of leasable space. And there were the superregional malls, totaling over 1,400,000 square feet of leasable space. At one place in New Jersey, citizens renamed their municipality "Cherry Hill" after the mall developed by James Rouse in 1961. Other localities were not so delighted. Malls eroded the economic base of older downtown department stores as well as stores on Main Streets in small towns and older suburbs, leaving empty storefronts. They privatized and commercialized public space. As historian Lizabeth Cohen has documented, mall owners were often anxious to restrict public access, and one of the ways of achieving this was to make access by public transit minimal, or to organize bus routes to reinforce market segmentation and racial segregation by race and class. Cohen suggests that malls also feminized public space: "they enhanced women's claim on the suburban landscape but also empowered them more as consumers than producers."[9]

By 2000, Americans had built almost twice as much retail space per citizen as any other country in the world: over nineteen square feet per person.[10] Most of it was in malls. A superregional such as the South Coast Mall in Orange County, California, claimed to do more retail business every day than all of downtown San Francisco.[11] The Mall of America (MOA) in Bloomington, Minnesota, is even more gigantic. A project of the Ghermezian brothers, with Melvin Simon and Associates as developer and managing partner, it opened in 1992. The largest superregional mall in the United States, in 2002 MOA included four anchor department stores and over 520 stores, 51 restaurants, 8 nightclubs, 14 theater screens, and theme park attractions. Its Camp Snoopy offers twenty-eight rides on seven acres, a virtual NASCAR speedway, a bowling alley, and a 1.2-million-gallon aquarium with three thousand marine animals, including sharks and stingrays. With a gross building area of 4.2 million square feet and leasable space of 2.5 million square feet, it draws between six hundred thousand and nine hundred thousand visitors weekly. Attractions include haircoloring demonstrations, children's fashion shows, cheerleader tryouts, mall walks for seniors, and a show of red, white, and blue flowers called "Great American Backyard." At 42.5 million visitors per year, the Mall of America claims to top Disney World, Graceland, and the Grand Canyon as the most popular tourist destination in the United States.[12]

# From the Mall to the Edge Node

Edge nodes expanded with the rise of malls, especially the superregionals with their surrounding seas of parking. In edge nodes, site plans are scaled to the truck or car, never to the pedestrian. Edge nodes have assumed different forms in various parts of the country since the 1970s, but many of them are in unincorporated areas rather than politically bounded towns. Many have a maze of overlapping jurisdictions such as county, town, and special service districts. Most nodes are "boomers" like Tysons Corner, exploding out of strip commercial areas on older arterials near freeway interchanges, where loose zoning and automotive uses have prevailed since the 1920s, and a new mall brought development to the area. Garreau uses the term "pig in the python" to describe the way some boomers are formed as big nodes within a linear strip.[13] Edge nodes can also be "uptown," that is, on the site of an older downtown, perhaps one that has been razed by urban redevelopment, with land then sold on favorable terms to new private investors. Such is the case in Stamford, Connecticut, where an industrial city making Yale locks gave way to a mall and corporate offices.[14] A third kind of edge node is "greenfield," located in open, undeveloped land, usually near a freeway exit.

The privately planned new towns and Title VII communities founded in the 1960s provide an exception to Garreau's typology. Urban planner Ann Forsyth notes that all were "highly designed—and designed with parking seen as 'landbank' for future expansion."[15] The developers, planners, architects, and landscape architects who worked on these projects saw themselves as providing an alternative to the sprawling suburbs of the 1950s. Columbia, Maryland, was developed by James Rouse beginning in 1963. With about fourteen thousand acres, Columbia held eighty-eight thousand residents in 2000. About one-fifth were African-American because Rouse had emphasized achieving racial integration. The Woodlands, outside of Houston, Texas, was developed by George Mitchell, beginning in 1964. He hired Ian McHarg to develop an ecological focus for the planning of 15,000 acres (now 27,305 acres). The Woodlands reached 55,649 inhabitants by 2000. The Irvine Company began to develop a new town in 1960 and hired William Pereira as master planner for more than ninety-three thousand acres in Southern California. The city of Irvine holds one hundred and thirty thousand people. These three planned developments included regional retail as well as neighborhood retail centers serving both single-family houses and apartments. All three managed to create long-term job development, including office parks, and by 1991 they appeared on Joel Garreau's list of edge cities, although they derived from consistent attempts to plan and develop large new suburban communities.

For the most part, edge nodes are uncomfortable and ugly places. Building is cheap; depreciation is accelerated; obsolescence is rapid. Money might be spent on a corporate headquarters when a corporation intends to stay, but developers of speculative office parks design for rapid turnover. There is little site design beyond inexpensive buildings with big signs and parking lots, although private security services and building maintenance services are often provided to tenants. Developers of industrial parks also build minimal buildings. Clustered around malls, offices, and industry are office services, such as lawyers, accountants, and printing, and other services, such as fast food, chain motels, cineplexes, and freeway churches. When geographer Peter Muller documented the growth of King of Prussia, Pennsylvania, in 1976, his diagram showed the Pennsylvania Turnpike, Interstate 76, and U.S. 202 wrapping a series of pods, with a mall, office parks, industrial parks, hotels, fast food, a freeway church, and a music fair.[16] It lacked the pedestrian structure of a traditional downtown, where sidewalks allowed pedestrians to walk from office to restaurant or from church to shopping. Despite Muller's optimism about the upscale King of Prussia mall providing "prestige" addresses for adjoining businesses, there was little public space. His diagram showed an edge node that could grow but could not improve with time. Each new single-use pod was surrounded by its own sea of parking.

The older building types that had been on the strips of the 1920s were replaced by newer facilities as the nodes grew, but they did not produce places with a pedestrian presence. Fast-food franchises disrupted sidewalks with drive-throughs that encouraged people to eat on the road. They also displaced public playgrounds with private ones to attract children and parents to fast food. Chain hotels and motels supplanted older hotels and tourist courts. Cineplexes, multiple-screen theaters housed in big, warehouselike buildings without sidewalks, replaced art deco single-screen Main Street theaters, whose slogan had been "the show starts on the sidewalk." Freeway churches drew large congregations to locations near offramps, surrounded by seas of parking, replacing churches on downtown corners. Over time, many evangelical freeway churches added sports facilities, fitness centers, and food courts to their sanctuaries. They were designed to look more like malls than churches.[17]

By the 1990s planner Robert Cervero noted that most edge nodes were being built at densities too low for the effective provision of public transport, yet high enough to cause traffic gridlock. Each new pod added to an edge node might be designed for internal traffic circulation, but the parcels tended to agglomerate with no consistent land use planning or traffic circulation beyond the property line.[18] "Suburbia may be paved with good intentions, but mainly it is paved," said architect Douglas Kelbaugh.[19] Introducing new urban design guidelines is uphill work; renovation of existing spaces is even harder.

## Big Boxes, Category Killers, and Outlet Malls

In the 1990s big-box discount stores of fifty thousand to two hundred thousand square feet began to undercut the older shopping malls that had been at the heart of the edge nodes. The largest big-box stores like Wal-Mart sell almost everything—drugs, hardware, linens, furniture, stationery, toys, clothing, electronics, plants, and eyeglasses. Their supercenters also include a full supermarket. Wal-Mart had over nine hundred thousand employees in 1999, which makes it the largest private employer in America, surpassing General Motors. Wal-Mart has claimed that 93 million Americans shop there every week. It also operates in many other countries, exporting American-style big-box retailing.[20] Category killers—slightly smaller big-box discount stores of twenty-five thousand to one hundred thousand square feet—attempt to dominate (or kill) a particular sales category. Toys "R" Us specializes in toys, Staples in office supplies, Home Depot in building supplies and hardware.

In the face of the big boxes' aggressive expansion, local drugstores, stationery stores, clothing stores, and hardware stores have disappeared by the tens of thousands, changing the shape of older suburbs and small towns.[21] In the ten years between 1983 and 1993, the state of Iowa lost 7,326 small retail businesses. Making the case against sprawl, activist Al Norman contended, "There's one thing you can't buy in a Wal-Mart. That's small town quality of life. And once you lose it, you can't get it back at any price."[22] Through the 1990s the big boxes "killed" older malls, chain supermarkets, chain drugstores, and small department stores, as well as little markets, pharmacies, and clothing stores. The scale of roadside commercial development became overwhelming. Less and less was local. Warehouselike buildings were dictated by management rules about "facilities" of twenty-five thousand to two hundred thousand square feet, with no interior columns, no windows, and parking for thousands of cars.[23] Most of these buildings had no relationship in siting or style to the character of the towns where they were located, although occasionally local planners were able to persuade chains to insert their operations into older structures.

Big boxes were tied to national or international chains, part of an expanding global economy often requiring port and airport access as well as access by truck. Ports such as Long Beach, near Los Angeles, were restructured to accommodate vast containers filled with manufactured goods headed to American discount stores from foreign farms and factories. Airports expanded their cargo areas. Highways were jammed with trucks hauling fifty-three-foot-long containers to speed four billion tons of "just-in-time" merchandise to retail outlets every year.[24] The trucking firms demanded wider arterials and bigger intersections. Trucks shook the foundations of older buildings when they tore into towns.

A few attempts have been made to disguise the bloated architectural scale of big boxes and outlet malls. Developers may present them as villages by decorating one facade of the warehouse or by putting a veneer of Victorian trim on the central public circulation, leaving the rear for the trucks. Sometimes old-fashioned items designed at the human scale, such as sailboats or train coaches, have been added to an outlet mall's design. Their purpose is to serve as "memory points," landmarks to keep thousands of customers from getting lost in rows of warehouses. More common is a lineup of two or three big boxes as a "power center" with no access designed for pedestrians at all. The trucks find this best. One big-box retailer, Target, has emphasized aesthetics in its advertising, hiring noted architects and industrial designers to create its lamps and tea kettles and bring order to store interiors. Unfortunately, they have not yet campaigned for better exterior and site design to modify the scale of the big boxes and parking lots.

Defenders of the big boxes and outlet malls argue that they attract customers. Wal-Mart underwear is cheap, and so is Home Depot's plastic paneling, and so are McDonald's hamburgers.[25] Outlets do beat smaller stores' prices, but quality is often low. Even if quality is the same for mass-produced products, such as flashlight batteries, the customer is missing the local experience the old neighborhood stores used to provide. The customer's time and the customer's automobile replace a neighborhood store's clerk and personal service. Once in the big box, self-service is usually the rule, as customers fill carts and lug purchases. Labor costs are low, compared with traditional department stores, hardware stores, or restaurants, because often workers are part-time and working at the minimum wage without benefits. Many big-box employers discourage unionization. However, Wal-Mart workers who claimed they were frequently forced to put in overtime without pay organized class-action suits across the country in 2002.[26]

Many of the giants are now under close scrutiny for their effects on American towns. Companies may argue that they compete to serve "the market," but federal subsidies for roads and commercial overbuilding have supported the rise of the giants and contributed to the demise of thousands of small local businesses. It is hard to find a small town or older suburb that has not been disrupted. Not only local restaurants but also family farms and small ranches which used to provide vegetables and meat have been displaced from the American landscape by the rise of gigantic global businesses purveying fast food. But not every transaction in the edge nodes is about making a profit on inexpensive goods and services. In a heavily franchised landscape, many calculations cycle back to real estate, and the rise of mass investments in Real Estate Investment Trusts (REITs). The Teachers Insurance and Annuity Association (TIAA) handles pension funds for professors and teachers across the United States. While researching malls I was disconcerted to discover that my own retirement savings helped to build the Mall of America.

## Legacies of Accelerated Depreciation

Although it has become the most visible of American suburban landscapes, the edge node has few architectural defenders. Even developers despair: "Shopping centers built only in the 1960s are already being abandoned. Their abandonment brings down the values of nearby neighborhoods. Wal-Marts built five years ago are already being abandoned for superstores. We have built a world of junk, a degraded environment. It may be profitable for a short-term, but its long-term economic prognosis is bleak."[27] Those who do speak in favor of edge nodes, like Joel Garreau, tend to idealize them as a temporary, rough "frontier" of economic growth. He admits most nodes are "as ugly as poison ivy."[28]

No one has yet done a definitive economic study of how much edge nodes have been subsidized by federal tax concessions and local government subsidies. Because of federal, state, and local giveaways, government has encouraged very large businesses to cannibalize smaller businesses, wiping out many Main Streets and older suburban commercial areas, but few Americans understand how their tax dollars have supported this destructive process. The end result has been a mall glut. About four thousand dead malls were empty or abandoned in the United States in 2002.[29] More failures are expected. Older big boxes and outlet malls have also been abandoned. Some developers and designers are working on plans for adding housing to retail in dying malls in order to redevelop older complexes. Meanwhile, the edge node has replaced Main Street, and both shoppers and workers are stuck in traffic.

Few Americans can describe the physical form or financial underpinnings of edge nodes like Tysons Corner or King of Prussia. Even scholars and design professionals are often unaware how complex, hidden subsidies have boosted their growth. Jobs and commerce have moved to edge nodes, but few people want to live in them. The presence of housing in edge nodes is often the result of spot builders filling in leftover sites with "affordable" housing units. Nearby freeways make many of these units undesirable. Occasionally expensive apartments for households without children are added near upscale mall areas, such as the Houston Galleria or the new Southdale Mall in Edina, near Minneapolis, but most affluent families prefer to live elsewhere. Ugly environments, cheap gas, and subsidized freeways mean that workers commute to residences far outside the edge nodes, scattering into less dense areas, creating one more suburban pattern, the rural fringes.

# NOTES

1. Victor Gruen and Larry Smith, *Shopping Towns USA: The Planning of Shopping Centers* (New York: Reinhold, 1960); also see Howard Gillette, Jr., "The Evolution of the Planned Shopping Center in Suburb and City," *American Planning Association Journal* 51 (Autumn 1985): 449–60.
2. Mark Jeffrey Hardwick, *The Mallmaker: Cities, Suburbs, and Architect Victor Gruen* (Philadelphia: University of Pennsylvania Press, forthcoming).
3. Margaret Crawford, "The World in a Shopping Mall," in *Variations on a Theme Park: The New American City and the End of Public Space*. ed. Michael Sorkin (New York: Hill and Wang, 1992), 3–30. On market segmentation and characterizations of malls, see Michael J. Weiss, *The Clustered World: How We Live, What We Buy, and What It All Means About Who We Are* (Boston: Little, Brown, 2000).
4. Hanchett, "U.S. Tax Policy," 1108.
5. A comic example of this is described in William Fulton, *The Reluctant Metropolis: The Politics of Urban Growth in Los Angeles* (Point Arena, Calif.: Solano Press, 1997), 255–82.
6. Mark Gottdiener, *Planned Sprawl: Private and Public Interests in Suburbia* (Beverly Hills, Calif.: Sage, 1977), 103.
7. Morton Paulson, *The Great Land Hustle* (Chicago: Henry Regnery, 1972); Leonard Downie, *Mortgage on America* (New York: Praeger, 1974).
8. International Council of Shopping Centers, http://www.icsc.com (March 23, 2002); William Leach, *Country of Exiles: The Destruction of Place in American Life* (New York: Pantheon, 1999), 55. On the design of malls and how they can work in Main Street situations, especially in Australia, see Ann Forsyth, "Variations on a Main Street; When a Mall is an Arcade," *Journal of Urban Design* 2 (Fall 1997): 297–307.
9. Lizabeth Cohen, "From Town Center to Shopping Center: The Reconfiguration of Community Marketplaces in Postwar America," *American Historical Review* 101 (October 1996): 1050–81; Lizabeth Cohen, A Consumers' *Republic*: The Politics of Mass-Consumption in Postwar America (New York: Knopf, 2003), 257–344.
10. Frank Jossi, "Rewrapping the Big Box," *Planning* 64 (August 1998): 16–18.
11. Benfield, Raimi, and Chen, *Once There Were Greenfields*, 15.
12. "Mall of America," http://www.mallofamerica.com (March 23, 2002).
13. Garreau, *Edge City*, 113–16.
14. Bettina Drew, *Crossing the Expendable Landscape* (Minneapolis: Graywolf, 1998), 11–31.
15. Ann Forsyth, personal communication, August 2002; Ann Forsyth, *Reforming Suburbia: Building New Communities in Irvine, Columbia, and The Woodlands* (Berkeley; University of California Press, forthcoming). She notes that The Woodlands was "the only one of the thirteen 'Title VII' new towns to be largely completed."

16. Muller, *Contemporary Suburban America*, 164.

17. Patricia Leigh Brown, "Megachurches as Minitowns," *New York Times,* May 9, 2002, F1. This recalls attempts around 1900 to make churches resemble urban settlement houses, with spaces for sports and meetings.

18. Benfield, Raimi, and Chen, *Once There Were Greenfields*, 36–40.

19. Douglas Kelbaugh, article in *Urban Land,* June 1999, quoted in Konsoulis and Sies, *Metropolitan Perspectives*, n.p.

20. Al Norman, *Slam-Dunking Wal-Mart* (Atlantic City, N.J.: Raphael Marketing, 1999); Bill Saporito and Jacqueline M. Graves, "And the Winner is Still . . . Wal-Mart," *Fortune* 129 (May 2, 1994): 62ff.

21. Constance E. Beaumont, *How Superstore Sprawl Can Harm Communities and What Citizens Can Do About It* (Washington, D.C.: National Trust for Historic Preservation, 1994); Constance E. Beaumont, *Better Models for Superstores* (Washington, D.C.: National Trust for Historic Preservation, 1997).

22. Al Norman, "The Case Against Sprawl," www. sprawlbusters. com (May 10, 2002).

23. Keller Easterling, *Organization Space: Landscapes, Highways, and Houses in America* (Cambridge, Mass.: MIT Press, 1999).

24. Leach, *Country of Exiles*, 32–35.

25. Schlosser, *Fast Food Nation*, 6–10, condemns McDonald's massive monopoly of beef and potatoes, processed according to the rules of headquarters, who freeze a standard product complete with flavor additives and "mouthfeel" texture.

26. *Ibid.*, 59–88; Steven Greenhouse, "Suits Say Wal-Mart Forces Workers to Toil Off the Clock," *New York Times*, June 25, 2002, A18.

27. Robert Davis, "Postscript," in Congress for the New Urbanism, *Charter of the New Urbanism* (New York: McGraw-Hill, 2000), 182.

28. Garreau, *Edge City*, 14–15.

29. Timothy Egan, "Retail Darwinism Puts Old Malls in Jeopardy," *New York Times* (January 1, 2000), A20.

# CHAPTER 6

# THE NEW POLITICS OF SPACE

## FEAR AND THE
## PRIVATIZATION OF URBAN SPACE

Many urban scholars have argued that fear is reshaping the geography and politics of urban America. In the twentieth century, affluent citizens escaped the problems of the city by moving to the suburbs. In the twenty-first century, people are finding new ways of separating themselves from the problems of urban life. Enclosed malls, gated communities, office parks, condominium towers, and tourist bubbles provide an escape from the public realm. What are the political consequences of this trend?

In Selection 18, Mike Davis asserts that urban inequalities and social tensions have resulted in the militarization of space in Los Angeles. In Davis's rendering, the militarization of space has taken various forms. There has been, first, the destruction of public spaces where people can freely mingle. Second, "mean streets" have become sharply segregated from the privatized spaces hidden behind facades and walls. Third, minority populations and the poor have been subjected to high-tech policy enforcement and a pervasive surveillance, creating a "carceral city"; by this phrase, Davis means to compare the city inhabited by the poor to a prison. For those readers who bridle at Davis's metaphor, it may be helpful to remember that the movie *Bladerunner* portrays Los Angeles in an even more negative light than does Davis.

In Selection 19, Margaret Kohn maintains that a basic daily activity, shopping, has become politicized in a way that undermines individual civil liberties. According to Kohn, public areas are disappearing in cities and suburbs as a result of the proliferation of shopping malls. Unlike familiar Main Streets, these privately owned shopping enclaves usually exclude or severely restrict opportunities for face-to-face politics that take place in the public sphere, including handing out political leaflets, gathering signatures for candidates or ballot issues, holding protests, and other forms of political communication. Nevertheless, in many suburbs the malls are virtually the only available sites for these political activities.

Do mall owners have the right to exclude political activities or is there a legitimate state interest in making these spaces accessible for free speech? Kohn argues that in a series of "shopping mall" cases the U.S. Supreme Court has closed its eyes to the privatization of public space by insisting that the first amendment

251

to the U.S. Constitution only limits what government agencies can do. Although some state courts have been more open to ensuring that private malls have public access responsibilities, there is no judicial consensus on this principle. Kohn contends that similar issues of exclusion arise in business improvement districts (BIDs), where business property owners essentially are entitled to control a private government in order to collect special revenues and to funnel the money into additional services for their own area. Although BIDs often exercise far-reaching governmental powers over public areas, they are largely beyond voter control. According to Kohn, they are also changing the nature of public space. BIDs mimic the suburban mall by transforming city streets into managed environments providing the same kind of security, order, and tidiness as suburban shopping malls.

Selection 20, by Peter Marcuse, examines the impact of the "war on terrorism" on cities after the attack on New York City's World Trade Center in 2001. He believes that governmental and private-sector responses to terrorism have undermined the quality of urban life and the health of democracy within cities. In Marcuse's account, the fear of terrorism has prompted a dispersal of business activities and services away from city centers and provoked moves to fortify and barricade urban space. Evaluating the trends since 9/11 in New York and several other cities, he describes how concern for security has been used to justify and expand legal and physical measures to scatter and fortify valued protected spaces while increasing their surveillance. The end result is the shrinking of public space, reduced access to the public spaces that remain, and violations of fundamental civil liberties.

In Selection 21, Dennis R. Judd observes that urban scholars have generally shared a gloomy prognosis of the urban future. The most recent version of this tendency is based on the argument that urban space—and cities in general—have become fragmented into exclusionary and often militarized enclaves. Judd challenges this view, arguing that urban scholars often indulge in excessively apocalyptic rhetoric about the urban condition. He argues that, at least in the case of tourist spaces, cities have become increasingly accessible and open; visitors to cities often go beyond enclaves and "tourist bubbles" and go into the larger city to experience the diversity and richness of urban entertainment, gastronomy, and culture. Judd concludes his essay by asking why urban scholars find apocalyptic visions of the city so attractive, and proposes that scholars often hark back to a "golden age" when cities allegedly were characterized by greater diversity, community, and free social interaction.

# 18

## *Mike Davis*

## FORTRESS LOS ANGELES

The city bristles with malice. The carefully manicured lawns of the Westside sprout ominous little signs threatening "ARMED RESPONSE*!*" Wealthier neighborhoods in the canyons and hillsides cower behind walls guarded by gun-toting private police and state-of-the-art electronic surveillance systems. Downtown, a publicly subsidized "urban renaissance" has raised a forbidding corporate citadel, separated from the surrounding poor neighborhoods by battlements and moats. Some of these neighborhoods—predominately black or Latino—have in turn been sealed off by the police with barricades and checkpoints. In Hollywood, architect Frank Gehry has enshrined the siege look in a library that looks like a Foreign Legion fort. In Watts, developer Alexander Haagen has pioneered the totally secure shopping mall, a latter-day Panopticon, a prison of consumerism surrounded by iron-stake fences and motion detectors, overseen by a police substation in a central tower. Meanwhile in Downtown, a spectacular structure that tourists regularly mistake for a hotel is actually a new federal prison.

Welcome to post-liberal Los Angeles, where the defense of luxury has given birth to an arsenal of security systems and an obsession with the policing of social boundaries through architecture. This militarization of city life is increasingly visible everywhere in the built environment of the 1990s. Yet contemporary urban theory has remained oddly silent about its implications. Indeed, the pop apocalypticism of Hollywood movies and pulp science fiction has been more realistic—and politically perceptive—in representing the hardening of the urban landscape. Images of prison-like inner cities (*Escape from New York, Running Man*), high-tech police death squads (*Bladerunner*), sentient skyscrapers (*Die Hard*), and guerrilla warfare in the streets (*Colors*) are not fantasies, but merely extrapolations from the present.

Such stark dystopian visions show how much the obsession with security has supplanted hopes for urban reform and social integration. The dire predictions of Richard Nixon's 1969 National Commission on the Causes and Prevention of Violence have been tragically fulfilled in the social polarizations of the Reagan era.[1] We do indeed now live in "fortress cities" brutally divided into "fortified cells" of affluence and "places of terror" where police battle the criminalized poor. The "Second Civil War" that began during the long hot summers of the late 1960s has been institutionalized in the very structure of urban space. The old liberal attempts at social control, which at least tried to balance repression with reform, have been superseded by open social warfare that pits the interests of the middle class against the welfare of the urban poor. In cities like Los Angeles, on the hard edge of post-modernity, architecture and the police apparatus are being merged to an unprecedented degree.

## The Destruction of Public Space

The universal consequence of the crusade to secure the city is the destruction of any truly democratic urban space. The American city is being systematically turned inward. The "public" spaces of the new megastructures and supermalls have supplanted traditional streets and disciplined their spontaneity. Inside malls, office centers, and cultural complexes, public activities are sorted into strictly functional compartments under the gaze of private police forces. This architectural privatization of the physical public sphere, moreover, is complemented by a paralleled restructuring of electronic space, as heavily guarded, pay-access databases and subscription cable services expropriate the invisible *agora*. In Los Angeles, for example, the ghetto is defined not only by its paucity of parks and public amenities, but also by the fact that it is not wired into any of the key information circuits. In contrast, the affluent Westside is plugged—often at public expense—into dense networks of educational and cultural media.

In either guise, architectural or electronic, this polarization marks the decline of urban liberalism, and with it the end of what might be called the Olmstedian vision of public space in America. Frederick Law Olmsted, the father of Central Park, conceived public landscapes and parks as social safety-valves, *mixing* classes and ethnicities in common (bourgeois) recreations and pleasures: "No one who has closely observed the conduct of the people who visit [Central] Park," he wrote, "can doubt that it exercises a distinctly harmonizing and refining influence upon the most unfortunate and most lawless classes of the city—an influence favorable to courtesy, self-control, and temperance."[2]

This reformist ideal of public space as the emollient of class struggle is now as obsolete as Rooseveltian nostrums of full employment and an Economic Bill of Rights. As for the mixing of classes, contemporary urban America is more like Victorian England than the New York of Walt Whitman or Fiorello La Guardia. In Los Angeles—once a paradise of free beaches, luxurious parks, and "cruising strips"—genuinely democratic space is virtually extinct. The pleasure domes of the elite Westside rely upon the social imprisonment of a third-world service proletariat in increasingly repressive ghettos and barrios. In a city of several million aspiring immigrants (where Spanish-surname children are now almost two-thirds of the school-age population), public amenities are shrinking radically, libraries and playgrounds are closing, parks are falling derelict, and streets are growing ever more desolate and dangerous.

Here, as in other American cities, municipal policy has taken its lead from the security offensive and the middle-class demand for increased spatial and social insulation. Taxes previously targeted for traditional public spaces and recreational facilities have been redirected to support corporate redevelopment projects. A pliant city government—in the case of Los Angeles, one ironically professing to represent a liberal biracial coalition—has collaborated in privatizing public space and subsidizing new exclusive enclaves (benignly called "urban villages"). The celebratory language used to describe contemporary Los Angeles—"urban renaissance," "city of the future," and so on—is only a triumphal gloss laid over the brutalization of its inner-city neighborhoods and the stark divisions of class and race represented in its built environment. Urban form obediently follows repressive function. Los Angeles, as always in the vanguard, offers an especially disturbing guide to the emerging liaisons between urban architecture and the police state.

## Forbidden City

Los Angeles's first spatial militarist was the legendary General Harrison Gray Otis, proprietor of the *Times* and implacable foe of organized labor. In the 1890s, after locking out his union printers and announcing a crusade for "industrial freedom," Otis retreated into a new *Times* building designed as a fortress with grim turrets and battlements crowned by a bellicose bronze eagle. To emphasize his truculence, he later had a small, functional cannon installed on the hood of his Packard touring car. Not surprisingly, this display of aggression produced a response in kind. On October 1, 1910, the heavily fortified *Times* headquarters—the command-post of the open shop on the West Coast—was destroyed in a catastrophic explosion, blamed on union saboteurs.

Eighty years later, the martial spirit of General Otis pervades the design of Los Angeles's new Downtown, whose skyscrapers march from Bunker Hill down the Figueroa corridor. Two billion dollars of public tax subsidies have enticed big banks and corporate headquarters back to a central city they almost abandoned in the 1960s. Into a waiting grid, cleared of tenement housing by the city's powerful and largely unaccountable redevelopment agency, local developers and offshore investors (increasingly Japanese) have planted a series of block-square complexes: Crocker Center, the Bonaventure Hotel and Shopping Mall, the World Trade Center, California Plaza, Arco Center, and so on. With an increasingly dense and self-contained circulation system linking these superblocks, the new financial district is best conceived as a single, self-referential hyperstructure, a Miesian skyscape of fantastic proportions.

Like similar megalomaniacal complexes tethered to fragmented and desolate downtowns—such as the Renaissance Center in Detroit and the Peachtree and Omni centers in Atlanta—Bunker Hill and the Figueroa corridor have provoked a storm of objections to their abuse of scale and composition, their denigration of street life, and their confiscation of the vital energy of the center, now sequestered within their subterranean concourses or privatized plazas. Sam

Hall Kaplan, the former design critic of the *Times*, has vociferously denounced the antistreet bias of redevelopment; in his view, the superimposition of "hermetically sealed fortresses" and random "pieces of suburbia" onto Downtown has "killed the street" and "dammed the rivers of life."[3]

Yet Kaplan's vigorous defense of pedestrian democracy remains grounded in liberal complaints about "bland design" and "elitist planning practices." Like most architectural critics, he rails against the oversights of urban design without conceding a dimension of foresight, and even of deliberate repressive intent. For when Downtown's new "Gold Coast" is seen in relation to other social landscapes in the central city, the "fortress effect" emerges, not as an inadvertent failure of design, but as an explicit—and, in its own terms, successful—socio-spatial strategy.

The goals of this strategy may be summarized as a double repression: to obliterate all connection with Downtown's past and to prevent any dynamic association with the non-Anglo urbanism of its future. Los Angeles is unusual among major urban centers in having preserved, however negligently, most of its Beaux Arts commercial core. Yet the city chose to transplant—at immense public cost—the entire corporate and financial district from around Broadway and Spring Street to Bunker Hill, a half-dozen blocks further west.

The underlying logic of this operation is revealing. In other cities, developers have tried to harmonize the new cityscape and the old, exploiting the latter's historic buildings to create gentrified zones (Faneuil Market, Ghirardelli Square, and so on) as supports to middle-class residential colonization. But Downtown Los Angeles's redevelopers considered property values in the old Broadway core as irreversibly eroded by the area's status as the hub of public transportation primarily used by black and Mexican poor. In the wake of the 1965 Watts Rebellion, whose fires burned to within a few blocks of the old Downtown, resegregated spatial security became the paramount concern. The 1960–64 "Centropolis" masterplan, which had envisioned the renewal of the old core, was unceremoniously scrapped. Meanwhile the Los Angeles Police Department (LAPD) abetted the flight of business from the Broadway–Spring Street area to the fortified redoubts of Bunker Hill by spreading scare literature about the "immigrant gang invasion" by black teenagers.[4]

To emphasize the "security" of the new Downtown, virtually all the traditional pedestrian links to the old center, including the famous Angels' Flight funicular railroad, were removed. The Harbor Freeway and the regraded palisades of Bunker Hill further cut off the new financial core from the poor immigrant neighborhoods that surround it on every side. Along the base of California Plaza (home of the Museum of Contemporary Art), Hill Street functions as the stark boundary separating the luxury of Bunker Hill from the chaotic life of Broadway, now the primary shopping and entertainment street for Latino immigrants. Because gentrifiers now have their eye on the northern end of the Broadway corridor (redubbed Bunker Hill East), the redevelopment agency promises to restore pedestrian access to the Hill in the 1990s. This, of course, only dramatizes the current bias against any spatial interaction between old and new, poor and rich—except in the framework of gentrification. Although a few white-collar types sometimes venture into the Grand Central Market—a popular emporium of tropical produce and fresh foods—Latino shoppers or Saturday *flaneurs* never ascend to the upscale precincts above Hill Street. The occasional appearance of a destitute street nomad in Broadway Plaza or in front of the Museum of Contemporary Art sets off a quiet panic, as video cameras turn on their mounts and security guards adjust their belts.

Photographs of the old Downtown in its 1940s prime show crowds of Anglo, black, and Mexican shoppers of all ages and classes. The contemporary Downtown "renaissance" renders such heterogeneity virtually impossible. It is intended not just to "kill the street" as Kaplan feared, but to "kill the crowd," to eliminate that democratic mixture that Olmsted believed was America's antidote to European class polarization. The new Downtown is designed to ensure a seamless continuum of middle-class work, consumption, and recreation, insulated from the city's "unsavory" streets. Ramparts and battlements, reflective glass and elevated pedways, are tropes in an architectural language warning off the underclass Other. Although architectural critics are usually blind to this militarized syntax, urban pariah groups—whether young black men, poor Latino immigrants, or elderly homeless white females, read the signs immediately.

Extreme though it may seem, Bunker Hill is only one local expression of the national movement toward "defensible" urban centers. Cities of all sizes are rushing to apply and profit from a formula that links together clustered development, social homogeneity, and a perception of security. As an article in *Urban Land* magazine on "how to overcome fear of crime in downtowns" advised:

> A downtown can be designed and developed to make visitors feel that it—or a significant portion of it—is attractive and the type of place that "respectable people" like themselves tend to frequent. . . . A core downtown area that is compact, densely developed and multifunctional, [with] offices and housing for middle- and upper-income residents ... can assure a high percentage of "respectable," law-abiding pedestrians. Such an attractive redeveloped core area would also be large enough to affect the downtown's overall image.[5]

# Mean Streets

This strategic armoring of the city against the poor is especially obvious at street level. In his famous study of the "social life of small urban spaces," William Whyte points out that the quality of any urban environment can be measured, first of all, by whether there are convenient, comfortable places for pedestrians to sit. This maxim has been warmly taken to heart by designers of the high corporate precincts of Bunker Hill and its adjacent "urban villages." As part of the city's policy of subsidizing the white-collar residential colonization of Downtown, tens of millions of dollars of tax revenue have been invested in the creation of attractive "soft" environments in favored areas. Planners envision a succession of opulent piazzas, fountains, public art, exotic shrubbery, and comfortable street furniture along a ten-block pedestrian corridor from

Bunker Hill to South Park. Brochures sell Downtown's "livability" with idyllic representations of office workers and affluent tourists sipping cappuccino and listening to free jazz concerts in the terraced gardens of California Plaza and Grand Hope Park.

In stark contrast, a few blocks away, the city is engaged in a relentless struggle to make the streets as unlivable as possible for the homeless and poor. The persistence of thousands of street people on the fringes of Bunker Hill and the Civic Center tarnishes the image of designer living Downtown and betrays the laboriously constructed illusion of an urban "renaissance." City hall has retaliated with its own version of low-intensity warfare.

Although city leaders periodically propose schemes for removing indigents *en masse*—deporting them to a poor farm on the edge of the desert, confining them in camps on the mountains, or interning them on derelict ferries in the harbor—such "final solutions" have been blocked by council members' fears of the displacement of the homeless into their districts. Instead the city, self-consciously adopting the idiom of cold war, has promoted the "containment" (the official term) of the homeless in Skid Row, along Fifth Street, systematically transforming the neighborhood into an outdoor poorhouse. But this containment strategy breeds its own vicious cycle of contradiction. By condensing the mass of the desperate and helpless together in such a small space, and denying adequate housing, official policy has transformed Skid Row into probably the most dangerous ten square blocks in the world. Every night on Skid Row is Friday the 13th, and, unsurprisingly, many of the homeless seek to escape the area during the night at all costs, searching safer niches in other parts of Downtown. The city in turn tightens the noose with increased police harassment and ingenious design deterrents.

One of the simplest but most mean-spirited of these deterrents is the Rapid Transit District's new barrel-shaped bus bench, which offers a minimal surface for uncomfortable sitting while making sleeping impossible. Such "bumproof" benches are being widely introduced on the periphery of Skid Row. Another invention is the aggressive deployment of outdoor sprinklers. Several years ago the city opened a Skid Row Park; to ensure that the park could not be used for overnight camping, overhead sprinklers were programmed to drench unsuspecting sleepers at random times during the night. The system was immediately copied by local merchants to drive the homeless away from (public) storefront sidewalks. Meanwhile Downtown restaurants and markets have built baroque enclosures to protect their refuse from the homeless. Although no one in Los Angeles has yet proposed adding cyanide to the garbage, as was suggested in Phoenix a few years back, one popular seafood restaurant has spent $12,000 to build the ultimate bag-lady-proof trash cage: three-quarter-inch steel rods with alloy locks and vicious out-turned spikes to safeguard moldering fishheads and stale french fries.

Public toilets, however, have become the real frontline of the city's war on the homeless. Los Angeles, as a matter of deliberate policy, has fewer public lavatories than any other major North American city. On the advice of the Los Angeles police, who now sit on the "design board" of at least one major

Downtown project, the redevelopment agency bulldozed the few remaining public toilets on Skid Row. Agency planners then considered whether to include a "free-standing public toilet" in their design for the upscale South Park residential development; agency chairman Jim Wood later admitted that the decision not to build the toilet was a "policy decision and not a design decision." The agency preferred the alternative of "quasi-public restrooms"—toilets in restaurants, art galleries, and office buildings—which can be made available selectively to tourists and white-collar workers while being denied to vagrants and other unsuitables. The same logic has inspired the city's transportation planners to exclude toilets from their designs for Los Angeles's new subway system.[6]

Bereft of toilets, the Downtown badlands east of Hill Street also lack outside water sources for drinking or washing. A common and troubling sight these days is the homeless men—many of them young refugees from El Salvador—washing, swimming, even drinking from the sewer effluent that flows down the concrete channel of the Los Angeles River on the eastern edge of Downtown. The city's public health department has made no effort to post warning signs in Spanish or to mobilize alternative clean-water sources.

In those areas where Downtown professionals must cross paths with the homeless or the working poor—such as the zone of gentrification along Broadway just south of the Civic Center—extraordinary precautions have been taken to ensure the physical separation of the different classes. The redevelopment agency, for example, again brought in the police to help design "twenty-four-hour, state-of-the-art security" for the two new parking structures that serve the *Los Angeles Times* headquarters and the Ronald Reagan State Office Building. In contrast to the mean streets outside, both parking structures incorporate beautifully landscaped microparks, and one even boasts a food court, picnic area, and historical exhibit. Both structures are intended to function as "confidence-building" circulation systems that allow white-collar workers to walk from car to office, or from car to boutique, with minimum exposure to the public street. The Broadway-Spring Center, in particular, which links the two local hubs of gentrification (the Reagan Building and the proposed Grand Central Square) has been warmly praised by architectural critics for adding greenery and art to parking. It also adds a considerable dose of menace—armed guards, locked gates, and ubiquitous security cameras—to scare away the homeless and the poor.

The cold war on the streets of Downtown is ever escalating. The police, lobbied by Downtown merchants and developers, have broken up every attempt by the homeless and their allies to create safe havens or self-governed encampments. "Justiceville," founded by homeless activist Ted Hayes, was roughly dispersed; when its inhabitants attempted to find refuge at Venice Beach, they were arrested at the behest of the local council member (a renowned environmentalist) and sent back to Skid Row. The city's own brief experiment with legalized camping—a grudging response to a series of deaths from exposure during the cold winter of 1987—was abruptly terminated after only four months to make way for the construction of a transit maintenance yard. Current policy seems to involve perverse play upon the famous irony about the equal rights of the rich and poor to sleep in the rough. As the former head of the city planning commission explained, in the City of the Angels it is not against the law to sleep in the street per se—"only to erect any sort of protective shelter."[7] To enforce this proscription against "cardboard condos," the police periodically sweep the Nickel, tearing down shelters, confiscating possessions, and arresting resisters. Such cynical repression has turned the majority of the homeless into bedouins. They are visible all over Downtown, pushing their few pathetic possessions in stolen shopping carts, always fugitive, always in motion, pressed between the official policy of containment and the inhumanity of Downtown streets.

## Sequestering the Poor

An insidious spatial logic also regulates the lives of Los Angeles's working poor. Just across the moat of the Harbor Freeway, west of Bunker Hill, lies the MacArthur Park district—once upon a time the city's wealthiest neighborhood. Although frequently characterized as a no-man's-land awaiting resurrection by developers, the district is, in fact, home to the largest Central American community in the United States. In the congested streets bordering the park, a hundred thousand Salvadorans and Guatemalans, including a large community of Mayan-speakers, crowd into tenements and boarding houses barely adequate for a fourth as many people. Every morning at 6 A.M. this Latino Bantustan dispatches armies of sewing *operadoras*, dishwashers, and janitors to turn the wheels of the Downtown economy. But because MacArthur Park is midway between Downtown and the famous Miracle Mile, it too will soon fall to redevelopment's bulldozers.

Hungry to exploit the lower land prices in the district, a powerful coterie of developers, represented by a famous ex-councilman and the former president of the planning commissions, has won official approval for their vision of "Central City West": literally, a second Downtown comprising 25 million square feet of new office and retail space. Although local politicians have insisted upon a significant quota of low-income replacement housing, such a palliative will hardly compensate for the large-scale population displacement sure to follow the construction of the new skyscrapers and yuppified "urban villages." In the meantime, Korean capital, seeking *lebensraum* for Los Angeles's burgeoning Koreatown, is also pushing into the MacArthur Park area, uprooting tenements to construct heavily fortified condominiums and office complexes. Other Asian and European speculators are counting on the new Metrorail stations, across from the park, to become a magnet for new investment in the district.

The recent intrusion of so many powerful interests into the area has put increasing pressure upon the police to "take back the streets" from what is usually represented as an occupying army of drug-dealers, illegal immigrants, and homicidal homeboys. Thus in the summer of 1990 the LAPD announced a massive operation to "retake crime-plagued MacArthur Park" and surrounding neighborhoods "street by street, alley by alley." While the area is undoubtedly a major drug market, principally for drive-in Anglo commuters, the police have focused not only on addict-dealers and gang members, but also on the industrious sidewalk vendors who have made the circumference of the park an exuberant swap meet. Thus Mayan women selling such local staples as tropical fruit, baby clothes, and roach spray have been rounded up in the same sweeps as alleged "narcoterrorists."[8] (Similar dragnets in other Southern California communities have focused on Latino day-laborers congregated at streetcorner "slave markets.")

By criminalizing every attempt by the poor—whether the Skid Row homeless or MacArthur Park vendors—to use public space for survival purposes, law-enforcement agencies have abolished the last informal safety-net separating misery from catastrophe. (Few third-world cities are so pitiless.) At the same time, the police, encouraged by local businessmen and property owners, are taking the first, tentative steps toward criminalizing entire inner-city communities. The "war" on drugs and gangs again has been the pretext for the LAPD's novel, and disturbing, experiments with community blockades. A large section of the Pico-Union neighborhood, just south of MacArthur Park, has been quarantined since the summer of 1989; "Narcotics Enforcement Area" barriers restrict entry to residents "on legitimate business only." Inspired by the positive response of older residents and local politicians, the police have subsequently franchised "Operation Cul-de-Sac" to other low-income Latino and black neighborhoods.

Thus in November 1989 (as the Berlin Wall was being demolished), the Devonshire Division of the LAPD closed off a "drug-ridden" twelve-block section of the northern San Fernando Valley. To control circulation within this largely Latino neighborhood, the police convinced apartment owners to finance the construction of a permanent guard station. Twenty miles to the south, a square mile of the mixed black and Latino Central-Avalon community has also been converted into Narcotic Enforcement turf with concrete roadblocks. Given the popularity of these quarantines—save amongst the ghetto youth against whom they are directed—it is possible that a majority of the inner city may eventually be partitioned into police-regulated "no-go" areas.

The official rhetoric of the contemporary war against the urban underclasses resounds with comparisons to the War in Vietnam a generation ago. The LAPD's community blockades evoke the infamous policy of quarantining suspect populations in "strategic hamlets." But an even more ominous emulation is the reconstruction of Los Angeles's public housing projects as "defensible spaces." Deep in the Mekong Delta of the Watts-Willowbrook ghetto, for example, the Imperial Courts Housing Project has been fortified with chainlink fencing, RESTRICTED ENTRY signs, obligatory identity passes—and a substation of the LAPD. Visitors are stopped and frisked, the police routinely order residents back into their apartments at night, and domestic life is subjected to constant police scrutiny. For public-housing tenants and inhabitants of narcotic-enforcement zones, the loss of freedom is the price of "security."

# Security by Design

If the contemporary search for bourgeois security can be read in the design of bus benches, megastructures, and housing projects, it is also visible at the level of *auteur*. No recent architect has so ingeniously elaborated or so brazenly embraced the urban-security function as Los Angeles's Pritzker Prize laureate Frank Gehry. His strongest suit is his straightforward exploitations of rough urban environments, and the explicit incorporation of their harshest edges and detritus as powerful representational elements. Affectionately described by colleagues as an "old socialist" or "street-fighter with a heart," Gehry makes little pretense at architectural reformism or "design for democracy." He boasts instead of trying "to make the best with the reality of things."[9] With sometimes chilling effect, his work clarifies the underlying relations of repression, surveillance, and exclusion that characterize the fragmented landscape of Los Angeles.

An early example of Gehry's new urban realism was his 1964 solution of the problem of how to insert luxurious spaces—and high property values—into decaying neighborhoods. His Danziger Studio in Hollywood is the pioneer instance of what has become an entire species of Los Angeles "stealth houses," which dissimulate their opulence behind proletarian or gangster facades. The street frontage of the Danziger is simply a massive gray wall, treated with a rough finish to ensure that it would collect dust from the passing traffic and weather into a simulacrum of the nearby porn studios and garages. Gehry was explicit in his search for a design that was "introverted and fortresslike," with the silent aura of a "dumb box."[10]

Indeed, "dumb boxes" and screen walls form an entire cycle of his work, ranging from the American School of Dance (1968) to his Gemini GEL (1979)—both in Hollywood. His most seminal design, however, was his walled town center for Cochiti Lake, New Mexico (1973): here ice-blue ramparts of awesome severity enclose an entire community, a plan replicated on a smaller scale in his 1976 Jung Institute in Los Angeles. In both of these cases architectural drama is generated by the contrast between the fortified exteriors, set against "unappealing neighborhoods" (Gehry) or deserts, and the opulent interiors, opened to the sky by clerestories and lightwells. Gehry's walled-in compounds and cities, in other words, offer powerful metaphors for the retreat from the street and the introversion of space that has characterized the design backlash to the urban insurrections of the 1960s.

Gehry took up the same problem in 1984 in his design for the Loyala Law School in MacArthur Park district. The inner-city location of the campus confronted Gehry with an explicit choice: to create a genuine public space, extending into the community, or to choose the security of a defensible enclave, as in his previous work. Gehry's choice, as one critic explained, was a neoconservative design that was "open, but not *too* open. The South Instructional Hall and the chapel show solid backs to Olympic Boulevard, and with the anonymous street sides of the Burns Building, form a gateway that is neither forbidding nor overly welcoming. It is simply there, like everything else in the neighborhood."[11] This description considerably understates the forbidding qualities of the campus's formidable steel-stake fencing, concrete-block ziggurat, and stark frontage walls.

But if the Danziger Studio camouflages itself, and the Cochiti Lake and Loyala designs are dumb boxes with an attitude, Gehry's baroquely fortified Goldwyn Branch Library in Hollywood (1984) positively taunts potential trespassers "to make my day." This is probably the most menacing library ever built, a bizarre hybrid of a drydocked dreadnought and a cavalry fort. With its fifteen-foot-high security walls of stuccoed concrete block, it's anti-graffiti barricades covered in ceramic tile, its sunken entrance protected by ten-foot-high steel stakes, and its stylized sentry boxes perched precariously on each side, the Goldwyn Library (influenced by Gehry's 1980 high-security design for the U.S. Chancellery in Damascus) projects nothing less than sheer aggression.

Some of the Gehry's admirers have praised the Library as "generous and inviting,"[12] "the old-fashioned kind of library," and so on. But they miss the point. The previous Hollywood library had been destroyed by arson, and the Samuel Goldwyn Foundation, which endows this collection of filmland memorabilia, was understandably preoccupied by physical security. Gehry's commission was to design a structure that was inherently vandalproof. His innovation, of course, was to reject the low-profile high-tech security systems that most architects subtly integrate into their blueprints, and to choose instead a high-profile, low-tech approach that foregrounds the security function as the central motif of the design. There is no dissimulation of function by form here—quite the opposite. How playful or witty you find the resulting effect depends on your existential position. The Goldwyn Library by its very structure conjures up the demonic Other—arsonist, graffitist, invader—and casts the shadow of its own arrogant paranoia onto the surrounding seedy, though not particularly hostile streets.

These streets are a battleground, but not of the expected kind. Several years ago the *Los Angeles Times* broke the sordid story of how the entertainment conglomerates and a few large landowners had managed to capture control of the local redevelopment process. Their plan, still the focus of controversy, is to use eminent domain and higher taxes to clear the poor (increasingly refugees from Central America) from the streets of Hollywood and reap the huge windfalls from "upgrading" the area into a glitzy theme park for international tourism.[13] In the context of this strategy, the Goldwyn Library—like Gehry's earlier walled compounds—is a kind of architectural fire-base, a beachhead for gentrification. Its soaring, light-filled interiors surrounded by barricades speak volumes about how public architecture in America is literally turning its back on the city for security and profit.

# The Panopticon Mall

In other parts of the inner city, however, similar "fortress" designs are being used to recapture the poor as consumers. If the Goldwyn Library is a "shining example of the possibilities of public-and private-sector cooperation," then developer

Alexander Haagen's ghetto malls are truly stellar instances. Haagen, who began his career distributing jukeboxes to the honkytonks of Wilmington, made his first fortune selling corner lots to oil companies for gas stations—sites since recycled as minimalls. He now controls the largest retail-development empire in Southern California, comprising more than forty shopping centers, and has become nationally acclaimed as the impresario of South-Central Los Angeles's "retail revival."

Haagen was perhaps the first major developer in the nation to grasp the latent profit potential of abandoned inner-city retail markets. After the Watts Rebellion in 1965, the handful of large discount stores in the South-Central region took flight, and small businesses were closed down by the banks' discriminatory redlining practices. As a result, 750,000 black and Latino shoppers were forced to commute to distant regional malls or adjacent white neighborhoods even for their everyday groceries. Haagen reasoned that a retail developer prepared to return to the inner city could monopolize very high sales volumes. He also was well aware of the accumulating anger of the black community against decades of benign neglect by City Hall and the redevelopment agency; while the agency had moved swiftly to assemble land for billionaire developers Downtown, it floundered in Watts for years, unable to attract a single supermarket to anchor a proposed neighborhood shopping center. Haagen knew that the Bradley regime, in hot water with its South-Central constituents, would handsomely reward any private-sector initiative that could solve the anchor-tenant problem. His ingenious solution was a comprehensive "*security-oriented* design and management strategy."[14]

Haagen made his first move in 1979, taking title to an old Sears site in the heart of the ghetto. Impressed by his success there, the redevelopment agency transferred to him the completion of its long-delayed Martin Luther King, Jr., Center in Watts. A year later Haagen Development won the bid for the $120 million renovation of Crenshaw Plaza (a pioneer 1940s mall on the western fringe of the ghetto), as well as a contract from Los Angeles County to build another shopping complex in the Willowbrook area south of Watts. In each case Haagen's guarantee of total physical security was the key to persuading retailers and their insurers to take up leases. The essence of security, in turn, was a site plan clearly derived from Jeremy Bentham's proposed Panopticon— the eighteenth-century model prison to be constructed radially so that a single guard in a central tower could observe every prisoner at all times.

The King Shopping Center in Watts provides the best prototype of this commercial Brave New World for the inner city:

> The King Center site is surrounded by an eight-foot-high, wrought-iron fence comparable to security fences found at the perimeters of private estates and exclusive residential communities. Video cameras equipped with motion detectors are positioned near entrances and throughout the shopping center. The center, including parking lots, can be bathed in bright [lights] at the flip of a switch.
>
> There are six entrances to the center: three entry points for autos, two service gates, and one pedestrian walkway. . . . The service area . . . is enclosed with a six-foot-high concrete-block wall; both service gates remain closed and are under

closed-circuit video surveillance, equipped for two-way voice communications, and operated by remote control from a security "observatory." Infrared beams at the bases of light fixtures detect intruders who might circumvent video cameras by climbing over the wall.[15]

The observatory functions as both eye and brain of this complex security system. It contains the headquarters of the shopping-center manager, a substation of the LAPD, and a dispatch operator who both monitors the video and audio systems and maintains communication "with other secure shopping centers tied into the system, and with the police and fire departments." At any time of day or night, there are at least four security guards on duty—one at the observatory, and three on patrol. They are trained and backed up by the regular LAPD officers operating from the observatory substation.[16]

The King Center and its three siblings (all variations on the Panopticon theme), as expected, have been bonanzas, averaging annual sales of more than $350 per leasable square foot, as compared to about $200 for their suburban equivalents.[17] Moreover, Haagen has reaped the multiple windfalls of tax breaks, federal and city grants, massive free publicity, subsidized tenants, and sixty- to ninety-year ground leases. No wonder he has been able to boast, "We've proved that the only color that counts in business is green. There are huge opportunities and huge profits to be made in these depressed inner-city areas of America that have been abandoned."[18]

# High-Rent Security

The security-driven logic of contemporary urban design finds its major "grassroots" expression in the frenetic efforts of Los Angeles's affluent neighborhoods to physically insulate their real-estate values and life-styles. Luxury developments outside the city limits have often been able to incorporate as "fortress cities," complete with security walls, guarded entries, private police, and even private roadways. It is simply impossible for ordinary citizens to enter the "cities" of Hidden Hills (western San Fernando Valley), Bradbury (San Gabriel Valley), Rancho Mirage (low desert), or Palos Verdes Estates (Palos Verdes Peninsula) without an invitation from a resident. Indeed Bradbury, with nine hundred inhabitants and ten miles of gated private roads, is so obsessed with security that its three city officials will not return phone calls from the press, since "each time an article appears, 1/4 it draws attention to the city, and the number of burglaries increases."[19]

Recently, Hidden Hills, a Norman Rockwell painting behind walls, has been bitterly divided over a Superior Court order to build forty-eight units of seniors' housing on vacant land outside the city gates. At meetings of the city's powerful homeowners' association (whose members include Frankie Avalon, Neil Diamond, and Bob Eubanks) opponents of compliance have argued vehemently that the old folks "will attract gangs and dope."[20]

Meanwhile, older high-income cities like Beverly Hills and San Marino have restricted access to their public facilities, using byzantine layers of regulations to build invisible walls. San Marino, which may be the richest and most Republican city in the country (85 percent), now closes its parks on weekends to exclude Latino and Asian families from adjacent communities. An alternative plan, now under discussion, would reopen the parks on Saturdays, but only to those with proof of residence or the means to pay daunting use fees. Other upscale areas (including thirty-seven Los Angeles neighborhoods) have minted similar residential privileges by restricting parking to local homeowners. Predictably such preferential parking ordinances proliferate mainly neighborhoods with three-car garages.

Affluent areas of the City of Los Angeles have long envied the autonomy of fortress enclaves like Hidden Hills and Palos Verdes. Now, with the cooperation of a pliant city council, they are winning permission to literally wall themselves off from the rest of the city. Since its construction in the late 1940s, Park La Brea has been Los Angeles's most successful experiment in mixed-income, high-rise living. Its urbane population of singles, young families, and retirees has always given a touch of Manhattan to the La Brea Tarpits area of Wilshire Boulevard. But its new owners, Forest City Enterprises, hope to "upgrade" the project image by sealing it off from the surrounding neighborhoods with security fencing and NO TRESPASSING signs. As a spokesperson for the owners blandly observed, "It's a trend in general to have enclosed communities."[21]

A few miles north of Park La Brea, above the Hollywood Bowl, the wealthy residents of Whitley Heights have won the unprecedented privilege of withdrawing their streets from public use. Eight high-tech gates will restrict access to residents and approved visitors using special electronic codes. An immediate byproduct of "gatehood" has been a dramatic 20 percent rise in local property values—a windfall that other residential districts are eager to emulate. Thus in the once wide-open tractlands of the San Fernando Valley—where a decade ago there were virtually no walled-off communities—homeowners are rushing to fortify their equity with walls and gates. Brian Weinstock, a leading local contractor, proudly boasts of the Valley's more than one hundred newly gated neighborhoods, and reports insatiable demand for additional security. "The first question out of [every buyer's] mouth is whether there is a gated community. The demand is there on a three-to-one basis."[22]

Meanwhile the very rich are yearning for unassailable high-tech castles. Where gates and walls will not suffice, the house itself is redesigned to incorporate state-of-the-art security. An important if unacknowledged motive for the current "mansionizing" mania on the city's Westside—the tearing down of $3 million houses to build $30 million supermansions—is the search for "absolute security." To achieve it, residential architects are borrowing design secrets from overseas embassies and military command posts. For example, one of the features currently in high demand is the "terrorist-proof security room" concealed in the houseplan and reached by hidden sliding panels or secret doors. Merv Griffin and his fellow mansionizers are hardening their palaces like banks or missile silos.

But technology is not enough. Contemporary residential security in Los Angeles—whether in the fortified mansion or the average suburban bunker—

depends upon the extensive deployment of private security services. Through their local homeowners' associations, virtually every affluent neighborhood from the Palisades to Silver Lake contracts its own private policing; hence the thousands of lawns displaying the little ARMED RESPONSE warnings. A recent Times want-ads section contained over a hundred ads for guards and patrolmen, mostly from firms specializing in residential protection. Within greater Los Angeles, the security-services industry is a Cinderella sector that has tripled its sales and workforce—from 24,000 to 75,000 guards—over the last decade. "It is easier to become an armed guard than it is to become a barber, hairdresser, or journeyman carpenter," reports Linda Williams in the Times. Although the patrolmen are mostly minority males earning close to minimum wage, their employers are often multinational conglomerates offering a dazzling range of security products and services. As Michael Kaye, president of burgeoning Westec, a subsidiary of Japan's Secom, Ltd., explains: "We're not a security-guard company. We sell a concept of security."[23]

What homeowners' associations contract from Westec—or its principal rival, Bel-Air Patrol (part of Borg-Warner's family of security companies, which include Burns and Pinkerton)—is a complete "systems package": alarm hardware, monitoring, watch patrols, personal escorts, and, of course, "armed response" as necessary. Although law-enforcement experts debate the efficiency of such systems in foiling professional criminals, there is no doubt that they are brilliantly successful in deterring unintentional trespassers and innocent pedestrians. Anyone who has tried to take a stroll at dusk through a neighborhood patrolled by armed security guards and signposted with death threats quickly realizes how merely notional, if not utterly obsolete, is the old idea of "freedom of the city."

## The LAPD as Space Police

This comprehensive urban security mobilization depends not only on the incorporation of the police function into the built environment, but also on the growing technopower of the police themselves. Undoubtedly the LAPD's pioneering substitution of technology for manpower was in part a necessary adaptation to the city's dispersed form; but it also expresses the department's particular relationship to the community. Especially in its self-representation, the LAPD appears as the progressive antithesis to the traditional big city police department with its patronage armies of patrolmen grafting off their beats. The LAPD, as reformed in the early 1950s by the legendary Chief Parker (who admired, above all, the gung-ho elitism of the Marines), would be incorruptible because unapproachable, a "few good men" doing battle with a fundamentally evil city. *Dragnet's* Sergeant Friday precisely captured the Parkerized LAPD's prudish alienation from a citizenry composed of fools, degenerates, and psychopaths.

Technology helped foster this paranoid esprit de corps, and virtually established a new definition of policing, where technologized surveillance and response supplanted the traditional patrolman's intimate folk knowledge of a specific community. Thus back in the 1920s the LAPD had pioneered the replacement of the flatfoot or mounted officer with the radio patrol car—the beginning of dispersed, mechanized policing. Under Parker, ever alert to spinoffs from military technology, the LAPD introduced the first police helicopters for systematic aerial surveillance. After the Watts Rebellion of 1965, this airborne effort became the cornerstone of a policing strategy for the entire inner city. As part of its Astro program LAPD helicopters maintain an average nineteen-hour-per-day vigil over "high-crime areas." To facilitate ground-air coordination, thousands of residential rooftops have been painted with large, identifying street numbers, transforming the aerial view of the city into a huge police grid.

The fifty-pilot LAPD airforce was recently updated with French Aerospatiale helicopters equipped with futuristic surveillance technology. Their forward-looking infrared cameras are extraordinary night eyes that can easily form heat images from a single burning cigarette a mile away, while their 30-million-candle-power spotlights, appropriately called "Night Suns," can turn night into day. Meanwhile the LAPD retains another fleet of Bell Jet Rangers capable of delivering SWAT units anywhere in the region. Their training, which sometimes includes practice assaults on Downtown high-rises, anticipates some of the spookier Hollywood images—as in *Blue Thunder* or *Running Man*—of airborne police terror.

But the decisive element in the LAPD's metamorphosis into a Technopolice has been its long and successful liaison with the military aerospace industry.[24] Just in time for the opening of the 1984 Los Angeles Olympics, the department acquired ECCCS (Emergency Command Control Communications Systems), the most powerful police communications system in the world. First conceptualized by Hughes Aerospace between 1969 and 1971, ECCCS's design was refined and updated by NASA's Jet Propulsion Laboratory, incorporating elements of space technology and mission-centered communication.

Bunkered in the earthquake-proof security-hardened fourth and fifth sublevels of City Hall East (and interconnecting with the police pentagon in Parker Center), the Central Dispatch Center coordinates all the complex itineraries and responses of the LAPD using digitalized communication to eliminate voice congestion and guaranteed the secrecy of transmission. ECCCS, together with the LAPD's prodigious information-processing assets, including ever-growing databases on suspect citizens, have become the central neural system for the vast and disparate security operations, both public and private, taking place in Los Angeles.

# The Carceral City

All these technologically advanced policing strategies have led to an invisible Haussmannization of Los Angeles. No need to clear fields of fire when you control the sky; no need to hire informers when surveillance cameras ornament every building. But the police have also reorganized space in far more straight-forward ways. We have already seen their growing role as Downtown urban designers, indispensable for their expertise in "security." In addition they lobby incessantly for the allocation of more land for such law-and-order needs as jail space for a burgeoning inmate population and expanded administrative and training facilities for themselves. In Los Angeles this has taken the form of a *de facto* urban-renewal program, operated by the police agencies, that threatens to convert an entire section of Downtown and East LA into a vast penal colony.

Nearly 25,000 prisoners are presently held in six severely overcrowded county and federal facilities within a three-mile radius of City Hall—the largest single incarcerated population in the country. Racing to meet the challenge of the "war on drugs"—which will double detained populations within a decade—authorities are forging ahead with the reconstruction of a controversial state prison in East Los Angeles as well as a giant expansion of County Jail near Chinatown. The Immigration and Naturalization Service, meanwhile, has been trying to shoehorn privatized "microprisons" into unsuspecting innercity neighborhoods. Confronting record overcrowding in its regular detention centers, the INS has commandeered motels and apartments for operation by private contractors as auxiliary jails for detained aliens—many of them Chinese and Central American political refugees.

The demand for more law-enforcement space in the central city, however, will inevitably bring the police into conflict with developers. The plan to add two high-rise towers with 2,400 new beds to County Jail on Bauchet Street, Downtown, has already raised the ire of developers hoping to make nearby Union Station the hub of a vast complex of skyscraper hotels and offices. One solution to the increasing conflict between carceral and commercial redevelopment is to use architectural camouflage to insert jail space into the skyscape. Ironically, even as buildings and homes become more like prisons or fortresses, prisons are becoming aesthetic objects. Indeed, carceral structures are the new frontier of public architecture. As an office glut in most parts of the country reduces commissions for corporate highrises, celebrity architects are designing jails, prisons, and police stations.

An extraordinary example, the flagship of the emergent genre, is Welton Becket Associates' new Metropolitan Detentions Center in Downtown Los Angeles. Although this ten-story Federal Bureau of Prisons facility is one of the most visible new structures in the city, few of the hundreds of thousands of commuters who pass by every day have even an inkling of its function as a holding center for what has been officially describe[d] as the "managerial elite of narco-terrorism." This postmodern Bastille—the largest prison built in a major U.S. urban center in decades—looks instead like a futuristic hotel or office block, with artistic flourishes (for example, the high-tech trellises on its bridge-balconies) that are comparable to Downtown's best-designed recent architecture. In contrast to the human inferno of desperately overcrowded County Jail a few blocks away, the Becket structure appears less a detention center than a convention center for federal felons—a "distinguished" addition to Downtown's continuum of security and design.

# The Fear of Crowds

In actual practice, the militarization of urban space tends to race far ahead of its theoretical representations. This is not to say, however, that the fortress city lacks apologists. Charles Murray, ideologue *par excellence* of 1980s antiwelfarism, has recently outlined ambitious justifications for renewed urban segregation in the 1990s. Writing in the *New Republic* (increasingly, the theoretical journal of the backlash against the urban poor), Murray argues that *landlords*—"one of the greatly maligned forces for social good in this country"—*not cops* are the best bet for winning the war on drugs.[25] Given the prohibitive cost of building sufficient prison space to warehouse the country's burgeoning population of inner-city drug users, Murray proposes instead to isolate them socially and spatially. In his three-prong strategy, employers would urine-test and fire drug-tainted workers at will; parents would use vouchers to remove their children from drug-ridden public schools; and, most importantly, landlords would maintain drug-free neighborhoods by excluding the "wrong kind of person."

Murray advocates, in other words, the restoration of the right of employers and landlords to discriminate—"without having to justify their arbitrariness." Only by letting "like-minded people . . . control and shape their small worlds," and letting landlords pursue their natural instinct "to let good tenants be and to evict bad ones," can the larger part of urban America find its way back to a golden age of harmonious, self-regulating communities. Murray is undoubtedly proud of all the Los Angeles suburbanites rushing to wall off their tract-home *gemeinschafts.*

At the same time, he unflinchingly accepts that the underclass—typified, in his words, by the "pregnant teenage[r] smoking crack" and the "Uzi-toting young male"—will become even more outcast: "If the result of implementing these policies is to concentrate the bad apples into a few hyperviolent, antisocial neighborhoods, so be it." Presumably it will be cheaper to police these pariah communities—where *everyone*, by definition, is a member of the dangerous class—than to apprehend and incarcerate hundreds of thousands of individuals. "Drug-free zones" for the majority, as a logical corollary, demand social-refuse dumps for the criminalized minority. Resurrected Jim Crow legislation, euphemistically advertised as "local self-determination," will insulate the urban middle classes (now including the Cosby family as well) from the New Jack City at their doorstep.

In this quest for spatial discrimination, the aims of contemporary architecture and the police converge most strikingly around the problem of crowd control. Cothinkers of Murray doubtless find the heterogeneous crowd a subversive anathema to their idyll of "like-mindedness." As we have seen, the designers of malls and pseudopublic space attack the crowd by homogenizing it. They set up architectural and semiotic barriers that filter out the "undesirables." They enclose the mass that remains, directing its circulation with behaviorist ferocity. The crowd is lured by visual stimuli of all kinds, dulled by Muzak, sometimes even scented by invisible aromatizers. This Skinnerian orchestration, if well conducted, produces a veritable commercial symphony of swarming, consuming nomads moving from one cash-point to another.

Outside in the streets, the task is more difficult. The LAPD continues to re-strict the rights of public assembly and freedom of movement, especially of the young, through its mass sweeps and "Operation Hammer," selective juvenile curfews, and regular blockades of popular "cruising" boulevards. Even gilded white youth suffer from the strict police regulation of personal mobility. In the former world capital of adolescence, where millions overseas still imagine Gid-get at a late-night beach party, the beaches are now closed at dusk, patrolled by helicopter gunships and police dune buggies.

A watershed in the local assault on the crowd was the rise and fall of the "Los Angeles Street Scene." Launched in 1978, the two-day annual festival at the Civic Center was intended to publicize Downtown's revitalization as well as to provide Mayor Bradley's version of the traditional Democratic barbecue. The LAPD remained skeptical. Finally in 1986, after the failure of the Ramones to appear as promised, a youthful audience began to tear up one of the stages. They were immediately charged by a phalanx of 150 police, including mounted units. In the two-hour melee that followed, angry punks bombarded the police cavalry with rocks and bottles; fifteen officers and horses were injured. The producer of the Street Scene, a Bradley official, suggested that "more middle-of-the-road entertainment" might attract less "boisterous crowds." The presti-gious *Downtown News* counterattacked: "The Street Scene gives Downtown a bad name. It flies in the face of all that has been done here in the last thirty years." The paper demanded "reparations for the wounded 'reputation of Downtown.' " The Mayor canceled the Scene.[26]

The demise of the Scene suggested the consolidation of an official consen-sus about crowds and the use of space in Los Angeles. Once the restructuring of Downtown eliminated the social mixing of groups in normal pedestrian circu-lation, the Street Scene (ironically named) remained one of the few occasions or places (along with redevelopment-threatened Hollywood Boulevard and the Venice boardwalks) where Chinatown punks, Glendale skinheads, Boyle Height lowriders, Valley Girls, Marina designer couples, Slauson rappers, Skid Row homeless, and gawkers from Des Moines could still mingle together in rel-ative amity. Moreover, in the years since the Battle of the Ramones, relentless police intimidation has ignited one youthful crowd after another into pande-monium, producing major riots in Hollywood on Halloween night in 1988, and in Westwood Village in March 1991 (during the premiere of *New Jack City*). Each incident, in turn, furnishes new pretexts for regulating crowds and "preventing the invasion of outsiders" (as one Westwood merchant explained in a TV inter-view). Inexorably, Los Angeles moves to extinguish [its] last public spaces, with all of their democratic intoxications, risks, and undeodorized odors.

# NOTES

1. National Committee on the Causes and Prevention of Violence. *To Establish Justice, to En-sure Domestic Tranquility* (Final Report. Washington D.C.: USGPO, 1969).

2. Quoted in John F. Kasson, *Amusing the Millions* (New York: Hill and Wang, 1978), p. 15.

3. *Los Angeles Times*, Nov. 4, 1978.

4. Ibid., Dec. 24, 1972.
5. N. David Milder, "Crime and Downtown Revitalization," *Urban Land*, Sept. 1987, p. 18.
6. Tom Chorneau, "Quandary over a Park Restroom," *Downtown News*, August 25, 1986.
7. See "Cold Snap's Toll at 5 as its Iciest Night Arrives," *Los Angeles Times*, Dec. 29, 1988.
8. Ibid., June 17, 1990.
9. "The old socialist" quote is from Michael Rotundi of Morphosis. Gehry himself boasts: "I get my inspiration from the streets. I'm more of a street fighter than a Roman scholar." (Quoted in Adele Freedman, *Progressive Architecture*, Oct. 1986, p. 99.)
10. The best catalogue of Gehry's work is Peter Arnell and Ted Bickford, eds., *Frank Gehry: Buildings and Projects* (New York: 1985).
11. Milfred Friedman, ed., *The Architecture of Frank Gehry* (New York: 1986), p. 175.
12. Pilar Viladas, "Illuminated Manuscripts," *Progressive Architecture*, Oct. 1986, pp. 76, 84.
13. See David Ferrell's articles in the *Los Angeles Times*, Aug. 31 and Oct. 16, 1987.
14. Ibid., Oct. 7, 1987.
15. Jane Bukwalter, "Securing Shopping Centers for Inner Cities," *Urban Land*, Apr. 1987, p. 24.
16. Ibid.
17. Richard Titus, "Security Works," *Urban Land*, Jan. 1990, p. 2.
18. Buckwalter, "Securing," p. 25.
19. *Los Angeles Daily News*, Nov. 1, 1987.
20. Interview, Fox News, Mar. 1990.
21. *Los Angeles Times*, July 25, 1989.
22. Jim Carlton, quoted in *Los Angeles Times*, Oct. 8, 1988.
23. Quoted in *Los Angeles Times*, Aug. 29, 1988.
24. Interviews with LAPD personnel; also Don Rosen, "Bleu Thunder," *Los Angeles Herald Examiner*, May 28, 1989.
25. Charles Murray, "How to Win the War on Drugs," *New Republic*, May 21, 1990, pp. 19–25.
26. *Los Angeles Times*, Sept. 22 and 25, 1986.

# 19

## *Margaret Kohn*

## THE MAULING OF PUBLIC SPACE

Bridgewater Township is a community of 40,000 located in New Jersey. Like earlier cities that were traditionally situated at the intersection of transportation routes, it owes its location to the confluence of Routes 287 and 78, two superhighways. Although Bridgewater was originally a bedroom community serving professionals who worked in New York, it gradually developed its own local economy with offices, businesses, and services. What it lacked was a sense of place. Local residents dreamed of a town center, some ideal composite of a New England village green and a Tuscan piazza, a place where old people could gossip, young people could *farsi vedere* (make themselves seen), mothers could bring young children while getting a latté, a sandwich, or some postage stamps. After over a decade of discussion, in 1988 they inaugurated Bridgewater Commons—a mall.[1]

The Bridgewater Commons Mall was not originally the initiative of commercial real estate developers. After years of research and debate, local government planners and community groups decided that a carefully designed shopping mall was the form of development best suited to maintaining the small town's quality of life and avoiding the strip mall aesthetic. Individual retailers could not provide the capital necessary to implement a comprehensive plan that included environmentally sensitive landscaping and rational traffic management. More importantly, a traditional downtown could not guarantee the most highly prized amenities: safety, cleanliness, and order.

The Bridgewater Commons and hundreds of supermalls like it have long troubled architects and critics who bemoan the homogeneity, sterility, and banality of the suburbs.[2] Approaching the mall primarily as an aesthetic or even a sociological issue, however, overlooks the enormous political consequences of the privatization of public space. Public sidewalks and streets are practically the only remaining available sites for unscripted political activity. They are the places where insurgent political candidates gather signatures, striking workers publicize their cause, and church groups pass out leaflets. It is true that television, newspapers, and direct mail constantly deliver a barrage of information, including political leaflets. But unlike the face-to-face politics that takes place in the public sphere, these forms for communication do not allow the citizen to talk back, to ask a question, to tell a story, to question a premise. The politics of the public sphere requires no resources—except time and perseverance. Public spaces are the last domains where the opportunity to communicate is not something bought and sold.

And they are rapidly disappearing. Such places are not banned by authoritarian legislatures. The public is not dispersed by the police. Their disappearance is more benign but no less troubling. The technology of the automobile, the expansion of the federal highway system, and the growth of residential suburbs has changed the way Americans live. Today the only place that many Americans encounter strangers is in the shopping mall. The most important public place is now private. And that is probably not an accident.

The privatization of public space poses a number of conceptual challenges for public policy makers. Does the ownership or use determine whether a particular place is truly private? How should the right to private property be weighed against the legitimate state interest in sustaining a public sphere? Does it violate the First Amendment right to free speech if a shopping mall prohibits orderly political speech? Are suburban malls meaningfully different from downtown developments?

The United States Supreme Court has tried to answer these questions in a series of decisions that have determined government policy defining the public sphere. The Supreme Court's doctrine in "the shopping mall cases" reflects a growing unwillingness to engage the broader political issues emerging from rapid social change. By insisting that the First Amendment only limits what government agencies can do, the Court has effectively closed its eyes to the privatization of public space.

## The Shopping Mall Cases

The Supreme Court addressed the implications of private ownership of quasi-public spaces in a series of cases decided between 1946 and 1980. The Court first considered the issue in 1946 in *Marsh v. Alabama*, which dealt with a Jehovah's Witness who was arrested for distributing religious pamphlets in the business district of a company-owned town. The majority decided that the arrest violated the freedom of the press and freedom of religion guaranteed by the First Amendment and applied to the states under the Fourteenth Amendment. The opinion written by Justice Black emphasized that all citizens must have the same rights, regardless of whether they live in a traditional municipality or a company-owned town. He noted that a typical community of privately owned residences would not have had the power to pass a municipal ordinance forbidding the distribution of religious literature on street corners. Why then, should a corporation be allowed to do so?

The company, Gulf Shipbuilding Corporation, based its argument on the common law and constitutional right to private property. If an individual does not have to allow Jehovah's Witnesses into her home, why should the company have to allow them on its property? The court, however, rejected this logic. It cited a long list of precedents—cases involving bridges, roads, and ferries—to establish that the right to private property is not absolute. Especially when a private company performs public functions, it opens itself up to greater government scrutiny and regulation. Given that the town was freely accessible to outsiders, it implicitly invited in the general public, thereby voluntarily incurring quasi-public obligations. The concept of "invitee" went on to play an important role in desegregation cases. According to the Court, "The more an owner, for his advantage, opens up his property for use by the public in general, the more do his rights become circumscribed by the statutory and constitutional rights of those who use it."

The opinion concluded that property rights must be weighed against other state interests. Justice Black emphasized that a democracy had a compelling state interest in maintaining free and open channels of communication so that all of its residents could fulfill their duties as citizens: "To act as good citizens they must be informed. In order to enable them to be properly informed their information must be uncensored." A concurring opinion by Justice Frankfurter stated that fundamental civil liberties guaranteed by the Constitution must have precedence over property rights.

Based on the reasoning in *Marsh v. Alabama*, it would seem likely that the right to free speech would apply to other private arenas that are similarly open to a broad public. In a 1972 decision, *Lloyd Corp. v. Tanner*, the Court considered whether First Amendment guarantees extended to the shopping mall.[3] This time, however, the majority upheld the mall's policy forbidding the distribution of handbills on its premises. The owners could exclude expressive conduct, even when it did not disrupt the commercial functions of the mall. Writing for the majority, Justice Powell argued that a shopping mall was not the functional equivalent of a company town, because it was not a space where individuals performed multiple activities. It was simply devoted to shopping. Although it was true that the shopping mall implicitly invited the general public onto its premises, this did not transform it into a public space. According to Powell, political activists misunderstood the invitation if they turned the mall into a public forum; the invitation to the public was only to shop. Moreover, because the First Amendment only limited "state action" there was no constitutional basis to apply it to private entities.

In *Lloyd v. Tanner* the Court did not overrule *Marsh v. Alabama*; instead it emphasized how the two cases differed. The mall was no company town. Basically, the Court concluded that activists had other opportunities to engage in political activity. They could make use of the public roads and sidewalks on the perimeter of the shopping mall. The assumption was that citizens had other chances to be exposed to diverse ideas and viewpoints. Because they presumably spent at most part of their day at the shopping mall, they could become informed citizens elsewhere.

Although the Court tried to emphasize the differences of fact between the two cases, it actually modified its view of the relevant doctrine. In the *Lloyd* decision there was no idealistic discussion of the free exchange of ideas necessary to maintain an informed citizenry. Rather than considering the goal of the First Amendment—presumably to foster the free expression characteristic of a democracy—the Court focused narrowly on the supposed absence of state action. It decided that private property does not "lose its private character merely because the public is generally invited to use it for designated purposes."

It is puzzling that the justices in *Lloyd* did not really analyze the logic of *Marsh v. Alabama* on the critical issue of state action. In *Marsh*, Justice Black suggested that the enforcement of state criminal trespass laws constituted state action. If the state may make no law abridging freedom of speech, then it cannot pass a criminal trespass statue penalizing a citizen simply for engaging in nondisruptive expressive conduct in a place where he or she would be legitimately allowed to enter. This same logic was used in a much more famous case, *Shelley v. Kraemer*, which was decided by the same court in 1948. In that case, the Supreme Court struck down a restrictive covenant preventing residents from selling their homes to blacks. The contract was undeniably private, however, it could not be enforced without "the active intervention of the state courts, supported by the full panoply of state power." According to this decision, private actors could not use the police and the courts to enforce practices that violate constitutional rights. In *Lloyd v. Tanner* (1972) the Supreme Court decided to overlook these precedents, assuming a much narrower definition of what constitutes state action.

The last shopping mall case, *Pruneyard Shopping Center v. Robins* (1980) dealt with a group of high school students who attempted to gather signatures for a petition protesting a U.N. resolution condemning Zionism. The California State Supreme Court originally found in favor of the students, ruling that the state's criminal trespass law would constitute state action for the purposes of the First Amendment. The shopping mall owners appealed to the United States Supreme Court, claiming that their Fifth Amendment right not to be deprived of "private property, without due process of law" was violated by the California decision. They argued that the mall was no public forum. To require that the mall allow political solicitation was tantamount to "taking without just compensation." The owners also claimed that the right to exclude others is an essential component of the definition of private property.

The *Pruneyard* decision, which governs to this day, articulated a mediating position. The Supreme Court rejected the mall owner's claim to absolute dominion over its property. Drawing upon a long history of precedents regarding public regulation of private property, the court concluded that the due process clause only required that the laws "not be unreasonable, arbitrary, or capricious and that the means selected shall have a real and substantial relation to the objective sought." The right to exclude others would only be decisive if the mall owners could prove that allowing orderly political speech would substantially decrease the economic value of their property.[4]

The Court, however, also rejected the students' claims to protection under the free speech clause of the First Amendment. Because the facts of the case were substantially the same as those in *Lloyd v. Tanner*, the Court saw no reason to reconsider the issue. They still insisted that the mall was private and therefore beyond the reach of the Bill of Rights. But there was a second issue at stake. The students had challenged the shopping center's policy under both the U.S. and the California State Constitution. The language of the California free speech clause was more expansive. Article 1, § 2, of the California Constitution provides:

> Every person may freely speak, write and publish his or her sentiments on all subjects, being responsible for the abuse of this right. A law may not restrain or abridge liberty of speech or press.

The U.S. Supreme Court found that there was no reason why a state or federal statute could not guarantee access to the public areas of private malls. In other words, the Court did not find any constitutional prohibition against legislation protecting political speech in places where citizens were normally allowed to be. This finding was consistent with an earlier decision, *Hudgens v. NLRB* (1976), which held that striking workers had no First Amendment right to picket in a mall, but they could assert such a right under federal labor laws protecting the processes associated with collective bargaining.[5] Since the decision fourteen states have considered whether their own state constitutions protect expressive conduct in shopping malls. Only five—California, Oregon, New Jersey, Colorado, and Massachusetts—recognized broader protections for speech.[6]

## Privatization and Public Policy

Over twenty years have passed since the Supreme Court's decision. Although the law has not changed in that period, society has. There is something quaint and anachronistic about reading the old shopping mall cases. They describe the world we take for granted as something new and marvelous and they could not even imagine the world in which we would soon live. Writing in 1972, Justice Powell described the Lloyd Center in Portland, Oregon like this:

> The Center embodies a relatively new concept in shopping center design. The stores are all located within a single large, multilevel building complex sometimes referred to as the "Mall." Within this complex, in addition to the stores, there are parking facilities, malls, private sidewalks, stairways, escalators, gardens, an auditorium, and a skating rink. Some of the stores open directly on the outside public sidewalks, but most open on the interior privately owned malls. Some stores open on both. There are no public streets or public sidewalks within the building complex, which is enclosed and entirely covered except for the landscaped portions of some of the interior malls.[7]

This futuristic mall had 60 shops and 1000 parking spaces. Compared to today's supermalls, the Lloyd Center is a neighborhood corner store. By 1990 there were over 300 mega-supermalls with at least five department stores and three hundred shops. The West Edmonton Mall has over 800 shops, 11 department stores, 110 restaurants, 20 movie theaters, 13 night clubs, a chapel, a large hotel, and a lake.[8] In the United States there are twenty-three square feet of shopping mall space for every person.[9]

In 1972, the Court concluded that this new concept in shopping, "sometimes referred to as the 'Mall'," in no way resembled a company town. It seemed obvious that a mall was simply devoted to a single activity, shopping, whereas a town was defined by the physical proximity of diverse spaces and activities, housing and services, leisure and work, consumption, education, and production. A mall is a place you visit; a town is a place you live. But this has been slowly changing.[10] Industry watchers report that the average visit to a "leisure time destination" (a mall with sophisticated design elements, restaurants, and movie theaters) lasted four hours as compared to just one hour at a conventional mall.[11]

The mall has become an entertainment mecca, a major employer, and a premier vacation destination. The Travel Industry Association of America (TIA) reported that shopping is the number one vacation activity in America. The Mall of America in Bloomington, Minnesota attracts 42.5 million visitors annually.[12] Its hundreds of retail establishments are not the only attraction: it has a wedding chapel, the nation's largest indoor amusement park, a post office, a police station, and a school.

The mall is also a workplace. The West Edmonton Mall has over 15,000 employees. Although they do not manufacture automobiles or aircraft carriers, they do produce the spiral of fantasy, desire, and consumption that is the basis of the North American service economy.

The mall is becoming not only a genuine multi-use facility, but a completely self-contained homotopia of suburban life. In the morning the doors open to waiting seniors, the famous mall-walkers who appreciate the controlled climate, cleanliness, and safety. At night the security guards have to herd out the lingering teenagers, who are in no rush to go home to their monotonous housing developments.[13] The mall is clearly the nodal point of social life, but is it the equivalent of a downtown business district?

Not exactly. The shopping mall is so attractive because it combines the pleasures of public life with the safety and familiarity of the private realm. Ironically, the suburban megamall was intended to be an oasis of urbanity and civilization. Victor Gruen, the Viennese architech who designed the prototype of the modern mall, was motivated by a progressive vision. He wanted to recreate a vibrant, pedestrian-oriented; multi-use area that captured the excitement of urban space. An immigrant from Vienna, he was inspired by the glass-enclosed atriums of Europe, particularly the gallerias of Milan and arcades of Paris. In 1956 he built Southdale in Edina, Minnesota, the first multi-level, enclosed; climate-controlled mall. He thought that the mall could serve as a community center and nodal point for civic identity in the suburbs.[14] He realized that many people long for the vitality, diversity, beauty, and stimulation of public space. Gruen astutely predicted that when public space is not available, people would flock to private simulacra. But the private provision of public places is a Faustian bargain. Once developers possess the power of property rights, they usually exercise them to create the highly orchestrated and controlled environments that eviscerate the diversity that animates public space.

Following in Gruen's footsteps, contemporary mall designers have used their formidable skills to simulate the old-fashioned downtown of our imaginations. Faux antiquarian signs suggest that shopping corridors are actually city streets and the central atrium is the town square.[15] Some malls, such as Faneuil Hall Marketplace in Boston, incorporate restored historical buildings in order to create the atmosphere of reassuring urbanity that many Americans identify with the past. Other malls play freely with period and place in order to incorporate images widely associated with a sophisticated and alluring public life. The Borgota, a mall in Scottsdale, Arizona, for example, was built to resemble a walled village in thirteenth-century Italy. Replete with an imitation church bell tower, bricks imported from Rome, and signs in Italian, it appeals to affluent consumers' fantasies about public space.[16] These design elements reflect the developers' claim that the mall is a "city within a city" (The Mall of America) or "an urban village" (Universal City Walk).[17]

When animal rights protesters went to court to gain access to the "public" areas of the Mall of America, they tried to make use of the mall's semiotic system for their own ends. They claimed that the mall presented itself as a multi-use downtown business district and therefore should be governed by the principles set out in *Marsh v. Alabama*. Faced with petitioners trying to engage in protest activity, the Mall of America, however, quickly retreated from the semiotics of "Main Street USA" and embraced a more conventional defense of private property.

In some cases, the claim that malls are contemporary community centers is based on more than imagineering.[18] Increasingly the mall is a civic center as well as a shopping destination. The local and county government in Knoxville, Tennessee, for example, has located essential government services in a shopping mall on the periphery of town, the Knoxville Center. In an effort to "take the services to the people," the city encourages Knoxville citizens to visit "City Hall at the Mall," where they can pay their property taxes, renew their drivers' licenses, mail letters, and apply for marriage licenses. There is also a police station and a community room.[19] The consequence of this convenience is that the shopping center effectively serves as a moat of private space that insulates public functionaries from protest activity. The leasing arrangement opens up a potentially Kafkaesque scenario in which the aggrieved citizens try vainly to gain access to the city hall only to be turned away at the gates of the mall by unaccountable private security forces. Lest this scenario seem fantastic, imagine a group of antiwar activists who want to deliver a petition to the city government, but they are turned away at the entrance to the mall because they are wearing T-shirts that say "Give Peace a Chance."

The "City Hall at the Mall" may be an extreme example, but it is emblematic of a trend toward multi-use malls. An April 1999 survey by the journal *Shopping Center World* found that half of the 150 new projects under construction are multi-use malls. Some of these are the New Urbanist-inspired developments that try to mimic the appeal of old-fashioned downtowns. . . . They link higher density housing with office and retail space, all unified by architectural cues evoking the turn of the century. Fifty of the new multi-use malls include office space, libraries, housing, or hotels.

One such project is the new Towers at Zona Rosa, a shopping mall situated ten minutes from downtown Kansas City. Although the plan relies on 30,000 foot department stores to anchor the retail plaza, it also includes loft-style apartments situated above boutiques and cafés. Underground parking, decorative street lamps, indigenous plants, and outdoor tables are among the lifestyle-enhancing amenities. As theme parks, megamalls, and gated communities merge, nostalgic recreations of the village green replace actual public space.[20]

Living at the mall might still seem unusual, but it is a culmination of a dynamic that has been accelerating throughout the 1990s—the emergence of what Joel Garreau has called Edge Cities. The growth of Edge Cities reflects a complete transformation of the spatial structure of postwar American life. The typical pattern of bedroom communities situated along the outskirts of urban cores is disappearing. He reports that Americans no longer sleep in the suburbs and work in the city. In dozens of cities including Houston, Boston, Tampa, and Denver, there is more office space outside the central business district than within it. This new office space is built in Edge Cities, suburbs that now incorporate millions of square feet of commercial development.[21]

There are undoubtedly positive sides of this development. As more companies relocate to the suburbs, the average American's commute time decreases. But as workplaces become more and more decentralized, the density needed to support public transportation such as commuter railroads also disappears. Your suburban office park may be closer to your home, but it is probably not served by the subway, which leads to greater automobile dependence, traffic congestion, pollution, and the blight of endless parking lots. It becomes increasingly commonplace to move from home to office to shopping mall in the automobile. The Edge City citizen need never traverse public space. It becomes possible to spend an entire day or lifetime without encountering street corners, bus stops, or park benches.

The new Edge City geography poses a challenge to the doctrine established by the Supreme Court. If private space takes on a public character in cases like the company town when it colonizes every aspect of life, then it is time to reconsider the character of the mall. But this is unlikely to happen. As recently as 1992, the Supreme Court held that labor organizers had no right to try to contact potential members by passing out leaflets in the parking lot of a Lechmere's store, this despite the fact that the only alternative space was a 46 foot wide grassy strip separating the lot from the highway.[22] In 1999 the Minnesota State Supreme Court heard a challenge from an animal rights group that was prevented from peacefully protesting in the common area of the 4.2 million square foot Mall of America. The protesters argued that the mall was a public space because it had been heavily subsidized by the state, which provided $186 million in public financing.[23] The Justices found that "neither the invitation to the public to shop and be entertained . . . nor the public financing used to develop the property are state action for the purposes of free speech" under the Minnesota Constitution.[24]

## Politics and the Public Space

This string of defeats is a setback for political activists and proponents of an active public life. But it could have the unintended consequence of channeling debate over privatization into the political arena and out of the closed chambers of the court. If judicial intervention will not protect the public sphere, then political action still presents an alternative. Congress or state legislatures could pass statutes mandating that malls of a certain size must provide access to community groups. They could also establish guidelines to extend broader protections for political activity. One way to do this would be to pass legislation applying speech and petition guarantees to the functional equivalents of traditional public forums. As indicated in the *Pruneyard* decision, there is no constitutional provision that would invalidate these kinds of laws. Because labor unions are dependent on tactics such as the picket line, they would be powerful proponents of such a law and useful allies for other activist groups fighting to maintain access to public space. As the Seattle-inspired euphoria wanes, the struggle for such legislation could unify labor and other social movements.

Even in areas where such tactics were unsuccessful at the state level, it would still be possible to adopt similar strategies at the local level. The obvious place to start is to support downtown business districts and other public places that still encourage diversity and invite political activity. But this individualist solution, by itself, is naïve. Collective action is also necessary. When new large-scale mall developments are proposed, citizens have the most leverage to demand some form of continued public access. The support of local government agencies, town councils, and planning boards is crucial for a project on the scale of the modern mall. By building and upgrading roads, modifying zoning, and approving permits, localities still have bargaining power over some aspects of development. They could negotiate a policy guaranteeing free access to a community booth or public courtyard in the mall.[25] For example, in 1991 the Hahn Company, which owns thirty malls in California, signed an agreement with the American Civil Liberties Union that allows leafletting and petitioning in most of its malls. In New York, Democratic state legislators have introduced a bill mandating that privately owned complexes with at least 20 stores and 250,000 square feet of commercial space designate an area where citizens can congregate to engage in non-disruptive political activity.[26] In 1988 a similar bill was defeated in the state legislature.[27]

Why are these tactics seldom even employed let alone successful? Although malls like the one in Bridgewater manage to preserve natural oases such as "Mac's Brook," they fail to protect oases of publicness in a privatizing world. And this is not only the fault of greedy developers. Most people do not value the disruption and unease caused by other people's political speech. One of the appeals of the mall is precisely that it provides an environment carefully designed to exclude any source of discomfort. As Benjamin Barber put it, shopping malls and theme parks sell a sanitized substitute for public life "where people can experience the thrill of the different without taking any risks."[28] The soothing lighting, polished surfaces, pleasant temperature, and enticing displays are not the only allure; part of the fantasy involves entering a world where no homeless person, panhandler, or zealot can disturb the illusion of a harmonious world. We appreciate free speech in the abstract but often avoid it in reality.

In this mauling of public space, democratic theorists have confronted extremely sophisticated marketing experts, and the democratic theorists have been the losers. The political theorists who are most concerned with democracy have failed to offer a compelling rationale to challenge the privatization of public space. By concentrating on the value of speech rather than the importance of space, they turn the public sphere into an abstraction. We need to engage in more careful reflection on the reasons why we should protect free speech *and* public space.

In academic circles, theorists argue that deliberation between citizens is the most promising way to reach rational political decisions. Moreover, they stress that rational, public-spirited discussions are necessary to legitimate democratic procedures and make sure that politics does not degenerate into mere struggles over power. These theories of deliberative democracy are indebted to Jürgen Habermas's influential work on the ideal speech situation. The basic idea of the ideal speech situation is something like this: when we engage in conversation we assume that other participants are telling the truth, speaking sincerely, and oriented toward mutual understanding. When these conditions are realized, then a rational consensus can emerge.[29]

I believe that one reason for the popularity of deliberative democracy is that it is based on a certain optimism about the efficacy of ideas. Although our convictions may also be resistant to change, they are much more malleable than the built environment. Confronted with a landscape filled with strip malls, decaying supermalls, forbidding seas of concrete parking lots, and urban high-rises isolated in unkempt wastelands, it is tempting to focus on democratic theories rather than the more intractable problem of democratic practices.

At first it seems as if this emphasis on "deliberative democracy" is precisely what is needed to reinvigorate our commitment to the public sphere, whether it is comprised of street corners with soap boxes and speakers or their modern equivalents. Deliberative democracy reinforces traditional justifications of the speech clause of the First Amendment. But the concept of deliberation will not be useful if it emphasizes the rationality that emerges from the ideal speech situation. Let's face it. Nothing approaching the ideal speech situation ever happens in the mall. The ideal speech situation is basically an extremely idealized depiction of the norms of scholarly journals or conferences. We need free speech and public places not because they help us, as a society, reach a rational consensus but because they disrupt the consensus that we have already reached too easily. Reasonable arguments often just reinforce distance, whereas public space establishes proximity. This proximity has distinctive properties that democratic theorists often overlook. We can learn something from facing our fears and evasions that we cannot learn from debating principles. The panhandler and the homeless person—they do not convince us by their arguments. Rather, their *presence* conveys a powerful message. They reveal the rough edges of our shiny surfaces. The union picketer and right-to-lifer confront us with meaningful and enduring conflict. Provocative speech cannot be something that happens elsewhere—in academic journals, conferences, mass mailings, and highly scripted town meetings. It must sometimes be literally in your face for it to have any impact. For a robust democracy we need more than rational deliberation. We need public places that remind us that politics matter.

In New Jersey, at least, malls will be part of this public. That is the implication of a decision reached by the New Jersey State Supreme Court on June 13, 2000. In a unanimous vote, the Court held that Mill Creek, another New Jersey mall, could not restrict free speech by forbidding political groups from leafletting. Although the owners could place reasonable restrictions on expressive conduct to make sure that politics did not disrupt the commercial activities of the mall, they could not deny access to the only place left in New Jersey where there is an opportunity for face-to-face contact with large groups of people. By a circuitous route, the dream of Bridgewater comes true and the residents will get a commons.[30]

# The Mall Goes Downtown: Business Improvement Districts

. . . Business Improvement Districts (BIDs) have been at the forefront of the attempt to apply the logic of the shopping mall to downtown centers. There are over 1000 BIDs in the United States and more than forty in New York City alone.[31] BIDs are geographically contiguous areas that vote to assess property owners a special fee in order to provide additional services. These services include sanitation, security, and landscaping. Some BIDs employ uniformed personnel to provide tourists with directions and discourage criminal activity.

Others install benches, enforce uniform exterior décor standards, and distribute maps featuring local businesses. They have been widely credited in the press for improving the quality of life in downtown commercial districts.

BIDs have been popular with both city officials and business owners. For government officials, they provide additional tax revenue to fund needed services in the most visible areas of the city. Business interests support BIDs because the structure allows them greater control over their own tax payments. Revenue collected through the BID is spent exclusively in the district and reflects the priorities of business owners. Because assessments are mandatory, setting up a BID overcomes the free-rider problem that plagues voluntary associations such as the Chamber of Commerce. At the same time, business interests maintain complete fiscal control, thereby avoiding the interference of government bureaucrats, local residents, and other citizens. With budgets in the tens of millions of dollars, these publicly regulated, private governments are reshaping the political landscape of downtown.

The proliferation of Business Improvement Districts (a phenomenon that goes by many names including special assessment district or business improvement zone) is a response to competition from the suburban shopping mall. The BID is, in effect, a centralized management structure that allows dispersed downtown retailers to imitate and incorporate successful elements of the mall. For a shopping mall it is fairly easy to provide common spaces, maintain cleanliness, and orchestrate a high degree of visual and spatial coherence. Because the entire mall is owned by a single developer who leases space to individual stores, centralized control is guaranteed through property rights, rules, and detailed lease restrictions.[32] In most downtown business districts, streets and plazas are public; small businesses coexist alongside large chains in buildings that they may either rent or own. The BID, unlike the mall, has to rely on governmental powers such as eminent domain, taxation, fines, and zoning in order to mimic the effects of centralized control. The enabling legislation in Arkansas gives some idea of just how wide-ranging the power of business improvement districts can be. They are allowed:

(1) To acquire, construct, install, operate, maintain, and contract regarding pedestrian or shopping malls, plazas, sidewalks or moving sidewalks, parks, parking lots, parking garages, offices, urban residential facilities including, without limitation, apartments, condominiums, hotels, motels, convention halls, rooms, and related facilities, and buildings and structures to contain any of these facilities, bus stop shelters, decorative lighting, benches or other seating furniture, sculptures, telephone booths, traffic signs, fire hydrants, kiosks, trash receptacles, marquees, awnings or canopies, walls and barriers, paintings or murals, alleys, shelters, display cases, fountains, child-care facilities, restrooms, information booths, aquariums or aviaries, tunnels and ramps, pedestrian and vehicular overpasses and underpasses; (2) To landscape and plant trees, bushes and shrubbery, grass, flowers, and each and every other kind of decorative planting; (3) To install and operate, or to lease, public music and news facilities; (4) To construct and operate childcare facilities; (5) To construct lakes, dams, and waterways of whatever size; (6) To employ and provide special police facilities and personnel for the protection and enjoyment of the property owners and the general public using the facilities of the district; (7)

To prohibit or restrict vehicular traffic on the streets within the district as the governing body may deem necessary and to provide the means for access by emergency vehicles to or in these areas; (8) To remove, by agreement or by the power of eminent domain, any existing structures or signs of any description in the district not conforming to the plan of improvement; and (9) To do everything necessary or desirable to effectuate the plan of improvement for the district.[33]

In other words, BIDs can exercise far-reaching governmental powers against individual property owners in order to transform an existing neighborhood into a "managed environment" with quaint matching signs and manicured plazas. In some cases they can even eliminate seedy businesses that might scare off the target consumer demographic. All this is done with minimal input from neighborhood residents, citizen groups, or even commercial tenants.[34]

Business Improvement Districts have imitated the environment of the suburban shopping mall as well as its management structure. The shopping mall, like the theme park, tries to create an atmosphere "in which the emphasis on safety and tidiness is supposed to make visitors feel secure and happy so they'll spend money and come back."[35] To this end, BIDs devote, on average, twenty percent of their budget to sanitation and twenty-five percent to security.[36]

These downtown shopping districts try to achieve a mix of urban and suburban values. Their appeal is due to the energy, variety, visual stimulation, architectural distinctiveness, and cultural opportunities distinctive of urban centers.[37] At the same time they mimic the safety, cleanliness, order, and familiarity that has proven such an effective formula in suburban malls. This allows consumers to enjoy the traditionally urban pleasures of proximity to diverse strangers in a setting where any risk of threat, disruption, disorientation, or discomfort has been removed.[38] This is a formula that was perfected in "festival market-places" such as Faneuil Hall in Boston, Riverwalk in New Orleans, the Cannery in San Francisco, and South Street Seaport in New York. Each project transformed a historic district into a zone of leisure and consumption, filled with restaurants, chain boutiques, and kiosks specializing in local color. Wildly successful from a commercial point of view, these projects have been criticized for transforming distinctive, mixed-use districts into formulaic, sanitized tourist traps.[39] Festival market-places sell a simulacra of the city as tableau or spectacle, something to be enjoyed visually but not experienced kinesthetically: the city without its smells, sensations, or dangers. They cleverly integrate design cues that evoke nostalgia for an imagined urban past with the safety, cleanliness, and familiarity of the suburban mall.

# Social and Political Consequences of Business Improvement Districts

Whereas most commentators have focused on an aesthetic critique of festival marketplaces and the Disneyfication of downtown, they overlook the political and social consequences of this transformation, particularly the impact of Business Improvement Districts on democratic governance. BIDs pose several challenges to a democratic polity. First, political influence in a Business Improvement District is usually directly proportional to the value of one's property, thereby violating the basic democratic principle of one-person, one-vote. Second, BIDs increase the impact of the already powerful business community on local government. Finally, BIDs, as private, nonprofit organizations, may be able to circumvent the constitutional provisions that require local governments to protect the civil liberties of their citizens.

In San Francisco, like most municipalities, the creation of a BID and its priorities depend on the support of the majority of property owners in the district. But all property owners do not have equal votes. Votes are apportioned in relation to the value of commercial property, therefore a very small cadre could effectively control the decisions of the BID. Although oligarchical control is acceptable, a monarchy is ruled out, at least in San Francisco, where the weighted vote of one individual cannot surpass forty percent.[40]

There have been several court cases challenging the anti-democratic decision-making structure of Business Improvement Districts. The most notable decision involves New York's Grand Central BID, which encompasses 71 million square feet of commercial space (nineteen percent of Manhattan's total office space) and has a budget of over $10 million. Robert Kessler, a shareholder in a co-op apartment building in the district, argued that the governance structure, which guaranteed thirty-one seats to property owners, seventeen seats to tenants, and four seats to government appointees, violated the constitutional principle of one-person, one-vote. In 1997 the United States District Court found in favor of the BID and the decision was upheld a year later by the Second Circuit Court of Appeals.

From a legal perspective, the issue was how to interpret the precedent established in *Avery v. Midland County*, the case in which the Supreme Court applied the doctrine of one-person, one-vote to local government. Although the Court clearly stated that cities and counties must guarantee personhood suffrage, it left open the question as to whether this doctrine applied to the myriad diverse and overlapping sub- and supra-local institutions. The Supreme Court noted that "a special-purpose unit of government assigned the performance of functions affecting definable groups of constituents more than other constituents" might be exempt from the principle of one-person, one-vote.[41] In subsequent litigation, the court recognized at least one such exception. It held that the governing board of a local watershed management district designed to provide irrigation could be elected exclusively by agricultural interests.[42] In *Kesslar*, United States Circuit Court Judge Kearse concluded that the Grand Central Business Improvement District (BID) was similar to the water management district: it existed for the purpose of promoting business. Due to its limited scope and disproprotionate impact on property owners, one-person, one-vote did not apply.[43]

Although it is certainly true that Business Improvement Districts exist in order to promote business interests, they still have a significant impact on local residents. The range of services provided by well-funded BIDs—security, sanitation, social services, and capital improvements—is similar to that of local government. Furthermore, the Grand Central BID's foray into social sevices illustrates some of the dangers that rise when a business lobby takes on quasi-governmental power. The controversy involved a program designed by the Grand Central Partnership (a Business Improvement District) to tackle the problem of homelessness by providing shelter and job training. There were two accusations levied against the program, which resulted in litigation.[44] Over forty participants in the job-training program claimed that the Partnership violated state and federal minimum wage laws. Under the auspices of "job training," homeless people were paid $1.16 per hour to serve as outreach workers.[45] The second accusation dealt with the nature of the work that fell under the category of "out-reach." Four former outreach workers claimed that they were told by supervisors to use all means necessary in order to remove homeless people from the district. They admitted to beating homeless people and destroying their belongings. These statements corroborated the stories of homeless people who claimed they had been beaten and threatened by Partnership employees.[46] After an investigation, the Department of Housing and Urban Development (HUD) requested that the BID return the unused portion of a $547,000 grant that had been awarded to subsidize its work with the homeless. Andrew Cuomo, assistant secretary of HUD, explained, "We are not in the business of subsidizing thuggery."[47]

The example of the HUD grant also illustrates another under-appreciated political consequence of the proliferation of BIDs. Although BIDs are widely lauded for raising additional tax revenue from businesses, they also are more effective at competing for scarce resources from city coffers. This is another lesson that BIDs have learned from shopping mall developers, who have been very successful at getting a variety of government subsidies in order to lure commercial development to a particular locality. In the suburbs, these subsidies usually include tax abatements and public funds for site development and roads. BIDs have made downtown more effective at lobbying for the enactment and enforcement of pro-business laws and gaining resources such as extra police protection or direct subsidies.[48] To take one example, the Wall Street BID offered to offset some of the costs (towards space and equipment) if New York City located a police substation in the district. Even though it was not an under-served area, the police department complied.[49] Decisions such as that one further exacerbate inequalities between neighborhoods in the distribution of essential services. Not only do Business Improvement Districts benefit from their ability to pay for higher levels of service, they may also receive a greater proportion of city resources, as cost-sharing rather than need becomes a criterion for distributing scarce resources. Although it is true that a voluntary Chamber of Commerce, large corporation, or interest group will also be effective at influencing local government, the BID formalizes this influence by creating a strong institutional mechanism.

BIDs aspire to imitate the controlled environment and unified management of the shopping mall but public ownership of the streets and common spaces imposes a serious limitation on their ability to do so. Unlike mall owners, local police officers are limited in their ability to eject homeless people, preachers, street performers, and leafletters from common spaces downtown.

But what happens if private security forces do so? Take, for example, the homeless people who were intimidated and forced to leave the Grand Central District. Had the police tried to evict them, they could have complained to the city review board in charge of police misconduct. The homeless victims also could have brought a complaint under a federal statute that provides redress to any citizen deprived of any right secured by the Constitution and laws. But because this statute only applies to rights violations undertaken by a person "acting under color of law,"[50] neither of these remedies is available to someone intimidated or threatened by a private security force.[51]

This raises the possibility that local governments may rely on private proxies to employ tactics that are forbidden to government actors. Although the Bill of Rights prevents the government from limiting individuals' right to free speech, movement, and assembly, it is unclear what would happen if a private government such as a BID tried to do so. Imagine a scenario in which a Business Improvement District adopted a code of conduct that banned skateboarding, lying on benches, loitering, and leafletting. A BID could claim that it was not a state actor, and therefore the Constitution did not apply. If this failed, the city could lease or give the streets, sidewalks, and plazas to the BID, which had already assumed the cost of policing and maintaining them. Armed with this designation as private property, the BID would be a step closer to its goal of transforming downtown into a specialty mall.

# Conclusion

The malling of America is not limited to the suburbs. The shopping mall is an icon of fantasy, leisure, and consumption at the same time as it is a symbol of homogeneity, sterility, market stratification, and social control. If Rem Koolhaas is right and shopping provides the only public space that still exists, then the difference between the city street and the suburban mall may be diminishing. . . .[52]

The growing influence of Business Improvement Districts is problematic for two reasons. The governance structure of most BIDs violates norms of democratic accountability by giving a disproportionate voice to property owners over other community interests and possibly by circumventing statues and principles ensuring the protection of civil liberties. BIDs also exacerbate existing inequalities in the provision of government services in order to create marketable "Brand Zones" within the city. It is not surprising that the wealthy and powerful would prefer to govern themselves without interference from everyone else. What is surprising is that a democracy is willing to let them.

# ENDNOTES

1. The story of Bridgewater is recounted in Joel Garreau's *Edge City: Life on the New Frontier* (New York: Doubleday, 1991), 42–45.
2. John Hannigan, "The Saturday Essay: Who Wants to Spend Their Life in a Theme Park?" *The Independent*, Nov. 28, 1998, T1.

3. In an earlier case, *Food Employees v. Logan Valley Plaza* 391 U.S. 308 (1968) the court ruled that a labor union could picket a supermarket located in a shopping mall, despite the objections of the mall manager. For a full discussion of the shopping mall cases, see Brady C. Williamson and James A. Friedman, "State Constitutions: The Shopping Mall Cases," *University of Wisconsin Law Review* (1998), 883–903; Curtis J. Berger, "Pruneyard Revisited: Political Activity on Private Lands," *N.Y.U. Law Review* 66 (1991), 663–691.

4. For a critical view of this argument, see Richard Epstein, "Takings, Exclusivity and Speech: The Legacy of *Pruneyard v. Robins*," *The University of Chicago Law Review* 64 (Winter 1997), 21–56.

5. *Hudgens v. NLRB* 424 U.S. 507 (1976) was an important decision because it overturned *Food Employees v. Logan Valley Plaza* 391 U.S. 308 (1968), the first shopping mall case. The decision held that striking workers did have a First Amendment right to protest unfair labor practices in front of their employer's store, even though it was located in a mall. In weighing the issues, the court concluded that the employees had no alternative place to protest, inasmuch as their message was directly linked to the commercial activity of a store located in the mall. In contrast, *Hudgens* stated that "property does not lose its private character merely because the public is generally invited to use it for designated purposes."

6. Mark Alexander, "Attenation, Shoppers: The First Amendment in the Modern Shopping Mall," *Arizona Law Review* 41 (Spring 1999), 1–47. Alexander notes that many of the nine states which have rejected petitioners' free speech claims rely on the Supreme Court doctrine of "state action" even though their own constitutional provisions provide a broader guarantee similar to the language in the California constitution.

7. *Lloyd Corp. v. Tanner* 407 U.S. 551 (1972).

8. Margaret Crawford, "The World in a Shopping Mall," in *Variations on a Theme Park: The New American City and End of Public Space*, ed. Michael Sorkin (New York: Hill and Wang, 1992), 3.

9. Eds. Chuihua Judy Chung, Jeffrey Inaba, Rem Koolhaas, and Sze Tsung Leong, *Harvard Design School Guide to Shopping* (Cologne: Taschen, 2001).

10. For a detailed account of the transformation of the shopping mall, see William Severini Kowinski, *The Malling of America: An Inside Look at the Great Consumer Paradise* (New York: Morrow,1985).

11. Jim Walker, "Visionary's Quest: Columbus-Based Developer Yaromir Steiner Determined to Build Better Shopping Center," *The Columbus Dispatch*, June 9, 2002, 1E.

12. Melissa Levy, "On the Road Again," *Minneapolis Star Tribune*, July 16, 2001, 1D.

13. Kowinski, *The Malling of America*, 26–52.

14. See Victor Gruen and Larry Smith, *Shopping Towns USA: The Planning of Shopping Centers* (New York: Reinhold, 1960). See also Witold Rybczynski, *City Life* (New York: Touchstone, 1995), 206–207.

15. Some of the Mall of America's promotional literature reads: "[The] Mall of America will be a city within a city, unlike other malls. . . . It will be divided into four distinctive city streets providing four unique shopping and visual environments." Brief of Amicus Curiae from the Minnesota Civil Liberties Union, presented in the case *State v. Wicklund*.

16. Kowinski, *The Malling of America*, 233.

17. "Universal City Walk: An Architect's Dream: A Conversation with Jon Jerde," Universal City Press Release, 1993. Cited in Adia Hozic, *Hollyworld: Space, Power and Fantasy in the American Economy* (Ithaca, NY: Cornell University Press, 2001), 6.

18. The term " imagineering" suggest " engineering and image" à la Disney. The term comes from Keally McBride, *Social Imagineering,* unpublished manuscript, 2002.

19. Jennifer Niles Coffin, "The United Mall of America: Free Speech, State Constitutions, and the Growing Fortess of Private Property, " *University of Michigan Journal of Law Reform* 33 Summer 2000), 615–649.

20. Craig Kellog, "Shopping and Housing Mix in New Kanas City Mall," *Architectural Record* 187, no. 2 (1999),56.

21. Garreau, *Edge City*.

22. *Lechmere, Inc. v. NLRB* 502 U.S. 526 (1992).

23. The mall is also protected by City of Bloomington police and the only police substation is located on mall property. For a more thorough discussion of this case see Coffin, "The United Mall of America."

24. Mike Kaszuba,"Megamall Not Public Space, Court Rules," *Minneapolis Star Tribune*, March 12, 1999, 1A.

25. Many other malls, including those operated by the Rouse Company (the developer of many visible projects such as Faneuil Hall in Boston), routinely provide a booth for community groups. See Witold Rybczynski, *City Life* (New York: Simon and Schuster, 1995), 209.

26. Anne Miller, "Mall Drops T–Shirt Charges," *The Times Union*, March 6, 2003, B1.

27. Anne Miller, "Mall, Main Street Intersect in Debate; As Anti-War Voices Seek a Public Outlet, Private Property Issue Arise, " *The Times Union*, March 7, 2003, A1.

28. Benjamin Barber, "Malled, Mauled and Overhaulded: Arresting Suburban Sprawl by Transforming the Mall into the Usable Civic Space," in *Public Space and Democracy*, ed. Marcel Hénaff and Tracy B. Strong (Minneapolis: University of Minnesota Press, 2001), 206.

29. See Jürgen Habermas, *Theory of Communicative Action, Vol 1*, tr. Thomas McCarthy (Boston: Beacon, 1984); Jürgen Habermas, "What is Universal Pragmastics," *Communication and the Evolution of Society*, tr. Thomas McCarthy (Boston: Beacon, 1979). For an excellent secondary source, see Simone Chambers, *Reasonable Democracy: Jürgen Habermas and the Politics of Discourse* (Ithaca, NY: Cornell Univesity Press,1996).

30. Molly J. Liskow, "Leafletting Rules to Balance Mall's and Speakers' Rights," *New Jersey Lawyer*, August 28, 2000, B8. For the full text of the decision, see *Green Party of New Jersey v. Hartz Mountain Industries, Inc.*, New Jersey Supreme Court, A-59, June 13, 2000.

31. Richard Briffault, "A Government for Our Time? Business Improvement Districts and Urban Governance," *Columbia Law Review* 99 (March 1999), 365–477.

32. Kowinski, *The Malling of America*, 53–63.

33. See Arkansas Statue 14-184-115 (1995). Cited in Clayton P. Gillette and Paul B. Stephan III, "Constitutional Limits on Privatization," *American Journal of Comparative Law* 46 (1998).

34. Some BIDs, for example, those in New York, guarantee representation to non-property owners, but even there business people, especially landlords, dominate the membership of the governing boards. One study of eight BIDs in New York City found that 67% of members were business people; in the five remaining BIDs 75% of the board members were either business people or legal professionals. (Briffault, "A Government for Our Time?" 412.)

35. Stephen C. Fehr, "Property Owners Commit to Revive D.C.: In Heart of District a $38.5 Million Push for Safety, Cleanliness," *The Washington Post*, July 27, 1997, A20 (citing views of downtown business owners).

36. Briffault, "A Government for Our Time?" 396.

37. Paul Goldberger, "The Rise of the Private City," in *Breaking Away: The Future of Cities: Essays in Memory of Robert F. Wagner*, ed. Julia Vitullo-Martin (New York: Twentieth Century Fund Press, 1996), 136–137.

38. On festival marketplaces, see M. Christine Boyer, "Cities for Sale: Merchandising History at South Street Seaport," in ed. Michael Sorkin, *Variations on a Theme Park: The New American City and the End of Public Space* (New York: Hill and Wang, 1992), 181–204.

39. Bernard Frieden and Lynne Sagalyn, *Downtown, Inc.: How America Rebuilds Cities* (Cambridge, MA: MIT Press, 1990).

40. Tom Gallagher, "Trespasser on Main St.: (You!)," *The Nation*, December 18, 1995.

41. *Avery v. Midland County et al.* 390 U.S. 474 (1968).
42. The courts decided that local school board elections were not exempt from one-person, one-vote. In *Salyer Land Co. v. Tulare Lake Basin Water Storage District,* the Court determined that the water storage district, by virtue of its limited purpose and financing structure, could be governed by affected property owners exclusively.
43. "Voting Scheme for Board Okayed," *City Law,* November/December, 1998.
44. A similar lawsuit was brought by homeless plaintiffs against the Fashion District BID in Los Angeles. The suit was settled out of court. Although the BID denied wrongdoing, it also promised that its security contractor, Burns International Security, would not search, harass, or order homeless people to "move along." See Marla Dickerson, "Fashion District Group Agrees to Settle Homeless Lawsuit," *Los Angeles Times,* August 14, 2001.
45. "Homeless Workers: BIDs Failed to Pay Minimum Wage," *City Law,* March/April 1998. The article reported that U.S. District Court Judge Sonia Sotomayor ruled that the program participants were entitled to the minimum wage.
46. Heather Barr, "More Like Disneyland: State Action, 42 U.S.C. 1 1983, and Business Improvement Districts in New York," *Columbia Human Rights Law Review* (Winter 1997), 399–404. The accuracy of these later accusations is a matter of controversy. At least one of the four workers retracted the accusations and another claimed that he was pressured to retract. The BID did settle at least two lawsuits by homeless people injured by outreach workers.
47. Thomas Lueck, "Grand Central Partnership Is Subject of U.S. Inquiry," *New York Times,* May 26, 1995, A7.
48. Briffault, "A Government for Our Time?" 427–428. To cite one specific example, the Riverhead Business Improvement District successfully lobbied the town board to enact legislation requiring that any social service agency wanting to relocate in the district must get a special permit. See Mitchell Freedman, "Riverhead to Govern Downtown Tenants," *Newsday,* May 9, 2002, A30.
49. Briffault, "A Government for Our Time?" 462–463.
50. Barr, "More Like Disneyland," 404, 408–411. The statute quoted is 42 U.S.C. 1 1983.
51. Of course, a homeless person who was physically injured or whose property was destroyed could bring a criminal complaint or a civil suit for damages. The former is difficult, given how closely private security forces work with police (sometimes sharing a substation). The latter has been pursued successfully by homeless individuals. One plaintiff won a $27,500 judgment against the Grand Central Partnership. See David Stout, "For a Troubled Partnership: A History of Problems," *New York Times,* November 8, 1995, B6.
52. Eds. Chuihua Judy Chung, Jeffrey Inaba, Rem Koolhaas, and Sze Tsung Leong, *Harvard Design School Guide to Shopping* (Cologne: Taschen, 2001).

# 20

*Peter Marcuse*

## LIFE IN CITIES AFTER SEPTEMBER 11, 2001

## Introduction

Not terrorism, but what has been done under the mantel of counter-terrorism, has had a significant effect on cities since the attack on the World Trade Center on September 11, 2001. The consequences are particularly noticeable in the United States, but their repercussions will be felt throughout the global economy. They suggest, not a change in direction, but a continuation of trends already well under way before September 11, reinforced and aggravated by the cover given by the so-called "war on terrorism." The war on terrorism needs to be read always as in quotes, because it is not in any conventional sense a war—no national enemy, no troops, no territorial goal as such, no confrontation in battles—with the war on Iraq having only the most tenuous connection to actual terrorism. Nor are the policies undertaken in the name of the war on terrorism rationally related to the prevention of terrorism—they do not deal with the relations that produce terrorism, they are not proportional to the actual threats from real terrorism, they are not based on reliable information, and they serve purposes that are quite independent of any danger of terrorism, strengthening policy directions already well under way before September 11.

Hearings before the US Congress as this is being written highlight some of the irrationalities of the intelligence services dealing with actual terrorism. The repeated "orange alerts" declared by the government ("highrisk," as compared to yellow alerts, which are only "elevated risks") lead to measures looking more like Ariel Sharon's reaction to Hamas than to any threats from Al-Qaeda:

> Attorney General John Ashcroft . . . identified "lightly secured targets" as the most vulnerable, especially hotels, shopping centers, and apartment complexes. The increased measures are particularly visible in New York, which Ashcroft indicated was a potential target area for terrorists. Ashcroft also pointed to so-called "soft targets," which are potential targets that are a symbol of American power or prosperity, such as the Statue of Liberty or the Golden Gate Bridge. (Government Security Solutions.com, 2003)

But of course Al-Qaeda saw the commercial towers of the World Trade Center and the military bastion of the Pentagon as the symbols of American power, not the Statue of Liberty.

From Peter Marcuse, "The 'War on Terrorism' and Life in Cities after September 11, 2001" in Stephen Graham, ed., *Cities, War, and Terrorism: Towards Urban Geopolitics.* Copyright © 2003 by Blackwell Publishing. Reprinted by permission of Blackwell Publishing.

The prognosis of the impact of the war on terrorism is not good, for those interested in urban life and democracy. Both are threatened by actions in the market, and governmental responses are likely to aggravate problems. The war on terrorism is leading to a continued downgrading of the quality of life in US cities, visible changes in urban form, the loss of public use of public space, restriction on free movement within and to cities, particularly for members of darker-skinned groups, and the decline of open popular participation in the governmental planning and decision-making process. The planning both for the reuse of the site of the attack in New York City, for the "revitalization" of its financial district, and for measures to deal with the proclaimed threat of terrorism in the future in many other areas, suggest these developments. They are only tangentially related to a serious and rational concern with the lives of those that were actually directly affected by the terrorism of the attack.

This chapter concentrates on the impact at the level of urban form. The net result might be described as a decentralization of key business activities and their attendant services, but to very concentrated off-center locations in close proximity to the major centers—*concentrated decentralization*—with earlier tendencies to move out lower-level activities accelerated. Within both the new and the old urban concentrations, there will be an increased *barricading* within the city, a *citadelization* of new construction for major businesses and upper-class residences, and actors on the demand side in the real estate market will move in this direction, and they will influence government to assist in the process. That assistance will come both through limited public subsidies and from an abdication of independent planning and regulatory action by government in pursuit of social welfare goals: governments will be pushed to see their role as simply smoothing the way for private forces to act in the market. *Deplanning* might be a good term for much of governmental planning in this process, since what is not done is frequently accompanied by a surrender even of previously instituted procedures and an abdication of regulatory powers. Property developers and owners in the central areas, the supply side of the real estate industry, will however press to maintain earlier levels of centralization, and paradoxically they will be the ones calling for the maximum of governmental action to help them in the effort.

What follows deals first with developments in the market and in governmental policy at the urban level, then looks at the array of forces producing those developments. But before examining these issues, a look at one of the most direct consequences of the war on terrorism—the exponential growth of the security industry—is necessary to give some indication of the direction of events.

## The Growth of the Security Industry

What the official war on terrorism means most directly is an enormous boon to particular sectors of industry, who have been quick to see its profit potentials. The Center for Responsive Politics has estimated that "businesses appeared to be focusing on the creation of the Homeland Security Department more than any other legislation in recent memory." And successfully: private security services, overwhelmingly in urban centers, are booming; they may well be the fastest growing sector in a sluggish economy. The figures are illuminating.

- Private security employment is already over 1.7 times the level of employment in public security agencies, and the ratio is expected to grow to 2.4 by 2010.
- Expenditures for private security in 2000 were already $103 billion, up from $20 billion in 1980 and $52 billion in 1990.
- There are now over 100,000 private security firms in business, up from less than 30,000 twenty years ago (Security Industry Association, 2003).

It is specifically public spaces in cities that are affected by this multiplication of devices of control and surveillance. In recent debates about the reconstruction of Pennsylvania Station in New York City—one of the city's two major rail and commuter terminals—Senator Schumer asked for more security. He was told security was already based on the Rail Security Program, which included increased policing, new K-9 (police dog) bomb teams, sensors to detect chemical, biological, and radioactive materials, explosive trace detection devices that scan the air for traces of bomb materials, bomb-resistant trash cans, intrusion alarms, and vehicle barricades. But he nevertheless asked for $450 million more to be spent on even further augmented "security."

The public costs incurred in the purported quest for security are substantial. A whole new bureaucracy has been created at the federal level, much of it under the new Department of Homeland Security. It includes the new Transportation Security Administration (TSA) and incorporates other agencies that formerly existed as separate government agencies: the US Customs Service, which was previously part of the Department of Treasury; the enforcement division of the Immigration and Naturalization Service, which was previously part of the Department of Justice; the Federal Protective Service, which was previously part of the General Services Administration; the Federal Law Enforcement Training Center, which was previously part of the Department of Treasury; and the Animal and Plant Health Inspection Service, which was previously part of the Department of Agriculture. Altogether, over 170,000 people are employed in this work.

And of course these expenditures are at the expense of others, and what are particularly short-changed are programs that affect cities. Housing subsidies are cut from a level already low by international standards, social service programs are curtailed, public education is left so short of money some cities are forced to close their schools early in the year to save money, urban infrastructure is neglected, public libraries are closed early, and fire stations are closed completely to save money.

All of this cannot be blamed on Al-Qaeda, or on any known real terrorist organization or threat, yet it is the propaganda of the war on terrorism that justifies it. It is part of a long-term policy approach that seeks to minimize the public sector, privatize every possible governmental function for private profit, and protect those people and business firms that rate the top of the urban hierarchy from any possible diminution of their privileges, whether it is from taxation, from internal discontent, or even from radical criticism. The connection to the invasion of civil liberties has been well documented elsewhere and is discussed below, but is part of the same long-term pattern.

In this context, then, what has been the impact of the war on terrorism on the shape of cities in the United States (Marcuse, 2002b: 591–6)?

# Urban Form I: Concentrated Decentralization in the Market

The spatial impulses that followed September 11 in New York City were not so much a change in direction as an intensification of what has been happening anyway, now accelerated and explained by reference to concern over terrorism. In the market, both business patterns and residential changes were involved. To give perspective: some 2,825 people were killed in the attack on the World Trade Center; up to 100,000 jobs, including those of small business persons (further breakdowns below) were directly affected; 13.45 million square feet of office space was destroyed (Bagli, 2001), 30 percent of the Class A space in the downtown area, and 3.6 percent of all office space in Manhattan (Glaeser and Shapiro, 2001). Just as major disasters permit reconstruction on a newer basis, that might earlier have been wished but could not be implemented, so the destruction in lower Manhattan permits a clearer view of some longer-term trends, which it in turn amplified.

Employment patterns have for some time been towards decentralization of almost all types of jobs, with only a very narrow band of activities remaining concentrated in the central business districts of major cities, and most activities focusing on less central areas of the city—the suburbs, edge cities—with a noticeable movement from primary cities to secondary and even tertiary (economically defined) cities. A number of factors came together to shape this trend: the availability of technology-to-make-both transportation and communication easier across greater distances; the pressure on central real estate prices in a market dominated by private land ownership; the costs of congestion and environmental degradation; and, last but hardly least, the social tensions and insecurities that result from increasing polarization of the population and continuing racial division tied, both in fact and even more in perception, to life in big cities. To these negative aspects of concentration there has been counterpoised the advantages of agglomeration: the efficiencies of shared services, the importance of face-to-face meetings, in some cases the reduced friction of transportation, the desirability of a creative, diverse, lively, urban milieu.

In this balance, the fear of terrorism now added a significant weight to the side of decentralization. Over-agglomeration is equated with danger. In the more "global" cities, this balance has hitherto been more on the side of concentration than it has in other cities; that balance has now changed. The centers of global cities will no longer be exempt, even to the extent that they ever were. The pattern is already visible in New York City. The New York Stock Exchange won't build its long-planned new trading floor and 900-foot tower across the street from its current headquarters, but may build a secondary trading site outside lower Manhattan. But many say it should move to trading on an electronic network. More shares are traded on the NASDAQ stock market, which exists only on computer systems and the screens of its dealers, than on the Big Board at New York's Stock Exchange on Wall St. "With faster computers and data transmission, traders no longer have to meet in person to buy and sell shares," says the chief executive of the Cincinnati Stock Exchange:

> "Outside the United States, floors are disappearing really quickly, and automated auctions are the wave of the future," Mr. Madhavan said, "The USA is the lone holdout, and it's the holdout because it has a strong group of dealers who are polit-ically connected." Mr. Madhavan is head of ITG, which operates a computer trad-ing system that competes with the Big Board. (*New York Times,* October 12, 2001: C4)

So one trend is for certain business activities to leave the concentrated cen-ter(s) of the city. Which activities? Those that are largely self-contained, that have internalized a large part of their externalities; and those that do not, with the use of modern communications and transportation technologies, need to be in the same physical location as the headquarters they serve. So the headquar-ters of major industrial firms and those directly marketing services to con-sumers may move out, and back offices will move out. Nothing new here. Yet the trends will accentuate, and the definition of back offices will expand. As Saskia Sassen (2002a: 24) has pointed out, the destruction in the financial dis-trict has permitted some firms that had previously massively concentrated their activities there to do what they had already begun to do, but now much more quickly: disaggregate their activities into those which really needed to stay agglomerated in a concentrated downtown, and those that could (increas-ingly as technology advances) be deconcentrated.

But those moving out of the concentrated center are not moving to just anywhere; they remain concentrated in specific locations away from the center, most but not all remaining within the metropolitan area. In the first place—and this is perhaps unique to New York City—there are two "downtowns," and there is a continuing competition within the real estate industry between them: Midtown and the "downtown" Financial District. (Midtown for this purpose is defined as between 34th and 59th Street, 8th Avenue to the East River, and downtown as Manhattan south of Canal Street—not the definition used by the Lower Manhattan Redevelopment Corporation, which takes in all of the area below Houston Street.) That competition has been going on for some time; esti-mates are that in 1950 downtown had more workers than Midtown, today Midtown has three times as many as downtown (Glaeser and Shapiro, 2001: 20). Even after the loss of space in the lower Manhattan financial district the of-fice vacancy rate has doubled between September and January, "leaving some analysts to wondering which companies will move into the empty space, let alone any new towers that might be built" (Bagli, 2002: 1; Heschmeyer, 2001).

The hyper-concentrations of jobs in service-oriented office buildings in the Central Business Districts (CBDs) of the more globalized large cities (and both the high- and the low-paying jobs associated with them) will shrink, as multina-tional businesses change their spatial strategies in the search for security in more outlying areas. The focus will initially be within the same metropolitan regions (e.g., American Express, Lehman Brothers, and others, renting—on long-term leases—spaces in Jersey City, Stamford, etc.). Estimates are that, even by November 2001, 23,000 jobs had already moved to the suburbs after September 11, and another 144,000 were in jeopardy of such a move (Bagli 2002: 1).

Many major firms already had large satellite offices in fringe locations, to which they quickly moved on September 11; in some cases decisions to move more operations out of New York City to those locations were simply accelerated by the attack. The Bank of New York had 3,000 employees in its headquarters building at 1 Wall Street; they're all back at work there now. But it had 4,000 employees at 101 Barclay Street at one of its data centers; they've been moved. "[We are] just too concentrated in Manhattan" (New York Times, October 6, 2002: C1). Long Island City in Queens is touted, not only by self-interested developers but also by Senator Charles Schumer of New York, as "an ideal location for creating a new central business district" (Grid Magazine, 2001). In fact; since his speech, a $700,000,000 contract has been awarded by the city's Economic Development Corporation for the construction of a major mixed-use development there, expected to bring 7,000 jobs to this location in Queens (Globest. Com, 2001). Empire Blue Cross took temporary quarters in Melville, Long Island. It had 460,000 square feet in the World Trade Center. It is proposing to lease 300,000 at Metrotech in downtown Brooklyn, and less than 100,000 square feet at 11 West 42 Street, Times Square, where the chief executive and other top executives will stay (New York Times, October 12, 2001: D6). Deutsche Bank is building a backup operation in Jersey City. Marsh & McLennan, a major tenant at the World Trade Center, has taken some space in Midtown, but is moving 2,000 employees across the river to Hoboken, in New Jersey (Bagli, 2002: B2). Goldman Sachs is moving its entire equity trading department to Jersey City, across the Hudson River, to a $1 billion complex it is building there (with, incidentally, the highest skyscraper in New Jersey). According to a major real estate firm, "Goldman's decision is a significant setback because it affects the downtown core of financial services. It's not so much the number of jobs that's significant, but the kind of jobs. Equity trading is the heart and soul of any investment bank" (Bagli, 2002: B2).

The movement out will be primarily to the immediately adjacent but somewhat less dense and less expensive fringes, the outer boroughs in New York City and across the Hudson. But there will also be a lesser move to the suburbs, and beyond them to the edge cities (not just in Joel Garreau's narrow sense): Stamford, White Plains, etc. And over time the effects may lead to an even wider dispersal to other regions or urban enclaves. TIAA-CREF, the largest pension fund in the United States, now has 4,600 employees in New York City, 1,320 in Denver, and 597 in Charlotte. Their planned expansion will be overwhelmingly in Charlotte, hardly a global city (TIAA-CREF, 2001: pers. comm., October 9). Residential patterns, as well as business and commercial patterns, will change. In particular, the trend towards recreating residential housing and residential environments in central business districts will suffer, despite the efforts of CBD real estate interests, existing residential tenants, and local governments. In Washington, DC, where the major business tenant is government, there will be a continuing trend to the decentralization of government offices, but the hopes for bringing multi-family residential development to the down-town are now given little chance (www.globalst.com 2001: October 19). The trend here is longer standing, as suburbs generate more and more of the accou-trements of urbanity that used to be confined to the centers of cities: the side-walk cafés, the art galleries, the cultural centers, the symphony orchestras, the theatres. The safety issue will accentuate the trend. As Paul Krugman, who holds himself out as a hard-headed economist and lives in the Jersey suburbs, wrote: "I felt perfectly safe on September 11; there are millions of people living and working nearby, but no obvious targets, because there's no there here." The "there" that isn't there is a traditional urban oriented form, with a central-ized CBD, and fewer will want that, given the trade-offs, than even before.

## Urban Form II: Citadelization, Barricading, and Governmental Deplanning

In the decentralized but concentrated locations that have been given a boost by September 11, the form of development has also been influenced by those events. Obtrusive skyscrapers lose some of their appeal. The towers in Kuala Lumpur and Frankfurt have already felt the threat, closing and evacuating the day after the World Trade Center collapse; workers in the Empire State build-ing in New York and the Sears Tower in Chicago were reportedly afraid to go up to their offices. At Sears Tower taxis are not allowed to idle at the entrance and lunch deliveries may not be made to offices. The observation deck is closed; security in the lobby gives a feeling of martial law, and security guards greet long-time employees by name but demand to see their IDs. A consultant working on the 44th floor is quoted as saying he's considering buying a para-chute, and found one on the Internet for $130 (*New York Times*, September 23, 2001: A36). Five months after September 11, a business newspaper headlines on its front page: "Empire State Emptying Out as Tenants Flee. Anxiety Lingers; Vacant Space Triples" (*Crain's New York Business*, February 2002: 1) (The story goes on to say: "Concerns about terrorism plague other trophy towers, as well. Some businesses have refused to consider sublets in the Chrysler Building since September 11 . . . Many companies seeking space are issuing a new man-date to their brokers—'find us anonymous buildings'—in a blanket disap-proval of all well-known properties.") The apparently unrelated crash of a light plane into the floors of the Pirelli tower in Milan added to the problem.

In lieu of going ostentatiously high-rise, the direction of development is to-wards protected, secured citadels, to internalize and shield the activities criti-cal to the top tiers of global and national businesses. The trend towards citadelization already exists, but is modified and accentuated. The new form is for citadels within buildings or fortified complexes, including more and more of the facilities necessary for daily life within the building itself. One will never have to leave the citadel for shopping, for meals, for entertainment, for per-sonal services. The mall at the World Trade Center was a prototype of the form: commuters from New Jersey could arrive underground, find all their personal and business needs catered for entirely within the Center and its mall and protected adjacent areas, and leave again underground, without ever having to step foot in the City itself. That pattern, preexisting the attack on this particular citadel, will be strongly accentuated, but in less high-rise, less representative, less "signature" fashion, and more heavily barricaded and secured even than before.

So the new citadels will be less ostentatious externally, less ultra-high-rise signature buildings. They will be larger, more comprehensive fortified centers, with high-tech metal detectors, fingerprint card entry, etc. The barriers to easy access will increase (see below). The move of Morgan Stanley, the largest securities company in Manhattan and the largest tenant in the World Trade Center, typifies the kind of exclusive citadel that will increasingly be characteristic. The firm is buying the Westchester County former 107-acre headquarters campus complex of Texaco (symbolic!). It is not keeping the office tower it had begun in Midtown Manhattan, which it sold to Lehman Brothers, a company displaced from the World Trade Center. Most of its 14,000 employees will stay in New York City, but at least 2,000 will go to the 750,000 square foot campus in Westchester (Bagli, 2002). As the president of Global Marketing Consultants, a Canadian firm, said at an Urban Land Institute meeting:

> The high density and mass urbanization resulting from skyscrapers is not necessary or desirable ... we will see more 24-hour, multi-use projects offering employees amenities such as full-service business centers and medical facilities, and which provide space that is communal, flexible, "media-rich," easily adaptable. (Heschmeyer, 2001)

And the polarization by income, by occupation, and by race that is an ongoing process in central cities will accentuate a further developing pattern: a barricading of segregated spaces. This will come about both as a result of residential developments and of changes in employment patterns. Those able to move out of town or to barricaded citadels will do so; those unable to do so will remain behind. The difference between the two groups will be both income and race related, with sharper dividing lines between and among groups. So segregation and quartering will increase. One can see the dynamic in miniature by looking at what was already the occupational and income distribution of those directly affected by the attack on the World Trade Center: the three largest industry groups, among the 108,500 jobs lost as a direct result of the attack are shown in Table 6.1.

**Table 6.1 The three largest sectoral job losses in New York City as a direct result of September 11, 2001**

| Industry | Employment | Compensation ($ millions) |
|---|---|---|
| Securities | 12,200 | 2,577.2 |
| Retail trade | 12,200 | 311.1 |
| Restaurants | 11,900 | 241.8 |

*Source*: Fiscal Policy Institute

The difference in relative compensation is apparent from the table ("Securities" includes low-paid clerical as well as high-paid professional jobs). Lay-offs thus disproportionately affect high and low end workers; those without accumulated resources will be particularly hard hit. Those at the bottom of the economic ladder end up in the soup kitchens (Ruiz, 2001); those at the top are producing a boom in the ex-urban real estate market in Connecticut and upstate New York, and a more comprehensive form of gentrification in town.

The newly appointed deputy mayor of New York argues:

> I don't think that anyone has disputed the fact that we have to do anything we can to ensure that lower Manhattan remains the financial center of the city. But the lower Manhattan of the future also has to be a 24-hour community filled not just with financial firms, but also with residences, arts, culture, and other things. (Bagli, 2002)

Clearly, the danger here is that the entire area will become an exclusive, citadelized community for those who can afford to live there, socially if not physically barricaded off from the rest of the city (as Battery Park City, adjacent to the World Trade Center, had been).

The barricading of the city is a good shorthand term to describe what public policy is leading to. It is readily visible in public space, near public buildings, in places of public assembly and use. "Public space" will become less public; free access and free use will be severely limited. By contrast, controlled spaces, such as malls, will increase their attraction. Some public spaces, like the park at the Federal Courthouse in Boston (Bagli, 2001) or the plaza before City Hall in New York City and its adjacent recently renovated park, will simply be barred for open use, or so tightly controlled as to inhibit activities normal to a democratic society. Mayor Guiliani had pioneered this conservative development with his restrictions on assemblies near City Hall (Davis, 2001: 43) and attempts to limit the use of streets for parades, in the name of "security." Less freely accessible public buildings and metal detectors and demands for identification are being normalized, a pattern reminiscent of Eastern European and Soviet public buildings before 1989. Many places, from railroad stations to bus terminals to public streets and squares, will be subject to pervasive surveillance. The attractiveness of guarded malls will increase (Davis, 2001: 45). That the danger is not one the war on terrorism is designed to meet is revealed by the most recent assassination in New York City, where a disgruntled would-be politician shot a member of the City Council from a balcony in its meeting room; an individual crime, not an act of terrorism.

The impact of the war on terrorism's urban policies on urban life is evident: in Los Angeles, for the Oscar ceremonies:

> Hundreds of officers from local and federal law enforcement agencies will ring central Hollywood on Sunday night, in at least three levels of security checks and keep guard on a traffic-free perimeter of nearly two square miles...what makes the new venue a particular security concern is that it is in the middle of one of the most congested and urban neighborhoods in Southern California...We're not allowing any of these Oscar-viewing parties in the complex this year. (*New York Times*, March 23, 2003: 10.)

Or:

The National Park service is planning to spend $2 to $3 million on closed-circuit television systems at the Washington Monument and the Lincoln, Jefferson, Franklin D. Roosevelt, Vietnam, and Korean War Memorials. (*New York Times*, March 23, 2003: 10)

This barricading will be particularly prominent whenever there are plans for any type of popular protest mobilization, rally, march, or protest (Warren, this volume). Mayor Guiliani had pioneered this with his attempts to prevent rallies such as that in Harlem that would attract a large number of African-American youth, but the courts had over-turned his refusal to give permits for such events; such a pro-democracy result is not likely to occur when restrictions are imposed in the name of preventing terrorism. Again, the trend was already visible in actions by conservative governments before September 11, and can include literal barricading. For instance, Washington DC police and Secret Service officials said there was no final design for the security barrier expected to be erected in anticipation of the World Bank/International Monetary Fund protests in mid-September, although reports say it will be 2.5 miles of 9-feet-tall chain-link Cyclone fence. "The fence hasn't been completely set. It could be Cyclone fence, but it also could include Jersey barriers [giant cement blocks], vehicles, even bicycle racks. All those things are possible," one official is quoted as saying (Orin, 2001).

Barricading can be accomplished by social and legal measures as well as by physical ones. The passage of what is called, officially, the United States Patriot Act of 2001 (HR 3162: 2001) will extend the restrictions on customary civil liberties even further, with the federal government centrally involved but local communities and their residents directly affected. Key provisions of the legislation allow investigators to use roving wiretaps, following a suspect rather than a particular phone. It also gives the government the power to detain immigrants for up to seven days if they're suspected of involvement with terrorists, up from two days. The bill calls for tripling the number of immigration and border patrol agents along the 3,000-mile border with Canada. The new measure also provides new tools to fight money laundering by terrorists, allow government agencies to better share information about suspects and more easily track their communications, and increase penalties for terrorism-related crimes (ABC News, 2001).

Such measures will disproportionately affect immigrant communities in large cities. But they will more broadly affect the active participation in democratic debate that has been a characteristic of life in cities. "Stadt Luft macht freie"—city air produces freedom—becomes less true. Both official and unofficial government actions and statements lead in the same direction.

Senator Trent Lott has already called publicly for a reduction in the weight given to civil liberties in the interests of security (National Public Radio, 2001). Rage against those who don't follow the prevailing line on the terror attacks was seen in the recent firing of Dan Guthrie of the *Grants Pass Oregon Daily Courier*, who criticized President Bush for hiding in a shelter during the assaults in New York and Washington. When Tom Gutting wrote a column titled

"Bush Has Failed to Lead the US" in the *Texas City Sun*, the newspaper terminated him and ran a front page apology. In covering a September 29 peace demonstration in Washington, DC, the *New York Times* chose this deliberately inflammatory and misleading headline: "Protesters Urge Peace With Terrorists." Comedian Bill Maher, host of television's "Politically Incorrect," lost many advertisers after he commented that the US was cowardly in "lobbing cruise missiles from 2,000 miles away." White House spokesman Ari Fleischer later denounced Maher and warned: "Americans need to watch what they say, [and] watch what they do." This comment was deleted from a White House transcript of the press conference, according to the *New York Times*.

Thus, "security" becomes the justification for measures that threaten the core of urban social and political life, from the physical barricading of space to the social barricading of democratic activity. Stephen Graham goes further, and speaks of the "accelerated militarization of urban civil society" and the concomitant "urbanization of the military" (Graham, 2001), as serious military concerns (not the Star Wars kind) focus more and more on cities, how to defend them and how to attack them (see Warren, Hillis, this volume).

## Conclusion

So, some years after the event, the impact of September 11 has become clear. Very little has actually happened to counteract terrorism at its roots, and what has been done to deal with its symptoms is disproportionate to the danger, at least from all the available evidence to date. On the other hand, under the mantle of the so-called war on terrorism, a number of trends, often summarized under the heading of a neoliberal turn, have been accentuated and legitimated:

- A concentrated decentralization of business activities in cities, largely to outlying locations within their metropolitan areas, but also further abroad.
- A citadelization of major centers of business activities, incorporating more and more of daily functions within enclosed and protected spaces in large planned developments.
- A move towards barricading sections of the city from each other, particularly evident in so-called sensitive areas, with restrictions on the normal uses of public spaces.
- An increased public investment in security and surveillance and control mechanisms, together with a diminution of the public sector in its social welfare function.
- Deplanning, transfer of planning functions from public to private hands and within the public sphere, from traditional planning considerations to priority for police and security inputs.
- A disproportionate growth of those industries providing real or perceived or mandated security for daily activities.
- A narrowing of the limits of public discussion, of the rights of immigrants, and of civil liberties generally.

All justified in the name of a war on terrorism in the cities.

Abdelhadi, M. (2003) "Iraq rumour mill grinds on," *BBC News*, Middle East, July 6. www.bbc.co.uk.

Bagli, C. (2001) "For downtown: Vacant offices and lost vigor," *New York Times*, November 19.

Bagli, C. (2002) "Seeking safety, downtown firms are scattering," *New York Times*, January 29.

Davis, M. (2001) "The flames of New York," *New Left Review*, 12, November/December.

Glaeser, E. and Shapiro, J. (2002) "Cities and warfare: The impact of terrorism on urban form," *Journal of Urban Economics*, 51, 205–24.

Globest.com (2001) "City picks developer for $700 Mil. Queens Project." www.Globest.com; accessed October 26, 2003.

Government Security Solutions.com (2003) "A clockwork response to orange alert." http://govtsecurity.securitysolutions.com/ar/security_clockwork_response_orange/; accessed June 2003.

Heschmeyer, M. (2001) "Attack magnified existing New York City office trends." www.costargroup.com; accessed October 16, 2001.

Marcuse, P. (2002b) "Urban form and globalization after September 11th: The View from New York," *International Journal of Urban and Regional Research*, Vol. 26 (3), 596–606.

Orin, D. (2001) *New York Post*, August 31.

Sassen, S. (2002a) "Correspondence with Saskia Sassen," *Quaderns d'arguitectura I Urbanisme*, January.

Security Industry Association (2003) http://www.siaonline.org.

# 21

# URBAN SCHOLARS AS END-TIMES PROPHETS*

## *Dennis R. Judd*

Urban scholars have long shared an assumption that the city is in great jeopardy from all sides. The love affair between urban scholars and *noir* interpretations of cities goes back a long way. It has appeared in its most coherent version in two storylines, one told by the Chicago school of the 1920s and 1930s, the other version articulated, more recently, by the L.A. school and scholars who share its premises. Though the particular theories of these schools differ, they share an assumption that the spatial dynamics of urban development can be interpreted to mean that urban life is becoming steadily worse.

In their classic work, *The City*, Robert Park, Ernest Burgess, Roderick McKenzie and other members of the Chicago school proposed an elegant, sweeping version of Social Darwinism to explain the main dynamics of urban spatial and social structure. The social Darwinists applied Darwin's theories of evolution to society, and were especially enthusiastic about the idea that in society, as in nature, the fittest survive and the weak eventually perish. The social Darwinists used this principle to argue that government should do nothing to help the weak. The members of the Chicago School utilized it to reach a different conclusion: when they applied the metaphors describing natural systems to

---

Adapted from Dennis R. Judd, "Everything Is 'Always Going to Hell': Urban Scholars as End-Times Prophets," *Urban Affairs Quarterly*, Vol. 41(2), pp. 230–255, copyright © 2005 by Sage Publications, Inc. Reprinted by permission of Sage Publications, Inc.

cities, they reached the conclusion that city life was threatened by the social chaos of outcast groups.

To Ernest Burgess, a leading light of the Chicago School, the ecology of the city was directly analogous to ecological processes found in nature: ". . . as in the plant communities successions are the products of invasion, so also in the human community the formations, segregations, and associations that appear constitute the outcome of a series of invasion. . . The general effect . . . is to give to the developed community well-defined areas. . ." (Burgess, 1967 [1925]: 74). This rhetorical strategy interpreted cities as constantly evolving organisms characterized by growth and decay, interdependence, competition and cooperation, health and disease.

Like nature, the human ecology of the city was—to use a phrase Darwin had applied to nature—red in tooth and claw. The scholars of the Chicago School announced their devotion to careful scientific observation of urban life, but their studies kept returning to the same theme—the cities produced and reproduced sick subcultures at every turn. Park was convinced that social breakdown was the norm rather the exception in industrial cities; as a result, he and his legions of graduate students took pains to document the life of hobos, prostitutes, and other flotsam and jetsam of urban life. His colorful language often seemed a far remove from the social-science methodology he emphasized. For example, Park, on the baleful effects of slums: "the slum areas that invariably grow up just on the edge of the business areas of great cities, areas of deteriorated housing, vice, and crime, are areas of social junk. . ." (Park, 1967 [1925]: 109).

The narrative power of the Chicago school can be traced to its foreboding mood of fecundity, decay, and violence: as Hans Christian Andersen's fables reveal, children, like their elders, are attracted to the tension introduced by these elements. In our own time, a similarly riveting narrative has emerged about urban life in the 21st century. In the 1980s several scholars who became known as the "L.A. School" began writing about Los Angeles as an urban dystopia, and a harbinger of what cities everywhere else are in the process of becoming. Like the Chicago School of the 1920s, the L.A. School's storyline derives its power from its sweeping and often dramatically bleak interpretation of urban life. ("Dramatically dismal": in Mike Davis's writings, balls of rattlesnakes wash up on the beaches of Los Angeles; there are "pentecostal earthquakes," "dead cities," and the question, "who killed L.A.?") (Davis, 2002).

One scholar often identified with the L.A. School (but who actually rejects the label) summed up the thesis in these words: "Los Angeles is the place where 'it all comes together.' . . . One might call the sprawling urban region . . . a prototopos, a paradigmatic place;" he has added elsewhere that Los Angeles "insistently presents itself as one of the most informative palimpsests and paradigms of twentieth-century urban development and popular consciousness . . ." (Soja, 1989: 191, 248). What does Los Angeles reveal about the future? That the stark inequalities of the Third World are being exported elsewhere, and that these are written on the urban landscape in a patchwork of prosperity and despair: "The luxury compound atop a matrix of impoverished misery, the self-contained secure community, and the fortified home can be found first in places such as Manila and São Paolo" (Dear and Flusty, 2002: 14).

The L.A. School's version of a dystopian urban future has swept through the community of scholars who study cities.[1] Consider a recent invitation to a conference on "Art and the Fragmentation of Urban Space: Gated Communities, Global Lands, and Non-Places," held on November 5, 2004, at the University of San Diego. The preamble to the conference invitation reads:

> The globalization of the world's economy and culture is coupled with radical fragmentation of urban spaces. Most urban centers, since the 1980's, have been built in an historical and geographical vacuum, detached from the social, political, and functional context of traditional cities. New urban developments are hermetically sealed from the actual locality, and yet connected to a vast network of "non-places," conspicuous in the uncanny repetition of identical malls, theme parks and airports across the world.

The language of this conference makes its purpose clear: The assumption that cities are becoming overwhelmed by "hermetically sealed" environments and Disneyfied "non-places" must be taken as the starting point of discussion. The overblown rhetoric paints a dire portrait of urban life: "radical fragmentation;" "geographical vacuum;" "uncanny repetition; " "identical malls . . ." These kinds of rhetorical indulgences may explain why a student in one of my recent seminars began a paper with the observation that, "Hyperbole may have become the principle methodology of today's urban scholarship." Amen.

Much of the scholarly writing about globalization invokes hyperbolic metaphor as a rhetoric strategy on behalf of the argument that global forces are inexorably overwhelming local difference. As Michael Sorkin describes it, the "new city replaces the anomaly and delight of [local] places with a universal particular, a generic urbanism inflected only by appliqué" (Sorkin: 1992: xiii). In his account, this new city is characterized by "rising levels of manipulation and surveillance" and "new modes of segregation," all put in the service of a "city of simulations, television city, the city as theme park" (Sorkin, 1992: xiii–xiv). Graham and Marvin predict the global proliferation of fantasy cities that bundle together retailing, restaurants and bars, performance halls, cinemas and IMAX theatres, hotels, video and virtual reality centers, and other diversions into an all-consuming environment of consumption and entertainment (Graham and Marvin, 2001: 265).

Chicago, where I live, does not resemble this version of the city. Neither do most cities. It is true that cities all over the world contain globalized spaces built from a common template. Downtown fortress buildings, gated communities, tourist bubbles, and enclosed malls have popped up on virtually all urban areas; their proliferation can be cited as evidence that the L.A. school has it right. But it requires a great leap of faith to conclude that sanitized, enclosed, privatized, fortified enclaves are replacing all public spaces. Only in small cities is the Walmart phenomenon taking place, wherein a new mall, megastore, or Disneyfied environment drains the life out of the businesses and public streets of the historic city. Instead, globalized spaces have become mixed into an increasingly complex spatial urban ecology.

The exceptions help to prove the rule. Baltimore, Maryland is emblematic of a type of redevelopment common in older industrial cities in the 1970s and 1980s. These cities were faced with a practical problem: How do you carve out a space for redevelopment in the midst of physical decay? Baltimore began by building Harbor Place, which is a virtual reservation for visitors who rarely experience the rest of a troubled city. Likewise, in Detroit, except for the twin cylindrical towers of the Renaissance Center and the nearby mall and a few blocks of what is called Greektown, the city is hostile to visitors. (In both cities, hotel doormen adamantly warned me not to leave the tourist bubble.) Las Vegas is equally segmented. The Strip, with its neon lights, fake renditions of the New York skyline and ancient Egypt, and 24-hour-a-day entertainment, provides a voyeuristic glimpse into a city that has been constructed as a facade of carnival and spectacle (Rothman and Davis, 2002).

But these are exceptional cases. The physical reconstruction of urban regions and of central cities in the past twenty years has been astonishing in scale; indeed, the closest parallel is probably the building of the industrial city a century ago, when cities invested in mass transit systems, paved streets, sewer and water systems, and parks. The latest round of investment has been equally comprehensive, ranging from massive investments in transportation systems to parks and open space to the facilities to promote tourism and culture. Virtually all central cities have been transformed, but nowhere are the changes as dramatic as in the cities of the industrial belt, in places like Cleveland, Cincinnati, Minneapolis-St. Paul, and Pittsburgh. At first small spaces opened up or were secured, but in recent years the revitalization has inexorably spread.

As a result of this remarkable reconstruction, cities all over North America have become safer, more pleasant environments for local residents and visitors alike. A traveler to cities in North America, Europe, and many other places can observe that cities are becoming more, not less, accessible to the tourist *flaneur*. Urban texture has become an object of fascination and consumption: "the large city has assumed the status of exotica. Modern tourism is no longer centered on the historic monument, concert hall, or museum but on the urban scene or, more precisely, on some version of the urban scene fit for tourism" (Sassen and Roost, 1999). The "scene" that local residents and visitors consume is composed of a kaleidoscope of experiences and spaces devoted to work, consumption, leisure, and entertainment (Featherstone, 1994: 394–397). Local residents and visitors are not confined within barricaded spaces and enclaves in most cities of the United States or in any city in Canada or Europe. With few exceptions, such an experience greets visitors only in the most dangerous and crime-ridden cities in the world.

It is important to note that I am not arguing that the city has become more just or equitable. Clearly, in American society generally (and thus in its cities), inequalities in wealth and income have increased rapidly; homelessness has been displaced but not reduced; crime rates have gone down in proportion to the extraordinary number of people in prison. And this is in the wealthiest nation on earth; conditions in the developing world are much worse (Davis, 2004). In his article "Planet of Slums," Mike Davis documents a truly frightening urban

future in the Third World, and for this piece he writes, for the most part, in a re-
markably restrained style. Perhaps that is because rhetorical excess is not required; the material truly speaks for itself—which is what makes it a compelling read.

## The Urban Future Redux

Why are fantastic tales about the Mad Max cities of the future accepted so enthusiastically and uncritically by urban scholars? Susan Fainstein has proposed
that post-structuralists (but, I add, urban scholars of all stripes) "assume that a
golden age—or at least a better one—once existed . . . ;" in this golden age,
cities promoted diversity, community, and free social interaction (Fainstein,
2001: 207). Such nostalgia is necessary to sustain dire prognostications of urban
life; otherwise the narrative of decline cannot work. This formula makes an appearance in Jane Jacobs' recent book, *Dark Age Ahead* (a perfect *noir* title!),
which is based on the premise that mass amnesia about a "functioning culture . . . so hard won by our forebears" may be pushing us (in North America
and Europe) "headlong into a Dark Age." She asks, "How and why can a people so totally discard a formerly vital culture that it becomes literally lost?" (Jacobs, 2004:4). Here are combined the *noir* triptych: tragedy, high drama, and
foreboding doom. Against such a riveting scenario less pessimistic interpretations of the future seem like drab fare indeed.

## NOTES

\*   This article is adapted from part of a previously published essay; see Dennis R. Judd,
    "Everything is 'Always Going to Hell': Urban Scholars as End-Times Prophets," *Urban Af-
    fairs Review* 40: 6 (November 2005).
1.  I want to emphasize that not all of the writings of the L.A. school employ such rhetorical
    excess. The difficulty of saying anything about the L.A. school is that its membership is
    ambiguous, at best, and the literature that might be ascribed to it runs the gamut from
    careful, empirically based social science to gleefully opaque postmodernism to rhetorical
    inflammation. Some of it is undoubtedly playful and tongue-in-cheek; cf., for example,
    some sections of Michael J. Dear and Steven Flusty, *The Spaces of Postmodernity: Read-
    ings in Human Geography* (who can *not* like something inspired by Calvin and Hobbes?).
    As a result, any critique of the L.A. school runs the significant danger of seeming overly
    earnest or missing the point (or, worse, misunderstanding someone's inside joke). The
    world of urban scholarship would be much the poorer without this brilliant, complex and
    sometimes maddening, fun, provocative literature. It is certainly robust enough to with-
    stand the critique I level at it in this article.

# REFERENCES

Burgess, Ernest W., in Robert E. Park, Ernest Burgess, and Roderick D. McKenzie. 1967 [1925]. *The City: Suggestions for Investigation of Human Behavior in the Urban Environment.* Chicago: University of Chicago Press.

Davis, Mike. 2002. *Dead Cities and Other Tales.* New York: The New Press.

Davis, Mike. 2004. "Planet of Slums," *New Left Review* 26 (March/April).

Dear, Michael J. and Steven Flusty, "The Resistible Rise of the L.A. School," in Michael J. Dear (ed.). 2002. *From Chicago to L.A.: Making Sense of Urban Theory.* Thousand Oaks, CA: Sage Publications.

Dear, Michael J. and Steven Flusty (eds.), *The Spaces of Postmodernity: Readings in Human Geography.* New York: Blackwell.

Fainstein, Susan S. 2001. The *City Builders: Property Development in New York and London, 1980–2000.* Lawrence, KS: University Press of Kansas.

Featherstone, Mike. 1994. "City Cultures and Post-modern Lifestyles." Pp. 387–408 in Ash Amin (ed.), *Post-Fordism: A Reader.* Oxford and Cambridge: Blackwell.

Graham, Stephen, and Simon Marvin. 2001. *Splintering Urbanism: Networked Infrastructure, Technological Mobilities and the Urban Condition.* London and New York: Routledge.

Jacobs, Jane. 2004. *Dark Age Ahead.* New York: Vintage Books.

Park, Robert E., Ernest Burgess, and Roderick D. McKenzie. 1967 [1925]. *The City: Suggestions for Investigation of Human Behavior in the Urban Environment.* Chicago: University of Chicago Press.

Rothman, Hal K., and Mike Davis (ed.) 2002. *The Grit Beneath the Glitter.* Berkeley: University of California Press.

Sassen, Saskia, and Frank Roost. 1999. "The City: Strategic Site for the Global Entertainment Industry." Pp. 143–154 in Dennis Judd and Susan S. Fainstein (ed.) *The Tourist City.* New Haven: Yale University Press.

Soja, Edward W. 1989. *Postmodern Geographies: The Reassertion of Space in Critical Social Theory.* New York: Verso.

Sorkin, Michael (ed.). 1992. *Variations on a Theme Park: The New American City and the End of Public Space.* New York: The Noonday Press.

# CHAPTER 7

# SPRAWL, REGIONALISM AND THE NEW URBANISM

## GOVERNING THE SPRAWLED METROPOLIS

Population movement outward from the urban core has been a central feature of urban development in the United States for decades. The old urban form, which found a central city surrounded by spreading suburbs, is giving way to a metropolitan pattern characterized by many nodes of activity. While there are advantages to this arrangement, the disadvantages have attracted a great deal of concern. Urban sprawl is blamed for everything from traffic congestion and gridlock to air pollution, the loss of open space and farmland, polluted water, and even obesity. As the readings in this chapter reveal, a lively debate is being waged about how to solve these problems—and also over whether sprawl is the precipitating cause.

For decades, urban reformers have said that the answer to the worst problems of the metropolis is to implement comprehensive governmental reform. They argue that the political fragmentation of metropolitan areas into hundreds of jurisdictions makes it extremely difficult to address issues that exist at a regional as much as a local level. A few places, such as Miami–Dade County, Florida, and Minneapolis–St. Paul, Minnesota, have forged metropolitan-wide political institutions that help coordinate service delivery. Portland, Oregon, alone stands as a region with a growth boundary and some record of curbing sprawl. Cooperation is commonplace in urban areas as a means of coordinating such services as 911-dialing and county-wide parks and recreation and library services. But except for such arrangements, the governance of metropolitan areas is extremely fragmented.

The essays that follow provide a profile of a movement called the New Regionalism. In the past, most attempts to establish regional governance have failed. They are usually opposed by suburban local governments fighting threats to their powers and citizens wishing to keep the problems of the cities out of their backyards. In Selection 22, Myron Orfield describes how a measure of regional coordination was achieved in the Minneapolis–St. Paul region on the important issue of tax sharing. Orfield acknowledges that regional reform is difficult and controversial, but he claims it is possible because of the emergence of a new political center of gravity in urban politics. In the past, attempts to build regional political coalitions in Minneapolis–St. Paul were built on weak foundations—notably leaders dedicated to

#22

good government ideals. Their initial success in building regional coalitions was short-lived because they neglected to mobilize powerful interests sufficiently. By contrast, practitioners of the New Regionalism persuaded central-city interests to join with older suburbs who shared similar problems of decaying neighborhoods, sagging tax bases, and a retrenching local economy. The Twin Cities success in building some measure of regional tax sharing was enabled by this new political coalition—a coalition that potentially exists in other metropolitan areas around the country.

The case for challenging sprawl through more comprehensive forms of regional governmental intervention is made in Selection 23 by David Rusk. He believes that the core regional issue is growth management. His discussion shows that the way local government is organized is closely linked with the problems of social division and the quality of life in metropolitan areas. Rusk argues that sprawl has enveloped urban communities all over the United States, but that the problems it causes are worst in so-called "inelastic" cities where central cities have been unable to annex surrounding suburban communities for many decades. In these areas, social problems are concentrated in the inner cities while suburban governments capture a disproportionate share of regional wealth. By contrast, "elastic cities," mostly located in the Western and Southwestern rim of the United States, have been permitted to extend their governmental boundaries more easily. According to Rusk, this allowed them to mitigate some of the consequences of sprawl, resulting in less segregated and socially healthier cities and suburbs. Yet Rusk warns that even elastic cities are no longer able to keep up with the continued sprawl of people and jobs. He concludes that the answer is to create "big box" regional governments that can contain unplanned growth.

Are there alternatives to regionalism as the answer to sprawl? The two remaining selections offer contrasting responses. In Selection 24, Fred Siegel argues that sprawl ". . . is not some malignancy to be summarily excised, but, rather, part and parcel of prosperity." Siegel claims that fragmented government offers abundant advantages. It enables people who live in badly governed central cities to escape to other jurisdictions that provide an array of alternative places to live, shop, and conduct business. Most of all, he believes that fragmented government avoids the dead hand of a single, powerful regional government that will restrict choice. Although Siegel concedes that there may be cases of successful regional governments, as in Portland, Oregon, time will tell if such examples can be copied elsewhere. In the meantime, he prefers to address common regional issues through one-off measures like tax sharing and the prohibition of public policies that favor suburbs over cities.

Another approach to sprawl seeks to counter its worst effects by introducing small-scale planning and architectural design as a way of reviving a sense of community identity and reducing reliance on the automobile. In the 1990s a movement called the New Urbanism came together in reaction to the segmentation of urban space in the form of shopping centers, office parks, massive subdivisions, and traffic-choked streets and freeways. Advocates of the New Urbanism contend that people increasingly wish to escape the sameness of cookie-cutter housing developments and dull suburban spaces. The developers of New Urbanism projects respond to this impulse by designing enclaves that slow traffic and encourage walking and a sense of community by re-creating the look and feel of

#23

#24

small-town neighborhoods. In Selection 25, Peter Calthorpe conveys the essence of this philosophy when he calls for a vision of a new Regional City. He argues that the old regionalism pulled everything apart—residential, retail, commercial, and civic activities became isolated from one another. The new regional form would be made up of small-scale development designed to human scale by bringing together the social, economic, and physical dimensions of the metropolis. He argues that urban regions should be viewed as complex ecologies that work best when the the several components of the system are seen as a unit; "treating each element separately is endemic to many of the problems we now face."

These perspectives are important voices in a continuing debate about how to manage the problems of urban regions in the twenty-first century. The debate will continue to be lively because the decentralization of metropolitan populations, whether called *sprawl* or some other name, will surely continue.

# 22

## *Myron Orfield*

## BUILDING CONSENSUS

# Forty Years of Minnesota Metropolitan Politics

Skeptics tell me that regional equity reform will never happen in America's metropolitan regions because the suburbs are now in charge of American politics. It may be true that the suburbs are in charge of American politics. But the politics of metropolitan reform is not about cities versus suburbs or, for that matter, about Democrats versus Republicans.

The suburbs are not a monolith, economically, racially, or politically. Surrounding America's central cities, with their high social needs and low per capita tax wealth, are three types of suburbs. First are the older suburbs, which comprise about a quarter of the population of U.S. metropolitan regions. These communities are often declining socially faster than the central cities and often have even less per household property, income, or sales tax wealth. Second are the low tax-base developing suburbs, which make up about 10–15 percent of U.S. metropolitan regions. They are growing rapidly in population, especially among school-age children, but without an adequate tax base to support that growth and its accompanying overcrowded schools, highway congestion, and ground water pollution. Both the central city and these two types of suburbs have small tax bases, comparatively high tax rates, and comparatively low spending. Median household incomes are also comparatively low: $25,000–30,000 in central cities in 1990, $25,000–40,000 in older suburbs, and $35,000–50,000 in low tax-base developing suburbs. Families in these communities are thus extremely sensitive to property tax increases. A third type of suburb is the high tax-base developing community. These affluent communities, with the region's highest median incomes, never amount to more than 30 percent of a region's population. They have all the benefits of a regional economy—access to labor and product markets, regionally built freeways and often airports—but are able to externalize the costs of social and economic need on the older suburbs and the central city.

Suburbs and cities can also be surprisingly diverse in their electoral results. Not all suburbs are Republican—or all cities Democratic. In Philadelphia, Republicans control almost all the suburbs and even the white working-class parts of the city. In Pittsburgh, Democrats control virtually all suburban seats except the highest property-wealth areas. In San Francisco, almost all suburbs are represented by Democrats, while in Los Angeles and Southern California, most of the white suburbs are represented by Republicans. In general, Democrats build their base in central cities, move to the older and low tax-base suburbs, and, if they are very effective, capture a few of the high tax-base suburbs. Republicans do just the opposite. In many states the balance of power rests on electoral contests in a few older suburbs or low tax-capacity developing suburbs.

Minnesota has been engaged in the politics of metropolitan regional reform for almost 40 years. Over the decades, three types of metropolitan coalitions have sought to move policy reforms through the state legislature. The first, a Republican-led bipartisan coalition, engaged in some bitter legislative fights; the second, a consensualist-led coalition, eschewed controversy; the third, a Democratic-driven bipartisan group, revived the real-world reform political style of their Republican predecessors. The following short history of metropolitanism in Minnesota suggests the complexity of coalition politics—and my own conviction that, while compromise and accommodation is the necessary essence of politics, regional reform, like all other real reform movements in U.S. history, necessarily involves some degree of controversy.

## The Progressive Republican Vanguard

In the 1960s and 1970s, metropolitan reform efforts in Minnesota's legislature were led by "good government" Rockefeller Republicans and reform Democrats—in a sense the progressives that Richard Hofstader wrote of in his *Age of Reform*. Joined by leaders of local corporations, they took aim at waste in government and set out to plan and shape a more cohesive, cost-effective, efficient, and equitable region. Though they sought rough metropolitan-wide equity in Minnesota's Twin Cities, they were not typical practitioners of class warfare. They valued equity because they knew from hard-headed calculation the costs of inequity and of destructive competition for development among municipalities in a single metropolitan region.

In some ways progressive Republican regionalism was an elegant, direct, limited-government response to growing sprawl and interlocal disparity. Joining Minnesota's Governor LeVander were Oregon's Tom McCall, Michigan's Miliken and Romney, and the great Republican mayor of Indianapolis, Richard Lugar. Had the country heeded their far-sighted strategy, the 1980s and 1990s might have been much different for the central cities and older suburbs.

In Minnesota the progressive Republicans and reform Democrats created regional sewer, transit, and airport authorities for the Twin Cities, as well as a Metropolitan Council of the Twin Cities with weak supervisory powers over these authorities. (Making the Met Council an elected body was a top goal, but it failed in a tie vote in 1967.) They also created a metropolitan land use planning framework and enacted Minnesota's famous tax-base sharing, or fiscal disparities, law, which, since 1971, has shared 40 percent of the growth of our commercial and industrial property tax base among the 187 cities, 49 school districts, and 7 counties in our region of some 2.5 million people.

The battle to pass the fiscal disparities act was brutal. Though the legislation, introduced in 1969, had its origins in the ethereal world of good government progressivism, its political managers were shrewd vote counters who made sure that two-thirds of the Twin City region's lawmakers understood that the bill would both lower their constituents' taxes and improve their schools and public services. Some of the progressives' key allies were populists who did not hesitate to play the class card with blue-collar voters in the low property-value suburbs. Probably not coincidentally, the populists collected most of the votes. The progressives pragmatically swallowed their compunctions.

The fiscal disparities bill that passed in 1971 was supported by a coalition of Democratic central-city legislators and Republicans from less wealthy suburbs—essentially the two-thirds of the region that received new tax base from the act. A few more rural Republicans who had a strong personal relationship with the bill's Republican sponsor went along. The opposition was also bipartisan—Democrats and Republicans representing areas in the one-third of the region that would lose some of their tax base. Debate over the bill was ugly. Republican Charlie Weaver, Sr., the bill's sponsor, was accused of fomenting "communism" and "community socialism" and of being a "Karl Marx" out to take from "the progressive communities to give to the backward ones." One opponent warned that "the fiscal disparities law will destroy the state." "Why should those who wish to work be forced to share with those who won't or can't help themselves?" demanded a representative of the high property-wealth areas. Amid growing controversy, after two divisive failed sessions, the bill would pass the Minnesota Senate by a single vote.

Not until 1975—after court challenges that went all the way to the U.S. Supreme Court (which refused to hear the case)—did the fiscal disparities law finally go into effect. The last legal challenge to the law came in 1981, a decade after passage. High property-wealth southern Twin Cities suburbs were finally rebuffed in the Minnesota Tax Court. But representatives and state senators from high property-wealth Twin Cities suburbs have tried to repeal the statute in virtually every legislative session for the past 25 years.

## A New Approach

The tough progressive reformers were followed by consensus-based regionalists whose preferred approach, it has often been joked, was to convene leaders from across metropolitan Twin Cities in the boardroom of a local bank to hum together the word "regionalism." Highly polished professional policy wonks, the new generation of leaders leaned more to touring the country extolling the virtues of regional reform, which many had no part in accomplishing, than to gritty work in city halls and the legislature to make it happen. To make matters worse, business support for regionalism began to erode. The rise of national and multinational companies created a cadre of rotating, frequently moving executives who, facing a more competitive business environment, eschewed controversy in favor of political action that would boost the bottom line.

By the 1980s, proponents of the regional perspective in Minnesota had dwindled to the chairman of the Citizens League, a local policy group financially supported by the region's big businesses; a half-dozen legislators; two or three executives of declining power; and the editorial board of the Minneapolis paper.

Meanwhile, some suburbs, particularly the high property-wealth developing ones that saw no gain but plenty of loss coming from metropolitan action, rebelled. Over the course of the 1980s, as the Twin Cities region rapidly became more like the rest of the nation—more racially and socially segregated—and as fundamental divisions hardened, those suburbs hired high-priced lobbyists and prepared for a fight to dismantle "regional socialism." Metropolitanism's opponents, tough and organized, began to control the regional debate.

During 1980–90, state lawmakers gradually dismantled the metropolitan authority that had been put in place in the 1960s and 1970s. They stripped the Met Council of its authority over major development projects: the downtown domed stadium, a new regional race track, and even the Mall of America—a local landmark that by its sheer size had a thunderous effect on the retail market in central Minneapolis and St. Paul and the southern suburbs. They severely weakened the land use planning statute by giving supercedence to local zoning. They also overturned the Met Council system of infrastructure pricing, abandoned a regional affordable housing system, and shelved well-conceived regional density guidelines. And they took a hard, well-financed run at the fiscal disparities system.

Sometimes the consensus-based regionalists would oppose the changes, but more often they seemed unable to stomach controversy. Their general response to the newly assertive high property-wealth suburbs was to seek accommodation. Meanwhile, developers in the high property-wealth suburbs and their lawyers obtained coveted seats on the Met Council itself.

The first generation of regionalists had fought bloody fights for land use planning, the consolidation of regional services, and tax equity. A decade later, the consensus-based regionalists were reduced to building regional citizenship through a proposal for a bus that looked like a trolley car to connect the state capital to downtown St. Paul. Times, and tactics, had clearly changed.

The proud legacy of the first-generation regionalists was in shambles. In 1967, the Twin Cities had created a regional transit system with a tax base that encompassed seven regional counties and 187 cities. By 1998, what had been one of the most financially broad-based transit systems in the nation was struggling with below-average funding per capita. The Met Council, now in thrall to developers, allocated virtually all federal resources to its large highway building program. Finally, the Citizens League and the consensus-based regionalists, perhaps to curry favor with the rebellious high property-wealth suburbs, used their influence both to defeat the development of a fixed-rail transit service and to fragment and privatize the transit system. By the early 1980s, the southwestern developing suburbs, the most prosperous parts of the region and those that benefited most from the development of a regional sewer and highway system, were allowed to "opt out" of funding the transit system that served the region's struggling core.

In 1991, the Met Council was on the verge of being abolished. A measure to eliminate the Council passed on the House floor, and the governor opined that the Council should either do something or disappear. The consensus-based regionalists, frustrated after a decade of difficulty, were not even grousing about legislative roadblocks. They had moved on to champion school choice and had joined the business community in an effort to cut comparatively high Minnesota business property taxes.

## The Third Generation

Out of this state of affairs emerged a new type of regionalist, of which I count myself one. Most of us were new to politics in the 1990s, and we were spurred to action by worrisome conditions in the Twin Cities, where concentrated poverty was growing—at the fourth fastest rate in the nation.

To address the growing concentration of poverty in the central cities, we began to investigate reforms, particularly in fair housing, at a metropolitan level. We began to wonder, in particular, whether the sprawl at the edge of the Twin Cities area was undermining the stability at the core and whether the older suburbs, adjacent to the city, were having equally serious problems. As we learned more about the region's problems, we came to appreciate the metropolitan structure that had been put in place 20 years before—a structure severely out of fashion and irrelevant in liberal circles. "What does land use planning in the suburbs have to do with us?" asked our central-city politicos. "We need more of a neighborhood-based strategy," they said. We were also received as fish out of water when we went to the Met Council and the Citizens League to discuss our regional concerns. "This is not what the Met Council is about," they said. "It is about land use planning and infrastructure, not about urban issues or poverty."

In addition to the concentration of poverty at the core, we grew interested in the subsidies and governmental actions supporting sprawl. We were inspired by the land use reforms in Oregon and the work of Governor Tom McCall, Henry Richmond, and 1,000 Friends of Oregon. We read the infrastructure work of Robert Burchell at Rutgers. We became aesthetically attached to New Urbanism and Peter Calthorpe, its proponent of metropolitan social equity and transit-oriented development.

Our third-wave regionalism gradually became broader based. We added environmentalism and the strength of the environmental movement to what had heretofore been a sterile discussion of planning and efficiency. We also brought issues of concentrated poverty and regional fair housing into an equity discussion that had previously been limited to interlocal fiscal equity. The dormant strength of the civil rights movement and social gospel also readied itself for metropolitan action and activism. In only a few years, hundreds of churches joined the movement for regional reform.

We also mobilized the rapidly declining, blue-collar suburbs—angry places unattached to either political party—to advance regional reform. Blue-collar mayors, a few with decidedly hostile views toward social and racial changes in their communities, united with African-American political leaders, environmentalists, and bishops of the major regional churches to advance a regional agenda for fair housing, land use planning, tax equity, and an accountable elected regional governance structure.

In fact, probably the most important element of the new regional coalition was the older, struggling, fully developed suburbs—the biggest prospective winners in regional reform. To them, tax-base sharing means lower property taxes and better services, particularly better-funded schools. Regional housing policy means, over time, fewer units of affordable housing crowding their doorstep. As one older-suburban mayor put it, "If those guys in the new suburbs don't start to build affordable housing, we'll be swimming in this stuff."

Winning over these suburbs was not easy. We had to overcome long-term, powerful resentments and distrust, based on class and race and fueled by every national political campaign since Hubert Humphrey lost the White House in 1968. But after two years of constant cajoling and courting and steady reminders of the growing inequities among the suburbs, the middle-income, working-class, blue-collar suburbs joined the central cities and created a coalition of great political clout in the legislature.

In 1994 this coalition of central-city and suburban legislators passed the Metropolitan Reorganization Act, which placed all regional sewer, transit, and land use planning under the operational authority of the Metropolitan Council of the Twin Cities. In doing so, it transformed the Met Council from a $40-million-a-year planning agency to a $600-million-a-year regional government operating regional sewers and transit, with supervisory authority over the major decisions of another $300-million-a-year agency that runs the regional airport. That same year, in the Metropolitan Land Use Reform Act, our coalition insulated metro-area farmers from public assessments that would have forced them to subdivide farm land for development.

In both 1993 and 1994 the legislature passed sweeping fair housing bills (both vetoed); in 1995 a weakened version was finally signed. In 1995 the legislature passed a measure that would have added a significant part of the residential property tax base to the fiscal disparities pool. While the measure passed strongly, it too was vetoed. In 1996 a statewide land use planning framework was adopted, and a regional brownfields fund created. Throughout the process, we restored to the Council many of the powers and prerogatives that had been removed from it during the 1980s in the areas of land use planning and infrastructure pricing. In each area of reform—land use planning, tax equity, and regional structural reform—we were initially opposed by the consensus-based regionalists as "too controversial," only to have our ideas adopted by them a few years later as the political center of gravity began to change.

## Worth Fighting For

Like all real reform, regional reform is a struggle. From the fight against municipal corruption and the fight against the trusts to the women's movement, the consumer movement, the environmental movement, and the civil rights movement, reform has involved difficult contests against entrenched interests who operated against the general welfare. Today, we are told that the Age of Reform is over. We are in an age of consensus politics, when calmer words— "collaboration," "boundary crossing," "win-win" strategies—carry more promise than "assertive" ones.

In every region of this nation, [roughly] 20–40 percent of the people live in central cities, 25–30 percent in older declining suburbs, and 10–15 percent in low tax-base developing suburbs. These communities, representing a clear majority of regional population, are being directly harmed by an inefficient, wasteful, unfair system. Studies indicate that the regions in the nation that have the least economic disparity have the strongest economic growth and those with most disparity are the weakest economically. The social polarization and wasteful sprawl that are common in our nation take opportunity from people and businesses, destroy cities and older suburbs, waste our economic bounty, and threaten our future.

Those who care about these problems must "assert" themselves to reverse these trends. We must engage in a politics that is free of personal attacks and sensationalism, that is conducted with a smile and good manners—like the progressives. At each roadblock, we must seek a compromise that moves equity forward, before we entrench unproductively. We must achieve the broadest possible level of good feeling, gather for our cause as many allies as we can from all walks of life and from all points of the compass. We must educate and persuade. However, if there are those who stand in our path utterly—who will permit no forward movement—we must fight. We must fight for the future of individuals, for the future of communities, and for the future of our country.

In the end, the goal is regional reform, not regional consensus.

# 23

## *David Rusk*

## GROWTH MANAGEMENT: THE CORE REGIONAL ISSUE

Urban sprawl is consuming land at almost three times the rate of population growth. On the threshold of the twenty-first century, the rate of outward expansion of low-density development is outstripping the ability of even the most annexation-minded central cities to keep pace. The leadership of almost all central cities (whether locked in like Cleveland or expansionist like Charlotte) faces a common challenge: defending their city's viability by controlling sprawl through regional growth management.

Regional growth management must also be a key target of the social justice movement in America. While barriers based purely on race are slowly coming down, barriers based on income are steadily rising in most metropolitan areas. Sprawling regional development patterns are closing off avenues of advancement for low-income minorities. Sprawl is leading to (1) greater dispersion of jobs, placing low-skilled jobs beyond the reach of many low-skilled potential workers; (2) growing fiscal disparities, which impair the quality of services in inner cities and older suburbs; and (3) greater concentrations of poverty, which have devastating impacts on the education of inner-city children.

Strong regional growth management practices, by themselves, will not be instant solutions for all these propblems. Growth management is the essential framework within which access to low-skilled jobs can improve, fiscal equity can be achieved, and greater economic integration can be promoted. The political coalitions necessary to secure, through state legislatures, effective regional growth management will also be the source of support for other policies (such as regional tax-base sharing or fair-share affordable housing) that can achieve greater social equity.

## Highways and Sprawl

Suburbanization has been a constant phenomenon in America, beginning with the first national census in 1790 that reported on the "suburbs" of Philadelphia.[1] America's urban experience has been a history of changes in transportation modes that constantly extended urban development outward from the core settlement. However, though suburbanization as we know it began in earnest with mass automobile ownership in the 1920s, it accelerated from the mid-1950s onward. Indeed, America's most influential urban planner may well have been President Dwight David Eisenhower.

In 1956 the Republican president convinced a Democratic Congress to launch the federal interstate highway system. In the midst of the cold war, the new law was styled the National Interstate and Defense Highway Act. In political myth, it was born out of young Major Eisenhower's experience in leading an army convoy coast to coast shortly after World War I—a journey of fifty-nine days!

From a vantage point four decades later, the interstate highway system has been militarily insignificant in our overcoming the Soviet Union. However, the interstate highway system has had a fateful impact on America's cities.

In order to build new interstate highways, federal highway appropriations were ratcheted up dramatically. In one decade, total federal highway outlays rose fivefold from $729 million (fiscal year 1956) to $4 billion (fiscal year 1966). By fiscal year 1996, the federal highway program had expended $652 billion (in 1996 dollars), compared to just $85 billion in federal mass transit aid (which was initiated in 1965).[2]

The great bulk of the 43,000-mile interstate system may be interurban—connecting different urban regions—but its primary impact has been *intra*urban—promoting low-density, sprawling development around core cities. With federal highway grants typically covering 90 percent of project cost, building sprawl-supporting highways was virtually cost-free for state governments. Other inducements to highway construction and sprawl were cheap gasoline (based on low federal and state taxes); easy, interest-deductible automobile loans; other federal infrastructure grants (such as $130 billion in wastewater treatment grants); and housing finance and tax systems that greatly favored homeowners over apartment dwellers.[3]

What picture emerges from calculating the growth of America's "urbanized areas" (as contrasted with the growth of county-defined metropolitan areas)? The 1950 census reported that 69 million people resided in 157 urbanized areas covering almost 13,000 square miles. By 1990 the population of these same 157 areas had grown to over 130 million people occupying almost 46,000 square miles. While urbanized population grew 88 percent, urbanized land expanded 255 percent (almost three times the rate of population growth). By 1990 the average resident of these 157 communities was consuming 90 percent more land area than just 40 years before.[4]

# Central Cities as Quasi-Regional Governments

Many political commentators and scholars may decry the absence of metropolitan government in America. However, at midcentury there was still an implicit system of quasi-regional governance in place in the great majority of America's metropolitan areas: the dominance of the central city that spread a de facto unity over its region. Almost 60 percent of the nation's metropolitan population lived in 193 central cities. Most area children attended the city school system. Most area residents used city parks and libraries. Most area workers rode city buses, streetcars, and subways to blue- and white-collar jobs within the city or occasionally, to nearby factories just outside the city limits. Most of the region's voters cast their ballots for the same set of local offices. Although there were often fierce rivalries among ethnic and racial groups, city-based public institutions were unifying forces (except in the legally segregated South with its sets of parallel institutions).

Annexation and merger, of course, were the tools of municipal expansion, and they had been used by even the oldest American cities in their youth. In the nineteenth century, Boston grew from the compact, colonial port town that was besieged by General Washington's rebel forces from Dorchester Heights to a metropolis of 48 square miles. In the process Boston not only absorbed Dorchester Heights itself but the city of Roxbury (1867) and, leaping Boston Harbor in 1874, the city of Charlestown as well.[5]

In one afternoon in 1854, by act of the Pennsylvania General Assembly, the city of Philadelphia grew twentyfold in territory, filling all of Philadelphia County. In the process five of the nation's most populous cities disappeared: Spring Garden (ninth), Northern Liberties (eleventh), Kensington (twelfth), Southwark (twentieth), and Moyamensing (twenty-eighth).

In 1897 the New York General Assembly enacted the most ambitious restructuring of regional governance yet. The state legislature abolished the cities of New York and Brooklyn (the nation's first and seventh most populous cities), combined them with three largely rural counties (Queens, Richmond, and Bronx), and created the 315-square-mile New York City, the nation's first metropolitan government.

By the mid-twentieth century, of course, the territorial expansions of Boston, Philadelphia, and New York were history (and largely forgotten history, at that). In fact, throughout New England, New York, New Jersey, and Pennsylvania, the political boundaries of 6,236 cities, boroughs, villages, towns, and townships were set in concrete. On the threshold of accelerated urban sprawl, the Northeast had become a region of "inelastic" cities.[6]

Growing territorial inflexibility was also settling in over much of the Middle West, which through the Continental Congress's enactment of the Land Act of 1785 had inherited New England's pattern of township government. State laws might provide for municipal annexation, but cordons sanitaires of incorporated suburbs already surrounded many cities, such as Detroit and Cleveland. Throughout the Middle West, townships hastened to incorporate as independent municipalities as to avoid annexation. After 1950 Chicago would succeed only in annexing twenty square miles for the new O'Hare Airport.

## Annexation Versus Highways

At midcentury, central-city officials in regions other than the Northeast or Middle West could reasonably anticipate that annexation and mergers would continue to maintain their "elastic" city status as near-regional governments. They

**Table 7.1** *Territorial Growth of the USA's 50 Most Elastic Cities, 1960–90*
Square miles unless otherwise specified

| City[a] | Area | | | |
|---|---|---|---|---|
| | 1960 | 1990 | Increase | Percent increase |
| Albuquerque | 56 | 132 | 76 | 135 |
| Anchorage-Anchorage | 13 | 1,698 | 1,685 | 13,482 |
| Austin | 50 | 218 | 168 | 339 |
| Bakersfield | 16 | 92 | 76 | 474 |
| Birmingham | 75 | 149 | 74 | 99 |
| Charlotte | 65 | 174 | 110 | 169 |
| Chattanooga | 37 | 118 | 82 | 223 |
| Colorado Springs | 17 | 183 | 167 | 997 |
| Columbus | 89 | 191 | 102 | 114 |
| Columbus-Muskogee | 26 | 216 | 190 | 719 |
| Corpus Christi | 38 | 135 | 97 | 257 |
| Dallas | 280 | 342 | 63 | 22 |
| Denver | 71 | 153 | 82 | 116 |
| Durham | 22 | 69 | 47 | 215 |
| Fort Worth | 141 | 281 | 141 | 100 |
| Fresno | 29 | 99 | 71 | 247 |
| Houston | 328 | 540 | 212 | 65 |
| Huntsville | 51 | 164 | 114 | 224 |
| Indianapolis-Marion | 71 | 362 | 291 | 408 |
| Jackson | 47 | 109 | 63 | 134 |
| Jacksonville-Duval | 30 | 759 | 729 | 2,412 |
| Kansas City | 130 | 312 | 182 | 140 |
| Knoxville | 25 | 77 | 52 | 204 |
| Las Vegas | 25 | 83 | 59 | 237 |

*continued*

often had other tools available to shape development patterns. Many cities owned and operated regional water and sewage treatment systems; some exercised extraterritorial planning jurisdiction. With such powers, most southern and western cities expected to successfully maintain their "market share" of regional development.

By the 1990s, they had been proven wrong. The highway system decentralized America's metropolitan areas so rapidly and relentlessly that almost no city's annexation or merger efforts were able to keep pace.

Table 7.1 charts the territorial growth of the country's fifty most annexation-minded central cities from 1960 to 1990. Each added at least forty-six square miles to its municipal jurisdiction—an area equal to the city of Boston or the city of San Francisco. City-county consolidation was the mechanism for most of the largest expansions: Nashville-Davidson (1964), Jacksonville-Duval (1968), Indianapolis-Marion (1970), Lexington-Fayette (1973), and

**Table 7.1 (continued)** *Territorial Growth of the USA's 50 Most Elastic Cities, 1960–90*
Square miles unless otherwise specified

| City[a] | Area | | | Percent increase |
|---|---|---|---|---|
| | 1960 | 1990 | Increase | |
| Lexington-Fayette | 13 | 285 | 272 | 2088 |
| Little Rock | 28 | 103 | 75 | 264 |
| Memphis | 128 | 256 | 128 | 100 |
| Montgomery | 32 | 135 | 103 | 325 |
| Nashville-Davidson | 29 | 473 | 444 | 1532 |
| Oklahoma City | 322 | 608 | 287 | 89 |
| Omaha | 51 | 101 | 50 | 97 |
| Orlando | 21 | 67 | 46 | 219 |
| Phoenix | 187 | 420 | 233 | 124 |
| Portland | 67 | 125 | 58 | 86 |
| Raleigh | 34 | 88 | 55 | 163 |
| Reno | 12 | 58 | 46 | 387 |
| Sacramento | 45 | 96 | 51 | 114 |
| Salt Lake City | 56 | 109 | 53 | 94 |
| San Antonio | 161 | 333 | 173 | 107 |
| San Diego | 192 | 324 | 132 | 68 |
| San Jose | 55 | 171 | 117 | 214 |
| Shreveport | 36 | 99 | 63 | 174 |
| Tallahassee | 15 | 63 | 48 | 316 |
| Tucson | 71 | 156 | 85 | 120 |
| Tulsa | 48 | 184 | 136 | 284 |
| Wichita | 52 | 115 | 63 | 122 |
| Total | 3,383 | 11,025 | 7,642 | 226 |

*Sources:* Author's calculations based on census reports.
a. Hyphenation indicates city-county consolidation.

Columbus (Georgia)-Muskogee (1977). The champion of territorial imperialists was Anchorage, which by merging with Anchorage Borough in the mid-1960s ballooned from 13 square miles to 1,698 square miles.[7] Oklahoma City, Phoenix, and Houston annexed the most territory by conventional means. Collectively, the fifty cities more than tripled their municipal territory in three decades.

## Running Hard but Falling Behind

Most of these fifty cities still lost market share of regional growth. . . . As a group, despite tripling their municipal territory, the percentage of the regions' urbanized populations that were city residents dropped from 65 percent in

1960 to 51 percent in 1990. The cities' share of metropolitan population de-clined more precipitously, from 60 percent in 1960 to 43 percent in 1990.

Over the three decades, only nine cities—Anchorage, Jacksonville, Nashville, Lexington, Columbus (Georgia), Colorado Springs, San Jose, Bakersfield, and Fresno—increased their market shares of both urbanized and metropolitan popu-lations. However, the high-water mark for the consolidated jurisdictions' market shares typically occurred at the moment of the city-county mergers. During the 1980s, for example, Jacksonville, Nashville, Lexington, and Columbus experi-enced slower population growth than surrounding counties.

Even though these fifty most annexation-oriented cities are slowly losing ground in the face of accelerating urban sprawl, there is still strong justification for continued annexation. As suburban subdivisions are built around central cities, elastic cities are able to absorb some of that growth within their expand-ing municipal boundaries. By capturing shares of new, middle-class subdivi-sions, elastic cities maintain greater socioeconomic balance. Average incomes of residents in elastic cities are typically equal to or even higher than average incomes of suburban residents. Tapping broad, growing tax bases, elastic-city governments are better financed and more able to rely on local resources to address local problems. Although no community is free of racial in-equities, minorities are more evenly spread out within the "big boxes" of elastic cities. Segregation by race and income class is reduced.

By contrast, "inelastic" central cities are frozen within fixed city limits and surrounded by growing, independent suburbs. By the 1990s, the downtown business districts of many inelastic cities may have revived as regional em-ployment and entertainment centers, but most inelastic-city neighborhoods are increasingly catch basins for poor blacks and Hispanics. With the flight of middle-class families, inelastic cities' populations have dropped steadily (typically by one-quarter to one-half). The income gap between city residents and suburbanites steadily widens. Governments of inelastic cities are squeezed between rising service needs and eroding tax bases. Unable to tap areas of greater economic growth (their independent suburbs), inelastic-city govern-ments rely increasingly on federal and state aid. Suburban areas around inelas-tic cities are typically fragmented into many "little boxes"—multiple smaller cities and towns and "mini" school systems. With, at best, a heritage of exclu-sionary practices or, at worst, continuing practice of such policies, the frag-mented governmental structure of these little-box regions reinforces racial and economic segregation.

## Big Boxes Versus Little Boxes

A comparison of the very elastic cities with twenty-three "zero-elastic" cities il-lustrates these characterizations (Table 7.2). As a group, in four decades (1950–90), these twenty-three zero-elastic cities expanded their municipal areas by an average of only 3 percent—in sharp contrast to the very elastic cities' record of more than tripling their municipal areas in just three decades (1960–90).

By the 1990 census, the average income of zero-elastic city residents had fallen to 66 percent of suburban levels, while the average income of residents in very elastic cities was 91 percent of suburban levels. Zero-elastic cities averaged lower bond ratings (A) than highly elastic cities (AA).

In 1990, by a common demographic measure, African Americans were much more segregated within the metropolitan housing markets in zero-elastic core cities (an index of 74) than within metropolitan housing markets in highly elastic core cities (an index of 53).[8] For the 1989–1990 school year, the school segregation index matched segregated housing patterns in the zero-elastic regions (74 for both indexes), whereas schools were significantly less segregated (an index of 46) than neighborhoods (an index of 53) in the highly elastic regions. Finally, poor households living in zero-elastic regions were more likely to be segregated away from middle-class households (an index of 42) than those residing in highly elastic regions (an index of 31).[9]

## Governance Structure Counts

A clear regional trend appears when the two groups of metropolitan areas are compared. Of the fifty very elastic cities, all but Indianapolis and Columbus (Ohio) are located in the South and West, while all twenty-three of the zero-elastic cities are in the Northeast and Middle West, except Baltimore, Washington D.C., St. Louis, and San Francisco.[10]

**Table 7.2  Comparing Socioeconomic and Fiscal Health of 23 Zero-Elastic Cities and 50 Very Elastic Cities and Their Respective Metropolitan Areas**

| Criteria | Zero-Elastic Cities/Metro Areas[a] | Highly Elastic Cities/Metro Areas |
|---|---|---|
| Income of city residents as a percentage of suburban income (1989) | 66 | 91 |
| City bond rating (1993)[b] | A | AA |
| Metropolitan Segregation Index[c] | | |
| Housing (1990) | 74 | 53 |
| Schools (1990) | 74 | 46 |
| Poor households (1989) | 42 | 31 |

*Sources:* Author's calculations based on census reports.

a. Zero-elastic cities are New York, Newark, Paterson, Boston, St. Louis, Providence, Detroit, Washington, D.C., Pittsburgh, Cleveland, Baltimore, Hartford, Minneapolis, Rochester, Syracuse, Jersey City, New Haven, Chicago, San Francisco, Philadelphia, Buffalo, Bridgeport, and Cincinnati.

b. Bond ratings are those assigned by Moody's investor Services in their 1991 Municipal Data Book.

c. For segregation indexes, 100 = total segregation.

However, the proceeding discussion on racial and economic segregation is not just a disguised way of describing Rust Belt versus Sun Belt sectional differences. Within an urban region, how local governance is organized has an impact on issues of social mobility.

The clearest impact is on school segregation. In the decades after the U.S. Supreme Court declared segregated schools unconstitutional, school desegregation suits were brought in both southern and northern courts. Southern states (such as Florida, North Carolina, and Tennessee) tend to have big-box school districts that often are countywide. Court-ordered school desegregation plans integrated schools not just within elastic central cities but across city boundaries into the central county's suburban areas.

In the North, however, little-box school districts mirror little-box city, village, and town governments. In its 1974 decision *Milliken v. Bradley,* the U.S. Supreme Court ruled that suburban school districts would not be required to participate with central-city districts in school desegregation plans unless it could be shown that state action had brought about such segregation. With white, middle-class anxiety about local schools intensifying the lure of new suburban homes, central-city school districts like Cleveland, Rochester, and Minneapolis were left to integrate systems that rapidly became heavily minority enrollment districts.

For example, with 115 independent suburban systems, metropolitan Detroit has the nation's most racially segregated public school systems. It is the unspoken mission of many little school boards to "keep our schools just the way they are for children just like ours"—whoever "our children" happen to be. That mission is more readily achieved with 115 separate school districts empowered to erect walls around themselves—a pattern repeated over and over again in little-box regions.

"Keeping our town just the way it is for people just like us"—whoever "us" happens to be—has also been the mantra of suburban town councils and planning commissions in little-box regions. Exclusionary zoning policies reign. By contrast, because planning commissions and city councils of big-box governments are accountable to more diverse constituencies, they are less likely to implement policies that divide residents as rigorously by income, with the attendant consequences for racial and ethnic segregation.

In the 1990s, southern metropolitan areas are less racially segregated than northern metropolitan areas, but not primarily because "black and white Southerners always lived closer together than Northerners did." That conventional wisdom doesn't stand up very well to historical analysis. In 1970 the average residential segregation index for eighteen major northern metropolitan areas (including San Francisco-Oakland and Los Angeles) was 85 compared to an average index of 79 for fourteen major southern metropolitan areas—hardly a major difference. By 1990 the northern average had edged down 7 points to 78, but the southern average had dropped 15 points to 64.[11] It is the dyanmics of housing markets within big-box central cities, reinforced by public school integration policies (and generally growing regional economies), that largely account for the greater pace of residential desegregation in the South.

Maintaining central-city elasticity is important both for the city's economic and fiscal health and for the region's social health. Wherever cities still have annexation powers, they should use them prudently. Whenever state legislatures or local voters can be persuaded to approve city-county consolidations, the effort should be made.[12]

However, even the most elastic central cities cannot hope to maintain their traditional role as quasi-regional governments that largely control regional development. Annexation strategies have been overwhelmed by the sprawl-inducing effect of the federal interstate highway system and the networks of state highways supporting it.

For example, Charlotte, North Carolina, has carried out successfully one of the most sustained annexation programs. From 1950 to 1996, Charlotte expanded from 30 square miles to 225 square miles. In the process Charlotte captured 83 percent of all population growth within Mecklenburg County, the boundary of its 1950 metropolitan area. However, in those same decades, Charlotte's actual metropolitan area expanded beyond Mecklenburg County to embrace seven counties and fifty municipalities covering 3,700 square miles in two states. Charlotte can no longer call the regional development tune. The Queen City must negotiate transportation and land-use issues with other local (and independent) governments.

If Charlotte could not annex new development fast enough to maintain regional hegemony, no elastic city can. Elastic cities of the South and West now face the same phenomenon of sprawling development beyond their grasp that in earlier decades victimized inelastic cities of the Northeast and Middle West.

# The Regional Agenda

Don Hutchinson, president of the Greater Baltimore Committee, the area's regional business leadership organization, laid out the regional challenge most succinctly. "If regionalism isn't dealing with land-use, fiscal disparities, housing, and education," the former Baltimore County executive stated, "then regionalism isn't dealing with the issues that count."

In pursuit of that philosophy, in July 1997 the Greater Baltimore Committee issued a policy statement, *One Region, One Future*, that urged adoption of three major initiatives:

—Regional growth management policies that lead to redevelopment and reinvestment in older neighborhoods and reduce the infrastructure costs to the governments and taxpayers of the region.

—Policies that result in a system of tax-base sharing in the region. Any system should focus on the growth in the tax base and could draw upon a number of different models that have been adopted across the country.

—A policy for developing affordable housing throughout the metropolitan area. A key goal of this policy should be to avoid creating concentrations of people living in poverty.[13]

Baltimore's *One Region, One Future* is a policy statement that should serve as a model for business leadership in all metropolitan areas.

# Land Use: The Key Issue

Land-use planning is the pivotal issue. Fiscal disparities, lack of affordable housing, and poor public schools all reflect uneven regional development patterns.

Fiscal disparities arise as new subdivisions, commercial areas, and office parks lead to devaluation and abandonment of older property. Wide fiscal disparities typically emerge most virulently in little-box regions where central cities and suburban jurisdictions alike have fixed jurisdictional boundaries. Elastic cities do not suffer from fiscal disparities. Indeed, elastic cities act as an internal revenue-sharing mechanism, taxing wealthier city neighborhoods to maintain adequate service levels in poorer city neighborhoods. (Highly elastic cities such as Charlotte, Lexington, and Albuquerque annex so much high-end new development that they are wealthier than their suburban neighbors.)

Growing economic segregation in most metropolitan housing markets is a reflection of postwar development patterns. Cities always have had richer and poorer neighborhoods. However, many older city neighborhoods contain a greater variety of housing types than typical postwar suburban subdivisions. As a result, many city neighborhoods contain households that range widely in income.

The greater economic homogeneity of suburban subdivisions partly reflects the fact that homebuilding has changed from a retail industry to a wholesale industry. Postwar homebuilders have learned to apply factory-like production techniques to building sites. Specialized crews (foundation layers, framers, plumbing and electrical installers, sheetrock hangers, roofers) move from site to site with factory-like precision. The result is that, within a given subdivision, a builder will erect large numbers of similar homes priced for a relatively narrow band of potential homebuyers.

Suburban planning and zoning policies often magnify the effect of such industry practices. By setting large minimum lot sizes, limiting the location of (or banning outright) townhouse complexes, apartments, and mobile home parks, local governments encourage economic segregation.

In too many urban regions, where a child lives largely determines the quality of the child's school experience. The problem is not primarily fiscal disparities among different local school districts—the target of many education reformers. The core issue is that a child's school performance is heavily influenced by the socioeconomic status of the child's family and classmates. For example, in communities across the country, 65 to 85 percent of the school-by-school variation in standardized test scores is explained by variations in the school-by-school percentage of low-income students.[14] The most effective education reform for improving poor children's school performance would actually be housing reform: mixed-income housing policies that integrate poor children into middle-class neighborhoods and middle-class neighborhood schools.

# Target: New State Growth Management Laws

Growth management is rapidly emerging as the top regional issue of the next decade. There are two key targets: state legislatures, which control land-use rules, and federally required metropolitan planning organizations, which shape the allocation of federal transportation grants.

There are only twelve states that have enacted statewide growth management laws. They vary in effectiveness from strong (Oregon) to almost purely exhortatory (Georgia). In 1999, however, the Georgia legislature created a powerful Georgia Regional Transportation Agency to take charge of transportation and land-use decisions in sprawl-choked metropolitan Atlanta.

The two most recent state land-use reform laws have been adopted in Maryland (1977) and Tennessee (1998). Maryland governor Parris Glendening's Smart Growth Act strengthens a weak state planning law adopted in 1993. The Smart Growth Act ostensibly does not place new mandates on local planning, which is controlled almost entirely by county governments in Maryland. However, it restricts state highway, sewage treatment, and other infrastructure grants (and the federal grants they match) to established urban areas.

Tennessee's new state planning law popped forth virtually unnoticed by growth management advocates nationally. It had an unconventional origin—an obscure amendment to another Tennessee law that was adopted by voice vote in the waning minutes of the 1997 legislative session. To the Tennessee Municipal League's consternation, the stealth amendment suspended Tennessee's annexation laws for one year, wiping out existing cities' powers to veto the incorporation of new municipalities within five miles of their city limits. To ensure against annexation, proposals to incorporate mini-municipalities (dubbed "toy towns" by opponents) sprang up like weeds. By the time the Tennessee Supreme Court declared that the amendment was unconstitutionally adopted by the legislature, residents of unincorporated areas had initiated proceedings to create forty-four toy towns (including one that was simply a condominium apartment building near Knoxville).

During the heated controversy, Tennessee's speaker of the house and the lieutenant governor (the presiding officer of the state senate who had created the stealth amendment) appointed a broad-based commission to review the state's annexation laws. Under the urging of the Tennessee Advisory Commission on Intergovernmental Relations, the commission expanded its mission to consider the broader need for regional land-use planning.

The result was enactment of the Annexation Reform Act of 1998—a title that reflects the law's origins but not its broad scope. Through a complex process, the new law requires counties to adopt comprehensive land-use plans. The plans must designate urban growth boundaries for existing municipalities (which will also be their twenty-year annexation reserve areas), rural preservation areas, and "planned growth areas" (which may allow some "new town" development).

Though undoubtedly not as rigorous a growth management directive as Oregon's law, the new Tennessee law has real teeth. Counties that fail to adopt a comprehensive land-use plan by July 2001 will no longer be eligible for a long list of state infrastructure funds, including participation in federal highway grants.

# New Allies

Tennessee's new growth management law may have been born under unique circumstances, but there is growing public pressure for antisprawl legislation developing in many states, particularly in the Middle West, where no state has yet adopted a statewide growth management law. New recruits to the legislative struggle—business leaders, church coalitions, and inner-suburb mayors—are joining forces with environmentalists and farmland preservationists, growth management's more traditional advocates. Some key examples:

—A new association of business leadership groups in Pennsylvania, the Coalition of Mid-Sized Cities, has targeted enactment of a smart-growth, antisprawl law as its top priority.

—In Missouri a coalition of eighty churches—Protestant and Catholic, black and white, city and inner suburb—is lobbying for a new state growth management law for Greater St. Louis.

—In Ohio the recently established First Suburbs Consortium, initially formed by ten suburban mayors from communities around Cleveland, told the Governor's Task Force on Agricultural Preservation in 1997 that a strong state land-use law might be desirable to save farmland, but it was essential for the survival of older suburban communities.

"Since the late 1940's, policies have consistently encouraged the abandonment of boroughs and cities in Pennsylvania, and discouraged the redevelopment of existing neighborhoods and established commercial and industrial sites," explains Tom Wolf, president of Better York, owner of a multistate chain of builders' supply yards, and a leader of the Coalition of Mid-Sized Cities.[15] In addition to Better York, the coalition includes a dozen business groups such as the Lehigh Valley Partnership, Lancaster Alliance, and Erie Conference on Community Development.

"In the end, no one wins in a system that makes prosperity a temporary and fleeting phenomenon," Wolf continues. "No one wins in a system that has already condemned our cities and older boroughs to economic stagnation and decline. And no one wins in a system that ultimately threatens to do the same thing to our townships. The point is that public policies that encourage sprawl are neither smart nor right.

"We need to change the rules of the game," Wolf concludes. "Most of all we need to change the rules governing land-use planning.". . .

# Land-Use Planning: The Portland Model

Across the continent, business and civic delegations, state and local politicians, and professional planners are flocking to Portland to see the practical results of nearly twenty-five years of operating under different rules of the game. In 1973 the Oregon legislature enacted the Statewide Land Use Law. It required that urban growth boundaries be drawn around cities throughout the state. Portland Metro, the nation's only directly elected regional government, is responsible for land-use and transportation planning in the 1.5-million-person metropolitan area. Anticipating a 50 percent growth of population over the next forty-five years, in November 1997 the Portland Metro Council voted 5–2 to add less than 8 square miles to Portland's existing 342-square-mile urban growth boundary. (The two dissenting votes felt the expansion was too little.)

Opposition to greater expansion was led by many local officials, like Mayor Gussie McRobert of suburban Gresham, as well as by many environmentally concerned citizens. Portland's urban growth boundary has succeeded in protecting farmland in Oregon's rich Willamette Valley. If the Metro Council sticks to its plans, over the next forty-five years, only about four square miles of current farmland will be urbanized—as much farmland as is subdivided in the state of Michigan every ten days.[16]

A big bonus is that shutting down suburban sprawl has turned new private investment back inward into existing neighborhoods and retail areas. Mayor McRobert's Gresham as well as Milwaukie, Oregon City, and other older suburbs are booming. Property values in Albina, Portland's poorest neighborhood, doubled in just five years. As Metro councilor Ed Washington, whose District 6 includes Albina, explained his vote for the small boundary expansion, "We are having redevelopment in my district for the first time in forty years; we don't want to lose it."

By the mid-1990s, Portland's economy had become superheated by a high-tech investment boom. With $13 billion in new, high-tech construction underway, workers flocked to the Portland area. From 1990 to 1996, the Portland area's population grew 16 percent, putting extreme pressure on the housing supply. Housing prices shot up 60 percent, and many area homebuilders and other allies launched a campaign against the region's tight land-use controls.[17]

In the midst of an affordable-housing crisis, the Metro Council adopted a wide-ranging package of regulatory actions and incentives to increase the production of affordable housing. A tough, mandatory inclusionary zoning ordinance (patterned on the successful program in Montgomery County, Maryland)[18] was deferred after several legal challenges before the state Land Conservation and Development Commission that regulates local growth management.

## Citizen Accountability: The Portland Model

Portland Metro is the joint creation of both the Oregon legislature (1979) and local citizens (through three separate referenda, including adoption of a home rule charter for Portland Metro in 1992). Covering three counties and twenty-four municipalities, Portland Metro is responsible for regional solid waste disposal, regional air and water quality, the regional zoo, and the Oregon Convention Center. In the new home rule charter, the area's citizens affirmed that long-range planning is Metro's "primary" function. Metro's long-range planning function includes responsibility for both land-use and transportation planning.

Portland area citizens know where the crucial decisions affecting the future of their region are made: Metro. They know when and how such decisions will be made: in well-advertised public meetings after extensive public hearings. (In revising the Portland 2040 plan, Metro held 182 public hearings and presentations.) And citizens know who will make the decisions: the seven Metro councilors and Metro chief executive who are directly elected by the region's citizens. Land-use and transportation decisions are the issues that dominate political campaigns for Metro's elected offices. The result is that there is a much higher level of knowledgeable citizen engagement in regional planning issues in the Portland area than in any other regional community in the United States.

# Transforming Metropolitan Planning Organizations

A Republican-controlled Congress dominated by self-anointed "conservatives" enacted in 1998 a $217 billion Transportation Efficiency Act (TEA-21). The country is poised for another massive round of federal transportation spending. Over the next six years, the federal government will spend almost one-third as much for highway and transit construction as was spent in the previous four decades. How this new generation of transportation investments will affect the growth and shape of America's urban areas will be determined largely by metropolitan planning organizations (MPOs).

For decades, deciding how federal transportation funds would be used was primarily the province of the Federal Highway Administration and state highway departments. That changed with the Intermodal Service Transportation Efficiency Act of 1991 (ISTEA). In the judgment of the National Association of Regional Councils, ISTEA "marked a radical and visionary transformation of the nation's transportation policy."[19]

Prior to ISTEA, local planning input was largely limited to prioritizing laundry lists of projects within narrow, federally prescribed program allocations. Under ISTEA, MPOs for all urbanized areas with at least 200,000 residents acquired broad discretion to allocate lump-sum federal funds among road, bridge, and transit projects.

About half of all MPOs are "regional councils," voluntary consortia of local governments with a variety of interests beyond transportation planning. Other MPOs are regional economic development organizations, transportation planning agencies, and arms of state highway departments.

In the years since ISTEA was enacted, most MPOs have not had as "radical" and "transforming" an impact as the National Association of Regional Councils originally anticipated. However, transportation planning certainly has acquired a much more local flavor. Had the MPO structure been eliminated (as several key congressional powers proposed), TEA-21 would have dealt a massive blow to the cause of regional planning; instead, TEA-21 will provide continued impetus to the evolution of regional land-use planning.

There has been a uniquely American asymmetry about the relationship between land-use planning and transportation planning. It is inconceivable that a land-use plan could largely ignore an area's network of roads and highways, yet transportation plans often have been developed as if they dealt only with transportation problems.

However, transportation decisions *are* land-development decisions. Who can doubt today that the primary impact of interstate beltways was not to route interstate traffic swiftly and conveniently around major cities (as originally justified) but was rather to generate major suburban commercial, industrial, and residential development? In urban areas the great majority of interstate highway users are local-origin cars and trucks.

Metropolitan planning organizations are federated bodies. Their boards are composed of individuals appointed by member governments and agencies. This raises two problems for organizations faced with increasingly tough, important decisions.

First, the primary loyalty of most board members is to their home jurisdictions. This is particularly true of local elected officials serving on MPO boards (who usually constitute all or a majority of board members). This makes it difficult to achieve an overall regional perspective. Second, federated boards can rarely survive judicial scrutiny when challenged under the "one person, one vote" standard.

# Precedents for Elected Regional Organizations

Very limited precedents suggest that voluntary regional structures like MPOs will evolve into limited-purpose regional governments directly elected by the region's citizens. Portland Metro began as the Metropolitan Services District, with a seven-member federated board of local elected officials—one each from the city of Portland and Clackamas, Multnomah, and Washington counties and three representing other cities in each of the three counties. A parallel organization, the Columbia Region Association of Governments (CRAG), started as a federated board of representatives from four counties and fourteen cities and grew to represent five counties and thirty-one cities. As one observer noted, "The difficulty in building consensus around a [comprehensive regional land-use plan] reflected a fundamental tension in using the council of governments model to develop regional policies. . . . [CRAG board members] were often torn between the imperatives of regional issues and the need to protect their own community from unwanted costs, programs, or development initiatives."[20]

In 1977 the Oregon legislature abolished CRAG, assigned its regional planning responsibilities to the Metropolitan Services District, and authorized replacing the federated, appointed board with a directly elected twelve-member council and elected chief executive. In 1978 the Portland area electorate approved the changes. (The voters reduced council membership from twelve to seven and renamed the organization "Portland Metro" when the home rule charter was adopted in 1992.)

During the postwar years, another regional organization had evolved in the Seattle metropolitan area. Seattle Metro was a well-respected regional wastewater and transit authority governed by a federated board. By 1992, however, with the growth of region's population, the Metro Council had grown from its original sixteen members to forty-five.

Controversy increasingly revolved around the makeup and power of the federated Metro Council. After a dozen abortive efforts by the state legislature to reorganize Metro, the debate took a decisive turn in 1990 when a federal district judge ruled that the Metro Council's federated structure violated the constitutional one-person, one-vote guarantee. After further local controversy, legislative debate, and missed court deadlines, Metro Council members proposed merging Metro into King County government. Under the merger proposal approved by voters in November 1992, a single legislative body—the Metropolitan County Council—replaced the King County and Metro Councils, in effect expanding the King County Council from nine to thirteen members elected by district.

To give cities "a voice and a vote" in developing countywide comprehensive planning policies, three new bodies were mandated in a charter amendment to the King County charter: the Regional Transit Committee, Regional Water Quality Committee, and Regional Policy Committee. Each committee has twelve voting members: six Metro County Council members and six members divided between Seattle and suburban cities. The Metro County Council is the only body that is legally empowered to enact plans and policies. However, the County Council can override a regional committee recommendation only if at least eight of the thirteen council members agree. Otherwise, a regional committee's recommendations automatically become law.

A third nationally recognized regional body—the Twin Cities Metropolitan Council—is on the brink of passing from appointed to elected status. Since its legislative creation in 1967, the "Met Council" has been governed by a seventeen-member board appointed by Minnesota's governor. Although members are residents of sixteen districts into which its seven-county jurisdiction is divided, they and their full-time chairman are, in practice, accountable to the governor that appointed them, not to their neighbors. The Met Council functions like another state agency.

For three decades the Met Council carried out land-use planning functions and exercised loose oversight over three regional wastewater and transit agencies. The regional agencies, however, pursued increasingly independent directions. In 1994, seeking greater regional unity, the Minnesota legislature abolished the three agencies and placed their functions directly under the Met Council. The Metropolitan Reorganization Act transformed the Met Council from a planning body with loose supervisory control into an operational agency with a budget of more than $400 million and supervisory control over the $300 million Metropolitan Airports Commission. "After Hennepin County," noted state representative Myron Orfield, leader of the legislature's regional reform bloc, "the Met Council was Minnesota's second largest unit of government in terms of budget, and perhaps its most significant in terms of authority."[21]

A regional public agency with so much authority and spending so many tax dollars, Orfield and other colleagues argued, ought to be directly accountable to the citizens of the region. A bill to convert membership on the Met Council from gubernatorial appointment to direct election was defeated narrowly in the 1996 legislative session but passed in 1997, only to be vetoed by the governor. There are strong prospects that a similar bill will pass and become law in the near future.

# Dealing with the Regional Issues That Count

The growing political support for state land-use planning laws and the increasing level of federal transportation grants are leading in the same direction: the evolution of stronger regional planning organizations. In some states existing regional planning organizations are likely to have their planning authority extended into housing policy, regional revenue sharing, and economic development policy. Some may also become vehicles for management of regionwide infrastructure programs formerly carried out by independent authorities.

I would like to offer some crystal ball gazing. Though there is little pragmatic evidence to date, I believe that as regional organizations become more operationally significant and the impact of their planning decisions becomes better understood, public demand may convert some of them into directly elected rather than appointed bodies.

Thus in coming decades, directly elected metropolitan governments are likely to evolve in a growing number of regions. They will not be unitary governments. (Anchorage is the country's only such example covering an entire metropolitan area.) They will not replace the mosaic of local governments as primary providers of local services. Their powers will appear limited but will be vitally important, since they will affect regional land-use and transportation planning, affordable housing, fiscal disparities, and major regional infrastructure investments—the "outside game." These evolving metropolitan governments will deal with the issues that count for the wealth and health of regions and the future of their central cities.

## NOTES

1. Unless otherwise noted, all data in this article are drawn from the author's calculations based on various decennial census reports; Department of Commerce, *Statistical Abstract of the United States,* various editions; and Department of Commerce, *Historical Statistics of the United States: Colonial Times to 1970 (1975).*
2. Executive Office of the President, *Budget of the United States Government, Historical Tables for Fiscal Year 1996,* table 8.7.

3. The outstanding value of all federally aided home mortgages (including Fannie Mae and Freddie Mac's portfolios) was $2.5 trillion in 1995. By contrast, the annual direct federal appropriation for rental housing assistance for low-income households was $26 billion. In 1996 the federal tax code provided $94 billion in tax incentives for homeowners compared to less than $9 billion in tax incentives for investors in rental properties.

4. Over the next three decades, the census recognized another 239 urbanized areas. By 1990, 396 urbanized areas contained 61,000 square miles of urbanized land—about 2 percent of our land mass.

5. By the centennial of the American Revolution, the site of the Battle of Bunker Hill (that is, Breed's Hill) and all other major landmarks of the siege of Boston lay well with Boston's city limits.

6. "Elastic cities" expand their boundaries through annexation or, more rarely, city-county consolidation to absorb many new suburban areas. "Inelastic cities" are trapped within fixed city limits by either bad state annexation laws or being surrounded by incorporated suburbs. For a full discussion of the consequences of city elasticity and inelasticity, see David Rusk, *Cities Without Suburbs*, 2d ed. (Johns Hopkins University Press, 1995).

7. As of 1990, less than one-tenth of the land within Anchorage's city limits was classified as "urbanized" by the Census Bureau.

8. The segregation indexes are "dissimilarity indexes" that describe the relative unevenness of the distribution of target populations. On a scale of 0–100, a score of 0 indicates an absolutely even distribution, or complete integration; a score of 100 indicates an absolutely uneven distribution, or complete segregation. The measurements are made on a census tract by census tract basis (that is, largely without regard to political boundaries). Dissimilarity indexes cited are drawn from a report by Roderick J. Harrison and Daniel H. Weinberg, *Racial and Ethnic Segregation in 1990* (Bureau of the Census, Department of Commerce, 1992).

9. With the assistance of the Urban Institute in Washington, D.C., I calculated dissimilarity indexes for attendance zones of all public high schools in 320 metropolitan areas, based on computer tapes provided by the National Center for Education Statistics, for the 1989–1990 school year:

10. The term *South* refers to the seventeen states and the District of Columbia that maintained legally segregated school systems until the U.S. Supreme Court's epochal *Brown v. Board of Education* decision in 1954.

11. See David Rusk, *Inside Game/Outside Game: Winning Strategies for Saving Urban America* (Century Fund and Brookings, 1999), p. 73.

12. In the 1990s, voters have approved three new city-county consolidations: Athens–Clarke County and Augusta–Richmond County, both in Georgia, and Kansas City–Wyandotte County, Kansas.

13. Greater Baltimore Committee, *One Region, One Future* (1997).

14. See David Rusk, *Abell Report: To Improve Poor Children's Test Scores, Move Poor Families* (Baltimore: Abell Foundation, July 1998).

15. David Rusk, "Renewing Our Community: The Rusk Report on the Future of Greater York," *York Daily Record* (November 20, 1997), p. 2.

16. The Michigan Society of Planning Officials estimates that Michigan is subdividing farmland at the rate of ten acres an hour.

17. Housing prices escalated rapidly in other regions of the booming Pacific Northwest and Rocky Mountain states. Without any urban growth boundary in effect, Albuquerque, for instance, experienced a similar increase in housing prices and for much the same reason. In both Albuquerque and Portland, Intel was building $4 billion chip factories.

18. In 1973 the Montgomery County Council adopted the Moderately Priced Dwelling Unit (MPDU) ordinance. It requires that in any new housing development of fifty or more units builders must make at least 15 percent of the units affordable for households in the lowest third of the county's income range. To compensate builders for lost profits from developing 15 percent of their property at less than market potential, the MPDU ordinance provides up to a 22 percent density bonus. In the twenty-five years under the policy, homebuilders have built over 10,000 affordable units in compliance with the MPDU policy. The county's Housing Opportunities Commission, which, by ordinance, has right of first purchase for one-third of the MPDU units, has purchased over 1,500 units as rental properties for very low-income tenants. While economic segregation has increased in most urban areas, Montgomery County's dissimilarity index for poor households has been stable at a low 27 rating—a direct consequence of the county's MPDU policy and other mixed-income housing initiatives.
19. National Association of Regional Councils, *Regional Reporter 3* (January 1992), p. 1.
20. Carl Abbott and Margery Post Abbott, "Historical Development of the Metropolitan Service District," prepared for the Metro Home Rule Charter Committee.
21. Myron Orfield, *Metropolitics* (Cambridge, Mass., and Washington, D.C.: Lincoln Institute of Land Policy and Brookings, 1997), p. 133.

# 24

## *Fred Siegel*

# IS URBAN SPRAWL A PROBLEM?

Suburban sprawl, the spread of low-density housing over an ever-expanding landscape, has attracted a growing list of enemies. Environmentalists have long decried the effects of sprawl on the ecosystem; aesthetes have long derided what they saw as "the ugliness and banality of suburbia"; and liberals have intermittently insisted that suburban prosperity has been purchased at the price of inner-city decline and poverty. But only recently has sprawl become the next great issue in American public life. That's because suburbanites themselves are now calling for limits to seemingly inexorable and frenetic development.

Slow-growth movements are a response to both the cyclical swings of the economy and the secular trend of dispersal. Each of the great postwar booms have, at their cyclical peak, produced calls for restraint. These sentiments have gained a wider hearing as each new upturn of the economy has produced an ever widening wave of exurban growth. A record 96 months of peacetime economic expansion has produced the strongest slow-growth movement to date. In 1998, antisprawl environmentalists and "not-in-my-backyard" slow-growth

Fred Siegel, "Is Regional Government the Answer?" Reprinted with permission from *The Public Interest,* No. 137 (Fall 1999), pp. 85–98. © by National Affairs, Inc.

suburbanites joined forces across the nation to pass ballot measures restricting exurban growth.

Undoubtedly, the loss of land and the environmental degradation produced by sprawl are serious problems that demand public attention. But sprawl also brings enormous benefits as well as considerable costs. It is, in part, an expression of the new high-tech economy whose campus-like office parks on the periphery of urban areas have driven the economic boom of the 1990s. And it's sprawl that has sustained the record rise in home ownership. Sprawl is not some malignancy to be summarily excised but, rather, part and parcel of prosperity. Dealing with its ill effects requires both an understanding of the new landscape of the American economy and a willingness to make subtle trade-offs. We must learn to curb its worst effects without reducing the wealth and freedom that permit sprawl to develop.

Rising incomes and employment, combined with declining interest rates, have allowed a record number of people, including minority and immigrant families, to purchase homes for the first time. Home ownership among blacks, which is increasingly suburban, has risen at more than three times the white rate; a record 45 percent of African Americans owned their own homes in 1998. Nationally, an unprecedented 67 percent of Americans are homeowners.

Sprawl is part of the price we're paying for something novel in human history—the creation of a mass upper middle class. Net household worth has been increasing at the unparalleled annual rate of 10 percent since 1994, so that while in 1970, only 3.2 percent of households had an annual income of $100,000 (in today's dollars), by 1996, 8.2 percent of American households could boast a six-figure annual income. The new prosperity is reflected in the size of new homes, many of whose owners no doubt decry the arrival of still more "McMansions" and new residents, clogging the roads and schools of the latest subdivisions. In the midst of the 1980's boom, homebuilders didn't have a category for mass-produced houses of more than 3,000 square feet: By 1996, one out of every seven new homes built was larger than 3,000 square feet.

## Today's Tenement Trail

Sprawl also reflects upward mobility for the aspiring lower-middle class. Nearly a half-century ago, Samuel Lubell dedicated *The Future of American Politics* to the memory of his mother, "who pioneered on the urban frontier." Lubell described a process parallel to the settling of the West, in which families on "the Old Tenement Trail" were continually on the move in search of a better life. In the cities, they abandoned crowded tenements on New York's Lower East Side for better housing in the South Bronx, and from there, went to the "West Bronx, crossing that Great Social Divide—the Grand Concourse—beyond which rolled true middle-class country where janitors were called superintendents."

Today's "tenement trail" takes aspiring working- and lower-middle class Americans to quite different areas. Kendall, Florida, 20 miles southeast of Miami, is every environmentalist's nightmare image of sprawl, a giant grid carved out of the muck of swamp land that encroaches on the Everglades. Stripmalls and mega-stores abound for mile after mile, as do the area's signature giant auto lots. Yet Kendall also represents a late-twentieth-century version of the Old Tenement Trail. Kendall, notes the *New Republic's* Charles Lane, is "the Queens of the late twentieth century," a place where immigrants are buying into America. Carved out of the palmetto wilderness, its population exploded from roughly 20,000 in 1970 to 300,000 today. Agricultural in the 1960s, and a hip place for young whites in the 1970s, Kendall grew increasingly Hispanic in the 1980s, as Cubans, Nicaraguans, and others who arrived with very little worked their way up. Today, it's half Hispanic and a remarkable example of integration. In most of Kendall, notes University of Miami geographer Peter Muller, "You can't point to a white or Latino block because the populations are so intermixed."

Virginia Postrel, the editor of *Reason*, argues that the slow-growth movement is animated by left-wing planners' hostility to suburbia. Others mock slow-growthers as elitists, as in the following quip:

Q: What's the difference between an environmentalist and a developer?
A: The environmentalist already has his house in the mountains.

But, in the 1990s, slow-growth sentiment has been taking hold in middle- and working-class suburbs like Kendall, as development turns into overdevelopment and traffic congestion becomes a daily problem.

# Regional Government

One oft-proposed answer to sprawl has been larger regional governments that will exercise a monopoly on land-use decisions. Underlying this solution is the theory—no doubt correct—that sprawl is produced when individuals and townships seek to maximize their own advantage without regard for the good of the whole community. Regionalism, however, is stronger in logic than in practice. For example, the people of Kendall, rather than embracing regionalism, are looking to slow down growth by *seceding* from their regional government. Upon examination, we begin to see some of the problems with regional government.

Kendall is part of Metro-Dade, the oldest major regional government, created in 1957. The largest of its 29 municipalities, Miami, the fourth poorest city in the United States, has 350,000 people; the total population of Metro-Dade is 2 million, 1.1 million of whom live in unincorporated areas. In Metro-Dade, antisprawl and antiregional government sentiments merge. Despite county-imposed growth boundaries, residents have complained bitterly of overdevelopment. The county commissioners—many of whom have been convicted of, or charged with, corruption—have been highly receptive to the developers who are among their largest campaign contributors. As one south Florida resident said of the developers, "It's a lot cheaper to be able to buy just one government." The south Florida secessionists want to return zoning to local control where developers' clout is less likely to overwhelm neighborhood interests.

When Jane Jacobs wrote, in *The Death and Life of Great American Cities*, that "the voters sensibly decline to federate into a system where bigness means local helplessness, ruthless oversimplified planning and administrative chaos," she could have been writing about south Florida. What's striking about Metro-Dade is that it has delivered neither efficiency nor equity nor effective planning while squelching local self-determination.

The fight over Metro-Dade echoes the conflicts of an earlier era. Historically, the fight over regional versus local government was an important, if intermittent, issue for many cities from 1910 to 1970. From about 1850 to 1910, according to urban historian Jon Teaford, suburbanites were eager to be absorbed by cities whose wealth enabled them to build the water, sewage, and road systems they couldn't construct on their own. "The central city," he explains, "provided superior service at a lower cost." But, in the 1920s, well before race became a central issue, suburbanites, who had increasingly sorted themselves out by ethnicity and class, began to use special-service districts and innovative financial methods to provide their own infrastructure and turned away from unification. Suburbanites also denounced consolidation as an invitation to big-city, and often Catholic, "boss rule" and as a threat to "self-government."

In the 1960s, as black politicians began to win influence over big-city governments, they also joined the anticonsolidation chorus. At the same time, county government, once a sleepy extension of rural rule, was modernized, and county executives essentially became the mayors of full-service governments administering what were, in effect, dispersed cities. But they were mayors with a difference. Their constituents often wanted a balance between commercial development, which constrained the rise of taxes, and the suburban ideal of family-friendly semirural living. When development seemed too intrusive, suburban voters in the 1980s, and again in the 1990s, have pushed a slow-growth agenda.

## The New Regionalism

In the 1990s, regionalism has been revived as an effort to link the problem of sprawl with the problem of inner-city poverty. Assuming that "flight creates blight," regionalists propose to recapture the revenue of those who have fled the cities and force growth back into older areas by creating regional or metropolitan-area governments with control over land use and taxation.

The new regionalism owes a great deal to a group of circuit-riding reformers. Inspired by the arguments of scholars like Anthony Downs, one of the authors of the Kerner Commission report, and sociologist William Julius Wilson of Harvard, as well as the example of Portland, Oregon's metro-wide government, these itinerant preachers have traveled to hundreds of cities to spread the gospel of regional cooperation. The three most prominent new regionalists—columnist Neil Peirce, former Albuquerque mayor David Rusk, and Minnesota state representative Myron Orfield—have developed a series of distinct, but overlapping, arguments for why cities can't help themselves, and why regional solutions are necessary.

Peirce, in his book *Citistates*, plausibly insists that regions are the real units of competition in the global economy, so that there is a metro-wide imperative to revive the central city, lest the entire area be undermined. Less plausibly, Orfield in *Metropolitics* argues that what he calls "the favored quarter" of fast-growing suburbs on the periphery of the metro area have prospered at the expense of both the central city and the inner-ring suburbs. In order both to revive the central city and save the inner suburbs from decline, Orfield proposes that these two areas join forces, redistributing money from the "favored quarter" to the older areas. Rusk argues, in *Baltimore Unbound*, that older cities, unable to annex the fast growing suburbs, are doomed to further decline. He insists that only "flexible cities"—that is, cities capable of expanding geographically and capturing the wealth of the suburbs—can truly deal with inner-city black poverty. Regionalism, writes Rusk, is "the new civil rights movement."

There are differences among them. Orfield and, to a lesser degree, Rusk operate on a zero-sum model in which gain for the suburbs comes directly at the expense of the central city. Peirce is less radical, proposing regional cooperation as the means to a win-win situation for both city and the surrounding region. But they all share a desire to disperse poverty across the region and, more importantly, recentralize economic growth in the already built-up areas. The latter goal is consistent with both the environmental thrust of the antisprawl movement and the push for regional government. In a speech to a Kansas City civic organization, Rusk laid out the central assumption of the new regionalism. "The greater the fragmentation of governments," he asserted, "the greater the fragmentation of society by race and economic class." Fewer governments, argue the new regionalists, will yield a number of benefits, including better opportunities for regional cooperation, more money for cash-strapped central cities, less racial inequality, less sprawl, and greater economic growth. However, all of these propositions are questionable.

## Better Policies, Not Fewer Governments

Consider Baltimore and Philadelphia, cities that the regionalists have studied thoroughly. According to the 1998 *Greater Baltimore State of the Region* report, Philadelphia has 877 units of local government (including school boards)—or 17.8 per 100,000 people. Baltimore has only six government units of any consequence in Baltimore City and the five surrounding counties—or 2.8 per 100,000 people. Greater Baltimore has fewer government units than any other major metro area in the United States. As a political analyst told me: "Get six people in a room, and you have the government of 2,200 square miles, because the county execs have very strong powers." We might expect considerable regional cooperation in Baltimore, but not in

Philadelphia. Regionalism has made no headway in either city, however. The failure has little to do with the number of governments and a great deal to do with failed policy choices in both cities.

Rusk does not mention the many failings of Baltimore's city government. He refers to the current mayor, Kurt Schmoke, just once and only to say that Baltimore has had "excellent political leadership." In Rusk's view, Baltimore is "programmed to fail" because of factors entirely beyond its control, namely, the inability to annex its successful suburbs. In the ahistorical world of the regionalist (and here, Peirce is a partial exception), people are always pulled from the city by structural forces but never pushed from the city by bad policies.

Baltimore is not as well financed as the District of Columbia, which ruined itself despite a surfeit of money. But Baltimore, a favorite political son of both Annapolis and Washington, has been blessed with abundant financial support. Over the past decade, Schmoke has increased spending on education and health by over a half-billion dollars. He has also added 200 police officers and spent $60 million more for police over the last four years. "His greatest skill," notes the *Baltimore Sun*, "has been his ability to attract more federal and state aid while subsidies diminished elsewhere." But, notwithstanding these expenditures, middle-class families continue to flee the city at the rate of 1,000 per month, helping to produce the sprawl environmentalists decry.

Little in Baltimore works well. The schools have been taken over by the state, while the Housing Authority is mired in perpetual scandal and corruption. Baltimore is one of the few cities where crime hasn't gone down. That's because Schmoke has insisted, contrary to the experiences of New York and other cities, that drug-related crime could not be reduced until drug use was controlled through treatment. The upshot is that New York, with eight times more people than Baltimore, has only twice as many murders. Baltimore also leads the country in sexually transmitted diseases. These diseases have flourished among the city's drug users partly owing to Schmoke's de facto decriminalization of drugs. According to the Centers for Disease Control and Prevention (CDC), Baltimore has a syphilis rate 18 times the national average, 3 or 4 times as high as areas where the STD epidemic is most concentrated.

# Flexible Cities

Rusk attributes extraordinary qualities to flexible cities. He says that they are able to both reduce inequality, curb sprawl, and maintain vital downtowns. Rusk was the mayor of Albuquerque, a flexible city that annexed a vast area, even as its downtown essentially died. The reduced inequality he speaks of is largely a statistical artifact. If New York were to annex Scarsdale, East New York's average income would rise without having any effect on the lives of the people who live there. As for sprawl, flexible cities like Phoenix and Houston are hardly models.

A recent article for *Urban Affairs Review,* by Subhrajit Guhathakurta and Michele Wichert, showed that within the elastic city of Phoenix, inner-city residents poorer than their outer-ring neighbors are subsidizing the building of new developments on the fringes of the metropolis. While sprawl is correlated with downtown decline in Albuquerque, in Phoenix it's connected with what *Fortune* described as "the remarkable rebound of downtown Phoenix, which has become a chic after-dark destination as well as a residential hot spot." There seems to be no automatic connection between regionalism and downtown revival.

Orfield's *Metropolitics* provides another version of an over-determined structuralist argument. According to him, the favored quarter is sucking the inner city dry, and, as a result, central-city blight will inevitably engulf the older first-ring suburbs as well. He is right to see strong pressures on the inner-ring suburbs, stemming from an aging housing stock and population as well as an influx of inner-city poor. But it is how the inner-ring suburbs respond to these pressures that will affect their fate.

When Coleman Young was mayor of Detroit, large sections of the city returned to prairie. But the inner-ring suburbs have done fairly well precisely by not imitating Detroit's practice of providing poor services at premium prices. "Much like the new edge suburbs," explains the *Detroit News*, "older suburbs that follow the proven formula of promoting good schools, public safety and well-kept housing attract new investment." Suburban Mayor Michael Guido sees his city's well developed infrastructure as an asset, which has already been bought and paid for. "Now," says Mayor Guido, "it's a matter of maintenance …and we offer a sense of history and a sense of community. That's really important to people, to have a sense of belonging to a whole community rather than a subdivision."

## Suburb Power

City-suburban relations are not fixed; they are various depending on the policies both follow. Some suburbs compete with the central city for business. In south Florida, Coral Gables more than holds its own with Miami as a site for business headquarters. Southfield, just outside Detroit, and Clayton, just outside St. Louis, blossomed in the wake of the 1960s' urban riots and now compete with their downtowns. Aurora, with a population of more than 160,000 and to the east of Denver, sees itself as a competitor, and it sees regional efforts at growth management as a means by which the downtown Denver elite can ward off competition.

Suburban growth can also help the central city. In the Philadelphia area, economic growth and new work come largely from the Route 202 high-tech corridor in Chester County, west of the city. While the city has lost 57,000 jobs, even in the midst of national economic prosperity, the fast growing Route 202 companies have been an important source of downtown legal and accounting jobs. At the same time, the suburbs are creating jobs for residents that the central city cannot produce, so that 20 percent of city residents commute to the suburbs while 15 percent of people who live in the suburbs commute to Philadelphia.

The "new regionalists" assume that the prosperity of the edge cities is a function of inner-city decline. But, in many cities, it is more nearly the case that suburban booms are part of what's keeping the central-city economy alive. It is the edge cities that have taken up the time-honored urban task of creating new work.

According to *INC* magazine, the 500 fastest growing small companies are all located in suburbs and exurbs. This is because local governments there are very responsive to the needs of start-up companies. These high-tech hotbeds, dubbed "nerdistans" by Joel Kotkin, are composed of networks of companies that are sometimes partners, sometimes competitors. They provide a pool of seasoned talent for start-ups, where engineers and techies who prefer the orderly, outdoor life of suburbia to the crowds and disorder of the city can move from project to project. Henry Nicholas, CEO of Broadcom, a communications-chip and cable-modem maker, explained why he reluctantly moved to Irvine: "It's hard to relocate techies to L.A. It's the congestion, the expensive housing—and there's a certain stigma to it."

Imagine what the United States would be like if the Bay Area had followed the New York model. In 1898, New York created the first regional government when it consolidated all the areas of the New York harbor—Manhattan, Brooklyn, Queens, the Bronx, and Staten Island—into the then-largest city in the world. The consolidation has worked splendidly for Manhattan, which thrives as a capital of high-end financial and legal services. But over time, the Manhattan-centric economy based on high taxes, heavy social spending, and extensive economic regulation destroyed Brooklyn's once vital shipping and manufacturing economy.

In 1912, San Francisco, the Manhattan of Northern California, proposed to create a unified regional government by incorporating Oakland in the East Bay and San Jose in the South. The plan for a Greater San Francisco was modeled on Greater New York and called for the creation of self-governing boroughs within an enlarged city and county of San Francisco. East Bay opposition defeated the San Francisco expansion in the legislature, and later attempts at consolidation in 1917, 1923, and 1928 also failed. But had San Francisco with its traditions of high taxation and heavy regulation succeeded, Silicon Valley might never have become one of the engines of the American economy. Similarly, it's no accident that the Massachusetts Route 128 high-tech corridor is located outside of the boundaries of Boston, even as it enriches the central city.

# The Portland Model

The complex and often ironic history of existing regional governments has been obscured by the bright light of hope emanating from Portland. It seems that in every generation one city is said to have perfected the magic elixir for revival. In the 1950s, it was Philadelphia; today, it's Portland. In recent years, hundreds of city officials have traveled to Portland to study its metropolitan government, comprehensive environmental planning, and the urban-growth boundary that has been credited with Portland's revival and success.

While there are important lessons to be learned from Portland, very little of its success to date can be directly attributed to the growth boundary, which was introduced too recently and with boundaries so capacious as not yet to have had much effect. Thirty-five percent of the land within the boundary was vacant when it was imposed in 1979. And, at the same time, fast growing Clark County, just north of Portland but not part of the urban-growth boundary, has provided an escape valve for potential housing pressures. The upshot, notes demographer Wendell Cox, is that even with the growth boundary, Portland still remains a relatively low-density area with fewer people per square mile than San Diego, San Jose, or Sacramento.

Portland has also been run with honesty and efficiency, unlike Metro-Dade. Blessed with great natural resources, Portland—sometimes dubbed "Silicon forest," because chipmakers are drawn to its vast quantities of cheap clean water—has conserved its man-made as well as natural resources. A city with more cast-iron buildings than any place outside of Manhattan, it has been a leader in historic preservation. Time and again, Portland's leadership has made the right choices. It was one of the first cities to reconnect its downtown with the riverfront. Portland never built a circumferential freeway. And, in the 1970s, under the leadership of Mayor Neil Goldschmidt, the city vetoed a number of proposed highway projects that would have threatened the downtown.

In 1978, Portland voters, in conjunction with the state government, created the first directly elected metropolitan government with the power to manage growth over three counties. Portland metro government has banned big-box retailers, like Walmart and Price Club, on the grounds that they demand too much space and encourage too much driving. This is certainly an interesting experiment well worth watching, but should other cities emulate Portland's land-management model? It's too soon to say.

Good government is always important. But aside from that, it's hard to draw any general lessons from the Portland experience. The growth boundaries may or may not work, and there's certainly no reason to think that playing with political boundaries will bring good government to Baltimore.

## Living with Sprawl

What then is to be done? First, we can accept the consensus that has developed around preserving open space, despite some contradictory effects. The greenbelts around London, Portland, and Baltimore County pushed some development back toward the city and encouraged further sprawl as growth leapfrogged the open space. The push to preserve open space is only likely to grow stronger as continued growth generates both more congestion and more wealth, which can be used to buy up open land.

Secondly, we can create what Peter Salins, writing in *The Public Interest*[1] described as a "level playing field" between the central cities and the suburbs. This can be done by ending exurban growth subsidies for both transportation as well as new water and sewer lines. These measures might further encourage the revival of interest in old fashioned Main Street living, which is already attracting a new niche of home buyers. State and local governments can also repeal the land-use and zoning regulations that discourage mixed-use development of the sort that produces a clustering of housing around Main Street and unsubsidized low-cost housing in the apartments above the streets' shops.

Because of our strong traditions of local self-government, regionalism has been described as an unnatural act among consenting jurisdictions. But regional cooperation needn't mean the heavy hand of all-encompassing regional government. There are some modest, but promising, experiments already under way in regional revenue sharing whose effects should be carefully evaluated. Allegheny County, which includes Pittsburgh, has created a Regional Asset District that uses a 1 percent sales tax increase to support cultural institutions and reduce other taxes. The Twin Cities have put money derived from the increase in as-sessed value of commercial and industrial properties into a pot to aid fiscally weaker municipalities. Kansas and Missouri created a cultural district that levies a small increase in the sales tax across the region. The money is being used to rehabilitate the area's most treasured architectural landmark, Kansas City's Union Station.

Cities and suburbs do have some shared interests, as in the growing prac-tice of reverse commuting which links inner-city residents looking to get off welfare with fast growing suburban areas hampered by a shortage of labor. Re-gionalism can curb sprawl and integrate and sustain central-city populations if it reforms the misguided policies and politics that have sent the black and white middle class streaming out of cities like Baltimore, Washington, and Philadelphia. Regional cooperation between the sprawling high-tech suburbs and the central cities could modernize cities that are in danger of being left fur-ther behind by the digital economy. In that vein, the District of Columbia's Mayor Anthony Williams seized on the importance of connecting his welfare population with the fast growing areas of Fairfax County in Northern Virginia. The aim of focused regional policies, argues former HUD Undersecretary Marc Weiss, should be economic, not political, integration.

Sprawl isn't some malignancy that can be surgically removed. It's been part and parcel of healthy growth, and curbing it involves difficult tradeoffs best worked out locally. Sprawl and the movement against sprawl are now a permanent part of the landscape. The future is summed up in a quip attributed to former Oregon Governor Tom McCall, who was instrumental in creating Portland's growth boundary. "Oregonians," he said, "are against two things, sprawl and density."

## REFERENCE

1. "Cities, Suburbs, and the Urban Crisis," *The Public Interest*, No. 113 (Fall 1993).

# 25

## Peter Calthorpe and William Fulton

## THE REGION IS THE NEIGHBORHOOD: SPRAWL AND THE NEW URBANISM

At the heart of creating concrete visions for the Regional City is the notion that they can be "designed." We use the term "design" not in the typical sense of artistically configuring a physical form but to imply a process that synthesizes many disciplines. Regional design is an act that integrates multiple facets at once: the demands of the region's ecology, its economy, its history, its politics, its regulations, its culture, and its social structure. And its results are specific physical forms as well as abstract goals and policies—regional maps and neighborhood urban design standards as well as implementation strategies, governmental policies, and financing mechanisms.

Too often we plan and engineer rather than design. Engineering tends to optimize isolated elements without regard for the larger system, whereas planning tends to be ambiguous, leaving the critical details of place making to chance. If we merely plan and engineer, we forfeit the possibility of developing a "whole systems" approach or a "design" that recognizes the trade-offs between isolated efficiencies and integrated parts.

The engineering mentality often reduces complex, multifaceted problems to one measurable dimension. For example, traffic engineers optimize road size for auto capacity without considering the trade-off of neighborhood scale, walkability, or beauty. Civil engineers efficiently channelize our streams without considering recreational, ecological, or esthetic values. Commercial developers optimize the delivery of goods without balancing the social need of neighborhoods for local identity and meeting places. Again and again we sacrifice the synergy of the whole for the efficiency of the parts.

The idea that a region or even a neighborhood could or should be "designed" is central to creating the Regional City. We need to acknowledge that we can direct our growth and that such action can include complex trade-offs as well as unexpected synergies. The common impression is that our neighborhoods, towns, or regions evolve organically (and somewhat mysteriously). They are the product of invisible market forces or the summation of technical imperatives. There also is the illusion that these forces cannot and should not be tampered with. Planning failed in the past; therefore it will fail in the future.

The real illusion, of course, is that we cannot control the form of our communities. Historically, design played a large role in shaping our forms of settlement. The template that underlies much of our suburban growth was designed in the thirties by Frank Lloyd Wright with his Broadacre Cities plans and Clarence Stein's Greenbelt towns. These were then bastardized and codified by the HUD minimum property standards of the 1950s. The template for urban redevelopment was developed about the same time by Le Corbusier and a European group of architects called CIAM (Congres Internationaux d'Architecture Moderne). Their vision of superblocks and high-rise development became the basis of our urban renewal programs of the 1960s.

The problem is not that our suburbs and cities are lacking design but that they are designed according to failed principles with flawed implementation. They are designed in accord with modernist principles and implemented by specialists. The modernist principles of specialization, standardization, and mass production in emulating our industrial economy had a severe effect on the character of our neighborhoods and regions.

At the neighborhood scale, specialization meant that each land use—residential, retail, commercial, or civic—was isolated and developed by "experts" who optimized their particular zones without any responsibility for the whole. Regional specialization meant that each area within the region could play an independent role: suburbs for the middle class and new businesses, cities for the poor and declining industries, and countryside for nature and agriculture.

As a complement to specialization, standardization led to the homogenization of our communities, a blindness to history and the demise of unique ecological systems. A "one size fits all" mentality of efficiency overrode the special qualities of place and community.

Mass production (in housing, transportation, offices, and so forth) upends the delicate balance between local enterprise, regional systems, and global networks. The logic of mass production moves relentlessly toward ever-increasing scales, which in turn reinforces the specialization and standardization of everyday life.

Against this modern alliance of specialization, standardization, and mass production stands a set of principles rooted more in ecology than in mechanics. They are the principles of diversity, conservation, and human scale. Diversity at each scale calls for more complex, differentiated communities shaped from the unique qualities of place and history. Conservation implies care for existing resources whether natural, social, or institutional. And the principle of human scale brings the individual back into a picture increasingly fashioned around remote and mechanistic concerns.

These alternative principles apply equally to the social, economic, and physical dimensions of communities. For example, the social implications of human scale may mean more police officers walking a beat rather than hovering overhead in a helicopter; the economic implications of human scale may mean economic policies that support small local business rather than major industries and corporations; and the physical implications of human scale may be realized in the form and detail of buildings as they relate to the street. Unlike the standard governmental categories of economic development, housing, education, and health services, each of these design principles incorporates physical design, social programs, and economic strategies. These principles, then, are the ones that we believe should form the foundation of a new regional and neighborhood design ethic.

## Human Scale

For several generations, the design of buildings, the planning of communities, and the growth of our institutions have exemplified the view that "bigger is better." Efficiency was correlated with large, centralized organizations and processes. Now the idea of decentralized networks of smaller working groups and more personalized institutions is gaining currency in both government and business. Efficiency is correlated with nimble, small working groups, not large hierarchical institutions.

Certainly, the reality of our time is a complex mix of both of these trends. For example, we have ever-larger retail outlets at the same time that Main Streets are making a comeback. Some businesses are growing larger and more centralized while the "new economy" is bursting with small-scale start-ups and intimate working groups. Housing production is diversifying home types at the same time that it consolidates into larger financing packages. Both directions are evolving at the same time, and the shape of our communities will have to accommodate this complex reality.

Yet people are reacting to an imbalance between these two forces. The building blocks of our communities—schools, local shopping areas, housing subdivisions, apartment complexes, and office parks—have all grown into forms that defy human scale. And we are witnessing a reaction to this lack of scale in many ways. People uniformly long for an architecture that puts detail and identity back into what have too often become generic, if functional, buildings. They desire the character and scale of a walkable street, complete with shade trees and buildings that orient windows and entries their way. They idealize Main Street shopping areas and historic urban districts.

Human scale is a design principle that responds simultaneously to simple human desires and the emerging ethos of the new decentralized economies. The focus on human scale represents a shift away from top-down social programs, from characterless housing projects, and from more and more remote institutions. In its most concrete expression, human scale is the stoop of a townhouse or the front porch of a home rather than the stairwell of a high-rise or the garage door of a tract home. Human scale in economics means supporting individual entrepreneurs and local businesses. Human scale in community means a strong neighborhood focus and an environment that encourages everyday interaction.

## Diversity

Diversity has multiple meanings and profound implications. It has the most challenging implications for the social, environmental, and economic dimensions of community planning. Perhaps its most obvious outcome is the creation of communities that are diverse in use and in population. As a planning axiom, it calls for a return to mixed-use neighborhoods that contain a broad range of uses as well as a broad range of housing types and people.

The four fundamental elements of community—civic places, commercial uses, housing opportunities, and natural systems—define the physical elements of diversity at any scale. As a physical principle, diversity in neighborhoods ensures that destinations are close at hand and that the shared institutions of community are integrated. It also implies an architecture rich in character and streetscapes that vary with place and use.

As a social principle, diversity is controversial and perhaps the most challenging of all. It implies creating neighborhoods that provide for a large range in age group, house-hold type, income, and race. As already stated, neighborhoods have always (to a greater or lesser degree) been defined by commonalties even if energized by differences. But today we have reached an extreme: age, income, family size, and race are all divided into discrete market segments and locations that are built independently. Complete housing integration may be a distant goal, but inclusive neighborhoods that broaden the economic range, expand the mix of age and household types, and open the door to racial integration are feasible and desirable.

Diversity is a principle with significant economic implications. Gone are the days when economic-revitalization efforts focused on a single industry or a major governmental program. A more ecological understanding of industry clusters has emerged. This sensibility validates the notion that a range of complementary but differing enterprises (large and small, local, regional, and global) are important to maintaining a robust economy, and that now more than ever, the quality of life and the urbanism of a place, as well as the more traditional economic factors, play a significant role in the emerging economy.

Finally, diversity is a fundamental principle that can help to guide the preservation of local and regional ecologies. Clearly, understanding the complex nature of the existing or stressed habitats and watershed systems mandates a different approach to open-space planning. Active recreation, agriculture, and habitat preservation are often at odds. A broad range of open-space types, from the most active to the most passive, must be integrated in neighborhood and regional designs. Diversity in use, diversity in population, diversity in enterprise, and diversity in natural systems are fundamental to the Regional City.

## Conservation

Conservation implies many things in community design beyond husbanding resources and protecting natural systems; it implies preserving and restoring the cultural, historic, and architectural assets of a place as well. Conservation calls for designing communities and buildings that require fewer resources— less energy, less land, less waste, and fewer materials, but it also implies caring for what we have and developing an ethic of reuse and repair—in both our physical and our social realms.

The principle of conservation and its complements, restoration and preservation, should be applied to the built environment as well as to the natural environment—not only to our historic building stock and neighborhood institutions, but also to human resources and human history. Communities should strive to conserve their cultural identity, physical history, and unique natural systems. Restoration and conservation are more than environmental themes; they are an approach to the way that we think about community at the regional and local levels.

Conserving resources has many obvious implications in community planning. Foremost are the quantities of farmlands and natural systems displaced by sprawling development and the quantity of auto travel required to support it. Even within more compact, walkable communities, conservation of resources can lead to new design strategies. The preservation of waterways and on-site water-treatment systems can add identity and natural amenities at the same time that they conserve water quality. Energy-conservation strategies in buildings often lead to environments that are climate responsive and unique to place.

Conserving the historic buildings and institutions of a neighborhood can preserve the icons of community identity. Restoring and enhancing the vernacular architecture of a place can simultaneously reduce energy costs, reestablish local history, and create jobs. Although the preservation movement has made great strides with landmark buildings, it is correct now in extending its agenda beyond building facades to the social fabric of neighborhoods and to the ecology of the communities that are the lifeblood of historic districts.

Conserving human resources is another implication of this fundamental principle. In too many of our communities, poverty, lack of education, and declining job opportunities lead to a tragic waste of human potential. As we have begun to see, communities are not viable when concentrations of poverty turn them into a wasteland of despair and crime. In this context, "conservation" takes on a larger meaning—the restoration and rehabilitation of human potential wherever it is being squandered and overlooked. There should be no natural or cultural environments that are disposable or marginalized. Conservation and restoration are practical undertakings that can be economically strengthening and socially enriching.

# Designing the Region Is Designing the Neighborhood

What happens to regions or neighborhoods if they are "designed" according to these principles? An interesting set of parallel design strategies emerges at both the regional and the neighborhood levels. First and foremost, the region and its elements—the city, suburbs, and their natural environment—should be conceived as a unit, just as the neighborhood and its elements—housing, shops, open space, civic institutions, and businesses—should be designed as a unit. Treating each element separately is endemic to many of the problems that we now face. Just as a neighborhood needs to be developed as a whole system, the region must be treated as an human ecosystem, not a mechanical assembly.

Seen as this integrated whole, the region can be designed in much the same way as we would design a neighborhood. That the whole, the region, would be similar to its most basic pieces, its neighborhoods, is an important analogy. Both need protected natural systems, vibrant centers, human-scale circulation systems, a common civic realm, and integrated diversity. Developing such an architecture for the region creates the context for healthy neighborhoods, districts, and city centers. Developing such an architecture for the neighborhood creates the context for regions that are sustainable, integrated, and coherent. The two scales have parallel features that reinforce one another.

Major open-space corridors within the region, such as rivers, ridge lands, wetlands, or forests, can be seen as a "village green" at a megascale—the commons of the region. These natural commons establish an ecological identity as the basis of a region's character. Similarly, the natural systems and shared open spaces at the neighborhood scale are fundamental to its identity and character. A neighborhood's natural systems, like the region's, are as much a part of its commons as its civic institutions or commercial center.

Just as a neighborhood needs a vital center to serve as the crossroads of a local community, the region needs a vital central city to serve as its cultural heart and as a link to the global economy. In the Edge City metropolis, both types of centers are failing. In the suburbs, what were village centers of human proportions are overcome by remote discount centers and relentless commercial strips. In the central cities, poverty and disinvestment errode historic neighborhood communities. Both fall prey to specialized enterprises oriented to mass distribution rather than the local community. Like the commons, healthy centers, both urban and suburban, are fundamental to local and regional coherence.

Regional and neighborhood design has other parallels. Pedestrian scale within the neighborhood—walkable streets and nearby destinations—has a partner in transit systems at the regional scale. Transit can organize the region in much the same way as a street network orders a neighborhood. Transit lines focus growth and redevelopment in the region just as main streets can focus a neighborhood. Crossing local and metropolitan scales, transit supports the life of the pedestrian within each neighborhood and district by providing access to regional destinations. In a complementary fashion, pedestrian-friendly neighborhoods support transit by providing easy access for riders, not cars. The two scales, if designed as parallel strategies, reinforce each other.

As we have pointed out, diversity is a fundamental design principle for both the neighborhood and the region. A diverse population and job base within a region supports a resilient economy and a rich culture in much the same way that diverse uses and housing in a neighborhood support a complex and active community. The suburban trend to segregate development by age and income translates at the regional level into an increasing spatial and economic polarization—the "secession of the successful," as Robert Reich articulated in *The Work of*

*Nations.* Both trends can be countered by policies that support inclusionary housing and mixed-use environments.

These parallels across scales are not merely coincidence. The fundamental nature of a culture and economy expresses itself at many scales simultaneously. Sprawl and our lack of regional structure is a manifestation of an older and quite different paradigm. Since World War II, our economy and culture have accelerated their movement toward the industrial qualities of mass production, standardization, and specialization. The massive suburbanization that marks this period is the direct expression of these qualities. As a counterpoint, the principles and concurrences just outlined define a new paradigm of community and growth, one that leads from the Edge City to the Regional City.

# CHAPTER 8

# FEDERAL-CITY RELATIONS
# AND THE CAPACITY TO GOVERN

## URBAN POLITICS IN A
## DECENTRALIZED FEDERAL SYSTEM

For more than two decades, federal policymakers have been shedding their responsibilities for urban programs and have been moving the responsibility for implementing important program onto cities. Local public officials are searching for ways of managing their new roles while absorbing the shock waves caused by profound changes in their populations, economies, and political environments. How can localities best respond? In what direction is intergovernmental politics evolving after years of decentralization?

The selections in this chapter provide some answers. In Selection 26, Peter Eisinger highlights the interdependency of local, state, and national politics. He examines the strength of the fiscal link between the federal government and municipal governments after years of devolution and concludes that a New Federal Order has emerged. He argues that changes in intergovernmental relations have forced mayors to focus more on making the most of the limited resources they have, making city hall less likely to attend to social, racial, and economic issues. Urban politics increasingly is focused on managing the political consequences of city hall's inability to solve many of their most pressing problems. Not surprisingly, in recent years many cities such as New York, Los Angeles, Philadelphia, Indianapolis, and others have witnessed the election of conservative mayors who stress public order and quality of life issues (such as clean streets) that are amenable to limited government.

Pietro Nivola examines a different aspect of the New Federalism in Selection 27. He points out that the hand of the federal government in local affairs remains a large and growing presence despite declining national financial assistance to localities. He argues that Congress is inclined to pass laws that force local governments to undertake new responsibilities without providing financial help in carrying out these mandates. Further, he argues that federal laws and judicial decisions are regulating matters that were left to local decision makers in the past.

He describes how national prescriptions frequently deal with the minutiae of local affairs, such as requiring bright, standard-size yellow lines to separate drivers and passengers on school buses. He concedes that some national prohibitions and regulations are necessary when problems spill over local governmental boundaries, but asserts that many federal mandates go beyond that. According to Nivola, one-size-fits-all federal standards are becoming so ubiquitous that they undermine the ability of local officials to find sensible and effective solutions to their problems. Nivola reaches the conclusion that less national government would be better for all cities, but especially for central cities that disproportionately pay the legal bills and compliance costs that are generated by misplaced national regulations.

In the wake of Hurricane Katrina, which struck New Orleans in August 2006, and the attack on the World Trade Center in New York on September 11, 2001, a debate has broken out concerning the question of how local, state, and federal governments should prepare for, respond to, and recover from such disasters. Stephen D. Stehr suggests in <u>Selection 28</u> that much is known about how to make cities and regions safer, but that political and economic calculations often make effective responses difficult. An inherent problem is that the mitigation of disasters is likely to be the responsibility of local governments, while the economic costs of recovery and reconstruction are borne by higher-level governments, especially the federal government. He asserts that local governments have few incentives to make preparedness for disasters or their mitigation high priorities because federal governmental programs and private insurance will provide assistance if and when the disaster occurs.

Stehr also believes that political pressures at all levels of government confound rational planning for disasters. The competition for local development encourages cities to give greater attention to economic growth, rather than to public safety and disaster recovery. Federal governmental attention to homeland security in an age of terrorism often diminishes interest of federal officials in planning for natural disasters even though they may be more likely to happen than terrorist events. Stehr concludes that the vulnerability of cities to disasters is essentially a political matter determined by the dominant narrative or interpretation of how such events should be managed.

What is the proper relationship between the federal government and the cities? Do cities possess the capacity to respond to all problems that may face them? Making cities face the burdens once shouldered by the federal government does not help them to generate the resources necessary for responding to such events as Hurricane Katrina and the terrorist attacks; clearly, much of New Orleans's problem can be traced to the chronically dire straits of the city budget. Sometimes local governments demonstrate the capacity to respond, sometimes they clearly do not. There are problems that can overwhelm any local government, no matter how competently it may be run. This is an important legacy of the American system of local government.

# 26

## Peter Eisinger

## CITY POLITICS IN AN ERA OF FEDERAL DEVOLUTION

The effort that began more than 25 years ago to construct what might be called a New Federal Order is still very much a work in progress. President Clinton and most members of Congress . . . clearly embraced some of the elements that differentiate this federal arrangement from its New Deal-Great Society predecessor such as diminishing federal intergovernmental aid, block grants, and formal devolution of federal responsibilities. But the scope and details of implementation of this latest iteration of the federal arrangement are not yet fully worked out. The bare walls of the edifice have been erected, but there is little interior decoration.

As members of the tripartite federal partnership that came to its fullest expression in the Great Society and the years immediately following, local governments have a deep interest in the process and outcomes of federal realignment. As the outlines of the New Federal Order of the 1990s have taken shape, it is clear that the implications for urban government are manifold. Nevertheless, even though many of the problems and issues that are reshaping federalism are concentrated in urban areas, much is uncertain about what precise role the cities will play in the emerging intergovernmental environment. Curiously, city representatives and city interests have been, according to Weir (1996, 1), "conspicuously absent from the congressional debate about devolution."

Certain developments in national politics make this an appropriate moment to take stock and to speculate about the future of the cities in the New Federal Order. In summer 1996, Congress passed, and the president signed, the new welfare law, converting cash support for the poor from an open-ended federal entitlement to a fixed block grant to the states. Devolution through block granting is the focus of debate in other areas of public policy, from law enforcement to highway funding and from job training to housing, all policy domains in which the local government role is clearer and more formalized than in the welfare realm. Not only is there now broad interest in devolving power through block grants but the intergovernmental aid reductions put in place in Republican Washington in the 1980s are no longer resisted by deficit-averse

Peter Eisinger, "City Politics in an Era of Federal Devolution," *Urban Affairs Review,* Vol. 33 (3), pp. 308–325, copyright © 1998 Sage Publications, Inc. Reprinted by permission of Sage Publications, Inc.

Democrats. In this article, then, I explore what is known about cities in the New Federal Order, what their future role might be, and what the effects on cities of the changes in the federal arrangement have been.

I suggest that to the extent that cities are increasingly cut off from federal aid and program initiatives, mayors must focus more and more on making the most of the resources they control. Thus the arts of public management are becoming the primary tasks of local political leadership. This represents an important change in the moral climate of local politics, because city hall is far less likely to be used these days as the bully pulpit from which mayors once sought to exercise leadership on major social, racial, and economic issues.

## The New Federal Order

I define the New Federal Order as that rearrangement of federal relationships that began with President Richard Nixon's efforts to devolve authority from Washington to subnational governments through block grants and general revenue sharing and continues today as Congress, the president, and the governors combine to contract the role of the federal government in domestic policy. Although the initial efforts in the 1970s to transform the New Deal-Great Society federal system were seen as partisan attempts to diminish Washington's influence, both parties seem to agree today not only that the era of big government is over but that the proper locus of policy invention and administration is at the state and local level. For example, even before the passage of the welfare reform bill of 1996, the Clinton administration had approved 78 state welfare demonstration projects. More generally, the president's urban policy, according to his assistant secretary of the Department of Housing and Urban Development (HUD) at the time, "recognizes that the most pressing problems facing older cities can no longer be addressed through countercyclical grant-in-aid programs" (Stegman 1996). Where do the cities fit, then, in the New Federal Order?

It is important to begin by distinguishing several different aspects of the process of creating the New Federal Order. One aspect is simply the contraction of federal intergovernmental aid. This trend represents the devolution by default of fiscal responsibility to states and localities. A second aspect is the formal devolution of power from Washington to subnational government, a rearrangement of responsibilities of city governments. A third feature concerns the indirect consequences of devolution to the states. These spin-off fiscal and political effects are manifold, and they affect the cities in important ways.

### Fiscal Contraction

Federal assistance to cities is much diminished since the late 1970s. The contraction of aid has been so dramatic that the federal government's loss of interest in urban affairs is one of the signal stories of the great transformation to the New

Federal Order. Yet a focus on the big picture alone may be somewhat misleading: Cities have not been entirely cut adrift fiscally to live on their own resources.

In 1977, the year before federal aid contraction began, municipal governments looked to Washington for 15.9% of their total revenues. By 1992, federal assistance had decreased to only 4.7% of local revenues. (Chernick and Reschovsky 1997; see also Wallin 1996). In 1991, combined federal grants in aid to state and local governments regained their high watermark of 1978 (in constant dollar terms), but the functional distribution of intergovernmental fiscal assistance had changed in ways particularly disadvantageous to the cities. Although grants for education, job training, and social services, many of which are allocated to local governments, accounted for 23.9% of federal intergovernmental aid in 1980, the figure had decreased to 15.8% by 1994. Community development assistance decreased during this period from 7.1% to 2.9% of federal aid, and grants for sewer and water construction and environmental cleanup went from 5.9% to 2.0%. Meanwhile, health-related grants, mainly Medicaid, which is channeled through the states to individuals, rose from 17.2% of all federal inter-governmental assistance to 42.1% (Advisory Commission on Intergovernmental Relations 1994, 31). In short, a much smaller proportion of federal aid is devoted to urban programs than was true just a decade and a half ago.

An analysis by the U.S. Conference of Mayors ([USCM] 1994) of funding of key urban programs shows how severe the cuts have been from the perspective of the cities. Between 1981 and 1993, funding of community development block grants, urban development action grants, general revenue sharing, mass transit aid, employment and training programs, clean-water construction, assisted housing, and the various programs of the Economic Development Administration decreased by 66.3% in real dollar terms (see Table 8.1).

Table 8.1   Federal Funds for Cities, 1981–1993 (in billions of constant 1993 dollars)

| Program | FY 1981 ($) | FY 1993 ($) | % Real Cut |
|---|---|---|---|
| Community Development Block Grant | 6.3 | 4.0 | −36.5 |
| Urban Development Action Grant | 0.6 | 0.0 | −100.0 |
| General revenue sharing | 8.0 | 0.0 | −100.0 |
| Mass transit | 6.9 | 3.5 | −49.3 |
| Employment and training | 14.3 | 4.2 | −70.6 |
| Economic Development Administration | 0.6 | 0.2 | −66.7 |
| Assisted housing | 26.8 | 8.9 | −66.8 |
| Clean-water construction | 6.0 | 2.6 | −56.7 |

*Source:* U.S. Conference of Mayors (1994).

State governments did little to make up for the evaporation of federal monies for their municipalities. Reeling from the losses of federal aid that they themselves were experiencing, especially with the end of the state portion of general revenue sharing in 1980, state governments significantly reduced the rate of growth of aid to their local governments. Altogether, state aid to local governments as a proportion of local revenues decreased from 25.4% to 21.2% of local revenues between 1977 and 1992 (Chernick and Reschovsky 1997).

Although urban-oriented federal aid had dropped substantially by the mid-1990s, the federal government in the Clinton era has not abandoned the cities. Beginning with fiscal year 1995, the USCM began tracking federal funding of a range of specific "municipal programs."[1] Of the 80 programs tracked over the three-year period by the USCM, 27 showed decreases, 8 were unchanged, and 45 received increases in funding. Of those 45, however, only 26 received funding increases that equaled or exceeded the inflation rate.

The data indicate, however, that with a few exceptions, municipal programs did not experience the huge cuts in the middle Clinton years that they had suffered in the earlier decade. Federal funding of programs that benefit cities could be described as approaching a steady state, with substantial changes only at the tails of the distribution. One implication for the cities is that although they do not stand to lose even more federal dollars, it is unlikely that a return to the patterns of the pre-Reagan era will occur. Nothing in the patterns of federal aid in the 1990s suggests that city governments will be able to relax their habits of fiscal self-reliance.

## Formal Devolution

The principal definition of the term devolution in the context of U.S. federalism is the reallocation of specific responsibilities and authority from Washington to subnational governments. Since 1980, devolution has primarily involved a shift from national to state government. Such a rearrangement lay at the heart of President Reagan's New Federalism, one of the elements of which involved a failed proposal to carry out the so-called Great Swap: Washington would assume full responsibility for Medicaid in return for complete state takeover of the Aid to Families with Dependent Children (AFDC) and Food Stamps programs.

Reagan's effort to shape the New Federal Order was not entirely in vain, however: He did succeed in persuading Congress to consolidate 77 categorical grants-in-aid into 10 broad block grants to the states. The consequence was to strip Congress of the authority to designate specific uses of federal assistance for a variety of mainly health and education programs. State governments could now establish their own priorities within the broad boundaries of these new block grants. As in the current era, however, the interests of cities were scarcely considered in this federal reordering. Indeed, the new state power came directly at the expense of the cities: Of the categorical programs consolidated into block grants to the states, 47 had previously delivered funds directly to local governments (Ladd 1994, 219).

The Reagan federalism reforms failed to stem the growth of categorical grants, the number of which had reached an all-time high of 618 by 1995. Yet, contrary to the legislative trend, interest in devolution has remained high, both in Washington and in the state houses, fueled by the increasingly bipartisan conviction that in most matters of domestic policy, government closest to the people governs best. For proponents of devolution, the decade of the 1990s began in a promising way with the passage of the Intermodal Surface Transportation Efficiency Act (ISTEA), which greatly expands the ability of state and local governments alike to reallocate transportation funds among specific modes. Thus, in 1995, for example, more than $800 million was shifted by subnational governments from one purpose to another, such as the New York City Transit Authority's transfer of money initially designated for highways to mass transit projects, including station upgrades and signal modernization.[2]

Another significant devolutionary initiative during the Clinton years was the 1996 Personal Responsibility and Work Opportunity Reconciliation Act, better known as welfare reform, which created the Temporary Assistance to Needy Families (TANF) block grant. Henceforth, states will receive a fixed amount of funding from which to provide income support and work programs. State governments will now be responsible for establishing eligibility requirements and time limits. The shift of welfare responsibility to the states creates no formal local role, however, although there are clearly indirect implications for the cities that will be discussed later.

In no analysis of the urban implications of the changing distribution of responsibilities and authority in the federal system can one ignore two other initiatives of the mid-1990s: the Empowerment Zone and Enterprise Cities Act of 1993 and the Unfunded Mandates Reform Act of 1995. Neither devolves specific powers to subnational governments that they did not have before, but unlike most earlier devolutionary reforms, they both promise to expand the scope of local self-determination.

Along with providing some tax and regulatory relief, the Empowerment Zone and Enterprise Cities Program offers selected communities grants under the Title XX Human Services block grant program that may be used for an expanded range of social services and economic development. The Title XX block grant is made to the states, which in turn pass the funds onto their winning communities. In the first round, the few big winners received grants of $100 million each over a 10-year period, and a larger number of cities won smaller grants.

The program does not represent a devolution of new programmatic authority and responsibility in the field of economic and community development; these already rest primarily at the subnational level. Rather, the empowerment zone program devolves additional *capacity* to facilitate initiatives devised at the local level. Indeed, HUD is explicit in its implementation guidelines that programs are to be the product of strategic plans developed in the neighborhoods rather than in Washington (U.S. Government Accounting Office 1996, 3, 5).

The Unfunded Mandates Reform Act of 1995 has less obvious consequences but holds out the potential for curbing the growth rate of federal intergovernmental regulation and oversight and the imposition on states and localities of enforceable duties, as they are called in the act. The relief from mandates provided by Congress is oblique: The purpose of the act is to "assist Congress in its consideration of proposed legislation . . . containing Federal mandates . . . by providing for development of information about the nature and size of mandates, [by promoting] informed and deliberate decisions by Congress on the appropriateness of Federal mandates in any particular instance, [and by requiring] that Congress consider whether to provide funding" to help subnational governments comply with the mandates (Unfunded Mandate Reform Act of 1995, P.L. 104–4). Members of Congress may be called upon to vote explicitly to include a mandate in a new program. The act is thus designed not so much to bar unfunded mandates as to discourage Congress by making the decision to impose a new mandate a thoroughly self-conscious and transparent action. If the intent of the act is realized, state and local governments may find over time that they may exercise unregulated governance over a slightly larger range of functions.

Although it is evident that little formal devolution from Washington to the cities has yet occurred, there are various proposals on the political agenda that would expand the urban role in the New Federal Order. During his term as the head of HUD, Secretary Henry Cisneros recommended creating a block grant through the consolidation of existing programs that would go to local governments to serve the homeless. Cisneros was said to believe that "homelessness is a local problem that is best solved . . . at the local level. . . . The most Washington can do is show the way" (Rapp 1994, 80). There has also been talk in Washington of consolidating 60 current HUD programs into three block grants for housing assistance, housing production, and community development. Another proposal, put forth by congressional Republicans after they won control of the House in the 1994 elections, was to eliminate the Community Oriented Policing Services program and substitute a $10 billion block grant to localities for law enforcement purposes, but President Clinton vetoed the appropriations bill that threatened to transform this signature program.

As these examples make clear, devolution is increasingly a shared goal of both political parties. Unlike the devolution of the Reagan years, the expansion of state authority is not the sole focus of federal reform. Although little formal authority has yet been transferred to local governments, some of the groundwork has been laid by forcing city governments to rely more heavily on their own resources. City governments may anticipate playing an even more central role in the federal rearrangement in the future.

## Indirect Consequences of Devolution

As federal devolution proceeds at the end of the century, cities are increasingly subjected to a variety of indirect effects. Some of these are a function of the increased burdens on state governments; others stem from the cities' growing fiscal self-reliance. There are at least three categories of indirect consequences. First, there are the looming fiscal effects of welfare devolution. Second, there will be some shifting of burdens in a variety of functional areas as federal aid reductions force cities to provide services now supported by shared funding. Finally, there are a number of consequences, already evident, for the nature of local politics and political leadership. In particular, political reputation and success increasingly rest on public management skills rather than on the ability to exercise moral suasion on matters of social policy or to promote a racial agenda. These latter effects, already strongly in evidence, are signs of a deep change in the texture of urban politics.

**Fiscal Effects** Weir (1996) offered the general prediction that states will adjust to reductions in federal funding by poaching on local revenue sources, although how widespread this might become and the particular forms it might take are not yet apparent. There is one modest fiscal challenge to local government revenues, however, and it derives from the new welfare law. Certain provisions of the bill are likely to reduce municipal tax collections, increase local government costs by creating greater demand for local public service jobs and education, and harm the consumer economy in high-poverty neighborhoods by reducing the disposable income of the poor.

The new law provides that after a maximum of two years on TANF, recipients must leave the welfare rolls and engage in some sort of work. Some will succeed, finding unsubsidized jobs in the private sector. Others, however, will not. Indeed, this outcome is the more likely in many cities, because there are simply not enough entry-level jobs to absorb the number of adults that will come off the welfare rolls. For example, if all the unemployed adults in Chicago—those on public assistance as well as those who are not—were to look for work, there would be six workers for every available entry-level job (Weir 1996, 4). In New York City, there are currently approximately 470,000 able-bodied adults on welfare. They will join the roughly 271,000 unemployed people not on welfare in the job search. These roughly three-quarters of a million people will be competing for employment in a local economy that is producing about 20,000 new jobs per year, and many of these require substantial skills and education (Finder 1996).

Of those who do not find work in the private sector, some will migrate from the state and others will fall back on relatives or friends. In either case, they will no longer have the steady, even if modest, spending power provided by cash welfare assistance. Pagano, Lobenhofer, and Dudas (1996) argued that one result of this loss of cash assistance by people otherwise not gainfully employed will be to lower the city's property and sales taxes and the local excise tax base by reducing both rental housing demand and consumer spending. With less cash—and fuel or food stamp benefits—flowing into poor urban communities, retail sales and employment dependent on welfare clients will suffer. Using an economy-wide model developed at the U.S. Department of Agriculture, Smallwood et al. (1995, 10) found that even a modest cut in food assistance will lead to more than 100,000 lost jobs in food processing, retail, and non-food sectors.[3]

Those who exhaust their welfare eligibility but who cannot find work in the private sector and who do not vanish from administrative view by moving in with relatives or leaving the state have several options, according to the law. They may seek subsidized employment in either the public sector or community service programs; they may seek job skills training directly related to employment; or, for high school dropouts, they may return to high school.[4] Although the block grant to the states may fund some of these options, it is also likely that local government resources may be called into play to create public service jobs or classroom training and education. This is so in large part because the new law does not provide enough funding to finance subsidized work and training. The Congressional Budget Office estimates the shortfall in support of the work requirement at $12 billion over the next six years (Super et al. 1996, 14). States may pick up some of these costs, but they are likely to push some of them onto the cities. The 1996 welfare reform, then, will not be free of cost for the cities.

**Service Shifting of Burdens** Some welfare recipients who reach their time limits will find neither work nor shelter with relatives or friends. Some will no doubt find themselves literally on the streets. Homeless programs that are funded locally will certainly feel the impact. Other unsuccessful job seekers will resort to crime, increasing the burden on the local criminal justice system.

Although anyone who would have been eligible for welfare on 16 July 1996 remains eligible for Medicaid, there is no guarantee that Congress will not change the entire Medicaid program. The House and the Senate were near agreement late in 1995 to create a Medicaid block grant to the states that would have provided reduced funding over the next seven years. If such a proposal is successfully revived, one effect on cities will surely be an increase in demand on public hospital emergency services (see Center on Budget and Policy Priorities 1996).

**Public Management as Urban Politics** The most important impact on the cities of the shifting balance in the federal arrangement has been to change what could be called the moral tenor of urban politics. In short, good public administration has displaced the urban social and racial agendas that had dominated local politics since the 1960s. By increasingly forcing local leaders to make do with less intergovernmental aid and by making them husband what resources can be raised locally, the New Federal Order has placed a premium on local public management skills and discouraged grand visions of social and racial reform. As an official from the USCM explained, "In the last few years, our attention has shifted from trying to increase aid to cities in any form to trying to streamline it and make it more effective. *Let's talk about how we can make better use of what we're getting*" (Stanfield 1996, 1802, emphasis added).

Some scholars see this simply as part of a broad national trend toward conservatism, one that, as Sonenshein, Schockman, and DeLeon (1996, 1) put it, reaches down "even into the generally safe Democratic and minority reaches of urban leadership." Others see a more complex phenomenon taking place; for example, Clark (1994, 23) argued that a New Political Culture has emerged in the cities, one that features lifestyle and consumption concerns (especially lower taxes) rather than redistribution and material issues like housing and community development for the disadvantaged. He traced the crystallization of this middle-class urban politics to the decline of federal and state grants, many of which were targeted to poverty clienteles. Thus the contraction of federal aid has not only meant less money for the cities, but less policy guidance.

In a political climate in which the fear of taxpayer revolts is always present and the continuing flight of the middle class is a constant threat to urban health, leaders must first and foremost demonstrate skills in managing scarce resources. Social issues may or may not be present on current mayoral agendas, but if they are a matter of concern, the new mayors make clear that they can best be addressed by better management. This set of management tasks contrasts significantly with the mayoral challenge of the 1960s and 1970s, the dimensions of which were laid out most clearly by the Kerner Commission (National Advisory Commission on Civil Disorders 1968, 298): "Now, as never before, the American city has need for the personal qualities of strong democratic leadership" to address racial polarization, slum clearance, housing, police misconduct, poverty, and unemployment.

The prototype mayors of this earlier period were people like John Lindsay of New York, Jerome Cavanagh of Detroit, Kevin White of Boston, and Richard Lee of New Haven. They excelled in grantsmanship, and they understood how to use city hall as a bully pulpit in their efforts to bridge racial and class divisions. As Sonenshein, Schockman, and DeLeon (1996, 5) described, "Sympathetic to the urban poor, supported by private philanthropy and federal aid, seeking redevelopment, these liberal mayors redefined the mayoral role." In the political climate of the 1990s, however, mayors seek guidance to accomplish their leadership tasks not first by reference to the moral compass of liberal reform but rather from the more neutral market. According to Gurwitt (1994, 26), Mayor Steven Goldsmith of Indianapolis, who exemplifies the new mayoral type, argues that market forces and competition ultimately serve the citizens of his city better than the government monopoly. Mastery of the market, he believes, requires the ingenuity of the entrepreneur and the management skills of a corporate executive officer (CEO).

The new mayors seem at ease with their fiscal self-reliance. The mayor of Nashville, quoted in an editorial in *The Wall Street Journal* ("Cities Discover Federalism" 1995), professed that "it's not all bad [that] Washington is busy extricating itself from . . . responsibility for well-being [in the cities]." Cities now have more freedom to experiment. John Norquist, mayor of Milwaukee, made a similar point about the freeing effects of federal divestment: Federal grants, he says, "are only costing us more money, because they force us to . . . do things we wouldn't otherwise do" (quoted in Osborne 1992, 63).

The new mayors speak the language of modern public management and run their administrations accordingly. They believe in reinvention, innovation, privatization, competition, strategic planning, and productivity improvements. They favor economic development and low taxes, partnership with the business sector, and good housekeeping. As Mayor Norquist reportedly said ("A Genuine New Democrat" 1996), his success is a function of performance, not ideology.

The issue of privatization illustrates how the commitment to the new public management crosses partisan and racial boundaries. Although Mayor Goldsmith, a Republican who once declared that he wanted to become the CEO of Indianapolis, is noted for his leadership in privatizing public services, the same policies have been pursued with equal fervor by Mayor Richard Daley, Jr. of Chicago, a Democrat, and by successive black mayoral administrations in Detroit (see Smith and Leyden 1996; Jackson and Wilson 1996). Daley has been particularly vigorous in contracting formerly public responsibilities to private firms, including, among others, the parking garage at O'Hare Airport, sewer cleaning, office janitorial services, the management of public golf courses, water customer billing, abandoned automobile collection, parking ticket enforcement, and tree stump removal.

The change in the moral tenor of urban politics is perhaps nowhere more evident than in the cities governed by black mayors. "New black leaders," such as Michael White of Cleveland, Kurt Schmoke of Baltimore, Marc Morial of New Orleans, and others, are characterized as "technopoliticians" in contrast to such "champions of the race" as Coleman Young of Detroit and Marion Barry of Washington (Barras 1996, 20). According to Barras (p. 19), "They have moved beyond rallies and protest marches, replacing talk with action and ushering in a new era of competent, professional stewardship in cities."

Young's successor in Detroit provides an example. Peirce (1993, 3013) wrote that Mayor Dennis Archer's agenda is to fashion a "reinvented" city government "that pays its bills on time," improves its low bond rating, and "picks up garbage on time and keeps the streetlights on all night." Archer, who established close ties to the white business establishment in pursuit of economic development objectives, is contrasted with Young for "rejecting the politics of class and race." Similarly, Barras (1996) compared Bill Campbell, mayor of Atlanta, to the civil rights giants Maynard Jackson and Andrew Young, who preceded him in city hall.[5] Although Campbell is a strong supporter of affirmative action, he reportedly sees himself

> as the vanguard of a new generation of black leaders who embrace a less conspicuous brand of racial politics. . . . His agenda is less about the fight for black empowerment than about paving potholes, encouraging job growth, making neighborhoods safer and building downtown housing. (Sack 1996)

Two decades ago, the social agendas of both black and white mayors captured the attention of the news media and urban observers, but today, the public spotlight is on the new public managers. Eggers (1993) claimed that "America's boldest mayors" were Edward Rendell of Philadelphia, Milwaukee's Norquist, and Indianapolis's Goldsmith. What was bold about these urban leaders was their management initiatives: Rendell's Private Sector Task Force on Management and Productivity, which saved the city more than $150 million; Norquist's strategic budget process; and Goldsmith's introduction of competitive bidding between city service providers and private firms.

Leadership as public management is what urban electorates apparently want in this age of local fiscal self-reliance. In fact, America's boldest mayors hardly stand out from their colleagues in other cities. Mayor Richard Riordan of Los Angeles, a businessman turned politician, runs his city in the style of a CEO—nonideological, managerial, eschewing the "arts of political leadership and public appeals" (Sonenshein, Schockman, and DeLeon 1996, 15). Even Rudolph Giuliani of New York, an aggressive and brash former public prosecutor, came to office promising to "reinvent" city government by cutting and streamlining its massive size (Gurwitt 1995, 23).

# The New Federal Order Brings New City Limits

In the New Federal Order, the fiscal links between Washington and the cities have become significantly attenuated. More than at any time since the early Great Society years, city governments can spend only what they can raise. It is possible to imagine several responses to this local fiscal autonomy. One response is to raise taxes to maintain the array of service responsibilities that people have come to expect. To some modest extent, this is what city governments have done. Beginning in 1982 and continuing through the decade, city governments increased per capita tax revenues to offset rising expenditure burdens (Bahl et al. 1991, Table 7). Another response is to engage vigorously in economic development activities, seeking to raise additional revenues by growing the indigenous tax base. There is strong evidence that this has been done in cities too (Clarke and Gaile 1989).

Another response, ever sensitive to citizen resistance to higher taxes, is to husband the resources that cities control through more careful management strategies characterized by contracting out, strategic planning, downsizing, and reorganizing. There is strong evidence that this, too, has been a major response in the cities to the New Federal Order.

The resultant emergence of a public management agenda in place of a social reform platform—what Sonenshein, Schockman, and DeLeon (1996) called the platform of multiethnic liberalism—might be seen as a narrowing of political vision. In a different light, better, more innovative management of the scarce resources under local control may be seen as simply a realistic response to a fiscal world very different from that of a quarter of a century ago. In a sense, the absence of a growing stream of federal dollars has meant that city political leaders cannot afford, fiscally or politically, to push an agenda of social and racial reform financed by local taxpayers alone. Nor can municipal leaders find much encouragement for defying these realities: Left to confront the great urban racial and economic polarities, few elected officials would be so foolhardy as to risk inevitable failure by initiating solutions based solely on the modest and limited resources that they themselves can raise. It is far easier—

and the outcome more certain—to lower taxes, reduce government employment, and fill potholes. City limits have never been more in evidence.

# NOTES

1. The definition of municipal is somewhat broad. In its analysis, the USCM included Food
   Stamps, AFDC, Headstart, and National Endowment for the Arts grants, none of which, by
   any account, would be regarded as particularly municipal in character. But it also included various homeless assistance grants, a broad range of assisted housing programs,
   mass transit, community policing, and other such programs that have a strong urban component. Prior to 1995, the USCM tracked funding for a mix of specific programs and general categories of programs (see Table 1).
2. Testimony of Secretary of Transportation Federico Peña in the *Reauthorization of ISTEA*
   hearings before the Committee on Transportation and Infrastructure, U.S. House of Representatives, 2 May 1996.
3. A $5 billion cut in federal food assistance would reduce food spending by $750 million
   per year, a .10% decrease. Smallwood et al. (1995) calculated that 3,600 farm jobs would
   be lost, as well as 14,000 jobs in food processing and another 103,000 jobs that are generated indirectly.
4. An excellent comparison of the features of the new welfare law with the old Aid to Families with Dependent Children program is contained in Burke (1996).
5. In a national survey of 1,211 black Americans conducted in 1992 for the *Detroit News*,
   researchers found that 94% of the respondents believed that the people who came to
   power during the Civil Rights era were out of touch with the real concerns of ordinary
   African-Americans. Such leaders continue to cite racism as the most pressing issue facing
   blacks, but the black citizenry is concerned about crime, employment, and economic
   prospects (Barras 1996, 19).

# BIBLIOGRAPHY

Advisory Commission on Intergovernmental Relations. 1994. *Significant features of fiscal federalism, 1994.*
     Vol. 2. Washington, DC Government Printing Office.
Bahl, R., J. Martinez, D. Sjoquist, and L. Williams. 1991. The fiscal conditions of U.S. cities at the beginning
     of the 1990s. Paper presented at the Urban Institute Conference on Big City Governance and Fiscal
     Choices, Southern California University, Los Angeles, June.
Barras, J. R. 1996. From symbolism to substance: The rise of America's new generation of black political
     leaders. *New Democrat* 8 (November-December): 19–22.
Burke, V. 1996. New welfare law: Comparison of the new block grant program with Aid to Families with
     Dependent Children. Congressional Research Service Report to Congress, 26 August.
Center on Budget and Policy Priorities. 1996 (22 March). The NGA Medicaid proposal will shift costs onto
     local governments. Washington, DC: Author.
Chernick, H., and A. Reschovsky. 1997. Urban fiscal problems: Coordinating actions among governments.
     In *The urban crisis: Linking research to action,* edited by B. Weisbrod and J. Worthy, 131–176.
     Evanston, IL: Northwestern University Press.
Cities discover federalism. 1995. *The Wall Street Journal,* 8 December.
Clark, T. N. 1994. Race and class versus the New Political Culture. In *Urban Innovation,* edited by T. N.
     Clark, 21–78. Thousand Oaks, CA. Sage Publications.

Clarke, S., and G. Gaile. 1989. Moving toward entrepreneurial economic development policies: Opportunities and barriers. *Policy Studies Journal* 17 (spring): 574–598.

Eggers, W. D. 1993. City lights: America's boldest mayors. *Policy Review* (summer): 67–74.

Finder, A. 1996. Welfare clients outnumber jobs they might fill. *The New York Times*, 25 August. A genuine new democrat. 1996. *The Wall Street Journal*, 21 March.

Gurwitt, R. 1994. Indianapolis and the Republican future. *Governing* 7 (February): 24–28.

———. 1995. The trials of Rudy Giuliani. *Governing* 8 (June): 23–27.

———. 1996. Detroit dresses for business. *Governing* 8 (April): 38–42.

Jackson, C., and D. Wilson. 1996. Service delivery in Detroit, Michigan. Paper presented at the annual meeting of the Midwest Political Science Association, Chicago, IL, April.

Ladd, H. 1994. Big-city finances. In *Big-city politics, governance, and fiscal constraints*, edited by G. Peterson, 201–66. Washington, DC: Urban Institute.

National Advisory Commission on Civil Disorders. 1968. *Report of the National Advisory Commission on Civil Disorders.* New York: Bantam.

Osborne, D. 1992. John Norquist and the Milwaukee experiment. *Governing* 5 (November); 63.

Pagano, M., J. Lobenhofer, and A. Dudas. 1996. Cities and the changing federal system: Estimating the Impacts of the Contract with America. Department of Political Science, Miami University of Ohio. Typescript.

Peirce, N. 1993. Motor City's "Mayor Realtor." *National Journal*, 18 December, 30–33.

Rapp, D. 1994. A program for Billy Yeager. *Governing* 7 (July): 80.

Sack, K. 1996. Mayor finds old issue emerging in new way. *The New York Times*, 15 July.

Smallwood, D. B. Kuhn, K. Hanson, S. Vogel, and J. Blaylock. 1995. Economic effects of refocusing national food-assistance efforts. *Food Review* 18 (January-April): 2–12.

Smith, D., and K. Leyden. 1996. Exploring the political dimension of privatization: A tale of two cities. Paper presented at the annual meeting of the Midwest Political Science Association, Chicago, IL, April.

Sonenshein, R., E. Schockman, and R. DeLeon. 1996. Urban conservatism in an age of diversity. Paper presented at the 1996 annual meeting of the Western Political Science Association, San Francisco, California, March.

Stanfield, R. 1996. Mayors are the soul of the new machine. *National Journal* 28 (24 August): 1801–1802.

Stegman, M. 1996. Speech presented at Rutgers University, Princeton, NJ, 28 February.

Super, D., S. Parrott, S. Steinmetz, and C. Mann. 1996. The new welfare law. Policy brief. Washington, DC: Center on Budget and Policy Priorities.

U.S. Conference of Mayors (USCM). 1994. *The federal budget and the cities.* Washington, DC: Government Printing Office.

———. 1995–1997. Funding levels for key municipal programs. Annual releases. Washington, DC: Author.

U.S. Government Accounting Office. 1996. Community development: Status of urban empowerment zones. Report to the chair of the Subcommittee on Human Resources and Intergovernmental Relations, Committee on Government Reform and Oversight, House of Representatives, Washington, DC, December.

Wallin, B. 1996. Federal retrenchment and state-local response: Lessons from the past. Paper presented at the annual meeting of the American Political Science Association, San Francisco, 30 August.

Weir, M. 1996. Big cities confront the New Federalism. Paper presented at Columbia University, New York, 12 April.

# 27

## Pietro S. Nivola

## FEDERAL PRESCRIPTIONS AND CITY PROBLEMS

It would be nice if America's local governments had a consistent history of good conduct. In reality much has gone wrong—at times so wrong any fair observer would have welcomed or at least understood an extensive federal usurpation of local powers. Think about the following episodes from various cities.

On the evening of May 31, 1921, a lynch mob in Tulsa, Oklahoma, descended on the municipal courthouse in search of a black man who had been charged with (and later acquitted of) raping a white woman.[1] After an altercation at the courthouse the mob invaded the city's black neighborhood, destroying thirty-five square blocks and murdering hundreds of residents. At one downtown location 123 blacks were found clubbed to death. How did city and state authorities respond as the bloodbath unfolded? The Tulsa police department deputized large numbers of the white vigilantes and, according to an account citing court records from the time, instructed them to "go out and kill." The state of Oklahoma appointed a Tulsa Race Riot Commission to launch an investigation—more than three-quarters of a century later.

In 1975 a strange thing happened: New York, the biggest city in the world's richest nation, neared bankruptcy. The sources of this fiscal crisis were complex, but at least one root cause was unmistakable: New York had spent beyond its means on redistributive social services.[2] This municipal welfare state could no longer be sustained by its vulnerable local tax base.

More recently the Atlanta metropolitan area has been experiencing a buildup of air pollution.[3] Along the eastern seaboard of the United States no metropolis belches more smog than Atlanta. It has one of the dirtiest coal-fired power plants in the country, and emission levels of nitrous oxides from motor vehicles have regularly exceeded the Environmental Protection Agency's (EPA) caps and projections. The local political establishment, however, has been slow to act. While Draconian steps such as ordering a four-day work week were rightly rejected, so were more modest proposals—like charging for parking spaces and converting to cleaner fuels. The idea of cleaner fuel, which implied a slight increase in energy prices, caused consternation in the Georgia legislature.

In 1989 a well-known journalist, staunchly committed to public education, described a problem his son experienced in a classroom of the public school system of the city in which they resided. "One of my children," the journalist

From *Tense Commandments: Federal Prescriptions and City Problems* by Pietro S. Nivola, pp. 15–24, 26–31, 32–33, 33–35, 36, 38–41, 45–47, 165–176. Copyright © 2002 The Brookings Institution. Reprinted with permission.

wrote, "spent a year with an elementary school science teacher who had been shifted from teaching English. She was fully 'qualified' to teach, since she had her credentials, but she knew less about science than most of the children did."[4] One of the things this qualified science teacher did not know was how the moon revolved around the earth.

# The Trouble with Localism

The derelictions of local government range from the barbaric to the regrettable, the irresponsible, and the merely ridiculous. What they imply, though, is that in the absence of enforced national standards some self-governed communities have proved capable of sinking below the most elementary regard for public competency, environmental safeguards, financial prudence, or even basic human rights.

The account about the public school teacher who did not understand the orbit of the moon was hardly unique. Reports of this sort or worse are sufficiently common to stir calls for national education standards. Nor was the Tulsa race riot of 1921 an isolated incident. In a wave of hysteria about rumored rapes of whites by blacks during the 1920s racial violence erupted in cities across the country.[5] The federal government may not have had at its disposal sufficient statutory powers to quell these atrocities or even to prosecute their perpetrators. Would that it had.

In the case of Atlanta's polluted atmosphere the argument for national "hammers" to compel an end to the local policy paralysis went beyond a need to protect the region's residents from possible health risks. Air pollution crosses boundaries. Concentrations of ozone can drift across hundreds of square miles. One place's foul air pollutes another region's water.[6] Why should people living in other jurisdictions have to inhale or swallow the poisons spewing from a neighboring urban area whose citizens year after year are not curtailing their wide-ranging effluents?

As Madison warned in *Federalist No. 10*, the inertia of local government has to do, at least in part, with the ability of entrenched interests to capture small polities: how can municipal school systems reinvent themselves when their administrations remain in the grip of obstructive teachers' unions? Will a one-company town, whose factory is the local economy's mainstay but also its worst polluter, put in a fix? Localism begets freeloading. When some jurisdictions become welfare magnets, others are tempted to lower their benefits below an acceptable minimum. A city or state whose contaminated air or water flows downstream to neighboring cities or states has little incentive to control the spillover for their sake. Indeed localities competing for business investment and taxable income might reciprocally "dumb down" standards.[7]

Clearly if interjurisdictional competition and externalities arbitrarily enrich certain communities at the expense of others or else draw too many into a "race to the bottom," or if local mismanagement is so endemic it corrupts the commonweal, or mischievous local factions egregiously violate the fundamental freedoms of citizens, the solution seems plain: "extend the sphere" of governance, as Madison recommended, shifting control from the "smaller" jurisdictions to "the Union."[8]

# Mandating without Spending

In the past half-century most of this remedial enlargement of the national ambit has been purchased with federal dollars. As of 1990 nearly $120 billion in grants to state and local governments was being disbursed to patch alleged shortcomings of local policies in transportation, environmental protection, economic development, job training, education, public safety, and much more.[9] Because the purpose of this funding has not been to distribute unrestricted handouts but largely to make up for local deficiencies, receipt of the funds has been conditioned on compliance with a plethora of federal requirements. In theory those requirements could be ignored if the grantees simply turned down the money. In practice this became almost impossible. He who pays the piper calls the tune. New federal instructions are often affixed after the grant programs have been institutionalized. By then their constituencies are so well organized the programs have all but ceased to be voluntary. And typically the federal rules remain firmly in place even if congressional appropriations fall far short of authorizations. The local provision of special education for students with disabilities, for instance, is essentially governed by federal law, even though Congress has never even come close to appropriating its authorized share of this $43 billion-a-year mandate.

Federal grants feature these bait-and-switch dynamics because, despite considerable weaning during the past couple of decades, local governments remain dependent on whatever aid they can get. There are far fewer federal aid junkies today than twenty years ago (when more than three-quarters of the revenues in cities such as Detroit came from Washington), but federal aid remains a substantial source of state and local revenue, still exceeding in many places the proceeds from sales taxes or property taxes.

## Going Off Budget

Paying the piper, however, is but one way of gaining influence. In recent decades the manner in which Washington exerts control changed. As the national government's deficits grew, and Congress's propensity to throw money at domestic programs bumped against budget caps, a tendency developed for the federal government to regulate local governments more stringently while aiding them less generously.[10] At the end of 1974 some forty federal mandates reflected this pattern. Twenty years later the number had grown by almost 160 percent (Figure 8.1).[11] Presidents Ronald Reagan and George Bush put up faint resistance to what the Advisory Commission on Intergovernmental Relations had come to call regulatory federalism, even in the realm of administrative rulemakings. Between 1981 and 1986 Reagan presided over the promulgation of some 140 agency rules that placed nearly six thousand new obligations on states and localities.[12]

To local entities, of course, many of these actions seemed unfair and irrational. To policymakers at the national level, however, there was method in the madness. Before a retrenchment commenced in the 1980s federal grant giving

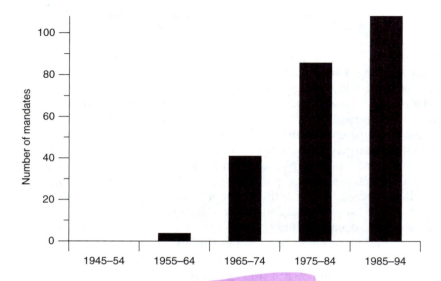

**Figure 8.1**   Federal Mandates on State and Local Governments, 1955–1994.
*Source:* National Conference of State Legislatures, as cited in Clyde Wayne Crews Jr., *Ten Thousand Commandments: A Policymaker's Snapshot of the Federal Regulatory State* (Washington: Competitive Enterprise Institute, September 1996), p. 17.

had gotten out of control. Between 1960 and 1980 expenditures increased one and a half times as fast as the growth of the economy. Funds were tossed hither and yon, sponsoring countless questionable "community development" needs—like the construction of a tennis complex in an affluent section of Little Rock, Arkansas, and the expansion of a municipal golf course in Alhambra, California.[13] Gradual curtailment of such waste after 1980 was a positive change regardless of whether a less profligate government might try to extend its influence by means of off-budget regulations.

Indeed, as the federal government applied the brakes to discretionary spending and eventually managed to bring a bloated budget into balance in the 1990s, inflation and interest rates fell, and the national economy surged. Federal austerity yielded by way of economic growth a large net gain for the nation and for the treasuries of most states and municipalities. With plenty of states and many cities now running surpluses there was something to be said for devolving to them more chores and expenses.[14]

Passing responsibilities to local authorities can be fiscally prudent not only for the federal fisc but for society.[15] If local public works are mostly funded by Washington, their costs are harder to contain. States, cities, and counties do not print money; to spend they have to tax. Local resistance to taxation encourages cost consciousness.[16]

## Stingy or Just Thriftier?

Local politicians wish Congress would simply shovel them cash and ask no questions. What the same politicians do not always acknowledge is that when Congress declines to write blank checks, and instead subjects state and local governments to uncompensated demands, some of the demands actually conform to local preferences.[17] A federal law that, say, asks states to administer particular licensing procedures for truck drivers using interstate highways is not an oppressive request if almost every state already has adopted, or willingly intends to adopt, essentially those same procedures. Hence, while the locals are often quick to say that, at a minimum, they should be paid back for the cost of meeting federal requirements, an indiscriminate policy of reimbursements would pose a moral hazard. States and municipalities that had been poised to take the desired actions anyhow would acquire an excuse to stop, sit back, and wait for federal payments.

Nor should taxpayers from afar be expected to indulge local governments that get themselves into trouble. In the early 1990s the governor of California, Pete Wilson, repeatedly complained that Washington was leaving his state too many of the burdens of servicing immigrants. In the next breath he insisted that his state had a rightful claim to hundreds of millions of dollars in federal disaster relief for property damage from earthquakes, floods, and mudslides, even in areas in which permissive California building regulations were substantially responsible for the losses.[18] The rotting rubbish at New York City's primary municipal dump discharges into the tri-state region not only one million gallons of polluted water each day but also large quantities of methane, a major contributor to global warming. People residing in Oregon or Oklahoma—or, for that matter, New Jersey and Connecticut—should not be taxed to detoxify the garbage New Yorkers generate. Efficiency and equity requires that the polluters pay. Most federal environmental regulations operate on that logical principle.

Besides, though federal grants for mandatory pollution abatement have shrunk, other parts of the federal welfare state continued to support the nation's cities. Even during the Reagan years, the social safety net frayed less completely than many observers feared. Measured in constant dollars, federal welfare payments, Food Stamps, Medicaid, child nutrition, and supplemental feeding for women and children—all programs essential to cities—held up reasonably well between 1980 and 1990.[19]

Some would argue that the ability to deduct local property taxes and to exclude interest income earned by state and local debt instruments from the federal income tax represents a $70 billion concession to local control.[20] In 1988 the Supreme Court decided that Congress was free, if it wished, to tax the interest on municipal bonds.[21] Their tax-free status nonetheless has remained intact and continues to favor the beneficiaries with preferential rates of interest. The deductibility of local income and property taxes enables localities to raise more revenue than they otherwise could. Along with these constants at least one other remains in the equation: about half of the billions of dollars in revenues received annually from the sale of minerals, timber, and other commodities on public lands is shared with states and localities.

In sum in the United States as in any other country exactly what the central government "owes" subnational jurisdictions is a debatable matter. And certainly there are times when the Union, in Madisonian terms, has reason to take charge of local affairs—and can legitimately do so even without further indemnifying local governments.

## The Yellow Line

But there also can be too much of a good thing.

Consider a small sample of the municipal functions now touched by national regulations. Federal law draws a line, commonly bright yellow, behind which passengers are forbidden to stand when they ride city buses. In many states, federal law may have a say in how firefighters should be deployed when fighting a fire. Federal law has influenced decisions about how long some unruly students in public schools can be suspended. Federal law has a bearing on how much a city pays for everything from snow removal services to contracts for sidewalk ramps. Federal law can affect whether the recruits for a police department are physically fit. Whether your child can walk to school or must commute by bus may depend on federal law. The degree to which a city's vacant industrial land parcels have to be cleared of toxic waste is dictated by federal law. The salary your child's teacher is paid may be affected by federal law that reaches well beyond the national minimum wage. Federal law addresses what protective measures must be taken to secure municipal landfills, school buildings that contain asbestos, and housing units with lead paint. Federal law determines how a city has to purify its drinking water.

None of these examples are flights of fancy.

When charges for basic municipal services rise, personnel costs are typically the reason. In the wake of the Supreme Court's opinion in the 1985 case of *Garcia v. San Antonio Metropolitan Transit Authority* the entire local public sector became liable for retroactive pay to employees filing claims for overtime compensation.[22] Before that time, Congress had moved in 1974 to include state and local governments under the minimum wage and overtime pay provisions of the Fair Labor Standards Act, but two years later this exercise of the commerce clause power had been overturned.[23] *Garcia*, and the subsequent statutory reinstatement of FLSA coverage in the local public sector, can help explain the high cost of operating a fleet of city snowplows during a Sunday night snowstorm.

The Americans with Disabilities Act of 1990 (ADA) tells every municipality to install ramps so that streets and sidewalks can be wheelchair accessible. But when any federal funds help construct these special accommodations (or any other local public works projects) the Davis-Bacon Act, a vestige of the New Deal, requires that the municipal contracts go not to the lowest bidders but to those who pay the "prevailing" (that is, union negotiated) wage of laborers working comparable projects in the geographic vicinity.[24]

Antibias suits brought under the auspices of federal statutes are now so pervasive they shape the employment practices of every municipal agency.

Sometimes this litigation appears to have discouraged police departments from testing rigorously for the physical qualifications of the men and women that apply for jobs. For example, after it interrupted such testing in 1986 because of legal challenges, the New York Police Department found itself with some hires who were unfit.[25]

The federally ordained special education program, frequently enforced in painstaking detail by judicial consent decrees, now takes so large a bite out of the budgets of urban school districts that many are unable to raise their regular classroom teachers' salaries, which lag behind those of wealthier suburban districts.

Beginning in the 1960s a number of federal court decisions greatly expanded the rights of students to appeal school suspensions.[26] Despite more modulated opinions by the Supreme Court in later years few teachers or principals can ignore the legal minefield they enter when they contemplate disciplinary actions, especially against students said to be suffering from learning disabilities.[27]

Whether children in a city attend neighborhood schools or are bused sometimes over great distances often hinges on whether and with what methods a federal court order is regulating the racial composition of the city's school system.

As for the instructions to firefighters and the federal pettifogging about where to stand on local public buses, the first fall under standard operating procedures formulated by the Occupational Safety and Health Administration (OSHA).[28] The second is a Department of Transportation (DOT) regulation, which reads as follows:

> Every bus which is designed and constructed so as to allow standees, shall be plainly marked with a line of contrasting color at least 2 inches wide or equipped with some other means so as to indicate to any person that he/she is prohibited from occupying a space forward of a perpendicular plane drawn through the rear of the driver's seat and perpendicular to the longitudinal axis of the bus. Every bus shall have clearly posted at or near the front, a sign with letters at least one half inch high stating that it is a violation of the Federal Highway Administration's regulations for a bus to be operated with persons occupying the prohibited area.[29]

## Crossing the Line

The immersion of the central government in most of these matters seems hard to understand. Why should a national cabinet department or regulatory bureaucracy concern itself with how "standees" ride city buses or with the deployment of firefighters? If local transit authorities or fire departments cannot be left to decide such minutiae, what, if anything, are local governments for? Surely few of the activities in question—putting out fires, riding buses, disciplining troublemakers in schools, hiring police officers, remunerating city workers or contractors—blow fallout across jurisdictions the way some forms of environmental pollution do. . . .

# One Size Does Not Fit All

The point of federalizing standards is to set norms for society as a whole and hence ensure uniformity. However, uniform rules of little significance for some jurisdictions can be onerous for others. The reach of the amended Fair Labor Standards Act is illustrative. It extends to public employers the mandatory minimum wage and other provisions that the FLSA originally reserved only for private firms. Not only does this generic regulation of workplaces carry different implications for municipalities than markets, its effects vary from one location to the next. The law would not have for most suburban towns, with no unionized employees, comparatively small payrolls, and bountiful tax bases, the same costly consequences it has had for some major cities.

A federal lawsuit that contests traditional fitness tests can pose difficulties for a big city's police force like New York's, which has to cope with crime-ridden slums. The same suit would be of little consequence for, say, Beverly Hills, a place so affluent and sheltered that, as the joke goes, the police department has an unlisted phone number.[30]

## Green Mandates

The unequal impacts of federal environmental regulations are sometimes notorious.[31] In 1987 Congress concluded that every municipality in the United States would have to treat storm water much the same as discharge of polluted water from industrial plants. This requirement, appropriate for humid climates, was ill-suited to arid regions such as much of the Southwest. Never mind that Phoenix averages only seven inches of rainfall a year. This city nonetheless was required to spend large sums each year monitoring the runoff from extremely infrequent rain storms.

Between 1974 and 1994 American taxpayers poured $213 billion into upgrading their municipal water-treatment plants. Now the EPA predicts that $200 billion more will be needed through the year 2014 to bring local wastewater systems up to newly specified design criteria. To that estimate must be added another $132 billion for the replacement of aging plants. The projected total, therefore, rises to $332 billion—a figure that does not include the soaring increases in operating and maintenance expenses associated with more advanced technologies. If the recent past is prologue, local governments will be expected to come up with more than 90 percent of the funding for these capital improvements, plus 100 percent of annual operating expenses.

And for at least some cities the bill will be needlessly steep. Under the Clean Water Act cities have to install secondary wastewater treatment facilities that remove the remaining organic matter not treated in primary facilities. While secondary treatment is usually necessary for landlocked communities, according to a 1993 study by the National Academy of Sciences, the same precaution may not be essential for many seaport cities. Tides at coastal cities help flush organic residue from water bodies. Although the EPA has granted a number of waivers, arguably more oceanside cities ought to receive dispensations.[32]

So stringent are the federal criteria for cleaning up local land containing toxic wastes, and so unsparing have been the liability provisions, that developers and lending institutions have resisted investing in many abandoned industrial and commercial sites. A recent survey of more than two hundred cities by the U.S. Conference of Mayors reported no fewer than 81,000 acres of brownfields, including some undoubtedly entangled in Superfund suits. These sites continue to languish in the inner cities, costing them possibly as much as $2.4 billion in lost property tax revenue each year and foreclosing opportunities to create as many as 550,000 jobs. Meanwhile policymakers bewail the "sprawl" wrought by businesses that, steering clear of the legal liabilities, opt to locate on virgin acreage in the suburbs.

Under the rules of the Safe Drinking Water Act localities everywhere have been busy examining their water supplies for pesticides and other toxic residues that pose substantial risks only in particular areas. Before it was finally relieved from some of this duty in the mid-1990s Columbus, Ohio, found itself guarding against approximately forty pesticides. Many of them had long since been discontinued in the vicinity, including one product used chiefly on pineapple plantations in Hawaii.[33]

At times the nationalized regulations appear to have created new problems at the regional level. New York, for instance, ran afoul of a national prohibition on ocean dumping of sewage sludge. Banned since 1988 from disposing of any sludge at sea, the city resorted to dewatering and composting its waste. But this practice emits nitrogen-rich effluents that endanger marine life in nearby estuaries. In March 1998 the state of Connecticut filed suit against the city for contaminating Long Island Sound.[34]

## Rights and Wrongs

If environmental standards often do not admit enough diversification, latitude, and cognizance of costs at the local level, the federal regulations that fall under the capacious category of civil rights permit even less. For the most part this is as it should be. "Rights tends to be viewed as absolutes," explains Robert A. Katzmann, "overriding considerations of cost effectiveness."[35] But no society can afford to extend "total justice" to an ever-increasing variety of petitioners.[36] What began in the 1960s as a long-awaited effort to secure equality of opportunity for African Americans has expanded into a vast apparatus of federally mandated protections and preferences for many additional groups. Whether every class of claimants has needed maximal compulsory remedies is a good question. So is whether each remedy should be determined from the top down.

Consider the rights of persons with disabilities. The ideal of accommodating the physically impaired is just and desirable, but should every municipality be told how to improve handicapped access in its public facilities? To modernize public buses and retrofit subways, as demanded by the Rehabilitation Act of 1973, New York concluded in 1980 that the requisite capital improvements and annual operating bills would amount to a budget-busting expense. Mayor Edward I. Koch figured, "It would be cheaper for us to provide every severely disabled person with taxi service than make 255 of our subway stations accessible."[37]

Mercifully, after pitched legal battles, the federal planners relented and lowered the costs. New York, with an old and extensive transit system, should never have been sidetracked from opting for alternatives to the federal retrofit policy. For this city it should have been obvious from the outset that investing in advanced paratransit or even subsidizing taxi rides would secure a greater net gain for the seriously disabled and for beleaguered local taxpayers.

In 1973 during the congressional debate on the Rehabilitation Act, the bill's authors seemed to have had no clue that in venues like New York the legislation's burdens might well exceed its blessings. One of the chief sponsors admitted afterward that neither he nor any of his colleagues "had any concept that it would involve such tremendous costs."[38] The deliberations were not altogether different sixteen years later when Congress took up the Americans with Disabilities Act of 1990, an even bolder piece of legislation mandating "fair and just access."[39] Local authorities pleaded for greater leeway or else for federal aid to cushion compliance costs, but Congress seemed untroubled. It wrote into the ADA a raft of requirements and almost no financial assistance.[40]

At congressional hearings on the ADA a representative of the Memphis Area Transit Authority guessed that the measure, if adopted, would force that city to eliminate hundreds of thousands of transit trips annually.[41] Dire warnings like this one about the fiscal havoc the bill portended proved mostly exaggerated. Nevertheless the law's seeming insouciance about local dissimilarities hit some communities hard. Faced with an ultimatum to construct some 65,000 wheelchair ramps by the mid-1990s the city of Phoenix reported that "it would be physically impossible to find enough skilled labor in the Valley to conduct such a massive construction program, even if the deadline were several years away.[42] Ordered to incorporate curb cuts and sidewalk ramps in its plans for downtown street repaving, officials in Philadelphia guessed that more than a third of its planned repavements would be unaffordable.[43] The Washington Metro in the nation's capital is America's most modern and beautifully designed subway system. Nonetheless it was directed to tear up parts of forty-five station platforms and install bumpy tiles along edges to accommodate the sight impaired. Interestingly the two leading organizations representing the blind—the American Council of the Blind and the National Federation of the Blind—disagreed about whether this multimillion dollar effort would protect sight-impaired transit users or perhaps endanger them.

## Zero Tolerance

How to handle municipal overtime pay, regulate the town water supply, or resurface city streets and sidewalks used to be judgments that local authorities dispatched. Now, more and more of these daily administrative duties are subject to federal guidance. Whatever the rationale for guiding so many quotidian decisions, however, the government's agenda would be less troublesome for many cities if its specifications sought to set only modest baselines. Alas the specifications are sometimes utopian.

## Environmental Perfection

A number of U.S. environmental mandates certainly seem to qualify for that description. Their targets, timetables, and technologies seem specified without regard to whether the perils the rules are meant to diminish are great or small. Indeed policy in important instances proceeds as if risk should be banished at any price. This feverish pursuit of environmental purification, sometimes tolerating virtually no margin of health risk, is unreasonable for many municipalities and thousands of businesses.

When the EPA revised its goals for curbing effluents from municipal incinerators in 1995, for instance, it ordered the virtual elimination of emissions of mercury and lead as well as dioxin.[44] Most of these toxic substances had already dropped dramatically; overall lead emissions, for example, were down 98 percent between 1970 and 1995. The city of Tampa, which had finished building a state-of-the-art incinerator only ten years earlier, now had to refit that modern installation with another round of pollution control equipment costing scores of millions of dollars.[45]

How much the latest incineration standards would improve public health was uncertain. In a review of epidemiological research on the health of persons living near city incinerators in the United Kingdom one study discerned no consistent pattern of ill health.[46] The findings were interesting because the studies surveyed relied primarily on data from the 1970s and 1980s when pollution controls on incinerators were underdeveloped. After at least a decade of stringent regulation it was likely that the remaining health hazards from these facilities would be small—especially in the United States where a person's average exposure to poisons such as mercury is now less than half the average in Europe.[47]

In 1994 the Congressional Budget Office estimated that under the Comprehensive Environmental Response, Compensation and Liability Act the expense of cleaning up the nation's toxic waste dumps would run between $106 billion and a staggering $463 billion.[48] How could this environmental project cost more than twice the entire gross domestic product of Sweden? The excesses of Superfund bear some responsibility. Costs escalate when sites have to be decontaminated so pristinely that a child playing on them could safely eat their dirt for seventy days a year.[49] Thus the program had completed merely 52 of 1,320 designated sites as of 1993. City governments have incurred directly only a fraction of the multibillion dollar Superfund bill. But the persistence of old brownfields, at least partly shadowed by Superfund liabilities, continues to be for inner cities a financial sinkhole. . . .

## Hypersensitivity

In bygone days almost anyone joining a big city police force, fire department, sanitation crew, or inner city school system understood that he or she would be entering an often unpleasant, indeed perilous, occupation. The clients of these tough "street-level bureaucracies" were not always polite company, and neither would be some of the supervisors and coworkers. Nasty or boorish encounters would occur; they went with the territory.

Expectations are rather different nowadays. U.S. legal theories have added new meanings to the pursuit of admissible and equitable employment conditions. "Hostile" work environments, unintentional discriminations ("disparate impacts"), even precautions misconstrued as insults or slights—all these imperfections and more are actionable.

Taxpayers, not philanthropists, pay the salaries of municipal employees. One would think that city officials accountable to voters might be permitted to set, say, basic health eligibility criteria and then unceremoniously ask prospective employees for their medical histories, especially if the jobs in question were physically demanding, stressful, or dangerous. Not so fast. To attain a bias-free environment for applicants with disabilities, such queries now have to be conducted with extreme delicacy, if indeed, they can be conducted at all. In one of many revealing vignettes in his 1997 book *The Excuse Factory*, Walter K. Olson relates what happened to a policeman in Boston who was disciplined after his superiors discovered that he had lied under oath about having received inpatient psychiatric care on five occasions. The policeman had to be reinstated, with back pay and damages.[50] What about the subway cleaner in New York who was refused a promotion to train operator because his corpulence prevented him from passing a basic stress test? He had standing to sue for alleged discrimination, did, and got the job.[51]

Sometimes the kinds of pains taken to ensure benign work environments are not without ironies. "A Los Angeles Police Department official," Olson recounts, "said the department was moving against a range of 'inappropriate' male doings even though 'very, very few' of them 'would rise to the level of true sex harassment.'"[52] But some years later misconduct of a different sort was disclosed in the LAPD: some members of the force had trafficked in narcotics and were accused of planting evidence, framing suspects, and shooting some unarmed ones.[53] What had been done to prevent *these* doings? Apparently too little according to newspaper accounts. Some of the officers implicated in the scandal seem to have been hired without adequately checking their backgrounds, which included histories of arrests and alcoholism.[54]

At all levels of government in the United States efforts to protect the civil rights of workers have moved beyond the original mission—to attain basic equality of opportunity for an oppressed minority in the labor force. State and local jurists often have been just as uncompromising as many federal ones in their efforts to sanitize employment procedures. (The Boston policeman took his grievance to a state court, though his could as easily have been a federal case.) The evolution of employment law at the federal level, however, has provided the legal foundation, and the main inspiration, for all concerned. . . .

# Adversarial Legalism

Which brings up a third feature of the ubiquitous federal presence: it has helped stoke a firestorm of litigation. Between 1991 and 1995 the cost of routine liability claims in New York City increased 57 percent in constant dollars.[55] By 1992 these legal bills were totaling more than the city's entire budget for its parks and libraries.[56] The trend in some other cities was worse. During the same period Minneapolis experienced a 187 percent increase in liability expenditures.[57]

And that was only one portion of the jagged legal landscape. Alongside the mounting malpractice complaints, traffic accident claims, zoning appeals, slip-and-falls, and countless other petty municipal torts came new causes to sue city governments, now increasingly in the federal courts. Several Supreme Court opinions had widened the general exposure of cities to civil actions.[58]

These and other stimulants made themselves felt.

## The Long Arm of the Lawsuit

Litigation in the federal courts exploded after 1960. That year there was a total of only 2,483 civil filings under the categories of civil rights-related cases, for example, whereas the number of such cases reached 98,153 by 1995.[59] Of these lawsuits, the ones that targeted the local public sector left virtually no facet of municipal administration undisputed. Major cities found themselves awash in court orders determining everything from the racial balancing of schools to the placement of foster children and the schooling of learning-disabled students, to the provision of shelters for the homeless, the use of city jails, buses, and even public fire alarm boxes.

Fire alarm boxes? In 1996 a federal judge halted the New York City Fire Department's plan to replace 16,300 antiquated alarm boxes with public telephones wired to an emergency system. The rationale: hearing-impaired persons might be unable to use the phones; the new system violated a federal guarantee of "equal access" to public facilities.[60]

For years a federal court had told New York how to run its jails. Conditions in the jails needed reform. But under the terms of its decree, active since 1978, the court-appointed "special masters" became fastidious. No particular was spared—down to the ratio of cups of borax per gallon of water required to mop the bathrooms.[61]

In 1996, at the other end of the country, the Los Angeles Metropolitan Transit Authority (MTA) settled a federal suit in which the MTA was accused of discriminating against minorities because city buses on certain routes were very crowded. One of the plaintiffs characterized the conditions on the MTA's buses as "a brutal violation" of civil rights. The terms of the consent decree got into specifics: there could be no more than an average of fifteen people standing during bus rides for any twenty-minute peak period by the end of 1997; then no more than an average of eleven people by June 2000; then no more than eight by June 2002.[62]

While court orders like those in Los Angeles and New York had delved into details those in some other cities were detailed—and drastic. To relieve overcrowding in Philadelphia's prisons, for instance, a federal judge barred pretrial detention of any suspect not charged with a violent crime. The long-range purpose of this shock treatment was to ameliorate the city's jails, but in the meantime, according to the court's critics, the result was that the number of fugitive drug dealers soared.[63] By one count more than three-quarters of Philadelphia's drug dealers became fugitives within ninety days of their arrests.

To be sure, most legal threats to city authorities would fizzle well short of producing judicial injunctions, usually because the underlying grievances simply could not stand up even by the standards of the world's most accommodating civil justice system. That did not mean, however, that cities could ignore the threats. To limit liabilities millions of dollars have been spent each year paying lawyers, keeping legally bullet-proof records, purchasing insurance, commissioning consultants, administering sensitivity training to personnel, and so forth. . . .[64]

## Litigious Workplaces

Employment cases, which already accounted for about a quarter of all civil suits against city governments by the mid-1980s, multiplied as well.[65] A growing number were brought by people expecting to be made whole by one or another of the federal civil rights statutes. Energized by various bold enactments, such as the Age Discrimination in Employment Acts of 1975 and 1986, the Americans with Disabilities Act of 1990, and the Civil Rights Act amendments of 1991, federal antibias suits fanned out to service a lengthening queue of clients. As in environmental advocacy cases plaintiffs acquired new incentives to sue. After 1991, for example, the burden of proof in cases of alleged racial or ethnic discrimination was tilted against defendants. The mere composition by race of an employer's payroll could be used as *prima facie* evidence of racism, leaving the truth to the accused, not the accusers, to establish. The accusers, moreover, could have the fees of their attorneys and expert witnesses recovered in multiples when prejudice was proved. And compensatory and punitive damages became available, with the odds of collecting large sums significantly improved by the use of jury trials.

Novel legal assaults on municipal employment practices also came from federal authorities acting directly. Closely scrutinized by the Equal Employment Opportunity Commission and the Department of Justice's Civil Rights Division have been the testing procedures for city job candidates. In city after city the physical fitness tests conducted by police and fire departments as well as other municipal agencies came under suspicion of victimizing some protected classes (women, for instance), while the pencil-and-paper examinations administered under typical civil service systems risked charges of excluding others (for example, blacks and Hispanics). Statistical discrimination was found even when respectable quotients of minorities ultimately made their way into hiring pools. Minority candidates were 30 percent of those who took a special civil service exam designed to increase minority representation in New York City's police department in the early 1980s. Nearly two thousand blacks and Hispanics reached the final pool. But that was not enough, according to a federal judge, who proceeded to set a standard for the department whereby half of all new hires had to be black or Hispanic until they reached at least 30 percent of the total force. . . .[66]

## Suing the Schools

While the municipal workplace became increasingly litigious other sources of legal strife engulfed the delivery of city services, most notably the schools. For decades numerous cities had grappled with court-ordered desegregation plans, many of which had the unwanted consequence of aggravating racial imbalances by accelerating the exodus of white families from urban school systems.[67] These ordeals had finally run their course by the late 1990s, although not everywhere. As of 1995 several major city school districts, including those of Nashville, Buffalo, Indianapolis, and Memphis, were still operating under their original court orders or were still being supervised by a federal court though their original desegregation plans had been revised.[68] And as late as 1998 the DOJ was filing additional briefs requesting continued judicial supervision of the decades-old desegregation case in St. Louis.[69] But even as most of the forced busing experiments receded legal activists pressured school systems to secure other entitlements—such as a right to asbestos-free classrooms and the right of all children with disabilities to receive special educational services.

In 1975 Congress passed the Education of All Handicapped Children Act.[70] The aim of the law was to nationalize standards and procedures by which schools educated the handicapped. Teachers, administrators, and parents were to design jointly "individualized educational programs" for these children. The extensive tests and evaluations needed to prepare the programs could not be "racially or culturally discriminatory." Parents dissatisfied with a program were entitled to appeal up the line, ultimately to the federal courts. Schools would have to mainstream students "to the maximum extent appropriate" and provide for them "related services" such as physical therapy, psychological counseling, and recreational facilities. No school could change the placement of a special education student without parental approval. School districts would be required to identify all possible candidates for special education. This so-called child-find process involved discovering not only the eligible children, but also figuring out which ones were already enrolled but inadequately served.

Enforcing so elaborate a national code stirred legal conflicts as inevitable local infractions pertaining to one provision or another were revealed or perceived. "Every decision you make in special education you ask, 'Am I going to get sued for this?'"[71] That fear, voiced by the principal of an elementary school in Dade Country, Florida, could have been expressed by any number of other school officials around the country in the mid-1980s, at least in districts with sizable special education enrollments. One survey of state and local education boards published in 1987 indicated that more than a quarter of them had been sued.[72]

As the level of disputation rose the Supreme Court tried repeatedly to set boundaries. A decision in 1984 denied parents the ability to recoup attorneys' fees and one in 1989 went so far as to invoke Eleventh Amendment immunity of states from certain federal suits.[73] However, Congress promptly reversed these setbacks. Reauthorizations of the handicapped education act in 1986 and 1990 further enfranchised its citizen litigants, covered their legal expenses (now for administrative hearings as well as trials), and extended the whole program to preschool children.[74]

Predictably the law, presently titled the Individuals with Disabilities Education Act (IDEA), ratcheted the volume of litigation another notch (Figure 8.2). As in other spheres of adversarial excess (certain environmental programs, for instance) IDEA raised some bizarre expectations, not just legitimate requests, in the nation's courts of law. The superintendent of one California school district reportedly described confronting plaintiffs' lawyers who demanded such "related services" as karate lessons for a kindergarten child with an immune system disorder, horseback riding lessons as rehabilitation therapy for a child who had had seizures, and school trips to Disneyland for a child who was depressed.[75]

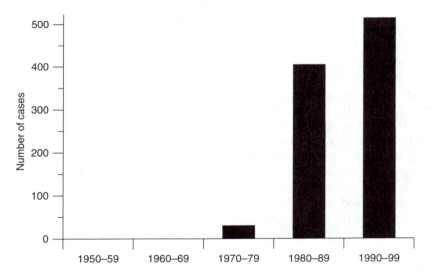

**Figure 8.2**   Special Education Litigation in Federal Courts, 1950–1999.[a]

*Source:* Perry A. Zirkel, "The 'Explosion' in Education Litigation: An Update," *West's Education Law Reporter,* no. 114 (1997), p. 348.

[a] Data for 1990–99 are a projection that is based on the actual number of cases through December of 1995.

And predictably the distribution of the legal troubles has been uneven: besieged disproportionately have been the districts with large special-ed constituencies—the school systems of cities like New York, Baltimore, and Washington, D.C., that would have to cope for years with laborious consent decrees.[76]

# Curing or Abetting the Mischiefs of Faction?

The Individuals with Disabilities Education Act is a monument to best intentions gone astray. Back in 1975, when Congress voted almost unanimously to plant this federal foothold in local public education, the lawmakers hardly anticipated what lay ahead. As its original title indicated the legislation was intended to assist the comparatively small number of children who were *handicapped*—that is, blind, deaf, paralyzed, or otherwise gravely impaired. In the ensuing quarter-century, however, definitions of disability widened to include categories of emotional, mental, or behavioral characteristics that had scarcely denoted a "handicap" in years past. Twenty-five years ago, for instance, there was no clinical classification for inattentive pupils. Now, diagnosed as suffering from "attention deficit disorder," they could be eligible for special services.[77] Twenty-five years ago underachieving students were simply called slow learners. Now, they, too, could qualify for special treatment; according to the U.S. Department of Education, "a severe discrepancy between achievement and intellectual ability" could signify that such students were learning disabled.[78] Partly in this fashion, IDEA eventually amassed about 6.1 million clients—and with them, colossal costs.[79]

The lawmakers of 1975 envisioned an expense that might rise to $8 billion nationwide, 40 percent of which would be defrayed by federal grants.[80] By the late 1990s the initiative's annual total was more than five times larger.[81] In the meantime, the federal contribution settled between 8 and 15 percent as congressional appropriators fled the oncoming budgetary behemoth.[82] State and local governments were left to confront it. New York City found itself allocating a quarter of its school budget to special-ed, an obligation so massive it crowded out more than $1 billion of other local priorities, from programs boosting gifted and talented kids to improved street lighting.[83]

Oversubscribed with students in special education, all of whom were entitled to customized "appropriate education" plans and some of whom required extraordinary facilities, many cities resorted to placing substantial percentages in private institutions. The premium for these schools, on top of the rest of the program's lopsided overhead, drove its average per pupil expenditures to twice the average for regular instruction, and in some cities (New York, for instance) to nearly three times the cost of instructing regular students.[84]

No affluent, civilized society can neglect the educational needs of disabled children. In 1975 the decision to assist them with what was supposed to be a large infusion of federal funds was decent and humane. But a responsible government also cannot, in effect, bring forth a blizzard of demands and then renege on its promise, shift the expense to communities that can least afford it, and run the risk of lowering the welfare of the remaining citizens in those communities. It is not too much to say that federal policy for special education has erred in just about all these ways. Its constraints on claims and eligibility are unclear; its appropriated funds have consistently fallen far below authorizations; and it has weighed most heavily on overtaxed cities with weak school systems. . . .

# Summary

If each of these federal interventions decidedly improved the quality of urban life, the misgivings expressed in these pages could be shrugged off. But there is a point at which routinely subjecting municipal decisions to national supervision and regimentation risks doing more damage than good.

Federal regulation today reaches into so many details of municipal administration that picayune concerns are nationalized alongside weightier ones. Much of this spectacle is merely a nuisance. A federal court that interferes with the ability of a city to test, say, municipal clerk-typists for grammar, spelling, and punctuation (as the Fifth Circuit ruled a number of years ago) might trifle with the local community's own valued standards but probably does not put it in jeopardy.[85] At times, however, the stakes have been higher. The safety of community residents can be compromised, for example, by rulings that limit the testing of would-be firefighters and police recruits for endurance, strength, or agility (as some of the opinions handed down by the federal courts have done), or by rulings that turn loose hundreds of arrested suspects, including some charged with robbery, stalking, carjacking, drug dealing, and manslaughter (as a federal injunction against pretrial detention did for several years in Philadelphia).

Some federal mandates sock cities with unnecessarily large costs. Costs can soar, for example, amid the national campaigns for risk-free environments—such as perfectly bias-free workplaces, toxin-free tap water, asbestos-free schools, lead-free housing, hazard-free redevelopment sites, and more. The persistence of some 21,000 brownfields languishing in cities is a stark example of the debacle that a zero-risk mentality can create.[86]

Federal law has also enmeshed municipalities in new litigation, some of which manacles their managers, demoralizes their personnel, and ties their budgets in knots. Due in no small part to federal policy, the terms and conditions of municipal employment are cited as the realm most roiled by legal disputes or the threat of them.[87] City schools used to be relatively simple and trusted neighborhood institutions. Since the 1960s, however, they have been buffeted by federal regulatory and judicial directives, leaving many preoccupied with legal bills and compliance issues more than with the quality of instruction for most students.[88]

By the early 1990s New York City's costs of complying with the ten largest court orders and mandates, specifying protocols for various municipal functions, were said to corner 26 percent of the city's tax revenue.[89] Even if every dollar earmarked in this litigious fashion were a dollar well spent (a dubious proposition), local taxpayers could fairly ask whether less adversarial means would have allocated the desired resources better, or at least without as much costly friction. By the early 1990s the cumulative cost of settling New York's liability claims had reached bewildering proportions.[90]

Alongside these considerable vexations lies the fact that some federal regulations are relatively rigid templates, superimposed on cities and towns regardless of their diverse circumstances. In certain locations, therefore, the mandated expenditures are simply a waste of money. (Should Phoenix really be made to spend significant sums to monitor the runoff from practically nonexistent rain storms?) In other instances the costs of meeting a given standard, though not pointless, will vary wildly among localities. For example, all municipalities will have to bring their groundwater treatment up to the nationwide standards of the Safe Drinking Water Act. The charges for households could vary by several thousand percent between small and large cities.[91]

U.S. environmental strictures are hardly the only ones that beget interjurisdictional inequities. Many central cities in the United States continue to contain disproportionate percentages of the low-income residents of metropolitan areas. Hence these cities bear a disproportionate share of poverty-related public expenditures. National regulations can contribute to the imbalance when their costs are not adequately reimbursed and are a function of local poverty rates. The federal special education mandate, as we have seen, falls into this category, but so do quite a few others.[92]

At the end of 1996 the District of Columbia was home to 45 percent of the Washington region's poor.[93] A consequence, as in other cities that have to shoulder comparable concentrations of poverty, is that the expense of administering almost any city service is inherently higher in the District than in the surrounding suburbs.[94] Whatever the other reasons for the District's extraordinary administrative cost structure, the heavy lifting is scarcely alleviated by some thirty-nine federal court decrees, some of which have compelled steep increases in the costliest of municipal items—like overtime compensation for city workers.[95]

## Race to the Bottom—or the Top?

It is generally assumed that Washington intervenes in local decisions primarily to prevent intergovernmental rifts and rivalries from degrading basic norms for public health, safety, or welfare. Federal authorities, the theory goes, chiefly step in to set suitable baselines—for Atlanta's air quality, or New York's fiscal practices, or the competence of school teachers in a bunch of cities. But in reality much federal preemption of local policies works the other way around. It subjects state and local governments to national directives even when those governments are emulating, indeed outdoing, one another to run standards up, not down.

In 1986 Congress moved to extend to preschoolers the universal right to special education for handicapped children. But forty-two states already had begun programs of this sort.[96] Similarly, by the time Congress proclaimed that no schoolchild should be exposed to asbestos risks most school districts already had programs to repair dangerous buildings. In 2001 a new administration in Washington proposed to coax the states to start rating the performance of all their local elementary and secondary schools. But less noticed during the national education reform debate was that seventeen states already assigned such ratings, four more were poised to initiate them in 2002, and at least two more planned to do so soon thereafter.[97] The concept of school accountability, in other words, was percolating and spreading at the local level well in advance of any coercive federal measures.

Proponents of central direction, however, frequently seem unimpressed. By their logic, if so many state and local initiatives have already blazed a trail, national standards only complete what the locals have started. The latter, it would appear, are as likely to have their independence shorn when they are proactive and progressive as when they are laggards.

Principled arguments are hard to advance for at least some of the specialized, coerced expenditures that have been pressed upon cities. But worthy or not, federally mandated programs, once established, are not easy to redesign. Program preservationists prevail.[98] The cementing of policies by vested interests was not what the framers of the Constitution had in mind when they sought to enlarge the orbit of national authority. What the founders intended was to check and counterbalance the power of calcified local elites. . . .

# NOTES

1. For a full account of the Tulsa riot on which this paragraph is based, see Brent Staples, "Unearthing a Riot," *New York Times Magazine*, December 19, 1999, pp. 64–69.
2. See Paul E. Peterson, *City Limits* (University of Chicago Press, 1981), chaps. 10, 11.
3. See David Goldberg, "Heads Up, Atlanta: Cities Are Scrambling to Comply with the Clean Air Act's Strict New Rules," *Planning*, vol. 64 (July 1998), pp. 20–23.
4. James Fallows, *More Like Us* (Houghton Mifflin, 1989), p. 169.
5. Racial violence, sparked by alleged black rapes, exploded in Omaha, Kansas City, Knoxville, Rosewood, Fla., Longview, Tex., and Washington, D.C., among other towns, at about this period.
6. Nearly all the PCBs flowing into the Great Lakes originate from the air. An estimated quarter of the nitrogen in the Chesapeake Bay derives from polluted air drifting from at least four neighboring states. Mary Graham, *The Morning After Earth Day: Practical Environmental Politics* (Brookings, 1999), p. 80.
7. Susan Rose-Ackerman, "Does Federalism Matter? Choice in a Federal Public," *Journal of Political Economy*, vol. 49, no. 1 (1981), pp. 152–63. See also John H. Cumberland, "Interregional Pollution Spillovers and Consistency of Environmental Policy," in M. Siebert and others, eds., *Regional Environmental Policy: The Economic Issues* (New York University Press, 1979), pp. 255–81.
8. James Madison, "Federalist No. 10," in Pietro S. Nivola and David H. Rosenbloom, eds., *Classic Readings in American Politics*, 3d ed. (St. Martin's, 1999), p. 34.
9. *Budget of the United States Government, Fiscal Year 1993*, 1, 5, pp. 164–65.
10. This was reflected in the nearly static level of aid to state and local governments between 1980 and 1995, excluding federal assistance for Medicaid, Annothy Conlan, *From New*

*Federalism to Devolution: Twenty-Five Years of Intergovernmental Reform* (Brookings, 1998), pp. 204–06, 219.

11. Conlan, *From New Federalism to Devolution*, p. 204.

12. James Q. Wilson and John J. Dilulio Jr., *American Government: Institutions and Policies*, 7th ed. (Houghton Mifflin Company, 1998), p. 70.

13. Bernard J. Frieden and Marshall Kaplan, *The Politics of Neglect: Urban Aid from Model Cities to Revenue Sharing* (MIT Press, 1977).

14. As early as 1994, the states were enjoying surpluses that totaled more than 7 billion.

15. On how devolution has been a cost-controlling mechanism for social programs such as Medicaid, see James R. Tallon Jr. and Lawrence D. Brown, "Who Gets What? Devolution of Eligibility and Benefits in Medicaid," in Frank J. and John J. Dilulio Jr., *Medicaid and Devolution: A View from the States* [Brookings, 1998], p. 237.

16. See generally, on the efficiency gains from interjurisdictional competition within federal systems, Michael S. Greve, *Real Federalism* (Washington: American Enterprise Institute Press, 1999). For the leading analysis of its disadvantages see Paul E. Peterson, *The Price of Federalism* (Brookings, 1995).

17. Paul C. Light, *The True Size of Government* (Brookings, 1999), p. 32.

18. In 1995, for instance, California collected $1.2 billion in federal disaster relief, much of it to compensate questionable "victims." Dan Morgan, "Governors Bit Helping Hand in Mandates Fight," *Washington Post*, January 1995, pp. A1, A6.

19. Demetrios Caraley, "Washington Abandons the Cities," *Political Science Quarterly*, vol. 107, no. 1 (1992), p. 13.

20. For the subsidy argument, see James R. St. John, "Unfunded Mandates: Financing State and National Needs," *Brookings Review*, vol. 13 (Spring 1995), 12–15.

21. *South Carolina v. Baker*, 485 U.S. 505 (1988).

22. *Garcia v. San Antonio Metropolitan Transit Authority*, 469 U.S. 528 (1985). Nine months later Congress responded by amending the Fair Labor Standards Act (FLSA), extending it again to all public sector employees. Public Law 99-150, November 13, 1985.

23. *National League of Cities v. Usery*, 426 U.S. 833 (1976).

24. On the impact of Davis-Bacon, see U.S. Advisory Commission on Intergovernmental Relations, *The Role of Federal Mandates in Intergovernmental Relations* (January 1996), p. 13.

25. See Walter Olson, *The Excuse Factory: How Employment Law is Paralyzing the American Workplace* (Free Press, 1997), p. 185.

26. For instance, *Tinker v. Des Moines Independent Community School District*, 393 U.S. 503 (1969); *Goss v. Lopez*, 419 U.S. 565 (1975). See Abigail Thernstrom, "Where Did All the Order Go? School Discipline and the Law," in Diane Ravitch, ed., *Brookings Papers on Education Policy*, 1999 (Brookings, 1999), p. 213. In a North Carolina school district, for instance, a student who broke a teacher's arm was given a mere two-day suspension.

27. In *Bethel School District No. 403 v. Fraser*, 478 U.S. 675 (1986) and several ensuing decisions, the court sought to nudge the balance of authority back from students to school officials. However, lower courts have tended to restrict removals and even suspensions of special-ed students.

28. According to the so-called "2-in, 2-out" procedure, at least two employees have to remain outside the site of an "interior structural fire" when two go inside (Standard Number 1910.134 (g) (4) (i) through (iii)). OSHA, *Regulations (Standards - 29 (CFR): Standard Number 1910.134*. The rule may apply to many fire departments that have federally approved occupational safety and health (OSH) plans in effect. Section 18(b) of the Occupational Safety and Health Act of 1970 (Public Law 91-596) stipulated that states operating under their own OSH plans are required to provide OSH protection to public as well as private sector workers. And the standards of each state OSH plan have to be at least as

stringent as those of the federal OSHA program, which covers all private sector workers. See U.S. Department of Labor, Office of Inspector General, *Evaluating the Status of Occupational Safety and Health Coverage of State and Local Workers in Federal OSHA States* (February 2000). Some two dozen states operate under federally approved OSH plans. Thus, California, as an example, follows the federal OSHA firefighting guideline verbatim. How much, if any, flexibility localities might have in such states is not entirely clear. A note attached to paragraph (g) of the OSHA regulations, however, adds this proviso: "Nothing in this section is meant to preclude firefighters from performing emergency rescue activities before an entire team has assembled."

29. Motor Carrier Safety Administration, Federal Highway Administration, Regulation no. 393.90.
30. I owe the Beverly Hills joke to James Q. Wilson and John J. Dilulio Jr., *American Government: Institutions and Policies* (Boston: Houghton Mifflin Company, 1998), p. 68.
31. The ensuing discussion is drawn from Pietro S. Nivola and Jon A. Shields, *Managing Green Mandates: Local Rigors of U.S. Environmental Regulation* (AEI-Brookings Joint Center for Regulatory Studies, 2001).
32. San Francisco concluded that it was simpler in the long run to build an oceanside secondary treatment plant than to count on obtaining periodic waivers. This city's experience illustrates the kinds of local complications that arise, even under EPA policies intended to increase local flexibility. San Francisco had obtained a waiver in the early 1980s, but it was only good for five years. If, one day, the city would have to build a second treatment plant, a particular site was referred. Rather than risk that subsequent waiver applications might be turned down, and that by then the land at the site might not be available, the city broke ground for the new facility in the late 1980s and opened it in September 1993.
33. At one time, however, the product in question had been in use near Columbus as well. For a breezy account of this and other incidents, see Thomas DiLorenzo, "Federal Regulations: Environmentalism's Achilles' Heel," *USA Today Magazine*, vol. 123 (September 1994), p. 48.
34. Mike Allen, "Connecticut Joins Lawsuit over Pollution in Sound," *New York Times*, March 24, 1998, p. A24.
35. Robert A. Katzmann, *Institutional Disability: The Saga of Transportation Policy for the Disabled* (Brookings, 1986), p. 189.
36. The phrase is from Lawrence M. Friedman, *Total Justice* (Russell Sage Foundation, 1988).
37. Edward I. Koch, "The Mandate Millstone," *Public Interest*, no. 61 (Fall 1980), p. 45.
38. Representative Charles Vanik, quored in Timothy Clark, "Access for the Handicapped," *National Journal*, October 21, 1978, p. 1673. The Congressional Budget Office estimated that section 504 of the 1973 Rehabilitation Act would require $6.8 billion to equip buses with wheelchair lifts, install elevators in subway systems, and take other measures to expand access to public transit systems for the physically disabled. Congressional Budget Office, *Urban Transportation for Handicapped Persons: Alternative Federal Approaches* (Washington, 1979), p. xi.
39. For a definitive treatment of this initiative see Thomas F. Burke, "On the Rights Track: The Americans with Disabilities Act," in Pietro S. Nivola, ed., *Comparative Disadvantages: Social Regulations and the Global Economy* (Brookings, 1997).
40. Stephen L. Percy, "ADA, Disability Rights, and Evolving Regulatory Federalism," *Publius*, vol. 23 (Fall 1993), p. 87.
41. *Hearings on the Americans with Disabilities Act* before the Subcommittee on Surface Transportation of the House Committee on Public Works and Transportation, 101 Cong. 1 sess. (Government Printing Office, 1989), p. 2721.
42. James H. Matteson, "Americans with Disabilities Act Requirements: Community Sidewalks and Curbs," *City Council Report*, City of Phoenix, January 24, 1997, pp. 1–2.

43. Percy, "ADA," p. 104.
44. Pursuant to the Clean Air Act amendments of 1990, "Standards of Performance for New Stationary Sources and Emissions Guidelines for Existing Sources," *Federal Register*, vol. 60, no. 243 (December 19, 1995), pp. 65378–436.
45. City of Tampa, *Mayor's Strategic Initiatives* (January 1999), pp. 51–52.
46. Medical Research Council, *Health Effects of Waste Combustion Products* (Leicester, UK: Institute for Environment and Health, 1997).
47. U.S. Environmental Protection Agency, *Mercury Study Report to Congress: Volume II* (December 1997).
48. Katherine N. Probst and others, *Footing the Bill for Superfund Cleanup: Who Pays and How?* (Brookings and Resources for the Future, 1995), p. 1995.
49. Cleaning up urban waste sites, rivers, air sheds, and so on, by 90 percent may be practicable, but erasing the remaining 10 percent can be prohibitive. Stephen Breyer, *Breaking the Vicious Cycle: Toward Effective Risk Regulation* (Harvard University Press, 1993), pp. 11–12, 29.
50. Olson, *The Excuse Factory*, p. 17.
51. James Rutenberg, "Long Weight's Over," *New York Daily News*, March 5, 1998, p. 8.
52. Olson, *The Excuse Factory*, p. 253.
53. Rene Sanchez, "LAPD Reeling as Corruption Cases Multiply," *Washington Post*, February 12, 2000, pp. A1, A14.
54. James Sterngold, "Los Angeles Police Officials Admit Widespread Lapses," *New York Times*, February 17, 2000, p. A12.
55. Charles Epp, "Litigation against Local Governments: Expenditures on Legal Services, 1960–1995," paper presented at the annual meeting of the American Political Science Association, 1997, p. 5.
56. Allen R. Myerson, "Soaring Liability Payments Burdening New York," *New York Times*, June 29, 1992, p. B1.
57. Epp, "Litigation against Local Governments," p. 5.
58. See, for instance, *Monell v. New York City Department of Social Services*, 436 U.S. 658, 56 2d 611, 98 S Ct. 2018 (1978); *Owen v. City of Independence*, 445 U.S. 622, 633n., 13m 100 S Ct. 1398, 1406–1407 (1980); and *Maine v. Thiboutot*, 448, 100 S Ct. 2502 (1980).
59. Richard A. Posner, *The Federal Courts: Challenge and Reform* (Harvard University Press, 1996), pp. 57, 60–61.
60. Don Vannatta Jr., "U.S. Judge Says Removing Alarm Boxes Discriminates against the Deaf," *New York Times*, February 14, 1996, p. B3.
61. Greg B. Smith, "City Asks for End to Jail Regs," *New York Daily News*, May 30, 1996, p. 22.
62. "MTA Officials Admit Violating Federal Court Order to Reduce Overcrowding, Report Says," Associated Press State and Local Wire, September 9, 1998.
63. See Sarah B. Vanderbraak, "Why Criminals Would Rather Be in Philadelphia," *Policy Review*, no. 71 (Summer 1995), pp. 73–75.
64. See Charles R. Epp, "Litigation Stories: Official Perceptions of Lawsuits against Local Government," paper prepared for the 1998 annual meeting of the Law and Society Association, Aspen, Colorado, pp. 9–11.
65. Yong S. Lee, "Civil Liability of State and Local Governments," *Public Administration Review*, vol. 47 (March–April 1987), p. 160.
66. Koch, "Mandate Millstone," p. 53.
67. White student enrollment in Milwaukee stood at 58.9 percent in 1976. After the city's desegregation plan took effect, the percentage dropped to 45.3 percent by 1980. White students had been leaving city schools all along, but the annual rate of departures accelerated by almost 62 percent as the desegregation process unfolded. Paul E. Peterson, Barry

G. Rabe, and Kenneth K. Wong, *When Federalism Works* (Brookings, 1986), p. 185. Forced busing in Charlotte-Mecklenburg had been in effect for decades. As of the late 1990s, it had still to achieve racial balance. In fact, forty-two of the district's schools were not in balance as of 1998, compared with only seven in 1979. Busing in Denver began in 1974. Parents responded by moving away to suburban districts, sharply reducing the number of white students in city schools. In 1995 a federal judge finally ordered the busing to stop. "Stopping the School Bus," *Economist*, May 29, 1999, pp. 25–26. Boston's busing program also began in 1974. Today, only 15 percent of the city's public school students are white, compared with 60 percent in the early 1970s. Carey Goldberg, "Busing's Day Ends: Boston Drops Race in Pupil Placement," *New York Times*, July 15, 1999, p. A1.

68. National School Boards Association, *Survey of Public Education in the Nation's Urban Districts* (Alexandria, Va., 1995), pp. 130–32.

69. Clegg, "Lee," p. A19.

70. For an excellent chronicle of this program's evolution, see R. Shep Melnick, *Between the Lines: Interpreting Welfare Rights* (Brookings, 1994), chaps. 7 and 8.

71. Peterson and others, *When Federalism Works*, p. 127.

72. Roberta Weiner and Maggie Hume, *And Education for All: Public Policy and Handicapped Education* (Alexandria, Va.: Capital, 1987), cited in Paul I. Posner, *The Politics of Unfunded Mandates: Whither Federalism* (Georgetown University Press, 1998), p. 132.

73. *Smith v. Robinson*, 468 U.S. 992 (1984); and *Dellmuth v. Muth*, 491 U.S. 223, 230 (1989).

74. See *Congressional Quarterly Almanac* (Washington: Congressional Quarterly, Inc., 1990), p. 616.

75. Lisa Gubernick and Michelle Conlin, "The Special Education Scandal," *Forbes*, February 10, 1997, p. 66.

76. Urban school systems naturally have disproportionate numbers of pupils in special education because learning disabilities are closely correlated with poverty. Jay Gottlieb and others, "Special Education in Urban America," *Journal of Special Education*, vol. 27, no. 4 (1994), pp. 453–65.

77. See Wade F. Horn and Douglas Tynan, "Revamping Special Education," *Public Interest*, no. 144 (Summer 2001), p. 38.

78. Under the wide-ranging category of students said to suffer a "specific learning disability" (SLD) are those who may have trouble listening, speaking, reading basic words, comprehending what they read, expressing themselves in writing, problem solving in mathematics, or doing mathematical calculations. According to the director of the University of Minnesota's National Center on Educational Outcomes, more than 80 percent of all schoolchildren in the United States could qualify as having SLD under one definition or another. Horn and Tynan, "Revamping Special Education," p. 38. See also Joseph P. Shapiro and others, "Separate and Unequal," *U.S. News & World Report*, December 13, 1993. Some diagnosed afflictions seem to have burst onto the scene in epidemic proportions. In the years 1994–99, for instance, the number of children considered autistic increased by 153.6 percent, David Brown, "Autism's New Face," *Washington Post*, March 26, 2000, p. A1.

79. The 6.1 million figure was for 1999–2000 and included children and youth ages three to twenty-one. In 1976–77 the number of children receiving special education services and accommodations had been 3.7 million. Horn and Tynan, "Revamping Special Education," p. 36. Jeffrey L. Katz, "Policy on Disabled is Scrutinized over Discipline Problems, Cost," *Congressional Quarterly Weekly Report*, May 11, 1996.

80. *Congressional Quarterly Almanac*, 1975, vol. 31 (Congressional Quarterly Inc., 1976), p. 651.

81. Tom Loveless and Diane Ravitch, "Broken Promises: What the Federal Government Can Do to Improve American Education," *Brookings Review*, vol. 18 (Spring 2000), p. 20.
82. U.S. Advisory Commission on Intergovernmental Relations, *The Role of Federal Mandates in Intergovernmental Relations* (January 1996). Loveless and Ravitch, "Broken Promises," give a more current 12 percent estimate. See also Jeffrey L. Katz, "Policy on Disabled Is Scrutinized," p. 1297.
83. Norm Fruchter and others, *Focus on Learning: A Report on Reorganizing General and Special Education in New York City*, New York University, Institute for Education and Social Policy, 1995; Sam Illon, "Special Education Absorbs School Resources," *New York Times*, April 7, 1994, p. A1; Scott Miner Brook, "The Cratering of New York," *U.S. News & World Report*, May 27, 1991, p. 31.
84. This distortion in New York was far worse than in the rest of the state. (Spending on special education grew much less rapidly elsewhere in New York State, and did not squeeze the resources available for regular students as badly.) Mark Lankgord and James Wyckoff, "The Allocation of Resources to Special Education and Regular Instruction," in Helen F. Ladd, ed., *Holding Schools Accountable: Performance-Based Reform in Education* (Brookings, 1996), p. 231. In the District of Columbia, as much as $49 million of the city's proposed $125 million special education budget in 1998 may have been claimed by the 17 percent of special education students that had to be sent to private schools. Beset by litigation, the District's program also anticipated paying between $6 million and $8 million in legal fees to plaintiffs' lawyers. Doug Struck and Valerie Strauss, "D.C. Special Ed System Still in Disarray, Report Says," *Washington Post*, July 20, 1998, p. B1.
85. Olson, *Excuse Factory*, p. 181.
86. U.S. Conference of Mayors, *Recycling America's Land: A National Report on Brownfields Redevelopment*, vol. 3 (February 2000), pp. 9–11.
87. Epp, "Litigation Stories," pp. 6–7.
88. Paul T. Hill, "Supplying Effective Public Schools in Big Cities," in Diane Ravitch, ed., *Brookings Papers on Education Policy, 1999* (Brookings, 1999), pp. 422–23.
89. Ross Sandler and David Shoenbrod, "Government by Decree—The High Cost of Letting Judges Make Policy," *City Journal*, vol. 4 (Summer 1994).
90. Allen R. Myerson, "Soaring Liability Payments Burdening New York," *New York Times*, June 29, 1992, sec. B, p. 1.
91. Congressional Budget Office, *Federalism and Environmental Protection: Case Studies for Drinking Water and Ground-Level Ozone* (GPO, November 1997), pp. 25–30.
92. Great variations in the intermediary roles of state governments translate into widely divergent federal impacts. The U.S. special education program does not pose the same financial complexities for the cities of Florida, say, as for the municipalities of New York. (Local districts in Florida are responsible for only 2 to 3 percent of special education spending.) Peterson, *When Federalism Works*, p. 156.
93. Brookings Center on Urban and Metropolitan Government, *A Region Divided: The State of Growth in Greater Washington, D.C.* (Brookings, 1999), p. 3.
94. For a general analysis of this unbalanced pattern in metropolitan areas, see Janet Rothenberg Pack, "Poverty and Urban Public Expenditures," *Urban Studies*, vol. 33, no. 11 (1998), pp. 1995–2020.
95. U.S. General Accounting Office, *District of Columbia Government: Overtime Costs Exceed Those of Neighboring Governments* (September 1997), pp. 21, 32. The GAO found the District paying more in overtime as a percentage of municipal salaries than did any of the city's surrounding counties. For some poverty-related services (corrections, for instance) nearly 18 percent of the District's salary base went to overtime, compared with 0.2 percent in Maryland's Prince George's County.

96. Posner, *Unfunded Mandates*, p. 64.

97. "School Accountability: How Are States Holding Schools Responsible for Results?" *Education Week*, vol. 20 (January 11, 2001), p. 80.

98. See, more generally, the delightfully readable Jonathan Rauch, *Government's End: Why Washington Stopped Working* (New York: Public Affairs, 1999), especially chap. 6.

# 28

## *Stephen D. Stehr*

# THE POLITICAL ECONOMY
# OF DISASTER ASSISTANCE

The devastation wrought in the cities of the Gulf coast by Hurricanes Katrina and Rita has once again cast a spotlight on disaster policy and administration in the United States. Although presidential disaster declarations over the past decade have averaged approximately one per week, many go unnoticed except by those directly affected. But so-called "megadisasters," characterized by significant loss of life, widespread physical and economic damage, and extensive media attention act as a catalyst for a reexamination of current policies and procedures. As the economic costs associated with disasters have grown (Cutter and Emrich 2005), these debates have increasingly focused on disaster relief and assistance programs and how urbanized regions might mitigate damages before they occur (Mileti 1999; Platt 1999). This is not an issue that is likely to go away anytime soon. Many of the nation's most populous urban areas are situated in coastal areas that are at high risk from naturally occurring events such as earthquakes or hurricanes. According to the Census Bureau, more than half of the nation's 297 million people live in coastal areas—most in major cities—and seven of the top 10 fastest-growing states are coastal. Cities nationwide are subject to an array of natural hazards such as riverine flooding, wildfires, ice storms, tornados, drought, and volcanic eruptions. In the post–September 11 environment, all cities are considered to be at some level of risk to terrorist attacks that have the potential of causing many of the same types of problems (e.g., large-scale evacuation of citizens; urban search and rescue; public health and environmental concerns; mass casualty management and victim identifica-

AUTHOR's NOTE: Portions of the research reported here were supported by a grant from the National Science Foundation (CMS 0234100). The opinions presented in this article are the author's and do not necessarily reflect those of the National Science Foundation. The author would like to thank the anonymous reviewers who provided useful comments on an earlier draft.

Stephen D. Stehr, "The Political Economy of Urban Disaster Assistance," *Urban Affairs Review,* Vol. 41 (4), pp. 492–500, copyright © 1998 Sage Publications, Inc. Reprinted by permission of Sage Publications, Inc.

tion; victim compensation; reconstruction of public infrastructure; business continuity) that are also associated with natural events.

Despite the increasing vulnerability of urban areas to catastrophic events, relatively little attention has been explicitly paid to issues that would inform both the literatures concerning urban studies and those that focus on the social science aspects of disaster.[1] This article represents a modest attempt to begin a dialogue between those who study more traditional topics in urban governance and those who study how communities prepare for, respond to, and recover from disasters. My primary focus is on two related questions: First, is it possible to reconcile the competing forces of economic development decisions and political calculations with hazard mitigation policies? Under the current structure, local officials have very few incentives to mitigate hazards secure in the knowledge that federal aid will be forthcoming following an event. Recovery from large-scale urban disasters also lays bare local political dynamics that may have been obscured prior to the event (Kantor 2002). But they also expose longer-term national political trends and priorities as they relate to disaster preparedness and response capabilities. A second question relates to the possibility of incorporating the idea of community resilience into discussions of sustainable development. As Savitch points out, our collective understanding of the life of cities goes through recognizable paradigmatic shifts (Savitch 2003). It remains to be seen if some of the forces discussed in this article have reached a critical mass and will launch a new paradigm focused on safe cities.

The history of disaster relief and assistance policy in the United States can be characterized as having brief periods of intense political activity typically following a major disaster or a series of disasters, followed by longer periods where interest in the subject wanes (May 1985). This has resulted in a fragmented set of policies that, over time, have significantly increased the financial exposure of the federal government (Platt 1999). There are four primary means through which postdisaster assistance is administered: (1) government programs (primarily implemented through the federal government); (2) charities and philanthropic organizations; (3) private insurance; and, (4) the court system chiefly through tort claims and bankruptcy filings.[2] Federal disaster assistance is provided through approximately 30 separate programs that offer aid to individuals and families, businesses, states and municipalities, special districts, and not-for-profit organizations (Jordan 2005). A wide range of financial strategies is utilized including direct grants to stricken communities and individuals, low interest disaster loans, federal public works programs to remove debris and rebuild public infrastructures, disaster unemployment benefits, mental health and legal services, environmental cleanup, and federal income tax deductions for uninsured casualty losses.

Federal aid is intended to be supplemental to funds dedicated by state and local governments. The Federal Disaster Assistance Act of 1988 (the Stafford Act)—the primary federal law governing disasters—specifies a 75/25 ratio of federal/nonfederal cost sharing of disaster assistance with state and local governments. However, recent presidents of both parties have raised the federal share or waived nonfederal contributions entirely (Platt 1999, p. 17). Although these waivers are no doubt motivated in part by compassion, presidents (and members of Congress) are also under intense political pressure to act quickly and generously, particularly in election years. Several recent studies have documented a connection between presidential elections, congressional politics, and level of disaster relief allocated to specific areas (Garrett and Sobel 2003; Reeves 2005).

Postdisaster response and recovery assistance has historically made up the vast majority of federal spending on disasters. According to a report issued by the Bipartisan Task Force on Funding Disaster Relief, approximately three-quarters of all federal spending on disasters between 1977 and 1994 was expended to pay for postdisaster recovery (U.S. Senate 1995). This same report charged that the federal government discourages state, local, and individual self-reliance by offering federal disaster assistance too readily. It seems reasonable to conclude that in some instances disaster assistance has become a form of political "pork barrel," particularly in cases where genuine need seems to be absent.[3]

The implementation of disaster assistance in New York City following the terrorist attacks of September 11 illustrates the basic structure of relief policies. According to a report completed by researchers at RAND, the total amount of direct disaster assistance delivered to victims, businesses, and government entities was $38.1 billion (Dixon and Stern 2004). Of this amount, slightly more than half ($19.6 billion, or 51%) was paid out by insurance companies. Through 2004, government programs accounted for $15.8 billion (42%) of total relief payments but this figure will grow as monies allocated but not yet expended are spent. Despite an unprecedented mobilization charitable distributions accounted for only 7% of total assistance.[4]

Soon after the attacks, President George W. Bush promised $20 billion in federal money to help the New York City area recover from 9/11. Although some may have interpreted this pledge to mean that New York City would receive a lump sum payment, in reality the aid package was structured to provide for both immediate needs as well as long-term assistance. The flow of federal aid to New York City and its inhabitants is being tracked by the New York City Independent Budget Office (IBO). By its accounting, approximately 30% ($6.3 billion) of the money was expended on emergency response activities. The majority of this money (approximately 70%) was provided to New York City to pay for debris removal and overtime costs for the police and fire departments and to establish an insurance pool to protect the city and its contract workers against lawsuits resulting from work at the World Trade Center site (IBO 2004). Only a small portion of the response funds (about 10%) were provided as direct aid to individuals or as low interest loans to property owners. About 20% ($4.4 billion) of $20 billion appropriated by Congress was designed to spur economic recovery in Lower Manhattan and to help alleviate the budget crisis the city faced in the wake of the attack. Most of these funds were provided directly to New York City government (38% or $1.7 billion) or for business assistance grants (26% or $1.2 billion). The remaining $9.7 billion (most of which have not yet been spent), will go for long-term rebuilding projects primarily in the area of transportation improvements.

Although care should be taken in generalizing from this admittedly un-precedented case, several lessons emerge nonetheless. First, insurance compa-nies provided about 50% of the total compensation provided. These monies went to individuals (mostly through life insurance policies) and affected businesses. As it turns out, there is empirical evidence to suggest that the 50% figure is a reasonable assumption in many natural disasters as well (Pielke 2005). Second, most of the assistance provided through federal programs was ad-ministered to New York City with a smaller portion going to businesses that were damaged, destroyed, or disrupted. In fact, aside from the approximately $7 billion that was expended through the VCF, a relatively small amount of direct assistance was provided to individuals. Finally, disaster recovery and reconstruction—even when the physical damage is relatively concentrated as it was in New York City—does not take place overnight. It is estimated that it will take approximately 10 years to fully expend the entire $20 billion authorized by Congress (IBO 2004).

Although disaster assistance is commonly thought to include only those activities that occur following an extreme event, a more comprehensive ap-proach also includes pre-event mitigation and preparedness activities designed to eliminate or reduce event impacts. As Lindell and Prater (2003) point out, there are strong and important linkages between hazard mitigation and pre-paredness practices, and community recovery and reconstruction outcomes. An inherent problem in the structure of disaster assistance is the fact that the mit-igation and preparedness are largely the responsibility of local governments while the economic costs of recovery and reconstruction are borne elsewhere. Subnational governments and individuals owning property in hazardous areas to a large extent control decisions that determine the ultimate effectiveness of mitigation and preparedness measures adopted at the local level; in most cases, these parties have few incentives to make these policies a high priority because federal programs will provide assistance should a disaster occur (May 1985; Stehr 1999). Adding to the problem is that well-intentioned government pro-grams sometimes undermine each other. Rutherford Platt argues that a vast ar-ray of federal spending and economic development programs such as highway construction, housing, urban renewal, shoreline stabilization, water pollution abatement, and river control projects may undercut the goals of hazard mitiga-tion by indirectly sponsoring development and redevelopment in areas of re-current hazard (Platt 1999). It remains to be seen if a "paradigm shift" from a political-economic logic of urban development to one based in public security and protection will inform decisions regarding the rebuilding of New Orleans (Savitch 2003).

Going beyond the pressures associated with local economic development decisions and the problems it creates in creating workable response and assis-tance policies, disaster policy is also a by-product of other, seemingly uncon-nected policy decisions. For instance, decisions made in the arenas of national security policy, urban policy, and social policy have traceable impacts on cur-rent disaster policy. Following September 11, planning to detect and prevent terrorist attacks all but eliminated federal interest in preparedness and response activities and funding for natural disaster mitigation projects (Holdeman 2005;

Tierney 2005). Significantly, the Federal Emergency Management Agency (FEMA), the agency established to coordinate hazard mitigation, and disaster response and recovery policies, was stripped of its cabinet-level status when it was placed within the newly created Department of Homeland Security. Project Impact, a hazard mitigation program started during the Clinton administration to provide grants to cities, was eliminated in 2001 although it was costing only about $20 million per year. This devolution of responsibility can be seen as merely one part of a "new" urban policy whereby cities are expected to take on additional responsibilities for protecting their citizens (Eisinger 2004). This is also part of a larger trend. As William Barnes recently reported, federal funds as a percentage of municipal revenues reached a high in 1978 at about 17% and have declined steadily since then to less than 5% (Barnes 2005). Some observers have interpreted the events in New Orleans as resulting from decades of federal urban disinvestment, exurbanization, and "white flight," which have left the central cores of many cities "abandoned" (Graham 2005), or as "exposing the unacknowledged inequalities" that are the result of years of failed social policies (Frymer, Strolovitch, and Warren 2005).

# Can We Create Resilient Cities?

For at least the past decade, community resilience has been a prominent topic among academic urban planners and natural disaster researchers. Dennis Mileti defines the concept this way: "Local resiliency with regard to disasters means that a locale is able to withstand an extreme natural event without suffering devastating losses, damage, diminished productivity, or quality of life and without a large amount of assistance from outside the community" (Mileti 1999, pp. 32–33). One aspect of community resilience focuses on hazard mitigation—that is, activities designed to reduce or eliminate long-term risk to people and property and break the cycle of damage, reconstruction, and repeated damage from disasters. These efforts include such actions as stricter building codes, engineering retrofits, land use planning, and property acquisition (Hardenbrook 2005; Godschalk et al. 1999; Burby 1998). How successful are these efforts likely to be? Certainly there will be localized success stories. However, as this article points out, there are strong political and economic forces at work that will make widespread urban hazard mitigation difficult to achieve. One promising avenue to pursue is the concept of "comprehensive emergency management." This idea is rooted in the notion that loss-reduction efforts should be oriented toward integrating mitigation, preparedness, response, and recovery activities suitable for a variety of localized hazards whether natural, technological, or human caused. But implementing this concept costs time and money and requires local political and administrative leadership. In the absence of national incentives to create resilient communities, the provision of public protection will continue to fall largely on urban governance structures.

In their recent book, *The Resilient City*, Vale and Campanella raise a number of important questions that could help inform a more robust dialogue between urbanists and those who study the social science aspects of disaster (Vale and Campanella 2005, pp. 12–13). For example, they pose the question: what does it mean for a "city" to "recover"? As regional hubs of economic, social, and cultural activities, cities recover to the extent that they return to some semblance of predisaster normalcy in human and economic relationships. But large-scale disasters also raise value-laden questions such as who will set the priorities for recovering communities? How will short-term recovery forces be balanced with long-range planning? Will predisaster inequities be replicated as part of the recovery process? Who will be displaced (and at what cost) as neighborhoods are rebuilt? What are the proper roles of local, state, and federal officials in an intergovernmental disaster assistance system? What dominant narratives will emerge to help us interpret what transpired and inform future hazard policies? By addressing these and many other important questions, a richer and more complete understanding of the vulnerability of cities to hazards could emerge that would serve to inform research from a variety of professional perspectives.

## NOTES

1. In the aftermath of the attacks of September 11, some urban scholars have turned their attention to issues related to homeland security (Gerber et al. 2005) and urban terrorism (Eisinger 2004; Kantor 2002).
2. This article will focus primarily on the governmental component of disaster assistance.
3. Reporters at the South Florida *Sun-Sentinel* examined 20 of the 313 disasters declared by the Federal Emergency Management Agency from 1999 to 2004. They concluded that 27% of the $1.2 billion paid out went to areas where official reports showed minor damage or none at all (Kestin 2005).
4. In exchange for establishing the September 11th Victim Compensation Fund (VCF) to provide compensation to families of those who were killed and to the seriously injured, Congress limited the role of the tort system in part to protect the airlines involved in the attacks and the owners of the World Trade Center.

## REFERENCES

Barnes, W. 2005. Beyond federal urban policy. *Urban Affairs Review* 40(5): 575–89.

Burby, R., ed. 1998. *Cooperating with nature: Confronting natural hazards with land-use planning for sustainable communities*. Washington, D.C.: Joseph Henry Press.

Cutter, S., and C. Emrich. 2005. Are natural disaster losses in the U.S. increasing? *EOS: Transactions, American Geophysical Union* 86(41): 381–96.

Dixon, L., and R. Stern. 2004. *Compensation for losses from the 9/11 attacks*. Santa Monica, CA: RAND.

Eisinger, P. 2004. The American city in the age of terror: A preliminary assessment of the effects of September 11. *Urban Affairs Review* 40(1): 115–29.

Frymer, P., D. Strolovitch, and D. Warren. 2005. Katrina's political roots and divisions: Race, class, and federalism in American politics. Understanding Katrina: Perspectives from the social sciences. Web site created by the Social Science Research Centre. University of Maryland, http://www.understandingkatrina.ssrc .org (accessed September 19, 2005).

Garrett, T., and R. Sobel. 2003. The Political Economy of FEMA Disaster Payments. *Economic Inquiry* 41(3): 496–509.

Gerber, B., D. Cohen, B. Cannon, D. Patterson, and K. Stewart. 2005. On the front line: American cities and the challenge of homeland security preparedness. *Urban Affairs Review* 41(2): 182–210.

Godschalk, D., T. Beatley, P. Berke, D. Brower, and E. Kaiser. 1999. *Natural hazard mitigation: Recasting disaster policy and planning.* Washington, D.C.: Island.

Graham, S. 2005. Cities under siege: Katrina and the politics of metropolitan America. Understanding Katrina: Perspectives from the social sciences. Web site created by the Social Science Research Center, University of Maryland, http://www.understandingkatrina.ssrc.org (accessed September 19, 2005).

Hardenbrook, B. 2005. The need for a policy framework to develop disaster resilient regions. *Journal of Homeland Security and Emergency Management* 2(3): Article 2.

Holdeman, E. 2005. Destroying FEMA. *Washington Post,* August 30, 2005.

Jordan, M. 2005. Federal disaster recovery programs: Brief summaries. CRS Report for Congress, Congressional Research Service. August 29, 2005.

Kantor, P. 2002. Terrorism and governability in New York City: Old problem, new dilemma. *Urban Affairs Review* 38(1): 120–27.

Kestin, S. 2005. FEMA battered by waste, fraud. South Florida *Sun-Sentinel,* September 18, A1.

Lindell, M. K. and C. Prater. 2003. Assessing community impacts of natural disasters. *Natural Hazards Review* 3(2): 176–85.

May, P. 1985. *Recovering from catastrophes: Federal disaster relief policy and politics.* Westport, CT: Greenwood.

Mileti, D. 1999. *Disasters by design: A reassessment of natural hazards in the United States.* Washington, D.C.: Joseph Henry.

New York City Independent Budget Office. 2004. Three years after: Where is the $20 billion in federal WTC aid? Inside the budget. August 11, 2004.

Pielke, R. 2005. Historical economic losses from hurricanes: Where does Katrina fit in? Center For Science and Technology Policy Research, University of Colorado, http://www.sciencepolicy.colorado.edu (accessed September 19, 2005).

Platt, R. 1999. *Disasters and democracy: The politics of extreme natural events.* Washington. D.C.: Island.

Reeves, A. 2005. Political disaster? Presidential disaster declarations and electoral politics. Department of Government, Harvard University (unpublished manuscript).

Savitch, H. 2003. Does 9–11 portend a new paradigm for cities? *Urban Affairs Review* 38(1): 120–27.

Stehr, S. 1999. Community recovery and reconstruction following disasters. In *The handbook of crisis and emergency management,* edited by A. Farazmand, 345–57. New York: Marcel Dekker.

Tierney, K. 2005. The red pill. Understanding Katrina: Perspectives from the social sciences. Social Science Research Center, University of Maryland, http://www.understandingkatrina.ssrc.org (accessed September 19, 2005).

U.S. Congress. Senate. Bipartisan Task Force on Funding Disaster Relief. Report of Senate task force on funding disaster relief. 104th Congress. Document No. 104–4.

The, L., and T. Campanella, eds. 2005. *The resilient city: How modern cities recover from disaster.* Oxford: Univ. Press.